Boater's Pocket Reference

Your Comprehensive Resource for Boats and Boating

Thomas McEwen

**First Edition
4th Printing Revised**

**Anchor Cove Publishing

www.anc

Boater's Pocket Reference
Your Comprehensive Resource
for Boats and Boating

Copyright © 2006 Thomas McEwen
Published by:

Anchor Cove Publishing Inc.
Post Office Box 270588
Littleton, CO 80127-0010
books@anchorcovepublishing.com
www.anchorcovepublishing.com

ISBN-10: 0-9774052-0-6
ISBN-13: 978-0-9774052-0-6
LCCN: 2005909125
Manufactured in the United States of America

Contents at a Glance

4

TABLE OF CONTENTS

QUICK REFERENCE TABLE OF CONTENTS

PREFACE—NOTE TO THE READER

This book is not meant to be a book you read from cover to cover, although anyone is certainly welcome to do so. Rather, it is intended as a reference, containing information ranging from very basic to advanced intermediate. Hopefully you will find facts and information that are new to you, and if not new, that will act as a refresher or memory jogger. There is a lot to know and remember if you wish to be a safe, responsible, and competent boater.

Many chapters in this book contain equations that require a basic knowledge of algebra to understand and a scientific calculator to evaluate. They have been included for those boaters who are interested in some of the more technical aspects of boating, but they can safely be ignored by those who are not so inclined. You do not have to be a mathematician to be a good boater. Tables have usually been included that evaluate these formulas and equations.

If you find errors or omissions in this book please email me at books@anchorcovepublishing.com so I can correct the next edition.

Phone numbers herein were correct at the time of publication. If you find errors in phone numbers or website addresses please let me know at the above email address.

ACKNOWLEDGMENTS

It is not possible to list all the sources used in this book; however, books referenced in the preparation of this guide are listed in the Information Sources chapter and photographs or illustrations are credited wherever they are used.

A special thanks to all the people who selflessly volunteer their time as officers or class instructors for the Boulder Valley Sail and Power Squadron. They include Dana and Gwen Andersen, Don Buddington, John and Pam Chatting, Bruce Crystal, Jack Euler, Carl Forsberg, Harry and Anne Hammond, John Harris, Steve Lawrence, Jerry LeCocq, Frank Locker, Phil and Barbara McLean, Stan and Nancy Roberts, Ron Schwiesow, Winston Scott, and Ed and Deanna Velie.

It was with a friend, Ken Sweet, that the idea to produce a book of this type was formed. There were times when I thought he was trying to get revenge for something I did to him, but now that it's finished, thank you, Ken.

Scott Henington gave lots of encouragement and helped persuade me that somebody might actually buy a book like this. Gerry and Glenna Travers provided invaluable hands-on experience aboard their boats. Sue Collier of Lead Dog Communications did a great job editing and Marilyn Ross of Self Publishing Resources gave excellent advice on getting this book finished and out to market.

I am particularly indebted to my wife, Dawn McEwen, who put up with me spending exponentially more and more time on this book, starting as a part time project and ending as an all-day, seven-day-a-week odyssey.

This book is dedicated to my wonderful wife Dawn and my three lovely daughters, Lianne, Shannon, and Stacey.

WHY THIS BOOK?

If you are a boater you are surely aware there have been hundreds, if not thousands, of books written about any and all aspects of boats and boating. Any bookstore has several shelves devoted to the subject and any good marine supply store has several rows of books on boating. There are books on such diverse topics as how to build a boat, how to buy a boat, how to operate a boat, how to tie knots, how to navigate, how to repair engines, how to repair fiberglass, and —well you get the idea. There are also some excellent books that do a great job of covering all aspects of recreational boating, in particular, *Chapman Piloting*[1], which is generally considered the "bible" of modern recreational boating. So why does the world need another book about boats?

As a boater seeking to increase his knowledge of boats and boating, the author attended a *Passagemaker Magazine* seminar at the Miami Boat Show some years ago and while learning a lot, also found out he had a lot more to learn about the subject. From there, a logical step was joining the Boulder Valley Sail and Power Squadron in Colorado (Yes, there's a Power Squadron in land-locked Colorado) and taking every course they offered, as well as reading innumerable books and magazines since that time.

All the while I compiled notes and data in three ring binders as a boating reference for myself, much as I did during a career as an engineer in the mining business.

As a mining engineer I have used the *Pocket Ref*[2] authored and published by Thomas Glover for over 16 years,

1. Maloney, Elbert S. *Chapman Piloting, Seamanship & Small Boat Handling*. New York: Hearst Marine Books, 2003

2. Glover, Thomas J. *Pocket Ref*, Littleton CO: Sequoia Publishing Inc.,2003

and have found it an invaluable reference source full of facts and figures useful both for work and home. This is a pocket sized book (it measures a little over 3"×5"×1" thick and has over 750 pages—it's like a small bible.

One day while driving to a Power Squadron sailing class with a friend, the idea occurred that a similar reference book might be useful for the boating community. This would be something helpful for beginners as well as more advanced boaters and physically small enough to always take with you. A little research at the local library and bookstore revealed no books quite like this. From there, it was a short step to deciding to put together such a book, especially since I had a lot of the stuff already compiled in the binders.

So here it is—some how-to-do-it information and reference facts, figures, formulas, graphs, and tables about most aspects of boating in a book small enough to fit in your pocket. The book ended up containing the kind of information I would like to have had, all in one place, when starting out to learn all about boating.

If you're reading this, hopefully you have bought this little book or intend to. I wish you the best in your boating experiences and hope this little reference helps make those experiences safer and more enjoyable. Happy cruising!

This Book Belongs To:

Name:	
Address 1:	
Address 2:	
City:	
State/Prov:	Zip/Postal:
Ph Work:	
Ph Home:	
Ph Cell:	
Email:	

Boat Data:

Name:	
Home Port:	
Boat Make and Type:	
Length:	Beam:
Draft:	Displacement:
Bridge Clearance Mast Up	Bridge Clearance Mast Down
State Registration # or Cdn License #:	
US Documentation # or Cdn Registration #:	
Hull Identification #:	

1 BOAT TYPES, DESIGN, AND CONSTRUCTION

INTRODUCTION

Before heading out in a boat, it's a good idea to have a basic understanding of how boats are designed and built, so you know what conditions it's capable of handling. This chapter discusses basic terminology, and design and construction aspects of boats.

Like a car or truck, boats are a compromise based on the intended purpose and the amount of money available. For example, a boat suitable for carrying heavy loads will not be a very fast boat. A boat designed for crossing oceans will not be very good for cruising inland waterways. Money always plays a major role in determining the size and type of boat you will acquire. Understanding the basics of boat design and construction will help you make a much more informed decision as to the type and size of boat to purchase with your available funds.

Boating has a vocabulary all its own, and anyone lacking knowledge of at least the basic terminology will have a difficult time communicating with other boaters, which could at times be a safety issue. The most common terms are defined in the illustrations on the next three pages, with a complete glossary of boating terms included in chapter 15.

This is followed by a discussion of the basic types and shapes of hulls as a prerequisite to reviewing some basic parameters and ratios used to design boats. Design parameters include such items as stability curves and stability types, as well as coefficients and ratios (such as the block coefficient or the displacement to length ratio). Construction materials and methods using wood, fiberglass, aluminum, and steel are described along with the relative advantages and disadvantages of each. The chapter ends with descriptions and illustrations of various types of recreational boats and sailing rigs.

BASIC TERMINOLOGY

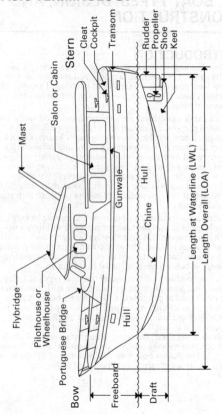

FIGURE 1-1: Powerboat Side View

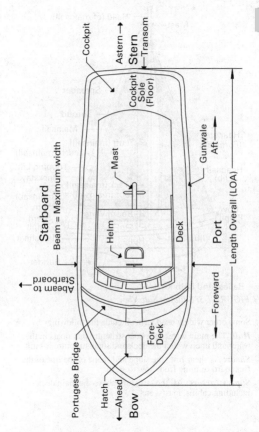

FIGURE 1-2: Powerboat Top View

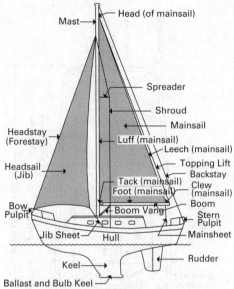

FIGURE 1-3: Sailboat Side View

Some other widely used terms include the following:

Hull: The main watertight boat structure that floats in the water and upon which the deck and superstructure is built.

Shear: As shear line; the slope and shape of the line of the freeboard running from bow to stern.

Superstructure: All the structure above the main deck including cabins, masts, etc.

HULL TYPES AND CHARACTERISTICS

DISPLACEMENT AND PLANING HULLS

Displacement

The fact that any body at rest in the water displaces its own weight of water is known as the Archimedes Principle and forms the basis for measuring displacement in boats.

For a boat, the ***displacement*** is defined as the weight of water the boat displaces when the boat is at rest, and it is simply equal to the weight of the boat (including everything in or on the boat).

Displacement Hulls

A boat that continues to displace her own weight in the water as she moves forward at speed is considered to have a displacement hull design. This is sometimes called full displacement to distinguish from semi-displacement (described later).

It is helpful to consider the ratio of boat speed to boat length, which is commonly called the ***speed to length ratio*** (**SLR**) and is expressed as in equation 1-1.

$$\text{SLR} = \frac{\text{S (Knots)}}{\sqrt{\text{LWL (Feet)}}} = \frac{\text{S (Knots)}}{\sqrt{\text{LWL (Meters)}} \times 3.28}$$

Where: SLR = Speed to Length Ratio
S = Speed
LWL = Length at Waterline

EQUATION 1-1: Speed to Length Ratio

A boat with a displacement hull moving through the water creates a wave that acts to limit its maximum speed. This speed is related to the distance between surface waves on water, where the waves advance at a speed of 1.34 times the square root of the distance between crests.

1.34 is, for all intents and purposes, the maximum SLR achievable in equation 1-1, and it can be used for calculating the maximum speed achievable by a typical full displacement hull. The maximum achievable displacement speed is commonly called the ***hull speed***.

This ratio (i.e., SLR = 1.34) is a general guideline in that some displacement boats, particularly those with long narrow hull designs, can achieve SLRs as high as 1.6 or even higher. For the average recreational boat, however, 1.34 is a good number. Keep in mind this is a maximum and not the most efficient speed. An efficient cruising speed will be at an SLR of something more like 1.0 to 1.2. Again, the boat design will affect these numbers. This is not an absolute number but it does represent a practical limit beyond which adding more horsepower does little or no good.

Substituting 1.34 for SLR and reorganizing equation 1-1, we get an equation that, when evaluated, will yield the approximate maximum displacement speed (hull speed) for a given hull length.

$$S \text{ (Knots)} = 1.34 \times \sqrt{\text{LWL (ft)}}$$
$$= 1.34 \times \sqrt{\text{LWL (m)}} \times 3.28$$

Where: S = Speed
LWL = Length at waterline

EQUATION 1-2: Hull Speed

From equation 1-2 we calculate that a 20-foot boat has a maximum displacement speed of around 6 knots, a 40-footer 8.5 knots, and an 80-footer 12 knots.

A displacement hull can be driven at such speeds with amazingly little power compared to a semi-displacement or planing hull type (described next). For example, a 50-foot boat displacing 55,000 pounds cruising at 7.8 knots (SLR 1.1) will require just 55 shaft horsepower. At 9.5 knots (SLR 1.34) it will require 100 horsepower. Tables showing achievable speeds with various displacement to horsepower combinations are given later in the Mechanical chapter.

The displacement hull form is the only choice for long-range offshore cruising because of both its ability to carry heavy loads—including lots of fuel—and to be thrifty with the use of that fuel.

Speed at Differing SLRs

Table 1-1 uses the SLR equation to calculate speeds achievable at different SLRs for various lengths of boat.

Planing Hulls

With adequate power and the correct hull shape, a boat can speed up enough to rise up out of the bow wave and plane on the top of the water using hydrodynamic lift. At this point, hydrodynamic lift rather than buoyancy is supporting the boat A hull that is designed for this purpose is a *planing* hull and is characterized by a relatively flat bottom aft.

Length		Speed (knots)							
		Full Disp		Semi Disp		Planing			
LWL (Ft)	LWL (M)	SLR 1.1	SLR 1.34	SLR 2.0	SLR 2.5	SLR 3.0	SLR 4.0	SLR 6.0	SLR 8.0
5	1.5	2.2	3.0	4.5	5.6	6.7	8.9	13.4	17.9
6	1.8	2.4	3.3	4.9	6.1	7.3	9.8	14.7	19.6
7	2.1	2.6	3.5	5.3	6.6	7.9	10.6	15.9	21.2
8	2.4	2.8	3.8	5.7	7.1	8.5	11.3	17.0	22.6
9	2.7	3.0	4.0	6.0	7.5	9.0	12.0	18.0	24.0
10	3.0	3.2	4.2	6.3	7.9	9.5	12.6	19.0	25.3
12	3.7	3.5	4.6	6.9	8.7	10.4	13.9	20.8	27.7
14	4.3	3.7	5.0	7.5	9.4	11.2	15.0	22.4	29.9
16	4.9	4.0	5.4	8.0	10.0	12.0	16.0	24.0	32.0
18	5.5	4.2	5.7	8.5	10.6	12.7	17.0	25.5	33.9
20	6.1	4.5	6.0	8.9	11.2	13.4	17.9	26.8	35.8
22	6.7	4.7	6.3	9.4	11.7	14.1	18.8	28.1	37.5
24	7.3	4.9	6.6	9.8	12.2	14.7	19.6	29.4	39.2
26	7.9	5.1	6.8	10.2	12.7	15.3	20.4	30.6	40.8
28	8.5	5.3	7.1	10.6	13.2	15.9	21.2	31.7	42.3
30	9.1	5.5	7.3	11.0	13.7	16.4	21.9	32.9	43.8
33	10.1	5.7	7.7	11.5	14.4	17.2	23.0	34.5	46.0
36	11.0	6.0	8.0	12.0	15.0	18.0	24.0	36.0	48.0
40	12.2	6.3	8.5	12.6	15.8	19.0	25.3	37.9	50.6
43	13.1	6.6	8.8	13.1	16.4	19.7	26.2	39.3	52.5
46	14.0	6.8	9.1	13.6	17.0	20.3	27.1	40.7	54.3
50	15.2	7.1	9.5	14.1	17.7	21.2	28.3	42.4	56.6
55	16.8	7.4	9.9	14.8	18.5	22.2	29.7	44.5	59.3
60	18.3	7.7	10.4	15.5	19.4	23.2	31.0	46.5	62.0
70	21.3	8.4	11.2	16.7	20.9	25.1	33.5	50.2	66.9
80	24.4	8.9	12.0	17.9	22.4	26.8	35.8	53.7	71.6
100	30.5	10.0	13.4	20.0					
120	36.6	11.0	14.7	21.9					
150	45.7	12.2	16.4						
200	61.0	14.1	19.0						
500	152.4	22.4	30.0						
600	182.9	24.5	32.8						
800	243.8	28.3	37.9						
1000	304.8	31.6	42.4						

TABLE 1-1: Speed to Length Ratios

Hydrodynamic lift is somewhat analogous to aerodynamic lift for an airplane. It is the same force that keeps a water skier on top of the water.

The planing boat requires much more power than the full displacement style of boat and also must be much lighter to enable it to "get out of the hole" and onto plane. As such, it will have much less load-carrying capacity, as well as much less range than a full displacement boat even if traveling at displacement speeds.

A planing hull will generally begin to come up onto plane at an SLR of around 2 to 2.5 and can achieve speeds much greater than that, given enough horsepower.

At speeds between SLRs of approximately 1.34 to 2.5, the boat is in transition from displacement to planing and is being supported by both buoyancy and hydrodynamic force. The hydrodynamic lift component increases as the speed increases.

Consider the 50-foot 55,000-pound boat we previously figured we could drive at an SLR of 1.35 or 9.5 knots with 100 horsepower. The boat would get on plane around 18 knots (SLR 2.5). Accomplishing this would require a planing hull design and about 700 horsepower. That's seven times the power needed to drive the boat from an SLR of 1.35 to an SLR of 2.0!

Semi-Displacement Hulls

Many recreational boats today are specifically designed to operate in the transition region between displacement and planing mode. This design is said to be a *semi-displacement* boat.

The idea here is to have a boat that has greater load-carrying capacity and range and better sea-keeping ability than planing designs while achieving greater speeds than the full displacement designs. This hull design will typically have more draft than a full planing design but not as much as a full displacement design.

Considerably more horsepower is required to drive one of these hulls at semi-displacement speeds than to drive at displacement speed (but less than for planing speeds). This naturally reduces the range of the vessel as compared to a displacement design.

Consider again our 50-foot 55,000-pound boat with the hull speed of 9.5 knots achieved with 100 horsepower. At a semi-displacement speed of, say, 14 knots (SLR 2.0) we would require about 370 horsepower. That's almost four times the power to get just a 50 percent speed increase!

HULL SHAPES

THREE BASIC HULL FORMS

Boat hulls are variations of three basic shapes: the *flat*, the *round*, and the *vee*. More complex hull forms are variations of these three types.

Round Bottom Hull

The round bottom is always a full displacement hull that is generally considered to have the softest ride in rough water. A round hull is, however, very susceptible to roll.

A properly designed round bottom hull will generally be the most efficient displacement hull and will achieve hull speed with the least horsepower, although the vee shape hull can be almost as efficient.

A round bottom hull with adequate ballast will not have a great deal of initial stability but can have very high ultimate stability. Initial and ultimate stability are explained in the next section of this chapter.

Flat Bottom Hull

Flat bottom hulls are found in both displacement and planing applications. Examples of flat bottom displacement hulls include a barge or some houseboats. Generally, flat bottom displacement boats confine themselves to calm inland waters. The flat bottom is usually the easiest hull type to get on plane but lacks directional stability and has a bumpy ride on rough water, with a tendency to slam.

Vee Bottom Hull

The vee bottom hull can be found in all three hull types—displacement, semi-displacement, and planing. A displacement hull with a vee bottom will not be subject to as much roll but will not have a soft a ride as the round bottom hull. The ride can be softened somewhat by rounding the chines. A chine, which has been rounded, is sometimes called a soft chine, and a chine with a sharp angle is called a hard chine.

The deadrise angle is the angle between the bottom of the boat and horizontal (level) and is normally in the range of 5 to 15 degrees.

For planing in very rough water, the **deep vee** was developed with a deadrise often greater than 20 degrees to allow the boat to cut through the waves. The deep vee requires more power to get on plane than flatter hull designs. It tracks very well in all types of seas, so much so that it can be difficult to turn.

Another development in vee shape hulls is the **modified vee**, which has a deadrise decreasing from forward to aft. This gives it a sharp entry for cutting through waves and a flatter stern section to aid in planing. When only one deadrise angle is specified for a modified vee, it is normally given as the deadrise at the stern.

OTHER HULL FORMS

Cathedral Hull

The cathedral hull is a planing hull that eliminates some of the slamming action associated with flat hulls while retaining much of the efficiency of the flat hull. This design also tracks well and provides high initial stability.

Sailboat Hull

The sailing monohull is characterized by a deep keel that reduces slipping sideways (leeway) from to the force of wind. It can be rounded or vee shape with a hard or soft chine.

Trimaran

The trimaran is usually associated with sailboats and consists of a main hull with two outriggers, one on each side, that provide high initial stability. The main hull and outriggers can be any of the three primary types of hull designs, and can be designed for displacement or planing use.

The outriggers allow the use of long slim hulls, which are faster than hulls that have a wide beam.

Type ⇒ Shape ⇓	Displacement	Semi-Displacement	Planing
Round Bottom			
Vee Bottom			
Flat Bottom			
S/L Ratio	< 1.35	1.35 - 2.5	> 2.5
D/L Ratio	> 300	225 - 300	180 - 225

TABLE 1-2: Hull Shapes Versus Hull Types

Catamaran

The catamaran eliminates the center hull of the Trimaran. It has two main hulls supporting a superstructure that spans the two hulls.

In recreational boats the catamaran has been mostly used in sailing, particularly in the charter trade, but power catamarans are quickly catching on in all sizes from runabouts to yachts.

Like the trimaran the catamaran has the advantages of high initial stability and with the long narrow hulls can achieve higher speeds than a wider hull with same amount of sail or engine horsepower.

Hull Type Considerations

The displacement hull is heavier than the semi-displacement hull, which in turn is heavier than the planing hull. The displacement to length ratios (DLRs) in table 1-2 are typical. (Note: DLRs are explained in the Design Ratios section on page 34).

The prospective boat buyer wants to be well aware of just what kind of hull he or she is buying. It is not unheard of for an underpowered planing boat to be marketed as a semi-displacement boat since it will only operate at semi-displacement speeds. The buyer is shortchanged because he or she is not getting the displacement, range, and load-carrying capacity of a true semi-displacement design.

Similarly, if you buy a semi-displacement design with just enough power to drive at displacement speeds, you lose the benefits of the full displacement design. This includes such things as more headroom in the engine room, more ultimate stability, and more weight-carrying capacity.

DESIGN PARAMETERS

DISPLACEMENT

As mentioned earlier, for a boat, the **displacement** is defined as the weight of water the boat displaces when the boat is at rest, and it is simply equal to the weight of the boat (including everything in or on the boat).

Displacement changes depending on how the boat is loaded with fuel, water, supplies, people, etc. Manufacturers will quite often quote displacement without fuel, water, or any other load, sometimes even excluding items such as an outboard engine. The actual or working displacement after loading the boat can be as much as 50 percent more than the dry displacement in some extreme cases, particularly with smaller boats. This has serious implications both for seakeeping ability as well as for trailering. This needs to be kept in mind when comparing boats, as they should be compared using the same basis for displacement.

Many of the equations and tables that follow use displacement as a variable, and if they are used to compare boats, it follows that the displacements used should be on the same basis.

These additional loads can be calculated with a fair degree of accuracy just by inventorying everything that is expected to be required for the typical voyage and adding up their weights. Weights for fuel and water can be derived from tables included later in this reference manual.

A brief checklist for some things to include when calculating total displacement is shown in table 1-3.

For weight of fuel see equation 1-15 on page 41. Water weighs 8.34 pounds per gallons. In addition to being useful

Additional optional equipment installed such as generator sets, water makers, washers, etc.	☐
Anchor and anchor rode.	☐
Any moveable furniture	☐
A tender (dinghy) if on board	☐
Water and fuel	☐
Crew —assume 160 lbs (73 kg) per person	☐
Food and supplies for number of days at sea —figure around 5 to 7 lbs (2.3 to 3.2 kg) per day per crew member.	☐
Personal items —about 5 lbs (2.3 kg) per day per crew member	☐
Miscellaneous	☐

TABLE 1-3: Displacement Calculation Checklist

for comparing boats, these numbers are also useful for determining the size and displacement of boat needed to meet your requirements.

STABILITY

Forces Affecting Stability

Stability refers to the ability of a boat to remain upright in the water under various conditions. Stability results from the interplay of two forces; these being the force of buoyancy upward, which is counteracted by the downward force of the boat's weight. It is primarily a function of the hull shape, the amount the boat is heeled, and the distribution of weight in the boat.

A boat together with its load has a *center of gravity* (**CG**), the point through which the boat's weight can be considered to act. This would be the point from which you could suspend the boat in any orientation and it would remain in perfect balance. This point does not move relative to the boat itself unless something on the boat shifts such as a load or water in the bilge.

Similarly, the *center of buoyancy* (**CB**) is a point through which the upward force of buoyancy can be considered to act. This point is dynamic and moves according to the shape of the water being displaced by the boat at any given angle of heel. Think of it as the center of gravity of the volume of

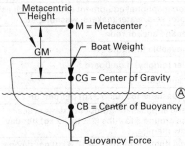

FIGURE 1-4: Stability of Upright Boat

water being displaced. Figure 1-4 shows these points on a boat that is perfectly upright.

Now consider a boat that has rolled to one side, as in figure 1-5. Here we see the CG has remained in the same place relative to the boat but the CB has moved to the right. Now, the CB exerts an upward force as before and the CG exerts a downward force as before, but the forces are not in line and a *righting arm* (**GZ**) has developed, which exerts a counter-clockwise torque acting to right the boat.

The righting arm is calculated as the displacement in pounds times the righting arm length in feet with resulting units of pound feet.

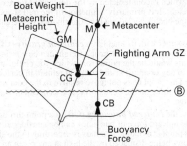

FIGURE 1-5: Stability of Heeled Boat

As the boat heels further to the right, the righting arm will increase up to a point and then will start to decrease as the center of gravity starts to move out over the center of buoyancy. As you can intuitively imagine, when the center of gravity has gone outside of the center of buoyancy, the boat will have a negative righting arm and the forces are now such that they will act to capsize the boat. Once this happens there is no going back!

Figure 1-6 shows a situation where too much load has been placed too high on the boat and the boat has rolled too far. CG is outboard of CB, and this boat is going the rest of the way over.

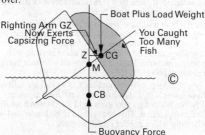

FIGURE 1-6: Stability of a Capsizing Boat

Water (or shifting loads) in the bilge can have a disastrous effect on the boat's stability since, as the boat heels, the water shifts sideways in the direction of heel, effectively shifting the center of gravity outwards and contributing to further heeling.

Metacentric Height

The *metacentric height* (**GM**), best seen in figure 1-5, is a term used by naval architects to help describe the relative stability of a boat. Again referencing figure 1-5, it is apparent that the metacentric height is the distance from the center of gravity to the *metacenter* (**M**), and that it will increase as the righting arm increases and vice-versa.

The metacentric height of an upright vessel can be increased by widening the hull (which moves the CB outward) or by adding ballast low in the hull to lower the center of gravity. In a sailboat ballast may be added to the bottom of a deep keel and may weigh more than a third of the total displacement.

Calculation of the appropriate ballast required for any boat is an extremely important part of the design and plays a most important part in determining the stability (and *safety*) of the boat.

Stability Types

There are two kinds of stability: *initial* (or *form*) stability and *ultimate* (or *reserve*) stability. In general, initial stability is the resistance to heel from an upright position, and ultimate stability is the stability at extreme angles of heel. The initial stability will tend to be influenced mostly by the shape (or form) of the hull in the water, while the ultimate stability will be influenced more by weight distribution or the location of the center of gravity of the boat.

A wide flat boat will have very high initial stability (long righting arm at upright position) and low ultimate stability (short righting arm) when the boat is tipped way over. This vessel is also said to be stiff and will resist heeling with sharp return motions, but if it gets beyond a certain point it will readily capsize.

Conversely, a deep, narrow boat such as a cruising sailboat will have lower initial stability but a very high ultimate stability. Such a design may even right itself from a totally upside down position. This boat is said to be tender and will resist heeling with a gentler return motion.

Comparing Stability

The naval architect calculates the righting moment at various degrees of heel ranging from 0 to 180 degrees (upside down) and from this can construct a graph showing the righting moment versus the amount of heel in degrees. This graph can be an effective way to compare various types of boat and hull designs.

The sketch in figure 1-7 shows hypothetical curves as they might look for four different types of boats. Note how the wide boats such as the catamaran and flat bottom boat show a large initial righting arm that goes rapidly to a negative righting arm as the boat passes 90 degrees.

The powerboat shown can heel to about 105 degrees and still recover. The sailboat shown with heavy ballast at the bottom of the keel will almost right itself from upside down. These curves, however, assume the boats do not have a major load shift or take on water at these extreme angles. If water gets into the hull then all bets are off.

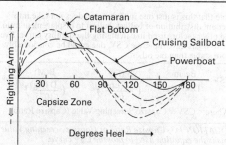

FIGURE 1-7: Stability Curves

Capsize Ratio or Capsize Screening Value

The *capsize screening value* (**CSV**) was developed after the 1979 "fastnet storm" in the Irish Sea where several boats capsized and several lives were lost.

Generally a boat is considered suitable for offshore use if the CSV is less than 2.0. The higher the CSV is above 2.0 the more likely a boat is to capsize in adverse conditions. Notice that this means the hull should not be too wide for a given displacement. The curve in figure 1-8 represents the CSV at 2.0. The safe area is below the curve. Boats that fall above the curve are considered unsafe for offshore use.

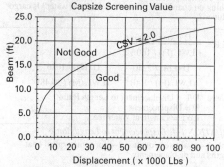

FIGURE 1-8: Capsize Screening Value = 2.0

Note that this is just one indicator and does not take into account distribution of ballast, ballast to displacement ratio, and other factors used in calculating the stability curve. Even if two boats have the same CSV, one could be considerably more stable than the other.

$$CSV = \frac{Beam}{Disp.\ Vol.^{1/3}} = \frac{B\ (Ft)}{\left(\dfrac{D\ (Lbs)}{64}\right)^{1/3}} = \frac{B(M)}{\left(\dfrac{D\ (Kg)}{1025}\right)^{1/3}}$$

Where: CSV = Capsize Screening Value (Capsize Ratio)

EQUATION 1-3: Capsize Ratio or Capsize Screening Value. This is the equation used to plot the CSV curve.

DESIGN RATIOS (COEFFICIENTS OF FORM)
Use of Ratios
In addition to the SLR discussed earlier on page 21, there are several other ratios used by designers that are also useful to the recreational boater seeking to compare one boat to another. When several boats are being compared and one has a ratio or ratios substantially different from the others, a red flag is raised as to why the difference exists.

Displacement to Length Ratio (DLR)
Displacement can be used to compare boats of differing length. Be careful that displacement is on the same basis for all boats being considered. Ask yourself: Is it design weight with nothing on board? Does it include fuel and water? Is cargo included?

$$DLR = \frac{D\ (Long\ Tons)}{(\ LWL\ (Ft)\ /\ 100\ )^3}$$

$$= \frac{D\ (Lbs)\ /\ 2240}{(LWL\ (Ft)\ /\ 100)^3} = \frac{D\ (Kg)\ /\ 1016}{(LWL\ (M)\ /\ 30.48)^3}$$

Where: D/L = Displacement to Length Ratio
        D = Displacement
        LWL = Length at Waterline

EQUATION 1-4: Displacement to Length Ratio

Table 1-4 evaluates equation 1-4 for some typical boat lengths and displacements.

LWL (Ft)	(M)	Disp (Lb)	(Kg)	DLR	LWL (Ft)	(M)	Disp (Lb)	(Kg)	DLR
15	4.6	760	340	100	36	11.0	10000	4500	100
15	4.6	1130	510	150	36	11.0	16000	7300	150
15	4.6	1510	680	200	36	11.0	21000	9500	200
15	4.6	1890	860	250	36	11.0	26000	11800	250
15	4.6	2270	1030	300	36	11.0	31000	14100	300
15	4.6	2650	1200	350	36	11.0	37000	16800	350
15	4.6	3020	1370	400	36	11.0	42000	19100	400
15	4.6	3400	1540	450	36	11.0	47000	21300	450
15	4.6	3780	1710	500	36	11.0	52000	23600	500
18	5.5	1300	590	100	45	13.7	20000	9000	100
18	5.5	2000	910	150	45	13.7	31000	14000	150
18	5.5	2600	1180	200	45	13.7	41000	19000	200
18	5.5	3300	1500	250	45	13.7	51000	23000	250
18	5.5	3900	1770	300	45	13.7	61000	28000	300
18	5.5	4600	2090	350	45	13.7	71000	32000	350
18	5.5	5200	2360	400	45	13.7	82000	37000	400
18	5.5	5900	2680	450	45	13.7	92000	42000	450
18	5.5	6500	2950	500	45	13.7	102000	46000	500
22	6.7	2400	1100	100	54	16.5	35000	16000	100
22	6.7	3600	1600	150	54	16.5	53000	24000	150
22	6.7	4800	2200	200	54	16.5	71000	32000	200
22	6.7	6000	2700	250	54	16.5	88000	40000	250
22	6.7	7200	3300	300	54	16.5	106000	48000	300
22	6.7	8300	3800	350	54	16.5	123000	56000	350
22	6.7	9500	4300	400	54	16.5	141000	64000	400
22	6.7	10700	4900	450	54	16.5	159000	72000	450
22	6.7	11900	5400	500	54	16.5	176000	80000	500
26	7.9	3900	1800	100	64	19.5	59000	27000	100
26	7.9	5900	2700	150	64	19.5	88000	40000	150
26	7.9	7900	3600	200	64	19.5	117000	53000	200
26	7.9	9800	4400	250	64	19.5	147000	67000	250
26	7.9	11800	5400	300	64	19.5	176000	80000	300
26	7.9	13800	6300	350	64	19.5	206000	93000	350
26	7.9	15700	7100	400	64	19.5	235000	107000	400
26	7.9	17700	8000	450	64	19.5	264000	120000	450
26	7.9	19700	8900	500	64	19.5	294000	133000	500
32	9.8	7000	3200	100	78	23.8	106000	48000	100
32	9.8	11000	5000	150	78	23.8	159000	72000	150
32	9.8	15000	6800	200	78	23.8	213000	97000	200
32	9.8	18000	8200	250	78	23.8	266000	121000	250
32	9.8	22000	10000	300	78	23.8	319000	145000	300
32	9.8	26000	11800	350	78	23.8	372000	169000	350
32	9.8	29000	13200	400	78	23.8	425000	193000	400
32	9.8	33000	15000	450	78	23.8	478000	217000	450
32	9.8	37000	16800	500	78	23.8	531000	241000	500

TABLE 1-4: D/L Versus Length and Displacement

Prismatic Coefficient (CP)

The CP is a ratio of the volume of water displaced by the boat to the volume of a prism like shape with a length = LWL and constant cross-section equal to the maximum cross-section of the boat (below the waterline).

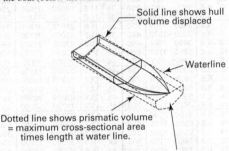

FIGURE 1-9: Prismatic Coefficient

To better explain this, figure 1-9 shows the two volumes used in calculating the prismatic coefficient. The numerator is represented by the solid line and indicates the volume actually displaced by the vessel. The denominator is represented by the dotted line and shows the volume of the maximum boat cross-section times the length of the boat at waterline.

Equation 1-5 is used to calculate the prismatic coefficient.

$$CP = \frac{D \text{ (Volume)}}{MS \times LWL}$$

$$= \frac{D \text{ (Lb)} / 64}{MS \text{ (SqFt)} \times LWL \text{ (Ft)}} = \frac{D \text{ (Kg)} / 1025}{MS \text{ (SqM)} \times LWL \text{ (M)}}$$

Where: CP = Prismatic Coefficient
   D = Displacement Volume (Seawater)
   MS = Midship Section = Underwater Area of
      the Maximum Hull Section
   LWL = Length at Waterline

EQUATION 1-5: Prismatic Coefficient.

Both the numerator and denominator are volumes and may be expressed as either imperial or metric units as long as both are on the same basis. The 64.0 and 1025.0 are densities of seawater; for fresh water use 62.4 and 1000.0, respectively.

A boat with a high prismatic coefficient will have a fairly constant cross-section along its length with a fairly blunt bow and full width transom. A low prismatic coefficient implies a fine tapered hull design with a gradual slimming to both ends of the boat.

Naval architects have established a relationship between the ideal SLR and the CP. In general, faster (i.e., planing) hulls will have higher CPs (0.7) and displacement hulls will have lower CPs (0.5 to 0.6). The CP provides yet another way to compare boats of supposedly similar types. Published values of these relationships differ somewhat, so figure 1-10 shows a curve based on an average of values from different sources.

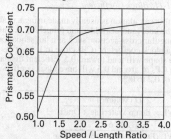

FIGURE 1-10: Prismatic Coefficient Versus SLR

You will need to obtain this number directly from the builder, or you will need design drawings showing the maximum cross-section so you can calculate the maximum cross-section area (MS) yourself.

Block Coefficient (CB)

The CB is similar in concept to the prismatic coefficient. It compares the volume displacement to the volume of a rect-angular block sized to contain the hull. The volumes used for the block coefficient calculation are illustrated in figure 1-11

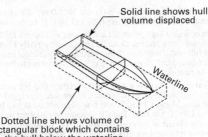

FIGURE 1-11: Block Coefficient

Note that this calculation is usually made using a draft that excludes the keel (and/or rudder and propeller). A hull with a very rectangular cross-section, such as a houseboat or barge, will have a block coefficient (CB) close to 1, whereas a hull with a vee shape will tend toward 0.5. Efficient displacement hulls with CPs of around 0.5 will have block coefficients in the range of 0.2 to 0.3.

$$CB = \frac{D \text{ (Volume)}}{LWL \times \text{Beam Waterline} \times \text{Draft}}$$

$$= \frac{D \text{ (Lb)} / 64}{LWL \text{ (Ft)} \times BWL \text{ (Ft)} \times DH \text{ (Ft)}}$$

$$= \frac{D \text{ (Kg)} / 1025}{LWL \text{ (M)} \times BWL \text{ (M)} \times DH \text{ (M)}}$$

Where: CB = Block Coefficient
D = Displacement (Seawater)
LWL = Length at Waterline
BWL = Beam at Waterline
DH = Draft of Hull (Excluding Keel)

EQUATION 1-6: Block Coefficient

Midship Section Coefficient (CM)

This is the ratio of the midship section area to the area of a bounding rectangle, which encloses the midship section area.

The barge or houseboat would have a CM above 0.90 and a deep vee hull could have a CM in the range of 0.55 to 0.60.

$$CM = \frac{MS}{BWL \times DH}$$

Where: CM = Midship Section Coefficient
MS = Midship Section = Maximum Cross-Sectional Area Below Waterline
BWL = Beam at Waterline
DH = Draft of Hull (Excluding Keel)

EQUATION 1-7: Midship Section Coefficient

A reasonable guess for the average hull would be in the 0.65 to 0.70 range.

Rearranging equation 1-7 for the **midship section** (**MS**) yields equation 1-8. You could use this equation to make a calculated guess at the midship section (MS) to use in equation 1-5 on page 36 to calculate the CP. Equation 1-8 shows 0.65 as an estimated CM.

$$MS = BWL \times DH \times CM = BWL \times DH \times 0.65$$

Where: 0.65 is your guess for the midship section CM

EQUATION 1-8: Calculate Midship Section by Guessing the midship section coefficient CM.

RATIOS FOR SAILBOATS

Sail Area to Displacement (SA/D)

Sail area varies as displacement volume to the 2/3 power. This ratio varies from about 15 to 30 with the higher number generally being the fastest boat. The ratio 15 to 18 is typical for cruising sailboats, the low twenties is fast, and 30 is very fast racing.

$$SA/D = \frac{Sail\ Area}{(Displacement\ Volume)^{2/3}}$$

$$= \frac{SA\ (Sq\ Ft)}{\left(\frac{D\ (Lb)}{64}\right)^{2/3}} = \frac{SA\ (Sq\ M)}{\left(\frac{D\ (Kg)}{1025}\right)^{2/3}}$$

EQUATION 1-9: Sail Area to Displacement

Note that raising the volume displacement to the 2/3 power yields an area that, when divided into the sail area, yields a true dimensionless ratio.

Sail Area to Length (SA/L)

Sail area can also be compared to the boat length squared.

$$SA/L = \frac{Sail\ Area}{Length^2} = \frac{SA\ (Sq\ Ft)}{LWL\ (Ft)^2} = \frac{SA\ (Sq\ M)}{LWL\ (M)^2}$$

EQUATION 1-10: Sail Area to Length

Sail Area to Wetted Surface Area

$$SA/WSA = \frac{Sail\ Area}{Wetted\ Surface\ Area}$$

Where: The areas are expressed as either Sq Ft or Sq M

EQUATION 1-11: Sail Area to Wetted Surface Area

Frictional resistance to movement through the water is related to the underwater surface area of the boat and all appendages such as keel, rudder, etc. A high SA/WSA is desirable in light winds since friction rather than wave action will be the dominant slowing force at slow speeds (SLR considerably less than 1.34). In light winds, an SA/WSA ratio under 2.0 tends to be slow, and above 2.5 is quite fast.

OTHER COMPARATIVE RATIOS

For purposes of comparing boats there are many other ratios or numbers that can be useful.

Length to Beam Ratio (LBR)

$$LBR = \frac{Length}{Beam}$$

EQUATION 1-12: Length to Beam Ratio

The LBR uses the length at waterline and the beam at waterline. They may be expressed in any units (feet or meters).

Ballast Ratio (BR)

$$BR = \frac{Weight\ Ballast}{Displacement}$$

EQUATION 1-13: Ballast Ratio

The ballast ratio is useful when comparing similar type boats but can be misleading in that a higher ballast ratio does not necessarily imply higher stability. Stability depends on placement of ballast as it affects the location of the overall center of gravity, and it also depends on hull shape, so don't use this for much other than comparative purposes.

Power to Weight Ratio (PWR)

$$PW = \frac{Horsepower}{Displacement}$$

EQUATION 1-14: Power to Weight Ratio

This is not a true dimensionless ratio but it is useful for comparisons.

Fuel to Displacement Ratio (FDR)

$$FDR = \frac{Weight\ fuel}{Displacement} = \frac{Gallons\ x\ d}{D\ (lbs)} = \frac{Litres\ x\ d}{D\ (kg)}$$

Where: d = 7.0 lbs per gallon for diesel
d = 6.0 lbs per gallon for gasoline
d = 0.84 kg per liter for diesel
d = 0.74 kg per liter for gasoline

EQUATION 1-15: Fuel to Displacement Ratio

This will yield the fraction of the boat's weight carried as fuel. Multiply by 100 to get the percentage.

Long-distance cruising boats will probably be greater than 5 percent, coastal cruising boats in the 3 percent range, and very fast boats 1 percent to 2 percent.

Fresh Water to Displacement Ratio (WDR)

This is the fraction of boat weight carried as fresh water. Multiply by 100 to get the percentage.

$$WDR = \frac{Weight\ Water}{Displacement} = \frac{Gallons \times 8.34}{D\ (lb)} = \frac{Liters}{D\ (Kg)}$$

EQUATION 1-16: Fresh Water to Displacement Ratio

Long-distance cruisers will be over 5 percent unless they have a watermaker, in which case they will be as low as 2 percent. Average boats are in the range of 2 percent to 5 percent depending on their usage.

RELATIVITY OF BOAT SIZES AND MEASUREMENTS

As boat size changes there are certain relationships between different boat measurements that generally remain constant. These have been called by various names, such as *Froude's Law of Comparison* or *the Law of Mechanical Similitude*. Some of these are:

- Linear dimensions (such as beam and draft) vary proportionally to length (L).
- Areas will vary as the length squared (L^2). This includes wetted surface area and sail area. Resistance varies with wetted surface area.
- Speed varies as the square root of length ($\sqrt{L}$).
- Weight, displacement, and volume vary as length cubed (L^3). *Corollary*: Cost varies with the displacement and therefore as the length cubed (L^3).

A boat that is twice as long as another boat will:

- Have twice the beam and twice the draft.
- Have four times the sail and wetted surface area.
- Travel $\sqrt{2}$ or 1.4 times faster (displacement hull speed)
- Displace eight times as much.
- *Cost eight times as much!*

BOAT CONSTRUCTION

HULL MATERIALS

General

Today most recreational boats are made from fiberglass, which in the last 50 years has all but replaced wood as the material of choice for hull construction. In addition, some recreational boats are constructed from either steel or aluminum, or a combination of both.

Wood

The structural properties of wood make it an ideal material for use in building boats. It is easy to work with and provides excellent strength for its weight without being too brittle (it will deform to some degree before shattering or failing).

Wood construction is skilled labor intensive, so it does not easily lend itself to assembly line construction techniques. In addition, wood is susceptible to damage by water, particularly rot. These two factors have led to the demise of wood as a primary construction material in most recreational boats. Usually its use is limited to small vessels such as dinghies.

Wood-epoxy construction is another story as it provides a method of constructing wooden boats without the usual problems associated with wood construction. This method is discussed below after the fiberglass topic.

Fiberglass

Introduction

Fiberglass is the dominant construction material for building recreational boats. It is much more resistant to water damage than other materials (although not entirely) and with proper design, construction and maintenance, can be expected to last for 50 years or more. It lends itself to assembly line construction techniques using molds that allow identical hulls to be mass-produced more economically than with any other material.

Fiberglass, although strong, is a relatively flexible material so it must be fairly thick to achieve the stiffness needed. Fiberglass does not handle point loading well, which translates into problems at joins with internal structural members, and greater susceptibility to getting holes punched in your boat. Another downside of fiberglass is that it burns quickly and fiercely.

Fiberglass is so named because it consists of fibers of glass impregnated with a plastic resin that, when cured, binds the glass fibers together. The glass fibers impart the tensile strength to the fiberglass composite. Three different types of resin are used as binder: these being *polyester*, *vinylester*, and *epoxy*. Polyester resin is the most common, primarily because it's cheaper than the others. However, polyester resin doesn't resist water damage as well as vinylester or epoxy, nor is it as strong. As one might expect, vinylester and epoxy are found in higher end and custom boats, although this is not always the case.

Fiberglass Boat Construction

To construct a fiberglass boat a *plug* is first made, which from the outside looks like a full size model of the hull. Around this, a structure is constructed that, when the plug is removed from the inside, produces a reusable mold, which is then used as a form for laying up one or more hulls. The mold is polished and all imperfections removed, since the surface of the mold is what determines the outside finish quality of the hull. The accurate construction of both the plug and mold is expensive and time-consuming, so this method is only economic when many boats are to be built using the same mold. A mold can run upwards of $500,000 to produce.

Once the mold is constructed the process of placing the fiberglass material in the mold begins. The first step is to spray a layer of **gelcoat** onto the mold to a uniform thickness of from two to three one-hundredths of an inch (0.5 to 0.8 mm). When the hull is removed from the mold, this gelcoat forms the outside (usually white) smooth surface of the hull you see that looks like paint. The gelcoat is a resin similar to the resin in the fiberglass and cures just like it. Vinylester or epoxy resins are preferred over polyester resin in gelcoat because of their superior resistance to water intrusion.

Layers of glass cloth are then placed onto the mold interspersed with and impregnated with resin binder. Properly done, each layer will be placed before the previous layer cures (sets), so the resin mixes together as one cohesive unit like a weld. If a layer is allowed to cure before the next one is placed then there will be a weak bonding between layers, much as if the layers were glued together. This applies to the application after the gelcoat as well. Needless to say, this whole process becomes a major quality control concern.

The glass layers usually consist of some form of glass cloth, the most common of which are **chopped strand mat** (**CSM**) and **woven roving**. CSM consists of 1- to 2-inch (2.5 to 5 cm) glass strands randomly combined to form a cloth of about 1/16 inch (3 mm) thickness. It looks much like the glass fiber insulation you use in your attic but compressed to a thick cloth. Woven roving is woven from much longer strands and will impart considerably more strength to the hull structure. **Fiberglass cloth** is also used in lay-ups and is similar to woven roving except the weave is much finer.

Chopped
Strand Mat

Woven
Roving

FIGURE 1-12: Chopped Strand and Woven Roving Glass Cloth

Figure 1-12 shows chopped strand and woven roving. There are many different types of cloth, however, including some where all the fibers are aligned in one direction, and yet others where the fibers in each direction are in separate layers rather being woven together.

In a well-built hull the first layer to be placed on the gelcoat is usually the smoother chopped strand cloth, so as to eliminate **print through**, where the pattern of the glass cloth shows through to the outside of the gelcoat. Subsequent layers will then usually be a combination of chopped strand and woven roving. Woven roving is more expensive than chopped strand so expect to find chopped strand used in lieu of roving in cheaper boats.

Another technique used is to spray on a kind of slurry with a **chopper gun**, which is a mix of the resin and chopped strands. This method of hull construction has developed a bad reputation, probably due more to lack of uniform application thickness than to the inherently weaker structure (relative to woven roving).

One of the major quality control issues in the laying up process is the elimination of voids both in and between the cloth layers. Quite often the resin is worked into the cloth by hand, which is labor intensive as well as being an environmental problem since the fumes from the resin are toxic.

One method developed to deal with this is a technique called **vacuum bagging**, wherein a layer of plastic film is placed over the resin and glass mat and air is pumped out to produce a vacuum of about –8 psi (–55 kPa). The plastic film pushes down and both irons down the cloth and squeezes out the voids. This method also drastically reduces the fumes, since they are contained by the plastic film and are sucked out by the vacuum pump.

Taking vacuum bagging a step further, a technique called **Seeman Composites Resin Infusion Molding Process** (SCRIMP™) was developed by Bill Seeman. The various layers of mat and roving are placed dry in the mold. A resin delivery system (infusion medium), which allows the vacuum infusion of resin into all parts of the lay-up, is also placed, and then all this is covered with plastic film much as in vacuum bagging. A vacuum is then applied, which draws the resin out of containers and into the lay-up. This results in higher glass to resin ratios and fewer voids, which translates to higher strength. The patent for this process is held by TPI Composites, Inc. Check out www.tpicomposites.com.

Another similar in concept technique is the ***Vacuum Infusion Process*** (**VIP**). This was developed as a sufficiently different alternative to SCRIMP so users would hopefully not have to pay fees to TPI. The cloth is laid and covered with plastic, but with channels left open in foam core material so a vacuum applied at one end will draw epoxy from a drum at the other end through the channels. Over a period of hours the lay-up becomes completely saturated with the resin.

The latest and most sophisticated system to be developed is the ***Virtual Engineered Composite*** (**VEC™**) system developed by Genmar (www.genmar.com). This system uses an inside mold as well as the usual outside mold. The VEC system allows placement of stringers and boat floor so the entire structure is constructed as one piece in one step. The inner mold is lowered and resin is then injected under pressure rather than by vacuum. Computer control of all aspects of the process throughout the injection and curing steps, with more than 500 variables being monitored, ensures high quality and consistency from one hull to the next. The method is being used to produce boats up to 24 feet (7.3m) in length.

Structural Properties of Fiberglass

Let's add an additional complication to fiberglass boat construction. Fiberglass is actually quite a heavy material, with stiffness much less than aluminum on a pound for pound basis. As a result, building boat hulls from solid fiberglass, especially in larger boat sizes, yields a heavier boat, which is not conducive to a planing or semi-displacement design. In order to solve this problem and add strength to the fiberglass hull form, a lightweight core is added in between two layers of fiberglass. So now we place a layer of gelcoat, a layer of fiberglass, a relatively thick layer of lightweight material, and a layer of fiberglass.

Note the deflection in the two different cases shown in figure 1-13. The sandwich construction bends much less, showing greater structural rigidity and strength.

FIGURE 1-13: Comparative Flexure of Solid and Cored Fiberglass

By adding a lightweight core, we can considerably reduce the amount of fiberglass used and end up with the same structural strength albeit with one major caveat. The thinner fiberglass is more susceptible to being punctured by a sharp object, and we all know punctures in boat hulls are not good.

Materials used for the lightweight cores include end grain balsa wood and porous plastic foams. Use of these materials requires considerably more care than solid fiberglass in the lay-up process, particularly within curved hull sections, as the coring material must be forced down in the concave hull shape so that it is in even contact with the outer layer throughout. To get a good bond (which is absolutely required) and to ensure water resistance, the core material must be completely saturated with the resin and applied before the resin is fully cured.

Problems have been encountered with cored construction with delaminating between layers, water rotting out and replacing the core (which also adds to boat weight), and puncturing. In my reading I have found expert opinions that differ to extremes as to whether and where the use of cored fiberglass is warranted. The most contentious issue is with the use of coring in the hull below the waterline.

Because of past problems boat manufacturers have generally moved away from the use of cored hulls below the waterline, but use it from the waterline up, and for decks and superstructure.

Wood-Epoxy

A tried and true method of constructing boats, which combines wood and epoxy to construct very strong light boats, is known as ***wood-epoxy composite*** or ***cold-molded*** construction.

As mentioned previously, wood has physical characteristics that make it one the best materials for building boats. But it also has the well-known problems of susceptibility to sea organisms, dry rot, and breakdown in the continued presence of water. Impregnating wood with epoxy can eliminate all these problems thus putting the construction of wood-epoxy boats on an equal footing with the other construction methods and materials. Certainly, for one-off construction, this material deserves serious consideration.

Epoxy is the strongest and most water resistant of the resins used in boat building and its use combined with wood provides superior resistance to water penetration as well as excellent impact and abrasion resistance. The wood provides natural insulation so that interior insulation may not be required as it is with steel, aluminum, and in some cases fiberglass.

A traditional wood boat has planking attached to the frame with some kind of metal fasteners. In wood-epoxy construction, the planking is attached with fasteners too, but it is also impregnated with the epoxy that, when it cures, effectively glues the planks to the frame as well as to each other. In the traditional boat the fasteners can corrode and work their way loose, but with the epoxy they will be much less likely to do so, and even if they do corrode or come loose, the epoxy bond is far stronger than the fasteners were in the first place. Ultimately, the fasteners are rendered unnecessary once the epoxy has set.

The fact that the wood planks are bonded to each other makes the hull behave as a single unit whereas the traditional wooden planks act independently of one another. This has a very positive effect on impact resistance since the epoxy bonded plank has the support of adjacent planks to prevent failure.

To appreciate how much this helps, try jumping on the center of an 8-foot long 2-inch by 4-inch board lying flat and supported at each end by a saw horse. You will almost certainly break the board, maybe without even jumping. If you fasten another 2-inch by 4-inch board securely to either side of it, and then jump on it, you probably can't break it no matter now hard you try.

There are different ways of actually carrying out this type of construction, but the most common method is to build an upside down mold of wooden frames (like bulkheads) with strips of wood that run longitudinally attached to the frames. The wood-epoxy hull is then constructed onto this frame with transverse framing members being saturated with epoxy and placed first. After this the planking is epoxied and fastened to the framing. Finally layers of fiberglass cloth are applied also using epoxy. This is a simplified description of this construction method, and you can find a much better one at www.coveyisland.com. This is the website for Covey Island Boatworks in Nova Scotia, which specializes in wood-epoxy boat building.

Steel

As a material for boat hulls, steel has the decided advantage of being the strongest. There are some new composites that might be stronger and some other metals like copper-nickel that can compete with steel in strength, but they are very expensive and generally not used in recreational boats.

Steel isn't used much in recreational boats under 40 feet (12 meters), and it isn't seen in mass-produced boats either. Steel boats tend to be custom designed and built, although do-it-yourself steel boat designs and kits have been popularized by designers such as Bruce Roberts-Goodson. His website at www.bruceroberts.com has designs for metal sail and power boats ranging from 20 feet (6 meters) to over 100 feet (30 meters).

For all intents and purposes, steel doesn't burn, a significant advantage in case of fire at sea. Also, when repairs to steel are needed, facilities with reasonably skilled welders can be found almost anywhere in the world.

Rust has been one of the main problems with steel in the past, and this as much as anything has tended to limit its use to commercial boats where a little rust showing doesn't get the owners nearly as upset as your average yacht owner. Modern protective coatings have largely mitigated this problem, although you still have to watch for scratches and scrapes through to bare steel and take corrective action.

The other main disadvantage of steel is that it is heavy; this fact alone tends to make it less desirable for semi-displacement and planing craft where weight is a major performance factor. Steel boats can plane, but they will generally be heavier and consequently require more power. The best fit for steel is in full displacement hulls where added weight doesn't carry anywhere near the penalty it does with planing designs.

Many custom yachts are built with steel hulls and aluminum superstructures to lessen weight with the added benefit of lowering the center of gravity. Special care must be taken at the juncture of the two dissimilar metals to prevent galvanic corrosion.

Steel, more than any other material, can withstand abuse like running aground on rocks or coral, being driven ashore in a storm, or even a collision with another vessel. Numerous examples exist of steel boats breaking loose from moorings in hurricanes along with fiberglass boats, where the glass boats were pounded to pieces and the steel boats were just banged up.

Aluminum

Aluminum has many of the advantages of steel without the disadvantages of heavy weight and rust. Pound for pound, aluminum is much stronger than steel, so aluminum hulls can be designed to be much lighter. In fact, aluminum hulls can be made as light as solid fiberglass hulls and this favors its use in semi-displacement and planing hulls.

Like steel, aluminum conducts heat (or cold) readily and will almost certainly require insulating on the insides of the hull and superstructure, particularly in colder climates or where air conditioning will be used.

Aluminum is much more fire resistant than fiberglass but less so than steel. Aluminum can melt at temperatures of about 1220 degrees Fahrenheit (660 degrees Celsius).

Unpainted aluminum does oxidize but the oxidation actually provides a sealing layer, which protects it from further oxidation. If you don't mind how it looks, you don't have to paint your aluminum boat and that can save considerable money on paint and future maintenance. The hull below the water-line still has to be painted with anti-fouling paint though. Aluminum is susceptible to galvanic and/or electrolytic corrosion action. Galvanic action occurs when two different metals come in contact and a small electrical current flows between them, inducing corrosion. Electrolytic action occurs primarily in marinas where either the shore power or the boat is improperly grounded. Nearby boats with improper wiring can induce problems also.

Aluminum can be cut much more easily than steel and much can be done with ordinary carpenters' tools. Welding aluminum is more difficult than welding steel and requires a higher level of expertise as well as more specialized equipment.

Aluminum can take considerable abuse (although not quite as much as steel), and because of this is used in many smaller production runabouts and canoes due to its toughness and resistance to puncturing. In these smaller sizes, some hulls or hull parts can almost be stamped into shape, which is con-ducive to mass production. In larger boats, aluminum tends to be used only in custom designs. Building a single boat in aluminum is probably cheaper than building an equivalent boat in fiberglass, since there is no need for the plug and mold needed for fiberglass construction.

Other Materials

Numerous alternatives to fiberglass are being developed, some of which are being used now both in racing sailboats as well as higher end yachts. The techniques are similar to fiberglass but instead of glass, materials such as graphite and Kevlar are used. For example, layers of Kevlar can be combined with layers of glass. Newer and better alternatives for the binding resins are also being developed.

Alternative metals include both bronze and copper-nickel. Both have the advantage of being almost completely corrosion resistant as well as not needing paint or even anti-fouling paint. Both materials are almost as strong as steel. Prohibitive cost is probably the primary reason these materials are not popular for building metal boats.

Characteristics of Boat Building Materials Compared

Tables 1-5 and 1-6 on page 52 show strengths of some typical, and some not so typical, materials used in building boats. This data is meant to give an idea of the relative strengths and stiffness of the various materials and also to show how these different materials compare on a weight adjusted basis.

The first columns, labeled Tensile Strength, show the range of forces per unit area required to cause failure in tension. This is like the force in pounds, pulling apart on each end of a cylinder or rope of 1-inch square cross-section, which causes the material to break. The equivalent metric unit is megapascals (mPa). A Pascal is 1 Newton (force) per square meter.

The columns labeled Stiffness (Modulus of Elasticity) give a range of values that are measures of the stiffness of the material. Higher values indicate increased stiffness, or less flexibility.

The four columns that show strength and stiffness to weight are simply the values in the first four columns divided by the Typical Density column.

The values in these tables are averages of values taken from several sources and they are meant for informative and comparative purposes only.

Some things to note:

- There are other measures of strength, including compressive strength, shear strength, resistance to point loading and impact, etc., all of which are considered in boat design just as in the design of any structure.
- E-Glass composite is the normal fiberglass used in boat construction.
- The values are given as ranges to demonstrate how composite and fiber strengths can vary substantially, depending on the orientation and length of fibers, along with many other factors. In particular, note the very wide range of strengths for the E-Glass composite.

Basic Properties of Fibers and Other Engineering Materials U.S. Units								
Material	Tensile Strength (psi x 1000)		Stiffness (Modulus of Elasticity) (psi x 1,000,000)		Typical Density Lb/CuFt	Tensile Strength to Weight		Stiffness to Weight x 1000	
	Fr	To	Fr	To		Fr	To	Fr	To
Metal and Wood									
Mild Steel	59	65	29.9	29.9	512	120	130	58	58
Stainless Steel	116		28.4		487	240	0	58	0
Aluminum Alloys	35	58	10.0	15.5	168	160	340	59	92
Titanium	65	145	16.0	16.2	281	230	520	57	58
Wood	3	28	0.7	2.0	35	90	800	20	56
Fiber and Resin Composites									
E-Glass Composite	15	167	1.2	6.5	94	160	1,780	13	69
S-Glass Composite	100	261	4.2	7.7	106	940	2,460	40	73
Kevlar Composite	58	247	3.2	9.4	88	660	2,810	36	107
Graphite Composite	110	357	11.5	23.5	100	1,100	3,580	115	235
Spectra Composite	168		9.4		82	2,050	0	115	0
Fibers only									
E-Glass Fiber	348	493	10.0	10.4	156	2,230	3,160	64	67
S-Glass Fiber	500		12.5		156	3,210	0	80	0
Aramid Fiber	450	522	8.7	26.1	94	4,810	5,580	93	279
Graphite Fiber	290	769	23.2	63.8	112	2,580	6,850	207	568

TABLE 1-5: Comparison of Properties of Various Construction Materials

- E-Glass composite is quite flexible (low stiffness) relative to other materials, which is why fiberglass hulls require more stiffening with stringers than metal hulls.
- Aluminum and fiberglass and better grades of wood have greater tensile strength than steel on a per unit weight basis.

Basic Properties of Fibers and Other Engineering Materials Metric Units									
Material	Tensile Strength (MPa)		Stiffness (Modulus of Elasticity) (Mpa)		Typical Density (g/cc)	Tensile Strength to Weight		Stiffness to Weight	
	Fr	To	Fr	To		Fr	To	Fr	To
Metal and Wood									
Mild Steel	410	450	206	206	8.2	50	50	30	30
Stainless Steel	800		196		7.8	100	0	30	0
Aluminum Alloys	240	400	69	107	2.7	90	150	30	40
Titanium	450	1000	110	112	4.5	100	220	20	20
Wood	20	190	5	13	0.6	40	340	10	20
Fiber and Resin composites									
E-Glass Composite	100	1150	8	45	1.5	70	770	10	30
S-Glass Composite	690	1800	29	53	1.7	410	1060	20	30
Kevlar Composite	400	1700	22	65	1.4	290	1210	20	50
Graphite Composite	760	2460	79	162	1.6	480	1540	50	100
Spectra Composite	1158		65		1.3	880		50	
Fibers only									
E-Glass Fiber	2400	3400	69	72	2.5	960	1360	30	30
S-Glass Fiber	3450		86		2.5	1380	0	30	0
Aramid Fiber	3100	3600	60	180	1.5	2070	2400	40	120
Graphite Fiber	2000	5300	160	440	2.5	1110	2940	90	240

TABLE 1-6: Comparison of Properties of Various Construction Materials.

BOAT STRUCTURAL CONSIDERATIONS

Keel

The *keel* is the boat's backbone and runs fore and aft down the bottom centerline of the hull. In traditional wood and metal boats, this is the structural member that bears the weight of the boat and is usually the first member to be laid in the construction process. The other structural members are then attached to the keel.

In fiberglass boat construction there is often no traditional type of keel, since the hull is molded in one piece, which together with the internal structure forms a *monocoque* structure. Even though there is no keel structural member, the bottom centerline of the hull is still called the keel.

This part of the boat must be reinforced and have greater thickness than the rest of the hull since it will take all the weight when the boat is grounded. The prospective boat buyer must pay particular attention to the construction and condition of the keel.

Bulkheads and Stringers

Except for very small craft, boats usually require internal *stringers*, which run fore and aft (lengthwise direction) to provide additional stiffening to the hull. This is particularly true for fiberglass boats because of the flexibility of fiberglass, although this need is offset somewhat by the use of cored fiberglass, which adds to stiffness.

Additionally, *bulkheads* that run athwartships (across the hull) are needed to reduce twisting motion in the hull as well as imparting transverse strength. They range from a solid wall, which may occupy the entire cross-section of the hull and may have openings for doors, to members called *ring frames* installed around the perimeter of the hull.

It is beyond the scope of this handbook (and the author's knowledge) to specify how many and of what size structural members (scantlings) like these should be. The only two books I have found that address this subject in a manner comprehensible to someone other than a naval architect are *The Nature of Boats* and *Elements of Boat Strength* (see bibliography). Both are written by Dave Gerr, who is a well-known and respected naval architect. Read *The Nature of Boats* first; it's an interesting book, and introduces structural aspects of boat design. Then if you are more technically inclined and really want to get into it, obtain the *Elements* book.

Deck

The deck is often thought of as something that just sits on top of the hull and only needs to be fastened well enough so it doesn't fall off. Nothing could be further from the truth; the deck is as much a part of the structure of the boat as the bulkheads and stringers. In fact, if you think about it, it is a bulkhead, except that it's horizontal instead of vertical.

When the boat encounters rough going, the forces on the hull are transmitted to the internal structural members and upwards to the deck as well. So the join between the hull, the bulkheads and the deck becomes an area that merits careful consideration. Also, the design and construction of the deck itself are important. If you're buying a used boat, this is an area where you should look closely for problems with cracking and failure of screws or bolts.

A good hull to deck join on a fiberglass boat will have both surfaces bolted (rather than screwed) together with a high-grade marine adhesive (3M-5200) between the surfaces. Screws are much easier to install but don't hold well in fiberglass and will work loose under constant flexing.

RECREATIONAL BOATS

BOAT TYPES

General

Boats cannot be classified nicely into just one "type" since there are so many styles and types of boats that several overlap. For example, a trawler can be an aft cabin, a double cabin, or a pilothouse type, and a sport fisherman is typically a flying bridge sedan type.

Here I classify boats as small power, medium size power, or sail, and then show some examples of specific types within those classifications.

Ship

There is no exact definition of what is a ship as opposed to a boat. The Collision Regulations differentiate between boats greater than or less than 20 meters (65.6 ft) in length. It seems to be generally accepted in the boating community that a ship is a boat greater than 20 meters (66 ft) in length.

Yacht

Again, no exact definition exists for a yacht, but generally a recreational sailboat or powerboat longer than say 50 feet (15 m) might be considered a yacht; certainly most people would call an 80-footer a yacht. As a rule a yacht will be a larger vessel while a medium size boat will be called a cruiser or trawler.

SMALL POWERBOATS

Here we'll consider small powerboats around 30 feet (9 m) in length or less. As a general rule, boats of this size are trailerable and are powered by outboard, sterndrive, or inboard engines. Water jet power has become more common in recent years. Usually boats in this size category use gasoline engines, rather than diesel.

Runabouts

The term runabout refers generally to smaller boats in the 15- to 25-foot (5 to 8 m) range. These typically are planing boats with outboard or sterndrive (also called inboard/outboard or outdrive) propulsion. There are many variations of these with special designs for such diverse activities as water skiing, river running, racing, fishing, etc. Some examples of runabouts follow.

Bowrider

Photo of an LXi 208 (Courtesy Larson Boats)

The ***bowrider*** is an all-purpose runabout with an open bow that allows seating forward in the bow. The boat in the picture is a sterndrive model. Outboards models are available as well, and jet drives have also become more popular in recent years. This type of boat can be used for skiing and fishing and is almost always made of fiberglass. This boat type with a sterndrive is the most popular model of runabout for general purpose use.

Cuddy

Photo of a Cabrio 220 (Courtesy Larson Boats)

The cuddy style of runabout has a forward enclosed ***cuddy*** cabin. In smaller boats this would contain vee berths and in larger models can include a toilet with shower as well as a small galley. Suitable for overnight camping but at the cost of the open space found in the bow riders or deck boats. These can be powered by an outboard or sterndrive and are almost always made with fiberglass.

Deck Boat

Photo of an Escape 214 (Courtesy Larson Boats)
The deck boat has an open single level deck from bow to stern that allows free movement fore and aft. The open bow area is wider and less vee shaped than that of a bowrider. Outboard or sterndrive powered. These are usually constructed from fiberglass but sometimes from aluminum.

Fishing Boat—All-Purpose

Photo of an aluminum 18 Pro Sport. (Courtesy Lund Boat Company)
The all-purpose fishing boat is suited to many types of fishing and will usually have an open bow like a bowrider, often with a raised swivel seat in the open bow and sometimes another raised swivel seat aft. It is equipped with equipment specific to fishing, such as live wells and rod holders and storage lockers. Small boats dedicated to fishing usually are outboard powered since this allows better access to the stern for retrieving fish, and the transom can be used to mount a

second smaller outboard motor (trolling motor) that is used for trolling at slow speeds. These are made of either aluminum or fiberglass.

Jon Boat

Photo of a Jon Boat (Courtesy Lund Boat Company)
The Jon Boat is a small economical outboard powered boat with a flat bottom hull used primarily by fishermen, hunters, and campers. They are not particularly fast and not suitable for open water. These are usually made of aluminum.

Bass Boat

Photo of a 185VX Tour Edition. (Courtesy Ranger Boats)
These are outboard powered and are designed to get to where the fish are in a hurry, as many of these are capable of speeds well in excess of 50 miles per hour (80 kph). The bass boat has a vee hull with a low deadrise and very shallow draft. It is usually made of fiberglass.

Center Console

This is a variation of the runabout, which has a console located in the center of the boat such that crew can move freely around both sides fore and aft. This style is favored by fishermen because of good access to all sides of the boat. It is

Photo of a 190 Nantucket Center Console (Courtesy Boston Whaler, Inc.)

also quite popular with police and park rangers. It is usually outboard powered.

Ski Boat

Photo of an Air Nautique 216 (Courtesy Correct Craft Ski Nautique)

Boats dedicated to water skiing or wake boarding are usually inboard powered, which allows the propeller to be well under the hull out of the way of skiers. This boat has lockers for ski/wakeboard and equipment storage as well as attachments for tow ropes. The boat in the picture has a tower for the tow rope, which aids wake-boarders performing aerial maneuvers.

Fish and Ski

The fish and ski boat is a boat designed for both purposes, and at minimum will include lockers for storing fishing and ski gear. Specific features for fishing such as a live well may also be included. Usually, as with most small fishing boats, this will be outboard powered.

Inflatable

Photo of a RIB 19 Deluxe (Courtesy Nautica International, Inc.)

Inflatable boats have become more and more popular in the last couple of decades, particularly for use as dinghies on larger craft. They have an inflatable tube around the perimeter, which provides the flotation. A variation of the inflatable (shown above) has a rigid bottom that provides for much better tracking and planing. These are commonly known as a rigid inflatable boat or RIB.

Personal Watercraft (PWC)

Photo of a Yamaha FX (Courtesy Yamaha Motor Corporation)

Jetskis or *WaveRunners* fall in the category of PWCs. These are small, fast, highly maneuverable, water jet powered boats. Capacity is typically from one to three people. Larger models (three person capacity required) of WaveRunners can pull a water skier.

Note that although jet powered boats are highly maneuverable, they are completely unable to steer without power. This has lead to many accidents since inexperienced operators tend to cut power when confronted by an obstacle, resulting in a complete loss of steerage.

Jet Boat

Photo of an 1875 Jetcraft (Courtesy HARBERCRAFT.COM)

A jet boat is any boat powered by a jet drive. These can range in size anywhere from a PWC to 40-foot plus express cruisers. Several fiberglass bow riders in the 18- to 22-foot range have become available in recent years. Aluminum jet boats like the one shown here have long been popular in the Pacific Northwest and Alaska where semi-submerged logs and debris are common, since they have no propellers or hardware extending below the hull. These are great for river running as well. Jet drives are not as efficient as propellers at speeds under 25 knots.

Pontoon Boat

*Photo of an 1885 Sport Classic Pontoon Boat
(Courtesy Crestliner, Inc.)*
The pontoon boat is basically a flat platform built on two
pontoons or **sponsons,** which provides plenty of deck space
for a given length of boat. The pontoons are usually made
of aluminum and are streamlined and shaped to reduce
resistance and to improve tracking and planing. These boats
are usually powered by outboard engines and some can get
up on plane and be quite fast. They have high initial stability
like a catamaran but they are not suitable for use on very
rough water.

MEDIUM SIZE POWERBOATS
Sport Cruiser

Photo of a 340 Sundancer (Courtesy Sea Ray Boats)
The sport cruiser design typically has streamlined modernistic styling with a planing hull design. This type of boat will

typically achieve speeds of 20 to 30 plus knots depending on engine size and displacement. Cabins, galley, and heads are forward and in some of these a berth is tucked aft under the cockpit floor.

Express Cruiser

Photo of a 43 Eastbay SX. (Courtesy Grand Banks Yachts)
The express cruiser is a higher speed boat usually built on a planing hull and capable of achieving speed to length ratios of 3 and beyond. These come in styles ranging from very modernistic to the more traditional down east look like the boat shown here. The Eastbay in the picture is capable of speeds over 28 knots.

Down East

Photo of a 36 Picnic Boat. (Courtesy Hinckley Boat Company)
The down east style boat has a traditional look reminiscent of Maine lobster boats, but the hulls and power trains may be anything but. Although some of these boats retain lobster boat hull designs, others are jet powered planing boats, like the one in the photo, capable of speeds over 30 knots. These are typically used as day boats for family outings, picnics, etc. There are usually bunks, a head, and a galley forward, which make it suitable for overnight trips as well. One could just as well call this an express cruiser.

Sportfisher

Photo of a 60 Convertible (Courtesy Hatteras Yachts)
Designed specifically for fishing offshore, this has a deep vee planing hull designed to get you to fishing grounds quickly. These are good rough water boats and although they are designed for fishing can make good recreational boats. Note the *tuna tower* on top, which is used for spotting fish and shoals. Duplicate controls are contained in the tower.

Trawler

Photo of a 37 Nordic Tug (Courtesy Nordic Tugs, Inc.)
Early recreational boats that were based on the fishing trawler displacement hull design became known as *trawlers*. The use of the name trawler has evolved to include many different styles of recreational boat, including ones with

semi-displacement hulls like the one shown in the photo. Many of the other boats shown in this section can also be considered to be trawlers. Trawlers come in pilothouse, sedan, and aft-cabin layouts. The boat shown here is a pilothouse model. Many of the boats that follow can also be considered trawlers.

Double Cabin

Photo of a 46 Heritage CL (Courtesy Grand Bank Yachts)
This classic double cabin design has two sleeping cabins, one forward and one aft, that are raised partially above the deck level. This type of cabin, which allows walking around the sides of the boat, is often called a trunk cabin.

Sundeck/Aft Cabin

Photo of a Heritage East 36 (Courtesy Yacht Registry)
The sundeck design has a sleeping cabin aft that spans the entire width of the boat as well as a cabin forward in the bow. The top of the aft cabin is the sundeck. This is sometimes called a double cabin. Note that the top of the aft cabin is higher than the forward deck.

Pilothouse

Photo of a Krogen 44 (Courtesy: Kadey-Krogen Yachts)
The pilothouse design is characterized by a raised pilothouse separated from the salon. Typically there will be a cabin in the bow as well as a guest cabin under the pilothouse. There may or may not be a flying bridge as shown in the above drawing. The Krogen 44 shown in the picture is a full displacement hull design and is suitable for ocean passages.

Sedan

Photo of a 390 Trawler (Courtesy Mainship Trawlers)
The sedan has the salon and cockpit on one level with the helm being located in the forward part of the salon. A second helm located on an open bridge above the main bridge,

as shown, is quite common on the sedan style boat, and is termed a *flying bridge* or *flybridge.* Sleeping accommodations and the head are in the bow.

Power Catamaran

Photo of a PDQ MV/34 (Courtesy PDQ Yachts)
Distinguished by their twin hulls, these are becoming increasingly popular in all sizes mainly because of increased resistance to rolling and faster speeds obtainable with less horsepower. They are also highly maneuverable because of the twin propellers spaced far apart. Usually catamarans will have more living space for a given length of boat.

Houseboat

Photo of a 92 Sharpe (Courtesy Sharpe Houseboats)
The houseboat has a rectangular design with a relatively flat full displacement hull or pontoons. These are not suitable for rough water and are normally used in relatively calm,

protected rivers and lakes. The boxlike design allows for the most living space of any boat for a given length and beam

Passagemaker

Photo of a Nordhavn 47 (Courtesy Nordhavn)

A passagemaker is a boat designed for crossing oceans and has a relatively strong and heavy full displacement hull design. A long cruising range is needed to cross vast expanses of ocean without refueling. She must have very reliable and sometimes redundant mechanical and electrical systems since it's hard to call for a tow in the middle of the Atlantic. For added reliability they will often be keel cooled with a dry stack exhaust (cooling and exhaust systems are discussed in the Mechanical chapter).

SAILBOAT TYPES

Introduction

Since the most noticeable difference between sailboats lies in their sail plans rather than the boat itself, the following data on sail boat types concerns itself mainly with different types of sail plans.

Sailboats greater than 20 feet generally have a cockpit aft and a cuddy or cabin forward, although in some cases the cockpit is placed amidships. Smaller sailboats have an open cockpit with perhaps a small storage locker in the bow.

Catboat

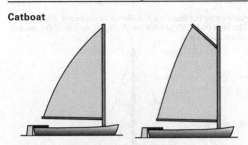

A *catboat* has a single sail on one mast. This rigging is quite common on smaller sailboats in the 10- to 20-foot range. The catboat on the left is sloop rigged and the one on the right is *lateen* rigged. Lateen rigging is very common on board small sailboats and catamarans.

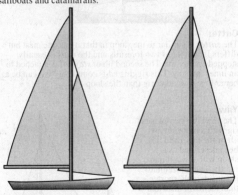

Sloop

The *sloop* is the most common type of recreational sailboat. It has a single mast with one mainsail and one headsail (jib). The mast is stepped further aft than the catboat. The sloop is also known as a *Bermudian* rig, a *Marconi* rig, or a *jib-headed* rig. The boat on the left is with the jibstay going only partway up the mast is a *fractional* or *standard* sloop rig. The boat on the right with the jibstay to the top of the mast is a *masthead* rig.

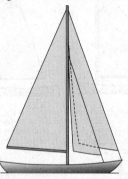

Cutter

The *cutter* is similar to the sloop in that it has one mast but differs in that it has two foresails and the mast is usually stepped further aft. The second jib or *staysail* is attached to an inner forestay. This rigging adds complexity but can be a better heavy-weather rig than the sloop.

Yawl

The yawl is a two-masted rig with a mizzenmast aft of the main and has been described as a sloop with a small mast far aft. The mizzenmast is considerably shorter than the main mast and is generally aft of the rudderpost. The mizzen sail has about a quarter of the area of the main sail.

Ketch

Like the yawl, the ketch is two masted and has a mizzenmast shorter than the main. The mizzenmast is taller than the mizzenmast of a yawl, is located forward of the rudderpost, and has a sail with up to half the area of the mainsail. Some have gaff rigged main and/or mizzen sails and often have more than one foresail (like a cutter).

Schooner

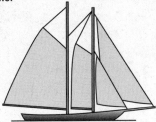

A schooner has two and sometimes more masts with the aft mast being the taller mast. The schooner usually has two or more headsails.

Ketch

Like the yawl, the ketch is two-masted and has a mizzenmast. It is stepped farther forward than the mizzenmast on the yawl. The mizzenmast is larger than the yawl's, and the foremost is positioned aft. Its position is behind the cockpit, and its mainsail is larger. The ketch is more easily handled because of its reduced sail area. The mizzen mast is stepped forward of the rudder post and the area of the mainsail and mizzen are about the same. The ketch is often used for long voyages.

Schooner

A schooner has two or more masts, with the forward mast shorter than the main. In the past, schooners usually had two or more mainsails.

2 BOATING RULES AND REGULATIONS

OWNERSHIP REGULATIONS

BOAT REGISTRATION

U.S. Registration and Documenting

In the United States vessels must be *registered* with the state in which the principal boating use takes place. As an alternative, vessels greater than 5 net tons may be *documented* by the U.S. Coast Guard; however, some states may nonetheless require state registration and display of a validation sticker. Applicable state and federal taxes apply to documented vessels.

Certificate of Number (U.S.)

A certificate of number and a state validating sticker will be issued by the state for vessels registered with the state. The certificate of number must always be carried on board the vessel when it is in use. The numbers must be displayed on the forward half of the boat on both sides and be at least 3 inches high. The state validating sticker must be level with and within six inches of the numbers. The number is preceded by a two-character state abbreviation (which is different than the state postal code). The state will usually provide more specific instructions for the location and placement of the registration numbers.

If the boat is moved to a new state, the certificate is valid for 60 days, after which, the boat must be registered in the new state of principal use. A new number will be issued by the new state. If boat ownership changes the owner must notify the state that issued the certificate within 15 days.

It is important to note that issuance of a certificate of number (registration) is not proof of clear title as with documentation.

State boating office addresses and phone numbers are given in the chapter on Boating Information Sources.

State Prefix Abbreviations

Table 2-1 lists the two character state abbreviations. Postal codes are included in the table to illustrate that the state boat prefix is not always the same as the postal code.

State	Postal	Boat	State	Postal	Boat
Alabama	AL	AL	Montana	MT	MT
Alaska	AK	AK	Nebraska	NE	NB
Arizona	AZ	AZ	Nevada	NV	NV
Arkansas	AR	AR	New Hampshire	NH	NH
California	CA	CF	New Jersey	NJ	NJ
Colorado	CO	CL	New Mexico	NM	NM
Connecticut	CT	CT	New York	NY	NY
Delaware	DE	DL	North Carolina	NC	NC
Distr. Of Columbia	DC	DC	North Dakota	ND	ND
Florida	FL	FL	Ohio	OH	OH
Georgia	GA	GA	Oklahoma	OK	OK
Hawaii	HI	HA	Oregon	OR	OR
Idaho	ID	ID	Pennsylvania	PA	PA
Illinois	IL	IL	Rhode Island	RI	RI
Indiana	IN	IN	South Carolina	SC	SC
Iowa	IA	IA	South Dakota	SD	SD
Kansas	KS	KA	Tennessee	TN	TN
Kentucky	KY	KY	Texas	TX	TX
Louisiana	LA	LA	Utah	UT	UT
Maine	ME	ME	Vermont	VT	VT
Maryland	MD	MD	Virginia	VA	VA
Massachusetts	MA	MS	Washington	WA	WN
Michigan	MI	MC	West Virginia	WV	WV
Minnesota	MN	MN	Wisconsin	WI	WS
Mississippi	MS	MI	Wyoming	WY	WY
Missouri	MO	MO			

TABLE 2-1: State Prefix Abbreviations

U.S. Documentation

The 5 net tons requirement for documenting, mentioned above, is actually a volume measurement rather than a weight measurement. In simplified form, it is gross tons (the cubic foot volume of the hull divided by 100) with a factor applied depending on the boat type (e.g. powerboat, sailboat, etc.). A vessel longer than 25 feet is likely to be greater than 5 net tons. Additional information on calculating tonnage and on documentation procedures is available from:

National Vessel Documentation Center
792 T J Jackson Drive
Falling Waters, WV 25419
Toll free: (800) 799-8362
www.uscg.mil/hq/g-m/vdoc/poc.htm

Documentation requires that the owner be a U.S. citizen and prove legitimate ownership of the vessel. Documentation shows that the vessel is free and clear of any encumbrances and proves ownership and nationality, which is advantageous when applying for financing. Documentation is preferred to registration and sometimes required when visiting foreign ports.

The documentation number must be carved into or fixed permanently to the inside of the vessel so that it cannot be removed or altered. The documentation number is preceded by the characters "No." and is to be a minimum of 3 inches high

The documented vessel will display the name and hailing port of the vessel on the hull exterior instead of the registration numbers. The letters must be at least 4 inches in height. The location on the hull of the name and port is not specified for recreational vessels; however, the transom or stern is the usual place for the name and port, and the name is sometimes placed on both sides of the bow.

Canada Licensing and Registration

In Canada *licensing* or *registration* is required for any vessel powered by greater than 10 horsepower (7.5 kilowatts). Note that the term license equates roughly to register in the United States, and the term register equates roughly to document in the United States.

Recreational vessels under 15 gross tons may be either licensed or registered. Vessels over 15 gross tons must be registered. Note that gross tons are a volume measurement, not a weight measurement. An 11-meter (36 foot) powerboat will survey around 15 gross tons.

License (Canada)

Effective April 1, 2006 boat licences are obtained from any of about 320 Service Canada Centres. The Canada Border Services Agency (formerly Customs and Revenue Canada) no longer issues boat licences. There is no charge for the license at the current time.

A two letter code (the postal abbreviation) for the province), which indicates the regional office that issued the license, precedes the license number and that number will stay with the boat throughout its life, even if the boat is moved to another province. The old numbering system used a single letter to indicate the issuing region. Existing old numbers may be retained or exchanged for a new one. The license number must be displayed on both sides of the bow of the vessel and be in block characters at least 7.5 centimeters (3 in) high.

The license serves only to identify the boat (like the certificate of number in the United States) but does not prove clear ownership that is free of third-party rights.

Province	New	Old	Province	New	Old
British Columbia	BC	K	Nova Scotia	NS	A
Alberta	AB	H	Newfoundland and	NL	M
Saskatchewan	SK	G	Labrador		
Manitoba	MB	F	Yukon	YK	J
Ontario	ON	E	Northwest	NT	F
Quebec	QC	D	Territories		
New Brunswick	NB	C	Nunavut	NU	F
Prince Edward Island	PE	B			

Regional office letters used in Canadian license numbers:

Registration (Canada)

Application for registration is with any Transport Canada Port of Registry office. Registration requires that the owner provide citizenship documents and prove legitimate ownership of the vessel. A tonnage survey will be required and is carried out by a government appointed surveyor.

Registration shows that the vessel is free and clear of any encumbrances and proves ownership and nationality, which is often needed when applying for financing. Registration is preferred to licensing and sometimes required when visiting foreign ports.

The registered vessel will display the name and hailing port of the vessel on the hull exterior instead of the registration numbers. The letters must be at least 10.3 centimeters (4 in) in height. The name and port of registry is placed on the stern and the name is placed on both sides of the bow.

HULL IDENTIFICATION NUMBER

All manufactured or imported boats must have a *hull identification number* (**HIN**). The HIN is required in both the United States and Canada and the format is the same in both countries. The HIN is analogous to the VIN on automobiles.

The manufacturer must permanently place the HIN on the hull in two places during construction. The characters in the HIN must be no less than ¼ inch (6 mm) in height.

The primary HIN must be placed:

- On the transom located in the upper starboard quarter. In the United States within 2 inches of the top of the transom.
- On vessels without a transom or where the transom is unsuitable, on the starboard aft part of the hull. In the United States within 2 inches of the top of the hull and within 1 foot of the stern.
- On vessels with removable hulls such as some multihulls, to the aft crossbeam within 1 foot of the starboard hull attachment.

A second duplicate HIN is placed somewhere else in an unexposed location on the boat such as underneath a fitting or piece of hardware.

There are actually three different HIN formats, one being the current format that was placed in use in January 1985, and the other two that were discontinued at the end of 1984. These formats are illustrated in figures 2-1 through 2-3 starting on page 78. All three formats have the following in common:

- They are 12 digits long.
- Characters 1 through 3 are the three-digit *manufacturer's identification code* (**MIC**).
- Five characters from 4 through 8 are the manufacturer's hull serial number.
- Four characters (9 to 12) indicate the month and year of manufacture (certification) and the model year. It is only these four characters that vary with the three different formats.

United States: The MIC is assigned by the U.S. Coast Guard, or in the case of home built (backyard boats) by the state boating agency where the boat was built. In this case the first two digits of the MIC will be the state code. The U.S. Coast Guard maintains a database that is available online where you can look up manufacturers and their codes or vice-versa. It also allows listing all manufacturers by states. This web page is currently located at http://www.uscgboating.org/recalls/mic_database.htm.

FORMAT #1: This is the current format that has been in use since January 1985. Note that this number may be preceded by a three-character code that indicates the country of manufacture. The country code is described below.

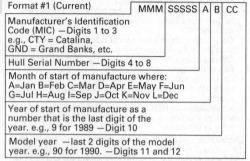

Format #1 (Current) | MMM | SSSSS | A | B | CC |

Manufacturer's Identification Code (MIC) —Digits 1 to 3 e.g., CTY = Catalina, GND = Grand Banks, etc.

Hull Serial Number —Digits 4 to 8

Month of start of manufacture where: A=Jan B=Feb C=Mar D=Apr E=May F=Jun G=Jul H=Aug I=Sep J=Oct K=Nov L=Dec

Year of start of manufacture as a number that is the last digit of the year. e.g., 9 for 1989 —Digit 10

Model year —last 2 digits of the model year. e.g., 90 for 1990. —Digits 11 and 12

FIGURE 2-1: Hull Identification Number in Current Use

FORMAT #2: Mostly used from the mid 1970s to the end of 1984 although the older format #3 was still used by some builders. Note only the last 4 digits are different from format #1; digits 1 through 8 remain the same.

Format #2 (Before Jan 1985) | MMM | SSSSS | M | 84 | D |

Manufacturer's Identification Code (MIC) e.g. CTY = Catalina, GND = Grand Banks, etc.

Hull Serial Number

The 9th character is always M

Characters 10 and 11 are the model year. 1984 is shown here.

The last character (12) is the month in which building began: A=Jan B=Feb C=Mar D=Apr E=May F=Jun G=Jul H=Aug I=Sep J=Oct K=Nov L=Dec

FIGURE 2-2: Hull Identification Number Pre-1985

FORMAT #3: Used primarily from the 1960s through the mid 1970s although some builders continued to use this format up through the end of 1984.

Format #3 (1960s – 1970s)	MMM	SSSSS	11	73

Manufacturer's Identification Code (MIC) e.g., CTY = Catalina, GND = Grand Banks, etc.

Hull Serial Number

Month of start manufacture. November is shown here.

Year of start manufacture. 1973 is shown here.

FIGURE 2-3: Hull Identification Number 1960s – 1970s

Country Code Prefix to HIN

The country code is used in countries outside the United States and Canada and is optional in Canada. It is a three-digit prefix to the HIN consisting of two alpha characters and a hyphen designating the country of manufacture. For example AU- for Australia, CA- for Canada, and US- for United States. This prefix is required for manufacturers in North America exporting to Europe and many other countries as well.

Argentina	AR	Israel	IL
Australia	AU	Italy	IT
Austria	AT	Japan	JP
Belgium	BE	Mexico	MX
Brazil	BR	Monaco	MC
Canada	CA	Netherlands	NL
Chile	CL	New Zealand	NZ
China	CN	Norway	NO
Denmark	DK	Portugal	PT
Estonia	EE	Russia	RU
Finland	FI	Singapore	SG
France	FR	South Africa	ZA
Germany	DE	Spain	ES
Greece	GR	Sweden	SE
Hong Kong	HK	Switzerland	CH
Hungary	HU	Taiwan	TW
Iceland	IS	Turkey	TR
India	IN	United Kingdom	GB
Ireland	IE	United States	US

TABLE 2-2: HIN Country Code Prefixes

The country codes used in table 2-2 are the country codes as designated by the alpha two-country code in ISO 3166.

RULES FOR BOAT OPERATION

OPERATING

Enforcement

United States

A vessel underway, when hailed by a Coast Guard vessel, is required to heave to or maneuver in such a manner that permits a boarding officer to come aboard. Other federal, state, and local law enforcement officials may board and examine the vessel, regardless of its numbering or documentation.

The Coast Guard may impose a civil penalty up to $1,000 for failure to comply with equipment requirements or other federal regulations, or to report a boating accident. Failure to comply with the Inland Navigation Rules Act of 1980 can result in a civil penalty up to $5,000.

Canada

An enforcement officer may, in order to verify and ensure compliance with regulations,

(a) go on board a vessel;

(b) examine a vessel and its equipment;

(c) require that the owner or the master or other person who is in charge or appears to be in charge of the vessel produce, forthwith,

    (i) personal identification, and

    (ii) any license, document or plate required by these Regulations; and

(d) ask any pertinent questions of, and demand all reasonable assistance from, the owner or the master or other person who is in charge or appears to be in charge, of the vessel

A contraventions act has changed the way boating regulations are enforced (in some provinces). Under the older system, offenses were processed in court the same way as criminal code offenses. This was felt to be too cumbersome for processing just regulatory offenses.

The contraventions act allows for ticketing of offenders much like ticketing for automobile driving offenses.

Provinces using the new contraventions system are British Columbia, Manitoba, Ontario, Quebec, Prince Edward

Island, New Brunswick, and Nova Scotia. Discussions are underway with the remaining provinces to do the same.

Boating Under the Influence

United States

Operating a vessel while intoxicated became a specific federal offense effective January 13, 1988. The final rule set standards for determining when an individual is intoxicated. If the blood alcohol content (BAC) is .08 percent (.10 percent in some states) or higher for operators of recreational vessels being used only for pleasure, violators are subject to a civil penalty not to exceed $1,000 or criminal penalty not to exceed $5,000, one-year imprisonment, or both.

Canada

Operating a vessel while impaired is an offense under the Canadian Criminal Code and convictions can result in heavy punishment (including first offenses). The minimum penalty is $600. Violators could be prohibited from operating a boat for up to three years and under certain circumstances could get life imprisonment.

Individual provinces have differing rules determining how and when alcohol can be consumed and transported.

Negligent Operation

United States

Negligent or grossly negligent operation of a vessel and/or interference with the safe operation of a vessel, so as to endanger lives and/or property, are prohibited by law. The Coast Guard may impose a civil penalty for negligent operation. Grossly negligent operation is a criminal offense and an operator may be fined up to $5,000, imprisoned for one year, or both. Some examples of actions that may constitute negligent or grossly negligent operation are:

- Operating a boat in a swimming area.
- Operating a boat while under the influence of alcohol or drugs.
- Excessive speed in the vicinity of other boats or in dangerous waters.
- Hazardous water skiing practices.
- Bowriding, also riding on seatback, gunwale, or transom.

Canada

No person shall operate a small vessel in a careless manner, without due care and attention or without reasonable consideration for other persons.

Shoreline Speed Restrictions

United States

Speed restrictions are imposed by individual states. *You are always responsible for damage caused by your wake, even if you are not in a no-wake zone.*

Canada

In British Columbia, Alberta, Saskatchewan, Manitoba, and Ontario there is an unposted speed limit of 10 kilometers per hour (5.4 knots) within 30 meters (98 ft) from shore, except where otherwise posted.

Exceptions:
- Rivers less than 100 meters (328 ft) wide, canals, or buoyed channels.
- Water skiing where the boat towing the skier pulls the skier to or from the shore.

Quebec has speed restrictions on certain bodies of water, and these will usually be posted.

Termination of Use

United States

A Coast Guard boarding officer who observes a boat being operated in an unsafe condition, specifically defined by law or regulation, and who determines that an especially hazardous condition exists, may direct the operator to take immediate steps to correct the condition, including returning to port.

Termination for unsafe use may be imposed for:

- Insufficient number of CG-approved personal flotation devices (PFDs).
- Insufficient fire extinguishers.
- Overloading beyond manufacturer's recommended safe loading capacity.
- Improper navigation light display.
- Ventilation requirements for tank and engine spaces not met.
- Fuel leakage.
- Fuel in bilges.
- Improper backfire flame control.
- Operating in regulated boating areas during predetermined adverse conditions (applies in 13th CG District only).
- Manifestly unsafe voyage.

An operator who refuses to terminate the unsafe use of a vessel can be cited for failure to comply with the directions of a Coast Guard boarding officer, as well as for the specific violations which were the basis for the termination order. Violators may be fined not more than $1,000, imprisoned not more than one year, or both.

Canada

An enforcement officer may, in order to ensure compliance with these Regulations or in the interests of public safety, direct or prohibit the movement of vessels or direct the operator of a vessel to stop it.

Every person shall comply with the requirements of an enforcement officer in the course of carrying out duties and functions under these Regulations.

Reporting Boating Accidents

United States

The operator or owner of any recreational boat is required to file a boating accident report (BAR) if the boat is involved in an accident that results in:

- Loss of life;
- Personal injury that requires medical treatment beyond first aid;
- Damage to the boat and other property damage of $2,000 or more; or
- Complete loss of the boat.
- Boat operators are required to report their accident to local authorities in the state where the accident occurred.

Fatal Accidents (U.S.): Immediate notification is required for fatal accidents. If a person dies or disappears as a result of a recreational boating accident, the nearest state boating authority must be notified without delay. The following information must be provided:

- Date, time and exact location of the accident;
- Name of each person who died or disappeared;
- Number and name of the vessel; and
- Name and address of the owner and operator.

Reporting Timelines (U.S.): If a person dies or disappears from the boat, or there are injuries requiring medical treatment beyond first aid, a formal report must be filed within 48 hours of the accident. A formal report must be made within 10 days for accidents involving property damage of $2,000 or more, or complete loss of a vessel.

Note: State requirements for reporting boating accidents may be more stringent than federal (i.e., some states require all boating accidents to be reported immediately). Check with the boating law administrator in the state where the accident occurred for proper reporting procedures.

If you need further information regarding accident reporting, please call the U.S. Coast Guard Infoline at 800-368-5647.

Canada

Accident Reporting and Timeline (Canada)

The following doesn't apply in all provinces. Check with local authorities to see what applies in your area.

> If a pleasure craft is involved in an accident that results in injury to a person that requires medical treatment beyond first aid but not admittance to a hospital, or that causes property damage estimated at more than $2,500, the person responsible for the care and control of the pleasure craft shall complete a Boating Accident Report Form and forward it to the Office of Boating Safety of the Canadian Coast Guard, not later than 14 days after the accident.

Serious Accidents (Canada)

> If a pleasure craft is involved in an accident that results in a fatality, injury to a person that requires admittance to a hospital, or property damage greater than $5,000 resulting from fire, an explosion or collision with another vessel or other floating or fixed structure, the person responsible for the care and control of the pleasure craft shall report the accident to the local police authority as soon as possible.

Rendering Assistance—"Law of the Sea"

> The master or person in charge of a vessel is obligated by law to provide assistance that can be safely provided to any individual in danger at sea. The master or person in charge is subject to a fine and/or imprisonment for failure to do so.

From U.S. Code "Good Samaritan Clause:

> An individual complying with the above or gratuitously and in good faith rendering assistance at the scene of a marine casualty without objection by an individual assisted, is not liable for damages as a result of rendering assistance or for an act or omission in providing or arranging salvage, towage, medical treatment, or other assistance when the individual acts as an ordinary, reasonable, and prudent individual would have acted under the circumstances.

Nondistress Call (U.S.)

When a boater contacts the Coast Guard on channel 16 VHF-FM and the situation is determined to be nondistress, the Coast Guard will offer to contact any assistance provider (commercial or friend) the boater requests. If the boater has no preference, the Coast Guard will issue a Marine Assistance Request Broadcast (MARB) to all local commercial assistance providers approved by the Coast Guard.

OPERATOR QUALIFICATIONS

U.S. Qualifications Requirements

At present there are no federal requirements for noncommercial operation of a recreational boat. Some states have enacted licensing requirements that require passing an exam or showing proof of some form of boating education, from organizations such as the U.S. Power Squadrons or the U.S. Coast Guard Auxiliary. Most of those states will allow a visitor to operate a boat for up to 60 days before requiring licensing in that state.

States known to require some type of universal boater licensing are Alabama, American Samoa, Connecticut, Indiana, New Jersey, and Oregon (this list may not be inclusive), and many others are in the process of enacting legislation. Many additional states have education and licensing requirements for minors.

If the operator is carrying passengers for hire he must pass a U.S. Coast Guard exam and obtain a license. These licenses vary as to purpose, number of passengers, tonnage, and geographical area.

From the Passenger Vessel Safety Act of 1993:

> Passenger for hire means a passenger for whom consideration is contributed as a condition of carriage on the vessel, whether directly or indirectly flowing to the owner, charterer, operator, agent, or any other person having an interest in the vessel.
>
> Consideration means an economic benefit, inducement, right, or profit including pecuniary payment accruing to an individual, person, or entity, but not including a voluntary sharing of the actual expenses of the voyage, by monetary contribution or donation of fuel, food, beverage, or other supplies.

Thus passengers can volunteer to share expenses of a trip and not be considered passengers for hire.

Canada Qualifications Requirements

In Canada the operator requirements are federally mandated and apply in all Canadian waters.

Operator Competency Requirement—Canada

The operator competency requirements are being phased in over time and the following persons are required to show proof of competency.

All operators born after 01Apr83. (Currently in effect -since 15Sep99).
Operators of craft less than 4 meters (13 feet) in length including personal watercraft. (Currently in effect -since 14Sep02).
Any and all operators starting on 15Sep09.

Proof of competency can be any of:

A pleasure craft operator card. Obtaining this card requires passing a Canadian Coast Guard approved test.
OR: Successful completion of a boating safety course prior to 01Apr1999.
OR: A rental powerboat checklist completed successfully.

Nonresidents operating their own boats in Canada must meet these requirements after 45 days. An equivalent to the operator card issued by the home country or state is considered proof of competency for this purpose.

Non-residents chartering Canadian registered boats must meet the competency requirement at once. The 45-day grace period does not apply.

Age-Horsepower Requirement (Canada)

The following table shows the age limits for operating boats of varying horsepower. Note the operator competency requirement applies regardless.

Unsupervised persons under the age of 12 may not operate boats with greater than 7.5 kilowatt (10 horsepower) engines. A person accompanied by and supervised by someone greater than 16 years of age may do so.
Unsupervised persons under the age of 16 may not operate boats with greater than 30 kilowatt (40 horsepower) engines. A person accompanied by and supervised by someone greater than 16 years of age may do so.
Persons under 16 years of age are not allowed to operate Personal Watercraft (PWC) under any circumstances.
There are no power restrictions on persons 16 years of age and over.

REQUIRED AND SUGGESTED EQUIPMENT

The tables that follow show the minimum on board equipment requirements for both the United States and Canada. This is the *minimum* requirement and following the tables are some suggestions for additional on board equipment, some of which common sense would dictate even though not required by law.

Note that in the United States many individual states have more stringent requirements, and it is your responsibility to know and comply with these requirements.

Visitors to Canada

A boat operating in Canada but registered or licensed in another country must comply with the safety equipment requirements of the registering or licensing country. A visitor to Canada operating a Canadian registered vessel must comply with the Canadian equipment requirements.

Required Equipment Tables and Notes

Four classes of boats are specified in U.S. federal regulations:

Class A: Less than 16 feet (4.9 meters)

Class 1: 16 feet to less than 26 feet

Class 2: 26 feet to less than 40 feet

Class 3: 40 feet to 65 feet

These classes are used to determine which equipment is required. Required equipment is shown in tables 2-3 through 2-6 starting on page 88.

Table clarification notes:

Note [1] The International Collision Regulations (Navigation Rules) specify that a vessel greater than 12 meters (39.4 feet) in length must carry a whistle or a horn as well as a bell. The requirements for frequency and loudness vary with the size of the vessel. Both the U.S. and Canada adhere to this rule.

Note [2] The ventilation requirement applies to all vessels with enclosed engine and /or fuel tank compartments.

In the U.S. all gasoline powered vessels built after 25Apr1940 must have natural ventilation with at least 2 ducts fitted with cowls. Vessels built after 31Jul1980 must also have a rated power exhaust blower.

The Canadian requirement is similar requiring both natural ventilation and a power exhaust blower.

Required Equipment	U.S Regulations				Canada Regulations			
	<16ft / <5m	16>26ft / 5<8m	26<40ft / 8<12m	40>65ft / 12<20m	<6m / <20ft	6<8m / 20<26ft	8<12m / 26<40ft	12<20m / 40>65ft
Licenses	State Registration or documentation required on board. numbers or name on outside of boat.				License or registration required onboard. Numbers or name on the outside of boat			
Wearable personal flotation devices (PFDs) or life jackets	One USCG approved Type I, II, III, or V PFD for each person on boat.				One CCG approved PFD or lifejacket for each person on boat.			
Throwable personal flotation devices (PFDs)			One Type IV throwable PFD in addition to the wearable PFD's		One buoyant heaving line > 15 m			
Canada — approved life-buoy diam. is 610 mm or 762 mm with buoyant line > 15 m						OR approved lifebuoy	AND approved lifebuoy	AND appr. lifebuoy w. light
Fire extinguisher (hand held)	One B-I with enclosed spaces or permanent fuel tanks	Two B-I or One B-II	Three B-I or one B-I plus one B-II		One 5BC if inboard or fixed fuel tanks or fuel burning appliance	One 5BC if power-driven or one 5BC if fuel burning appliance	One 10BC if power-driven & one 10BC if fuel burning appliance	10BC at each location specified in note [1]
Ventilation	All gasoline powered vessels with enclosed tanks or engine must have natural ventilation with at least 2 ventilation cowls as well as an approved exhaust blower. See note [2]				On gasoline engines in enclosed spaces			
Backfire flame arrestor	On all gasoline engines except outboards				On gasoline engines in enclosed spaces			

TABLE 2-3: Required Equipment (Table 1 of 4)

Required Equipment	U.S Regulations				Canada Regulations			
	<16 ft (<5 m)	16<26 ft 5<8 m	26<40 ft 8<12 m	40>65 ft 12<20 m	<6 m <20 ft	6<8 m 20<26 ft	8<12 m 26<40 ft	12<20 m 40<65 ft
Visual distress signals	1 approved electric distress light or 3 day/night flares. [3] [4]	1 orange distress flag & 1 electric distress light OR 3 orange smoke signals and 1 electric distress light OR 3 day/night red flares are all acceptable combinations. See 2-8 for further explanation of combinations [4]			1 watertight flashlight OR 3 type A, B, or C approved flares	1 watertight flashlight AND 6 type A, B, or C approved flares [5]	1 watertight flashlight AND 12 type A, B, or C approved flares [5]	1 watertight flashlight AND 12 type A, B, C, or D approved flares [5] [6]
Sound signals	A whistle or horn or other device to produce an efficient sound signal. Human voice not acceptable.		A whistle or horn AND A bell that satisfy ColRegs [7]		A sound signalling device (pealess whistle or a compressed gas or electric horn) or sound-signaling appliance (a whistle or horn that satisfy ColRegs).	A whistle or horn AND A bell that satisfy ColRegs [7]		
Navigation lights	Lights that meet the standards prescribed in the collision regulations — must be displayed from sunset to sunrise or in conditions of poor visibility.							
Copy of Navigation Rules (Collision Regulations)				Required on board				
Navigation charts					Required unless the navigator is familiar with the charted area.			

TABLE 2-4: Required Equipment (Table 2 of 4)

Required Equipment	U.S Regulations				Canada Regulations			
	<16 ft / <5 m	16<26 ft / 5<8 m	26<40 ft / 8<12 m	40>65 ft / 12<20 m	<6 m / <20 ft	6<8 m / 20<26 ft	8<12 m / 26<40 ft	12<20 m / 40>65 ft
Reboarding device (Ladder or hoist)						Required If freeboard > 0.5 m (1.6 ft)		Required
Manual propelling device (paddle)					Required unless anchor is on board			
Anchor					Req'd If no paddle. Min 15 m (50 ft) rode		Min 30 m (98 ft) rode	Min 50 m (164 ft) rode
Bailer or pump					1 bailer OR 1 manual pump [8]	1 bailer OR 1 manual pump	1 bailer AND 1 manual pump	Bilge pumping system
Other								1 axe AND 2 buckets >= 10 L
Toilet (if installed)	Must be a Type I, II, or III MSD (Marine Sanitation Device)				A pleasure craft that is fitted with a toilet shall be fitted with a holding tank.			
Oil pollution placard (5 x 8 inch minimum size)			Display in machinery space or bilge station					
Garbage placard (4 x 9 inch minimum size)			Display in a prominent location					

TABLE 2-5: Required Equipment Table (3 of 4)

Required Equipment (Canada Only)	Sailboard	Paddleboats and Watercycles < than 6 M length	Rowboats, Canoes, Kayaks, Shells<6 M length	Personal Water Craft
Licenses				License required & on board
Wearable personal flotation devices (PFDs) or life jackets	One CCG approved PFD or lifejacket for each person on boat.			
Sound signals	A sound signaling device (pealess whistle or a compressed gas or electric horn) or sound-signaling appliance (a whistle or horn that satisfy ColRegs).			
Throwable personal flotation devices	One buoyant heaving line > 15 m if not wearing PFD		One buoyant heaving line > 15 m	One buoyant heaving line > 15 m
manual propelling device (e.g., paddle)	Required if not wearing PFD		Required unless anchor is on board	Not req if wearing PFD or anchor is on board
Anchor			Required unless paddle is on board	Not required if wearing PFD or paddle is on board
Visual distress signals	1 watertight flashlight OR 3 type A, B, or C approved flares if not wearing PFD			1 watertight flashlight OR 3 type A, B, or C approved flares if not wearing PFD
Navigation lights	If operating between sunset and sunrise require lights that meet the standards prescribed in the Collision Regulations			
Water pump or bailer			Required	Required if not wearing PFD

TABLE 2-6: Required Equipment Table (4 of 4) —Canada

Note [3] *United States:* Visual Distress Signals on a boat less than 16 ft (5 M) are only required between sunset and sunrise.

Note [4] *United States:* Visual Distress Signals Visual distress signals are required on the Great Lakes, territorial seas of the United States, waters connected to the Great Lakes, and territorial seas to a point where the distance between shorelines is less than 2 nautical miles wide.

Note [5] *Canada:* Flares are not required if boating on Canadian waters in which the boat can at no time be more than one nautical mile from shore or is engaged in an official competition or in final preparation for an official competition and has no sleeping arrangements.

Note [6] *Canada:* No more than 6 of the 12 flares may be type D flares.

Note [7] The frequencies and approximate range of audibility for whistles and bells are specified in Annex III of the Collision Regulations as follows:

BELL
A bell or gong must produce a sound pressure level of not less than 110 dB at a distance of one meter from it. This would equate to being audible at a distance of somewhat less than one half a nautical mile.

The mouth of the bell must have a diameter of at least 300 millimeters (11.8 in) for a vessel of more than 20 meters length and at least 200 millimeters (7.9 in) for a vessel between 12 and 20 meters length.

WHISTLES

Vessel Length	Frequency Hz	Approximate Range Nautical Miles
> 200 M (61 ft)	70 to 200 Hz	2 .0 nm
75 to 200 M (246 to 656 ft)	130 to 350 Hz	1.5 nm
20 to 75 M (66 to 246 ft)	250 to 700 Hz	1.0 nm
12 to 20 M (39 to 66 ft)	250 to 700 Hz	0.5 nm

U.S Inland Modification—the frequency range on vessels less than 75 meters (246 ft) is reduced to 250 to 525 Hz.

Canada Modification—the frequency range on vessels between 12 and 20 meters is expanded to 250 to 2100 Hz.

LIFE JACKETS AND PFDS
It takes about 7 pounds of buoyancy to keep a typical adult afloat with a sufficient portion of the head out of the water.

Life Jackets and PFDs: United States

PFD is the acronym for a *personal flotation device*. PFDs achieve buoyancy either through the use of some buoyant material, usually foam, or through inflation with air, or some combination of the two. There are minimum buoyancy requirements for each of these three buoyancy methods in combination with the different Types of PFD.

PFDs are classified as Types I through IV. All PFDs must be marked as U.S. Coast Guard approved along with the type.

A *Type I PFD* (life jacket) is designed for off shore use and is useable in all waters. It is designed to turn most unconscious persons face up in the water. This type meets International Convention for Safety Of Life At Sea (SOLAS) standards for life jackets.

A *Type II PFD* (near shore buoyancy vest) is for calm waters expected on smaller inland bodies of water. These are also designed to turn an unconscious person face up but are not as effective as a Type I. An inflatable Type II will usually turn a person face up as well as a Type I.

A *Type III PFD* (flotation aid) assumes a conscious user in calm water where quick rescue is at hand. The wearer may have to take action such as tilting the head back to keep the face out of the water. These come in different styles suitable for such diverse activities as water skiing or fishing. Coats that float are made as Type III PFDs as well.

The *Type IV PFD* (throwable device) is not designed to be worn but is a throwable device for use in calm water where immediate help is at hand. These are not inflatable.

A *Type V PFD* (special use device) is designed for a specific purpose. A vest combined with a safety harness or a deck suit

| Size | Type | Buoyancy (lbs) | | Inflatable and Foam (Hybrid) | |
		Foam	Inflatable	Inherent	Inflated
Adult	I	22 lb	34 lb		
Adult	II	15.5 lb	34 lb	10 lb	22 lb
Adult	III	15.5 lb	22.5 lb	10 lb	22 lb
Adult	V	15.5 – 22 lb	22.5 – 34 lb	7 lb	22 lb
Youth	II	11 lb	n/a	9 lb	15 lb
Youth	III	11 lb	n/a	9 lb	15 lb
Youth	V	11 – 15.5 lb	n/a	7.5 lb	15 lb
Child	II	7 lb	n/a	7 lb	12 lb
Infant	II	7 lb	n/a	n/a	n/a

TABLE 2-7: PFD Minimum Buoyancy Requirements

is a Type V PFD. A Type V PFD is marked on its label as, and will provide the performance of, a Type I, II, or III PFD. The U.S. Coast Guard has not tested and has not approved the safety harness aspect of the Type V combined vest and harness.

An inflatable PFD is a Type V PFD and must be worn when on deck to count as a lifejacket or flotation device.

Life Jackets and PFDs: Canada

Three main types of lifejackets are the *SOLAS lifejacket*, the *standard type lifejacket*, and the *small vessel lifejacket*. In addition **PFDs** are available.

The *SOLAS lifejacket* conforms to the standards set by SOLAS and has the highest performance standard of any of the flotation devices. Among other things it requires an unconscious person to be turned face up with mouth out of the water within five seconds. These can be substituted for any of the other jackets or flotation devices. Two sizes are available, one for persons who weigh more than 35 kilograms (70 lbs) and a smaller version for persons weighing less than 35 kilograms. Must be red, orange, or yellow.

The *standard lifejacket* is less bulky than the SOLAS lifejacket but sacrifices some of the performance. It is also designed to turn the wearer face up in the water. Two sizes are available, one for persons who weigh more than 40 kilograms (80 lbs) and a smaller version for persons weighing less than 40 kilograms. Must be red, orange, or yellow.

Small vessel lifejackets are approved for use on small vessels and are available in both vest and keyhole styles. It will turn a person face up in the water but not particularly efficiently. This would be for use in calm waters where rescue is close at hand. Three sizes are available, one for persons more than 41 kilograms (90 lbs), one for persons from 18 kilograms (40 lbs) to 41 kilograms (90 lbs), and one for persons under 18 kilograms (40 lbs). Must be red, orange, or yellow.

Approved *PFDs* (**personal flotation devices**) may be worn instead of a lifejacket on any pleasure craft. They are usually more comfortable than the lifejackets but they don't perform as well. For example, they may not have much turning capability, although they must not tend to turn the wearer face down. These are available in all colors. Some are for specific purposes such as water skiing, kayaking, and hypothermia protection.

In Canada as in the United States, PFDs are available as *inherently buoyant* and *inflatable*.

Inherently buoyant PFDs come in sizes for persons weighing:
- More than 41 kilograms (90 lbs)
- 2 –41 kilograms (59–90 lbs)
- 14–27 kilograms (31–60 lbs)
- 9–14 kilograms (20–31 lbs)

The inherently buoyant PFD must provide at least 7 kilograms (15.5 lbs) buoyancy.

Inflatable PFDs must be worn when on deck to count as a lifejacket or flotation device. They are not approved for use in white water paddling or for personal water craft (PWCs) or for persons less than 16 years of age. The most common type is the vest or suspender type, which can be manually or automatically inflated when the wearer goes into the water. They provide 15.3 kilograms (33.7 lbs) buoyancy. The pouch or belt-type PFD is manually activated and after inflation requires the wearer to slip the inflated pouch over their head. This type provides 10.2 kilograms (22.5 lbs) buoyancy.

A pleasure craft is not required to carry a personal flotation device or lifejacket of appropriate size for any infant who weighs less than 9 kilograms (19.8 lb) or person whose chest size exceeds 140 centimeters (55 in). Nevertheless, a lifejacket must be carried for these individuals.

A person, who ordinarily resides in a country other than Canada, may bring aboard a pleasure craft a wearable personal flotation device or lifejacket that conforms to the laws of that (other) country. This will count as one of the one-per-person requirement.

FIRE EXTINGUISHERS

Fire Extinguishers General Discussion

The basic types are as follows:

Type A: For wood, cloth, paper, trash, and other common materials. These fires are put out by "heat absorbing" water or water based materials or smothered by dry chemicals.

Type B: For oil, gasoline, grease, paints, and other flammable liquids. These fires are put out by smothering (depriving the oxygen supply), preventing the release of combustible vapors, or stopping the combustion chain. Use Halon, dry chemicals, carbon dioxide, or foam.

Type C: For "live" electrical equipment. These fires are put out by the same process as Type B, but the extinguishing material must be electrically nonconductive. Use Halon, dry chemicals, or carbon dioxide.

Type D: For combustible metals such as magnesium. These fires are put out by smothering or heat absorption.

Combinations of the above letters indicate the extinguisher will put out more than one type of fire. For example a type ABC will put out all three types of fire. Type D is not combined with other types. A number in front of the Type, such as 10B, shows the "size" of the fire an extinguisher will put out. The base line numbers are as follows:

Class 1A: The number 1 is equivalent to the fire extinguishing capacity of 1.25 gallons (4.7 l) of water.

Class 1B: Will put out an area of flammable liquid that is 1.0 square foot (929 sq cm) in size.

Any number other than "1" simply indicates the extinguisher will put out a fire that many times larger, for example "10A" will put out a fire 10 times larger. A number does not precede type C.

Even though type A is not required on a boat in either the United States or Canada, a type ABC makes sense since you never have to think about what type of fire you are using it on.

USCG Fire Extinguisher Ratings

Unlike the Underwriters Laboratories (UL) ratings, the U.S. Coast Guard uses a rating system where Class B is divided into Size I or Size II, based on the weight of the extinguishing agent.

USCG Classification -Type and Size	B-I	B-II
UL Listed equivalent (approximate as this will not always match)	5B	10B
Carbon Dioxide (minimum pounds)	5.0	15.0
Dry Chemical (minimum pounds)	2.0	10.0
Halon (minimum pounds)	2.5	10.0

Canada Fire Extinguisher Ratings

Canada recently switched from the Size I, II, or III rating system to the UL system described above. Extinguishers approved by any of the following agencies are recognized by Canada: UL of Canada, Transport Canada, British Board of Trade for Marine Use, or U.S. Coast Guard.

VISUAL DISTRESS SIGNALS

Visual Distress Signals: United States

Combinations of Visual Distress Signals for Boats Greater Than 16 feet (5m).

A least one signal approved for day use and one signal approved for night use must be carried. Pyrotechnic signals require a quantity of three to meet the requirement as one signal. Table 2-8 shows types of signals approved for this purpose under 46 CFR (46 Code of Federal Regulations).

Signal Device	Meets Reqmnt For		Number Required	Height	Burn Time	46CFR Number
	Day	Night				
Orange Flag	✓		1			160.072
Electric Distress Light		✓	1		6 hrs	161.013
Hand Held Red Flare		✓	3		2 min	160.021
Floating Orange Smoke Signal 40CFR160.022	✓		3		5 min	160.022
Floating Orange Smoke Signal 40CFR160.057	✓		3		15 min	160.057
Pistol Projected Parachute Red Flare	✓	✓	3	45 m (150 ft)	30 sec	160.024
Hand-Held Rocket Propelled Parachute Red Flare	✓	✓	3	150 m (500 ft)	30 sec	160.036
Hand-Held Orange Smoke Signal	✓		3		50 sec	160.037
Distress Signal for Boats —Red Aerial Pyrotechnic Flare	✓	✓	3	n/a	5.5 sec	160.066

TABLE 2-8: Visual Distress Signals (United States)

Orange Distress Flag

The approved orange distress flag is at least 3 by 3 feet with a black square and ball on the orange background.

Electric Distress Light

Must be marked as U.S. Coast Guard approved. Will automatically flash the Morse SOS distress signal. The short flashes are at 1/3-second intervals and the long flashes are 1-second intervals.

Pyrotechnic Distress Signals

These are to be marked as U.S. Coast Guard approved and must not be older than the expiration date, although expired signals may be carried but cannot be counted toward the requirement. In table 2-8 the column labelled "Number Required" specifies the number of devices needed to qualify as one signal.

Visual Distress Signals: Canada

Pyrotechnic Distress Signals

Type of Device	Height	Burn Time
A: Parachute—single red star	300 meters (984 ft)	40 seconds
B: Multi star—two red stars	100 meters (328 ft)	4 seconds
C: Handheld red flare		1 minute
D: Handheld smoke signal		3 minute

TABLE 2-9: Pyrotechnic Distress Signals: Canada

Pyrotechnic signals must be less than four years old from the marked date of manufacture. They must be approved by Canada Coast Guard, Transport Canada, or SOLAS. Types of pyrotechnic signals used in Canada are shown in table 2-9.

EQUIPMENT NOT LEGALLY REQUIRED
Essential Equipment

Some items such as VHF radios are not required in either the United States or Canada on smaller vessels. Others are not required in the United States, although they are required in Canada.

Consider visual distress signals, which generally are not required where the body of water is less than 2 miles wide. It's because it will be difficult to attract attention with only a sound signaling device if you are a mile off shore. A 3-foot-square orange flag a mile out isn't going to help much either, even though it meets the daytime visual signal requirement. Table 2-10 lists equipment items that could or should be considered essential equipment.

Equipment	Comments
VHF Radio	Acquire a VHF radio regardless of vessel size or type if you are operating in an area where VHF is in use. Even Kayakers have been rescued only because they had a hand held VHF with which to call for help.
First Aid Kit	Size and comprehensiveness depend on the nature of the voyage.
Orange Smoke Signals	For daytime use these will attract attention from a long way off far better than a flag.

Equipment	Comments
Red Flares	For night use these will attract more attention more than a flashlight. On larger bodies of water an aerial flare will be seen from a further distance.
USCG certified electric distress light.	For night use the nice thing about these is, in addition to automatically flashing SOS; they keep operating for a minimum of 6 hours.
Waterproof flashlight	On any vessel out between sunrise and sunset —so you can see, or signal if you lose power.
GPS	On a larger body of water –when you make that VHF call for help you can tell people exactly where you are. Newer VHF radios with DSC capability accept coordinates from a GPS and signal for help at the push of a button (if they've been set up properly).
Anchor	Should be on all but the smallest of specialty craft.
Reboarding Device	On any vessel with more than about 1-1/2 ft (0.5m) of freeboard, a ladder, or a block and tackle, or other means of getting a person out of the water. On larger vessels plan for a way to recover an unconscious person.
Oars or Paddles	On smaller boats
Bailing Equipment	On smaller craft this can be as simple as a bucket or manually powered bilge pump. On larger vessels at least two bilge pumping systems; one automatic and one manually operated high volume.
Compass	On all but the smallest bodies of water.
Charts	Anywhere outside of completely familiar waters or on any larger waters.
Radar Reflector	The purpose of the radar reflector is to ensure that other boats, particularly large ones, can see you on their radar. Needed in waters and situations where fog is possible. These should be considered by anyone venturing offshore. Rule 40 of the Canadian Collision Regulations requires these for boats that are made of non-metallic (read non radar reflective) material. This does not apply where compliance is not essential for the safety of the vessel or in areas where radar navigation is not used.
Radar	Should be considered a requirement for running at night and/or in fog. Highly recommended for vessels offshore.

TABLE 2-10: Essential Equipment

Suggested Equipment
Other equipment that should be on board

Binoculars	❏
Boat hook	❏
Dock lines	❏
Equipment	❏
Fenders	❏
Spare anchor	❏
Spare parts	❏
Spare propeller	❏
Spare tiller	❏
Spotlight	❏
Throwable horseshoe buoy or lifebuoy with line	❏
Tools	❏
Towline	❏

TABLE 2-11: Suggested Equipment

Essential Offshore Equipment
For safety offshore, additional equipment is essential. The equipment type and performance will depend on how far off-shore you plan to go, as crossing an ocean is obviously different than fishing 5 miles off. The following table shows only the most essential items, as there is a lot of other equipment that needs to be considered when venturing far offshore.

Satellite EPIRB (406 MHz)	When activated will send an emergency radio distress signal via geostationary satellite. An EPIRB with GPS will send an accurate position as a part of the distress message. These must be registered with NOAA. EPIRB = Emergency Position Indicating Radio Beacon
Inflatable Life Raft	These should be Coast Guard approved and be of sufficient size for everyone on board.
SSB Marine Radio	This is a short wave radio used for long distance communication where you are beyond the range of VHF radio.

TABLE 2-12: Essential Offshore Equipment

ENVIRONMENTAL REGULATIONS
POLLUTION PREVENTION REGULATIONS: UNITED STATES
Discharge of Refuse From Vessels
The International Convention for the Prevention of Pollution from Ships 1973 (MARPOL Annex V) deals with disposal of refuse including sewage from boats and ships. The United

States passed the Act to Prevent Pollution from Ships, which implements the Convention.

Any U.S. ship must comply with the act worldwide. Any non–U.S. ship must comply within the U.S. Exclusive Economic Zone 200-mile limit.

It is illegal to discharge any refuse in United States navigable waters including the Great Lakes and inland waters.

Minimum Distance from Nearest Land (Nautical Miles)	Garbage Type
3 nm	Paper, rags, glass, food waste, ground to less than 25 mm (1 in) mesh size
12 nm	Paper rags, glass food waste greater than 25 mm (1 in) size
25 nm	Dunnage, lining and packing materials
Disposal prohibited	Plastics including so-called biode-gradable plastics.

TABLE 2-13: Refuse Discharge Rules

Sewage Disposal

The Clean Water Act (33 USC 1322) prohibits the dumping of untreated sewage within 3 miles of shore. All vessels, including foreign flag vessels, are required to have USCG certified MSDs (marine sanitation devices) designed to prevent discharge of inadequately treated sewage (fecal coliform count greater than 200 per 100 ml or suspended solids greater than 150 mg/l).

Type I MSD —a discharge device that treats sewage with chemical or other means. Discharge coliform count must be less than 1000 / 100 ml and suspended solids less than 150 mg / l.
Type II MSD —a discharge device that treats sewage to a higher standard than the Type I device. Treatment is usually biological although some physical treatment units (incineration, etc.) are approved. Discharge coliform count must be less than 200 / 100 ml and suspended solids less than 150 mg / l.
Type III MSD —This is a zero discharge MSD. All sewage is stored on board in holding tanks until if can be pumped out at a pump out facility or at sea.

TABLE 2-14: Types of MSD

The states can implement laws and regulations that completely prohibit treated or untreated sewage discharge, and many states have already done so.

Vessels under 65 feet must have a type I, II, or III MSD if toilets are installed.

Oil Discharge

The Federal Water Pollution Control Act (FWPCA) prohibits the discharge of oil or oily waste into U.S. waters. This includes any discharge which causes a film or discoloration of the surface of the water or causes a sludge or emulsion beneath the surface of the water.

Vessels longer than 26 feet (8 m) must display an oil pollution placard which measures at least 5 inches by 8 inches (13 cm by 20 cm), placed in each machinery space and which states:

DISCHARGE OF OIL PROHIBITED

The Federal Water Pollution Control Act prohibits the discharge of oil or oily waste into or upon the navigable waters of the United States, or the waters of the contiguous zone, or which may affect natural resources belonging to, appertaining to, or under the exclusive management authority of the United States, if such discharge causes a film or discoloration of the surface of the water or causes a sludge or emulsion beneath the surface of the water. Violators are subject to substantial civil penalties and/or criminal sanctions including fines and imprisonment.

POLLUTION PREVENTION REGULATIONS: CANADA

Discharge of Refuse

Generally no ship may discharge garbage into Canadian waters or fishing zones of Canada. Garbage is defined as solid galley waste, food waste, paper, rags, plastics, glass, metal, bottles, crockery, junk, or similar refuse. Canadian waters means the territorial sea of Canada and all internal waters of Canada. Per *Canada Shipping Act—Regulations Respecting the Prevention of the Pollution of Waters by Garbage From Ships*.

Sewage Disposal

Discharge of treated or untreated sewage is prohibited by Federal Law in certain specified waters of British Columbia and Manitoba. There are no specific provisions for treated sewage as opposed to untreated sewage as in the United States. Per *Canada Shipping Act—Pleasure Craft Sewage Pollution Prevention Regulations*.

Provinces may have their own more stringent laws and regulations regarding sewage disposal. For example, discharge of treated or untreated sewage is prohibited in any Ontario waters. A vessel with a toilet on those waters where sewage discharge is prohibited must have a holding tank installed and any means of discharge disconnected. Portable toilets are not permitted on Ontario waters.

CUSTOMS AND IMMIGRATION

ENTERING AND LEAVING THE UNITED STATES

Entering the United States

Boats entering the United States must clear U.S. Customs and Immigration at a *Port of Entry* (**POE**). All persons aboard must present themselves and must have proof of citizenship identification, such as a passport or birth certificate. Driver's licenses are usually unacceptable.

Alternative means of reporting include using the OARS system, or having an I-68 Canadian Border Boat Landing Program form or having a NEXUS member proximity card. All three of these alternatives are described below.

Any vessel over 30 feet (9.1 m) must also have or must purchase a *customs decal* that is good for one year. Cost is $25 for the year. At some ports vessels less than 30 feet may be required to purchase the decal since local rules can apply for customs as well as immigration.

Customs decals may be obtained by completing form CF-339V which can be obtained by:

*   Calling Decal Inquiries at (317) 298-1200, ext. 1245
*   From a local U.S. Customs port
*   By downloadable form via the forms links on the right side of the web page: http://www.customs.gov/travel/travel.htm
*   You can also apply online at the same website

It's a good idea to get the decal in advance since you could be subject to considerable delays getting one while entering at a POE. Also, you must have the decal if you plan on using the I-68 program or OARS system (both described below) for travel between the United States and Canada.

Leaving the United States

It is a little known fact that the captain of a boat leaving the United States must clear the vessel and all guests out of the country. In particular, any non–U.S. citizens aboard must be cleared by the U.S. Immigration and Naturalization service. Failure to do so may result in the foreign citizen not being allowed to re-enter the United States and can also result in a large fine for the captain. Here is some wording from the regulation:

Sec. 231.2 Departure manifest for passengers.

The master, captain, or agent of every vessel or aircraft departing from the United States for a foreign place or outlying possession of the United States shall present a departure manifest to the immigration officer at the port of departure. The manifest must be in the form of a properly completed departure portion of Form I-94, Arrival/Departure Record, for each person on board except for United States citizens, and lawful permanent resident aliens of the United States. No manifest is required for a vessel or aircraft departing on a trip directly for and terminating in Canada, or departing from the United States Virgin Islands directly to the British Virgin Islands on a trip terminating in the British Virgin Islands

Sec 231.3 Exemptions for private vessels and aircraft.

The provisions of this part relating to the presentation of arrival and departure manifests shall not apply to a private vessel or private aircraft not engaged directly or indirectly in the carriage of persons or cargo for hire.

Section 231.3 seems to exempt recreational boaters; however, you would be wise to check with Customs and Border Protection before departing. Also note that there is similar requirement for an arrival manifest. A Google search for "Sec 231.2 Departure Manifest" will bring up all the relevant language.

U.S. Ports of Entry

The following list of ports of entry was compiled from United States Homeland Security, Customs and Border Protection websites. This information (particularly phone numbers) changes frequently so you would be wise to verify these locations and numbers in advance.

Hawaii		Friday Harbor	360-378-2080
Honolulu	808-522-8012	Point Roberts	360-945-2314
Alaska		Tacoma	360-332-7650
Anchorage	907-271-2675	Aberdeen	360-310-0109
Juneau	907-586-7211	Everett	425-259-0246
Ketchikan	907-225-2254	Moses Lake	509-762-2667
Kodiak	907-271-2675	Port Angeles	360-457-4311
Skagway	907-983-2325	Port	360-385-3777
Sitka	907-747-3374	Townsend	
Valdez	907-835-3597	Oroville	509-476-3132
Wrangell	907-874-3415	**Oregon**	
Washington		Astoria	503-325-5541
All Ports	800-562-5943	Coos Bay	541-267-6312
Blaine	360-332-6318	Newport	541-265-6456
Seattle	206-553-4406	Portland	503-325-5541
Lynden	360-354-2183	**California**	
Bellingham	360-734-5463	Eureka	707-442-4822
Anacortes	360-293-2331	Los Angeles	562-366-5555

San Diego	619-557-5370	Myrtle Beach	843-884-2367
San Fransisco	415-782-9200	Morehead City - Beaufort	252-726-5845
San Luis Obispo	805-595-2381	Wilmington	910-772-5900
Texas		**Virginia**	
Most Ports	800-973-2867	Newport News	757-533-4211
Brownsville/ Los Indios	956-548-2744	Norfolk (Portsmouth)	757-533-4211
Corpus Christi	361-888-3352	Richmond (Petersburg)	757-533-4211
Port Aransas	512-888-3352	Alexandria	
Port Lavaca	512-888-3352	**Maryland**	
Port O'Connor	512-888-3352	Baltimore	410-962-2666
Rockport	512-888-3352	**Delaware**	
Freeport	979-233-3004	Both Places	800-743-7416
Houston	281-985-6700	Wilmington	215-597-4648
Galveston	409-766-3624	Dover	215-596-1972
Houston Seaport	281-671-7701	**Pennsyvania**	
Port Arthur	409-727-0285	Philadelphia	215-597-4648
Louisiana		**New Jersey**	
All Places	504-589-3771	New York / Newark	201-443-0110
New Orleans	504-589-4522	Perth Amboy	201-443-0415
Baton Rouge	225-389-0261	**New York (Atlantic)**	
Gramercy	225-869-3765	New York / Newark	201-443-0110
Lake Charles	337-439-5512	Pier 92 North River	212-399-2901
Morgan City	985-384-6658	Rosebank Staten Island	718-816-0469
Florida Gulf		**Connecticut**	
Fort Myers	941-561-6205	Bridgeport	203-367-9487
Key West	305-296-5411	New Haven	203-773-2040
Panama City	850-785-4688	New London (Hartford)	203-442-7123
Pensacola	850-432-6811	**Rhode Island**	
Port Everglades	954-356-7240	Providence	401-941-6326
Port Manatee	941-634-1369	Newport	401-847-2744
St. Petersburg	727-536-7311	**Massachusetts**	
Tampa	813-228-2385	Boston	
Florida Atlantic		Fall River (New Bedford)	508-994-5158
Cape Canaveral	321-783-2066	Gloucester	978-921-0782
Fernandina Beach	904-261-6154	Lawrence (Gloucester)	978-921-0782
Jacksonville	904-360-5020	New Bedford	508-994-5158
Miami Seaport	305-536-5261	Plymouth (New Bedford)	508-994-5158
South Florida	800-432-1216	Salem (Gloucester)	978-921-0782
Georgia			
Brunswick	912-262-6692		
Savannah	912-447-9400		
South Carolina			
Charleston	843-884-2367		
Georgetown	843-884-2367		

New Hampshire	
Portsmouth	603-433-0737
Maine	
Portland	207-771-3600
Bar Harbor	207-288-4675
Bath	207-771-3605
Belfast	207-338-3954
Eastport	207-853-4313
Jonesport	207-454-3621
Rockland (Belfast)	207-338-3954
Vermont	
Highgate Springs	802-868-2778
New York (St Lawrence)	
Champlain	518-298-8346
Rouses Point	518-297-2441
Alexandria Bay	315-482-2472
Massena	315-769-3091
Ogdensburg	800-827-2851
Buffalo	800-927-5015
Rochester	877-833-0880
Pennsylvania	
Erie	814-833-1355
Ohio	
Ashtabula/ Conneaut	440-998-3073
Cleveland	440-891-3800
Toledo/San- dusky	888-523-2628

Michigan	
Algonac	810-794-3321
Detroit	313-226-3140
Marine City	810-795-5454
Bay City / Saginaw/Flint	989-695-2871
Drummond Island	906-493-5232
Freeland	517-695-2871
Port Huron	810-985-7125
Rogers City	517-734-3160
Sault Ste. Marie	906-632-7221
Battle Creek (Inland)	616-965-3349
Grand Rapids	616-456-2515
Illinois	
Chicago	312-983-1100
Waukegan	847-336-2136
Wisconsin	
Milwaukee	414-571-2860
Racine	262-633-0286
Green Bay	920-496-0606
Minnesota	
Grand Portage	218-475-2244
Duluth	218-720-5203
Grand Marais	218-387-1148
International Falls	218-283-2541
Baudette	218-634-2803
Warroad	218-386-2796

U.S. I-68 Canadian Border Boat Landing Program

The *I-68 program* allows persons entering the United States from Canada in small recreational boats to obtain a boating permit for an entire season. The permit allows multiple entries into the United States with only a phone call to the INS being required to clear each entry. There are specific phone numbers to call for various geographic areas.

The I-68 program is most widely used in the Great Lakes and St Lawrence River area, and although available, is not used much between Alaska and Canada, or in the Pacific Northwest.

Note that the I-68 program does not work if even one person on the vessel does not have an I-68. In that event clearing in person or by the OARS system is required. Also the I-68 program is suspended during Orange or higher alert levels.

United States citizens or lawful permanent residents and Canadian citizens or landed immigrants of Canada are eligible to apply for Form I-68. Persons who are not U.S. citizens or permanent residents must stay in the shoreline area and for no more than 72 hours each visit.

Applicants for the I-68 must appear in person for an interview at an INS facility that issues them. Cost is $16 per person with a cap of $32 per family. Children under 14 years of age are listed on the parents' form and those 14 and over will have their own I-68 issued. This information changes frequently so check before going to one of these locations.

U.S. I-68 Application Locations

Washington	
Blaine	360-945-2314
Point Roberts	800-562-5943
Minnesota	
Rainy Lake, International Falls,	218-283-8611
Warroad	218-386-2796
Lake Superior, Grand Portage, Highway 61 POE	218-475-2494
Lake Superior, Duluth, Office 515 E 1st Street	218-720-5207
Michigan	
Lake Superior, Sault Ste. Marie, International Bridge	906-632-8822
Detroit River, Detroit, Ambassador Bridge	313-963-4408
Detroit River, Detroit, Detroit Tunnel	313-568-6019
St Clair River, Port Huron, 1410 Elmwood St -Bridge	810-982-0133
Illinois	
Lake Michigan, Chicago, O'Hara Intl Terminal 5	773-894-2940
Ohio	
Lake Erie, Cleveland, Burke Lakefront Airport	216-522-2265
Lake Erie, Sandusky, 158 E Market Street	419-625-2194
Lake Erie, Toledo, 420 Madison Ave	419-259-6474
Pennsylvania	
Lake Erie, Erie, Erie Airport	814-833-8267
New York	
Niagara River, Buffalo, Peace Bridge POE	716-885-3367
Niagara River, Buffalo, Rainbow Bridge POE	716-282-3141 x323
Niagara River, Buffalo, Lewiston POE	716-285-1676
St Lawrence, Thousand Islands, I-81 POE (Bridge)	315-482-2681
St Lawrence, Ogdensburg, POE (Bridge)	315-393-0770
St Lawrence, Massena, POE (Bridge)	315-764-0310
St Lawrence, Toronto, Pearson Intl Airport	905-676-2563
St Lawrence, Ottawa, Ottawa Intl Airport	613-523-2105
St Lawrence, Montreal, Dorval Airport	514-631-2098

Lake Champlain, Champlain, POE Highway 187	518-298-7900
Lake Champlain, Rouses Point, POE Route #11	518-297-7521
Lake Champlain, Swanton, POE Highway 189	802-868-3349
Maine	
Border NB, Houlton, Route 95	207-532-2906
Vermont	
Border QB, Derby Line,I-91 South	802-373-3316

U.S. Canadian Border Outlying Area Reporting Stations (OARS)

The *Outlying Area Reporting Station* (**OARS**) was developed as an alternative to the I-68 program described above. Currently the OARS system is available only in INS regions east of Minnesota.

The OARS system allows persons arriving by boat from Canada to clear U.S. immigration by using one of approximately 30 videophones located at various docks and marinas. All persons on board the vessel must present themselves for inspection and clearance at the videophone. The applicant and the immigration officer can see and converse with each other and documents are presented to a document camera.

The OARS program uses videophones, typically located at public docks or marinas, which boaters may use to report to U.S. immigration inspectors.

The OARS system is suspended when the alert level is Orange or higher.

U.S. citizens, Lawful Permanent Residents of the United States, Canadian citizens, Landed Commonwealth Residents of Canada, and nationals of designated Visa Waiver Pilot Program countries with a valid, stamped I-94 or I-94W, Arrival/Departure Record are eligible to participate in this program. These locations change with time so call ahead to a nearby POE to verify the location still exists.

Locations of OARS Videophones

Minnesota—Lake of the Woods	
Northwest Angle	Grumpy's Resort
Northwest Angle	Young's Bay
Northwest Angle	Jim's Corner (Drive In)
Rainey Lake	Bohman's Landing (Land)
Michigan—Lake Huron	
Mackinac Island	Mackinac Island (not operational 15Aug03)
Ohio—Lake Erie	
Ashtabula	Ashtabula City Dock
Cleveland	East 55th Street Marina

Eastlake	Chagrin Lagoon Yacht Club
Fairport Harbor	Grand River Marina
Mentor	Mentor Lagoons Marina
Port Clinton	Brand's Dry Dock
Sandusky	Cedar Point Marina
South Bass	Put-in Bay Dockmaster's Office
Pennsyvania—Lake Erie	
Erie	Lampy Marina
Erie	Public Dock—Dobbins Landing
Erie	Perry's Landing Marina—Fuel Dock
Presque Isle	Presque Isle State Park
New York—Lake Erie	
Buffalo	Erie Basin Marina
New York—Lake Ontario	
Lewiston	Near Riverside Inn
North Tonawanda	Pinocle Park
Olcott	Public Dock Building
Oswego	Oswego Marina
Sackets Harbor	Navy Point Marina
Wilson	Tuscarora State Park
Youngston	Youngstown Yacht Club
New York—St Lawrence River	
Alexandria Bay	
Clayton	Front Public Dock
Morristown	Public Town Dock
Ogdensburg	Edwin Dobisky Recreation Bldg. City Marina
Waddington	Public Town Dock
Maine—East Grand Lake	
Orient	Dickensen's Marina
Vermont—Lake Memphremagog	
Newport	Newport City Dock

Western U.S. Small Boat Reporting System (SBRS)

In the Pacific Northwest an alternative to the I-68 program exists which is known as the *small boat reporting system* (**SBRS**). An I-68 can be obtained at the Blaine POE, but SBRS has been much more widely used in the northwest for repeated returns to the United States from Canada. It appears the SBRS is now being phased out and participants in the SBRS are now encouraged to enroll in either the I-68 or Nexus program.

The NEXUS Member Proximity Card

The *NEXUS* card is part a joint United States and Canada program which allows for entry to both Canada and the U.S. This program has definite advantages over the I-68 and Canpass (described below) programs. The primary advantage for recreational boaters is that it allows boaters to enter the United States or Canada by placing a phone call in lieu of reporting in. All persons on board must have a NEXUS card for this to work, otherwise the boat must report in at a port of entry.

All the language quoted below is taken from a document titled Pleasure Boat Fact Sheet available at the Department of Homeland Security/Customs and Border Protection website at www.cbp.gov.

> The NEXUS alternative inspection program allows pre-screened, low-risk travelers to be processed with little or no delay by United States and Canadian border officials. Approved applicants are issued a photo-identification/proximity card. Participants cross the border in a dedicated lane, where they present their membership identification and proximity card, and make a declaration. They are then released, unless chosen for a selective or random secondary referral.

> A NEXUS member will have the benefit of the expedited processing in both marine and highway modes. Becoming a member of the NEXUS alternative inspection program simplifies border crossings for pre-approved, low-risk travelers. As NEXUS members, recreational boaters have the privilege of entering the United States from Canada for recreational purposes with only the need to report their arrival to CBP by placing a telephone call. Boaters can use their NEXUS membership in lieu of the I-68 for reporting purposes.

Who Qualifies for NEXUS?

Individuals may qualify to participate in NEXUS if they are a citizen or permanent resident of the United States or Canada, or are a non-permanent resident who can demonstrate a need to use the NEXUS lanes. However, individuals may not qualify if they:

• Are inadmissible to the United States or Canada under applicable immigration laws;
• Provide false or incomplete information on their application;
• Have been convicted of a criminal offense in any country for which they have not received a pardon;
• Have been found in violation of customs or immigration law; or
• Fail to meet other requirements of the NEXUS program.

To participate, an individual's application must be approved by both the United States and Canada. If an individual does not meet the requirements of the program, their application will be denied.

What are the Benefits of NEXUS?

Individuals approved to participate in NEXUS receive an identification card to use at the border that allows them to:

- Use NEXUS-dedicated lanes in the United States and Canada; and
- Cross the border with a minimum of routine customs and immigration questioning.
- NEXUS membership allows recreational boaters the privilege of entering the United States from Canada for recreational purposes with only the need to report their arrival to CBP by placing a telephone call.

Because NEXUS is a harmonized program, applicants complete a single application form.

NEXUS also allows United States and Canadian Customs and Immigration officials to concentrate their efforts on potentially higher-risk travelers and goods, which helps to ensure security and integrity at our borders.

Finally, there is a cost benefit compared to other existing alternate inspection programs.

- Recreational boaters now pay $40 CAD for a 5-year membership in the CANPASS Private Boat Program.
- Recreational boaters must pay an additional $16 USD yearly for an I-68 permit.
- NEXUS will cost $50 USD or $80 CAD for 5 years.

Over a five year period recreational boaters would pay approximately $110 USD . The total cost of the NEXUS program is $50 USD for five years. This represents a significant cost saving of $60 USD.

The Nexus toll-free information line (both U.S. and Canada) is:

1-866-NEXUS 26 (1-866-639-8726)

Application forms are obtained from the Canada Border Services Agency (CBSA) website at http://www.cbsa-asfc. gc.ca/travel/nexus.

ENTERING AND LEAVING CANADA
Entering Canada

Recreational boats entering Canada must report to Canada customs immediately upon arrival or proceed to an authorized telephone reporting marine site and call the telephone reporting center at 1-888-CANPASS (1-888-226-7277). No one except the captain may leave the boat until authorized. You may be instructed to wait for an inspector or to move the boat to another location.

CANPASS Private Boats Permit

The CANPASS program allows persons entering Canada from the United States in small recreational boats to obtain a boating permit for five years. The permit allows multiple entries into the Canada with a phone call to customs and immigration at 1-888-CANPASS (1-888-226-7277) at least four hours before arrival.

Note that this does not work if even one person on the vessel is not enrolled in the CANPASS program. In that event clearing at a designated reporting station is required.

United States citizens or lawful permanent residents or Canadian citizens or landed immigrants of Canada are eligible to apply for CANPASS.

The cost is $40CDN per applicant over 18 years of age. Apply by completing form E672 and forwarding it to one of the following offices:

Western Canada
CANPASS Processing Centre
28-176th Street
Surrey BC V4P 1M7
Phone: (604) 535-9346

Ontario
CANPASS Processing Centre
P.O. Box 126
Niagara Falls ON L2E 6T1
Phone: (905) 371-1477
Toll free: 1-800-842-7647

Quebec and Atlantic Canada
CANPASS Processing Centre
400 Place d'Youville
Montréal QC H2Y 2C2
Phone: (514) 350-6137

Canada Ports of Entry

Because there are so many locations, they are not individually listed in the table below. These locations are not permanently staffed, rather they are marinas and yacht clubs where you may be directed to report in. Call the CANPASS number to find a specific location.

British Columbia, Vancouver Island	
Port Hardy	1
Rupert Inlet	1
Campbell River	3
Courtenay	1
Port Alberni	1
Nanaimo	5
Sidney	7
Victoria	4

British Columbia, Gulf Islands	
Bedwell	1
South Pender Island (summer only)	1
British Columbia, Mainland	
Prince Rupert	5
Vancouver Area	33
Surrey	1
White Rock	1

Crescent Beach	1
Osoyoos	2
Rossland	1
Creston	

Alberta, Waterton Lakes

Chief Mountain	1

Ontario, Lake of the Woods

Kenora	1
Rainy River	1

Ontario, Lake Superior

Thunder Bay	1
Sault Ste Marie	15
Gore Bay	1

Ontario, Lake Huron

Manitoulin Island	2
Port Severn	1
Owen Sound	2
Goderich	1
Sarnia	5
Lake Huron shoreline	22
Port Lambton	1

Ontario, Detroit River Area

Windsor and Omstead	38

Ontario, Lake Erie

Shoreline	8
Port Dover	3
Port Colborne	3
Fort Erie	14
Niagara River Area	15

Ontario, Lake Ontario

Hamilton	46
Oakville	3
Mississauga	3
Toronto	27
Whitby	2
Oshawa	3
Port Hope	2
Cobourg	
Trenton	12
Kingston	13

Ontario, St Lawrence River

Gananoque	2
Thousand Islands	26
Brockville	5
Prescott	2
Cardinal	1
Summerston	2
Morrisburg	2
Long Sault	1
Cornwall	6

Quebec, St Lawrence River

Montreal	1
Shoreline	9
Saguenay	2

Quebec, Gulf of St Lawrence

Gaspe Peninsula	2
Gaspe	1

Quebec Lake Champlain Area

Philipsburg	3
Notre Dame du Mont-Carmel	1
Stanstead	1

New Brunswick, Gulf of St Lawrence

Bathurst	1
Gulf 2 marinas	2

New Brunswick Bay of Fundy

Saint John	1
St Andrews	1
Deer Island	
Grand Manan Island	1

New Brunswick Interior

St Leonard	1
Fosterville	1

Prince Edward Island

Charlottetown	1
Summerside	1

Nova Scotia - Gulf of St. Lawrence

New Glasgow	1

Nova Scotia - Atlantic

Port Hawkesbury	1
Halifax	1
Halifax	1
Lunenburg	1
Liverpool	1
Shelburne	1

Nova Scotia, Bay of Fundy

Yarmouth	1
Kentville	1

Labrador

Goose Bay	1

Newfoundland

St John's	1
Other coastal locations	6

3 NAVIGATION RULES

RULES—GENERAL

BASIS FOR RULES

The *International Rules* were formalized at the Convention for Preventing Collisions at Sea of 1972. These International Rules were ratified in 1977 and are generally known as *72 COLREGS* (**Collision Regulations**). These rules apply on the high seas as well as on territorial waters outside of lines of demarcation called COLREGS Demarcation Lines. These Demarcation Lines are shown on charts and are also described in Coast Guard publications.

The *Inland Rules* for the United States are based on the International Rules and are for the most part the same language, but with some additions and modifications.

Similarly, the *Canadian Collision Regulations* are based on 72 COLREGS with some additions and modifications.

ABOUT THIS NAVIGATION RULES CHAPTER

This chapter either quotes directly, or paraphrases, the 72 COLREGS and USCG Navigation Rules International and U.S. Inland, as well as the Canadian Collision Regulations.

This section includes *most* but *not all* of the rules from 72 COLREGS or the U.S. Inland Rules. But there is nothing in this section that is not in the navigation rules. Thus you can assume that everything in this section are rules that apply to you and your vessel.

Every U.S. registered vessel over 12 meters (39.4 feet) in length is required to carry on board at all times a copy of the USCG Inland Navigation Rules.

> This Pocket Reference does not, and is not meant to, meet this requirement as a copy of the Navigation Rules. All of the rules are NOT included herein and many rules have been rephrased or recast into tabular form.

APPLICATION AND DEFINITIONS

Application of Rules

The U.S. Inland Rules apply to vessels on the inland waters of the United States. The Inland Rules apply to all U.S. vessels, except where the vessel is in the territorial waters of another country in which case the regulations of that country apply where they differ from the Inland rules.

The Inland Rules usually do not apply to landlocked bodies of water that commonly come under the jurisdiction of the states although generally the states tend to follow the Inland Rules.

The Canadian Collision Regulations apply to all Canadian registered vessels except where the vessel is in the territorial waters of another country in which case the regulations of that country apply if they differ from the Canadian regulations.

The Canadian Collision Regulations apply to every vessel located within Canadian waters or fishing zones.

This chapter on Navigation Rules will paraphrase or quote parts of the International Rules and only mention the U.S. Inland Rules or Canadian Collision Regulations where they differ from the International Rules. Also the Inland Rules will be referred to as the "U.S. Inland Rules" to prevent any confusion with Canadian Collision Regulations.

Definitions: General (Rule 3)

Definitions of some terms used in the rules:

1. The word *vessel* includes every description of water craft, including nondisplacement craft and seaplanes.
2. *Power-driven vessel* means any vessel propelled by machinery.
3. *Sailing vessel* means any vessel under sail and not under power. A sailing vessel under power is considered a power-driven vessel.
4. The term *vessel engaged in fishing* means any vessel fishing with nets, lines, trawls, or other fishing apparatus that restrict maneuverability, but does not include a vessel fishing with trolling lines or other fishing apparatus, which do not restrict maneuverability.
5. The term *vessel not under command* means a vessel that through some exceptional circumstance is unable to maneuver as required by these rules.
6. The term *vessel restricted in her ability to maneuver* means a vessel which from the nature of her work is restricted in her ability to maneuver as required by these rules.
7. **International and Canada only:** The term *vessel constrained by her draft* means a power-driven vessel, which, because of her draft in relation to the available width and depth of navigable water, is severely restricted in her ability to deviate from the course she is following.

8. The word *underway* means that a vessel is not at anchor, made fast to the shore, or aground.
9. The words *length* and *breadth* of a vessel means her length overall and greatest breadth.
10. Vessels must be deemed to be *in sight of one another* only when one can be observed visually from the other.
11. The term *restricted visibility* means any condition in which visibility is restricted by fog, mist, falling snow, heavy rainstorms, sandstorms, or any other similar causes.

Definitions: Sound and Light Signals (Rule 32)

The word *whistle* means any sound signaling appliance capable of producing the prescribed blasts and that complies with Annex III to the International Regulations or Annex III to the U.S. Inland Rules (not included in this book).

A *short blast* is a blast of about one second duration.

A *prolonged blast* is from four to six seconds in duration.

Equipment for Sound Signals (Rule 33)

A vessel of 12 meters (39.4 ft) or more must have both a whistle and a bell. A vessel of 100 meters (328 ft) or more also must be provided with a gong, the sound of which cannot be confused with the bell. Other devices may be substituted for the bell or the gong provided they sound the same and may be manually sounded.

A vessel less than 12 meters (39.4 ft) is exempted from this rule but must have some means of making an efficient sound signal.

Canada addition: In Canadian waters a vessel less than 12 meters (39.4 ft) and whose purpose is pushing or pulling and is not solely employed in yarding or warping operations must carry the whistle and bell described above for vessels of more than 12 meters.

CONDUCT IN ANY VISIBILITY

RESPONSIBILITY (RULE 2)

Avoiding a collision or danger is the primary responsibility of the vessel operator and as such may require a departure from the rules to avoid such collision or danger. In addition, neglect of any precaution that is not included in these rules, but which is normal practice at sea, does not exonerate the operator from responsibility. Due regard must be paid to all dangers of navigation and collision and to any special circumstances, including the limitations of the vessels involved, which may make a departure from the rules necessary.

For example, a small vessel crossing paths at sea with a large ship. Although the small boat might have right of way, the ship is unable to effectively maneuver to avoid collision. The small boat is responsible for avoidance when the limitations of the vessels involved is taken into account.

LOOK-OUT (RULE 5)

Every vessel must maintain a proper look-out by sight and hearing. Additionally all other available means, such as radar, must be used when conditions warrant.

SAFE SPEED (RULE 6)

Any vessel must proceed at a safe speed so that proper and effective action to avoid collision can be taken, and to allow stopping within a distance appropriate to the prevailing circumstances. Determination of safe speed must take into account factors such as, visibility, traffic density, vessel maneuverability, vessel draft, weather, and nearby navigational hazards. At night the presence of background lights is be taken into account.

In addition vessels with operational radar are to take account of the following factors:

1. Characteristics of the radar equipment.
2. Effect on the radar of weather and sea state or other sources of interference.
3. The possibility that small vessels and/or objects might not be detected by the radar.
4. The number of vessels detected by the radar.
5. Radar can be used to better assess visibility by determining the range of other objects in the vicinity.

Canada addition: In the Canadian waters of a roadstead, harbor, river, lake, or inland waterway:

- Every vessel passing another vessel or work that includes a dredge, tow, grounded vessel, or wreck must proceed with caution at a speed that will not adversely affect the work being passed.
- Every vessel must navigate with caution and comply with any Notice to Mariners or Notice to Shipping where abnormal water levels, ice conditions, or a casualty to a vessel or aid to navigation may make navigation difficult or hazardous, or cause damage to property, or block the navigational channel.

RISK OF COLLISION (RULE 7)

Every vessel must use all available means to determine if risk of collision exists. If in doubt, then such risk must be deemed to exist.

If radar is installed and operational, proper use of the radar must be made, including long-range scanning, and radar plotting or systematic observation of detected objects.

If the compass bearing of an approaching vessel does not change, that vessel must be considered to be on a collision course. Even if the bearing of the approaching vessel is changing, the risk of collision still exists, particularly when the vessel is very large, is a tow, or is at close range.

ACTION TO AVOID COLLISION (RULE 8)

If possible, action to avoid a collision must be positive, made in ample time, and use good seamanship. Alteration of course and/or speed should be large enough to be readily apparent to another vessel observing visually or by radar. A succession of small alterations of course and/or speed should be avoided.

If there is sufficient sea room, alteration of course alone may be the most effective action to avoid a close-quarters situation provided that it is made in good time, is substantial, and does not result in another close-quarters situation. Passing must be at a safe distance. If necessary, a vessel must slow or come to a stop.

The *stand on vessel* (the vessel with the right of way) also remains fully obliged to comply with the rules of this part when the two vessels are approaching one another so as to involve risk of collision.

DANGER SIGNAL (RULE 34)

This applies to vessels in sight of and approaching one another. If either vessel is in doubt as to the intentions of the other, or as to whether sufficient action is being taken by the other, then five short and rapid blasts must be given on the whistle. This signal may be accompanied by a corresponding light signal. This signal is used to indicate disagreement with the proposed overtaking signals as well as to meeting or crossing situations.

U.S. inland and Canada addition: Use of Radio Instead of Sound or Light Signals (Rule 34) A vessel that reaches agreement with another vessel by radio, in a meeting, crossing, or overtaking situation does not have to use the sound signals prescribed, but may do so. If agreement is not reached then whistle signals must be used and will prevail.

U.S inland and Canada addition: Signal Leaving Dock. When leaving a dock or berth, a power-driven vessel must sound one prolonged blast (4 to 6 seconds).

NARROW CHANNELS (RULE 9)

A vessel in a narrow channel must keep as far to the starboard side of the channel as is safe and practicable.

U.S. inland and Canada addition: The vessel proceeding with the current or tidal stream is the stand-on vessel and must propose the place of passage and must indicate the side on which she intends to pass by sounding the appropriate signals prescribed by Rule 34 as follows:

* One short blast (one second) to mean "I intend to leave you on my port side."
* Two short blasts to mean "I intend to leave you on my starboard side."
* Three short blasts to mean "I am operating astern propulsion."
* The upstream vessel is the give-way vessel and must promptly reply to the signal with the same signal if in agreement, or with the danger signal (five short blasts) if in doubt.
* The (give-way) vessel proceeding against the current or tidal stream must keep out of the way of the vessel proceeding with the current or tidal stream and must hold as necessary to permit safe passing.

A vessel of less than 20 meters (66 ft) in length or a sailing vessel must not impede the passage of a vessel that can safely navigate only within a narrow channel or fairway.

A vessel engaged in fishing must not impede the passage of any other vessel navigating within a narrow channel or fairway.

A vessel must not cross a narrow channel or fairway if such crossing impedes the passage of a vessel that can safely navigate only within such channel or fairway.

* If the latter vessel is in doubt as to the intentions of the crossing vessel, she may use the five short blast danger signal.
* **Canada addition:** In the waters of the Great Lakes Basin, if the latter vessel is impeded by a crossing vessel, she *must* use the five short blast sound signal.

In a situation where overtaking can only take place if the vessel to be overtaken has to take action to permit safe passing, the vessel intending to overtake must indicate her intention by sounding the appropriate signal (one or two whistles) as described in the section on overtaking. The vessel to be overtaken must indicate agreement with the appropriate (one or two whistles) signal or disagreement with the danger (five whistle) signal. This rule does not relieve the overtaking vessel of her obligation to keep out of the way of the vessel being overtaken (Rule 13 on Overtaking).

Canada addition: Notwithstanding the preceding paragraph, in the waters of the Great Lakes Basin a vessel must indicate its intention to overtake or its agreement to being overtaken, as the case may be, by sounding the appropriate one or two whistle signals.

Any vessel must avoid anchoring in a narrow channel if at all possible.

Canada addition: In Canadian waters a barge or an inconspicuous, partly submerged vessel or object must not be navigated, moored, or anchored so as to impede the safe passage of any other vessel or object using those waters.

SIGNALS FOR BENDS AND VISUAL OBSTRUCTIONS IN CHANNELS AND FAIRWAYS (RULE 34-E)

A vessel nearing a bend where other vessels may be obscured by an intervening obstruction must sound one prolonged (four- to six-second) blast. Any approaching vessel must respond with a prolonged blast.

TRAFFIC SEPARATION SCHEMES (RULE 10)

A vessel using a traffic separation scheme must:
- Proceed in the general direction of traffic flow for the lane.
- Keep clear of traffic separation lines or zones, as far as is practicable.
- Normally try to leave or join at the termination of the lane, but when joining or leaving from either side try to do so at as small an angle to the general traffic flow as practicable.

A vessel must avoid crossing traffic lanes if possible; but if necessary, it should cross on a heading as close as possible to a right angle to the traffic flow.

Canada addition: The above two paragraphs do not apply to vessels engaged in fishing (as defined by the rules—not recreational fishing) in or near a routing system located in Canadian waters or fishing zones.

A vessel should not use an inshore traffic zone when she can safely use a traffic lane within an adjacent traffic separation scheme.

- Vessels less than 20 meters (66 ft), sailboats, and boats engaged in fishing are exempted from this requirement.
- A vessel may use an inshore traffic zone when en route to or from a port or any place within the inshore zone, or to avoid immediate danger.
- **Canada addition:** Power vessels longer than 20 meters (66 ft) *must* use the traffic separation scheme or a routing system by which she can safely proceed to her destination.

A vessel not crossing or joining or leaving a lane should not enter a separation zone except to avoid immediate danger or to engage in fishing within a separation zone. Vessels should avoid anchoring in a traffic separation scheme or near its terminations. A vessel not using a traffic separation scheme should avoid it by as wide a margin as possible.

Canada modification: Fishing boats as defined in the rules are exempted.

Vessels less than 20 meters (66 ft), sailboats, and vessels engaged in fishing must not impede traffic in a traffic lane.

Vessels restricted in their ability to maneuver and engaged in:

- Maintenance of safety of navigation within a traffic separation scheme, or
- Laying, servicing, or picking up of a submarine cable within a traffic separation scheme

are exempted from complying with this rule to the extent necessary to carry out the operation.

Canada addition: This rule does not generally apply to vessels laying, servicing, or picking up a navigation mark, submarine cable or pipeline, dredging, surveying, underwater operations or launching, or recovering aircraft in or near a routing system located in Canadian waters or fishing zones, where that vessel does not prevent other vessels from using the route safely, and identifies herself to approaching vessels as to the location and nature of the operations and her intentions

CONDUCT OF VESSELS IN SIGHT OF ONE ANOTHER

RESPONSIBILITIES BETWEEN VESSELS (RULE 18)

Except where Rules 9 (Narrow Channels), 10 (Traffic Separation Schemes), and 13 (Overtaking) otherwise require:

In the following hierarchy the vessels lower in the list must keep out of the way of vessels higher in the list.

1	Vessel not under command (highest).
2	Vessel restricted in her ability to maneuver.
3	Vessel constrained by her draft exhibiting the signals in Rule 28 for same (International and Canada only).
4	Vessel engaged in fishing (fishing as defined by the rules).
5	Vessel under sail (but not under power).
6	Vessel power-driven (includes sailing vessels under power).
7	Seaplane on the water (lowest).

ACTION BY GIVE-WAY VESSEL (RULE 16)

The give-way vessel must, as far as possible, take early and substantial action to keep well clear.

ACTION BY STAND-ON VESSEL (RULE 17)

Where one of two vessels is to keep out of the way the stand-on vessel is to keep her course and speed.

The stand-on vessel may take action to avoid collision as soon as it becomes apparent that the give-way vessel is not taking action. In this case, in a crossing situation, the stand-on vessel should not alter course to port if possible.

When the stand-on vessel finds that collision cannot be avoided by the give-way vessel alone, she must take action to avoid collision.

HEAD-ON SITUATION (RULE 14)

When two power driven vessels are meeting head on or nearly so, each must alter course to starboard so as to pass port to port. The head-on situation is deemed to exist if at night the masthead lights of the other are nearly in a line or both sidelights can be seen. When in doubt, act as if this condition exists.

U.S. inland addition: A power-driven vessel operating on the Great Lakes, western rivers, or other specified waters, and proceeding downbound with a following current must have the right-of-way over an upbound vessel, must propose the manner of passage, and must initiate the appropriate maneuvering signals. These signals are described in Signals for Meeting or Crossing.

THE CROSSING SITUATION (RULE 15)

When two vessels are in a crossing situation, the vessel with the other to starboard is the give-way vessel and must keep out of the way of the other stand-on vessel and normally will avoid crossing ahead of the other vessel. In simple terms, the boat on your right has the right of way.

U.S. inland and Canada addition: On the Great Lakes, western rivers, Canadian waters, or other specified waters, a vessel crossing a river must keep out of the way of a power-driven vessel traveling up or down river. **Canada:** Except on the St. Lawrence River northeast of Ile Rouge.

SIGNALS FOR VESSELS IN SIGHT OF ONE ANOTHER (RULE 34)

International only: Power driven vessels underway when in sight of one another indicate maneuvers with whistle signals as follows:

- One short blast (one second) to mean "I am altering my course to starboard."
- Two short blasts to mean "I am altering my course to port."
- Three short blasts to mean "I am operating astern propulsion."

The sound signals may be supplemented by light signals that correspond to the whistle blasts described. For example, a one-second light flash means "I am altering my course to starboard." The light used for these signals must be an all-round white light visible for 5 miles.

No response is given by the other vessel.

U.S. inland and Canada substitution: Power driven vessels underway when in sight of one another and meeting or crossing at a distance within a half-mile of each other must indicate maneuvers with whistle signals as follows:

- One short blast (one second) to mean "I intend to leave you on my port side."

- Two short blasts to mean "I intend to leave you on my starboard side."
- Three short blasts to mean "I am operating astern propulsion."

If in agreement with the proposed maneuver, the other vessel must then sound the same whistle signal and take steps necessary to effect a safe passing.

If the other vessel doubts the safety of the proposed maneuver she must sound the danger signal: five short and rapid blasts.

The sound signals may be supplemented by light signals that correspond to and are synchronized with the whistle blasts described. For example, a one second light flash means "I intend to leave you on my port side." The light used for these signals must be an all-round white light visible for 2 miles.
U.S. inland addition: The light may alternatively be an all-round yellow light visible for 2 miles.

SAILING VESSELS (RULE 12)

When two sailboats, both under sail, are approaching one another one must yield to the other as follows:

- When each is on a different tack (wind on different sides) the vessel on the port tack (wind on the port side) must keep out of the way of the other.
- When both have the wind on the same side, then the vessel to windward keeps out of the way of the leeward vessel.
- If a vessel with the wind on the port side sees a vessel to windward and cannot determine whether the vessel has the wind on the port or starboard, she must keep out of the way of the other.

OVERTAKING (RULE 13)

A vessel is deemed to be overtaking when coming up with another vessel from a direction more than 22.5 degrees behind a line perpendicular to her direction of travel (22.5 degrees abaft her beam). At night this corresponds to only being able to see the sternlight, but not the sidelights of the vessel being overtaken.
Canada addition: In the Great Lakes Basin, a vessel must be deemed to be overtaking another vessel when at night she can see the all-round white lights but not the sidelights of:

- A vessel under 20 meters exhibiting a single all-round white light, or
- A vessel carrying a single all-round white light instead of the second aft masthead light and the sternlight as permitted by Canada (Rule 23e).

If a vessel is in doubt as whether she is overtaking then she must act as if she is overtaking.

Any vessel overtaking another must keep out of the way of the vessel being overtaken.

Any subsequent alteration of the bearing between the two vessels does not make the overtaking vessel a crossing vessel or relieve her of the duty of keeping clear until she is past and clear.

OVERTAKING SIGNALS: INTERNATIONAL ONLY (RULE 34)

A vessel intending to overtake another, in a narrow channel or fairway, must indicate her intention by the following signals:

*   Two prolonged (four to six seconds) blasts followed by
    One short (one second) blast to mean
    I intend to overtake you on your starboard side.
*   Two prolonged blasts followed by
    Two short blasts to mean
    I intend to overtake you on your port side

The vessel to be overtaken must indicate agreement with:

*   One prolonged blast
    One short blast
    One prolonged blast
    One short blast

OVERTAKING SIGNALS: U.S. INLAND AND CANADA SUBSTITUTION (RULE 34)

A vessel intending to overtake another (**Canada only:** in a narrow channel or fairway), must indicate her intention by the following signals:

*   One short (one second) blast to mean
    I intend to overtake you on your starboard side.
*   Two short blasts to mean
    I intend to overtake you on your port side

The vessel to be overtaken must indicate agreement with the same sound signal, that is one or two short blasts. If in doubt the five blast danger signal is given.

CONDUCT IN RESTRICTED VISIBILITY

CONDUCT OF VESSELS IN RESTRICTED VISIBILITY (RULE 19)

This rule applies to vessels not in sight of one another when in or near an area of restricted visibility.

Every vessel must proceed at a safe speed appropriate to the circumstances and visibility.

A vessel that detects using radar alone the presence of another vessel must determine if risk of collision exists and if so take avoiding action in ample time.
- If possible the vessel should avoid an alteration of course to port for a vessel forward of the beam, other than for a vessel being overtaken.
- Also the vessel should try not to alter course toward a vessel abeam or abaft (behind) the beam.

Except where it has been determined that a risk of collision does not exist:
- Every vessel which hears a fog signal forward of her beam or which cannot avoid a close quarters situation must reduce speed to the minimum needed to stay on course. If necessary she must come to a stop.

SOUND SIGNALS IN RESTRICTED VISIBILITY (RULE 35)

In or near an area of restricted visibility, day and night, the signals prescribed in this rule must be used. This normally refers to fog but applies to any other conditions of restricted visibility.

A vessel of less than 12 meters (39.4 ft) in length is not required to give these signals but must at least make some other efficient sound signal at intervals of not less than 2 minutes.

Canada addition: A vessel of less than 12 meters (39.4 ft) whose purpose is for pushing or pulling any floating object, and is not located within a recognized mooring, storage, or booming area, must sound the signals prescribed for vessels of greater than 12 meters in length.

Power-Driven Vessel Underway—Restricted Visibility

A power-driven vessel underway must sound one prolonged (four to six seconds) blast every two minutes.

Power-Driven Vessel Underway But Stopped—Restricted Visibility

A power-driven vessel underway but stopped and making no way must sound two prolonged blasts every two minutes. There should be a one-second interval between the two prolonged blasts.

Vessels in Special Situations—Restricted Visibility

Vessels under the conditions listed below must sound one prolonged and two short blasts in succession at intervals of two minutes.

- Vessels not under command.
- Vessels restricted in ability to maneuver.
- Vessels constrained by draft.
- Sailing vessels.
- Vessels engaged in fishing.
- Vessels engaged in towing or pushing.

International rule only: The following also use this signal instead of the restricted visibility signals prescribed for vessels at anchor

- Vessels engaged in fishing while at anchor, and
- Vessels restricted in ability to maneuver when carrying out work at anchor.

Towed Vessels—Restricted Visibility

The last vessel of a tow must sound in succession one prolonged and three short blasts at intervals of two minutes. If possible this signal should be made immediately after the signal made by the towing vessel.

Composite Vessels—Restricted Visibility

A pushing vessel and a vessel being pushed ahead, connected as one unit, are regarded as a power-driven vessel and give signals accordingly.

Vessel at Anchor—Restricted Visibility

A vessel at anchor must ring a bell for rapidly for about five seconds at intervals of not more than one minute.

A vessel of more than 100 meters (328 ft) in length sounds the bell in the forepart of the vessel, and immediately afterward sounds a gong in the after part of the vessel for about five seconds.

Vessel Aground—Restricted Visibility

A vessel aground gives the same signals as a vessel at anchor but also gives three distinct and separate strokes of the bell immediately before and after the rapid ringing of the bell.

U.S. inland rule exception: The following vessels are not required to sound signals as prescribed by this rule when anchored in a special anchorage area designated by the secretary:

- A vessel of less than 20 meters (65.6 ft) in length.
- A barge, canal boat, scow, or other nondescript craft.

SIGNALS TO ATTRACT ATTENTION (RULE 36)

If necessary, to attract attention, any vessel may make light or sound signals that cannot be mistaken for any signal authorized elsewhere in these rules, or may direct the beam of her search light in the direction of the danger, in such a way as not to embarrass any vessel.

International and Canada addition: Any light to attract the attention of another vessel must be such that it cannot be mistaken for any aid to navigation. For the purpose of this rule the use of high-intensity, intermittent or revolving lights, such as strobe lights, must be avoided.

DISTRESS SIGNALS (RULE 37)

When a vessel is in distress and requires assistance she must use or exhibit the signals in Annex IV of the International Regulations. The text of Annex IV follows:

The following signals, used or exhibited either together or separately, indicate distress and need of assistance:

- A gun or other explosive signal fired at intervals of about a minute.
- A continuous sounding with any fog-signaling apparatus.
- Rockets or shells, throwing red stars fired one at a time at short intervals.
- A signal made by radiotelegraphy or by any other signaling method consisting of the group •••−−−••• (SOS) in Morse Code.
- A signal sent by radiotelephony consisting of the spoken word "Mayday."
- The International Code Signal of distress indicated by N.C. (Code flags November Charlie)
- A signal consisting of a square flag having above or below it a ball or anything resembling a ball.
- Flames on the vessel (as from a burning tar barrel, oil barrel, etc.).
- A rocket parachute flare or a hand flare showing a red light.
- A smoke signal giving off orange-colored smoke.
- Slowly and repeatedly raising and lowering arms outstretched to each side.
- The radiotelegraph alarm signal
- Signals transmitted by emergency position-indicating radio beacons.
- Signals transmitted by radio communication systems.
- **U.S. inland addition:** A high-intensity white light flashing at regular intervals from 50 to 70 times per minute.

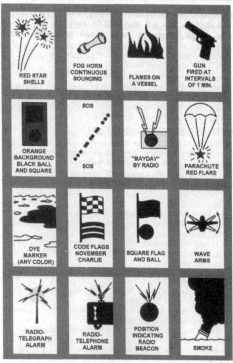

FIGURE 3-1: Distress Signals Illustrated (From United States Coast Guard Navigation Rules)

LIGHTS AND SHAPES

LIGHTS AND SHAPES APPLICATION (RULE 20)

Navigation lights are to be used from sunset to sunrise including in restricted visibility and in all weathers. The rules concerning shapes must be complied with during the day.

During such times no other lights are to be exhibited except where they cannot be mistaken for navigation lights and where they do not impair the visibility of the navigation lights. These lights may also be used at other times whenever deemed necessary.

LIGHTS AND SHAPES DEFINITIONS (RULE 21)

Masthead light means a white light placed over the center-line of the vessel showing an unbroken light over a horizontal arc of 225 degrees, so as to show from right ahead to 22.5 degrees abaft the beam on either side of the vessel. See figure 3-2 on the next page.

Sidelights means a green light on the starboard side and a red light on the port side each showing an unbroken light over a horizontal arc of 112.5 degrees, so as to show from right ahead to 22.5 degrees abaft the beam on either side of the vessel (figure 3-2 next page).

- On a vessel of less than 20 meters (66 ft) the sidelights may be combined in one lantern carried on the centerline of the vessel.
- **U.S. inland rule addition:** On a vessel of less than 12 meters (39 ft) in length combined sidelights must be placed as near as practicable to the centerline of the vessel.

Sternlight means a white light placed as near as practicable to the stern showing an unbroken light over a horizontal arc of 135 degrees so as to show from 67.5 degrees from aft forward on each side of the vessel. See figure 3-2 on the next page.

Towing light means a yellow light placed as near as practicable to the stern showing an unbroken light over a horizontal arc of 135 degrees so as to show from 67.5 degrees from right aft on each side of the vessel (same as Sternlight, only yellow).

All-round light means a light showing an unbroken light over a horizontal arc of 360 degrees.

Flashing light means a light flashing at regular intervals at a frequency of at least 120 flashes per minute.

U.S. inland and Canada addition: *Special flashing light* means a yellow light flashing at a regular frequency of 50 to 70 flashes per minute, placed as far forward and as close to centerline of the vessel as practicable. It is to cover a horizontal arc of not less than 180 and not more than 225 degrees so as to show from right ahead to abeam and no more than 22.5 degrees abaft the beam on either side of the vessel.

Canada addition: *Blue flashing light* means a blue all-round flashing light flashing at regular intervals of 50 to 70 flashes per minute.

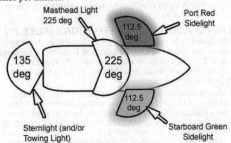

FIGURE 3-2: Visibility Arcs of Basic Navigation Lights.

Lights and Right of Way

The visible arcs of navigation lights correspond to the different situations: overtaking, head-on, and crossing.

If you see a single white light only, then you are in an overtaking situation and must act accordingly.

If you see a white (masthead) light over both green and red lights, then you are in a head-on situation and must take action accordingly. See figures on the following pages.

If you see a white (masthead) light above a green light (but not the red light) of another vessel you are in a crossing situation, where you are the stand-on vessel (have right of way). Think of green as a sort of go, but be careful, light.

If you see a white (masthead) lights over a red light (and not the green light) of another vessel you are also in a crossing situation, but here you are the give-way vessel. Think of red as yield.

VISIBILITY OF LIGHTS (RULE 22)

Lights must have an intensity so as to be visible at the ranges shown in table 3-1.

LIGHTS ON POWER DRIVEN VESSELS UNDERWAY (RULE 23)

Table 3-2 on page on page 134 summarizes the lights required on power-driven vessels underway.

Type of Light	Length of Boat			
	Less than 12 meters (39.4 ft)	12 meters (39.4 ft) or longer	20 meters (65.6 ft) or longer	50 meters (164 f) or longer
Masthead light	2 miles	3 miles	5 miles	6 miles
Sidelight	1 mile	2 miles	2 miles	3 miles
Sternlight	2 miles	2 miles	2 miles	3 miles
Towing light	2 miles	2 miles	2 miles	3 miles
All-round light-white, red, green, yellow	2 miles	2 miles	2 miles	3 miles
U.S. inland and Canada: Special flashing light	2 miles	2 miles	2 miles	2 miles
Canada: Government or police vessel blue flashing light	2 miles	2 miles	2 miles	2 miles
Inconspicuous, partly submerged vessel or object being towed white all-round light	3 miles	3 miles	3 miles	3 miles

TABLE 3-1: Visibility of Lights (Rule 22)

Power Vessel Over 50 Meters (164 Ft)

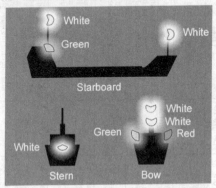

A vessel over 50 meters must have a masthead light forward and a second masthead light abaft of and higher than the forward one. Sidelights and a sternlight are also required.

Vessel Length From (>=)	Vessel Length To (<)	Masthead Light	Second Masthead Light	Sidelights	Sternlight
50 meters (164 feet)		Required forward	Required abaft of and higher than the forward one	Required	Required
20 meters (66 feet)	50 meters (164 feet)	Required forward	Optional	Required	Required
12 meters (39 feet)	20 meters (66 feet)	Required Forward. **Inland Only:** does not need to be forward or at amidships but shall be as far forward as possible	Optional	Required	Required
7 meters (23 feet)	12 meters (39 feet)	May exhibit an all-round white light in lieu of masthead and sternlights	Optional	Required	May exhibit an all-round white light in lieu of masthead and sternlights
International and Canada Only: 7 meters (23 feet)	12 meters (39 feet)	Masthead light may be off centerline if centerline fitting not practicable and if sidelights are combined in one on centerline	Optional	May be combined on centerline	May exhibit an all-round white light in lieu of masthead and sternlights
International Only: 0 meters (0 feet)	7 meters (23 feet) and speed less than 7 knots	May exhibit an all-round white light in lieu of masthead and sternlights	Optional	Shall be exhibited if practicable	May exhibit an all-round white light in lieu of masthead and sternlights
Inland Only: Great Lakes		May exhibit an all-round white light in lieu of the second masthead light and sternlight. This light shall be carried in the position of the second masthead light.			

TABLE 3-2: Lights on Power Vessels Underway Summarized

Power Vessel Less Than 50 Meters (164 Ft)

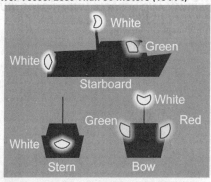

In addition to sidelights and a sternlight, a power vessel less than 50 meters requires one masthead light as far forward as possible and optionally a second masthead light abaft of and higher than the forward one.

Power Vessel Less Than 12 Meters (39 Ft)

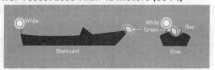

A power vessel less than 12 meters in length may have one all-round light and combined sidelights as shown.

Air Cushion Vessel

An air-cushion vessel when operating in the nondisplacement mode must, in addition to the normal power vessel navigation lights, exhibit an all-round flashing yellow light where it best can be seen.

LIGHTS AND SHAPES ON SAILING VESSELS UNDERWAY AND VESSELS UNDER OARS (RULE 25)

Sailing Vessel Underway

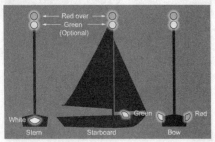

A sailing vessel underway must exhibit sidelights and a sternlight. A sailing vessel may also exhibit two all round lights near the top of the mast, the upper being red and the lower being green.

Note: there are no white masthead lights as on power vessels.

Sailing Vessel Underway Less Than 20 Meters (66 Ft)

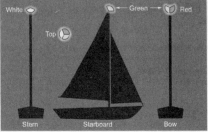

A sailing vessel of less than 20 meters (66 ft) in length may combine the sidelights and sternlight in one light near the top of the mast. In this case the red over green mast lights shown in the previous illustration may not be used.

Sailing Vessel Less Than 7 Meters (23 Ft)

A sailing vessel of less than 7 meters (23 ft) in length must if practicable exhibit lights as described in the previous paragraph.

If she does not do so, then she must have available an electric torch or lighted lantern which must be exhibited in time to prevent collision.

White

Vessels under oars may display lights as described in this rule for sailing vessels. If she does not then she must have available an electric torch or lighted lantern which must be exhibited in time to prevent collision.

A sailboat under power and sail must exhibit forward where it can best be seen, a conical shape apex downward. **U.S. inland and Canada:** Sailboats less than 12 meters (39 ft) are exempted.

TOWING AND PUSHING LIGHTS AND SHAPES (RULE 24)

Table 3-3 on page on page 138 summarizes most of the rules for lighting and shapes for towing and pushing.

Some other rules and considerations not covered in the table are as follows:

When a pushing vessel and a vessel being pushed ahead are rigidly connected in a composite unit, they must be regarded as one power-driven vessel and exhibit lights according to the rules for power-driven vessels in Rule 23. In other words, they will not be lighted according to towing and pushing Rule 24.

An inconspicuous, partly submerged vessel or object, or combination of such vessels or objects being towed must exhibit:

- If less than 25 meters (82 ft) in breadth, one all-round white light near the forward end and one near the after end. Dracones need not exhibit a light forward. (A dracone is a flexible cylinder that carries liquids such as petroleum products, that are lighter than water.)
- If 25 or more meters (82 ft) in breadth, two additional all-round white lights at or near the extremities of its breadth.

Vessel or Object	Length of Tow Stern of Towing to Stern of Tow	Type of Tow	Mast-head Lights	Towing Light	Other
Towing or Pushing Vessel	<= 200 meters (656 feet)	tow astern	2 vertical	1 in vertical line above sternlight	
	> 200 meters (656 feet)	tow astern	3 vertical	1 in vertical line above sternlight	Diamond shape, where it can best be seen
		pushing or alongside	2 vertical	U.S. inland and Canada: 2 vertical in lieu of sternlight	
		pushing or alongside	none	U.S. inland: 2 vertical in lieu of sternlight	Western Rivers and Mississippi above Huey P. Long Bridge
Towed or Pushed Vessel/s or Object/s		tow astern	none	none	Sidelights, sternlight see Canada only comments on next page
	> 200 meters (656 feet)	tow astern	none	none	Sidelights, sternlight -diamond shape where it can best be seen
		alongside	none	none	Sidelights, sternlight. Any number of towed alongside vessels lighted as one
		push	none	none	Sidelights forward. Any number of pushed vessels lighted as one. U.S. inland and Canada: special flashing light on bow

TABLE 3-3: Summary of Towing and Pushing Lights

- If it is more than 100 meters (328 ft) in length then intermediate pairs of all-round lights are required at spacing not exceeding 100 meters (328 ft).
- A diamond shape near the aft end and if the tow is greater than 200 meters (656 ft) an additional diamond shape near the forward end.

U.S. inland only: The towing vessel may direct a searchlight in the direction of the tow to indicate its presence to an approaching vessel.

Vessels involved in towing generally exhibit the same navigation lights as described in Rule 23 for power-driven vessels underway. Summary table 3-3 shows the differences specific to towing vessels and objects or vessels being towed.

If it is impracticable for a tow to exhibit lights as specified, then all possible measures must be taken to the light the vessel or object, or at least indicate the presence of the tow.

Canada only: In Canadian waters or fishing zones, if it is impracticable for a barge being towed to display the sidelights and sternlight, then every barge must carry one all round light at each end of the barge.
- Where two or more barges are grouped together, the group may be lighted as one barge. If the group is longer than 100 meters then an additional all-round white light is required near the middle point of the group.
- A barge being pushed ahead must carry, instead of the all-round white lights, white lights that show an unbroken arc of 225 degrees from forward to 22.5 degrees abaft the beam on both sides of the boat.

Vessels not normally engaged in towing operations are not required to display these lights when towing another vessel in distress or otherwise in need of assistance. All possible measures must be taken to indicate the fact that towing is taking place, in particular by illuminating the towline.

Towboat Greater Than 50 Meters (164 ft) in Length Towing Astern—Tow Less Than 200 Meters (656 Ft)

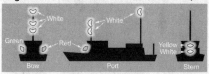

Note the second masthead light (aft) is higher than the forward masthead lights to satisfy the requirement for power driven boats longer than 50 meters (164 ft). Also the two masthead lights and the yellow towing light differentiate this boat from a non towing boat.

Tow Astern: Vessel Less Than 50 Meters (164 ft): Tow Less Than 200 Meters (656 Ft)

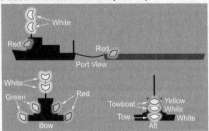

Towing vessel has two masthead lights and a yellow towing light over a sternlight. The tow has sidelights and sternlight as does the towing vessel.

Tow Astern: Tow Greater Than 200 Meters (656 Ft)

Lighting is the same as for the tow less than 200 meters except there are three masthead lights arranged in a vertical line.

Towing Alongside: International Only: Vessel Less Than 50 Meters (164 Ft)

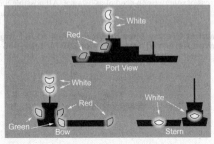

Towing vessel has two masthead lights. Notice there is no yellow towing light on the stern in the international case. The tow has sidelights and sternlights as does the towing vessel.

Towing Alongside: U.S. Inland, Canada: Vessel Less Than 50 Meters (164 Ft)

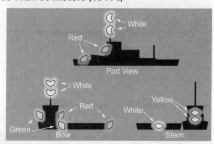

Lights are the same as for the previous international case, except there are two yellow towing lights instead of the sternlight.

Tow—Pushing: International Only: Vessel Less Than 50 Meters (164 Ft)

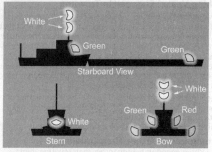

No yellow towing light at stern. Sidelights on the tow and towing vessel. Two masthead lights.

Tow—Pushing: U.S. Inland And Canada: Vessel Less Than 50 Meters (164 Ft)

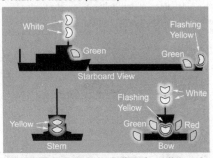

Note: Two yellow towing lights in lieu of sternlight and special flashing yellow on bow of tow. Sidelights on both the towing and towed vessels.

FISHING VESSELS LIGHTS AND SHAPES (RULE 26)

Whether underway or at anchor a vessel engaged in fishing must display the lights and shapes described in this rule.

Fishing Vessel Engaged In Trawling

Trawling means towing a dredge net or other apparatus used as a fishing appliance. Trawling is not trolling. A boat that is trolling is not considered a fishing vessel under these rules. A vessel when trawling must display, instead of masthead lights, two all-round lights in a vertical line, the upper being green and the lower being white. If greater than 50 meters (164 ft), the vessel must also display a masthead light aft of and higher than the all-round green light.

When lights are not displayed then a shape consisting of two cones must be displayed with their apexes together in a vertical line one above the other. When underway the fishing vessel must also display sidelights and a sternlight.

Fishing Vessel Other Than Trawling

A vessel engaged in fishing, other than trawling, must display, instead of masthead lights, two all-round lights in a vertical line, the upper being red and the lower being white. Also, if longer than 50 meters (164 ft), the vessel must also

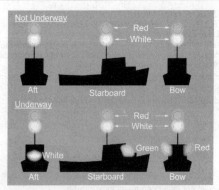

display a masthead light aft of and higher than the all-round red light.

When lights are not displayed, a shape consisting of two cones must be displayed with their apexes together in a vertical line one above the other.

U.S. inland only: A vessel of less than 20 meters (66 ft) in length may instead of this shape exhibit a basket.

When there is outlying gear extending more than 150 meters (492 ft) from the vessel, then an all-round white light or cone apex up must be displayed in the direction of the gear.

When underway, the fishing vessel must also display sidelights and a sternlight.

Vessels engaged in fishing in close proximity to other vessels engaged in fishing must also display additional signals as specified in Annex II of the regulations (not included in this book).

Canada only: May display the additional signals in Annex II if less than 20 meters in length or fishing with purse seine gear.

VESSELS NOT UNDER COMMAND OR RE-STRICTED IN THEIR ABILITY TO MANEUVER (RULE 27)

Vessels of less than 12 meters (39.4 ft) in length, except those engaged in diving operations, are not required to exhibit the lights and shapes prescribed in this rule.

The signals described are not distress or request for assistance signals. These are described elsewhere.

Vessel Not Under Command—Not Making Way

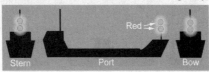

A vessel not under command must exhibit:
* Two red all-round lights in a vertical line where they can best be seen.
* Two balls or similar shapes in a vertical line where they can best be seen.

Additionally when underway, sidelights, and a sternlight must be exhibited as for a power vessel.

Restricted In Ability To Maneuver—Making Way

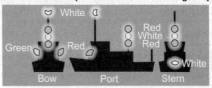

A vessel restricted in her ability to maneuver must show:
* All-round red, white, and red lights arranged vertically.
* Ball-diamond-ball shapes displayed vertically
* In addition when underway, sidelights, and a sternlight as for a power vessel.
* Additionally when at anchor, the lights and shapes prescribed for boats at anchor (Rule 30) described elsewhere.

Towing And Restricted In Ability To Maneuver (Rules 24 And 27)

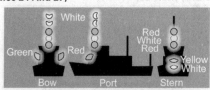

A vessel engaged in a towing operation, and which is also restricted in her ability to maneuver, must display lights both for towing (Rule 24) as well as for restricted maneuverability (this Rule 27).

Dredging or Underwater Operations and Restricted in Ability to Maneuver

A vessel that is restricted in her ability to maneuver and is also engaged in dredging or underwater operations must exhibit the lights and shapes previously described for restricted maneuverability (vertical red-white-red all-round lights, vertical ball-diamond-ball shapes, and running lights).

In addition, when an obstruction exists, she must also exhibit:

- Two all-round red lights or two balls in a vertical line to indicate the side on which the obstruction exists.
- Two all-round green lights or two diamonds in a vertical line to indicate the side on which another vessel may pass.
- When at anchor the lights described in this paragraph are used instead of the lights prescribed for vessels at anchor.

Diving Vessel Too Small to Display Restricted Maneuvering Lights

If the size of a vessel engaged in diving operations makes it impracticable to display all the lights and shapes for restricted ability to maneuver, then at least the following minimum must be displayed:

- Three all-round vertical red over white over red lights where they can best be seen.
- A rigid replica of the international code flag "A" not less than 1 meter (39.4 in) in height, displayed where it can be seen all round.

Vessels Constrained By Their Draft: International Rule Only (Rule 28)

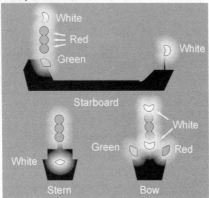

In addition to the lights prescribed for power-driven vessels, a vessel constrained by her draft may exhibit three all-round red lights in a vertical line or a cylinder.

Canada modification: In Canadian waters of a roadstead, harbor, river, lake, or inland waterway, no vessel may exhibit three all-round red lights in a vertical line or a cylinder.

U.S. inland: Rule 28 for vessels constrained by draft is not specified and is marked as reserved.

PILOT VESSELS (RULE 29)

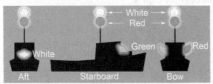

A pilot vessel on duty displays vertically, two all-round white over red lights near the masthead. Additionally, when underway sidelights and a sternlight are displayed. At anchor, lights for a vessel at anchor are also displayed.

When not on duty, a pilot vessel displays the normal running lights for a power driven vessel.

ANCHORED VESSELS AND VESSELS AGROUND (RULE 30)

Vessel At Anchor Greater Than Or Equal To 50 Meters (164 Ft)

A vessel at anchor which is greater than 50 meters (164 ft) in length must display a white light or one ball in the forepart of the ship.

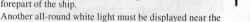

Another all-round white light must be displayed near the stern, and it must be lower than the light at the fore.

A vessel of greater than 100 meters (328 ft) must also use available working or other lights to illuminate her decks. A shorter vessel may optionally do this.

Vessel At Anchor Less Than 50 Meters (164 Ft)

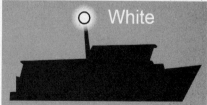

A vessel at anchor that is less than 50 meters (164 ft) in length may display just one all-round white light where it can best be seen, instead of the two lights discussed above.

Vessels less than 7 meters (23 ft) in length are exempted from this requirement as long as they are not in or near a channel, fairway, anchorage, or place where vessels normally navigate.

Canada modification: In Canadian waters a barge at anchor may instead display the alternative lights specified for barges underway in Canada, and an inconspicuous, partly submerged object when anchored may alternatively display the lights such an object displays when underway.

These barges or objects do not have to display any lights when located in a recognized mooring, storage, or booming area that is not an area in or near a narrow channel or fairway or where other vessels normally navigate.

Vessel Aground Greater Than Or Equal To 50 Meters (164 Ft)

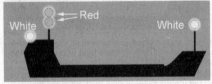

A vessel that is aground must display all the lights specified for anchoring as well as two all-round red lights in a vertical line where they can best be seen, and three balls in a vertical line.

A vessel aground of less than 12 meters (39.4 ft) length is exempted from displaying the two all-round red lights and the three balls specified in this rule.

4 SEAMANSHIP

SEAMANSHIP GENERAL

GENERAL DISCUSSION

Seamanship relates to the science (and art) of operating a boat. It includes such diverse activities as steering, docking, anchoring, sailing, fueling, handling rough seas, etc. Some of the other chapters of this book also cover seamanship subjects, such as marlinespike seamanship, although this chapter is limited to operating a boat and the skills for doing that.

Pivot point, rudder behavior, and prop walk are discussed first since they play such an important role in determining how the single-screw boat behaves at slow (docking) speeds, and because getting a boat docked, with some degree of elegance, is one of the most challenging aspects of "driving" a boat.

Checklists are included at the end of this section, as in other sections, and are meant to provide a starting point for those you develop for your own boat. Airline pilots use checklists for good reason, and boat owners can benefit from using checklists too. The systems and procedures on a boat are quite complex and the captain is guaranteed to forget something without them. There are checklists in other chapters for planning multiday cruises, checklists for launching from a trailer, departure checklists, arrival checklists, maintenance checklists, equipment checklists, etc. Updating and using these lists on an ongoing basis is just as important as making them in the first place.

CLOSE QUARTERS BOAT OPERATION

SLOW SPEED MANEUVERING

Controlling a boat in a crowded area, and getting it docked without mishap, is one of the more challenging aspects of boating for the less experienced boater. Unlike a car, a boat doesn't always go in the direction you steer it and it does not have brakes. The slower the boat's speed, the more pronounced the effect of wind and current on the movement of the boat.

Docking operations should be carried out at the slowest possible speed that still allows some control over the motion of the boat. The more wind or current, the more difficult it is to maintain control at slower speeds, so the operator ends up in a balancing act between slower speeds needed for safe docking and higher speeds to maintain steerageway.

The skills needed for these operations can't be learned by reading a book like this, any more than one can learn to drive a car by reading a book. In both cases, hands-on practice and repetition is required to get an intuitive "feel" for the vehicle, and handling a boat in close quarters requires considerably more practice than that learning to drive a car. People learning to fly an airplane spend a considerable amount of time doing "touch and goes" for good reason. Getting it safely on the ground is the most difficult part, just as getting the boat into the slip is.

Most of the maneuvers described in this section require considerable practice, even in smaller boats.

> *Common sense dictates that these maneuvers should not be attempted for the first time in a crowded marina by an inexperienced captain and crew! Remember, as captain you are responsible not only for your own actions but also those of your crew.*

New boaters do themselves—and everyone around them—a favor by spending a few days practicing slow speed maneuvers (touch and goes) in a quiet place to achieve the required competence and confidence before attempting to maneuver in a crowded anchorage or marina.

Rudder Behavior at Slow Speed

The rudder on an inboard boat is usually of sufficient size that some amount of steerage is obtained even at very slow speeds. This is particularly true of sailboats, since the rudder is relatively large in comparison to that of a typical powerboat. Generally, when moving aft, the rudder has less effect and is not very useful for steering.

An inboard powered boat has the rudder purposely placed behind the propeller so that in forward gear, the backflow from the propeller is over the rudder. As a result, a boat that is still or moving very slowly can kick her stern in either direction by applying short bursts of power with the propeller flow deflected appropriately by the rudder.

In figure 4-1-B the rudder is turned to starboard, so as power is applied the stern begins to move forward and to port, and the boat begins to turn to starboard. In reverse, at slow speed, or at rest, the rudder will have little or no effect, since the

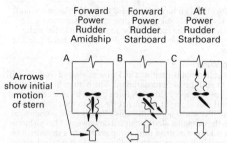

Forward Power Rudder Amidship   Forward Power Rudder Starboard   Aft Power Rudder Starboard

Arrows show initial motion of stern

FIGURE 4-1: Effect of Rudder on Thrust

propeller flow is now forward and not across the rudder, as in figure 4-1-C. However, as sternway increases, some ability to steer is gained from the flow of water over the rudder. By making use of these characteristics, even a single-screw boat can be made to turn in pretty much its own length (description of how to do this below) in still water with no wind.

Pivot Point

The pivot point is one of the most important concepts of boat behavior for the beginning boater to understand. When the boat is turned to, say, starboard, the stern swings out to port while the bow moves to starboard a lesser amount.

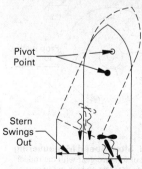

Pivot Point

Stern Swings Out

FIGURE 4-2: Pivot Point

In effect, the boat is swinging about its pivot point, which is found somewhere in the fore-word half of the boat, usually about two-thirds of the way forward. The pivot point location will vary with boat design and will move forward or backward with changes in speed.

As a practical application of this concept, if you are port side to a pier or lock wall and you turn your wheel to starboard and go forward to leave the wall (like you would a car), you'll only succeed in dragging the stern along the port side since the rudder is forcing the stern to the wall. You might get away from the wall eventually but it won't be pretty.

Prop Walk

A propeller that is rotating clockwise as viewed from aft will tend to pull the stern to starboard. The bottom blade moving left generates more sideways force than the top blade nearest the hull moving right, so the net force is to the right or starboard. It is worth noting that this effect is more pronounced when the propeller shaft is angled downward. This phenomenon is known as **_prop walk_**. Prop walk with a sterndrive or outboard will not be as noticeable as with an inboard, since the propeller shaft is nearly horizontal. Therefore, a single engine boat with a right-hand propeller (clockwise from aft) will tend to walk the stern to starboard when in forward gear, and walk the stern to port when in reverse. The prop walk effect will be more noticeable at slow speeds and in reverse, since the rudder is having relatively little effect. All the examples herein use a right-hand propeller, because this is what is most common on single engine boats.

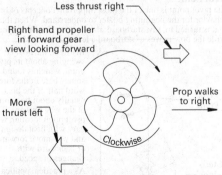

FIGURE 4-3: Prop Walk

Single-Screw Inboard, Slow Speed Maneuvering

Briefly shifting in and out of forward gear with the rudder hard to starboard will cause the stern to kick out to port before the boat begins any significant forward motion. Subsequently shifting into reverse gear with a right-hand screw counteracts the forward motion but will continue the stern to port because of the prop walk effect.

Turning the Boat in Its Own Length—Single Prop

By making use of these two characteristics, we can make the boat turn in its own length. With right-hand propeller rotation, it is easier to rotate the boat clockwise because the prop walk effect in reverse helps move the stern to port.

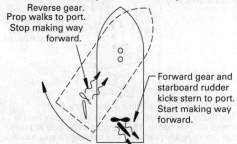

Reverse gear.
Prop walks to port.
Stop making way forward.

Forward gear and starboard rudder kicks stern to port. Start making way forward.

FIGURE 4-4: Turning a Single-Screw Boat in Its Own Length

To accomplish this with a right-hand screw, first turn the rudder hard to starboard, as shown in figure 4-4, and then leave it there for the remainder of this maneuver. Leave the throttle at idle and shift into forward for about two or three seconds. Then shift into reverse for a similar amount of time. The boat will begin rotating clockwise. Just keep repeating this until the boat is turned.

This also may work in the opposite direction, although it's more difficult because the prop walk works against the turn. It will ultimately depend on the boat.

Backing the Boat in a Straight Line—Single Prop

This operation is somewhat similar to turning the boat in its own length as discussed above.

Assume that we are backing with a right-hand screw. The rudder is turned to port and the throttle is left at idle for the entire operation. Shift to reverse until making way aft. The stern should be swinging to port because of prop walk.

Now shifting to forward will counteract this by kicking the stern to starboard. Alternating backward and forward should enable the vessel to move backward in some semblance of a straight line.

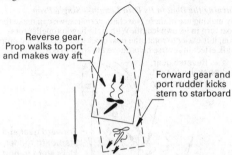

Reverse gear.
Prop walks to port
and makes way aft

Forward gear and
port rudder kicks
stern to starboard

FIGURE 4-5: Backing With a Single-Screw Boat

Note that in reverse with enough way on, you may be able to steer with the rudder. This depends on the boat and only experimenting and practicing will tell how the boat handles.

Twin-Screw Slow Speed Maneuvering

The twin-screw vessel is significantly easier to maneuver at slow speeds than the single-screw vessel. For one thing, a two-engine boat in forward normally has the starboard propeller rotating clockwise and the port propeller rotating counterclockwise so they counteract each other and eliminate prop walk effect.

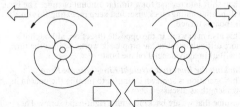

FIGURE 4-6: Aft View Twin-Screw Showing Counter Rotation

Maneuvers such as turning and backing are much easier than with a single-screw boat (assuming no bow thruster on the single).

Turning the Boat in Its Own Length—Twin

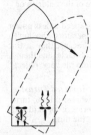

A turn in place is accomplished by placing one propeller in forward and the other in reverse. Since the propellers are offset from the centerline of the boat they induce a turning moment. If the port propeller is in forward and the starboard in reverse, then the turn will be to starboard. By working the throttles the boat can be turned in place or be made to make a very short turn. Starboard rudder through the starboard turn may accentuate the turn.

FIGURE 4-7: Twin Turning in Place

Backing the Boat in a Straight Line—Twin

For this maneuver both engines are placed in reverse at idle throttle with the rudder straight. If the boat begins to veer to one side, then the throttle on that side is increased momentarily to correct.

Crabbing Sideways—Twin

With some twin-engine boats it is possible to move the boat sideways with little or no forward or backward movement.

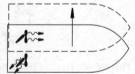

FIGURE 4-8: Twin Crabbing to Port

To move to port the rudder is placed to starboard, the starboard engine ahead, and the port engine astern. The counter rotating props should tend to push the bow to port while the starboard rudder tends to push the stern to port, with the net result that the boat moves to the side.

Outboards, Outdrives, and Jet Drives (Directed Thrust)

All of these have the characteristic of being able to direct thrust by changing the direction of the propeller or jet. In addition, the direction of thrust is controllable when in reverse, a feature not available to the inboard boat operator. Thus, to back up with a directed thrust drive, the operator steers in the direction of the turn similar to backing a car.

A less desirable characteristic of these drives is that without power applied, steering is minimal at slow speeds since there is no rudder other than the surface of the outdrive or outboard.

A jet drive has no steering ability at any speed unless power is applied. Personal watercraft (PWC) operators who don't understand this often get into accidents because they instinctively cut power when encountering an obstacle, and then without steerageway continue straight into the very object (or person) they are trying to avoid.

Turning the Boat in Its Own Length—Directed Thrust

The procedure to spin the boat is somewhat similar to turning the single-screw inboard in that a series of forward and reversing motions are required to effect the turn.

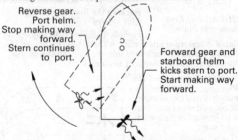

Reverse gear.
Port helm.
Stop making way forward.
Stern continues to port.

Forward gear and starboard helm kicks stern to port. Start making way forward.

FIGURE 4-9: Directed Thrust Turn in Place

Assuming we wish to turn the boat clockwise, first turn the drive hard to starboard and with the throttle at idle, shift into forward for about two or three seconds. The boat should begin a clockwise rotation without starting to make way. Shift into neutral, quickly turn the drive all the way in the opposite direction to port, and then shift into reverse for a similar amount of time. This should accentuate the clockwise turn and arrest any forward movement. The helmsman keeps alternating these two operations until the boat is rotated the desired amount.

Wind and Current Effect at Slow Speeds

Current will affect a heavy full displacement boat more than wind at slow speeds because of the deeper hull and keel. In a sailboat (sails down) with a large deep keel this behavior will be even more pronounced. Conversely, a lightweight planing hull will easily be blown about by the wind. This will lead to problems with the bow being blown to one side or the other while operating at slow speeds.

In the discussions that follow, the term wind will refer to either wind or current, whichever has the strongest effect on the boat. Also the use of a single engine boat with no bow thruster is assumed. In many of the docking situations discussed below, the use of spring lines is obviated by the use of twin engines or bow thrusters.

LEAVING THE DOCK

Strictly speaking, a dock is an area, sometimes enclosed, where a boat can be tied up. That is, it is the area occupied by the boat and not the pier, jetty, quay, wharf, or landing to which the boat is made fast. It is fairly common, however, to use dock as a generic term for whatever the boat is tied to. We'll sometimes use the term in this generic sense because it's just simpler to say something like "tie to the dock" rather than "tie to the pier, wharf, quay, jetty, or float."

Considerations for Leaving the Dock

It is usually easier to get the boat away from the dock than it is to dock the boat, especially with adverse conditions such as high winds and currents or tight maneuvering space.

Some things to consider before leaving the dock or pier:

- Check to see all equipment is on board. Some equipment checklists are included at the end of other chapters.
- Check the systems on the boat. This includes the obvious things like, is there enough gas and oil as well as controls working properly. Samples of detailed departure and arrival checklists are included later in this chapter and sample mechanical checklists are provided in the mechanical chapter of this book.
- Check gasoline engines for fumes in the engine compartment before starting!
- Get the engine warmed up before casting off.
- Check for other boats underway before leaving. Don't pull out into the path of an already moving boat.
- One last check before leaving: Are all dock lines and electrical cables detached?

In general, the goal in leaving the dock is to get the bow out and clear of any obstructions so the vessel can proceed straight ahead without the stern swinging into anything. The alternative approach is to get the stern swung out so as to allow backing out until the boat is clear to move forward. Keep in mind that there is less control when backing out than going forward.

Note: If you are not familiar with terms for dock lines such as "forward quarter spring," then skip forward to the section on tying the boat to the dock on page 172 where these terms are defined.

Leaving—Forward Stern Breast or Forward Quarter Spring

This can be used for almost all wind (or current) directions.

To get the bow away from the pier a boat hook may do the trick in a smaller boat, but power will be usually be required in a larger boat, particularly with wind.

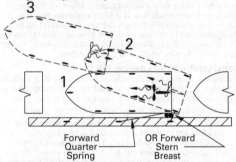

Forward Quarter Spring OR Forward Stern Breast

FIGURE 4-10: Leaving—Forward Quarter Spring

1. Place good fenders (a buoy or ball fender would be best) at the stern. Take off all dock lines but a forward stern line or forward quarter spring line.

2. If the wind is ahead or off the pier, let the wind blow the bow out. For no wind or wind from other directions, gently apply reverse power, keeping the rudder amidships.

3. Once the bow has swung clear of the boat in front, shift into forward and proceed out of the dock. Remember to disconnect the line.

Leaving—After Bow Breast or After Bow Spring

This can also be used for most wind directions, but it's generally less desirable because it requires backing the boat out, which affords less control than proceeding leaving forward maneuver.

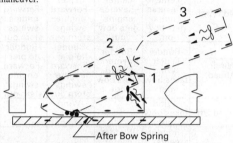

FIGURE 4-11: Leaving With After Bow Spring

1. Place good fenders (a buoy or ball fender would be best) at the bow. Take off all dock lines but a bow breast line or after bow spring line.

2. If the wind is aft or off the pier, let the wind blow the stern out.

For no wind or wind from other directions, gently apply forward power with the rudder to the pier to get the stern away from the pier.

3. Once the stern has swung clear of the boat aft, shift into reverse and proceed out of the dock.

Table 4-1 on page 160 is a quick reference table for leaving a side tie. This table provides ideas for leaving from a parallel to dock position between two other boats.

Keep in mind that if the wind is off the pier, an alternative is to just cast off all lines and let the wind blow the boat clear. Just be careful not to drift forward or aft into the other boats.

Leaving a Slip With No Wind and Adequate Clearance

Leaving a slip under these conditions should be a fairly easy process that will involve taking the boat straight out forward or aft. The main consideration here: Don't try to turn until after the boat is clear of the slip since the stern will swing

	Forward Stern Breast	Forward Quarter Spring	After Bow Breast	After Bow Spring
No Wind	-Rudder center -Reverse engine gets bow out	-Rudder center -Reverse engine gets bow out	-Rudder to pier -Forward engine swings stern out	-Rudder to pier -Forward engine swings stern out
Wind Ahead	-Rudder center -Wind takes bow out	-Rudder center -Wind takes bow out	-Rudder to pier -Forward engine swings stern out	-Rudder to pier -Forward engine swings stern out
Wind Off	-Wind takes bow out		-Wind takes stern out	
Wind Astern	-Rudder center -Reverse engine gets bow out	-Rudder center -Reverse engine gets bow out	-Wind takes stern out	-Wind takes stern out
Wind On	-Rudder center -Reverse engine gets bow out	-Rudder center -Reverse engine gets bow out	-Rudder to pier -Forward engine swings stern out	-Rudder to pier -Forward engine swings stern out

TABLE 4-1: Leaving With Wind or Current From Various Directions

sideways into whatever is adjacent. Complications arise when there is insufficient clearance to get the boat turned after leaving or, there is a significant crosswind. In this case the correct use of spring lines may be necessary (assuming no bow thrusters or twin-screws).

Leaving a Slip With Little Clearance

Consider using spring lines in this case. If there is no wind or current, however, you should be able to exit the slip and turn in your own boat length using the techniques described earlier.

Leaving a Slip Forward With a Spring Line

The object here is to get the boat out of the slip without being blown into pilings and also to get the boat turned into the wind if there is little clearance forward.

This is a difficult maneuver requiring practice and skill on the part of both the captain and the crew. It should not be attempted unless both the captain and the crew together have perfected this maneuver in a place away from other boats. This should not be attempted if the wind is blowing even partially onto the slips. Experimenting may lead to variations

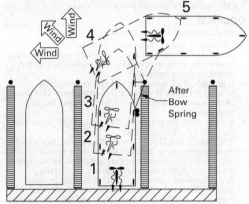

FIGURE 4-12: Leaving Slip Forward Using a Spring Line

such as using a line from the midships instead of the bow, or a combination of both.

For this example assume that the boat is to be turned to starboard on leaving the slip.

1. Get fender boards on the bow area that is likely to rub the piling on the starboard side. Cast off all lines except the bow spring that should be led around the piling and back to the boat so you can release it and bring it on board later. This requires plenty of line so be sure you have a long enough line before you start. Begin moving very slowly forward, using gentle bursts of power.

2. The crew must shorten the bow spring line as shown as you inch forward. Use port rudder to keep the wind from swinging the stern out to port.

3. Continue forward using port rudder to keep the stern from blowing out to port. Note that the bow spring is now being let out.

4. Once the stern is clear, stop letting the bow spring line out and apply some power with starboard rudder to swing the stern out to port. Note that if the wind is as shown, it will tend to swing the stern out even without power.

5. Release the bow line and proceed forward.

DOCKING

General Considerations for Docking

Some things to keep in mind when docking:

- Get ready well ahead of time. Get fenders out and docking lines ready. If the docking side isn't known then fenders should be out on both sides.
- If possible, dock up current and upwind or against whichever has the strongest effect on the boat. This should enable power to be maintained, which allows for better maneuvering.
- Keep in mind the prop walk effect on a single-screw boat particularly when reversing.
- The captain should talk through the docking plan with the crew in advance, so that each knows his or her role in the operation. This should have the right people in the right place at the right time and eliminate a lot of yelling.
- Radio earphone sets are available and on larger boats greatly enhance the docking experience by allowing communication between the captain and the crew without needing to yell or use difficult to understand hand signals.
- Take it slow and easy. Small bursts can change direction without moving forward or aft too quickly.
- Never fend off by hand; hands should be kept inside the boat.
- Consider using mid-ship docking lines first, both as spring lines and for initially making fast, since a mid-ship line will hold both ends of the boat from swinging away. This can be particularly useful if there is only one line handler.

Since the bow is the end of the boat that has no means of steering (remember the stern pivots sideways), the most common approach is to get the bow in first and then swing the stern in.

The docking methods below are meant to suggest ideas for getting a boat in rather than being a specific cookbook for every situation. These situations assume only a single engine with no bow or stern thrusters. Twin-screws or bow thrusters offer considerably more control of the bow in difficult docking situations but the basic techniques for getting in remain the same.

Normal Docking—Little or No Wind

1. Approach the pier at about 30 degrees at the slowest speed that still maintains steerageway.

2. When the bow is in close to the dock, a burst in forward with the rudder to starboard begins the rotation of the stern to the dock. Keep in mind that when the stern moves left, the bow moves right; so if this maneuver is begun with the bow not close enough to the dock, the boat will end up parallel but too far out to step off.

3. Stop the boat with a burst in reverse.

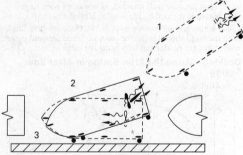

FIGURE 4-13: Normal Docking Alongside

Note that if the boat has a right-hand screw, the reverse thrust burst will further kick the stern into the dock, which will make the docking easier in tight quarters. Keep in mind that docking a right-hand screw to port will make it harder to swing the stern away to leave the dock later on.

Docking—Wind Ahead

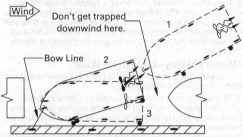

FIGURE 4-14: Docking With Wind Ahead

1. Come in at as shallow an angle (15 to 20 degrees) as possible with enough speed to keep the bow from yawing in the wind. Aim the boat well forward, as you don't want to get your port side trapped by the wind against the boat aft.

2. Get a bow line on as soon as possible. Once the bow line is on the wind should bring the stern in. Some forward power with starboard rudder can help bring the stern in.

Docking—Using the After Spring or After Bow Spring

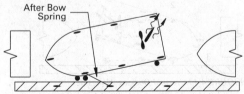

FIGURE 4-15: Docking With After Bow Spring

This can be one of the most useful techniques for docking in an adverse situation, such as high winds, strong currents, or very close quarters. The idea here is to get the bow in and get an after bow spring attached as soon as possible. Once this is done the stern may be powered in with propulsion forward and the rudder away from the pier. This keeps the boat from moving forward or backward until the stern and other lines can be secured.

Note that you can use this regardless of wind direction. If the wind is blowing you onto the dock, then forward propulsion with the rudder into the dock can keep you from arriving at dock with a bang.

The spring line could also be led further aft than shown to a cleat on the pier nearer the stern, or it could be cleated amidships and led aft to the pier. Some experimenting will help determine which works best for a particular boat. Also, like any other docking technique, it's best not to be trying this for the first time in an adverse docking situation.

Warning: Use of a spring line to power into a dock places very high stresses on the boat cleats, dock cleats, the spring line, and the hull against the pier. Make sure the cleats being used are strong enough with properly fastened backing plates and are able to take the load. Liberal use of fenders around the bow area is a must.

Keep in mind the force applied to the spring line is at least equal to the forward thrust of the propeller at dead slow plus an allowance for overcoming the inertia of the moving boat.

Docking—Wind Off Pier

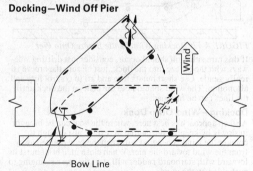

FIGURE 4-16: Docking With Wind Off Pier

Make the approach at a steep enough angle to keep the bow from blowing away from the wind. Get the bow line on as soon as possible making sure the line is long enough for the boat to come in parallel along side the pier without forcing the side of the bow into the pier. Use gentle bursts of forward power with the rudder away from the pier as shown to bring the stern in.

This is similar to using the after bow spring described above, however, with the wind keeping the bow off the pier there should be less likelihood of the forward part of the boat hull pushing against the pier. The difference is that you are not powering forward against the line but rather using gentle bursts to bring the stern in sideways without placing undue strain on the bow line.

Docking—Gentle Breeze Onto Pier

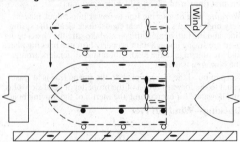

FIGURE 4-17: Docking With Gentle Breeze Onto Pier

If this rare situation should occur, consider just drifting sideways with the breeze into the dock; just be sure the breeze is really gentle. Use short bursts fore and aft to control fore and aft motion. The wind should hold the boat on the dock until the lines can be fastened.

Docking—Wind Onto Dock

A steep approach is best here, where the boat can be brought in slowly by keeping the engine in reverse just enough to counter the wind. The wind will keep the bow pointed away from the wind toward the pier. When close in, a brief burst in forward with starboard rudder will start the stern swinging to port aided by the wind.

Once the bow is near the pier, get someone off to fasten the bow line. Now with the bow under control you can reverse to keep the bow off the pier. Brief forward bursts with port rudder will keep the stern from blowing hard onto the pier, though the forward hull fenders are going to absorb some

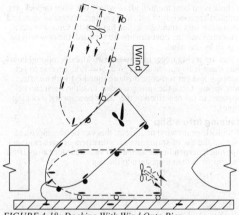

FIGURE 4-18: Docking With Wind Onto Pier

force as the boat rotates in parallel to the pier. Needless to say, have plenty of fenders around the bow area.

Docking—Downwind

Try to avoid docking downwind if there is any way to turn and come in against the wind. With the wind aft or with a following current, it will probably be necessary to reverse thrust to slow the boat, and there is virtually no ability to steer when in reverse. Conversely, if the boat is in forward gear to get steerageway, the boat will end up coming in too fast. Twin-screws or a bow thruster, either of which provide steering in this circumstance, will make this docking much easier.

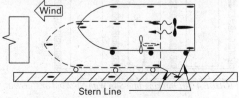

Stern Line

FIGURE 4-19: Docking With Wind Following

If there is no boat moored aft of where you want to dock, the simplest approach is to get close enough, reverse to stop, and get a stern line on the dock. See figure 4-19. Once the stern is secured and the boat can't move forward, the bow will be kept in by the wind.

If you are trying to get in between two already moored boats, then there is no choice but to go in bow first, reverse to get stopped, and get someone onshore (quickly) with an after bow spring. Once the spring is made fast, the stern can be powered in (as described in the "after bow spring" docking topic).

Backing Into a Slip

With little or no wind or current, this can be accomplished without the use of spring lines (or thrusters or twin engines). Approach perpendicular to the slip and then steer away from the slip so as to end up stern to the slip.

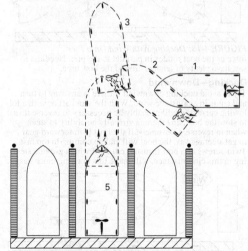

FIGURE 4-20: Backing Into Slip With No Wind or Current

If your boat allows, you may be able to back up with some steering control, in which case you simply back and steer your way in slowly and carefully. If not, the backing technique described earlier in this section works quite well in this situation, with alternate gentle bursts forward with the rudder to the appropriate side and gentle bursts in reverse to keep moving aft into the slip.

Backing Into a Slip With a Forward Quarter Spring Line

Usually this docking procedure can be used when there is a wind or current or current perpendicular to or away from the slip. The preferable approach in this case would be into the wind.

The warning given earlier for leaving a slip using spring lines bears repeating here. This is a difficult maneuver requiring practice and skill on the part of both the captain and the crew. It should not be attempted unless both the captain and the crew have perfected this maneuver in a place away from other boats. This should not be attempted if the wind is blowing even partially onto the slips.

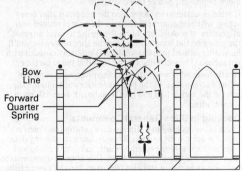

Bow Line

Forward Quarter Spring

FIGURE 4-21: Backing Into Slip With Forward Quarter Spring

Maneuver to a position perpendicular to the slip alongside the piling that the boat is to back around. Get a forward quarter spring line around this piling and back to the boat so that it can be easily let out and released. The length of this spring line must initially be short enough so that the boat will not swing into the piling opposite aft. Also place a bow line on this piling.

Gently apply some reverse power and the boat will pivot around the piling to align with the pier. As the boat continues aft into the slip, the forward quarter spring line can be released and brought aboard once the stern is partway in. The bow line is taken in as the boat moves back into the slip. Rigging a fender board would be a smart idea since the boat will likely rub the piling while pivoting around it.

If boats in the adjacent slips have either their bow or stern extending beyond the outside pilings then this maneuver is made much more difficult. It is hard to get a line on the piling from further out, not to mention fear of hitting one of those boats.

Docking Forward Into a Slip

Going forward into a slip should be easier than backing in simply because you have much better control of steering than when moving backwards. Try to get aligned with the slip as much as possible before proceeding in.

If wind or current is a factor then the use of an after bow spring will help control the bow as the boat is rotated into alignment. If possible try to rig the spring to pivot around the piling on the windward side of the slip; otherwise you'll be sliding around the piling (which is probably covered with barnacles). The stern line can be rigged at the same time.

Gentle forward power will begin the pivoting around the piling into the slip. As the boat moves forward into the slip, release the spring line and take it on board; keep taking in the stern line.

Docking in Slips General Comments

Quite often docking in a slip involves getting lines onto pilings that are too high or too far away. Consider having dock lines with eyes large enough to easily get over a piling and then tying the free end to the boat. This allows adjustments to be made more easily and also facilitates leaving more easily. The large eyes can also be dropped over cleats more easily.

An alternative is to run the line around the piling and make both ends fast on the boat. This will be the easiest way to leave the slip as the end to be released is within reach (on the boat) and the line is then pulled in around the piling.

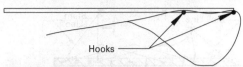

Hooks

FIGURE 4-22: Boat Hook Rigged for Pilings

A boat hook is almost a necessity for getting lines over and around pilings. Some boaters rig two hooks spaced a couple of feet apart on their boat hook to help keep the eye open for dropping over the piling. Use hose clamps to fasten the hooks. This can also be used to get a line on that returns to the boat.

Fenders by themselves are of little use around pilings since they will slip off the piling to one side or the other. Fender boards can be rigged to protect the boat in these situations. Fender boards are simply horizontal boards suspended to the outside of two cylindrical fenders. The fender board can be made from 2-inch by 6- to 10-inch lumber.

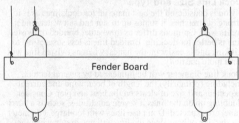

Fender Board

FIGURE 4-23: Fender Board

MAKING FAST

Dock Line Terminology

Dock lines are named first by their direction, then where they fasten to the boat, then by the type of line.

Figure 4-24 just gives examples of dock line names. (No one would actually tie this many lines to their boat.)

A spring line is approximately parallel to the boat, leading forward or aft to prevent forward and backward movement.

A breast line leads sideways and limits sideways motion. This isn't used much on recreational sized boats.

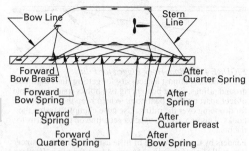

FIGURE 4-24: Examples of Dock Line Names

The bow line above leads forward enough that it could also be called a forward bow spring, but it's usually just called the bow line.

Dock Line Size and Type

Nylon is considered the best material for dock lines as is it strong, it stretches, it stands up to sun and salt water, and it wears well. Opinions differ as to whether braided or twisted line is better for docking. Braided line is less susceptible to kinking and is easier on the hands, whereas twisted line will have more elasticity.

Dock line diameter will be influenced by several factors, including (primarily) the length of boat, wind and current expected, and size of cleats on the boat and pier. Consider doubling up on the lines if severe conditions, such as a hurricane, are expected. Don't use lines with too large a diameter for the size of boat since the line will not stretch when the boat heaves on it.

Chafing is an issue with dock lines particular if the boat is to be tied up in rough water or for weeks at a time. The line should be protected where it leads through chocks or rubs on any surface. Chafing gear, which is a sleeve of cloth or rubber around the rope, can be purchased from the chandlery or rubber hose can be slipped over the rope for this purpose.

The dock line size table included herein is averaged from several sources that varied quite widely in their recommendations so keep in mind that it is just a guideline. Note that line less than 3/8 inch, even for a very small boat, is not recommended because of its susceptibility to chafing through. In its catalog, West Marine mentions a rule of thumb of 1/8 inch of diameter for every foot of boat length.

Line Size (in)	Boat Length				Displacement			
	From (ft)	To (ft)	From (m)	To (m)	From (lbs)	To (lbs)	From (kg)	To (kg)
3/8	0	24	0	7	0	6200	0	2800
1/2	16	33	5	10	4600	16000	2100	7300
5/8	29	42	9	13	14000	33000	6400	15000
3/4	36	50	11	15	31000	56000	14000	36000
7/8	44	58	13	18	55000	87000	25000	39000
1	50	64	15	20	84000	117000	38000	53000

TABLE 4-2: Dock Line Size

Tie Up Alongside Pier

Typically a recreational boat will be tied up with a bow line, a stern line, and one or two spring lines as shown in figure 4-25.

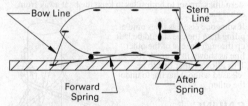

FIGURE 4-25: Typical Tie Up

The bow and stern lines are always used and are the minimum required for a small boat. Note the stern line leading from the far side of the boat to the pier to allow for up and down tidal motion.

If a high tidal range is expected, an after bow spring and forward quarter spring <u>might be used</u> as shown in figure 4-26.

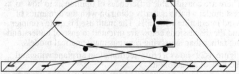

FIGURE 4-26: Tie Up For a High Tidal Range

The bow and stern lines must have enough length to allow for the rise and fall expected. This may require allowing the boat to drift away from the pier as shown.

Tie Up in a Slip

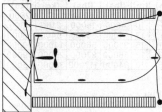

FIGURE 4-27: Slip Tie Up

The use of lines for making fast in a slip is similar to making fast along side a pier where bow and aft lines are used along with spring lines to limit fore and aft movement. In figure 4-27, finger piers are on both sides and bow and

stern lines are set to both sides to keep the boat away from either pier.

If someone else has lines onto a piling then the eye should be led up through the eye of the other line as shown in figure 4-28. This allows either line to be released without having to undo the other.

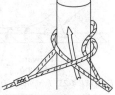

FIGURE 4-28: Two Lines on Same Piling

SAILING
BASIC PRINCIPLES

The forces of wind acting on a sail are similar to those acting on an airplane wing and much of the aerodynamic theory applied to sailing comes from the field of aeronautical engineering.

There are considerable differences of opinion as to how to best model what is actually going on with the dynamics of wind interacting with sails. The math used is quite complex and the discussions below are oriented to ease of understanding rather than satisfying rigorous mathematical models.

Figure 4-29 shows a cross-section of an airplane wing and the flow of air across it.

The trailing end of the wing is tilted slightly downward. The angle between horizontal and a straight line drawn from the

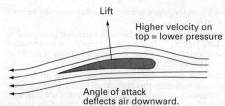

FIGURE 4-29: Cross-Section of Airplane Wing
leading edge bottom to the trailing edge bottom is called the
angle of attack.

The air flowing over the top of the wing must travel a longer
distance, and consequently must travel at a higher velocity
than the air below the wing. Bernoulli's principle states that
a fluid moving at a higher speed will have lowered pressure,
so in the case of our wing, lift is generated by virtue of the
relatively higher pressure below the wing versus the lower
pressure on top. The upward force is *lift*, which is a term applied to sailing as well.

With a positive angle of attack, the airflow is directed downward and additional lift is created by the opposing reaction
to this deflection. In general, the majority of lift is created
by the lowered pressure on top of the wing, per the Bernoulli
principle.

Figure 4-30 shows a view looking down from above a properly trimmed sail (where the angle of attack to the apparent
wind is optimum). Optimum trim for a sail will have an
angle of attack approximately 20 degrees from apparent wind

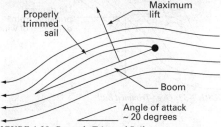

FIGURE 4-30: Properly Trimmed Sail

regardless of the boat's orientation (except running before the wind).

As with the airplane wing, lift is produced perpendicular to the chord (boom) by both reduced pressure on the lee side of the sail, and reaction forces from the deflection of the wind by the angle of attack.

Since the Bernoulli effect produces most of the lift, the object is to maximize this component of the lift. Basically this happens at an angle of attack just short of the leading edge of the sail luffing. *Luffing* is a fluttering of the leading edge (luff) of the sail that occurs when the angle of attack is too small. When the angle of attack is zero, the entire sail will be luffing as shown in figure 4-31, and there is no lift whatsoever.

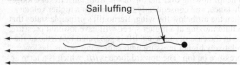

FIGURE 4-31: Sail Luffing

As the sail is trimmed in to a larger than optimum angle of attack, the lift from reduced pressure decreases and more of the lift comes from the reaction to the increased angle of attack.

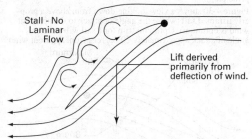

FIGURE 4-32: Over-Trimmed Sail

In figure 4-32 note how the airflow over the lee side of the sail is no longer laminar, but rather turbulent flow instead, which degrades the lift obtained from the Bernoulli effect.

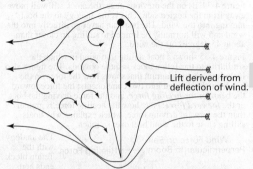

Lift derived from deflection of wind.

FIGURE 4-33: Wind on Sail Running Before the Wind

In the extreme case of running before the wind the angle of attack is set near 90 degrees and the maximum lift from wind deflection as in figure 4-33.

Sailing Into the Wind

An easy way to visualize how a sailboat can sail into the wind is to imagine a slippery triangular-shaped Teflon block set against a wall as shown in figure 4-34(A).

When a stick is pushed into the angled side of a block perpendicular to the wall, the block moves away from its angled side. Think of the stick as the wind and the angled side of the block as the sail. The block moving is the boat moving.

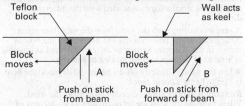

Teflon block

Wall acts as keel

Block moves

Block moves

Push on stick from beam

Push on stick forward of beam

A

B

FIGURE 4-34: Teflon Block on a Reach

The sailboat has a keel that acts much like the wall does for the block in that it resists sideways movement away from the wind. When we push the stick from forward of the block as in figure 4-34(B) on the previous page, the block still will move away from the angled side. This is the analogy to the boat moving into the wind. The boat can never go directly into the wind and will normally be limited to sailing no closer than about 45 degrees off the wind.

Figure 4-35 shows a boat sailing into wind in which the similarity to the Teflon block is quite obvious. The figure also includes a vector diagram that shows how the force on the boom can be divided into two components; the force toward the beam or the *heeling force*, and the force driving the boat or the *forward force*. Note how the heeling force is greater than the forward driving force, which explains why boats sailing close to the wind heel over so much.

The analogy with the Teflon block ends here since in the real world things are much more complex. We must deal with such things as apparent

FIGURE 4-35: Sailing Into the Wind

wind, true wind, and leeway. Leeway is the sideways slippage of the boat away from the wind.

Points of Sail

Points of sail are directions of sail relative to the true wind and there is terminology associated with the different directions.

A *reach* is sailing with the wind from the side from about 50 degrees off the bow to about 155 degrees off the bow as shown in the diagram. Sailing as close to the wind as possible at around 45 degrees is *close hauled* or *beating*.

When the wind is directly off the beam (90 degrees) the boat is said to be on a *beam reach*.

Running is sailing almost directly away from the wind. When running the sails are let out to almost 90 degrees so the sails are flat to the wind (as in figure 4-33).

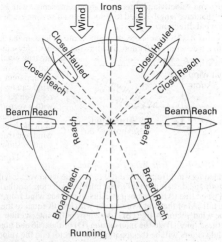

FIGURE 4-36: Points of Sail

The **close reach** is a point of sail anywhere from about 5 degrees off close hauled to a beam reach and a **broad reach** is a point of sail between a beam reach and running. The beam reach is usually the fastest point of sail and the boat will travel faster than at any other point of sail including running before the wind.

True and Apparent Wind

True wind is the actual wind that is experienced when one is motionless.

As the boat moves forward we experience another type of wind we'll call **boat wind**. If there is no true wind and the air is still then the boat wind is the only wind we would experience. The boat wind velocity would be equal to the boat speed and its direction directly onto the bow.

A boat moving directly into a true wind of 5 knots at a speed of 6 knots would experience an **apparent wind** of 11 knots. Conversely a boat running directly away from a true wind of 5 knots at a speed of 6 knots would experience an apparent wind of 1 knot off the bow.

The wind velocity and direction can be represented with vectors that have length scaled to velocity and direction equal to the wind direction.

In figure 4-37 a boat is traveling at 5 knots on a beam reach with a true wind of 10 knots. By drawing vectors represent-

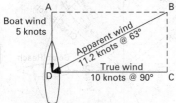

Boat wind
5 knots

ing true wind and boat wind, the apparent wind can be represented with a vector that combines both the boat wind and true wind as shown.

FIGURE 4-37: True Wind From Beam

A dashed line (BC) is ex-

tended forward from the tail (C) of the true wind vector with length and direction equal to the boat wind vector. Similarly, a dashed line (AB) is drawn parallel to the true wind from the tail (A) of the boat wind vector with length equal to the true wind vector. A line (BD) drawn from the intersection of these lines (B) to the intersection (D) of the true and boat wind vectors will be the apparent wind vector and the velocity and direction of the apparent wind can be scaled from this vector.

In the case of figure 4-37 the boat is moving forward at 5 knots creating a boat wind of 5 knots. The true wind is 10

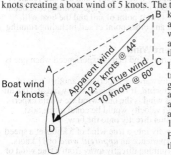

Boat wind
4 knots

knots off the beam and the apparent wind is 11.2 knots at 63 degrees off the bow.

In figure 4-38 the true wind is 60 degrees off the bow at 10 knots and the apparent wind is at 44 degrees and 12.5 knots.

Figure 4-39 shows the true wind from abaft the beam.

FIGURE 4-38: True Wind Ahead—Close Reach

From the diagrams it is clear that the apparent wind will always be forward of the true wind (except when the true wind is directly from the bow or stern). Conversely, the true wind is always abaft the apparent wind.

Also evident in the vector diagrams is the fact that on a close or beam reach, the apparent wind is always greater than the true wind. The apparent wind can also be greater than true wind in some instances of a broad reach. For example, in figure 4-39

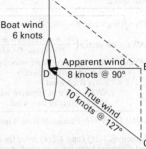

FIGURE 4-39: True Wind Abaft the Beam —Broad Reach

if the true wind of 10 knots comes from a relative bearing of 95 degrees then the apparent wind will be 10.4 knots from 72 degrees. It is also obvious that on a beam or close reach, the apparent wind will increase as the boat speed increases.

The point of all this is that it is the apparent wind, not the true wind, the sails feel, and it is the apparent wind direction and velocity that exert the driving force on the sails. It follows that the faster the boat goes, the greater the apparent wind and the greater the driving force. In fact, in the absence of any resistance or friction, the boat would go faster and faster as the apparent wind kept increasing as the speed kept increasing. An ice boat provides an excellent example of this phenomenon where the low friction of the blades on the ice allows the boat to attain speeds of several times the true wind speed.

Since it is the apparent wind the sails feel, then it is the apparent wind to which the sails are trimmed. As mentioned previously, the properly trimmed sail will have an angle of attack of about 20 degrees to the apparent wind.

For the technically inclined

The vector diagrams can also be solved using the following equations (you'll need either a scientific calculator or a spreadsheet program with trigonometry functions):

Equations 4-1(1) and 4-1(2) solve for true wind speed and direction knowing apparent wind speed and direction and boat speed.

$$Wt = \sqrt{[Wa \times \cos(90-AWa)]^2 + [(Wa \times \sin(90-AWa))-Wb]^2} \quad (1)$$

$$AWt = 90 - \arctan\left(\frac{Wt \times \sin(90-AWa)-Wb}{Wa \times \cos(90-AWa)}\right) \quad (2)$$

Where: Wa = Apparent wind velocity
Wt = True wind velocity
Wb = Boat wind
AWa = Angle of apparent wind
AWt = Angle of true wind

EQUATION 4-1: Calculate True Wind Speed and Direction

Equations 4-2(3) and 4-2(4) solve for apparent wind speed and direction knowing true wind speed and direction and boat speed.

$$Wa = \sqrt{[Wt \times \cos(90-AWt)]^2 + [Wt \times \sin(90-AWt)+Wb]^2} \quad (3)$$

$$AWa = 90 - \arctan\left(\frac{Wt \times \sin(90-AWt)+Wb}{Wt \times \cos(90-AWt)}\right) \quad (4)$$

EQUATION 4-2: Calculate Apparent Wind Speed and Direction

Heeling Versus Driving Force

Figure 4-40 shows the resultant forces for a boat with the apparent wind off the beam and for a boat on a close reach. W represents the direction of wind force on the sail, H is the heeling force component, and F is the forward driving force.

Intuition might lead one to believe the boat would heel away

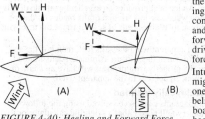

FIGURE 4-40: Heeling and Forward Force Vectors

from the wind the most when the wind is blowing directly from the side. This is not the case, however, as the most heeling force occurs when sailing closest to the wind.

Note how in both cases (A) and (B) of figure 4-40 the angle of attack is maintained at about 20 degrees to the apparent wind. For both boats, the force on the sail (perpendicular to the chord or boom) is resolved into a forward component parallel to the boat centerline and a heeling component perpendicular to the centerline

The first boat (A) has the sails trimmed in further with the result that the forward force component is relatively small compared to the heeling force, which results in less speed and more heel.

The second boat (B) has the sail out further so that the forward component is considerable greater than the sideways (heeling) component, which translates into less heel and more speed.

In general, as the apparent wind direction moves further aft, the heeling force decreases until it reaches zero when the wind is directly off the stern.

Sailing Into the Wind

Since the sailboat cannot sail directly into the wind, it must **tack** back and forth as shown in figure 4-41 to reach a destination that is less than about 45 degrees into the wind.

FIGURE 4-41: Tacking Upwind

The tack is a **port tack** when the wind is from the port side of the boat and is a **starboard** tack when the wind is from the starboard side. The process of turning from one tack to the other into the wind is **coming about**.

Coming about is initiated by turning the helm smartly to the direction of the turn. As the boat turns directly through the wind, the sails may flutter violently and will fill from the opposite side as the turn is completed. The boat must have enough speed to carry it through the complete turn since not coming completely about will result in the boat being stopped with a heading directly into the wind in a condition known as in ***irons***. In this condition, the sails luff through their entire surface (as in figure 4-31 on page 176) and the boat stops making way and will even begin to move backward in the water. As the boat presents a different side to the wind, the boom can swing quickly across to the lee side of the boat, which can be dangerous for crew members not paying attention.

The ***sheets*** are lines to the end of the mainsail boom and to the clew of the foresail and are used to control the angle of attack of the sails by trimming the sails in or out. When coming about, the jib sheet is released to allow the jib to blow to the lee side, where it is then trimmed and re-cleated. The simplest (most basic) way to trim the sails is to sheet out the sail until the luff (leading edge) of the sail begins luffing (fluttering), then trim back in just enough to stop the luffing.

To assist in better trimming the sails, ***telltales*** can be installed on the sail. These are commonly pieces of yarn or some light material, a few inches long that are installed about a foot back from the luff of the sails on both sides of the sail and sometimes near the leach (trailing edge) of the mainsail. Typically, one telltale would be installed somewhere in the top third of the sail, one around midpoint, and one near the foot of the sail. The idea is that when the sail is trimmed correctly (laminar flow), the telltales on both sides will stream straight aft, and when the sails are trimmed in too much or too little, the more turbulent airflow will cause the telltales to flutter and/or droop on one side or the other.

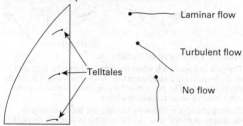

FIGURE 4-42: Telltales

There are numerous adjustments to the sails other than just letting the sheets in or out. For example, the ***boom vang*** is used to pull the boom down, which keeps the mainsail taut. Without it, the main fills too much and pulls up the boom.

In general, all this adjusting has the goal of creating laminar flow and maximum lift over the entire area of the sail.

Sailing Before the Wind

Sailing before the wind can be more difficult than one might think, and it can be trickier and potentially more dangerous than sailing into the wind.

With the wind directly on the stern, the mainsail is set at about 90 degrees to the wind on either the port or starboard side. In this situation, the jib will be shielded from the wind by the main and may flutter uselessly. To avoid this condition, the jib may be set on the opposite side to the main at as close to 90 degrees to the wind as possible in a configuration called **wing on wing**. A **whisker pole** may be used to hold the jib out and prevent it from collapsing. A whisker pole is a pole with a spike on one end and a jaw or fastening device on the other such that the spike goes through the jib's clew and the jaw end is fastened to the mast.

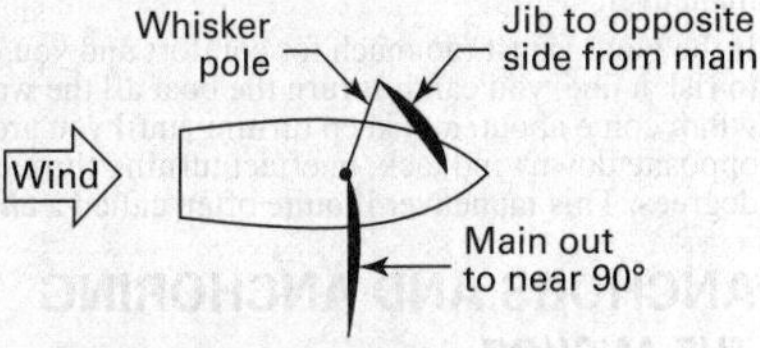

Since running directly before the wind is often a relatively slow point of sail, better overall speed made good may

FIGURE 4-43: Sailing Wing on Wing

often be achieved by tacking downwind even though the distance covered may be greater. This will involve sailing in a direction such that the foresail stays filled when set to the same side as the main.

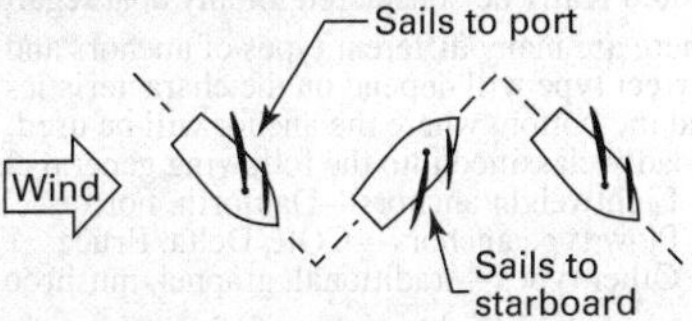

When turning from one tack to the other with the wind astern, as the wind catches the mainsail

FIGURE 4-44: Tacking Downwind

from aft, it can flip the sail and boom from one side to the other in a much more violent and uncontrolled manner than when coming about. Coming across with the wind astern like this is called a *jibe*, and you want this to be a controlled jibe rather than an uncontrolled jibe. An uncontrolled jibe can seriously injure crew who are in the way, it can do considerable damage to the boat and even cause a broach (capsize).

To control the jibe the main sheet must be drawn in as far as possible to the centerline before the jibe so that the boom is not free to swing. After the jibe, the boom is let out on the opposite side in a controlled manner. Control over the jib sheets

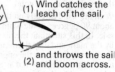

(1) Wind catches the leach of the sail,

(2) and throws the sail and boom across.

FIGURE 4-45: Uncontrolled Jibe

should also be maintained since letting go of both sheets at the same time will allow the jib to fly out ahead. With practice this can actually become a smooth and graceful maneuver.

If the wind is just too much for comfort and you don't want to risk a jibe, you can just turn the boat all the way into the wind, come about, and keep turning until you are on the opposite downwind tack, in effect turning through about 300 degrees. This maneuver if quite often called a *chicken jibe.*

ANCHORS AND ANCHORING
THE ANCHOR
General

An appropriately sized anchoring system or ground tackle is an absolute necessity on any size boat. For coastal or offshore use, at least two anchors of differing types are necessary and should really be considered for any boat regardless of use.

There are many different types of anchors and picking the correct type will depend on the characteristics of the anchor and the bottom where the anchor will be used. They can be broadly classified into the following general classes:
- Lightweight anchors—Danforth, Fortress, West
- Plow type anchors—CQR, Delta, Bruce
- Other types—traditional, grapnel, mushroom

In general, the lightweight and plow types of anchors are the ones used by recreational boaters.

Anchor Terminology

Figure 4-46 shows terminology for the parts of a traditional anchor. Where applicable, this same terminology is used on other anchor types.

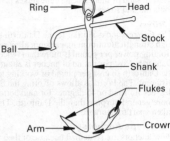

FIGURE 4-46: Parts of the Anchor

The purpose of the stock, which is perpendicular to the crown, is to keep the fluke pointed downward into the bottom. Some anchors are stockless and rely on the arrangement of the flukes to orient the anchor correctly in the seabed.

Lightweight Anchors

Most of the lightweight types of anchor are modeled after the Danforth anchor shown below. Other well-known makes are the Fortress anchor, and the West anchor. Both the Fortress and the West attempt to improve on the original Danforth design.

There are many other models and makes modeled after the Danforth anchor so there are lots to choose from. An anchor may seem like a simple device and the buyer may be tempted to go with the cheapest, but this could be a costly mistake if the anchor fails in a critical situation.

The lightweight anchor type is very popular on runabouts and small sailboats without bow rollers since it is light and can be easily stowed in a relatively small space.

Danforth

The **Danforth** anchor is the original lightweight anchor with long flukes that pivot 32 degrees away from the shank to provide good holding in most conditions. It works best in a sandy bottom but not quite as well in a mud bottom. Holding in rock, grass, and clay is limited. With enough horizontal tension on the rode, this anchor can bury itself in sand or mud. Because the flukes pivot, this anchor folds flat and stows well.

Fortress

The **Fortress** looks similar to the Danforth but is made of a high strength aluminum magnesium alloy rather than steel. Holding power per pound is more than twice that of the Danforth. Cost per pound of anchor is about twice that of the Danforth so cost per pound of working load is not much different. The Fortress allows pivoting the flukes to either 32 degrees for sand or 45 degrees for mud bottom thus making it more general purpose than the Danforth. The Fortress can be taken apart for storage.

Plow Type Anchors

Plow anchors are so named because of their resemblance to a plow. The most well-known types are the CQR, the Delta, and the Bruce, examples of which are shown below. As with the lightweight anchors there are plenty of models and makes of this type of anchor.

CQR

The **CQR** works well on a variety of bottom materials and is a favorite with many cruising yachtsmen. The sharp toe penetrates sand, mud, pebbles, weeds, kelp, and rocks. Pulling harder causes it to dig deeper. The unique hinged shank allows for changes in direction of wind and tide but makes if harder to handle on deck. It stores well on bow rollers. This is the most expensive of the plow type anchors.

Delta

The **Delta** anchor is quite similar to the CQR but without the hinged shank. The Delta anchor works well on a variety of bottom materials. Good for sand, mud, pebbles, weeds, kelp, and rocks. Pulling harder causes it to dig deeper. It is designed to be self-launching, which allows it to be let out with a windlass without manual intervention. It also stows nicely on a bow roller, being awkward to stow other than over the bow. It is moderately expensive.

Bruce

The **Bruce** is Scottish designed for anchoring floating oil rigs in the North Sea. It has no moving parts since it's made from one piece of cast steel. It will reset easily in different directions when wind or tide change. It sets even on short scope (up to a 30-degree angle), although this is not good anchoring practice. Scope is explained later in this section. It will work better on rocks or coral (do not ever anchor in coral except in extreme emergencies) than the other plow types since with the three points it will act somewhat like a grapnel or fisherman type anchor.

Other Anchor Types

Kedge Anchor

This is the traditional type of anchor seen in nautical artwork. Variations of the traditional kedge are the *yachtsman*, *fisherman*, and *Herreshoff* anchors. Getting the kedge to dig in depends more on anchor weight than the lightweight and plow designs, thus for a given amount of holding power these anchors will weigh much more. If the flukes are kept sharp, this anchor will hold well on rock if it can catch a crevice. It also penetrates grass well. It retrieves well with a trip line if caught on the bottom.

Mushroom Anchor

The **mushroom** anchor depends almost completely on weight for its holding properties. The heavy weight of the mushroom anchor will cause it to work its way into the bottom over time and will provide good holding power as a result. It is used primarily for permanent anchoring and is commonly used to anchor mooring buoys, and floating structures. Because of its weight, this anchor is inappropriate for use on a boat.

Grapnel Anchor

The *grapnel* is not efficient for boat anchoring; however, folding grapnels are sometimes used on dinghies and very small boats. They also can be used to try and snag items lost on the bottom. Shown here is a small folding grapnel.

THE ANCHORING SYSTEM
Anchoring Setup and Arrangement

The anchoring system and its components are often referred to as *ground tackle*. Figure 4-47 is a typical anchoring system showing the major components.

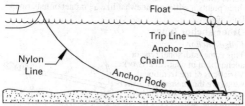

FIGURE 4-47: Typical Ground Tackle Arrangement With Trip Line

The anchor line is the *rode* and can be either all chain, or part synthetic and part chain, with the chain at the anchor end of the rode as shown. The heavy chain lies on the bottom to keep the pull on the anchor as horizontal as possible. This maximizes the holding power of the anchor and minimizes the possibility of pulling the anchor upwards and out of the bottom.

How much chain is needed in a mixed chain and nylon rode? One common opinion is 15 feet (5 m) of chain should be used at the anchor end of the nylon. Another rule of thumb is 1 or ½ foot of chain per foot of boat length (yes, I've seen both). Yet another suggests that the weight of chain should be at least equal to the weight of the anchor.

Is all chain rode better than all nylon rode? As might be expected there is no right answer. Each has its advantages, particularly in different cruising areas, and with different sizes and types of boats.

Chain has the advantage of being resistant to chafing and cutting from abrasive or sharp materials such as coral, barnacles, or rock. It can be re-galvanized every few years and can be expected to last 10 to 15 years and more with proper care and storage. The major disadvantage of chain is weight. Carrying enough chain to anchor in some areas with deep anchorages, can adversely affect the performance of lighter boats because of excess weight in the bow. Nylon line is both cheaper and lighter and will tend to be favored where a long rode is required for deep anchoring. It's also a lot easier on the hands if the rode must be lowered by hand. Disadvantages are susceptibility to cutting and chafing, and nylon line will not last nearly as long as chain.

The trip line shown is optional and can either be run to a float as shown, or can just be run back to the boat alongside the rode. It is used to free a wedged or otherwise stuck anchor and its use is recommended if you think there's any chance of the anchor getting caught. If a vertical trip line is run up to a float, the trip line should be just long enough to reach the float with allowance for tide, and the float should be highly visible so other boaters entering the anchorage will readily see it.

Figure 4-48 on page 192 shows detail of how the anchor is fastened to the rode. The anchor is attached to the chain with a shackle that has the pin wired to prevent the pin from working loose. The chain attaches to the nylon rode section with a swivel that has removable pins at each end, although a shackle is quite often used. A metal thimble is used in the eye of the nylon line to prevent chafing through the line. It's a good idea to seize the thimble in place on either side of the eye.

If a swivel is used on an all chain rode, it should never be attached directly to the anchor but rather to a shackle attached to the anchor to avoid sideways twisting forces on the swivel that might result in failure. With an anchor being raised or lowered with a *windlass*, the chain will be moved by a *gypsy* on the windlass. A gypsy is a sprocket that fits the chain links and is sized for particular chain types and sizes.

If a combination nylon line and chain rode is used with a shackle to fasten the two, the shackle or swivel cannot be run over the gypsy so the chain *stopper* must be set while the line is transferred to the capstan. To alleviate this manual

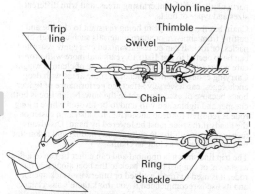

FIGURE 4-48: Anchor Fastening Detail

transfer step, combination windlass designs have a gypsy that contains a groove sized to the line so the chain and line can be run over the windlass without repositioning it. To accomplish this, the shackle must be eliminated and the rope spliced directly to the chain.

Advertisements claim that the splice will retain 90 percent of the nylon rope strength. The main danger with this arrangement will be chafing of the nylon splice through the chain loop, so this should be inspected frequently and periodic resplicing is recommended. The splice in three-strand twisted line is not particularly difficult to do yourself; however, prespliced rodes are available for purchase.

FIGURE 4-49: Rode Chain to Nylon Line Splice

To minimize tugging on the bow of the boat, twisted nylon rope is used for the synthetic portion of the rode, since twisted nylon has the most elasticity of the synthetic ropes and will provide the most cushioning effect to counteract surge from wave action. Nylon can stretch up to 15 percent of its length when tensioned to working load and up to 40 percent when tensioned to near breaking strength.

If any sort of wave action is expected and an all chain rode is used, then a nylon "snubbing line" of at least 30 feet (9 m) is needed to provide a cushioning effect, since chain has no give other than that provided by the catenary.

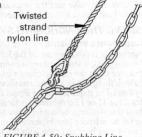

Twisted strand nylon line

Note in figure 4-51 that under the most severe conditions, the rode is pulled tight and the cushioning effect of the catenary (sag) is not available when it is needed most.

FIGURE 4-50: Snubbing Line

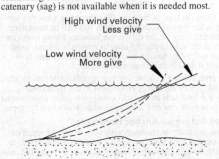

FIGURE 4-51: Catenary at Various Wind Velocities

The anchor is attached to the bow of the boat either over a **bow roller**, through **chocks**, or down a **hawsepipe**. On a runabout it may simply be attached to a deck cleat. The anchor is never attached to the stern in open water since the rode can hold the stern down and into oncoming seas, which could easily swamp the boat.

In most boats over, say, 25 feet (8 m) an electrically or hydraulically powered windlass is used for raising or lowering anchor. The rode usually stacks in a **chain locker** below deck. In smaller boats the anchor and rode may be kept in a bag and the anchor is simply thrown overboard and lowered by hand. Just make sure the bitter end is attached to a fitting on the boat before letting go the anchor.

SIZING THE ANCHORING SYSTEM
Comments on Sizing

Anchoring is probably one of the least scientific aspects of boating. Yes, science and engineering are involved, but in practice there are just too many variables here to just be able to look things up in a table, and pick and size an anchoring system. The requirement for a boat crossing oceans (prepared for force 11 or 12 conditions) is totally different than for a boat that will only be out for a few hours during the day and never be offshore (maybe force 7 conditions). In any case, the fate of your boat and even your life may at sometime depend on your having an appropriate size and type of anchoring system and knowing how, through having practiced, to use it.

Aside from the type of boating, the other huge source of variability is the type of bottom in which you will be anchoring. Anyone can imagine the difference between trying to get an anchor to set in hard packed sand to gravel, soft sand, loose mud, or rock. And having managed to set the anchor, how well will it hold in these various materials?

In the end, although you may get an approximate feel for the size and type of anchoring equipment to use from reading tables, the final *best advice will come from other experienced boaters in your cruising area* as to what works best for them.

Forces Acting on Anchor Hardware

The forces acting on the anchoring system are the result of wind, current, and wave surge on a boat of particular length, windage, and displacement, with wind usually being the most significant of these.

Most catalogs and books provide tables that match a particular anchor type and weight to boat length, with a second column for boat beam. The idea is to enter the length column and go down until your boat length is found, and then check to make sure the beam specified in that row is greater than yours. If it's not, then move down the beam column until a beam greater than your boat is reached and read your drag values or anchor size from that row.

Unfortunately, wind drag on a boat is not primarily related to length, but rather to cross-sectional area of the boat as viewed from the bow. Most tables are presented with length as the entry column, since most people know their boat length, but don't readily know its cross-sectional area. To construct the table, a typical cross-section is assumed for the particular length of boat listed, and the force is calculated from that cross-section.

The equation used to calculate the wind-induced drag on a boat is commonly in a form similar to that in equation 4-3:

$$D = C \times Fa \times A \times V^2$$

Where: D = Drag expressed as pounds (or kilograms force)
C = Coefficient taking into account density of air and other factors.
Fa = Factor for area depending on the type and shape of boat.
A = Area as beam times height (excluding rigging) expressed as square feet or meters.
V = Wind velocity in knots

EQUATION 4-3: Wind-Induced Drag

The value of C used here is based on an average from several publications and works out to about C = 0.009. C will differ for metric units and is C = 0.04394 (assumes V expressed in knots). The value allows for additional forces such as current and wave surge.

Table 4-3 on page on page 196 evaluates the equation for various areas and wind velocities. Note: We use kilograms (force) rather than Newtons to express drag, in metric units, since this seems to be the more familiar usage.

Fa varies from 0.7 to 1.5 depending mostly on the windage and displacement of the boat. The lower value of 0.7 might be used for a very fine and streamlined entry that provides less resistance to wind on the bow. The higher value would be used for a boat presenting a square blocky area to the wind like a houseboat or a sailboat with lots of rigging or a relatively heavy full displacement boat.

The wind tables presented here are not meant to be used to size your anchor system precisely, although they can help you get in the ball park. Rather, the tables are provided to give an appreciation for the relative forces involved, particularly at higher wind speeds and larger boat sizes.

Note how the drag or force exerted on the boat (and consequently on the anchoring system) goes up as the square of the wind velocity. As an example a 40-foot boat with an area factor of 1.5 goes from a force of 390 pounds with a 14 knot wind to 6300 lbs with a 60-knot wind.

Area	Typical			Fa	Moderate Breeze Force 3	Moderate Gale Force 7	Strong Gale Force 9	Storm Force 11
	B	H	L		15 knots	30 knots	42 knots	60 knots
Sq Ft	Ft	Ft	Ft		Lbs	Lbs	Lbs	Lbs
1				0.7	1.42	5.67	11.11	22.68
				1.0	2.03	8.10	15.88	32.40
				1.5	3.04	12.15	23.81	48.60
8	4	2	10	0.7	11	45	89	180
				1.0	16	65	127	260
				1.5	24	97	190	390
18	6	3	15	0.7	26	102	200	410
				1.0	36	146	290	580
				1.5	55	220	430	870
32	8	4	20	0.7	45	180	360	730
				1.0	65	260	510	1040
				1.5	97	390	760	1560
45	9	5	25	0.7	64	260	500	1020
				1.0	91	360	710	1460
				1.5	137	550	1070	2200
77	11	7	30	0.7	109	440	860	1700
				1.0	160	620	1220	2500
				1.5	230	940	1830	3700
96	12	8	35	0.7	140	540	1070	2200
				1.0	190	780	1500	3100
				1.5	290	1170	2300	4700
130	13	10	40	0.7	180	740	1400	2900
				1.0	260	1050	2100	4200
				1.5	390	1580	3100	6300
154	14	11	45	0.7	220	870	1700	3500
				1.0	310	1250	2400	5000
				1.5	470	1900	3700	7500
195	15	13	50	0.7	280	1100	2200	4400
				1.0	390	1600	3100	6300
				1.5	590	2400	4600	9500
272	17	16	60	0.7	390	1500	3000	6200
				1.0	550	2200	4300	8800
				1.5	830	3300	6500	13200
380	19	20	70	0.7	540	2200	4200	8600
				1.0	770	3100	6000	12300
				1.5	1150	4600	9000	18500

TABLE 4-3: Anchor Load Versus Wind Strength

Area	Typical			Fa	Moderate Breeze Force 3	Moderate Gale Force 7	Strong Gale Force 9	Storm Force 11
	B	H	L		**15 knots**	**30 knots**	**42 knots**	**60 knots**
Sq M	M	M	M		Kg	Kg	Kg	Kg
1				0.7	7	28	54	111
				1.0	10	40	78	158
				1.5	15	59	116	237
0.7	1.3	0.5	3.0	0.7	5	19	38	78
				1.0	7	28	54	111
				1.5	10	42	81	166
1.7	1.8	0.9	4.6	0.7	12	47	92	188
				1.0	17	67	132	269
				1.5	25	101	198	403
3.0	2.4	1.2	6.1	0.7	21	83	163	332
				1.0	30	119	233	475
				1.5	44	178	349	712
4.2	2.7	1.5	7.6	0.7	29	116	228	465
				1.0	42	166	326	664
				1.5	62	249	488	997
7.2	3.4	2.1	9.1	0.7	50	199	391	797
				1.0	71	285	558	1139
				1.5	107	427	837	1708
8.9	3.7	2.4	10.7	0.7	62	246	483	985
				1.0	88	352	690	1408
				1.5	132	528	1035	2112
12.1	4.0	3.0	12.2	0.7	84	335	657	1340
				1.0	120	479	938	1914
				1.5	179	718	1407	2871
14.3	4.3	3.4	13.7	0.7	99	396	776	1583
				1.0	141	566	1108	2262
				1.5	212	848	1663	3393
18.1	4.6	4.0	15.2	0.7	125	501	982	2004
				1.0	179	716	1403	2863
				1.5	268	1074	2104	4295
25.3	5.2	4.9	18.3	0.7	175	700	1373	2801
				1.0	250	1001	1961	4002
				1.5	375	1501	2942	6003
35.3	5.8	6.1	21.3	0.7	244	977	1915	3909
				1.0	349	1396	2736	5584
				1.5	523	2094	4104	8376

TABLE 4-4: Anchor Load Versus Wind Strength (Metric)

The table should be entered in the area column although length, beam, and height are presented and can provide alternative entry to the table. The length, beam, and height presented are average proportions calculated from dimensions of several actual boats in each length category.

When reading the table keep in mind that convention has it that a *lunch hook* is designed for a 15-knot wind, a *working anchor* system for 30 knots (moderate gale), and a *storm anchor* system for 42 knots (strong gale). Also note how going from 30 to 42 knots doubles the wind force and going from 42 to 60 knots (storm force 11) doubles it again.

Rode Size

Typically the anchor rode is sized by reading a table such as the one above to get the loading required, and then selecting the line or chain size with a *working load limit* (WLL) equal to or greater than that load. The breaking strength is not used and is only presented here for information's sake.

Nylon Line Size

Table 4-5 for nylon line shows strengths for both twisted 3 strand as well as double braid rope, although twisted 3 strand is the usual choice for anchor rode. Convention uses the 9 to 1 safety factor to size the line for a rode, although some

Size in	Average Break (lbs)	Average Working at 9:1 sf (lbs)	Average Working at 5:1 sf (lbs)	Size (mm)	Average Break (kg)	Average Working at 9:1 sf (kg)	Average Working at 5:1 sf (kg)
Twisted 3 Strand							
3/8	3840	430	770	10	1740	200	350
1/2	6810	760	1360	13	3090	340	620
5/8	10580	1180	2120	16	4800	540	960
3/4	15140	1680	3030	19	6870	760	1370
7/8	20500	2280	4100	22	9300	1030	1860
1	26650	2960	5330	25	12090	1340	2420
Double Braid							
3/8	4900	540	980	10	2220	240	440
1/2	8680	960	1740	13	3940	440	790
5/8	13500	1500	2700	16	6120	680	1220
3/4	19330	2150	3870	19	8770	980	1760
7/8	26200	2910	5240	22	11880	1320	2380
1	34090	3790	6820	25	15460	1720	3090

TABLE 4-5: Nylon Line Strength Versus Diameter

experts suggest that 5 or even 4 to 1 is adequate for determining a working load.

No sizes under 3/8 inch are shown since anything smaller, although it might be strong enough for the application, would be subject to failure through abrasion and/or cutting action and it's also harder on the hands.

Chain Rode Size

Chain used for rode is usually either **proof coil** or **BBB** (grade 30), which is less expensive or **high test** (grade 40), which is stronger but more expensive. High test is a little lighter per foot since the links are slightly longer and a smaller size can usually be used to get a specific working strength. For a given WLL, the cost per foot may be about the same as BBB chain so to save weight it may make sense to go with the higher quality chain if there is a choice.

In practice, the anchor windlass on the boat may require a particular type of chain, so there may be no choice short of replacing the windlass.

Table 4-6 on page 200 shows chain and shackle sizing. Something to be aware of in the chain size table is the WLL for BBB is 24 percent of breaking strength, and the WLL for high test is 33 percent of breaking strength. If you want to be conservative you might want to consider using a WLL of 25 percent (4:1) for high test just as for BBB.

Shackles are also selected from the chain table; however, inspection of the table shows that selecting a shackle with the same pin diameter pin as the chain diameter, will yield a shackle with a WLL less than the chain WLL (especially with high test), thus making the shackle the weakest link in the system. For this reason, the inside width is provided in the chain table so the largest shackle that will fit inside the chain loop can be selected. The shackles should always have the WLL stamped on them! Stainless steel shackles with higher WLLs are available but are probably not a good idea since the dissimilar metal in contact with the chain may encourage galvanic action.

The comments regarding shackle sizing also apply to swivel sizing, which is also shown in the chain table.

Anchor Sizing and Type Selection

Now let's open the real can of worms: comparing and selecting anchor types and sizes. An ideal anchor sets and holds in all types of bottoms but unfortunately that ideal anchor just doesn't exist. An anchor that sets easily in say grass may have

Size	Proof Coil BBB Grade 30				Grade 40 High Test				Steel Shackles		Swivel	Size Dec.
	Wt / 100 ft	Avg Break-ing	Avg Work-ing	Inside Width	Wt / 100 ft	Avg Break-ing	Avg Work-ing	Inside Width	Avg Break-ing	Avg Work-ing	Avg Work-ing	
in	lbs	lbs	lbs	in	lbs	lbs	lbs	in	lbs	lbs	lbs	in
1/4	72	5200	1300	0.43	75	7800	2600	0.40	5000	1000	850	0.25
5/16	111	7600	1900	0.50	110	11700	3900	0.48	7500	1500	1375	0.31
3/8	164	10600	2650	0.62	150	16200	5400	0.57	10000	2000	2125	0.38
7/16	210	14000	3500	0.75	211	21600	7200	0.65	15000	3000	3300	0.44
1/2	268	18000	4500	0.81	247	27600	9200	0.74	20000	4000	5200	0.50
5/8	438	27600	6900	1.01	369	34500	11500	0.82	32500	6500	7200	0.63
3/4	567	42400	10600	1.10	567	48600	16200	1.02	47500	9500		0.75
7/8	748	51200	12800	1.32					60000	12000		0.88
1	1025	71600	17900	1.50					75000	15000		1.00
mm	kg/100m	kg	kg	mm	kg/100m	kg	kg	mm	kg	kg	kg	mm
6	107	2360	590	11	112	3540	1180	10	2270	450	390	6
8	165	3450	862	13	164	5310	1770	12	3400	680	620	8
10	244	4810	1202	16	223	7350	2450	14	4540	910	960	10
11	313	6350	1588	19	314	9800	3270	17	6800	1360	1500	11
13	399	8160	2041	21	368	12520	4170	19	9070	1810	2360	13
16	652	12520	3130	26	549	15650	5220	21	14740	2950	3270	16
19	844	19230	4808	28	844	22040	7350	26	21550	4310		19
22	1113	23220	5806	34					27220	5440		22
25	1525	32480	8119	38					34020	6800		25

TABLE 4-6: Chain and Shackle Sizing

little or no holding power in mud; another may set and hold in sand but won't work at all in grass or rocks. To complicate things further the weight to holding ratio, or so-called *anchor efficiency*, will also vary with both the type of anchor and in many cases with the size of anchor.

Set refers to getting the anchor to dig in and hold in the first place and it's important to remember that this is just as important as holding power. It should be pretty obvious that if the anchor won't set then it won't hold. The related ability of the anchor to reset when the boat swings around and twists out the anchor is also important.

The holding power of the types of anchors used for recreational boats is related more to surface area and shape than weight. The general idea is to get the anchor flukes to set at or near perpendicular to the bottom with the pull of the anchor rode being as near horizontal as possible. An anchor with long thin flukes, like the traditional anchor, might set easily but will have little holding power in a soft bottom. Conversely, an anchor with a wider fluke area like the Delta may not set as easily but will hold better in a soft bottom.

Numerous studies and in-water tests have been carried out to determine the relative effectiveness of different anchors. Unfortunately the tests use differing methodology, use different weights of anchors, and are conducted in different bottoms and depths. As a result, the findings—particularly for holding power—vary widely. Some writers denigrate these tests for this reason; however, I believe the tests provide valuable information to the recreational boater.

First, the tests all tend to rank the anchors similarly for similar conditions, and tend to confirm what experienced boaters know from word of mouth in the boating community. Second, the tests often involve less well-known anchor types and models and often show that some anchors just don't work, while other new models show great promise. Third (I know this is really generalizing), the *old standby* anchors, which are the ones diagrammed and described earlier, tend to come out on top in most of the tests.

Some of the tests easily found on the web using a Google search are as follows:

- 1990 San Francisco Mud Test
- 1990 Miami Sand Test
- 1990 Vryhof Ankers Tank Test
- 1992 French Regulatory Test
- 1994 San Francisco Sand Test

- 2003 Gulfport Mud Test
- 1998—ongoing Practical Sailor Tests
- And there are lots of others

Some anchors, other than the ones we showed earlier, that do well in tests include **Supermax**, **Spade**, **Bulwagga**, and **Barnacle**. The *Practical Sailor* tests are up to date and ongoing, with recent anchor entries included. The test results can be ordered on their website for a nominal fee (www.practical-sailor.com).

The different test results differ too much to be tabulated for comparison so we have not applied for permission to use any of the test result data and consequently we don't summarize the results. Rather, if you really want to get more information on anchoring, search out the test results and read them.

Now that I've copped out on providing that comparison, I still want to present a comparison of some kind, if only because most books on recreational boating don't do so. Most of the manufacturers of anchors, with the exception of Fortress, don't publish **working load limits** (WLLs) for each of their anchor sizes, which is quite understandable since the WLL depends on very specific bottom characteristics. For example, holding force in mud can be as little as 10 to 30 percent of holding in firm sand.

On the other hand, the manufacturers and retailers do publish recommended maximum boat lengths for each size of anchor. So if we rearrange the formula for wind drag discussed previously, along with typical boat length, width, and height, we can back-calculate an implied WLL for each anchor. Table 4-7 shows the results of evaluating that equation for various anchor types and sizes. Also in the right-hand column is an implied efficiency ratio, which is simply WLL divided by anchor weight. Note that although the Fortress WLLs are the advertised WLLs and not the implied WLLs, the implied WLLs I calculated agree closely with the published WLLs used.

The purpose of including this table is to compare various types and weights of anchors rather than to look up a specific anchor size, although it can be used to get in the size ballpark.

It should also be noted that the relative efficiencies of the different anchor types are in general agreement with the results found in most of the tests. Some of the sand test results were remarkably close to the implied WLLs presented here. Again, I can't emphasize enough the value of consulting

Wt	Max Boat Length	Implied WLL From Length	Wt	Max Boat Length	Implied WLL From Length	Implied Efficiency
lb	ft	lb	kg	m	kg	ratio
Danforth Standard						
5	17	280	2	5	127	56
9	27	710	4	8	322	79
14	31	940	6	9	426	67
16	36	1270	7	11	576	79
25	40	1560	11	12	708	62
43	45	1960	20	14	889	46
West Performance						
6	25	610	3	8	277	102
14	35	1200	6	11	544	86
25	44	1880	11	13	853	75
40	50	2400	18	15	1089	60
70	70	4500	32	21	2041	64
Fortress						
4	27	700	2	8	318	175
7	32	900	3	10	408	129
10	38	1250	5	12	567	125
15	45	2000	7	14	907	133
21	51	3000	10	16	1361	143
32	58	4000	15	18	1814	125
47	68	5250	21	21	2381	112
69	150	6750	31	46	3062	98
Bruce						
11	23	520	5	7	236	47
16.5	28	770	7	9	349	47
22	32	1000	10	10	454	45
33	39	1480	15	12	671	45
44	46	2050	20	14	930	47
66	57	3080	30	17	1397	47
110	72	4740	50	22	2150	43
176	90	7050	80	27	3198	40
242	106	9340	110	32	4237	39
CQR						
15	30	880	7	9	399	59
20	40	1560	9	12	708	78
25	50	2400	11	15	1089	96
35	50	2400	16	15	1089	69
45	60	3390	20	18	1538	75
60	70	4500	27	21	2041	75
75	80	5720	34	24	2595	76
Delta						
9	30	880	4	9	399	98
14	30	880	6	9	399	63
22	40	1560	10	12	708	71
35	60	3390	16	18	1538	97
44	60	3390	20	18	1538	77
55	70	4500	25	21	2041	82
88	80	5720	40	24	2595	65

TABLE 4-7: Anchor Sizing. (Note: The WLL for Fortress is per Fortress Marine Anchor's Website.)

other boaters in your cruising area as to what works best for your size and type of boat. The needs of a boater in the Pacific Northwest with deep anchorages are dramatically different from those of a boater in Florida with a typical anchorage depth under 15 feet (5 m) in sand bottom.

A least squares fit on the implied efficiency ratio versus the anchor weight allows one to calculate an implied ratio for a specific anchor weight for comparison purposes. In table 4-8 the efficiency ratio shown is for a hypothetical 20-pound anchor weight. This is done because not all the anchors are available in an actual 20-pound size. The table shows the general characteristics of the differing anchor types.

The lightweight anchors, which include the Danforth, West, and Fortress, hold well in sand but poorly in other bottoms.

Anchor	Relative Set / Reset Sand	Eff. Ratio Firm Sand	Holding			
			Sand	Mud	Grass	Rock
Danforth	3	0.8	Good	Poor	Poor	Poor
West	3	1.0	Good	Poor	Poor	Poor
Fortress	2	1.7	Best	Best	Poor	Poor
Bruce	1	0.6	Good	Fair	Fair	Good
CQR	4	0.9	Good	Best	Fair	Fair
Delta	4	1.0	Good	Best	Fair	Fair
Traditional	5		Fair	Poor	Best	Best

TABLE 4-8: Anchor Type Comparison

They set and reset better than the others except for the Bruce. The Fortress anchor will be much lighter for its size since it's made of aluminum, hence the much higher efficiency ratio. The Fortress does well in mud because the flukes can be adjusted from the 32-degree angle used by most of the lightweight anchors, to 45 degrees for mud.

The CQR and Delta behave similarly, holding well in sand, and they do much better than the lightweight anchors in mud and are just okay in grass and rock.

The Bruce ends up being a good all round performer and is known for its ability to set almost instantly, even on short scope (defined below).

Scope
The ratio of the rode length to the depth of the anchor is the *scope*. As figure 4-52 shows, the depth must include the distance from the water to the bow roller or chock. In determining scope, allowance must be made for high tide as well.

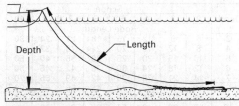

FIGURE 4-52: Scope = Length ÷ Depth

Since these anchors depend on pull being horizontal, it follows that letting out more rode will result in a flatter pull, which in turn will help the anchor do its job. Most literature advocates a scope of at least 7:1 for nylon rode and 4:1 or 5:1 for chain rode to obtain the best setting and holding power. For serious holding in a storm 10:1 is recommended.

Figure 4-53 shows how the angle from the horizontal changes as a function of varying scopes, assuming a perfectly straight rode with no catenary (sag).

FIGURE 4-53: Effect of Scope on Horizontal Angle

It's apparent from the diagram that the angle changes in ever smaller increments as the scope is increased much beyond 7:1. In practice, if you are anchoring among other anchored boats, you will need to keep your scope down to the same as theirs, to avoid swinging into one of them as the wind shifts. The generally accepted practice is the first boat to anchor sets the tone for those following (assuming the captain knows what he or she is doing). In crowded anchorages, 3:1 scopes are quite common, and at 3:1 you only get about 50 percent of the holding of 7:1. In this case, consider using an anchor a size or two heavier.

To get all this to work, you must know the depth and you must measure how much rode to pay out. The rode should be marked every 10 to 30 feet so you have a means of measuring its length.

Table 4-9 tabulates rode length versus depth. Note that either feet or meters can be entered and read since this is nothing

Depth	Scope							
	2	3	4	5	6	7	8	10
	Rode Length							
3	6	9	12	15	18	21	24	30
4	8	12	16	20	24	28	32	40
5	10	15	20	25	30	35	40	50
6	12	18	24	30	36	42	48	60
7	14	21	28	35	42	49	56	70
8	16	24	32	40	48	56	64	80
9	18	27	36	45	54	63	72	90
10	20	30	40	50	60	70	80	100
11	22	33	44	55	66	77	88	110
12	24	36	48	60	72	84	96	120
13	26	39	52	65	78	91	104	130
14	28	42	56	70	84	98	112	140
15	30	45	60	75	90	105	120	150
16	32	48	64	80	96	112	128	160
17	34	51	68	85	102	119	136	170
18	36	54	72	90	108	126	144	180
19	38	57	76	95	114	133	152	190
20	40	60	80	100	120	140	160	200
22	44	66	88	110	132	154	176	220
24	48	72	96	120	144	168	192	240
26	52	78	104	130	156	182	208	260
28	56	84	112	140	168	196	224	280
30	60	90	120	150	180	210	240	300
32	64	96	128	160	192	224	256	320
34	68	102	136	170	204	238	272	340
36	72	108	144	180	216	252	288	360
38	76	114	152	190	228	266	304	380
40	80	120	160	200	240	280	320	400
45	90	135	180	225	270	315	360	450
50	100	150	200	250	300	350	400	500
55	110	165	220	275	330	385	440	550
60	120	180	240	300	360	420	480	600
65	130	195	260	325	390	455	520	650
70	140	210	280	350	420	490	560	700
75	150	225	300	375	450	525	600	750
80	160	240	320	400	480	560	640	800
85	170	255	340	425	510	595	680	850
90	180	270	360	450	540	630	720	900
95	190	285	380	475	570	665	760	950
100	200	300	400	500	600	700	800	1000

TABLE 4-9: Rode Length Versus Depth and Scope

more than a multiplication table, multiplying depth times scope.

ANCHORING PROCEDURE
Where to Anchor

Since sand generally provides the best holding, it follows that you should seek out sand to anchor in—assuming you have any choice in the matter. Your charts describe the bottom type and depth and should be helpful in selecting an anchorage.

Obviously you want to find shelter from wind and waves, if possible, taking into account wind shifts that occur at night. About 15 to 20 feet of depth is ideal as it lets enough rode out to provide enough flexibility to protect against heaving or pitching in waves but not so much as to have a large swing radius.

If anchoring among other boats, then allowance must be made so as not to swing into them when the wind changes. Again, the best practice is to use the techniques and tackle used by other boaters in the area.

Setting the Anchor

Approach the selected spot upwind at dead slow until the bow is directly over the spot where the anchor is to be set. Lower the anchor to the bottom then either drifting with the wind or at dead slow back away from the anchor while paying out the rode. When the desired scope has been paid out and the rode made fast, the rode should tighten noticeably as the anchor begins to set. A little burst of power at this point should ensure a good set. If it pulls out, then repeat the whole procedure until you get a good set.

At this point it is a good idea to take compass bearings on a couple of landmarks and write them down. After an hour or two, take the same bearings to see if you are dragging anchor. Some GPS units allow an alarm to be set if the boat moves beyond a preset distance. If you can do both, so much the better.

Weighing Anchor

Weighing anchor is pretty much the opposite of setting the anchor. Approach the anchor at dead slow while taking in the rode until the rode is vertical. With any luck a little vertical tug will break the anchor free and you can raise it the rest of the way. If the anchor won't break free, try applying some force in forward using engine power. Or better yet, if you had the foresight to attach a trip line, you should be able to back it out by pulling on the trip line.

OTHER ANCHORING TECHNIQUES

Bahamian Moor

The **Bahamian Moor** uses two anchors placed at 180 degrees apart, both off the bow. With the two rodes tensioned, the movement of the boat is limited to swinging around the bow where both rodes are attached.

The Bahamian Moor is so named because of its use in crowded Bahamian anchorages to limit swing. It is also useful for use in narrow channels to keep the boat from swinging into shore where current or wind might reverse.

FIGURE 4-54: Bahamian Moor

Set the first anchor in the usual manner, and then back off to a distance twice that of the desired rode length and drop the second anchor. Haul in the first rode until the boat is at the midway point between anchors. Tension both rodes to ensure both anchors are set then let the rodes fall to their normal catenary so they will be below the keel and running gear to allow the boat to swing.

An alternative method is to drop the aft anchor first and continue forward twice the desired rode length and drop the up wind anchor. Since the aft anchor rode is trailing behind and you are moving forward under power, be particularly careful not to tangle the aft rode in the propeller. Then let out the forward rode and bring in the aft rode until the boat is positioned halfway between the two anchors.

Two Anchors Forward

Two anchors may be deployed forward in anticipation of a significant storm or the bottom is just not good. Two anchors set out at angles will also help keep the boat from swinging from side to side in the wind.

The anchor rodes should be angled 30 to 40 degrees apart to keep them from entanglement.

The first anchor is set in the normal fashion including backing away. To deploy the second anchor, proceed forward and to the side, to keep enough tension on the first rode to keep it in sight but not pull the anchor out. When the rode to the

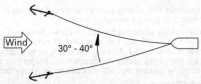

FIGURE 4-55: Two Anchors Forward

first anchor extends at about 90 degrees the second anchor
is dropped. If the first rode is nylon it can be carefully taken
in as you proceed forward to the second anchor to help avoid
fouling the propeller. Back off and set the second anchor.

Anchors Fore and Aft

The usual reason for using fore and aft anchors is to orient
the bow into oncoming waves that are at angles to the wind.
The bow anchor is set to hold against the wind and the stern
anchor is then set to pull the boat into the desired orientation.

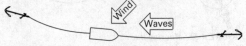

FIGURE 4-56: Fore and Aft Anchors

Rafting

Rafting involves two or more boats tied alongside each other
with one boat setting anchor. The purpose is usually social
and is done in quiet anchorages where there is little or no
wind or wave action.

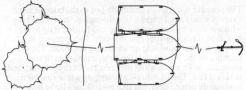

FIGURE 4-57: Rafting

Only one boat anchors and that is normally the largest boat.
The anchored boat should be the center of more than two
rafted boats. The anchored boat anchors in the normal fash-

ion, sometimes also setting a stern anchor or fastening to an object ashore to prevent swinging about.

The boats rafting to the anchored boat come abeam and get lines across to pull themselves alongside. Generous use of fenders is recommended. Making fast is similar to making fast at the pier, using spring and breast lines. Prepare for the unexpected by making sure all lines can be let go in a hurry.

Mooring Buoys

Mooring buoys are permanently installed and usually attached with a chain to a large block of concrete or a mushroom anchor that has been allowed to settle into the bottom. The chain will extend through to the top of the buoy to a ring where a pennant is usually attached. The pennant is a line that floats and may have a small float at its free end.

FIGURE 4-58: Mooring Buoy

Mooring buoys are used at yacht clubs, marinas, parks, etc., to provide mooring in addition to slips or as an alternative to anchoring. They are becoming much more prevalent in areas with coral reefs to alleviate damage to coral from boat anchors. Mooring buoys have the additional advantage of using less scope thus allowing more boats to safely moor in a given area.

The pennant is retrieved and made fast to the bow. In some cases you may need to get a line through a ring on the buoy, which is done by hooking the ring and pulling it up to the bow then threading your line through. The approach to a buoy is upwind similar to an anchoring approach. The crew member on the bow signals the helmsman when to stop, move aft, or forward, while the crew hooks the pennant, and makes it fast. The likelihood of dragging a mooring buoy is virtually nonexistent, but like everything else in boating, don't bet the farm on it.

SPECIAL SITUATIONS

GROUNDING

Safety First

In the event of grounding, everyone not already in lifejackets should immediately get them on. Before trying anything to get off, check for any holing or damage that is allowing water in. If you are holed you will be better off grounded until you can fix the leak. Check for fuel leakage!

Getting Off

Don't try to back off by reversing engines without knowing just how and where the boat is grounded on the bottom since damage to running gear, especially the rudder can result. Reversing with power can also throw sand and debris forward, burying your keel further, and it could plug your cooling water intake.

Take a little time to think about your situation as some common sense can go a long way here. If you have wind or waves driving you further on, then get a kedge anchor out as soon as you can. If you're in tidal water first figure out if the tide is coming in or out. If it's coming in then you probably just need to wait a few minutes although you may still need a kedge to keep from being pushed further aground as the water rises. If you can determine that just the bow is aground and the running gear is well clear of the bottom, then it's probably okay to use reverse engine to try to back out.

If the tide is going out then you are likely stuck for the duration and will probably have to take some precautions. If the boat is going to list to one side, make sure it leans shoreward, away from incoming surf, to prevent water entering when the tide comes in again. If you can brace the boat to keep it upright, so much the better. Check for and take precautions for possible spillage from fuel or water tanks.

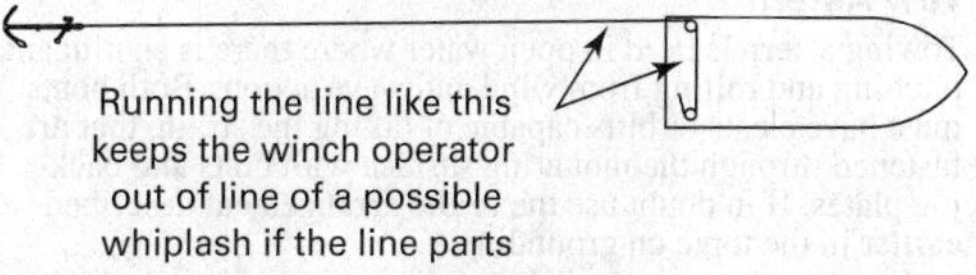

Running the line like this keeps the winch operator out of line of a possible whiplash if the line parts

FIGURE 4-59: Boat Aground Kedging Off

In nontidal water (or if you can act quickly enough in an outgoing tide), putting out a kedge astern and winching against it may work on a lighter boat. Rocking the boat from side to side, using any means you can think, of may help break it loose while applying tension with the winch.

If all else fails a tow may be necessary. The primary consideration when attaching a towline is finding a piece of hardware able to take the strain of the pull, which can be considerable. Consider placing a bridle all around the hull to distribute the strain and save your deck hardware.

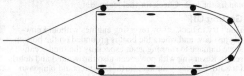

FIGURE 4-60: Bridle Arrangement for Towing

The towline should be braided nylon because of its strength and ability to absorb shock. The flexibility of nylon also means that, in the event of failure, it will whip back with dangerous force and anyone near or in line with it can be severely—even fatally—injured. *Stay well clear of the towline when it's under tension!*

TOWING

Towing General

Don't try to tow another boat unless you are of a size and power to do so. The exception to this might be with dead calm conditions and only a short distance to tow.

If the towing boat is larger than the towed boat then be careful not to tow the towed boat at more than its hull speed. I suggest towing at a speed to length ratio (SLR) of 0.7 or less. (An SLR table is found in chapter 1 on page 23 of this book.)

Tow Astern

Towing astern is used in open water where there is significant pitching and rolling from wind and wave action. Both boats must have cleats or bitts capable of taking the strain, that are fastened through the mounting surface with bolts and backing plates. If in doubt use the bridle arrangement described earlier in the topic on grounding.

During research for this book, I found contradictory recommendations made by diverse reputable organizations and publications advocating the use of twisted strand nylon line, or woven nylon line, or polypropylene line as being the best for use in towing. The basis for recommending twisted strand nylon was its combination of strength and high elasticity. The recommendations for woven nylon are strength, but not such high elasticity, so as to minimize snap back in the event of a break. Polypropylene line, though weaker, was recommended because it has little stretch and thus is safer in terms of snap back. Furthermore, it floats, and this was deemed less likely to foul the propeller. I tend toward nylon since the elasticity substantially reduces strain on deck fittings in less than perfect conditions, and the line is less likely to part in the first place. This may well be decided by what you have on board at the time you undertake the tow. In any case, this bears repeating: *Stay well clear of the towline when it's under tension!*

Except when well offshore, the towed boat should have an anchor at the ready in case the towline parts or there is some other difficulty. Since a boat turns by swinging the stern about the pivot point forward, it will be difficult if not impossible to turn the towing vessel if the towline is fastened at the stern and under tension. For this reason, the towline should be fastened as far forward on the towing vessel as possible. Distance between boats should be at least twice the length of the towed boat, at least two wavelengths apart and such that both boats tend to crest the waves at the same time.

Tow Alongside

Towing alongside is used in placid conditions, particularly when maneuvering near other boats and slips. The towing boat is fastened alongside with its stern aft of the towed boat.

Make liberal use of fenders and keep the lines between the boats tight. Make use of both spring and breast lines.

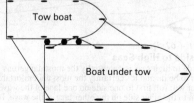

FIGURE 4-61: Towing Alongside

ADVERSE CONDITIONS

Head Seas

Usually heading within a few degrees off directly into the waves will provide the safest and most comfortable ride. Speed is adjusted to prevent pounding and in extreme conditions may have to be reduced to just making headway.

Running Before High Seas

This can be dangerous, particularly in a boat with a square transom and the waves directly aft. The danger in running before heavy seas is surfing down the front of a wave and burying the bow in the trough of the wave. At this point the oncoming wave may push the stern up and to the side causing the boat to yaw sideways and over in a roll, which can result in a ***broach*** (capsize). In an extreme case, as the bow buries itself, the stern is tossed up and over the bow as the boat ***pitchpoles***.

Running before the seas might be okay if the boat can be kept under control. Some faster boats might be able to adjust their speed to stay with the waves. Try proceeding at an angle to the seas.

Offshore cruising boats will often carry a drogue that is put out astern to keep the stern into the seas, to prevent surfing down the wave front, and to prevent the boat from broaching. The drogue is a cone or parachute shaped device similar to that shown in figure 4-62. Use of a drogue is only recommended on some boats, usually those designed specifically for offshore cruising.

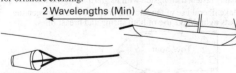

2 Wavelengths (Min)

FIGURE 4-62: Drogue

Broadside to High Seas

Broadside to high seas is potentially the most dangerous position to be in, and it's certainly the most uncomfortable. The boat will roll first to one side on one face of the wave, and then to the other side on the other face of the wave. In the extreme, the boat capsizes.

The usual approach to this situation is to tack into and away from the oncoming seas, which at least keeps the boat making headway in the desired direction. The tacking may be as much as 45 degrees to either side.

Heaving To

When things get so bad that trying to make way becomes outright dangerous, or you just can't physically take any more, then heaving to is an option.

In a sailboat, heaving to involves (1) lashing the tiller or helm so the rudder is to windward, a storm jib is raised and backed into the wind, and a storm trysail is raised and sheeted in. (2) In this configuration, when the boat falls off the wind, she will begin to make way and the rudder will turn her back into the wind. (3) As she heads back into the wind, she loses way, and the jib will start the boat falling off the wind again. This cycle then repeats itself with the boat making little or no way overall. Some experimenting will be needed to determine just how much rudder and sail setting are needed to make this work comfortably. This is something that is worth practicing in calmer conditions to build confidence.

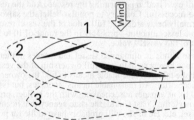

FIGURE 4-63: Sailboat Hove To

A powerboat can't really heave to. About all it can do is reduce speed to the minimum required to maintain steerage-way and keep headed within a few degrees of directly into the oncoming waves.

Storm Anchor

The storm anchor is similar to the drogue but is larger and looks similar to a parachute. It is put out off the bow much like a conventional anchor. The purpose is to keep the bow into the waves without the need for power and to minimize making way aft. See figure 4-64 on the next page.

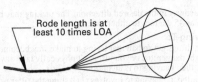

Rode length is at
least 10 times LOA

FIGURE 4-64: Storm Anchor
Like the drogue, the storm anchor is only to be used on boats
capable of withstanding the high forces imparted by the
storm anchor.

SALVAGE

Unlike on land, when at sea a person who successfully assists
and rescues a vessel in distress and in danger of being lost or
seriously damaged, can usually make claim for some portion
of that vessel's value.

Generally, the awards will be related to the danger, difficulty,
and skill exercised in performing the rescue. And the rescue
must be successful. Contrary to popular belief, the salvor will
not normally be awarded the full value of the vessel rescued
but some lesser amount—probably in the range of 10 to 30
percent of the vessel's value.

If a person finds an unmanned vessel and rescues it, then he
or she may have a right to take full ownership of the vessel
if he or she takes all reasonable means to find the owner but
is unsuccessful. "All reasonable means" includes, but is not
limited to, newspaper ads, checking with the builder, previous owners, the Coast Guard, the state agency that licensed
the vessel, etc. He or she will probably have to file for possession in court.

Be careful here: You may think you are doing someone a
favor by hauling some derelict floating downriver to shore,
but you may wind up owning it and being responsible for its
proper disposal. Towing a vessel not in danger of sinking or
being lost or seriously damaged will probably not be considered salvage, although there are plenty of individuals—including unscrupulous towboat operators—who have brought
exorbitant salvage claims for doing just that.

Have a salvage agreement, such as the Boat U.S. Standard
Form, on board so that if you need towing or rescue, you
and the salvor can agree in advance, in writing, on how the
compensation is to be paid. If there is time, call your insur-

ance company and have them negotiate the terms or arrange an alternate service.

In any case, thoroughly read and understand any form a towboat captain may ask you to sign, before you sign it. Better yet, join an organization such as Boat U.S. and purchase one of their towing packages. Boat U.S. also sells boat insurance.

Salvage laws in the United States and Canada are similar in that they conform, for the most part, to the International Convention on Salvage (London 1989).

CHECKLISTS

Use of checklists will minimize undesirable surprises and help ensure that your trip will be both safe and enjoyable. Consider the lists provided in this book as a starting point for developing your own lists.

All the lists shown here are available for download as Excel spreadsheets or Adobe Reader (.pdf) files from www. anchorcovepublishing.com. The spreadsheets have the advantage that you can modify them to suit your own needs.

Similarly, all forms in this book, such as the Float Plan shown below, are available as Adobe Reader files.

The Float Plan

Before leaving on a cruise make out a Float Plan and leave it with a reliable friend (not the Coast Guard). Then check in at the predetermined times specified on the form. If you don't check in, the friend then informs the appropriate authorities. See the sample Float Plan on the next page.

The sample float plan shown here is too small to use; however, a full size version is available for download from www.anchorcovepublishing.com.

Float Plan

Person Filing This Form

Name		Phone Number

Vessel Information

Name	Home Port	Make and Year

Country/Flag	Registration/Documentation/License No.	Length	Range	Fuel Capacity	Hull Color	Cabin Color	Trim Color

Type: Sail○ Power○ Fuel: Diesel○ Gas○ Drive: Inboard○ Outboard○ Outdrive○ No Engines: 1○ 2○ Hull Type: Monohull○ Multihull○

Communication Equipment	Nav Eqpt	Survival Eqpt	Other Information
Freq / Number	Compass □	Life Jackets □ Horn □	
VHF	GPS □	Flares □ Dinghy/Raft □	
SSB	Charts □	Mirror □ Paddles □	
Cell Phone	Radar □	Smoke Signal □ EPIRB 121.5/243.0 □	
Sat Phone	Loran □	Anchor □ EPIRB 406 □	
CB		Flashlights □ EPIRB 406 w GPS □	

Auto / Trailer

Make / Model	Year	Color	License	Trailer License
Parked At				

Persons on Board

Name	Phone	Age	Sex	Medical or Other Info

Itinerary

Location	Arrive Date	Arrive Time	Depart Date	Depart Time	Check In Deadline Date	Check In Deadline Time

Contacts

Name	Phone Numbers

A web search will find lots of other float plan forms available for download. You can also type or draw up your own plan.

The following float plan checklist includes the items that should be included in the plan.

FLOAT PLAN CHECKLIST	
Person filing this form	
Name	❏
Phone number	❏
Vessel information	
Vessel name	❏
Home port	❏
Make and year	❏
Registered country	❏
Registration or documentation or license number	❏
Length	❏
Range	❏
Fuel capacity	❏
Hull color	❏
Cabin color	❏
Trim color	❏
Specify sail or power	❏
Specify diesel or gas	❏
Specify inboard, outboard, or outdrive	❏
Specify number of engines	❏
Specify monohull or multihull	❏
Communications equipment —frequency monitored or number	
VHF	❏
SSB	❏
Cell phone	❏
Sat phone	❏
CB	❏
Navigation equipment	
Compass	❏
GPS	❏
Charts	❏
Radar	❏
Loran	❏
Survival equipment	
Life jackets	❏
Flares	❏
Mirror	❏
Smoke signal	❏
Anchor	❏

FLOAT PLAN CHECKLIST	
Flashlights	☐
Horn	☐
Dinghy/raft	☐
Paddles	☐
EPIRB 121.5/243.0	☐
EPIRB 406	☐
EPIRB 406 w GPS (GPIRB)	☐
Automobile and trailer information	
Make and model of automobile	☐
Model year	☐
Color	☐
License	☐
Trailer license	☐
Location where parked	☐
Persons on board—list all	
Name	☐
Phone	☐
Age	☐
Sex	☐
Medical and other info	☐
Itinerary—list all ports	
Locations	☐
Arrival dates and times	☐
Departure dates and times	☐
Check-in deadlines [the whole point of this form]	☐
Contacts to call in event of emergency	
Name	☐
Phone numbers	☐

Before Leaving Home

Adequate planning before leaving home is particularly important for a boat trip since leaving out even one critical item can result in serious delays or inconvenience when you are ready to leave the dock.

BEFORE LEAVING HOME CHECKLIST	
Boat related	
File the float plan with a reliable friend!	☐
Extra keys	☐
All manuals not already onboard	☐
Check predeparture list for items you may need to take	☐
Check mechanical section checklists	☐

BEFORE LEAVING HOME CHECKLIST	
Check trailering section checklist	☐
Check navigation section checklists	☐
Check insurance coverage for where you are going	☐
Very important	
Wallet and keys	☐
Passport or passport copies	☐
Airline tickets	☐
Domestic currency	☐
Foreign currency	☐
Insurance info	☐
Boat registration	☐
Credit cards	☐
Boat organization memberships	☐
Proof of operator qualification	☐
Other organization memberships	☐
Miscellaneous personal items	
Boater's Pocket Reference [this book]	☐
Toiletry kit	☐
Prescription drugs	☐
Alarm clock	☐
GPS, cords, instructions	☐
Corkscrew	☐
Camera and spare battery	☐
Tripod	☐
Extra watch	☐
Reading glasses	☐
Sunglasses	☐
Books to read	☐
Games	☐
Maps	☐
Mapping software	☐
Misc instruction manuals	☐
Small personal flashlight	☐
PDA	☐
Personal computer	☐
Appointment book	☐
Phone lists	☐
Cell phone and charger	☐
Modular phone cable	☐
Ethernet cable	☐
AM/FM radio	☐

BEFORE LEAVING HOME CHECKLIST	
CDs and CD player	☐
Casual clothing	
Pants	☐
Shorts	☐
Shirts	☐
Belt	☐
Sports socks	☐
Jacket or coat	☐
Sweaters	☐
Sweatshirt	☐
Tee shirts	☐
Shoes	☐
Deck shoes	☐
Running shoes	☐
Other clothing	
Undergarments	☐
Bathing suit	☐
Flipflops	☐
Pajamas	☐
Bathrobe	☐
Outdoors	
Rain gear	☐
Hats	☐
Hiking boots	☐
Insect repellent	☐
Sunscreen	☐
Water bottles	☐
Backpack	☐
Waist pack	☐
Fishing rods and equipment	☐
Scuba	
BC	☐
Mask, fins, snorkel	☐
Dive knife in checked bag	☐
Log book	☐
PADI card	☐

Predeparture Checklist

This is the checklist to use when you have arrived at the boat and are getting ready to depart.

PREDEPARTURE CHECKLIST	
Safety equipment check	
PFDs or life jackets for everyone	☐
Throwable flotation device	☐
Distress signals	☐
Fire Extinguishers	☐
Ground tackle—anchor, rode, etc.	☐
VHF and other radios operating	☐
First aid kit	☐
All safety equipment stowed and available	☐
Navigation equipment check	
Compass	☐
Hand-bearing compass	☐
Horn	☐
Bell	☐
GPS	☐
Radar	☐
Navigation lights	☐
Binoculars	☐
Flashlight	☐
Charts	☐
Cruising guides	☐
Approved copy of navigation rules	☐
Calculators	☐
Computer	☐
Sextant	☐
Check for local hazards or rules	☐
Miscellaneous equipment	
Boater's Pocket Reference [this book]	☐
Documents—registration, licenses, etc.	☐
Cell phone	☐
Spare batteries for everything	☐
Boat hook	☐
Tool kit (Tool checklist is in Mech section)	☐
Systems checks	
Adequate fuel for trip	☐
Potable water tanks full (check not fuel)	☐
Black water holding tanks pumped out	☐
Engine coolant level	☐

PREDEPARTURE CHECKLIST	
Engine oil level check	❏
Transmission oil level usually with engine running	❏
Fan belts—tension and condition	❏
Check battery fluid levels and SG	❏
Check fuel filters	❏
Check engine raw water filter	❏
Check generator raw water filter	❏
Look for leaks, oil, etc., in bilge area	❏
All required seacocks open	❏
Hoses condition and clamps tight	❏
Tapered plugs tied at each through hull	❏
Bilge pump test	❏
Rigging check	❏
Steering check	❏
Tilt and trim check	❏
Shifting check	❏
Operational	
Float plan completed and left with reliable friend	❏
Check weather forecast	❏
Guest safety review	❏
Guest expectations review	❏
Captain's emergency replacement—boat and radio operation	❏
Close head valves	❏
Cabinets locked closed	❏
Secure all loose items	❏
Propane turned off at tank	❏
Gas powered check for fumes—blower four minutes before start	❏
Controls in neutral and at idle	❏
Run engine to operating temperature before leaving	❏

Fueling

Follow these steps for safe fueling

FUELING CHECKLIST	
Tie off to the fuel dock	❏
All power systems off	❏
All stoves or open flames off	❏
All guests and crew ashore	❏
No smoking	❏
Close all openings to prevent fumes from entering boat	❏
Fire extinguisher at the ready	❏

FUELING CHECKLIST	
Double check to be sure you're filling the gas tank and not the water tank	❏
Double check to see you're holding the gas hose	❏
Portable tanks on dock for filling	❏
Don't fill to top—allow for expansion	❏
After fill replace filler cap	❏
Open closed openings	❏
Bilge blower on four minutes	❏
Check for vapors in engine room and bilge	❏

Departure Checklist

This list is for casting off and getting underway.

DEPARTURE	
Leaving	
Shore power breaker to off	❏
Unplug shore end of shore power	❏
Run engine to operating temperature before leaving	❏
Bring in dock lines not needed for leaving	❏
Check for other boats in waterway	❏
One prolonged blast before leaving (per Nav Rules)	❏
Dock lines off	❏
Underway	
Fenders in	❏
Dock lines coiled and stowed after leaving	❏
Keep checking engine temp, oil pressure, voltage	❏

Checklists for Arriving at Dock

Use this list starting before arrival and for ending the trip.

ARRIVAL CHECKLIST	
Before arrival	
Discuss docking procedure with crew	❏
Safety reminder—keep all body parts inside boat	❏
Safety reminder—no jumping ashore	❏
Fenders out on correct side	❏
Dock lines ready	❏
Pilothouse and cabin doors locked open	❏
After arrival	
Make fast with breast and spring lines	❏
Connect shore power cable boat end	❏
Connect shore power cable shore end	❏
Switch over to shore power	❏

ARRIVAL CHECKLIST	
Post-trip	
Empty holding tanks	☐
Shut off propane	☐
Flags inside	☐
Fresh water wash down	☐
Remove perishables from refrigerator and elsewhere	☐
Empty trash on shore	☐
Refrigerator on dock power if any food left	☐
Turn off all switches—except bilge pumps!	☐
Bilge pump power on!	☐

5 PILOTING AND NAVIGATION

INTRODUCTION TO PILOTING AND NAVIGATION

Navigation

Generally speaking, marine navigation is the science of determining the position of a vessel, the position of its destination, and how to proceed from the current position to the destination safely and efficiently. Although the science of navigation can be learned in the classroom, the practical application of navigating on the water is as much an art, learned through practice and experience, as it is a science.

This section introduces only the concepts and tables needed to get one started and to provide some refresher information for those who have already studied the subject. Navigation is a complex mathematical subject that cannot be adequately covered in a little handbook such as this. Plenty of books have been written that are entirely devoted to the subject, the definitive volume being *The American Practical Navigator* commonly referred to as *Bowditch*, so named after the original writer, Nathaniel Bowditch (1773–1838) of Salem, Massachusetts.

Bowditch

Bowditch was both a ship's master and owner, but more important, he was an outstanding mathematician who was able to substantially advance the science (and art) of navigation on a practical basis. He is considered one of the best (if not the best) mathematicians in the United States of his time.

The copyright to *American Practical Navigator* is now held by the U.S. government and the book is made available through purchase, and also as a free download as an Adobe Acrobat (.pdf) file from http://pollux.nss.nima.mil/pubs/.

Types of Navigation

Traditional types of navigation include:

Dead reckoning (**DR**) is where position is determined using estimated distance and direction from a known starting point.

Piloting is navigation with visual reference to land, objects, or structures with known positions.

Celestial navigation uses stars and other heavenly bodies to determine position. The sextant is the instrument used for accurate celestial navigation. It is now relegated to use as backup for modern electronic navigation systems

Electronic forms of navigation include:

Radio Navigation uses several types of systems including direction finding beacons and LORAN. Most of these have been, or soon will be, shut down in favor of GPS although LORAN may get a new lease on life as a backup to GPS.

Radar is used similarly to visual observation to plot bearings and distances to objects with known positions.

Satellite navigation determines position from satellite radio transmissions. Older satellite systems have been shelved in favor of the now-familiar *Global Positioning System* (**GPS**).

Phases of Navigation

Bowditch defines four distinct *phases* of the navigation process.

1. The *Inland Waterway Phase* involves piloting in narrow bodies of water such as rivers and canals. This is somewhat similar to driving your car down the highway and is sometimes called conning. Position plotting is usually not carried out, since it serves no useful purpose, any more than it would while driving down the highway.
2. As the name *Harbor/Harbor Approach Phase* implies, this involves finding your way to a harbor entrance and then in through harbor approach channels.
3. The *Coastal Phase* is navigation off a coastline and in open bays and inlets.
4. *Ocean Phase* refers to navigation at sea, generally out of sight of land.

The accuracy, equipment, and methods used in each phase differ. Table 5-1 from *Bowditch* shows the types of navigation and the phases in which they are used.

	Inland Waterway	Harbor/ Approach	Coastal	Ocean
DR	✔	✔	✔	✔
Piloting	✔	✔	✔	
Celestial			✔	✔
Radio		✔	✔	✔
Radar	✔	✔	✔	
Satellite	✔*	✔	✔	✔
* With SA off and/or using DGPS				

TABLE 5-1: Types and Phases of Navigation

PUBLICATIONS FOR NAVIGATION

CHARTS

Introduction

Charts are needed for successful navigation, just as road maps are necessary to find your way on land. Unlike land maps, nautical charts show features near, on, and under the water. Charts show water depths, navigation aids such as buoys and lighthouses, channels, hazards, etc. Nautical charts use latitude and longitude as the coordinate system.

In the United States, coastal and foreign charts are produced by two government agencies; the *National Imaging and Mapping Agency* (**NIMA**) and the *National Ocean Service* (**NOS**).

The NOS is a part of the *National Oceanic and Atmospheric Administration* (**NOAA**) and produces charts for coastal regions of the United States and its possessions. NIMA is part of the Department of Defense and produces charts covering the rest of the world. Note that NIMA recently changed its name to the *National Geospatial-Intelligence Agency* (**NGA**). Chart catalogs are available that list all charts available for civilian use, from both agencies. The U.S. Army Corps of Engineers produces charts of inland rivers, canals, and lakes.

In Canada, all charts are produced by the *Canadian Hydrographic Service* (**CHS**), which is part of the Department of Fisheries and Oceans.

NOAA has *Electronic Navigational Charts* (**ENCs**) in vector form that are available for free download from their website at http://chartmaker.ncd.noaa.gov/. Links to free viewers for these charts are also on the NOAA site. These ENCs conform to the international S-57 standard of the *International Hydrographic Organization* (**IHO**). S-57 is the acronym for Special Publication Number 57 and specifies the internationally accepted standard for digital hydrographic data.

Latitude and Longitude

As we all know, there are 360 *degrees* (360°) in a circle. Each degree is further subdivided into 60 *minutes* and each minute is further subdivided into 60 *seconds*.

Latitude and *longitude* are angular measurements expressed in degrees, minutes, and seconds and are used to specify position on the earth's surface.

Symbols used for each are: Examples
     Degrees: °   105° 53' 20"
     Minutes: '   or
     Seconds: "   105° 53.33'

Most large-scale charts use decimal minutes rather than
seconds, but be careful since some still use seconds.

Parallels of latitude circle the globe in an east west direction
parallel to the equator and are measured north and south
from the equator ranging from 0 degrees at the equator to
90 degrees at the poles. Parallels are usually written in the
form: **L 35° 12.3' N** where the **L** specifies latitude and the **N**
specifies north from the equator. **S** is used for direction south.
Parallels of latitude are evenly spaced and 1 *nautical mile* is
defined (for all intents and purposes) as the distance covered
by 1 minute of latitude. Since there are 60 minutes in a degree, it follows that 1 degree of latitude = 60 nautical miles.

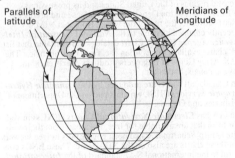

Parallels of latitude   Meridians of longitude

FIGURE 5-1: Latitude and Longitude

It is worth noting that a minute of latitude expressed to one
decimal place equates to nautical miles expressed to one
decimal place, which is a precision of 608 feet, or 185 meters.
Two decimals gets you within 60 feet and three decimals
within 6 feet.

Meridians of longitude start from zero at Greenwich
(London, England) and run east and west to 180 degrees (the
International Date Line). At the equator only, a minute of
longitude is equal to 1 nautical mile. Meridians are of the
form **Lo 105° 05.4' W** where **Lo** specifies longitude and **W**

specifies direction west from the Greenwich meridian. **E** is used for direction east.

The Mercator Projection

Almost all nautical charts use the ***Mercator projection***, which is constructed by projecting the globe onto a cylinder (figure 5-2) so that the lines of latitude (NS) and longitude (EW) appear as straight lines on the flattened chart. Since on the globe the meridians of longitude converge at the poles and on the projection they remain parallel, the actual distance represented by the distance between the longitude lines on the projection is less toward the poles. Also, although the physical distance between parallels of latitude is constant on the globe, on the Mercator projection the lines for the parallels are shown further apart away from the equator.

FIGURE 5-2: Mercator Projection

This can be seen on the Mercator world projection shown in figure 5-3 on the next page.

The distance on the chart between the lines of latitude is proportional to the distance between the lines of longitude, so the chart keeps the proportion of vertical to horizontal constant and geographic features retain their correct shape even though they appear larger toward the poles. The most important characteristic of the Mercator projection is that it is ***conformal***, which means that within any smaller area, direction and distance can be measured correctly on the map.

On larger scale maps (see scale topic on page 234) typical of those used for coastal navigation, the change of scale from top to bottom is almost unnoticeable and a scale bar showing distance is often provided.

The ***polyconic*** projection is another type of projection that was used in the past for charts of the Great Lakes and some inland waters; however, these are being replaced by charts that use the Mercator projection.

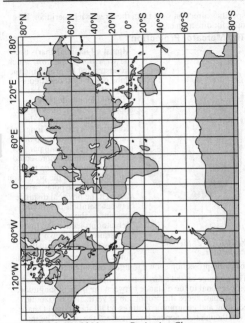

FIGURE 5-3: World Mercator Projection Chart

Measuring Latitude and Longitude on the Chart

To find latitude use dividers to measure the distance from a latitude line and transfer it to the latitude scale at the side of the chart. Similarly, transfer longitude to the top or bottom of the chart to find longitude. See figure 5-4.

Chart Title Block

The title block is the first thing to look at on a new chart.

Every chart has a title block that specifies:
* The area covered by the chart
* The scale at a specified latitude
* The projection used (usually Mercator)

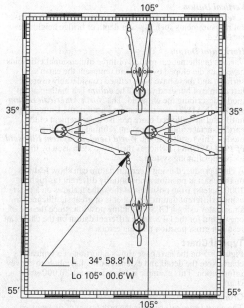

FIGURE 5-4: Finding Latitude and Longitude of a Point

- Depth units
- Horizontal and vertical datums
- Chart creation and update dates
- Symbols used on the chart
- Other useful information

In particular, the depth units should be noted. If depth units are in feet and you think they're in meters or fathoms, then running aground is definitely in the cards.

The horizontal datum is particularly important if you are using a GPS (it must be set to the correct datum) to plot positions on the chart. Most new charts use the WGS 84 datum. This is further explained later in the GPS Navigation topic.

Vertical Datum

A **vertical datum** is a reference elevation from which vertical measurements such as water depth or bridge height are measured.

Horizontal Datum

Various mathematical models of three dimensional ellipsoids have been developed over time to represent the earth's surface, and these have been refined considerably over the last couple of hundred years. The **datum** is a mathematical model describing the ellipsoid. The **North American Datum of 1927** (**NAD27**) was the standard used in the United States until satellites allowed more precise measurement of the earth's surface and a consequent refining of the ellipsoid model. This resulted in the **World Geodetic System Ellipsoid of 1984** (**WGS84**), which is the base system used by the global positioning system.

A chart produced using a certain datum can show features on the chart at positions substantially different (as high as 1000 meters) from positions of the same features on a chart using a different datum. This fact is of great significance to a navigator using a GPS for finding position, since the use of one datum for the GPS and a different datum on the chart can result in gross position plotting errors.

Typical Chart

Figure 5-5 on the next page shows a portion of a typical chart. Note the detail and extensive use of symbols to convey information. This example is taken from a 1:80,000 scale chart.

Chart Scale

The chart (**natural**) **scale** is the proportion of distance on the chart to distance on the earth's surface. Charts come in different scales for different purposes and range from approximately 1:2500 (**large scale**) to 1:15,000,000 (**small scale**). This naming is somewhat opposite to what intuition might suggest; so just keep in mind that $1 \div 2500 = 0.0004$ is a much larger number than $1 \div 15,000,000 = 0.00000007$. Another way to keep this straight is to *think of a small-scale chart as one on which geographic features are very small compared to those on a large-scale chart.*

Remember that scale on a Mercator chart varies with latitude and will be quite noticeable on very small-scale charts and not noticeable on the largest-scale charts.

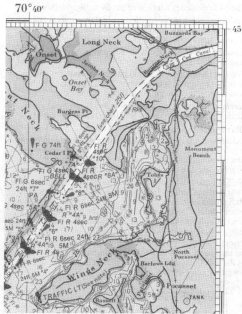

FIGURE 5-5: Typical Nautical Chart

Scale can also be expressed by other means such as miles (actual) per inch (of chart) or kilometers per centimeter. To convert divide the (ratio) scale described above by the number of chart units (say, inches) in the actual surface unit (say, miles). Some examples:

- Land miles/inch = natural scale ÷ 63360
- Nautical miles/inch = natural scale ÷ 72913
- Kilometers/centimeter = natural scale ÷ 100,000
- Nautical miles/centimeter = natural scale ÷ 185,200

Tables of scale conversions are included at the end of this chapter starting on page 346.

The NOS classifies nautical charts by scale as follows:

Sailing charts are the smallest scale (largest area) and are used for navigating on the open sea. Scale is generally smaller than 1:600,000.

General charts are for coastal navigation offshore. Scales range from 1:150,000 to 1:600,000.

Coastal charts are for coastal navigation inshore. These will be used in large bays and harbors and large inland bodies of water. Scale is from approximately 1:50,000 to 1:150,000.

Harbor charts are used in harbors and small waterways. Scale is usually larger than 1:50,000 (smallest area).

Distance Measurement

Distance at sea is usually measured in *nautical miles* (**nm**) regardless of whether English or metric units are used for other measurements such as depth, displacement, etc. Speed is expressed in nautical miles per hour and is termed *knots*.

Note: In this book, just the word "miles" or the abbreviation "nm" will sometimes be used instead of "nautical miles." References to statute miles will always be preceded by the word "statute," unless it is clear from the context to which kind of miles we are referring.

Since 1 minute of latitude equals 1 nautical mile; to measure distance on a chart spread dividers between the two points to be measured and then place the dividers on the latitude scale at the side of the chart to read the distance. Do not use the longitude scale to measure distance!

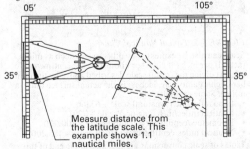

Measure distance from the latitude scale. This example shows 1.1 nautical miles.

FIGURE 5-6: Measurement of Distance on a Chart

Direction Measurement

Direction is usually expressed as the clockwise angle from true north to the direction line and can range from 0 to 360 degrees. This angle is called the **bearing**. Note: The term *azimuth* refers to the direction to a celestial body rather than to an earthbound object but it sometimes is used (incorrectly) instead. True north is almost always shown to the top of the chart. Strip charts for use along rivers and canals are an exception since they are aligned with the river or channel by necessity.

Figure 5-7 shows part of a compass rose from a chart. The outer ring measures direction from geographic (true) north and the inner ring measure from magnetic north. Direction of a reference line on the chart can be determined by moving a parallel rule from the line to the rose. Direction can also be determined with the use of a protractor.

Note the comments in the center of the rose that specify magnetic variance from true north for a particular year and

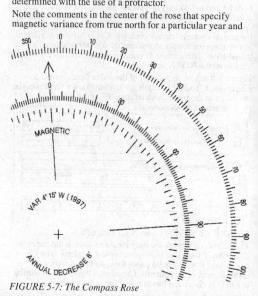

FIGURE 5-7: The Compass Rose

the annual decrease (or increase) in that variance. This year being 2005, the decrease would be (8' × (2005 − 1997) = 64'. The variation in 2005 would, therefore, be 4° 15' N less 64' = 3° 11'. The variance occurs because the earth's magnetic poles are moving.

Symbols and Color

Symbols and colors are used on charts to convey information such as, features on land, depths, bottom type, rocks, lights, buoys, etc. Land is usually shown with a tan or gray tint; shallow water with a blue tint; and deeper water as white. Areas that are uncovered at low tide sometimes will have a light green tint. Use caution when venturing into areas marked in blue and consider going to a larger-scale chart if one is available.

Chart No. 1, Symbols Abbreviations and Terms is actually a booklet and not a chart and shows most of the symbols and abbreviations used on nautical charts. *Chart No. 1* is country specific and the particular *Chart No. 1* used should be from the country where you are cruising. *Chart No. 1* is available in most marine supply stores and should be considered a "must-have" publication. It is also available as a free download from the NOAA website.

Figure 5-8 below shows part of the index page from U.S. *Chart No. 1*. To find symbols for landmarks, for example, you would go to the pages with a large "E" at the top.

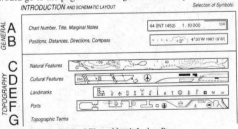

FIGURE 5-8: Part of Chart No. 1 *Index Page*

The following figures are only meant to show what pages in *Chart No. 1* look like with some typical symbols. The *Chart No. 1 book* is actually 96 pages long, so this is only a very small sample of its contents. Canadian Chart No. 1 is similar to the U.S. chart and has many of the same symbols.

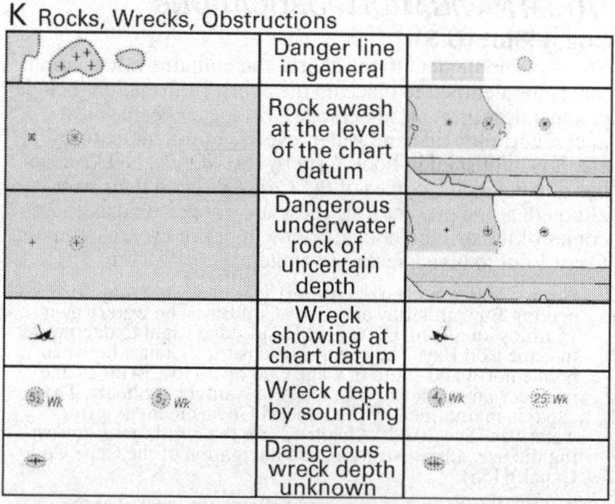

K Rocks, Wrecks, Obstructions

	Danger line in general	
	Rock awash at the level of the chart datum	
	Dangerous underwater rock of uncertain depth	
	Wreck showing at chart datum	
Wk Wk	Wreck depth by sounding	Wk 25 Wk
	Dangerous wreck depth unknown	

FIGURE 5-9: Some typical symbols from U.S. Chart No. 1. The left most column shows NOS and NIMA symbols and the right most column shows IHO (International) symbols.

Some of the more important chart symbols for navigation marks and hazards are included in the color plates section included in this book.

There are also many abbreviations used on charts, which are described in *Chart No. 1*. Some abbreviations used in "J Nature of the Seabed" are shown in table 5-2.

S	Sand
M	Mud
Cy; Cl	Clay
Si	Silt
St	Stones
G	Gravel
P	Pebbles
Cb	Cobbles
Rk; rky	Rock, Rocky
Co	Coral and coraline algae
Sh	Shells
S/M	Two layers sand over mud
Wd	Weed (including kelp)

TABLE 5-2: Some Common Seabed Abbreviations from Chart No. 1

OTHER NAVIGATION PUBLICATIONS

Coast Pilot (U.S)

This is a supplement to the charts and contains information that is too detailed to place on the chart. Information includes channel descriptions, anchorages, bridge and cable clearances, currents, tide and water levels, prominent features, etc. It is published in book form by the NOAA. NOAA also has downloadable copies of the *Coast Pilot* on their website although at the present time these are not certified as exact copies of the printed books. Following is an excerpt from the Coast Pilot to give a feel as to content:

> **Cape Cod Canal** is a deep-draft sea-level waterway connecting Buzzards Bay and Cape Cod Bay. The waterway is 15 miles long from Cleveland East Ledge Light to deep water in Cape Cod Bay. The canal shortens the distance between points north and south of Cape Cod by 50 to 150 miles and provides an inside passage to avoid Nantucket Shoals. The canal is maintained by the Federal Government as a free waterway.(See 207.20, chapter 2, for the regulations governing the use, administration, and navigation of the Cape Cod Canal.)(155)

> **Traffic lights** (red, green, and yellow) are located at the easterly canal entrance at Sandwich; at the Canal Electric Terminal basin on the south side of the canal at Sandwich; and at the westerly entrance of Hog Island Channel at Wings Neck. These signals apply to all vessels over 65 feet in length that desire to transit the canal.(See **207.20 (h)**, chapter 2, for detailed information on signals.)(156) Cleveland East Ledge Light.

Sailing Directions

Produced by NIMA these are similar to the *Coast Pilot* but are for ocean voyaging and include information from foreign pilots and sailing directions.

The *Sailing Directions* in Canada (sometimes called the *Pilots*) are the equivalent to the U.S. Coast Pilot and contain all the detailed information for each area.

Light Lists

The USCG *Light List* enumerates all lights and navigation aids in U.S. territorial waters. The lists include information supplemental to nautical charts, such as location, light characteristics, detailed descriptions, visibility, etc.

The Canadian *List of Lights, Buoys, and Fog Signals* is produced by the Canada Coast Guard and is available for purchase or download from http://www.charts.gc.ca/pub/.

Notice to Mariners

The *Notice to Mariners* is issued to provide updates to charts, light lists, coast pilots and other publications. *All applicable updates should be applied to any charts or other publications you plan to use*; furthermore, you should ensure that you are updating the latest chart. If newer charts are available these should be procured.

In the United States there are two *Notices to Mariners*, these being the *Local Notice to Mariners* (**LNM**) published by the USCG and the *Notice to Mariners* produced by NIMA for use outside the United States. The local notices are produced weekly and are available on the Internet, or they may be ordered free of charge from the appropriate Coast Guard district.

In Canada the *Notice to Mariners* is issued monthly by the Canadian Coast Guard.

Tide tables

The *tide tables* are used to determine the height of water and direction and speed of tidal currents at a given time and location. Use of tide tables is discussed elsewhere in this chapter.

In the United States, the information for the tide tables is produced by NOS and supplied to private companies that then publish and distribute the tables in book form.

In Canada the tide tables are compiled by CHS and are sold in book form.

Reed's Nautical Almanacs

This is an all-in-one book that contains not only information similar to the *Sailing Directions* (Pilots) and tide tables but much additional information on approaches, radio call signs and frequencies, marinas, anchorages, etc. These are very useful for piloting in coastal areas around the United States and Canada. *Reed's* has almanacs for the East Coast, West Coast, Caribbean, and Europe.

THE COMPASS

Introduction

A good compass, installed and functioning correctly, is arguably the most important navigation instrument on the boat. Although some might argue that radar or GPS is the most important, the compass remains the primary fallback when all else fails. For this reason, the compass must be accurately adjusted. If your compass is reading incorrectly, say, by 5 degrees, then you will be about 5 miles off course after traveling an easy day's run of just 60 miles.

A compass card has a magnet attached and is free to rotate in any direction such that the magnet aligns itself with the earth's magnetic field and points to the magnetic north pole. Usually, the card is suspended in a fluid to dampen its motion and to allow the card to stay horizontal regardless of the boat's movement.

A magnetic compass points to the magnetic north pole which is not located at the geographic north pole but is a few hundred miles away, and it is constantly moving such that it's bearing from true north changes by a few minutes a year, depending on your location. In 2005 the north magnetic pole will be located at approximately L 82.7° N and Lo 114.4° W (in the Arctic Ocean north of Canada) and is moving about a degree west and a third of a degree north each year (about 22 nm) per year.

The most important function of the compass is to steer the boat in the desired direction, with a secondary, but also very important, function of determining position by taking bearings on surrounding objects and features. Useful accuracy of a properly adjusted mechanical compass is around +/–2 degrees. This includes errors in both the compass itself as well as in reading the compass.

The Ship's Compass

The ship's compass will be permanently affixed to the boat, preferably mounted directly ahead of the helm. There are two primary types of compass cards, these being the flat card style where the heading is read at the back of the compass bowl (forward toward the bow), and the direct read where the heading is read from the front of the compass. The advantage of the flat card is that the azimuths are clockwise on the card, which is more intuitive. The direct read style allows reading from the front without peering inside, but the azimuths are counterclockwise, which can sometimes be confusing.

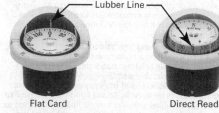

FIGURE 5-10: Fixed Mount Ship's Compass (Photos Courtesy Ritchie Navigation)

The compass has a lubber line that must be precisely aligned with the vessel's keel and is used to read the heading.

Hand Bearing Compass

A boat should also have onboard a hand bearing compass that is used to take bearings on navigation aids and other objects to aid in position determination. The hand bearing compass has other uses as well, which are described elsewhere in this chapter.

Bearings are taken with the hand bearing compass by sighting the object through the sights or across the lubber line and reading the compass dial at the sight or lubber line.

FIGURE 5-11: Hand Bearing Compass

Fluxgate Compass

Often a boat will also have a *fluxgate* compass installed, which is basically an electronic compass with components that sense the earth's magnetic field electronically (no moving parts). This type of compass is most often used to feed direction to an autopilot system or to other onboard instruments such as radar.

The makers of fluxgate compasses claim an accuracy on the order of +/−0.5 degrees, which is somewhat better than mechanical compasses. The actual sensor may be mounted remotely away from electrical and other magnetic influences, which further increases accuracy

Also a fluxgate compass is self-compensating, which eliminates the need to construct a deviation table (compensating is discussed later in this section). Compensating the fluxgate compass is accomplished by sailing the boat in a number of circles while the compass compensates itself, a much simpler procedure than constructing the deviation table for a conventional compass.

The variation (defined next topic) for a particular location can be entered into some fluxgate compasses such that the compass can read true headings rather than magnetic headings. This can considerably simplify the whole process of transferring information to and from paper charts. Since the fluxgate compass is more accurate and eliminates the need to refer to deviation tables, consider using a fluxgate compass as the main ships compass, with a traditional mechanical type compass as backup in case of electrical failure.

Variation

The angle between magnetic north and true north at any given position is the variation and must be taken account of in determining true bearing. Landlubbers call this declination; however, the term always used in marine navigation is variation.

The amount of variation can be determined from the compass rose (see example in figure 5-7 on page 237) on the chart for the cruising area and correcting for the annual change from the date specified on the rose. It is also available from other sources or can be approximated from the variation chart figure 5-13 on page 246.

If, from a given position, magnetic north is to the west of true north then variation is westerly and when magnetic north is to the east the variation is easterly. Figure 5-12 shows how

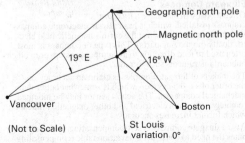

FIGURE 5-12: Magnetic Variation East and West

variation east or west looks from different points in North America.

The process of converting a bearing from magnetic to true is **correcting** and converting from true to magnetic is **uncorrecting**. To correct a westerly magnetic bearing to a true bearing, the variation is subtracted from the magnetic bearing; to correct an easterly magnetic bearing to a true bearing, the variation is added.

Deviation

Deviation Introduction

A compass is affected by magnetic influences on the boat and will not usually read an accurate true magnetic heading. The angle between the compass heading and the true magnetic heading is known as deviation and is westerly if the compass north points west of magnetic north and easterly if the compass north is east of magnetic north.

In order to minimize deviation errors, the compass must (1) be zeroed in a place free of magnetic influences, and then (2) adjusted after installation to minimize deviation. Finally (3) a table or graph is constructed that tabulates the remaining deviation for all headings. Note that (1) and (2) can't be done by the amateur adjuster if the compass doesn't have internal compensating magnets.

It is best to have your compass adjusted by a professional, but you can perform a do-it-yourself adjustment (unless you have a steel boat, in which case professional adjustment is a must). *Bowditch* includes more than 30 pages on compass adjustment, including the procedure used on steel vessels.

Compass Zeroing

Zeroing the compass is the first step taken to minimize deviation error. A new compass must be zeroed in at a location away from the boat, which is free of interference with the earth's magnetic field caused by nearby ferrous objects or electrical fields. A quality new compass should have been zeroed at the factory, so you might consider skipping this step, although "trust but verify" is an apt slogan here.

In its simplest form, zeroing involves placing the compass on a flat surface, away from the boat or any magnetic influences, and orienting the lubber line to compass north. Mark the alignment on the flat surface and then turn the compass exactly 180 degrees using the alignment marks. The compass should read exactly 180 degrees or south. If it is off, then the north-south adjusting screws are adjusted with a nonmagnetic

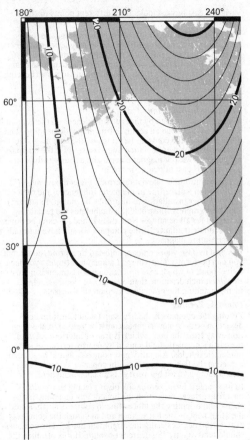

FIGURE 5-13: Magnetic Variation Americas 2005

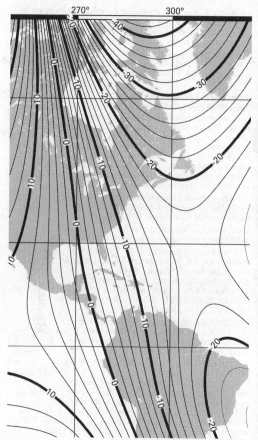

FIGURE 5-14: Magnetic Variation Americas 2005

screwdriver, to remove about half the error; the compass is turned rotated back 180 degrees, and the adjustment process is repeated. This back and forth process is repeated until both the north and south readings are zeroed.

The same process is then repeated but with the compass oriented in the east west direction and using the east west adjusting screws. The compass is now ready to be installed in the boat.

Adjusting the Installed Compass

After the compass is properly installed and aligned in the boat, a similar process to zeroing is carried out, except now to turn the compass 180 degrees, the entire boat is turned 180 degrees. Start with the east west direction adjusting the compensating screws half way as was done in zeroing. This is followed by the north south adjustment. In this case all the error probably cannot be completely adjusted out of the compass due to magnetic influences on the boat so the goal here is just to minimize the error.

All the electronics that are normally on during cruising *should be turned on* for this procedure, even though you may have mounted the compass well away from them.

On a fiberglass boat the deviation should be able to be adjusted down to a couple of degrees or less.

The main difficulty with this process is how to precisely measure the 180 degree swing (it's hard to draw a reference line on the water). Probably the best approach, for accurate alignment, is to use a *pelorus* in conjunction with a *range* on shore. A pelorus is a device that is used to measure angles to objects relative to the heading of the boat.

A range consists of two marks or objects on a chart with a known bearing between them. If you position your boat so they are aligned visually one behind the other, the bearing from the boat to the range is same as the bearing between the two objects.

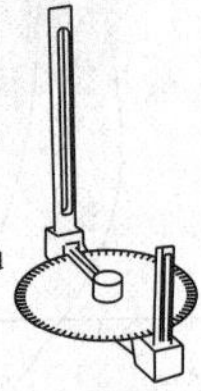

FIGURE 5-15: Pelorus

When the boat aligned with the range and is turned to compass heading north, the pelorus is used to read the relative bearing of the range.

In the example of figure 5-16, the relative bearing from the pelorus is 76 degrees. The boat is then turned exactly 180 degrees, so the pelorus relative azimuth to the range is 76 plus $180 = 256°$.

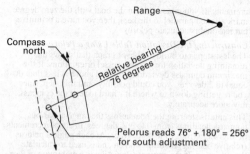

FIGURE 5-16: Zeroing the Installed Compass Using a Pelorus and a Range

A pelorus can cost anywhere from $60 to $700, depending on size and precision. An alternative to a pelorus is to mount a stick on a 1- to 2-foot square piece of plywood with a screw through the center of the stick and the center of the plywood so that the stick can be rotated to any direction. A vertical pin or nail is placed at opposite ends of the stick. This apparatus is then fixed to the boat and the two pins lined up with the range. To get the exact 180 degree reversal just sight the other way across the pins.

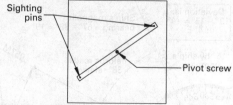

FIGURE 5-17: Simple Pelorus Alternative

It doesn't take too much imagination to see that once you've built this gizmo, you could then draw a circle by placing a pencil at the end of the stick and rotating the stick until a complete circle is drawn. Then with a protractor and a ruler, the circle can be divided into 5-degree (or even 1-degree) increments. If you mount this on the boat with the zero degree mark aligned parallel to the keel, then you have a primitive but reasonably accurate pelorus.

Constructing the Deviation Table Using a Pelorus

The last step is to build a table or graph that shows the remaining deviation for various vessel orientations. If the maximum compass deviation achieved above is less than or equal to 2 degrees, you could possibly omit this step, since you're getting down to where it's hard to read the compass any more accurately.

This entails steering the boat across the range at various compass headings from 0 to 360 degrees, in equal increments of anywhere from 15 to 45 degrees. At each angle a pelorus (relative bearing) reading is taken and is used to calculate the deviation. If the compass deviation is a maximum of 2 or 3 degrees then every 45 degrees will be adequate, but if it's high—5 or more degrees—then smaller increments, such as 15 or 30 degrees, are preferred. If the maximum deviation is less than 2 degrees then constructing the deviation table is probably unnecessary.

Figure 5-18 shows a pelorus (relative bearing) sighting of 38 degrees to a range when the vessel is on a heading of 15 degrees compass and is crossing the range. The magnetic bearing of the range is 57 degrees as determined from a chart, so subtracting the pelorus reading from the magnetic bearing yields the vessel's magnetic heading. The magnetic

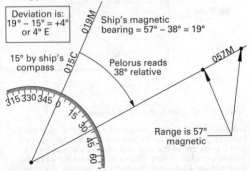

Deviation is:
$19° - 15° = +4°$
or 4° E

Ship's magnetic
bearing = $57° - 38° = 19°$

15° by ship's compass — 015C

Pelorus reads 38° relative

019M

057M

Range is 57° magnetic

FIGURE 5-18: Calculation of Deviation

heading minus the compass heading gives the deviation. As with variation, deviation is expressed as a positive angle if it is east and negative if it is west.

Table 5-3 gives an example of a table used to calculate deviation using the pelorus and a range. Note that precision for expressing deviation is to the nearest whole degree.

Compass Deviation Table Construction				
Compass Heading	Range Magnetic Bearing	Pelorus Relative Bearing On Range	Magnetic Heading	Deviation E(+)/W(−)
0	57	54	3	3
15	57	38	19	4
30	57	23	34	4
•••	•••	•••	•••	•••
•••	•••	•••	•••	•••
315	57	102	315	0
330	57	86	331	1
345	57	70	347	2

TABLE 5-3: Example Tabulation of Deviation

Table 5-4 is the final table that would be used to determine the magnetic headings from the compass headings when the boat is underway.

Compass Heading	Deviation E(+)/W(−)	Compass Heading	Deviation E(+)/W(−)
0	3	180	−3
15	4	195	−4
30	4	210	−4
45	5	225	−5
60	4	240	−4
75	4	255	−4
90	3	270	−3
105	2	285	−2
120	1	300	−1
135	0	315	0
150	−1	330	1
165	−2	345	2

TABLE 5-4: Final Compass Deviation Table

Some boaters prefer to use a graph rather than a table to read deviation. Figure 5-19 is a graph of Compass Deviation Table 5-4 on the previous page.

Note how at 180 degrees apart the deviations are approximately the same absolute value, but with opposite signs.

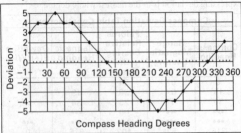

FIGURE 5-19: Compass Deviation Table

The Deviation Table Using a Hand Bearing Compass

An alternate but less accurate method to using the pelorus and range involves using a hand bearing compass to take readings on the boat's heading to compare to the ship's compass headings.

The first step is to find a location on the boat where the hand bearing compass can be used without showing deviation in any direction. Start in a location as far as possible from any known magnetic influences and have the helmsman take the boat in a circle while you keep sight on a distant landmark with the hand compass. If the bearing indicated by the hand compass remains the same throughout 360 degrees, then this location can be considered deviation free, and headings taken with the hand compass can be considered magnetic headings.

As with the pelorus method, we now proceed in 15- (or 30- or 45-) degree ship's compass heading increments. The hand compass lubber line is aligned with the vessel's heading and the ship's compass heading is subtracted from the hand compass (magnetic) heading to get the deviation.

The Deviation Table Using a Fluxgate Compass

If you have a fluxgate compass that has been properly compensated (see previous fluxgate compass discussion), and you feel it is working correctly, then the same procedure as for the hand bearing compass could be used. This should be somewhat easier and more accurate than using the hand bearing compass, since the readout is digital and the fluxgate compass display is located near the ships compass being compensated.

The Deviation Table Using a GPS

If conditions can found where there is *absolutely no wind or current*, such that the boat will head exactly in the direction it's pointed, a GPS can be used to construct the deviation table.

(For those not familiar with GPS, the topic is covered later in this chapter and should be reviewed before proceeding further.)

As with the previous methods, we now proceed in 15- (or 30- or 45-) degree ship's compass heading increments. Try to run at least 5 knots since the GPS course won't be as accurate at lower speeds. Read the course from the GPS, adjust for variation to get the magnetic course, and compute the difference (deviation).

Note that you can set the GPS to directly display the magnetic course eliminating the correction for variation step. But verify by comparing to the variation shown on your local chart to verify the GPS is computing variation correctly for your location.

If you are unsure whether your boat might be drifting with current or wind you can set a GPS "GOTO" waypoint on a landmark you can see and is also shown on a chart. Starting from a point due north or south of the waypoint, steer directly toward the waypoint. Watch for crosstrack error on the GPS. If there is no crosstrack error, there is no drift and the direction readings from the compass, and GPS can be considered reliable enough to construct the deviation table.

GPS can still be used in the event that there is crosstrack error. *The Weekend Navigator* (see bibliography) by Bob Sweet describes some techniques for constructing the deviation table with a GPS in the presence of drift.

Compass Error

Compass error is defined as the algebraic sum of variation and deviation and represents the total angular error from compass heading to true (geographic) heading.

As mentioned previously, *correcting* is the process of converting bearings to true and *uncorrecting* away from true. Figure 5-20 depicts this relationship. A commonly used mnemonic is shown in the right-hand column of the table to help remember the TVMDC sequence, although it's probably just as easy to reason out by looking at the compass rose on the chart.

West (-)			East (+)		Mnemomic
Correcting ↑ (-)	Uncorrecting ↓ (+)	T (rue) V (ariation) M (agnetic) D (eviation) C (ompass)	Correcting ↑ (+)	Uncorrecting ↓ (-)	True Virgins Make Dull Companions

FIGURE 5-20: Correcting and Uncorrecting

To help remember the signs used in correcting and uncorrecting consider the following:

1. In figure 5-20, west is shown to the left and east to the right as they would be looking at a map with North up.

2. If you think of west as being left of the y-axis in a negative x direction on a number line or graph, then it follows that it is negative, and east being in the positive x direction is positive. The signs derived thusly are used for correcting. Reverse them when uncorrecting.

Another quick aid for remembering the direction of correction is to just memorize table 5-5.

	West (-)	East (+)
Correcting	−	+
Uncorrecting	+	−

TABLE 5-5: Signs Used for Correcting and Uncorrecting

ELECTRONIC NAVIGATION EQUIPMENT

INTRODUCTION TO ELECTRONIC NAVIGATION

Electronic tools such as GPS and radar have become available and affordable for recreational boaters in the last 15 years and have completely revolutionized navigation on the water. In particular, GPS navigation has completely replaced celestial navigation as a means of navigating on the high seas.

Piloting in coastal waters, where navigation was traditionally carried out by visual reference to landmarks and navigation aids, has been dramatically transformed by the advent of GPS.

FIGURE 5-21: Electronic Navigation Equipment. This helm has a large multi-function display in the center (Garmin), which can display GPS position on marine charts, as well as radar and fishfinder images. Lower left is a depth sounder with digital readout. The display on the upper left displays comprehensive engine data (Cummins). The upper right unit is the autopilot (SIMRAD), which displays the heading from a fluxgate compass and allows setting a course for the autopilot to steer. Lower right is the fixed mount VHF radio. (Courtesy: Gerry Travers)

GPS combined with chartplotters and/or personal computer based charting programs has had the effect of enhancing both safety and enjoyment on the water, since the crew no longer needs to spend hours doing tedious navigation calculations. GPS is reliable, easy to use, and accurate. Positioning accuracy is measured in meters instead of miles as is typical with a sextant.

Radar lets the boater see in the dark and fog, which considerably decreases chances of collision under those conditions.

Unfortunately, reliability, simplicity, and accuracy have a dark side. Many new boaters never learn what to do in the event of GPS failure, precisely because it's so reliable and easy. For this reason, traditional piloting methods that can be used as a fallback in the event of electronics systems failures, or as adjuncts to electronic systems, need to be learned by the recreational boater. Along with electronics based navigation, these traditional methods are described in this chapter.

GPS

How GPS Works

NAVSTAR is the name of the ***Global Positioning System*** (**GPS**) developed and implemented by the U.S. government for military purposes starting in the 1970s, and later made available for civilian use. Most people refer to the NAVSTAR system as the Global Positioning System or just "GPS," and since that's what most people call it, this book will follow that convention. Just keep in mind that there are other GPS systems in this world. Russia has a GPS satellite navigation system called the ***Global Navigation Satellite System*** (**GLONASS**), which is also available for civilian use although it's not particularly useful for recreational boating activities at this time. In addition, Europe is developing ***Galileo***, which will be a third satellite navigation system that is supposed to be operational in 2008.

The ***space segment*** of NAVSTAR has 24 satellites, including three spares, orbiting in six separate orbital planes inclined at 55 degrees to the equator. The satellites orbit at an altitude of about 12,500 miles (20,000 km) and are spaced so that at least six satellites are always in view from any location on earth.

The GPS receiver constitutes the ***user segment***. By measuring the time for a radio signal to reach the GPS receiver from each satellite the receiver is able to calculate its distance from each satellite. To accomplish this, accurate clocks are used in the receivers and extremely accurate atomic clocks are used in the satellites.

If the exact location of the satellite is known and the distance from the satellite is known, then the position of the user can be determined as somewhere on a sphere of radius equal to the distance from, and centered on, the satellite. The underlying principal used to calculate position, once the distances are known, is similar to the use of intersecting circles of position described later in this chapter, although in this case we are actually dealing with intersecting spheres.

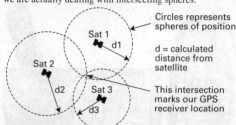

FIGURE 5-22: GPS Intersecting Circles (Spheres)

The GPS, although it keeps accurate time, is not precise enough to reliably measure the satellite-to-user distance with sufficient accuracy, which creates a problem with four unknowns: three unknowns or dimensions for position and one dimension for time. For this reason, the GPS unit requires a signal from at least four satellites to achieve a good three-dimensional fix. If elevation is assumed to be zero (sea level), then a two-dimensional fix can be obtained with three satellites although it won't be as accurate.

GPS Receivers

GPS receivers come in two flavors: handheld units and fixed-mount units. The fixed-mount units are usually installed at the helm and use an externally fixed antenna, which ensures good reception, whereas the handheld units often need to be taken topsides to get good reception.

Strictly speaking, a GPS receiver only determines latitude and longitude; however, most units, whether handheld or fixed mount, have additional features such as "GOTO" directions, and distance and speed calculations.

Some handheld receivers, and almost all currently available fixed-mount marine GPS receivers, include the ability to display maps or marine charts along with the current location plotted on the chart. The fixed units that incorporate charts are *chartplotters*, which are discussed later in this chapter.

Almost all modern GPS receivers, whether handheld or stationary, are capable of communicating using NMEA 0183 protocol with other devices such as auto piloting systems, separate chartplotters, or personal computers.

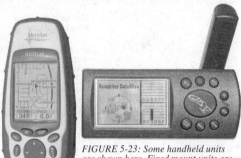

FIGURE 5-23: Some handheld units are shown here. Fixed mount units are generally combined with a chartplotter (shown later).

GPS Accuracy

As one can readily imagine, any changes in the propagation speed of the transmitted radio signal, or clock errors in either the satellites or the receiver, will result in errors that reduce the accuracy of the fix. In addition, error is introduced based on satellite geometry with respect to the user's receiver. According to *Bowditch*, the optimum geometry would be three satellites spaced at 120 degrees around the user with the fourth directly overhead as in A in figure 5-24. A worst case geometry would have all four satellites grouped closely together as in B.

A three-dimensional fix with four satellites should result in static horizontal position accuracy of approximately 10 meters (33 ft) 95 percent of the time anywhere on the globe. Elevation accuracy is somewhat less, on the order of +/– 30

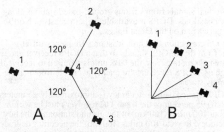

FIGURE 5-24: Satellite Geometry. The satellite geometry on the left will give a more accurate fix than the satellite geometry on the right.

meters (100 ft); however this is of little concern to the boater, since most boaters prefer to do their boating on the surface of the water. This system is referred to as the ***Standard Positioning Service*** (**SPS**).

Note that a two-dimensional fix will be substantially less accurate and should not be relied on for any coastal piloting work. On the water where lines of sight to the satellites are not obscured, there should be no reason not to always get a good three-dimensional fix.

Most GPS units will display an ***estimated positional error*** (**EPE**) to indicate position accuracy at any given time and location. EPE is computed based on satellite geometry and is not necessarily calculated in the same way by different vendors. In general though, it should provide a pretty good indication of how accurate your fix is.

To enhance accuracy, ground stations at known locations have been set up by both private and government agencies that measure the difference between the calculated location and the actual location at any given time. They then broadcast a correction signal to appropriately equipped GPS receivers, which the receivers can factor into their calculations to achieve much greater accuracy.

There are two correction systems of interest to the recreational boater: DGPS and WAAS.

The ***Differential Global Positioning System*** (**DGPS**) was developed to enhance accuracy for marine navigation and is operated by the U.S. Coast Guard. The Canada Coast Guard operates DGPS stations as well. DGPS broadcasts correctional signals from various ground-based stations along the coastlines. DGPS is available on both coasts of North America and on the Great Lakes.

DGPS corrections are broadcast on a frequency different from that of GPS signals so that a DGPS receiver and antenna separate from the GPS unit is required to receive the signals. DGPS receivers are readily available from marine supply stores.

DGPS Static Position Accuracy is approximately ±5 meters (16 ft) 95 percent of the time. The receiver must be within about 100 miles (160 km) of the ground station for the best accuracy. Beyond 100 miles (160 km) the accuracy degrades by about 3 feet per 100 miles (0.6 m per 100 km) further from the ground station.

Wide Area Augmentation System (**WAAS**) was developed for aviation use and uses two geosynchronous (stationary) satellites instead of a ground station to broadcast the correctional signals. A network of ground stations across the U.S. provides the correction data to the satellites. This signal is broadcast on the same frequencies as the GPS signals so most of the more recent GPS receivers are able to receive and process this signal. WAAS can be received and used over most of the North American continent.

When the GPS receiver is successfully processing a WAAS signal it will usually indicate so.

WAAS Static Position Accuracy is approximately ±3 meters (10 ft) 95 percent of the time.

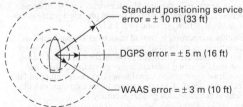

FIGURE 5-25: SPS, DGPS, and WAAS Positioning Error. This diagram shows typical 95 pevrcent probability positioning error relative to a 30 foot boat.

Although WAAS is *not certified* for use in a marine environment, it is commonly used for piloting in coastal waters because of its high accuracy.

Distance, Direction, and Speed on a GPS

A GPS figures distance covered simply by calculating the distance between the coordinates of a starting and ending point. Similarly, the direction or ***course over ground*** (COG) is calculated from a starting position and ending position along the line of travel. By repeatedly updating these on a continuing basis, the distance and direction of travel can be calculated and displayed as the boat moves.

Since two points are required to calculate direction the boat must be moving in order to calculate the direction of travel. The important principle to note here is that *a GPS cannot figure out which way is north (or any other direction for that matter) unless it is underway.*

A couple of exceptions: Some handheld GPS units have a built-in fluxgate (magnetic) compass and thus can indicate direction without being in motion however these do not actually use GPS to calculate direction when not underway. There are also some fixed-mount GPS units that use two or three antennas, spaced a few feet apart that can calculate direction even if the boat is at rest. These are still quite expensive and therefore not available to the average recreational boater.

Since a GPS has a very accurate clock, it is a simple matter to calculate speed over a particular distance and time between two points. By updating this repeatedly as the GPS moves, we get a continuous readout of speed in addition to the heading. The distances, directions, and speed obtained by a moving GPS are very accurate since the error in calculating relative distance between points is quite small.

The accuracy discussed earlier is ***static horizontal position error***, which is the accuracy of determining the coordinates of a specific geographic location. If we set one point and then move a short distance to another point then there will be a different accuracy associated with the relative distance between the these two points, since the two points will have similar errors in position.

For example, if two points are 100 feet apart and the first is off by 30 feet to the northwest, the second point will likely be off by about 30 feet northwest. That is, we have a horizontal position error of about 30 feet in the same direction for both points. On the other hand, the relative error in distance between the two points will be much less, perhaps less than a foot or so. For this reason, if the boat is moving at 5 knots or better, the speed registered by the GPS can be considered accurate to 0.1 knots, more accurate than the log or knotmeter. Keep in mind that the GPS measures *speed over ground* (**SOG**) and the log measures speed through the water.

Waypoints

A *waypoint* is just a geographic location (point) with an identifier and/or name along with the coordinates of the location expressed in latitude and longitude. Most modern GPS units allow the user to store the current location as a waypoint or enter waypoints from the keypad. In addition, waypoints can

be uploaded to or downloaded from a personal computer.

Although different brands of GPSs operate in slightly different ways, the general operating principles of models from different vendors are similar. To enter the current location on a typical handheld, the user just holds down the appropriate key until

FIGURE 5-26: A GPS waypoint. A waypoint has been entered and is ready to save. (Courtesy Garmin International, Inc.)

a waypoint entry screen is displayed with the latitude and longitude of the current location already filled in. The user can then accept the default name for the waypoint or key in another name and press "enter" to store the point.

To manually enter a waypoint, such as one determined from a chart, the coordinates must be keyed by scrolling around the screen to pick the digits one at a time. See figure 5-27 for an example of a display used to enter data. Keying in waypoints from the keypad can be tedious and

FIGURE 5-27: GPS data entry screen. Using the arrows on the keypad, navigate to each letter or number and press "enter" to enter each character. (Courtesy Garmin International, Inc.)

error prone, so it's preferable to enter and download them from a personal computer if possible. Tip: Record the current location and then modify it to save keying.

GOTO Function

Once several waypoints have been stored, by whatever method, the user can select one using the **GOTO** function or key and then display the bearing and distance to that waypoint from the current location. Note: Different makes of GPS may term the GOTO function differently. We use "GOTO" here because it's commonly used and is intuitive.

GOTO: SlipChat
BEARING
133°
TRACK
146°
DISTANCE
2.29 mi

FIGURE 5-28: Bearing and Distance to Waypoint

If the boat is moving then the track and speed can also be displayed and compared with the bearing to the selected waypoint. Alter the course to match the bearing to sail toward the waypoint. In figure 5-28, the destination has a bearing of 133 degrees and our current track is 146 degrees, so we'll have to alter course to port by 13 degrees to get to our destination.

Crosstrack Error

As the boat proceeds toward the next destination waypoint, a cross current or wind can move the boat to one side or the other of the intended track. If this happens, the GPS continuously calculates new bearings to the destination so that you will ultimately arrive at the destination, but along a curved path rather than the intended straight line track. ***Crosstrack error*** (**XTE**) is the distance the boat is off the intended track to the destination waypoint.

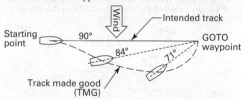

FIGURE 5-29: Effect of Wind or Current on Track Made Good. The Crosstrack Error gradually increases and then decreases as the boat nears the destination (GOTO waypoint).

For example, if the boat is blown to starboard the bearing to the GOTO waypoint will gradually decrease. To reach the destination the helmsman will continuously alter the heading (figure 5-29 on the previous page) to match the decreasing bearing. As a result the boat will actually follow a curved track (the ***track made good*** or ***TMG***) to the destination waypoint.

Most GPS units can display the intended track visually, usually with a representation of a road, as shown in figure 5-30. If the boat moves away from the intended track it displays as off the road to one side or the other. The helmsman can then adjust heading to get back on track (on the road) and stay there. This allows the boat to avoid the curved track situation and proceed straight along the intended track to the destination.

FIGURE 5-30: The Road Screen. In this situation, the boat must turn to port so that the road will lead straight up the center of the display. (Courtesy Garmin International, Inc.)

Routes

Whereas the GOTO function calculates a straight track to the destination waypoint, in actual practice we cannot usually travel in a straight line (as the crow flies) to the destination. For purposes of navigating safely to our destination without encountering obstructions, we plot a series of connected ***legs*** on a marine chart from the starting point to the destination, all of which connected together constitute a ***route***. At each intersection of two legs is a waypoint.

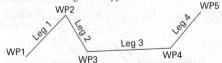

FIGURE 5-31: A Route. This is a route with four legs with a waypoint at the end of each leg.

The coordinates of each waypoint are then read from the chart and entered into the GPS unit. The route is then programmed into the GPS by connecting the waypoints along the direction of travel. Once this is done and the route is activated, the GPS will guide you leg by leg to the destination by routing you to each individual waypoint in sequence. The exact method of connecting the dots (waypoints) is specific to different makes of GPS, but all are similar.

To create a route in the GPS, the waypoints must already have been entered in the unit. Usually you start by naming the route and then selecting and adding waypoints in the intended travel sequence until they have all been entered.

FIGURE 5-32: Creating a Route on a GPS. The illustration shows selection of a waypoint to add to a route. (Courtesy Garmin International, Inc.)

Navigating a route is carried out by navigating to each individual waypoint in sequence. As each waypoint is reached, the GPS will automatically set the next waypoint as a GOTO waypoint.

RADAR

Introduction

Radar, an acronym for "radio detection and ranging," was developed during World War II to allow the early detection of enemy ships and aircraft. Initial installations were very large, very immobile and very expensive but now radar has come down, both in size and cost, to the extent that it is within reach of the average recreational boater.

While a GPS unit does a marvelous job of telling you where you are relative to fixed objects on a chart even in fog or at night, it does not show moving or noncharted objects at all. Radar is the answer to this problem. Not only does it help you to establish where you are on a chart, but it literally allows you to "see in the dark" to identify those moving and uncharted objects.

- Radar can help you navigate safely through the thickest fog and rain.
- Radar can pick out objects and land that the eye cannot see, even in clear weather with the aid of binoculars.

- Radar can measure distance and bearing to other boats, land masses, and other objects.
- Radar can be used establish the direction and speed of other boats relative to your boat to see if they might be on a collision course.

Unfortunately using radar isn't as intuitive as one might think. The screen doesn't always display what you might consider a nice clear picture of you and your surroundings. Some study and lots of practice is required to achieve the competence needed, to interpret what's on the screen, and to navigate confidently and safely at night or in fog. Almost every article or book on the subject emphasizes "practice makes perfect," and therefore, the radar should always be switched on and in use, even in the clearest weather. Learning to interpret what is on the radar display relative to what you see in clear weather, gives you that extra edge when the fog rolls in.

What follows here only touches on the basics of radar operation. If you are acquiring and installing radar on your boat, it would behoove you to obtain a good book that deals specifically with radar operation. The operating manuals get one up and going and tell you how to make the basic adjustments but really don't help with interpreting the strange stuff you are going to see on the display.

The Radar Book by Kevin Monahan, listed in the bibliography, provides excellent practical advice on interpreting and using what you see on the radar display.

Also the *StarPath Radar Trainer* computer program is an excellent radar simulator that is quite popular and comes highly recommended by lots of publications and organizations. Check it out at www.starpath.com.

Radar Operating Principles—How Radar Works

A radar set transmits short pulses of radio waves from an antenna, which are reflected from objects such as ships, boats, buoys, land, etc. (Strictly speaking the pulses aren't really reflected; rather they stimulate re-radiation but reflection is a good enough way to visualize the process.) After each pulse, the radar then switches to receive mode, to detect any reflections of the pulse. By measuring the time it takes for the radio wave to travel out and back, the radar can determine the distance to any targets. The term *target* was coined by the military during WWII since what they were trying to detect with their radar was enemy targets.

The pulse is approximately 1/2 to 1 millionth of a second long and about 1000 to 2500 pulses per second are sent and received as the antenna rotates.

The radar antenna is actually made up of an array of smaller antennas arranged in a horizontal line so as to generate a narrow beam of radio energy anywhere from 1 to 6 degrees in width and up to 35 degrees in height. The antenna rotates about 25 to 30 revolutions per minute, *painting* targets as it goes. The targets are displayed on a CRT or LCD screen in an imaginary line that continuously sweeps in a circle around the screen in concert with the rotation of the antenna..

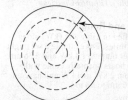

Imaginary line sweeps around and illuminates the screen as the antenna rotates 20 to 30 times per minute.

FIGURE 5-33: Radar Display Screen

Safety Note: The frequency of the radio pulses are in the microwave band so it's not a good idea to stand in front of an operating radar antenna. It follows that the radar should not be operated when tied up at the marina, so as not to irradiate the people around you. It also follows that the radar should be mounted in a location on the boat well above any areas where the crew or passengers will be.

The basic radar setup consists of the display unit and the antenna unit connected by a special cable. Figure 5-34 on the next page shows a typical hookup. The transmit and receive (transceiver) unit is housed along with the antenna.

A compass or GPS may be attached to the display unit to provide heading information so that the screen can be oriented to north up instead of heading up. Screen orientation is discussed later in the radar operation topic.

Some display units allow the overlay of electronic chart data on the radar screen, which can be very helpful in identifying objects on the screen. For example, it becomes much easier to determine which blips are buoys, since the blips will overlay the buoys on the chart.

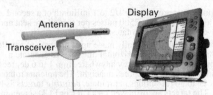

FIGURE 5-34: Basic Components of a Radar System. The photos are of a Raymarine open array antenna connected to an E120 Multifunction Display. (Photos Courtesy Raymarine, Inc.)

Radar Power, Resolution and Range

Radar transmit power is specified in kilowatts (kW) along with a range given in nautical miles. For example a set might be advertised as having a power output of 4 kW and a 36 nm range. Radars for recreational boats normally come with transmission power ratings from 2 kW to 4 kW and have an advertised range from about 16 nm to 48 nm.

In general, power relates to range:
• 2 kW radars have nominal ranges from about 15 to 20 miles.
• 4 kW radars have nominal ranges from about 35 to 50 miles.

The power required to operate the radar is very much less than the transmission power since the transmit pulses are so short (about a millionth of a second) relative to the interval between the pulses (about a thousandth of a second). In other words the radar is only transmitting about a thousandth of the time. Most small boat radars actually only consume around 20 to 75 watts of power continuously.

Radar transmits in a straight line, and therefore the distance the radar can function depends on both the height of the radar and the height of the target above sea level.

FIGURE 5-35: Radar and the Horizon

The following equation from *Bowditch* can be used to calculate the geographic radar range knowing both the height of the antenna and the height of target.

$$\text{Distance (nm)} = 1.22 \times \left(\sqrt{\text{Ht Antenna (ft)}} + \sqrt{\text{Ht Target (ft)}} \right)$$

EQUATION 5-1: Radar Geographic Range. This equation uses 1.22 as a factor whereas the equation for visual geographic range found later in this chapter uses 1.17. This is because the radar horizon is further than the visual horizon owing to the different refractive properties of microwaves versus light waves.

Considering that for a height of antenna of 15 feet (5 m), the radar horizon is only 4.7 nm away, that advertised 36 nm range is not going to be realized. If the target is also 15 feet (5 m) above sea level, then it can be detected from 9.4 nm—still much less than the advertised range.

Why would you want a radar with a range much greater than the distance allowed by the horizon? Here are a few reasons:

- Rain and fog absorb some of the microwave energy, so a more powerful radar will penetrate the rain and fog better.
- More powerful radar will perform noticeably better over similar distances.
- It will get a return from smaller objects that a less powerful unit will miss.

The advice encountered doing research for this book consistently recommends going to a 4 kW radar if you can afford it, and mounting the antenna as high as possible on the boat so as to maximize the geographic range. The other factor affecting radar performance is the angular width of the transmitted radar beam, which, as mentioned previously, ranges from approximately 1 to approximately 6 degrees, depending on the antenna design and length. In general, a longer antenna results in a narrower radar beam.

The vertical beam angle is around 25 to 35 degrees primarily to allow the radar to operate when the boat rolls. On some sailboats the radar is mounted on a gimbal arrangement so that the radar stays level when the boat is heeled over. As one

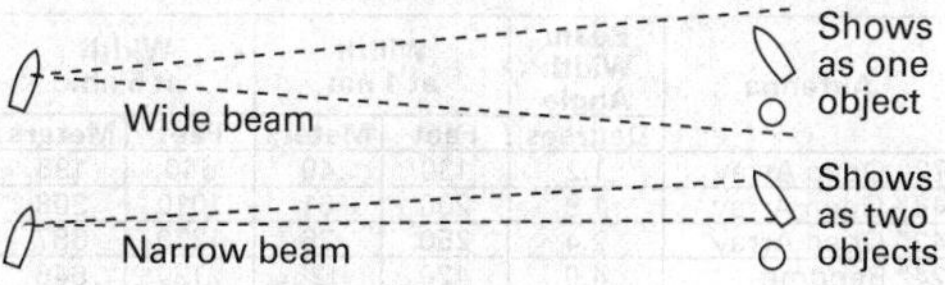

FIGURE 5-36: Difference Between Wide and Narrow Radar Beams.

might expect, the narrower beam will better discern between two objects close together. For example, a small boat and a nearby buoy might show up as one blob on radar with a wide beam, but show up as two distinct objects on radar with a narrower beam. A narrower beam also means that relative bearings are more accurate.

Radar antennas for small boats come in two main types: a **radome** or an **open array** antenna.

The radome type actually has a horizontal antenna array revolving inside the dome. The dome itself is made of material that is transparent to the radar waves. The radome style has two primary advantages over the open array style: (1) it is easier to seal against the entry of water since it is totally enclosed, and (2) since the rotating antenna is enclosed there is less likelihood of anything snagging on it. Generally, the radome type of antenna is the only type found on sailboats because of all the rigging that might get tangled in an open array type.

The open array style has the antenna array rotating without any covering dome. The primary advantage of the open array style is that much longer antennas can be obtained, which results in a narrower beam.

FIGURE 5-37: Radome and Open Array Radar Antennas. This illustration shows a radome antenna on the left and an open array antenna on the right.

To give you an idea of the effect of antenna size on beam width, table 4.1 lists some typical antenna sizes along with their angular beam width and the width of the beam out at 1 nm and 5 nm.

Antenna	Beam Width Angle	Width at 1 nm		Width at 5 nm	
	Degrees	Feet	Meters	Feet	Meters
72" Open Array	1.2	130	40	640	195
48" Open Array	1.9	200	61	1010	308
42" Open Array	2.4	250	76	1270	387
24" Radome	4.0	420	128	2120	646
18" Radome	5.3	560	171	2820	860

TABLE 5-6: Radar Beam Width Versus Antenna Size

As one might expect, the open array types of antennas are more expensive. Shopping around and looking through catalogs can yield some interesting results. Get the biggest antenna that you can afford and that is practical for your boat.

Radar Installation

Installing radar is best left to a professional; however, it can be done by a dedicated do-it-yourselfer. Installation basically involves the following steps:

- Mount the transceiver antenna unit.
- Mount the display unit.
- Run the cable between them.
- Hook up the power supply.
- Adjust and calibrate.

If the radar is to receive input from a GPS or electronic compass then these must be connected as well.

The antenna should be mounted as high as possible to:

- Eliminate obstructions on the boat interfering with the radar beam.
- Increase the geographic operating range.
- Keep microwaves away from personnel. For this reason it should be at least 5 feet (1.5 m) overhead.

Radar Operation

Radar Startup

Starting up radar is a two-step process. First an "on/off" switch must be switched to on which initiates a warmup and self-test. Once the unit is warmed and ready, the "standby/transmit" switch is moved to "transmit" to begin actual operation.

The Display Screen

Figure 5-38 on the next page shows a typical radar display with the boat at the center of the display and the direction of travel (heading) at the top. This is known as a head-up or heading-up display, which is the most common and intuitive orientation. An alternative orientation is the north-up display, which requires input from a GPS or compass and is normally used to orient the on screen information to match that of a chart.

The returns or echoes from targets show as blobs on the screen rather than as sharp images and require some practice to interpret.

In addition to the radar image, there are several digital data fields that display useful information on the screen. Bearing marks from 0 through 360 degrees are marked clockwise around the circumference of the screen with zero starting at the top on a head-up display.

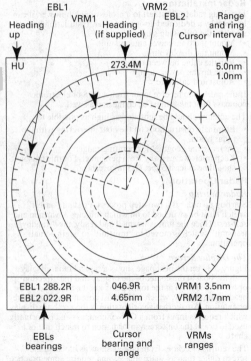

FIGURE 5-38: Typical Radar Display

The radar can be set to operate at different ranges such as 1 mile, 3 miles, 5 miles, etc. These ranges correspond to the distance from the center (your boat) to the outside edge of the display. The range rings are evenly spaced at a distance that is specified in one of the data fields on the screen and are used to judge distance of targets from the boat.

Modern radar sets automatically adjust to a longer pulse length for the longer ranges and down to shorter pulses for the closer in range settings. This is a tradeoff between getting stronger return echoes for the longer distances, and increased accuracy in measuring distance at closer ranges.

The *variable range marker* (**VRM**) is a circle, usually dashed, whose radius can be varied by the operator so as to intersect the circle with a target. A data field indicates the radius of the circle, which is the distance to the target. This distance measurement is fairly accurate and can be used to determine distance from a charted object and to determine a circle of position (described later in this chapter).

The *electronic bearing line* (**EBL**) is simply a line out to the circumference from the center of the display that can be rotated around the circle by the operator to intersect a target. An on screen data field indicates the relative bearing of the line to the target. By adding the relative bearing to the compass heading, a bearing to the target is obtained. The accuracy of this bearing depends on the beam width discussed earlier and is not as accurate, for purposes of position determination, as the distance measured with the VRM.

A cursor can also be displayed and moved about the screen of some radars. A data field shows the distance and bearing to the cursor, so this provides another way to determine distance and bearing to a target.

When a GPS is connected to the radar display, the active GOTO waypoint can be shown on the display as a *lollipop*, which consists of a small circle indicating the waypoint and a line from the center (the boat's position) to the circle (which looks something like a small lollipop).

Interpreting the Display

The radar only reflects from the front of objects so that any front to back depth is not shown. Basically you cannot discern the shape or orientation of an object with radar. Furthermore, the beam cannot reflect off objects that are shielded from view by things in the foreground since these objects are in *radar shadow*. For example, an inlet behind a headland will not show on the display. Land shows as a narrow strip along the shoreline; the land behind doesn't show like it does on a chart (figure 5-39).

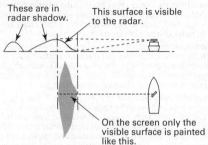

FIGURE 5-39: Radar Shadow

Also, a wider radar beam will make individual targets look larger than they really are since the target is being illuminated for a longer time as the antenna rotates.

Most modern radars have a setting that allows the onscreen blips representing targets to have some persistence over two or more rotations of the antenna. This has the effect of showing a little tail behind moving objects and gives an indication of their speed and direction. Usually the user is able to set the number of rotations the images persist.

Radar Adjustments
Adjusting the radar correctly is critical to proper operation and should be performed every time the radar is turned on, or better yet every time the range is changed.

Radar *gain*, which is an overall sensitivity adjustment, is normally the first adjustment made with the radar set to maximum range and all other controls such as sea-clutter and rain-clutter turned off. If you have a choice between manual and automatic adjustment, the manual adjustment should be performed, turning the gain up until small speckles just begin to appear all over the screen. This is the correct adjustment. Any less gain and you may miss small targets.

The next adjustment is the anti-*sea-clutter* control. Rough water can reflect radar waves particularly from close by the boat. Figure 5-40 shows what sea-clutter on the display looks like. The idea here is to adjust the sea-clutter control until most of the sea-clutter disappears, being careful not to over adjust to the extent that small nearby objects and boats are lost. The sea-clutter control basically adjusts gain for close in distance while leaving longer range alone.

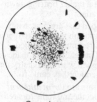 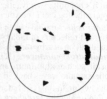

Sea-clutter
close to boat

After anti-sea-clutter
adjustment

FIGURE 5-40: Anti-Sea-Clutter Control

The other major adjustment is the anti ***rain-clutter*** control. Rain can reflect radar waves and obscure the real returns. Adjust this to remove the effects of rain, while keeping targets on the display.

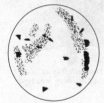 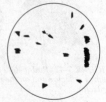

Rain-clutter
before adjustment

After anti-rain-clutter
adjustment

FIGURE 5-41: Anti-Rain-Clutter Control

Most small craft radar adjust pulse length automatically when the range setting is changed, switching to shorter pulses at closer range settings. Remember, shorter pulses result in better distance measurements. Some radar sets allow manual adjustment of pulse length that you can sometimes use to your advantage, switching down to a lower pulse length to get better distance measurement.

RADAR REFLECTORS

Small boats made of fiberglass or wood tend to absorb rather than reflect radar waves, which makes them quite stealthy. This might be an advantage for a car you're driving too fast, but it's not quite so advantageous if a tanker bearing down on you in the fog can't see you on its radar.

Radar reflectors have been developed that are reasonably efficient reflectors of radar waves and can make a small boat stand out on nearby radars. These are sometimes called ***radar target enhancers*** (**RTEs**). The reflectors are made of metal, such as aluminum, and designed with a geometry that reflects radio waves back in the direction they came from.

The two main types of radar reflectors are the ***octahedral reflector*** and the ***Luneberg lens***. Octahedral reflectors reflect strongly in certain directions but much less in others, which results in an inconsistent return, particularly if the boat is pitching and rolling. The Luneberg lens presents a more consistent return in all directions and orientations but it weighs and costs quite a bit more.

FIGURE 5-42: Radar Reflectors. On the left is an octahedral reflector and on the right is a Luneberg lens type reflector.

Radar reflectors found on recreational boats are typically in the 12-inch (30-cm) to 18-inch (45-cm) diameter size range. Seeing one on a boat, you are left wondering how such a small device can reflect more than the boat itself, but they can and do. The ***radar cross section*** (**RCS**) of a reflector is the cross sectional area of a metal sphere, expressed in square meters, that presents an equivalent target. The important thing to note is that the radar cross section increases by a power of 4 as the diameter of the reflector increases, so that a reflector with twice the size will have a radar cross section 16 times greater.

You should get the largest radar reflector you can afford and that will fit on your boat. You definitely should have one if you boat in commercial shipping lanes or you will cruise in fog or at night. A good octahedral type can be purchased for about $50 to $300, and a lens type will run from around $250 to $600.

DIGITAL CHARTS

Digital charts are charts that have been scanned or digitized into computer readable form from the original masters used to make paper charts. Various vendors then incorporate this information into chartplotters and various computer programs for personal computers. There are two types of digital charts: raster and vector charts.

Raster Charts

A raster chart is scanned into a computer and stored as a series of closely spaced lines of very small dots or rasters, each dot having its own color or brightness. When the chart is viewed on screen, it appears exactly like the paper chart, except that only a small section of the chart is viewed at a time due to limitations of screen size relative to the size of the original paper chart (actually the whole chart could be viewed on screen but everything would be so small as to be unreadable).

A raster chart can be thought of as a large photograph of the paper chart that you can pan around and zoom in and out of on the computer screen. Note that if you zoom close enough, the individual dots or rasters that make up the image become visible. Many experienced boaters prefer rasterised digital charts because they have the look and feel of the original paper charts.

Raster charts require relatively large amounts of memory to store and for that reason are usually found only on personal computers, which have the necessary disk storage space and memory.

Vector Charts

A vector chart is so named because all the graphics on the chart are made up of vectors. A vector is a straight line with a specific length, direction, and location on the chart. A curve on a vector chart is made up of series of small vectors strung together and having a certain color. A shaded area is described mathematically as color between curves. Numbers and letters are stored as numbers or letters with a coordinate attached to them.

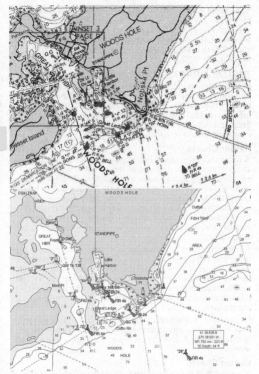

FIGURE 5-43: Compare Digital Raster and Vector Charts. These two screen captures from Nobeltec Visual Navigation Suite show a raster (top) and vector chart (bottom) of the same area. (Courtesy: Don Buddington)

To produce a vector chart from the original master, the chart is digitized by someone carefully tracing all the lines and objects from the original master on a digitizing board. Also some data is entered directly from aerial photography and surveys of objects.

The main point of all this is that the vector chart is described mathematically, rather than as a picture, and this requires far less computer memory and storage capacity than does a raster chart.

Since the chart is being digitized by hand, different types of features on the chart can be entered into different layers. For example, navigation aids can all be on one layer and depths on another, such that the user can turn layers on and off to eliminate unnecessary information or clutter on the screen.

As one zooms out of the chart on the screen, characters and symbols can stay the same size rather than getting smaller, so they stay readable, which can be helpful in some cases.

Zooming in too much is a danger with vector charts, since everything will continue to look good even when zoomed in past the accuracy inherent in the original chart, leading to a false sense of confidence.

Vector charts are used on chartplotters primarily because of the more limited computing power, storage capacity and memory of chartplotters. Vector charts are used on personal computers as well.

PERSONAL COMPUTERS

Introduction to Personal Computers for Navigation

The availability of sophisticated digital charting software, able to display real-time position on a digital chart using data from a GPS, has dramatically transformed the whole process of trip planning and navigating underway.

The digital charting programs on a PC are used to perform two primary functions for the navigator:

1. They are used for ***trip planning*** either before the trip or while underway. This is the process of laying out the legs that will be followed during the journey, so as to proceed efficiently to a destination while keeping clear of obstacles and hazards.

   Trip planning with a PC or chartplotter as well as with paper charts is discussed later in this chapter.

2. They can be used to ***navigate*** during the trip. Once underway, with a GPS connected to the PC, you can monitor your boat's position plotted directly on a digital chart. Furthermore, you can follow the legs and waypoints of the trip plan, with the navigation program showing the way and indicating where you are deviating from the plan.

Types of Personal Computer

PCs used for planning and navigating are usually either desktop or laptop/notebook systems; however, marinized versions are available for more permanent installations aboard. To my knowledge, all of the navigation software for these systems only run on the Windows operating system.

Laptop computers tend to be the most commonly used since one can do their trip planning at home, then simply pick up the laptop and bring it onboard. Set it by the helm, connect it to a GPS, and you have a real-time navigation system (assuming you have the appropriate navigation software installed). When you're anchored at night, you can take it below to answer your email or do some more trip planning.

A desktop system is used primarily at home for trip planning, but some larger vessels may have room for a desktop system onboard. Desktop systems are rarely found around the helm, but rather are found in some kind of office setup elsewhere on the boat.

Ruggedized notebooks are available that are sealed against moisture and are also able to withstand rough handling. Many of these also have daylight readable displays so they eliminate most of the problems associated with conventional laptops.

FIGURE 5-44: Computer System Running Maptech Digital Charting Software. Expect to pay at least double what you would pay for a conventional notebook of similar size and capacity and even more for one built to milspec (military specifications). Fortunately, prices are coming down.

Marinized PCs and LCD displays are now on the market but are still quite expensive, particularly the displays. I have found 15-inch XGA daylight readable waterproof displays priced between $2000 and $4400. Prices for this kind of equipment are also coming down rapidly.

One interesting note regarding PCs for navigation: Maptech has come out with the i3 System, which is a PC-based (Windows XP), networked system that is ruggedized and daylight readable meant to be mounted at the helm. The system uses Maptech digital charts and optionally includes radar and radar overlay and a fishfinder, among other things. It's still expensive but prices will drop, particularly if more vendors enter the market with similar PC-based systems.

Planning and Navigation Software for PCs

As we noted previously, both trip planning and active naviga-

FIGURE 5-45: Maptech i3 PC-Based System. (Courtesy Maptech, Inc.)

tion can be carried out with a PC. The prospective navigator should be aware that most charting software is differentiated in much the same way. Each vendor usually has one version that does only trip planning, and another more expensive type that does navigation as well. Note that regardless of the type, the same charts must be purchased for the appropriate region.

The charting software communicates with a GPS through the computer's serial port using NMEA-0183 protocol. NMEA is the National Marine Electronics Association, which developed the protocol in the 1970s to standardize communication between marine electronic devices.

The planning software is able to download waypoints to a GPS and usually can upload them from the GPS as well. The navigation software can, in addition, accept continuous positioning data and display the current position on the digital chart while underway.

Charts for the PC usually come on a CD; however, some companies who manufacture chartplotters make a reader for the PC such that the chart cartridges used in their chartplotter can also be used in the PC. The PC software can be used to do the trip planning and then the waypoints can be downloaded into a GPS or chartplotter, which is used for the actual navigation underway.

If the PC has the software that will do the navigation as well, the PC can act as a backup to the chartplotter (of course, you need a functioning GPS to connect to the PC). Or you can just carry out both functions using only the personal computer.

FIGURE 5-46: PC Display Underway. The boat is navigating a multi-leg route. This screen capture is from the Offshore Navigator program. (Courtesy Maptech, Inc.)

Personal Computers—The Reliability Issue

PCs running older versions of Windows have been notorious for freezing or rebooting in the middle of a job; most of us have seen the "blue screen of death" at least a few times. This has been much improved in the newer versions of Windows based on NT technology, namely Windows 2000 and Windows XP. Windows XP is really quite stable; I have been working on this book on a machine running Windows XP and haven't had a freeze up or forced reboot in a year. And I concurrently run a lot of compute-intensive programs like Adobe Photoshop and some of the charting software we talk about here.

There are a few things that can be done to enhance reliability of a personal computer for use in active navigation:

1. Get a new computer with a Pentium processor and at least 1 GB (gigabyte) of RAM (memory).
2. Partition the hard drive and install Windows XP and the charting programs in a partition by themselves. When you want to run navigation, boot, and run from that partition. If you don't know what a partition is or how to do this, find someone who does. If you're really planning to trust your PC to help you navigate, this is well worth doing.
3. If you really want to be safe—and you can afford it—install and run *only* the navigation software on this computer. Don't install any other programs after installing the navigation software. In this case, the partitioning step above is unnecessary.

Advantages and Disadvantages of Personal Computers

Disadvantages

Both conventional laptops and desktop systems have three main disadvantages for use in navigation underway:

1. The displays are virtually unreadable in direct sunlight. Even inside the pilothouse they can be difficult to see if the sun is shining in. Some kind of shroud must be put over the screen to make it visible.
2. Except on larger boats, there is not enough room for them. Even on larger boats, there often won't be enough room up on the flybridge.
3. Anywhere around saltwater, there are always saltwater droplets or particles in the air and this noxious (to electronics) mixture is continuously drawn into the computer by the cooling fan, where it then deposits itself on the circuitry. This can cause mysterious, sometimes intermittent problems with the computer, and will shorten the computer's useful life.

Advantages

Compared to a chartplotter, a PC-based system has far more horsepower, both in terms of speed as well as memory. More charts can be stored on the hard drive along with such extras as aerial photographs, and USGS topographic maps. The number of waypoints, routes, and tracks that can be stored is essentially unlimited.

If you have a laptop, you can pick it up and take it home with you with all the historical data from a trip. Conversely, it's easy to bring onboard and set up; just hook it to a GPS, and you're ready to go. There is no need to upload or download waypoints and trip plans to a chartplotter.

CHARTPLOTTERS

Introduction to Chartplotters

A dedicated *chartplotter*, whether linked to or having an integrated GPS unit, is becoming more commonplace on recreational boats. It offers unparalleled ease of use and accuracy, giving a constantly updated plot of the vessel's position, and it works day in and day out, and equally well in the dark. *This is a good thing*, since it doesn't make as many mistakes as humans, and it allows the captain to concentrate on other tasks like driving the boat and keeping a lookout for hazards.

There is a negative aspect in that inexperienced vessel operators are lulled into a false sense of security, failing to see the need for maintaining position plots on paper charts.

A chartplotter does pretty much what its name implies; it plots position on marine charts that are displayed on a LCD screen. Screen sizes typically range from a couple of inches on a handheld to around 12 inches (30 cm) on larger fixed-mount units. Some display black-and-white images, while

FIGURE 5-47: Chartplotter. The chartplotter in this illustration is an MFD concurrently displaying in color, a chart window, a fishfinder window, and a digital data window. The model shown here is a 3010C. (Courtesy Garmin International, Inc.)

larger more expensive units usually have color displays. The difference in cost between black-and-white and color displays, which was quite large in the past, is now only about a 20 percent premium for color. The larger units that are designed to be permanently mounted near the helm usually are color and have sunlight viewable displays; all the fixed-mount units are waterproof as well.

Chartplotter Planning and Navigation Software

The planning and navigation programs for a chartplotter are permanently installed and delivered as part of the unit. The charts themselves come in cartridges or cards that slide into a receptacle on the side of the plotter.

Usually a particular brand of chartplotter will only accept a particular kind of card, so once you acquire the chartplotter you will use the installed charting program and buy only the cards that work with it. Usually the charts used in a chartplotter are vector rather than raster charts.

The chart cards cover a "region" and cost about $200. A region will cover an area like the Great Lakes or the Gulf of Mexico. This may seem expensive, but it's a lot cheaper than all the paper charts for the same region and the card contains all the same data to the same level of detail.

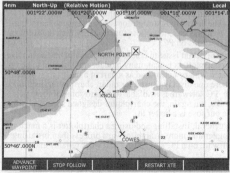

FIGURE 5-48: Chartplotter Display Underway. The boat is on course for the first waypoint (North Point) of a multi-leg route. This screen capture is from an E-Series Networked Display. (Courtesy Raymarine, Inc.)

Like the PC navigation programs, the chartplotter program allows both trip planning as well as position plotting (navigating) underway. Trip planning on a fixed-mount chartplotter is similar to trip planning with a PC program and is discussed later in the Trip Planning topic.

Navigating is also quite similar to navigating with a PC program in that position is continuously updated and displayed on the chart based on GPS input. Since the trip plan is displayed too, any departure from the trip plan is shown clearly.

The chartplotter displays any of the GPS screens previously discussed in the GPS topic. For example, highway view, crosstrack error, speed, distance and bearing to next waypoint, etc., can be displayed.

Advantages and Disadvantages of Chartplotters

Advantages

Chartplotters are designed and constructed for the sole purpose of navigating aboard, which yields some of the following benefits:

- They are waterproofed to marine standards, which ensures that dust and salt spray stay out of the electronics.
- The displays are designed to be readable in direct sunlight.
- The navigation software is built in and cannot be corrupted by the user, which enhances reliability.
- The software is straightforward and easy to learn, partially because it has less functionality than the software that runs on PCs.

An important issue to consider when evaluating advantages of chartplotters is that many models are designed to be integrated with or networked as a part of a multi-input system, where one display is used for radar, chartplotter, fishfinder, etc. PC software is available to fit into some of these networks, but again, the chartplotter designed specifically for the purpose is a better fit.

In general, installing and using a chartplotter is a much simpler and more straightforward process than installing software on a PC and getting it to work reliably and properly.

Disadvantages

Generally, because chartplotters lack the power and capacity available in personal computers, such niceties as aerial photography, three-dimensional views of the bottom, USGS topography, etc., are not available, although some of these features are starting to show up on some units. A computer has both a keyboard and a mouse for input devices, which makes some more complicated tasks easier to carry out. Some obvious examples include entry of text, such as when naming and describing waypoints, and moving the cursor around the screen to find information or enter points. In particular, trip planning is generally easier on a PC.

A chartplotter has less capacity in terms of the number of waypoints and routes that can be stored, but in practice this is unlikely to be a limitation for the average boater.

DEPTH SOUNDERS, FISHFINDERS AND SCANNING SONAR

Depth sounders, *fishfinders* and *scanning sonar* are all types of sonar. Sonar is included in the navigation chapter because:

- Sonar returns depth information that can be used to aid in position determination.
- Sonar is used to avoid running aground and that's what navigation is at least partly about —to get there safely without running into things.

How Sonar Works

Sonar (from **so**und **n**avigation **a**nd **r**anging) operates on a principle similar to that of radar, where the time a transmitted pulse takes to travel through the water from the boat to an object, reflect off the object and return, is used to calculate distance.

Transducer

In the case of sonar, a *transducer* mounted in the hull transmits sound pulses through water, which strike a target and are echoed back from the target to the transducer. The time out and back is used to determine the distance. Depth sounders, fishfinders, and scanning sonar are all sonar devices since they all operate the same way by sending and receiving sound pulses with a transducer.

Transducers are available in three different mounting styles. The first type is designed to be mounted as a through hull, which requires boring a hole through the hull. These generally work the best and are used on larger boats and ships.

Since fiberglass transmits sound fairly well, another type is designed to be mounted inside the hull and can be used if the fiberglass is not too thick. These need to be vertically aligned, so some sort of wedge shaped base may need to be installed on the inside of the hull. Also, if the transponder is not in solid contact with the hull, the bottom of the transponder will need to be immersed in a water or oil bath to ensure efficient transmission of the sound waves.

The third type is meant to be mounted on the outside of the transom, which is common on smaller fishing boats. These have the disadvantage of being aft rather than forward; in shallow water the bow could run aground while there is still clearance under the transponder. Also the transponder efficiency is affected by turbulence when the boat is on plane.

When transmitting, the transducer converts electrical impulses to sound and when receiving echoes, converts the sound back to electrical impulses. Most transducers operate

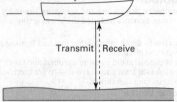

FIGURE 5-49: Sonar Transmit Receive

at a frequency of 200 kHz; however, some operate at either 200 kHz or 50 kHz. The higher frequency will return more detail, while the lower frequency will penetrate deeper water and will usually have a wider beam. As with radar, more power yields better resolution and more likelihood of detecting smaller targets.

Display Head

The other component of sonar is a display head mounted near the helm, which, in addition to the display, incorporates a small microcomputer and transceiver. The transceiver transmits and receives electrical impulses to and from the transducer, which are processed through the microcomputer for display on the screen. The screen can either be a CRT or LCD, but almost all screens today are of the LCD variety.

Types of Sonar

The three types of sonar for small boats, in increasing order of technical sophistication are depth sounders, fishfinders, and scanning sonar.

Depth Sounder

The depth sounder is sonar in its most basic form. It has a simple digital display that indicates the distance from the transponder vertically to the bottom.

Some depth sounders allow adjusting the digital display to read depth of water from surface, or depth from bottom

FIGURE 5-50: Depth Sounder Display

of keel, rather than from the transponder. Alarms can be set to go off when depth falls below a preset limit.

Fishfinder

Like the depth sounder, the fishfinder also displays depth; however it also traces trailing depth as the boat moves. To show this, the depth is displayed graphically in a side view and is scrolled from right to left as the boat moves forward. The rightmost part of the screen shows the depth where you are now and to the left is where you have been.

FIGURE 5-51: Fishfinder. This display shows depth has increased but now is decreasing as the boat moves to the right. The inverted U shapes (correct term "fish arches") are fish. The unit shown is an X136 Sonar. (Courtesy Lowrance Electronics, Inc.)

Patterns and color are used to indicate the type of bottom—hard, soft, etc. Fish or any other objects above the bottom are displayed as small arches at their relative distance above the bottom. Some fishfinders will optionally display the arches as little fish symbols if preferred. Some can even display depth by the fish.

Many fishfinders are available that are an integrated with a chartplotter. On these one has the choice of side by side display of the fishfinder and chart data, or just displaying one or the other.

Scanning Sonar

The best way to think of **scanning sonar** (also called **forward looking sonar**) is like radar for underwater use. While scanning sonar has been used for years on military and commercial ships, it has only recently become affordable for the recreational boater.

Scanning sonar uses a phased-array transponder that emits a narrow beam scanning either horizontally or vertically ahead. Horizontal mode units scan from 45 to 90 degrees each side of dead ahead depending on the model. Vertical mode sonar scans from horizontally ahead down to directly below the boat. Some of the newer units are capable of both vertical and horizontal scanning and can be switched between either mode by pressing a button.

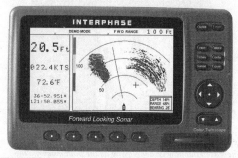

FIGURE 5-52: Scanning Sonar. The model shown is a Color Twinscope. (Courtesy Interphase Technologies, Inc.)

The display screen for a horizontal sweep looks somewhat similar to a radar display except the coverage is only 45 or 90 degrees to either side instead of a full 360-degree circle.

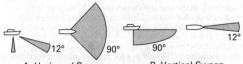

A. Horizonal Sweep   B. Vertical Sweep

FIGURE 5-53: Scanning Sonar Beam. The left half of the figure shows typical coverage of a 90 degree horizontal beam and the right half shows coverage of a vertical beam. (Adapted from an Interphase drawing)

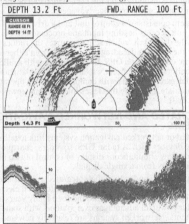

FIGURE 5-54: Screen Captures of a Horizontal and Vertical Display. The top part shows a typical horizontal mode display. The bottom part shows a vertical mode display to the right with a conventional fishfinder window to the left. For the vertical sweep, the screen displays a side view with the boat at the upper left and the water ahead to the right. Note that these are actually color displays that convey much richer information than these small black and white images. These screen shots are from an iScan180. (Courtesy Interphase Technologies, Inc.)

Units such as the one shown in figure 5-52 on page 290 can be purchased for around $2000 (not installed). Other less expensive forward looking sonars are available for under $1000. These make a lot of sense for larger boats, particularly for those boating in shallow waters since avoiding just one grounding will likely pay for the equipment several times over.

AUTOPILOT

An *autopilot* is a system that steers the boat automatically on a preset heading. Its main purpose is to relieve the helmsman of having to constantly steer the boat, which can be quite fatiguing, particularly on longer voyages.

The system consists of a control unit and a drive unit. The control unit accepts heading input and processes this to control the drive unit, which actually moves the rudder to provide the steering. Heading input comes from either an electronic compass or a GPS. By interfacing with a GPS the autopilot can steer directly to a waypoint without any crosstrack error, whereas with compass input the operator must calculate a heading that takes into account leeway and current drift.

INTEGRATED AND NETWORKED NAVIGATION SYSTEMS

Integrated or networked navigation systems link together separate devices such as radar, GPS, sounders, chartplotters, etc., and allow simultaneous display or control of two or more functions from a single display.

It is important to understand that integrated systems and networked systems are not the same thing. Integrated electronic navigation systems have been around for a many years and they offer powerful advantages over systems with standalone components. Networked systems are relatively new and enjoy all the advantages of integrated systems plus some.

Integrated Systems

A combination fishfinder, GPS, and chartplotter that allow display and control of the fishfinder and chartplotter from a shared display is an example of an integrated system. Another example is a radar system integrated with a GPS and chartplotter. Integrated systems share a common LCD display so that radar, chartplotter, sounder, and GPS information can be shown on the one screen. The screen can be split to show two functions such as radar and charts side by side and some can overlay radar and charts one over the other.

Integrated systems are cheaper than networks but lack their flexibility.

Networked Systems

A networked system is a network, much like an Ethernet computer network, where individual devices can be plugged into and out of the network as needed.

Network systems use *multifunction displays* (**MFDs**) that include chartplotter capability as the central part of the network. More than one MFD can be connected to the network so that devices such as radar can be controlled from various locations such as the pilothouse or flybridge. Some systems combined with NMEA compatible sensors can monitor information such as speed, engine temperature, RPM, and voltage directly on the MFD, although one could argue that these functions should be monitored independently of the network.

Currently, networked systems are available from Furuno, Garmin, and Raymarine, and each uses a proprietary network protocol so that devices compatible with one brand are not compatible with another. This generally means that once you decide on one manufacturer's hardware, any devices that will be hooked into the network must also come from the same vendor.

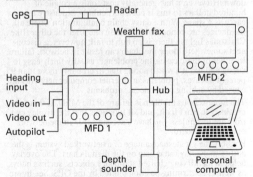

FIGURE 5-55: A Networked Navigation System

Most MFDs now accept composite video (television) input so video from remote cameras, a VCR, or even broadcast television can be displayed. For example, a camera can be mounted to monitor the engine room or video from an underwater camera could be displayed. A camera facing aft in the cockpit area could be useful backing into a slip.

Advantages and Disadvantages of Networked Systems

The most oft-quoted criticism of networked or integrated systems is that you are putting all your eggs in one basket; if the system fails then all networked functions such as radar, GPS, sounder, and autopilot are lost. The primary argument against integration is that totally separate systems and instrumentation for each function are safer and more reliable since failure of one system will still leave the others running. This argument is not quite true and is mitigated by the fact that with a networked system, failure of a remote device, such as a radar transceiver, will not normally bring the entire system down, but rather will result in the loss of just that one function.

Usually with a network, only a failure of the network itself will truly bring down the whole system. In a star-type network configuration, where all the devices are connected to a central hub, failure of the hub can take the entire system down. However, a hub generally costs only a couple of hundred dollars so this is not a particularly expensive item to carry as a spare. With a daisy chain configuration where all the devices are connected in a chain one after the other (like Christmas lights), there is no hub to fail; however, a disconnect somewhere along the chain can result in network failure. In either of these cases, the problem is usually fairly easy to debug and fix. It's worth noting that in probably more than 95 percent of cases, problems in ethernet computer networks are caused by cabling or connector problems.

The more serious problem is failure of the MFD. If that breaks, you can't fix it, and all functions that the display controls are lost unless you have a second MFD in the network or a spare onboard.

Possibly the greatest advantage of a networked system is the ability to overlay radar data on the digital chart. The overlay helps in identifying charted stationary objects, such as buoys, as well as confirming position plotted by the GPS. See figure 5-56 for an example of a digital chart with a radar overlay. It's a little hard to see in such a small picture, but note how the radar returns reflect the edge of the shoreline.

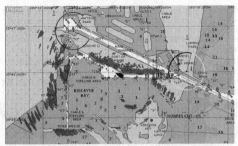

FIGURE 5-56: Radar Overlay on a Digital Chart. The boat is the black object at the center and the radar returns are the dark areas along the shoreline. This screen capture is from an E-Series Networked Display. (Courtesy Raymarine, Inc.)

To Network or Not to Network?

So what to do? I can't really answer that since everyone has his or her own preferences and circumstances, but here are some things to consider.

Offshore Passagemaking

The further from shore you venture, the more important your electronic navigation systems become, although some parts of the system will be more critical than others. For example, in the middle of the Atlantic Ocean, a functioning GPS will be more important than a working radar, depth sounder or chartplotter. Also, one can get along without an autopilot, although this will mean a lot more work for the crew. On a powerboat, engine RPM and temperature are something else that needs to be monitored no matter where you are.

The GPS problem is easy to rectify; just spend a hundred bucks and carry a spare handheld. Personally, I wouldn't go offshore without at least two spare handhelds, one of which is kept in a closed metal container to protect against lightning damage. A sextant and at least one person who knows how to use it should be onboard too.

Coastal Piloting

Near shore, the functions of the radar, chartplotter, and depth sounder become of more commensurate value, the relative degree of which depends on the situation at hand. One can argue that the chartplotter function is not as critical as that of radar or sonar since this function can be accomplished using paper charts and a handheld GPS. This leaves the radar and sounder as the two critical networked devices that can't be easily replaced by some manual procedure like the chartplotter can.

If you really feel redundancy of these two systems is critical, then there are always the options of either installing a second sonar system or installing the sonar separate from the networked system.

Two Helms

Where there is a flybridge as well as a pilothouse from which the boat can be controlled, the networked system with an MFD at each helm has the obvious advantage of providing display and control of all functions at both locations. In addition, since there are at least two MFDs in this situation, redundancy has been achieved, since failure of one MFD still leaves the other functioning.

AIDS TO NAVIGATION

INTRODUCTION TO AIDS TO NAVIGATION

The *Aids to Navigation* (**ATON**) System uses *marks* or *markers*, which are usually either *beacons* or *buoys* that may or may not be lighted. In addition, some other aids may be used such as lights of specific color and arrangement on bridges and other structures.

Beacons are marks that are permanently affixed to land, and include marks in the water that are rigidly fixed to the bottom by some means such as a piling or on some kind of foundation substructure.

Buoys, on the other hand, float on the water and are anchored to the bottom. Unlike a beacon, a buoy may move small amounts horizontally as the length of the anchor chain allows, with rising and falling tides and varying currents and winds. In extreme conditions the buoy may end up dragging the anchor, which can result in a misleading indication of position. Although not a very likely event, this should nevertheless be kept in mind when piloting using buoys in hazardous or shallow waters.

The ATON System uses specific color, sound, and light color and flash sequences to distinguish markers used for different purposes.

Aids are used for several purposes:

- As *lateral* marks used to define channels of safe navigation. These are the most common and useful marks and virtually all boaters have encountered and are familiar with these types of aids.
- As *cardinal* marks, which indicate the cardinal direction of both dangerous and safe water.
- To indicate *isolated danger*.
- To indicate *safe water*, fairways, and mid-channels.
- As *ranges*, a pair of beacons, which when in alignment indicate the vessel is on a desired line of position. Ranges are described in more detail on page 316.
- *Information* and *regulatory* marks.
- Other *special* marks.

In general, a beacon with no light is called a *daybeacon* or *dayboard*, and a beacon with a light is called a *light* or just a *beacon*. A *lighthouse* is a mark and is a beacon and a light.

The color plates section near the center of this book has color illustrations of the different types of marks and describes their color schemes and lighting characteristics. Also included in the color plates are some of the more common nautical chart symbols (from *Chart No. 1*) used to represent the navigation aids. International, U.S., and Canadian symbols are shown beside each other for quick reference.

Abbreviations for lights and beacons are included in tables below.

IALA REGIONS

Most countries now conform to the *International Association of Lighthouse Authorities* (**IALA**) system of buoyage. The IALA has defined two regions A and B as shown on the map on page 1 of the color plates. Region A covers Europe, Asia, and Africa except for Japan, Korea, and the Philippines. Region B covers North and South America, Japan, Korea, and the Philippines.

Lateral marks in both systems define the conventional sense of direction, which is generally returning from the sea, upriver, or clockwise around large land masses.

Lateral marks

The two IALA systems are fairly similar except for the color of lateral marks that are opposite from each other. In region A, red marks define the port side and green marks define the starboard side of the channel in the conventional direction (returning). In region B, green marks define port and red marks define starboard in the conventional sense of direction.

In North America the conventional sense of direction is south along the Atlantic coast, west across the gulf, and north up the Pacific coast.

On the Great Lakes, the conventional sense of direction can be considered as the direction that takes one further (by water) from the Atlantic Ocean, so Lakes Ontario and Erie are westward, Huron is northward, Michigan is southward, and Superior is westward.

In region B (i.e., United States and Canada), the mnemonic commonly used to remember the convention is the 3 Rs: *red-right-returning*. In other words, when travelling in the conventional sense of direction, the red marks will be to the right.

Cardinal Marks

Cardinal marks indicate in which direction the deepest or safest water lies. They are used extensively in IALA region A, to a lesser extent in Canada, and not in the United States. They are colored yellow and black and indicate the cardinal direction —north, east, south, or west —of the safest water. The opposite direction will be the hazard or danger to be avoided.

Obviously, to safely navigate around cardinal marks, you must be aware of direction, which will often require the use of the magnetic compass, particularly on foggy or cloudy days (another argument for having a well adjusted and cali-brated compass on which you can rely).

Color Abbreviations

Abbr.	Color	Abbr.	Color
W	White	Vi	Violet
R	Red	Y	Red
G	Green	Or	Orange
Bu	Blue	B	Black

TABLE 5-7: Color Abbreviations Used on Charts to De-scribe Marks

Daymarks Standard Designations

The first letter describes the shape or purpose of the beacon. Table 5-8 lists the letters used as the first letter. Note: Western Rivers is a name that refers to the Mississippi River and its tributaries. It does not refer to rivers in the western United States.

Letter	Description
S	Square used to mark the port hand of a channel
T	Triangle used to mark the starboard hand side of channel
J	Junction—square or triangle to mark preferred channel junctions (bifurcations)
M	Safe water octagonal marks fairway or mid channel
C	Crossing (Western Rivers only) diamond to indicate where channel crosses river.
K	Range daybeacon
N	No lateral significance—special purpose

TABLE 5-8: Daymarks Designation Letters Used on Charts

Table 5-9 shows additional information used on beacons on the Intracoastal Waterway. These are appended to the abbreviations listed in table 5-8 above.

The second letter indicates the main color of the beacon.

A third letter is on range boards only and indicates the color of the center vertical stripe.

Abbr.	Description
-I	Suffix—A yellow reflective horizontal strip on a dayboard indicates the aid marks the intracoastal waterway.
-SY	Suffix—A yellow reflective square on the dayboard indicating a port hand mark for the ICW.
-TY	Suffix—A yellow reflective triangle on the dayboard indicating a starboard hand mark for the ICW.

TABLE 5-9: Additional Letters Used on Charts for ICW Beacons

Light Abbreviations and Characteristics of Flashes

Abbr.	Type	Description
F	Fixed	Light shows continuously. No flashing.
Fl	Flashing	Light flash on duration longer than off duration. Flashes at 15 to 30 per minute.
LFl	Long Flashing	Light flashes on >= 2 seconds about every 10 seconds.
Q	Quick Flash	Flashes at about 60 flashes per minute.
VQ	Very Quick	Flashes at 80 to 160 (usually about 120 flashes per minute).
UQ	Ultra Quick	Flashes at 160 or more flashes per minute.
Oc	Occulting	Light shows longer than light is off.
Iso	Isophase	Durations of light and dark are the same.
Mo(A)	Morse A	Short flash followed by a long flash.
Al.WR	Alternating	Alternating two or more colors.

TABLE 5-10: Light Flash Abbreviations and Characteristics

Examples of Light Descriptions

Here are a couple of examples of light descriptions as found on a typical nautical chart.

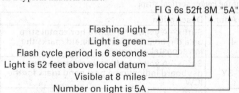

Fl G 6s 52ft 8M "5A"

Flashing light
Light is green
Flash cycle period is 6 seconds
Light is 52 feet above local datum
Visible at 8 miles
Number on light is 5A

FIGURE 5-57: Typical Light Description—Lateral Mark

This is for a flashing green light with a six-second cycle. The light is 52 feet above the local datum of mean high water and nominal visibility is 8 miles.

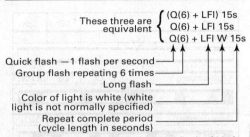

FIGURE 5-58: Typical Light Description—Cardinal Mark

This light flashes a group of six quick flashes, then eclipse, then a long flash, then eclipse. The total duration of cycle is 15 seconds. This example is for a South Cardinal Mark.

Graphical Representation of Light Cycles

Figures 5-59 and 5-60 on the next two pages illustrate graphically the light cycles used on lighted marks

USCG REMARKS ON AIDS TO NAVIGATION SYSTEM

USCG Dialogue on Western Rivers Marking System

The following dialogue is quoted from the USCG publication, *U.S. Aids to Navigation System*.

> The **Western Rivers Marking System** is a variation of the standard U.S. Aids to Navigation System and is found on the Mississippi River and tributaries above Baton Rouge, and on certain other rivers that flow toward the Gulf of Mexico. Red daybeacons, lights, and buoys mark the starboard banks and limits of channels as vessels "return from sea" or proceed upstream. Green daybeacons, lights, and buoys mark the port banks and limits of navigable channels while going upstream. The Western Rivers System varies from the standard U.S. system as follows:

1. Buoys are not numbered.

2. Beacons are not numbered but normally have an attached "mile marker" board that indicates the distance in statute miles from a fixed point (normally the river mouth).

3. Diamond-shaped nonlateral dayboards checkered red-and-white or green-and-white, similar to those used in the U.S. Aids to Navigation System, are used as crossing daybeacons where the river channel crosses from one bank to the other.

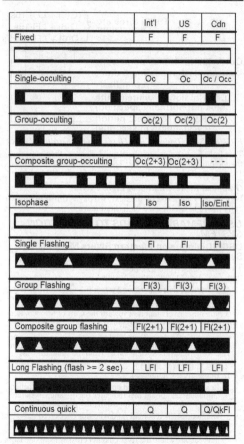

	Int'l	US	Cdn
Fixed	F	F	F
Single-occulting	Oc	Oc	Oc / Occ
Group-occulting	Oc(2)	Oc(2)	Oc(2)
Composite group-occulting	Oc(2+3)	Oc(2+3)	- - -
Isophase	Iso	Iso	Iso/Eint
Single Flashing	Fl	Fl	Fl
Group Flashing	Fl(3)	Fl(3)	Fl(3)
Composite group flashing	Fl(2+1)	Fl(2+1)	Fl(2+1)
Long Flashing (flash >= 2 sec)	LFl	LFl	LFl
Continuous quick	Q	Q	Q/QkFl

FIGURE 5-59: Light Cycles Used on Lighted Marks

	Int'l	US	Cdn
Group Quick 	Q(3)	Q(3)	Q(3)
Interrupted Quick 	IQ	IQ	IQ
Continuous Very Quick 	VQ	VQ	VQ
Group Very Quick 	VQ(3)	VQ(3)	VQ(3)
Interrupted Very Quick 	IVQ	IVQ	IVQ
Continuous Ultra Quick 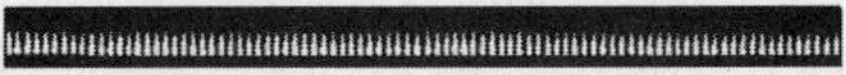	UQ	UQ	UQ
Interruped Ultra Quick	IUQ	IUQ	IUQ
Morse Code A 	Mo(A)	Mo(A)	Mo(A)
Fixed and Flashing	FFI	F FI	FFI
Alternating	Al.WR	AIWR	Al / Alt

 R	W	R	W	R	W

FIGURE 5-60: Light Cycles Used on Lighted Marks

4. Lights on green buoys and on beacons with green day-marks show a single flash, which may be green or white.

5. Lights on red buoys and on beacons with red daymarks show a double flash [Group Flashing (2)], which may be red or white.

6. Isolated danger marks and safe water marks are not used.

River Bank Names: When traveling downstream the banks are named right and left. The right bank has green aids and the left bank has red aids, thus the west bank of the Mississippi is its right bank and it has green aids. To avoid confusion, commercial river traffic often calls the right bank the *right descending bank* and the left bank the *left descending bank*, expressed in this way leaves no room for doubt.

Mile Markers: These markers are some of the most useful aids on a river. They are attached to beacons or displayed in other easily seen places and indicate distances in statute miles, the unit of measurement on the Western Rivers System. With the exception of the Ohio River, mile markers indicate the distance up stream from the mouth of a river. Ohio River markers start at its headwaters and indicate the distance downstream. Mile markers also help a vessel operator locate his or her position on a river chart.

Crossing Daybeacons: Because the navigable channels of rivers swing from bank to bank as the river bends; diamond-shaped crossing daybeacons are used to assist river traffic by indicating where the channel has changed from one side of the river to the other. Crossing daybeacons are always on the opposite side of the river. When a diamond-shaped crossing daybeacon is sighted, the vessel operator should head for the diamond, and treat the color of the daybeacon as a channel mark (i.e., red mark keep to the left bank when traveling downstream).

River Buoys: Changes in river channels caused by fluctuations in water level, current speed, and shifting shoals make buoy maintenance a continuous task for the Coast Guard. In wintertime where rivers freeze, buoys are lost or moved from position. Because of their somewhat temporary nature, river buoys do not have letters or numbers and are not usually shown on river charts.

USCG Dialogue on Bridge Clearances and Signals

The following dialogue is quoted from the USCG publication *U.S. Aids to Navigation System*.

Clearance gauges are extremely valuable to vessel operators because they indicate the vertical distance (clearance) between the "low steel" of the bridge channel span and the waterline. (They do not indicate the depth of water under the

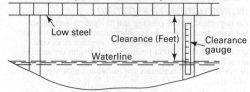

FIGURE 5-61: Bridge Clearance

bridge.) These gauges are permanently fixed to the bridge pier or structure and located on the right side of the channel facing approaching vessels. Each gauge is marked by black numbers and foot marks (lines) on a white background board.

Drawbridge Opening Signal: The Operator of a vessel requesting a drawbridge to open shall signal the bridge tender, and the bridge tender shall acknowledge that signal. The following are the most common types of signals a vessel operator should use to request an opening;

Radiotelephone Communications—Most bridges monitor VHF-FM channels 13 and 16 with the exception of bridges in Florida. In June 1996, the FCC published a notice stating that all boaters throughout the State of Florida should hail bridge tenders on VHF channel 9 to reduce the high amount of traffic on channel 13. Boaters operating in Georgia and South Carolina are encouraged to follow the same procedures. Note: Boaters should always use "low power (1 watt) output" on their VHF marine radio when hailing a bridge tender.

Sound Signals—These signals shall be made by whistle, horn, megaphone, or hailer. To request an opening, the vessel operator shall give the "opening signal" consisting of one prolonged blast (4 to 6 seconds duration) followed be one short blast (about 1 second operation). The draw bridge tender shall reply with the same sound signal (one prolonged followed by one short) acknowledging that the draw can be opened immediately. When a vessel approaches a drawbridge with the draw in the open position, the vessel shall give the opening signal. If no acknowledgment is received within 30 seconds, the vessel may proceed, with caution, through the open draw. When a draw cannot be opened immediately, or is open and must be closed promptly, the draw tender shall give five short blasts sounded in rapid succession after the vessel's opening signal request.

Further information on drawbridge regulations and opening signals for bridges over the Navigable Waterways can be found in the U.S. Coast Pilots.

POSITION PLOTTING

INTRODUCTION TO PLOTTING

An important part of piloting and navigation is maintaining an up to date plot of current position on the appropriate chart. When the GPS or chartplotter or other electronic systems fail, the current position plot provides the starting point for navigation by dead reckoning (explained below) or determining what landmarks or navigation aids you might be looking at.

Plotting Conventions, Symbols, and Terminology

Certain conventions and symbols are used when plotting position and these are described in *Bowditch* and other literature.

Some definitions and terminology used when plotting must be understood when looking at lines and points plotted on charts. As mentioned previously, ***direction*** expresses the angular position of one point relative to another from some reference direction, usually north and is expressed in degrees.

The ***bearing*** (**B**) of a point is the angle in degrees from north to some point with the vertex at the observer and is measured clockwise from 000 degrees at north around a full circle to 360 degrees (also north). B is normally plotted with three digits so that an angle with less than three digits, such as 14 degrees, would be represented as 014. Occasionally, bearing is also termed azimuth; however, strictly speaking azimuth is properly used in celestial navigation.

The direction can also be expressed as a ***bearing angle***, which measures an angle only to 90 degrees or 180 degrees from north or south with appropriate descriptors to describe the starting reference direction (N or S) and the direction (E or W) in which the angle is measured. e.g. S75°W. (See the examples on page 308 and figure 5-64 on page 309.)

A ***relative bearing*** is a bearing relative to the boat's heading. The ***heading*** is the direction the boat pointed in at any point in time. The bearing and heading may also be expressed as magnetic instead of true.

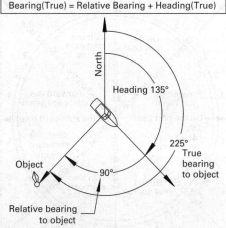

FIGURE 5-62: Relative and True Bearing of an Object

An alternative system of expressing relative bearings uses a 32-point system (figure 5-63 on the next page). This is a traditional system and isn't commonly used in navigation and piloting.

Examples using the 32-point system:

- 2 points on the starboard bow = relative bearing 22.5°
- 3 points on the starboard quarter = relative bearing 146.25°

The course (C) is the direction that a boat is steered or planned to be steered and it can be designated with reference to compass (C), magnetic (M), or true (T). When plotting course numbers it important to designate which of these is the reference. Generally, the lack of a designator implies that the course plotted is true.

Example: **C 075 = C 075 T = C 071 M= C 073 C** assuming variation is 4°E and deviation is 2°W.

Since magnetic north is a local phenomenon and is constantly moving over time, it is recommended that all course plotting be done with reference only to true north. Some texts now

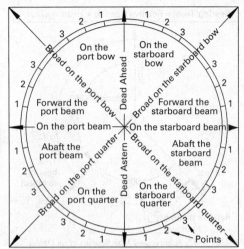

FIGURE 5-63: The 32-Point System of Direction

teach plotting using magnetic north as the reference, which simplifies some plotting tasks, and this is just fine as long as you are careful to designate which reference is being used. The main thing is to consistently use one method.

All examples and diagrams in this book show angular measurements such as course and bearing always with reference to true north.

Like bearings, the course is also sometimes expressed as an angle from 0 degrees to 90 degrees or 180 degrees. A couple of examples of these alternate expressions for course follow:

1. C 097 = C N97°E = C S83°E (180° – 97°)

2. C 255 = C N105°W (360° – 255°) = C S75°W (255° – 180°)

Figure 5-64 illustrates (2) graphically.

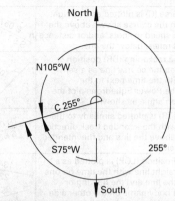

FIGURE 5-64: Alternatives for Expressing Course (C)

The **track** (**TR**) is the intended direction of travel and is not necessarily the same as the course, since the course may be different from the track to compensate for wind or current in an effort to end up at end of the track.

The **track made good** (**TMG**) is the actual track line from a departure fixed position to a destination fixed position. TMG is also termed **course made good** (**CMG**), which is commonly used rather than TMG. Since the American and Canadian Power Squadrons favor CMG, we'll use that here too.

A **line of position** (**LOP**) is a straight line plotted on a chart that indicates the vessel is somewhere on that line. A **circular line of position** (**COP**) is a circle that indicates the vessel is somewhere on that circular line. These are discussed further in the Position Determination topic.

Table 5-11 on the next page shows the symbols and conventions used for course plotting. It is important to adhere to these conventions so that other personnel can pick up and instantly understand the plot.

The course (C) is plotted as a straight line with the course shown above the line and speed in knots, and/or distance in nautical miles, below the line.	C 057 / S 53 D 26.8
The dead reckoning (DR) position is plotted on the course line as a semi-circle with the time next to the circle. The Power Squadrons plot the time at an angle as shown.	0548
A track (TR) is plotted similarly to the course with the intended track direction plotted above the line and the intended speed below.	TR 097 / S 63
Line of Position (LOP) is plotted as a solid straight line with the time on one side of the line and the bearing or celestial body name on the other side of the line. Here we show the time always on top.	1346 / 225 —— 0548 / Kochab
LOP advanced -shows the original time of the LOP and the time the LOP was advanced.	1638 - 1705 / 272
Plot a fix from the intersection of two LOPs as a circle of about 3/16 inch (50 mm) diameter with the time of the fix horizontally to the side of the circle. Suffix "R" for a running fix as 1756 R. Some use the suffix "FIX" after the time.	1756
Other types of fix are labelled with a suffix after the time to identify the type of fix. ie. RADAR, LORAN, etc.	0900 GPS
Estimated position (EP) is marked as a square on the LOP. Time may also be included if it not readily apparent from a DR or LOP.	1542
The Power Squadrons use a triangle to designate a known position.	

TABLE 5-11: Symbols Used in Plotting

Time, Speed, Distance

Time of day is expressed and plotted using the 24-hour military clock where the 24 hours start at midnight. Time of day is always shown as four digits using leading zeroes where necessary. Running time in coastal piloting is generally calculated to the nearest minute.

Examples:

12 Hour Expressed As:	24 Hour Expressed As:	12 Hour Expressed As:	24 Hour Expressed As:
12:13 AM	0013	12:13 PM	1213
1:13 AM	0113	1:13 PM	1313
8:37 AM	0837	8:37 PM	2037
11:05 AM	1105	11:05 PM	2305

TABLE 5-12: Examples of Military (24-Hour) Time

Distance on the water is normally in nautical miles rather than statute miles or kilometers, although statute miles are used on some rivers such as the Mississippi and tributaries, and kilometers are used on most inland waters in Canada. As mentioned previously, 1 nautical mile is equal to 1 minute of latitude.

Speed or ***velocity*** is expressed as ***knots*** (not knots per hour) where 1 knot is equal to 1 nautical mile per hour.

The following formulas relate time, speed, and distance where time is expressed in hours.

$$D = S \times T \quad \text{or} \quad S = \frac{D}{T} \quad \text{or} \quad T = \frac{D}{S}$$

Where: D = Distance in nautical miles
S = Speed in knots
T = Time in hours

EQUATION 5-2: Speed, Time (Hours), and Distance

The following equations are equivalent but express time in minutes rather than hours.

$$D = \frac{S \times T}{60} \quad \text{or} \quad S = \frac{D \times 60}{T} \quad \text{or} \quad T = \frac{D \times 60}{S}$$

Where: D = Distance in nautical miles
S = Speed in knots
T = Time in minutes

EQUATION 5-3: Speed, Time (Minutes), and Distance

DEAD RECKONING

Dead reckoning (**DR**) involves plotting a course line in the planned or actual sailing direction with DR positions marked at measured distances along the line. Distance along the course line is calculated using the speed and time formulas above or if the boat has a log, then the distance can be read directly from the log at any point. (The log is a device that performs a similar function to the odometer in a car.)

Dead reckoning (deduced reckoning) involves calculating position without reference to external objects, using just a starting point and course direction, speed, and travel time. When the GPS and the radar fail and you are out of sight of any landmarks, dead reckoning will be your fallback if you have been keeping your current position plot up-to-date.

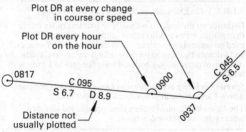

FIGURE 5-65: Dead Reckoning Plot

Example DR Calculations

1. In the DR plot in figure 5-65, the vessel is to travel 8.9 nautical miles at 6.7 knots on a course of 95° to the location of the planned course change to 45°. Using the equation for deriving time in minutes we get:

$T = (D \times 60) / S = (8.9 \text{ nm} \times 60) / 6.7 \text{ knots} = 79.7 \text{ min} \cong 80$ minutes to cover the distance.

0817 plus 80 minutes = 0937 is the estimated time for the course change.

2. Alternatively if we are underway and it is now 0937, then we calculate distance traveled with the distance equation:

0937 − 0817 = 80 minutes is the time underway.

$D = (S \times T) / 60 = (6.7 \text{ knots} \times 80 \text{ minutes}) / 60 = 8.9 \text{ nm}$ is the distance traveled by 0937.

PILOTING AND POSITION DETERMINATION

TRIP PLANNING

Planning With Paper Charts

Planning a trip on a paper chart consists of plotting a series of connected legs (straight lines) directly on the chart that lead from the point of departure to the destination. The legs are plotted such that each line avoids obstacles or hazards while providing an efficient route from start to finish.

The vertex of each pair of legs is a waypoint whose coordinates can be scaled from the chart for entry into a GPS. It is

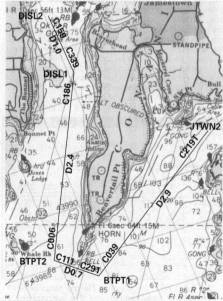

FIGURE 5-66: Trip Plan on a Paper Chart

helpful to label the waypoint with some meaningful identifier as in the example, where "BTPT" is used as a prefix for waypoints near Beavertail Point.

The heading for each course leg is plotted above each leg near the start of the leg and the inverse course is plotted above and near the other end of each leg. In the example of figure 5-66 on the previous page, the northward leg from BTPT2 to DISL1 will have the course of C006 plotted near the bottom and the inverse course of C186 (6° + 180°) near the top of the leg.

The distance is plotted below the leg as shown in the example of figure .

Planning With Computer or Chartplotter Charts

The procedure for trip planning on a computer or chartplotter is essentially the same as planning with paper charts, where individual legs are constructed and linked to provide a path from departure to destination. The main procedural difference is that successive waypoints are set by moving the cursor to an appropriate location on the digital chart and clicking or entering. The computer program draws the legs from waypoint to waypoint. Also, the coordinates are automatically calculated by the charting software so they don't need to be scaled off as from the paper charts. Figure 5-67 gives an example of a tabular display of a trip plan.

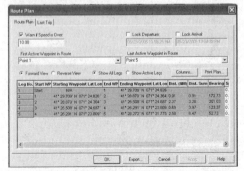

FIGURE 5-67: Trip Plan Window. The trip plan can be viewed in tabular format and printed. The bearings and distances of each leg are displayed here.

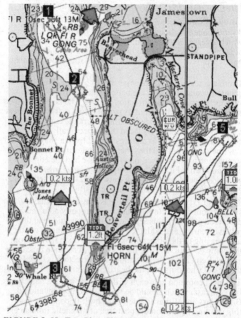

FIGURE 5-68: Trip Plan Chart Using Maptech Chart Navigator Computer Program. Note the course and distance are not plotted for each leg as on the paper chart, but are available as a separate tabulation.

To alter a path, waypoints can be moved by dragging with the mouse. Waypoints can be inserted into a leg to subdivide the leg into smaller legs, which can then be moved by dragging them as well.

This ease of inserting and moving waypoints leads to a simplified trip planning process, whereby a single leg is constructed from the starting departure point to the final destination point and then waypoints are inserted into the line and dragged into position to construct a multileg plan.

LINES OF POSITION

Line of Position

As mentioned earlier a *line of position* (**LOP**) is a line on which a vessel is located, and it may either be a straight line or a circle. A single plotted line of position whether linear or circular only tells us that the vessel is somewhere on that line.

There are several ways to arrive at a line of position. In general, visual sightings are better than electronic means such as radar and radio direction finding. The best method is to use a range of some kind. A *range* is two marks or objects with a known bearing between them. A range can either be a pair of navigation aids placed there specifically as a range, or it can be two cultural features picked from a chart that you can line up one behind the other. Examples include a church steeple and a water tower, or a lighthouse and the edge of headland behind it. The advantage of using a range is that no bearing need be taken, since a straight line plotted on the chart through the two features is the LOP.

The next best estimate of the LOP is to use a pelorus, assuming your ship's compass has been properly adjusted as described earlier in this section. Here you would read the relative bearing and add it to the vessel's heading to get the true bearing to the object. Make the correction to true from the compass course, using the TVMDC correction discussed earlier. Remember, the deviation (D) correction is based on the vessel's heading, *not* the bearing direction.

The most common approach will likely be using a hand bearing compass, which should be standard equipment aboard. Binoculars are also available with a built-in compass. For this you find a place on the boat free of magnetic influences and take a compass bearing on the object from there. In this case you only need correction for variation to get the true bearing to the object. Note that on a steel boat this isn't going to work very well.

Another alternative is to sight over the ship's compass if it is mounted in a binnacle or other suitable place. Hardware or other markings or fittings on the boat can often be used as a makeshift pelorus.

Bow on bearings can be taken with the ship's compass by stopping the boat and turning the bow to line up on the object in question. In this case the deviation correction will be for the direction of the bearing.

In figure 5-69, a bearing of 284 degrees true to the feature at A has been taken from the boat. To plot the line of position (LOP) the reciprocal angle is calculated and the line drawn from A in the reciprocal direction, in this case 104 degrees. To calculate the reciprocal angle, add 180 degrees if the bearing is less than 180 degrees and subtract 180 degrees if the bearing is more than 180 degrees.

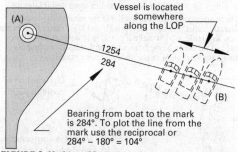

FIGURE 5-69: Line of Position

An alternative method of plotting the line is to use a parallel rule to transfer the bearing angle from the compass rose on the chart.

Line of Position Using Radar

Electronic means such as radar and radio direction finding are also used when conditions warrant, but are generally not as accurate as visual sightings, and are more subject to major errors and mistakes.

One of the problems with using radar for a direction fix is discerning on the display the object on which the fix is being taken. In figure 5-69, tower A probably cannot be differentiated from the land around it. On the other hand, a buoy will stand out on the screen if there are no other objects or land near it.

Note that you are not able to take a true bearing directly with radar, unless the radar has been interfaced with a fluxgate compass or GPS. As with the pelorus, the relative bearing obtained from (noninterfaced) radar is added to the boat's heading to get the bearing to the object being sighted.

Circular Line of Position by Distance Off

The *circular line of position*, also called a *circle of position* (COP), establishes a circle on which a vessel is located. It is plotted on the chart as an arc with a radius equal to the distance from the feature in question. Distance from an object can be determined reasonably reliably with radar but as with the straight LOP, a visual is the better way if possible. Obtaining a fix with radar is discussed in more detail later on.

There are various devices available for measuring distance directly, most of which are optical, and laser range finders are now available, which make it possible to determine distance even in the dark. Some binoculars with a built-in compass also have an optical range finding device built in.

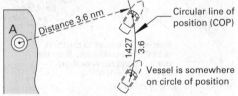

FIGURE 5-70: Circular Line of Position

Many rangefinders require knowing the elevation of the top of an object being sighted. Some of these distance measuring devices allow you to specify the height of the object and the device then returns the distance directly. Other range finding devices only allow you to measure the angle between the top of the object and the waterline at the bottom, and then calculate the distance off from a formula or table. A sextant can be used for this purpose although it is normally used for celestial navigation. The elevation of navigation aids is usually specified on charts and is specified in the light lists.

The following equations can be used to calculate the distance of an object from a vertical angle. Tables for tabulating the distance off using the vertical angle are given at the end of this chapter. These tables were constructed using these equations.

Equation 5-4 is from *Bowditch* and yields distance off, knowing the vertical angle between the waterline at object and the top of the object. Note that this equation can be used for an angle between any two objects with a known distance between them and that are equidistant from the observer, thus a horizontal angle between two features on a chart can be measured and used to calculate distance off.

$$D = \frac{H\ (ft)}{\tan(A) \times 6076} \qquad D = \frac{H\ (m)}{\tan(A) \times 1852}$$

Where: D = Distance off in nautical miles
H = Known height of the object above waterline
A = Vertical angle from top to waterline

EQUATION 5-4: Distance Off from Vertical Angle and Height

The formula for distance off by vertical angle between the sea horizon and the top of an object beyond the sea horizon is given in equation 5-5 (also from *Bowditch*).

$$D = \sqrt{\left(\frac{\tan(A)}{0.0002419}\right)^2 + \frac{H-h}{0.7349}} - \frac{\tan(A)}{0.0002419}$$

Where: D = distance off in nautical miles
A = Vertical angle from top of object to the sea horizon
H = Height of the object in feet
h = Height of the observer's eye

EQUATION 5-5: Distance Off Using Vertical Angle From Horizon to Top of Object Beyond the Horizon.

Circular Line of Position With Radar

Radar probably cannot discern object "A" in figure 5-70 because it will be obscured by the image of the land around it on the display. The sighting has to be of a recognizable feature that can be correlated with a feature on a chart. Examples include a buoy in open water or a shoreline return that has a shape that can be matched with a shoreline on a chart.

An example figure is given later that uses two intersecting circles of position obtained with radar to obtain a fix.

Circular Line of Position by Horizontal Angle

A circular line of position can also be established by measuring a horizontal angle between two objects with known distance between them. A marine sextant can be used for this purpose. There are a couple of ways to do this, both of which make use of the fact that the boat is located somewhere on a circle that passes through all three points (the boat and the two objects sighted).

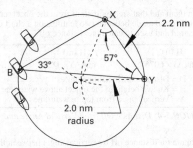

FIGURE 5-71: COP by Horizontal Angle

Method 1

The first method involves looking up or calculating the sine of the horizontal angle and evaluating the formula

R = D / (2 × sin A)

Where:

R is the calculated radius of the circle.

D is the distance in nautical miles from object X to object Y as determined from the chart.

A is the angle between the two objects

In the example of figure 5-71:

R = D / (2 x sin A) = 2.2 nm / (2 x sin 33) = 2.0 nm

With a compass or dividers draw an arc with radius 2.0 nm from each of X and Y. The intersection of the two arcs is the center of the COP, which can now be drawn.

Method 2

Calculate the complement of the horizontal angle. The complement is 90 degrees minus the angle. In this case in figure 5-71 the complement is: 90° – 33° = 57°

Using a protractor, plot lines from X and Y at an angle of 57 degrees, as shown. The intersection of the two lines will be the center of the circle, which can now be drawn.

ESTIMATED POSITION

One LOP is inadequate for a position fix but will allow an *estimated position* (**EP**) to be plotted when combined with a DR plot. An EP is considered better than a DR position but not as accurate as a fix.

Figure 5-72 shows an LOP of bearing 284 degrees taken at 1236 on the object at A. The 1236 DR is plotted and then a dashed line is extended perpendicular to the LOP, to the LOP from the DR position. The intersection of the line with the LOP is the EP.

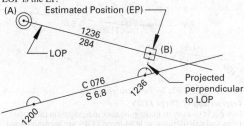

FIGURE 5-72: Plot Estimated Position

THE FIX

Fix Introduction

A *fix* is a relatively accurate determination of position that is determined independently of the DR position. There are several ways of getting a fix including but not limited to:

- The intersection of two or more lines or circles of position.
- Passing close by a charted navigation aid.
- With a GPS (accuracy ± 10 meters or 30 feet)
- LORAN—may be phased out in the next few years in favor of GPS.
- Using a sextant to make celestial observations (accuracy ± 2 to 5 nautical miles) when out of sight of land—today used only as a backup to GPS (or as a fun learning experience).

Intersection of Two or More LOPs

The intersection of at least two straight LOPs constitutes a fix. The closer the angle between the LOPs is to 90 degrees, the more accurate the fix.

In figure 5-73, one LOP has been determined and plotted with a bearing taken on the light, and the other LOP using a Range. Note the DR plot discontinued at 1128 and now starting from the new fix at 1128.

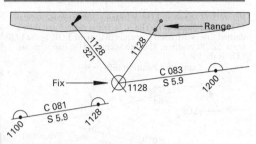

FIGURE 5-73: Fix by Two Straight LOPs

Intersection of Three LOPs

Since it is so easy to make mistakes in navigation observations and calculations, at least three LOPs are recommended if they can possibly be taken and plotted.

Figure 5-74 shows three LOPs. In almost all cases there will be a small triangle formed at the intersection of the three LOPs, the size of which indicates the accuracy of the fix. The smaller the triangle, the more accurate the fix.

Positioning the fix in the triangle is a matter of some judgment. If one of the LOPs is considered less accurate than the others then the fix might be placed nearer the intersection of the better ones. Or it might just be placed in the center of the triangle.

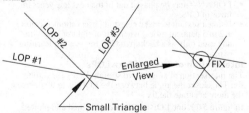

FIGURE 5-74: Intersection of Three LOPs

Intersection of Circular LOPs (COPs)

The intersection of two COPs constitutes a fix. They are plotted as shown in figure 5-75. They can be COPs derived either by distance off or by horizontal angle.

Both fixes were taken at 1356 and were at 2.5 nautical miles and 3.6 nautical miles, respectively.

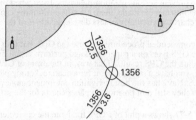

FIGURE 5-75: Intersection of Two COPs

Intersection of a COP and a LOP

The intersection of a COP and a LOP constitutes a fix. Figure 5-76 shows a plot of this type of intersection where the LOP is to a light on a bearing of 293 degrees. The COP is to a fixed navigation aid at a distance of 2.6 nautical miles.

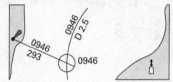

FIGURE 5-76: Intersection of a COP and a LOP

GPS Fix

The GPS provides fixes, which are both accurate and reliable. Since GPS units contain a radio receiver and a small computer, they do fail, and they sometimes give erroneous or spurious readings of position. This happened to me once while driving along in a car. The GPS had us driving down the highway and suddenly jumped to a position about 20 miles south. I have no idea why this happened, and it hasn't happened since, but it serves as a reminder of how, if things can go wrong, they probably will.

Potentially more serious than that, is the fact that the charts themselves are quite often not as accurate as the GPS position determination. Most charts in North America will at least specify the chart datum (usually WGS 84) and it is imperative that the GPS unit be set to the same datum as the chart to prevent serious positioning errors. Even when this datum adjustment is made, there are still positioning errors on the charts, particularly in less developed areas of the world.

The recommended procedure is to use the GPS, but also plot the GPS fixes on a paper chart and perform visual fixes to validate the GPS results. That way, in the event of GPS failure, you have a starting point for a dead reckoning plot. The U.S. Navy has the best navigation equipment money can buy but they still plot position on paper charts for the same reason.

Figure 5-77 shows a plot of a GPS fix. Note the characters GPS appended to the time of the fix. As with any other type of fix the new DR track restarts from the fix.

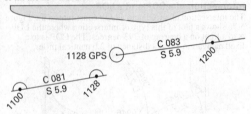

FIGURE 5-77: GPS Fix

Since GPS fixes are available easily and at any time, an alternative to maintaining DR plots is to just keep plotting GPS fixes at frequent intervals, the interval being determined by distance from shore, or obstructions. Just be sure you know how to maintain the DR plot when the GPS fails in the fog or the dark, and take visual fixes whenever possible.

The Two Horizontal Angle Fix With Common Leg

This is one of the better methods for taking a visual fix since it doesn't involve the use of the compass and its attendant errors.

Horizontal angles from object 1 to object 2 (A) and from object 2 to object 3 (B) are taken and then set on a three-arm protractor like the one shown below.

The protractor is then placed on the plot and moved around until the three arms pass through each of the objects on the chart. The point at the center of the protractor is then the

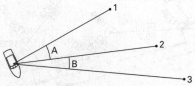

FIGURE 5-78: Fix With Two Horizontal Angles

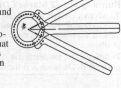

vessel's position. You can also draw the angles on something transparent like tracing paper and accomplish the same thing.

There is one catch with this procedure: In the unlikely event that the vessel and the three objects all happen to lie on a circle then there is no unique solution and no fix.

Running Fix—LOP 2 Marks

Often only one feature can be found on a chart that can be seen from a particular location, so that only one LOP can be plotted, which doesn't provide a fix. The solution, sometimes, is to advance the LOP to the time the next LOP on another object can be taken.

In figure 5-79 on the next page, at 1735 a bearing of 040 to the first object is determined and later at 1833 a bearing of 321 to the second object is taken. The LOP at 1735 is advanced to the 1833 LOP using a parallel ruler by a distance equal to the DR advance (X) between 1735 and 1833. The advance must be in a direction parallel to a straight line between the two DRs as shown.

The intersection of the advanced (1735-1833) LOP and the 1833 LOP is the fix and it is labeled with R Fix.

This type of fix relies on the accuracy of the DR track and the more legs in the DR plot, the more error is likely to be introduced into the advance of the LOP. If set and drift are known they can also be used to correct the final DR position before advancing the LOP.

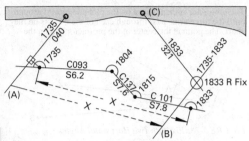

FIGURE 5-79: Running Fix on Two Features

Running Fix—2 Marks COP and LOP

To advance a COP, it is easiest to advance the feature to which the distance was measured and then draw a new advanced arc of the same radius with the center at the advanced position.

In figure 5-80, the feature at A is advanced by distance X to position B. Distance X is the DR advance from 1200 to 1240.

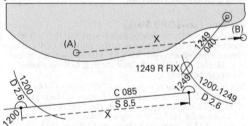

FIGURE 5-80: Running Fix With COP and LOP

The advanced COP is plotted from the advanced feature at B with radius 2.6 nautical miles. The intersection with the 1249 LOP is the running fix.

Running Fix—Using 1 Mark

This is basically the same as the running fix using two objects, except the second LOP is taken on the same object as the first LOP.

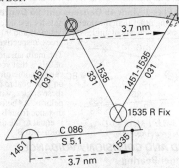

FIGURE 5-81: Running Fix on One Object

Here the 1451 LOP is advanced by the 3.7 mile DR advance, to intersect the second 1535 LOP on the same object.

Running Fix—1 Mark Double Angle

This is a special case of the running fix, which relies on the fact that if an LOP is established at a given relative bearing. Then a second LOP is established at twice the relative bearing of the first, then the distance off is equal to the distance run between the two LOPs.

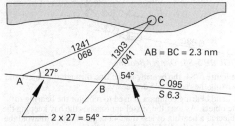

FIGURE 5-82: Double Angle Fix

In figure 5-82, the vessel advanced 2.3 nautical miles from A where the relative bearing was 27 degrees to B where the relative bearing was double that at A or 54 degrees. The distance from B to C is the same as from A to B or 2.3 miles.

Running Fix—1 Mark 45 Degrees and 90 Degrees

This is nothing other than the double angle fix just discussed, but using more convenient angles of 45 degrees and 90 degrees, respectively.

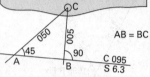

FIGURE 5-83: 1 Mark 45-Degree and 90-Degree Angle Fix

AB = BC

The main advantage of this is that you can rig something on your boat to sight these angles, without a pelorus. As before, the distance from B to C is equal to the distance from A to B.

HAZARD AND COLLISION AVOIDANCE

The Danger Bearing

The danger bearing is derived by drawing a straight line from a known feature, along the edge of the danger or obstruction. The bearing is plotted with not more than (NMT) or not less than (NLT) prefixed to the bearing angle.

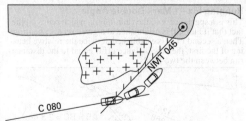

FIGURE 5-84: Danger Bearing

In figure 5-84, the bearing of the line through the object and skirting the rocks is 45 degrees.

A hand bearing compass is used to monitor the bearing to the object. As long as the vessel approaches the bay keeping the object at a bearing of less than 45 degrees, she will avoid the rocks, hence the NMT 45 degrees label.

Danger Bearing With GPS

The bearing to a known or charted feature is most easily determined with a hand bearing compass, however, a GPS can be used for this purpose as well. This technique can be used in situations where only a handheld GPS with no chartplotter is available and also as a check on the bearings taken with the hand bearing compass.

To monitor the bearing to the object, obtain the coordinates of the known feature from the chart and enter these into the GPS as a waypoint. Now when a GOTO for this waypoint is set in the GPS, the bearing to that waypoint will be continuously updated and displayed as the boat moves. As with the compass in the example of figure 5-84, the bearing must be NMT 45 degrees at any time, as the boat approaches the destination.

Note that with GPS there is no need to actually see the object or feature, since the GPS is just pointing to the waypoint coordinates and not a real physical object. In fact, the waypoint doesn't really need to be set on a real feature or object. Draw a line that avoids the hazard on the chart and set an arbitrary waypoint at the end of the line. Set the waypoint as a GOTO in the GPS and proceed as before.

Using GPS Crosstrack Error to Avoid Danger

The perpendicular distance from a leg to a hazard can be measured on a chart, and when underway treated as the maximum allowable crosstrack error. Some GPS units can be made to set off an alarm if a preset maximum crosstrack error is exceeded.

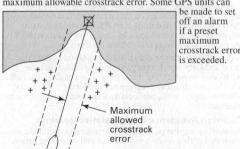

Maximum
allowed
crosstrack
error

FIGURE 5-85: Using Crosstrack Error to Avoid Danger

Danger Circles using GPS or Radar

If GPS and/or radar are available, a technique can be used for avoiding hazards using danger circles. A danger circle is simply a circle drawn on a chart that encompasses some charted hazards, the purpose being to keep the boat outside the circle.

If radar is to be used, the circle must be centered on some feature or object that is recognizable on the radar screen. A VRM (variable range marker) is set to the radius of the circle scaled from the chart. In the example of figure 5-86 the VRM will be set to 0.4 nm. Once the VRM is set, the helmsman must keep the target object outside the danger circle.

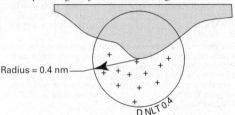

FIGURE 5-86: Danger Circle Plotted on Chart

With GPS, a danger circle may be drawn be centered anywhere, although it can be useful to center the circle on a charted object. A waypoint is set on the center and then distance to the point is monitored using the GPS. The distance to the waypoint (circle center) must be kept at not less than (NLT) the radius of the circle scaled from the chart.

A danger circle can be drawn to be monitored by both the radar and GPS unit, keeping in mind the center must be positioned on something that will be discernible on the radar. This has the obvious advantage of introducing redundancy, which is always wise, particularly when piloting near treacherous areas.

Collision Avoidance Using Relative Bearings

A vessel on a collision course with your vessel will have a constant bearing relative to your boat and corrective action must be taken to avoid collision.

A vessel whose relative bearing is decreasing (C in figure 5-87) will pass ahead and a vessel whose relative bearing is increasing will pass behind. Determining whether the

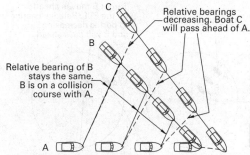

FIGURE 5-87: Collision Course Relative Bearings

relative bearing is increasing or decreasing is usually just an eyeball operation where the position of the other boat is observed relative to something like a cabin window frame. If it appears to be moving aft from the frame, then the bearing is increasing. Conversely, if it's moving forward, the bearing is decreasing. No change, and you're on a collision course.

If there is some land far behind the other boat, then a quick determination of change of relative bearing is to observe the movement of the boat relative to the land. If the boat appears to me moving aft against the land, then relative bearing is increasing and the boat will pass behind. If it's moving forward (toward the bow) the relative bearing is decreasing, and the other boat will pass ahead. As before, no movement indicates you are on a collision course.

Collision Avoidance With Relative Bearings using Radar

One of the primary reasons for having radar aboard is for collision avoidance; however, the fact of having the radar aboard and running certainly doesn't guarantee an absence of collisions. The display should constantly be monitored for targets that look like they might be on a collision course with your boat. See figure 5-88 on the next page for how this would look on the radar screen.

The electronic bearing line (EBL) can be set on the radar display to pass through a boat whose course you wish to monitor closely. If the target stays on the EBL then the boat is on a collision course. If it is moving forward or aft of the line, then the boat should pass forward or aft accordingly.

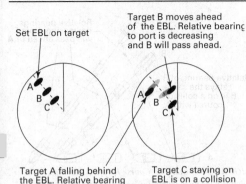

Set EBL on target

Target B moves ahead of the EBL. Relative bearing to port is decreasing and B will pass ahead.

Target A falling behind the EBL. Relative bearing to port is increasing and A will pass behind.

Target C staying on EBL is on a collision course.

FIGURE 5-88: Collision Avoidance With Radar

SET AND DRIFT

Introduction to Set and Drift

Current is tidal, ocean or other horizontal movements of water, and it can have a significant effect on the movement of the boat over the ground. *Set* is the direction of the current and *drift* is the speed of the current in knots. A vessel is also affected by *leeway*, which is motion of the boat away from the wind As the boat proceeds along a specific course, she also deviates from the course steered, through helmsman error, compass error, and other factors.

With the possible exception of current, these errors are difficult if not impossible to estimate individually, so estimates of combined set and drift from all these factors are made based on actual experience. The combined set and drift is usually referred to as just set and drift, as for current.

Determining Set and Drift

An approximation of leeway can be deduced by comparing the direction the boat is steered with the direction of the wake. The angle between the two can be used to correct the course steered to try to achieve the desired track (TR).

In some cases where leeway is not a significant factor and tide, and current tables are able to provide the speed and direction of currents, then this can provide an initial estimate of set and drift.

To derive an estimate of the (combined) set and drift while underway, the vessel is steered on a straight course at a constant speed from a known location (A) to the time of the next fix and then the DR at the time of the fix is compared to the fix to determine the set and drift. In theory there could be more than one leg in the DR plot until the fix is taken but the more changes there are, the more chance of error being introduced into the set and drift estimate. Figure 5-89 is a plot showing how set and drift are derived.

Note the line from A to B is the actual course over ground achieved and is called the course made good (CMG).

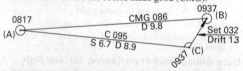

FIGURE 5-89: Determination of Set and Drift

In the example of figure 5-89, the vessel is steered on a course of 95 degrees true until 0937 when a fix is taken. The fix (B) and the DR (C) are plotted and the distance and direction from the DR (C) to the fix (B) are scaled from the plot. Often this is plotted to a larger scale on graph paper to achieve more accuracy. In the example, the set is read as 32 degrees using a protractor or the compass rose.

The drift was calculated as follows:

D = distance scaled off plot = 1.7 nautical miles

T = 0937 – 0817 = 80 minutes

Drift = S = (D x 60) / T = (1.7nm x 60) / 80 min = 1.3 knots

Determining Course From Track, Set, and Drift

Having determined the set and drift, the course can be adjusted to try to achieve the desired track (TR).

In the example of figure 5-90 on the next page, the set and drift vector is plotted from A to B, with the line in a direction of 32 degrees from north and with a length of 1.3 nautical miles, which is the amount the current and other effects, will move the vessel in one hour. Then set a divider or compass to the distance the vessel will move in one hour, in this case 6.7 nautical miles, and set one end of the dividers at B and mark the point C on the track (TR). The direction of the line from

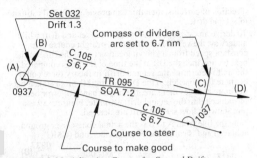

FIGURE 5-90: Adjusting Course for Set and Drift

B to C (105 degrees) is the course (C) to steer to try for the TR of 95 degrees.

Determining Track From Course, Set, and Drift

An alternative approach to using set and drift is to proceed on a specified course and then use the set and drift to calculate an estimated position (EP).

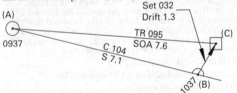

FIGURE 5-91: Estimate Track From Known Set and Drift

In the example of figure 5-91 the vessel proceeds on a course of 104 degrees at a speed of 7.1 knots. At the end of one hour the set and drift vector is plotted from B to C, with a direction of 32 degrees and a length of 1.3 nautical miles, the distance the current moves in 1 hour.

This estimate can also be made for sailing times other than one hour but the length of the set and drift vector will have to be calculated using the $D = (S \times T) / 60$ formula.

TIDES AND TIDAL CURRENTS

Introduction

Tides are changes in sea level due to forces of the moon and sun acting upon the earth as it rotates. Of the two, the moon exerts about twice the influence on tides as the sun. In addition to the rise and fall, tidal currents also exist and it is important to note that though these phenomena are related, they must be considered separately.

Tide refers to the vertical rise and fall of the sea and tidal current refers to the horizontal movement of the water.

In most locations, the tide occurs twice daily; that is, there will be two high and two low tides per day. This is a *semidiurnal* tide. In other areas there will only be one high and low tide per day and these are termed *diurnal* tides.

The tide rises and falls in a manner similar to a sine wave. Figure 5-92 shows an example from *Bowditch* of a semidiurnal tide.

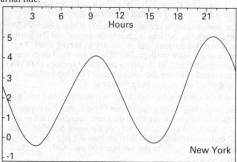

FIGURE 5-92: Tide Rise and Fall

Note how the rise and fall rate is slower at the highs and lows, and is faster in between.

Tidal Datums

Tide levels, depths, and overhead clearances are measured from averaged tide levels called *tidal datums*.

The *mean low water* (**MLW**) is the low tide averaged over many years. If one of the day's low tides is lower than the other, then only the lower level is averaged and we term this

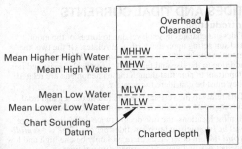

FIGURE 5-93: Tidal Datums

the *mean lower low water* (**MLLW**). The *mean high water* (**MHW**) and *mean higher high water* (**MHHW**) are arrived at in similar fashion. MHHW will normally be used as the datum for overhead clearances to bridges, etc.

The lows and highs are more pronounced twice each 29.53 days, when the moon is aligned with the sun and the Earth (new and full moons), and are known as *spring tides*. The *mean high water springs* (**MHWS**) is averaged from the high spring tides and the *mean low water springs* (**MLWS**) is averaged from the low spring tides. The high and low datums are sometimes based on these.

The tidal *range* is the difference between high and low water.

The important thing to understand here is that the depths indicated on charts, are from the chart sounding datum and tides lower than the datum are rare but quite possible. Once the estimated tide level is derived from the tide tables, this is added algebraically to the sounding on the chart.

Tide Tables

Tide tables are produced by the NOS in four volumes, each of which covers a particular area of the world. NOS no longer prints and distributes these directly but supplies data to private companies who in turn publish the volumes. These companies are listed on the NOS NOAA website and as of late 2005 included *International Marine*, *REED'S Nautical Almanac*, and *ProStar Publications*.

Online tidal predictions are available from NOS and many other sources. Marinas and yacht clubs often have small local tide table booklets available for free.

Each volume of the *Tide Tables* contains several tables, the first three of which are used to estimate tide levels.

Tide Table 1 contains daily predicted times and heights of tides for locations known as reference stations. The table is good for one year. *Tide Table 2* gives ratios or differences (corrections) used to adjust the times and heights derived from table 1 to locations known as subordinate stations. Once the tidal low and high elevations and times are derived, then *Tide Table 3* can be used to estimate tidal level for times between the bracketing high and low tides.

An alternative to *Tide Table 3* is to use the **Rule of Twelve**. To use the rule of 12 divide the time from low to high into six equal intervals then apply the change in height of tide as per table 5-13. If the time from low to high is about six hours, then the interval can be assumed to be an hour. This level of accuracy should suffice for most purposes.

Time interval	Tidal Change Fraction of Range	Cumulative Fraction	Cumulative Percent	Mnemonic
Interval 1	1/12 of range	1/12	8%	1
Interval 2	2/12 of range	3/12	25%	2
Interval 3	3/12 of range	6/12	50%	3
Interval 4	3/12 of range	9/12	75%	3
Interval 5	2/12 of range	11/12	92%	2
Interval 6	1/12 of range	12/12	100%	1

TABLE 5-13: Rule of Twelve

Computer Programs for Predicting Tides

The data is also made available in digital form for use in computer programs that perform the tidal calculations. Additionally, tables can be generated from some websites at no cost for specific days and locations of interest. Many GPS units have built-in tide prediction programs.

Tidal Current Tables

Tidal Current Tables are also produced by NOS in volumes for the Pacific and Atlantic coasts of North America and are used in a manner similar to using the tide tables.

Current Table 1 lists predicted times and velocity of maximum currents and times of slack water for reference stations. The number of tidal current reference stations is less than the number of tidal reference stations. *Current Table 2* has differences, ratios, and data relating to a larger number of subordinate stations to adjust the times and velocities derived from *Current Table 1*. *Current Table 3* assists in interpolat-

ing current velocity values to specific times between the
maximum current velocity (drift) and slack water. Tidal
current charts are also available that show current direction
and speed as small vectors (arrows) at various times after
slack water.

CELESTIAL AND OTHER MEANS OF NAVIGATION

The navigation methods discussed so far are by no means the
only methods used; however, they are the most commonly
used by the recreational boater.

LORAN

LORAN (**lo**ng **ra**nge **n**avigation) is a ground-based system
that uses chains of ground stations that transmit precisely
timed pulses. The receiver in the boat measures the difference in time between the pulses received from master and
secondary stations and position can be determined from this
information either manually on a chart, or with a computer
built in to the loran receiver. Accuracy is in the ±0.2 nm
range depending on location relative to the chain. Repeat-
ability (the ability to return to a previous position) is within
50 meters or better. The GPS system has largely replaced
the LORAN system, to the extent that LORAN electronics
are no longer available for purchase at major marine supply
stores and chains. The government continues to evaluate the
need for continuing LORAN operation, and it will likely be
shut down in the next few years, although some consideration
is being given to upgrading the system to provide more accuracy and a backup to the GPS.

Radio Direction Finding

Radio direction finding is yet another method of establishing
an LOP. A directional antenna is rotated until a maximum
signal is achieved for a station of known location and frequency. This is not commonly used in recreational boats and
has also been supplanted by GPS.

Celestial Navigation

The use of celestial navigation (navigation by the stars) for
positioning at sea has been supplanted in the last 20 years
by the use of GPS, which is both much easier to use and far
more accurate. If you can consistently get within 3 nautical
miles with a sextant, you are doing well, which doesn't even
begin to compare with the ±10 meter accuracy of the GPS
system. In addition, a fix can only be taken when an appro-

priate celestial body and the horizon is visible. If it's foggy, overcast, or too dark (no horizon) then you're out of luck.

As a result celestial navigation has largely been relegated to use as a backup means of navigation and as an excellent learning tool for gaining a deeper understanding of global navigation. The U.S. and Canadian Power Squadrons have excellent courses in celestial navigation I highly recommend for anyone desiring to learn more about this subject.

This book won't discuss celestial navigation any further than we have so far because:

1. The subject is sufficiently complex that entire books are dedicated to it, and plenty of books are available on the subject.

2. The calculations can't be carried out (manually) without the use of a *Nautical Almanac* for the current year, which also contains detailed instructions for doing the calculations, so there isn't any point to including instructions here.

For purists who want to do sight reductions entirely without the use of scientific calculators or computers, *Publication 229* sight reduction tables are available for free as downloadable Adobe Acrobat (.pdf) files at http://pollux.nss.nima.mil/pubs/. The nice thing about these is you only need to print and take the pages for the area in which you'll be cruising, rather than the whole volume.

NAVIGATION BOOKS, CHECKLISTS, AND FORMS

Some Recommended Navigation Books

I have recently become acquainted with three excellent books on modern navigation:

Sweet, Robert J. *The Weekend Navigator*, 1st ed. Camden, ME: International Marine, 2005.

Sweet, Robert J. *GPS for Mariners*, 1st ed. Camden, ME: International Marine, 2003.

Monahan, Kevin. *The Radar Book*, 1st ed. Anacortes, WA: FineEdge.com LLC, 2004.

All these books explain effective piloting and navigation with electronic equipment with far more extensive diagrams and examples, and much greater detail than this book.

Index to Navigation Checklists, Forms, and Tables

Navigation Checklist

Use this as is or as a starting point for you own checklist. This list is downloadable in Excel format at www. anchorcovepublishing.com.

NAVIGATION CHECKLIST	
Permanently Installed Navigation Equipment	
Ship's magnetic compass installed and adjusted properly	❏
Ship's compass deviation curve or table current	❏
Fluxgate compass calibrated	❏
Autopilot adjusted/checked	❏
Pelorus installed/aligned	❏
GPS checked out and functioning correctly	❏
Chartplotter check	❏
Computer with charting software	❏
Depth sounder check	❏
Tachometer calibrated with speed curves (include even if knotmeter installed)	❏
Knotmeter calibrated (GPS or measured mile)	❏
Log (odometer equivalent) calibrated	❏
Same check all nav equipment on second bridge	❏
Loran electronics check	❏
Radio direction finding equipment check	❏
Portable Navigation Equipment	
Calculator, two each, preferably scientific	❏

NAVIGATION CHECKLIST	
Hand bearing compass	❏
Binoculars (with or without built-in compass)	❏
Portable GPS (two if no installed GPS)	❏
Laptop computer with charting software	❏
Lots of spare batteries for all this equipment	❏
Publications	
Charts (legal requirement in Canada)	❏
Tide tables	❏
Current tables	❏
Light lists	❏
Coast pilots and or sailing directions	❏
Reed's Nautical Almanac for the area	❏
Cruising guides for the area	❏
Paper and Plotting Equipment	
Scratch pads, plotting sheets	❏
Navigation deck log (samples included in this section)	❏
Pencils	❏
Dividers	❏
Set squares	❏
Protractor	❏
Three-arm protractor	❏
Parallel rules	❏
Red light for night work	❏
Offshore	
Backup third GPS kept in sealed metal container for protection against lightning	❏
Sextant as back up for GPS	❏
Nautical Almanac for current year	❏
Starfinder reference	❏
Accurate, calibrated timepieces (digital watch okay)	❏
Radio capable of receiving time signal	❏
Scientific calculators (mandatory)	❏
Publication 229 tables (or excerpts for your area)	❏
Sight reduction forms you like	❏
Navigation computer (optional but nice to have)	❏

Daily Navigation Log

The sample deck log page that follows is probably too small to read unless you use a magnifying glass and is meant to be a sample or guide for you to design your own. A full size downloadable Adobe Acrobat (.pdf) version is available on the www.anchorcovepublishing.com website.

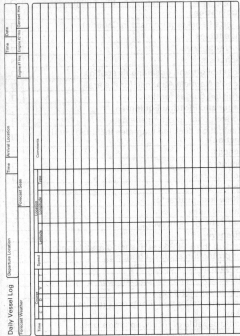

NAVIGATION TABLES

Conversion of Meters, Feet and Fathoms								
M	Ft	Fa	M	Ft	Fa	M	Ft	Fa
0.30	1.00	0.17	10.97	36.00	6.00	21.34	70.00	11.67
0.61	2.00	0.33	11.00	36.09	6.01	21.64	71.00	11.83
0.91	3.00	0.50	11.28	37.00	6.17	21.95	72.00	12.00
1.00	3.28	0.55	11.58	38.00	6.33	22.00	72.18	12.03
1.22	4.00	0.67	11.89	39.00	6.50	22.25	73.00	12.17
1.52	5.00	0.83	12.00	39.37	6.56	22.56	74.00	12.33
1.83	6.00	1.00	12.19	40.00	6.67	22.86	75.00	12.50
2.00	6.56	1.09	12.50	41.00	6.83	23.00	75.46	12.58
2.13	7.00	1.17	12.80	42.00	7.00	23.16	76.00	12.67
2.44	8.00	1.33	13.00	42.65	7.11	23.47	77.00	12.83
2.74	9.00	1.50	13.11	43.00	7.17	23.77	78.00	13.00
3.00	9.84	1.64	13.41	44.00	7.33	24.00	78.74	13.12
3.05	10.00	1.67	13.72	45.00	7.50	24.08	79.00	13.17
3.35	11.00	1.83	14.00	45.93	7.66	24.38	80.00	13.33
3.66	12.00	2.00	14.02	46.00	7.67	24.69	81.00	13.50
3.96	13.00	2.17	14.33	47.00	7.83	24.99	82.00	13.67
4.00	13.12	2.19	14.63	48.00	8.00	25.00	82.02	13.67
4.27	14.00	2.33	14.94	49.00	8.17	25.30	83.00	13.83
4.57	15.00	2.50	15.00	49.21	8.20	25.60	84.00	14.00
4.88	16.00	2.67	15.24	50.00	8.33	25.91	85.00	14.17
5.00	16.40	2.73	15.54	51.00	8.50	26.00	85.30	14.22
5.18	17.00	2.83	15.85	52.00	8.67	26.21	86.00	14.33
5.49	18.00	3.00	16.00	52.49	8.75	26.52	87.00	14.50
5.79	19.00	3.17	16.15	53.00	8.83	26.82	88.00	14.67
6.00	19.69	3.28	16.46	54.00	9.00	27.00	88.58	14.76
6.10	20.00	3.33	16.76	55.00	9.17	27.13	89.00	14.83
6.40	21.00	3.50	17.00	55.77	9.30	27.43	90.00	15.00
6.71	22.00	3.67	17.07	56.00	9.33	27.74	91.00	15.17
7.00	22.97	3.83	17.37	57.00	9.50	28.00	91.86	15.31
7.01	23.00	3.83	17.68	58.00	9.67	28.04	92.00	15.33
7.32	24.00	4.00	17.98	59.00	9.83	28.35	93.00	15.50
7.62	25.00	4.17	18.00	59.06	9.84	28.65	94.00	15.67
7.92	26.00	4.33	18.29	60.00	10.00	28.96	95.00	15.83
8.00	26.25	4.37	18.59	61.00	10.17	29.00	95.14	15.86
8.23	27.00	4.50	18.90	62.00	10.33	29.26	96.00	16.00
8.53	28.00	4.67	19.00	62.34	10.39	29.57	97.00	16.17
8.84	29.00	4.83	19.20	63.00	10.50	29.87	98.00	16.33
9.00	29.53	4.92	19.51	64.00	10.67	30.00	98.43	16.40
9.14	30.00	5.00	19.81	65.00	10.83	30.18	99.00	16.50
9.45	31.00	5.17	20.00	65.62	10.94	30.48	100.00	16.67
9.75	32.00	5.33	20.12	66.00	11.00	31.00	101.71	16.95
10.00	32.81	5.47	20.42	67.00	11.17	32.00	104.99	17.50
10.06	33.00	5.50	20.73	68.00	11.33	33.00	108.27	18.04
10.36	34.00	5.67	21.00	68.90	11.48	34.00	111.55	18.59
10.67	35.00	5.83	21.03	69.00	11.50			

TABLE 5-14: Conversion of Meters, Feet, and Fathoms

Conversion Nautical Miles, Statute Miles, Kilometers Sheet 1 of 2								
nm	sm	km	nm	sm	km	nm	sm	km
0.54	0.62	1.00	13.00	14.96	24.08	25.38	29.20	47.00
0.87	1.00	1.61	13.03	15.00	24.14	25.92	29.83	48.00
1.00	1.15	1.85	13.50	15.53	25.00	26.00	29.92	48.15
1.08	1.24	2.00	13.90	16.00	25.75	26.07	30.00	48.28
1.62	1.86	3.00	14.00	16.11	25.93	26.46	30.45	49.00
1.74	2.00	3.22	14.04	16.16	26.00	26.94	31.00	49.89
2.00	2.30	3.70	14.58	16.78	27.00	27.00	31.07	50.00
2.16	2.49	4.00	14.77	17.00	27.36	27.00	31.07	50.00
2.61	3.00	4.83	15.00	17.26	27.78	27.54	31.69	51.00
2.70	3.11	5.00	15.12	17.40	28.00	27.81	32.00	51.50
3.00	3.45	5.56	15.64	18.00	28.97	28.00	32.22	51.86
3.24	3.73	6.00	15.66	18.02	29.00	28.08	32.31	52.00
3.48	4.00	6.44	16.00	18.41	29.63	28.62	32.93	53.00
3.78	4.35	7.00	16.22	18.64	30.00	28.68	33.00	53.11
4.00	4.60	7.41	16.51	19.00	30.58	29.00	33.37	53.71
4.32	4.97	8.00	19.26	19.26	31.00	29.16	33.55	54.00
4.34	5.00	8.05	17.00	19.56	31.48	29.55	34.00	54.72
4.86	5.59	9.00	17.28	19.88	32.00	29.70	34.18	55.00
5.00	5.75	9.26	17.38	20.00	32.19	30.00	34.52	55.56
5.21	6.00	9.66	17.82	20.51	33.00	30.24	34.80	56.00
5.40	6.21	10.00	18.00	20.71	33.34	30.41	35.00	56.33
5.94	6.84	11.00	18.25	21.00	33.80	30.78	35.42	57.00
6.00	6.90	11.11	18.36	21.13	34.00	31.00	35.67	57.41
6.08	7.00	11.27	18.90	21.75	35.00	31.28	36.00	57.94
6.48	7.46	12.00	19.00	21.86	35.19	31.32	36.04	58.00
6.95	8.00	12.87	19.12	22.00	35.41	31.86	36.66	59.00
7.00	8.06	12.96	19.44	22.37	36.00	32.00	36.82	59.26
7.02	8.08	13.00	19.98	22.99	37.00	32.15	37.00	59.55
7.56	8.70	14.00	19.99	23.00	37.01	32.40	37.28	60.00
7.82	9.00	14.48	20.00	23.02	37.04	32.94	37.90	61.00
8.00	9.21	14.82	20.52	23.61	38.00	33.00	37.98	61.12
8.10	9.32	15.00	20.86	24.00	38.62	33.02	38.00	61.16
8.64	9.94	16.00	21.00	24.17	38.82	33.48	38.52	62.00
8.69	10.00	16.09	21.06	24.23	39.00	33.89	39.00	62.76
9.00	10.36	16.67	21.60	24.85	40.00	34.00	39.13	62.97
9.18	10.56	17.00	21.72	25.00	40.23	34.02	39.15	63.00
9.56	11.00	17.70	22.00	25.32	40.74	34.56	39.77	64.00
9.72	11.18	18.00	22.14	25.48	41.00	34.76	40.00	64.37
10.00	11.51	18.52	22.59	26.00	41.84	35.00	40.28	64.82
10.26	11.81	19.00	22.68	26.10	42.00	35.10	40.39	65.00
10.43	12.00	19.31	23.00	26.47	42.60	35.63	41.00	65.98
10.80	12.43	20.00	23.22	26.72	43.00	35.64	41.01	66.00
11.00	12.66	20.37	23.46	27.00	43.45	36.00	41.43	66.67
11.30	13.00	20.92	23.76	27.34	44.00	36.18	41.63	67.00
11.34	13.05	21.00	24.00	27.62	44.45	36.50	42.00	67.59
11.88	13.67	22.00	24.30	27.96	45.00	36.72	42.25	68.00
12.00	13.81	22.22	24.33	28.00	45.06	37.00	42.58	68.52
12.17	14.00	22.53	24.84	28.58	46.00	37.26	42.87	69.00
12.42	14.29	23.00	25.00	28.77	46.30	37.37	43.00	69.20
12.96	14.91	24.00	25.20	29.00	46.67	37.80	43.50	70.00

TABLE 5-15(1): Convert Between Nautical Miles, Statute Miles, and Kilometers. Also convert Knots, MPH, and km/hr.

Conversion Nautical Miles, Statute Miles, Kilometers Sheet 2 of 2								
nm	sm	km	nm	sm	km	nm	sm	km
38.00	43.73	70.38	50.40	58.00	93.34	70.39	81.00	130.36
38.23	44.00	70.81	50.76	58.41	94.00	71.00	81.71	131.49
38.34	44.12	71.00	51.00	58.69	94.45	71.26	82.00	131.97
38.88	44.74	72.00	51.27	59.00	94.95	72.00	82.86	133.34
39.00	44.88	72.23	51.30	59.03	95.00	72.13	83.00	133.58
39.10	45.00	72.42	51.84	59.65	96.00	72.99	84.00	135.18
39.42	45.36	73.00	52.00	59.84	96.30	73.00	84.01	135.20
39.96	45.98	74.00	52.14	60.00	96.56	73.86	85.00	136.79
39.97	46.00	74.03	52.38	60.27	97.00	74.00	85.16	137.05
40.00	46.03	74.08	52.92	60.89	98.00	74.73	86.00	138.40
40.50	46.60	75.00	53.00	60.99	98.16	75.00	86.31	138.90
40.84	47.00	75.64	53.01	61.00	98.17	75.60	87.00	140.17
41.00	47.18	75.93	53.46	61.52	99.00	76.00	87.46	140.75
41.04	47.22	76.00	53.88	62.00	99.78	76.47	88.00	141.62
41.58	47.85	77.00	54.00	62.14	100.00	77.00	88.61	142.60
41.71	48.00	77.25	54.02	62.14	100.01	77.34	89.00	143.23
42.00	48.33	77.78	54.75	63.00	101.39	78.00	89.76	144.46
42.12	48.47	78.00	55.00	63.29	101.86	78.21	90.00	144.84
42.58	49.00	78.86	55.61	64.00	103.00	79.00	90.91	146.31
42.66	49.09	79.00	56.00	64.44	103.71	79.08	91.00	146.45
43.00	49.48	79.64	56.48	65.00	104.61	79.95	92.00	148.06
43.20	49.71	80.00	57.00	65.59	105.56	80.00	92.06	148.16
43.45	50.00	80.47	57.35	66.00	106.22	80.81	93.00	149.67
43.74	50.33	81.00	58.00	66.75	107.42	81.00	93.21	150.01
44.00	50.63	81.49	58.22	67.00	107.83	81.68	94.00	151.28
44.28	50.95	82.00	59.00	67.90	109.27	82.00	94.36	151.86
44.32	51.00	82.08	59.09	68.00	109.44	82.55	95.00	152.89
44.82	51.57	83.00	59.96	69.00	111.04	83.00	95.51	153.72
45.00	51.79	83.34	60.00	69.05	111.12	83.42	96.00	154.50
45.19	52.00	83.69	60.83	70.00	112.65	84.00	96.67	155.57
45.36	52.20	84.00	61.00	70.20	112.97	84.29	97.00	156.11
45.90	52.82	85.00	61.70	71.00	114.26	85.00	97.82	157.42
46.00	52.94	85.19	62.00	71.35	114.82	85.16	98.00	157.72
46.06	53.00	85.30	62.57	72.00	115.87	86.00	98.97	159.27
46.44	53.44	86.00	63.00	72.50	116.68	86.03	99.00	159.33
46.92	54.00	86.90	63.44	73.00	117.48	86.90	100.00	160.93
46.98	54.06	87.00	64.00	73.65	118.53	87.00	100.12	161.12
47.00	54.09	87.04	64.30	74.00	119.09	88.00	101.27	162.98
47.52	54.68	88.00	65.00	74.80	120.38	89.00	102.42	164.83
47.79	55.00	88.51	65.17	75.00	120.70	90.00	103.57	166.68
48.00	55.24	88.90	66.00	75.95	122.23	91.00	104.72	168.53
48.06	55.30	89.00	66.04	76.00	122.31	92.00	105.87	170.38
48.60	55.92	90.00	66.91	77.00	123.92	93.00	107.02	172.24
48.66	56.00	90.12	67.00	77.10	124.08	94.00	108.17	174.09
49.00	56.39	90.75	67.78	78.00	125.53	95.00	109.32	175.94
49.14	56.54	91.00	68.00	78.25	125.94	96.00	110.47	177.79
49.53	57.00	91.73	68.65	79.00	127.14	97.00	111.63	179.64
49.68	57.17	92.00	69.00	79.40	127.79	98.00	112.78	181.50
50.00	57.54	92.60	69.52	80.00	128.75	99.00	113.93	183.35
50.22	57.79	93.00	70.00	80.55	129.64	100.00	115.08	185.20

TABLE 5-15(2): Convert Between Nautical Miles, Statute Miles, and Kilometers. Also convert Knots, MPH, and km/hr.

Natural and Numerical Chart Scales (Similar to *Bowditch* Table 5) Sheet 1 of 2						
Natural Scale	Naut. Miles /Inch	Inch/ Naut. Mile	Naut. Miles / cm	Cm / Naut Mile	Stat. Miles /Inch	Inches/ Stat. Mile	Feet /Inch
1:500	0.01	145.83	0.00	370.40	0.01	126.72	41.67
1:600	0.01	121.52	0.00	308.67	0.01	105.60	50.00
1:1000	0.01	72.91	0.01	185.20	0.02	63.36	83.33
1:1200	0.02	60.76	0.01	154.33	0.02	52.80	100.00
1:1500	0.02	48.61	0.01	123.47	0.02	42.24	125.00
1:2000	0.03	36.46	0.01	92.60	0.03	31.68	166.67
1:2400	0.03	30.38	0.01	77.17	0.04	26.40	200.00
1:2500	0.03	29.17	0.01	74.08	0.04	25.34	208.33
1:3000	0.04	24.30	0.02	61.73	0.05	21.12	250.00
1:3600	0.05	20.25	0.02	51.44	0.06	17.60	300.00
1:4000	0.05	18.23	0.02	46.30	0.06	15.84	333.33
1:4800	0.07	15.19	0.03	38.58	0.08	13.20	400.00
1:5000	0.07	14.58	0.03	37.04	0.08	12.67	416.67
1:6000	0.08	12.15	0.03	30.87	0.09	10.56	500.00
1:7000	0.10	10.42	0.04	26.46	0.11	9.05	583.33
1:7200	0.10	10.13	0.04	25.72	0.11	8.80	600.00
1:7920	0.11	9.21	0.04	23.38	0.13	8.00	660.00
1:8000	0.11	9.11	0.04	23.15	0.13	7.92	666.67
1:8400	0.12	8.68	0.05	22.05	0.13	7.54	700.00
1:9000	0.12	8.10	0.05	20.58	0.14	7.04	750.00
1:9600	0.13	7.60	0.05	19.29	0.15	6.60	800.00
1:10000	0.14	7.29	0.05	18.52	0.16	6.34	833.33
1:10800	0.15	6.75	0.06	17.15	0.17	5.87	900.00
1:12000	0.16	6.08	0.06	15.43	0.21	5.28	1000.00
1:13200	0.18	5.52	0.07	14.03	0.21	4.80	1100.00
1:14400	0.20	5.06	0.08	12.86	0.23	4.40	1200.00
1:15000	0.21	4.86	0.08	12.35	0.24	4.22	1250.00
1:15600	0.21	4.67	0.08	11.87	0.25	4.06	1300.00
1:15840	0.22	4.60	0.09	11.69	0.25	4.00	1320.00
1:16000	0.22	4.56	0.09	11.58	0.25	3.96	1333.33
1:16800	0.23	4.34	0.09	11.02	0.27	3.77	1400.00
1:18000	0.25	4.05	0.10	10.29	0.28	3.52	1500.00
1:19200	0.26	3.80	0.10	9.65	0.30	3.30	1600.00
1:20000	0.27	3.65	0.11	9.26	0.32	3.17	1666.67
1:20400	0.28	3.57	0.11	9.08	0.32	3.11	1700.00
1:21120	0.29	3.45	0.11	8.77	0.33	3.00	1760.00
1:12600	0.17	5.79	0.07	14.70	0.20	5.03	1050.00
1:22800	0.31	3.20	0.12	8.12	0.36	2.78	1900.00

TABLE 5-16(1): Natural and Numerical Chart Scales

Natural and Numerical Chart Scales (Similar to *Bowditch* Table 5) Sheet 2 of 2							
Natural Scale	Naut. Miles /Inch	Inch/ Naut. Mile	Naut. Miles / cm	Cm / Naut Mile	Stat. Miles /Inch	Inches/ Stat. Mile	Feet /Inch
1:24000	0.329	3.04	0.13	7.72	0.38	2.64	2000
1:25000	0.343	2.92	0.13	7.41	0.39	2.53	2083
1:40000	0.549	1.82	0.22	4.63	0.63	1.58	3333
1:48000	0.658	1.52	0.26	3.86	0.76	1.32	4000
1:50000	0.686	1.46	0.27	3.70	0.79	1.27	4167
1:62500	0.857	1.17	0.34	2.96	0.99	1.01	5208
1:63360	0.869	1.15	0.34	2.92	1.00	1.00	5280
1:75000	1.029	0.97	0.40	2.47	1.18	0.84	6250
1:80000	1.097	0.91	0.43	2.32	1.26	0.79	6667
1:100000	1.371	0.73	0.54	1.85	1.58	0.63	8333
1:125000	1.714	0.58	0.67	1.48	1.97	0.51	10417
1:200000	2.743	0.36	1.08	0.93	3.16	0.32	16667
1:250000	3.429	0.29	1.35	0.74	3.95	0.25	20833
1:400000	5.486	0.18	2.16	0.46	6.31	0.16	33333
1:500000	6.857	0.15	2.70	0.37	7.89	0.13	41667
1:750000	10.286	0.10	4.05	0.25	11.84	0.08	62500
1:1000,000	13.715	0.07	5.40	0.19	15.78	0.06	83333

- To convert natural scale to meters per centimeter divide by 100 (move decimal 2 places left).
  Example: 1:2400 natural = 2.4 meters / cm

- To convert natural scale to kilometers per centimeter divide by 100,000 (move decimal 5 places left).
  Example: 1:125,000 natural = 1.25 km / cm

- Divide natural scale by 72913.39 to get nautical miles / inch.

- Divide natural scale by 63360 to get statute miles / inch.

- Divide natural scale by 185200 to get nautical miles / centimeter.

- Divide natural scale by 12 to get feet / inch

TABLE 5-16(2): Natural and Numerical Chart Scales

Distance by Vertical Angle Measured Between Waterline at Object and Top of Object
(Similar to *Bowditch* Table 16)   Sheet 1 of 4

Angle		Height of object above the sea (Ft / M)								
		10	15	20	25	30	40	45	50	55
		3.05	4.57	6.10	7.62	9.14	12.19	13.71	15.24	16.76
Deg	Min				Nautical Miles					
0	10	0.57	0.85	1.13	1.41	1.70	2.26	2.55	2.83	3.11
0	11	0.51	0.77	1.03	1.29	1.54	2.06	2.31	2.57	2.83
0	12	0.47	0.71	0.94	1.18	1.41	1.89	2.12	2.36	2.59
0	13	0.44	0.65	0.87	1.09	1.31	1.74	1.96	2.18	2.39
0	14	0.40	0.61	0.81	1.01	1.21	1.62	1.82	2.02	2.22
0	15	0.38	0.57	0.75	0.94	1.13	1.51	1.70	1.89	2.07
0	20	0.28	0.42	0.57	0.71	0.85	1.13	1.27	1.41	1.56
0	25	0.23	0.34	0.45	0.57	0.68	0.91	1.02	1.13	1.24
0	30	0.19	0.28	0.38	0.47	0.57	0.75	0.85	0.94	1.04
0	35	0.16	0.24	0.32	0.40	0.48	0.65	0.73	0.81	0.89
0	40	0.14	0.21	0.28	0.35	0.42	0.57	0.64	0.71	0.78
0	45	0.13	0.19	0.25	0.31	0.38	0.50	0.57	0.63	0.69
0	50	0.11	0.17	0.23	0.28	0.34	0.45	0.51	0.57	0.62
0	55	0.10	0.15	0.21	0.26	0.31	0.41	0.46	0.51	0.57
1	00		0.14	0.19	0.24	0.28	0.38	0.42	0.47	0.52
1	10		0.12	0.16	0.20	0.24	0.32	0.36	0.40	0.44
1	20		0.11	0.14	0.18	0.21	0.28	0.32	0.35	0.39
1	30			0.13	0.16	0.19	0.25	0.28	0.31	0.35
1	40			0.11	0.14	0.17	0.23	0.25	0.28	0.31
1	50			0.10	0.13	0.15	0.21	0.23	0.26	0.28
2	00				0.12	0.14	0.19	0.21	0.24	0.26
2	15				0.10	0.13	0.17	0.19	0.21	0.23
2	30					0.11	0.15	0.17	0.19	0.21
2	45					0.10	0.14	0.15	0.17	0.19
3	00						0.13	0.14	0.16	0.17
3	20						0.11	0.13	0.14	0.16
3	40						0.10	0.12	0.13	0.14
4	00							0.11	0.12	0.13
4	20							0.10	0.11	0.12
4	40								0.10	0.11
5	00									0.10

TABLE 5-17(1): Distance by Vertical Angle from Waterline to Top of Object

Distance by Vertical Angle Measured Between Waterline at Object and Top of Object
(Similar to *Bowditch* Table 16)   Sheet 2 of 4

Angle		Height of object above the sea (Ft / M)									
		60	65	70	75	80	85	90	95	100	105
		18.3	19.8	21.3	22.9	24.4	25.9	27.4	29.0	30.5	32.0
Deg	Min	Nautical Miles									
0	10	3.39	3.68	3.96	4.24	4.53	4.81				
0	11	3.09	3.34	3.60	3.86	4.11	4.37	4.63	4.89		
0	12	2.83	3.06	3.30	3.54	3.77	4.01	4.24	4.48	4.71	4.95
0	13	2.61	2.83	3.05	3.26	3.48	3.70	3.92	4.13	4.35	4.57
0	14	2.42	2.63	2.83	3.03	3.23	3.44	3.64	3.84	4.04	4.24
0	15	2.26	2.45	2.64	2.83	3.02	3.21	3.39	3.58	3.77	3.96
0	20	1.70	1.84	1.98	2.12	2.26	2.40	2.55	2.69	2.83	2.97
0	25	1.36	1.47	1.58	1.70	1.81	1.92	2.04	2.15	2.26	2.38
0	30	1.13	1.23	1.32	1.41	1.51	1.60	1.70	1.79	1.89	1.98
0	35	0.97	1.05	1.13	1.21	1.29	1.37	1.45	1.54	1.62	1.70
0	40	0.85	0.92	0.99	1.06	1.13	1.20	1.27	1.34	1.41	1.49
0	45	0.75	0.82	0.88	0.94	1.01	1.07	1.13	1.19	1.26	1.32
0	50	0.68	0.74	0.79	0.85	0.91	0.96	1.02	1.07	1.13	1.19
0	55	0.62	0.67	0.72	0.77	0.82	0.87	0.93	0.98	1.03	1.08
1	00	0.57	0.61	0.66	0.71	0.75	0.80	0.85	0.90	0.94	0.99
1	10	0.48	0.53	0.57	0.61	0.65	0.69	0.73	0.77	0.81	0.85
1	20	0.42	0.46	0.49	0.53	0.57	0.60	0.64	0.67	0.71	0.74
1	30	0.38	0.41	0.44	0.47	0.50	0.53	0.57	0.60	0.63	0.66
1	40	0.34	0.37	0.40	0.42	0.45	0.48	0.51	0.54	0.57	0.59
1	50	0.31	0.33	0.36	0.39	0.41	0.44	0.46	0.49	0.51	0.54
2	00	0.28	0.31	0.33	0.35	0.38	0.40	0.42	0.45	0.47	0.49
2	15	0.25	0.27	0.29	0.31	0.34	0.36	0.38	0.40	0.42	0.44
2	30	0.23	0.25	0.26	0.28	0.30	0.32	0.34	0.36	0.38	0.40
2	45	0.21	0.22	0.24	0.26	0.27	0.29	0.31	0.33	0.34	0.36
3	00	0.19	0.20	0.22	0.24	0.25	0.27	0.28	0.30	0.31	0.33
3	20	0.17	0.18	0.20	0.21	0.23	0.24	0.25	0.27	0.28	0.30
3	40	0.15	0.17	0.18	0.19	0.21	0.22	0.23	0.24	0.26	0.27
4	00	0.14	0.15	0.16	0.18	0.19	0.20	0.21	0.22	0.24	0.25
4	20	0.13	0.14	0.15	0.16	0.17	0.18	0.20	0.21	0.22	0.23
4	40	0.12	0.13	0.14	0.15	0.16	0.17	0.18	0.19	0.20	0.21
5	00	0.11	0.12	0.13	0.14	0.15	0.16	0.17	0.18	0.19	0.20
5	20	0.11	0.11	0.12	0.13	0.14	0.15	0.16	0.17	0.18	0.19
5	40	0.10	0.11	0.12	0.12	0.13	0.14	0.15	0.16	0.17	0.17
6	00		0.10	0.11	0.11	0.12	0.13	0.14	0.15	0.16	0.16
6	20		0.10	0.10	0.11	0.11	0.12	0.13	0.14	0.15	0.16
6	40			0.10	0.10	0.11	0.11	0.12	0.13	0.14	0.15
7	00				0.10	0.11	0.11	0.11	0.12	0.13	0.14
7	20				0.10	0.10	0.11	0.11	0.12	0.12	0.13
7	40					0.10	0.10	0.11	0.11	0.12	0.12
8	00						0.10	0.10	0.11	0.11	0.12
8	20							0.10	0.10	0.11	0.11
8	40								0.10	0.10	0.11
9	00									0.10	0.10
9	30										0.10
10	00										0.10

TABLE 5-17(2): Distance by Vertical Angle from Waterline to Top of Object

Distance by Vertical Angle Measured Between Waterline at Object and Top of Object
(Similar to *Bowditch* Table 16)   Sheet 3 of 4

Angle Deg	Min	Height of object above the sea (Ft / M)									
		110	115	120	125	130	135	140	145	150	155
		33.5	35.1	36.6	38.1	39.6	41.1	42.7	44.2	45.7	47.2
		Nautical Miles									
0	10	6.22	6.51	6.79	7.07	7.36	7.64				
0	11	5.66	5.92	6.17	6.43	6.69	6.94	7.20	7.46		
0	12	5.19	5.42	5.66	5.89	6.13	6.37	6.60	6.84	7.07	7.31
0	13	4.79	5.01	5.22	5.44	5.66	5.88	6.09	6.31	6.53	6.75
0	14	4.45	4.65	4.85	5.05	5.25	5.46	5.66	5.86	6.06	6.26
0	15	4.15	4.34	4.53	4.71	4.90	5.09	5.28	5.47	5.66	5.85
0	20	3.11	3.25	3.39	3.54	3.68	3.82	3.96	4.10	4.24	4.38
0	25	2.49	2.60	2.72	2.83	2.94	3.06	3.17	3.28	3.39	3.51
0	30	2.07	2.17	2.26	2.36	2.45	2.55	2.64	2.73	2.83	2.92
0	35	1.78	1.86	1.94	2.02	2.10	2.18	2.26	2.34	2.42	2.51
0	40	1.56	1.63	1.70	1.77	1.84	1.91	1.98	2.05	2.12	2.19
0	45	1.38	1.45	1.51	1.57	1.63	1.70	1.76	1.82	1.89	1.95
0	50	1.24	1.30	1.36	1.41	1.47	1.53	1.58	1.64	1.70	1.75
0	55	1.13	1.18	1.23	1.29	1.34	1.39	1.44	1.49	1.54	1.59
1	00	1.04	1.08	1.13	1.18	1.23	1.27	1.32	1.37	1.41	1.46
1	10	0.89	0.93	0.97	1.01	1.05	1.09	1.13	1.17	1.21	1.25
1	20	0.78	0.81	0.85	0.88	0.92	0.95	0.99	1.03	1.06	1.10
1	30	0.69	0.72	0.75	0.79	0.82	0.85	0.88	0.91	0.94	0.97
1	40	0.62	0.65	0.68	0.71	0.74	0.76	0.79	0.82	0.85	0.88
1	50	0.57	0.59	0.62	0.64	0.67	0.69	0.72	0.75	0.77	0.80
2	00	0.52	0.54	0.57	0.59	0.61	0.64	0.66	0.68	0.71	0.73
2	15	0.46	0.48	0.50	0.52	0.54	0.57	0.59	0.61	0.63	0.65
2	30	0.41	0.43	0.45	0.47	0.49	0.51	0.53	0.55	0.57	0.58
3	00	0.35	0.36	0.38	0.39	0.41	0.42	0.44	0.46	0.47	0.49
3	30	0.30	0.31	0.32	0.34	0.35	0.36	0.38	0.39	0.40	0.42
4	00	0.26	0.27	0.28	0.29	0.31	0.32	0.33	0.34	0.35	0.36
4	30	0.23	0.24	0.25	0.26	0.27	0.28	0.29	0.30	0.31	0.32
5	00	0.21	0.22	0.23	0.24	0.24	0.25	0.26	0.27	0.28	0.29
5	30	0.19	0.20	0.21	0.21	0.22	0.23	0.24	0.25	0.26	0.26
6	00	0.17	0.18	0.19	0.20	0.20	0.21	0.22	0.23	0.23	0.24
6	30	0.16	0.17	0.17	0.18	0.19	0.20	0.20	0.21	0.22	0.22
7	00	0.15	0.15	0.16	0.17	0.17	0.18	0.19	0.19	0.20	0.21
7	30	0.14	0.14	0.15	0.16	0.16	0.17	0.18	0.18	0.19	0.19
8	00			0.13	0.14	0.15	0.15	0.16	0.16	0.17	0.18
8	30			0.13	0.13	0.14	0.14	0.15	0.15	0.16	0.17
9	00			0.12	0.13	0.14	0.14	0.15	0.15	0.16	0.16
9	30				0.12	0.13	0.13	0.14	0.14	0.15	0.15
10	00				0.12	0.12	0.13	0.13	0.14	0.14	0.14
10	30					0.12	0.12	0.12	0.13	0.13	0.14
11	00						0.11	0.12	0.12	0.13	0.13
11	30						0.11	0.11	0.12	0.12	0.13
12	00							0.11	0.11	0.12	0.12
12	30								0.11	0.11	0.12
13	00									0.11	0.11
13	30									0.10	0.11
14	00										0.10

TABLE 5-17(3): Distance by Vertical Angle From Waterline to Top of Object

Distance by Vertical Angle Measured Between Waterline at Object and Top of Object
(Similar to *Bowditch* Table 16)   Sheet 4 of 4

Height of object above the sea (Ft / M) — Nautical Miles

Angle Deg	Min	160 / 48.8	165 / 50.3	170 / 51.8	175 / 53.3	180 / 54.9	200 / 61.0	225 / 68.6	250 / 76.2	275 / 83.8	300 / 91.4
0	20	4.53	4.67	4.81	4.95						
0	25	3.62	3.73	3.85	3.96	4.07	4.53				
0	30	3.02	3.11	3.21	3.30	3.39	3.77	4.24	4.71		
0	35	2.59	2.67	2.75	2.84	2.91	3.23	3.64	4.04	4.45	4.85
0	40	2.26	2.33	2.40	2.48	2.55	2.83	3.18	3.54	3.89	4.24
0	45	2.01	2.07	2.14	2.20	2.26	2.51	2.83	3.14	3.46	3.77
0	50	1.81	1.87	1.92	1.98	2.04	2.26	2.55	2.83	3.11	3.39
0	55	1.65	1.70	1.75	1.80	1.85	2.06	2.31	2.57	2.83	3.09
1	00	1.51	1.56	1.60	1.65	1.70	1.89	2.12	2.36	2.59	2.83
1	10	1.29	1.33	1.37	1.41	1.45	1.62	1.82	2.02	2.22	2.42
1	20	1.13	1.17	1.20	1.24	1.27	1.41	1.59	1.77	1.94	2.12
1	30	1.01	1.04	1.07	1.10	1.13	1.26	1.41	1.57	1.73	1.89
1	40	0.91	0.93	0.96	0.99	1.02	1.13	1.27	1.41	1.56	1.70
1	50	0.82	0.85	0.87	0.90	0.93	1.03	1.16	1.29	1.41	1.54
2	00	0.75	0.78	0.80	0.82	0.85	0.94	1.06	1.18	1.30	1.41
2	15	0.67	0.69	0.71	0.73	0.75	0.84	0.94	1.05	1.15	1.26
2	30	0.60	0.62	0.64	0.66	0.68	0.75	0.85	0.94	1.04	1.13
2	45	0.55	0.57	0.58	0.60	0.62	0.69	0.77	0.86	0.94	1.03
3	00	0.50	0.52	0.53	0.55	0.57	0.63	0.71	0.79	0.86	0.94
3	20	0.45	0.47	0.48	0.49	0.51	0.57	0.64	0.71	0.78	0.85
3	40	0.41	0.42	0.44	0.45	0.46	0.51	0.58	0.64	0.71	0.77
4	00	0.38	0.39	0.40	0.41	0.42	0.47	0.53	0.59	0.65	0.71
4	20	0.35	0.36	0.37	0.38	0.39	0.43	0.49	0.54	0.60	0.65
4	40	0.32	0.33	0.34	0.35	0.36	0.40	0.45	0.50	0.55	0.60
5	00	0.30	0.31	0.32	0.33	0.34	0.38	0.42	0.47	0.52	0.56
5	20	0.28	0.29	0.30	0.31	0.32	0.35	0.40	0.44	0.48	0.53
5	40	0.27	0.27	0.28	0.29	0.30	0.33	0.37	0.41	0.46	0.50
6	00	0.25	0.26	0.27	0.27	0.28	0.31	0.35	0.39	0.43	0.47
6	20	0.24	0.24	0.25	0.26	0.27	0.30	0.33	0.37	0.41	0.44
6	40	0.23	0.23	0.24	0.25	0.25	0.28	0.32	0.35	0.39	0.42
7	00	0.21	0.22	0.23	0.23	0.24	0.27	0.30	0.34	0.37	0.40
7	30	0.20	0.21	0.21	0.22	0.23	0.25	0.28	0.31	0.34	0.38
8	00	0.19	0.19	0.20	0.20	0.21	0.23	0.26	0.29	0.32	0.35
9	00	0.17	0.17	0.18	0.18	0.19	0.21	0.23	0.26	0.29	0.31
10	30	0.14	0.15	0.15	0.16	0.16	0.18	0.20	0.22	0.24	0.27
11	00	0.14	0.14	0.14	0.15	0.15	0.17	0.19	0.21	0.23	0.25
12	00	0.12	0.13	0.13	0.14	0.14	0.15	0.17	0.19	0.21	0.23
13	00	0.11	0.12	0.12	0.12	0.13	0.14	0.16	0.18	0.20	0.21
14	00	0.11	0.11	0.11	0.12	0.12	0.13	0.15	0.17	0.18	0.20
15	00	0.10	0.10	0.10	0.11	0.11	0.12	0.14	0.15	0.17	0.18
16	00			0.10	0.10	0.10	0.11	0.13	0.14	0.16	0.17
17	00					0.10	0.11	0.12	0.13	0.15	0.16
18	00						0.10	0.11	0.13	0.14	0.15
19	00						0.10	0.11	0.12	0.13	0.14
20	00							0.10	0.11	0.12	0.14

TABLE 5-17(4): Distance by Vertical Angle From Waterline to Top of Object

Distance by Vertical Angle Measured Between Sea Horizon and Top of Object Beyond Sea Horizon
(Similar to *Bowditch* Table 15) Sheet 1 of 3

Angle		Height of Top of Object Above Sea Level less Height of Eye of Observer (in Feet with Meters Below)									
Deg	Min	25	30	35	40	45	50	60	70	80	90
		7.6	9.1	10.7	12.2	13.7	15.2	18.3	21.3	24.4	27.4
0	00	5.8	6.4	6.9	7.4	7.8	8.2	9.0	9.8	10.4	11.1
0	01	4.8	5.3	5.8	6.3	6.7	7.1	7.9	8.6	9.3	9.9
0	02	3.9	4.4	4.9	5.4	5.8	6.2	6.9	7.6	8.3	8.9
0	03	3.3	3.7	4.2	4.6	5.0	5.4	6.1	6.8	7.4	8.0
0	04	2.8	3.2	3.6	4.0	4.4	4.7	5.4	6.1	6.7	7.3
0	05	2.4	2.8	3.1	3.5	3.9	4.2	4.8	5.5	6.0	6.6
0	06	2.1	2.4	2.8	3.1	3.4	3.7	4.3	4.9	5.5	6.0
0	07	1.8	2.2	2.5	2.8	3.1	3.4	3.9	4.5	5.0	5.5
0	08	1.6	1.9	2.2	2.5	2.8	3.1	3.6	4.1	4.6	5.0
0	09	1.5	1.7	2.0	2.3	2.5	2.8	3.3	3.8	4.2	4.7
0	10	1.3	1.6	1.8	2.1	2.3	2.6	3.0	3.5	3.9	4.3
0	15	0.9	1.1	1.3	1.5	1.6	1.8	2.1	2.5	2.8	3.1
0	20	0.7	0.8	1.0	1.1	1.2	1.4	1.6	1.9	2.2	2.4
0	25	0.6	0.7	0.8	0.9	1.0	1.1	1.3	1.5	1.8	2.0
0	30	0.5	0.6	0.7	0.7	0.8	0.9	1.1	1.3	1.5	1.7
0	35		0.5	0.6	0.6	0.7	0.8	1.0	1.1	1.3	1.4
0	40			0.5	0.6	0.6	0.7	0.8	1.0	1.1	1.3
0	45				0.5	0.6	0.6	0.7	0.9	1.0	1.1
0	50				0.5	0.5	0.6	0.7	0.8	0.9	1.0
0	55					0.5	0.5	0.6	0.7	0.8	0.9
1	00						0.5	0.6	0.7	0.8	0.8
1	10							0.5	0.6	0.6	0.7
1	20								0.5	0.6	0.6
1	30									0.5	0.6
1	40									0.5	0.5
1	50										0.5

TABLE 5-18(1): Distance by Vertical Angle From Horizon to Top of Object Beyond Horizon

Distance by Vertical Angle Measured Between Sea Horizon and Top of Object Beyond Sea Horizon
(Similar to Bowditch Table 15) Sheet 2 of 3

Angle		Height of Top of Object Above Sea Level less Height of Eye of Observer (in Feet with Meters Below)										
		100	120	140	160	180	200	250	300	350	400	450
Deg	Min	30.5	36.6	42.7	48.8	54.9	61.0	76.2	91.4	106	121	137
0	00	11.7	12.8	13.8	14.8	15.7	16.5	18.4	20.2	21.8	23.3	24.7
0	01	10.5	11.6	12.7	13.6	14.5	15.3	17.3	19.0	20.7	22.2	23.6
0	02	9.5	10.6	11.6	12.5	13.4	14.3	16.2	17.9	19.6	21.0	22.5
0	03	8.6	9.7	10.7	11.6	12.5	13.3	15.2	16.9	18.5	20.0	21.4
0	04	7.8	8.8	9.8	10.7	11.6	12.4	14.3	16.0	17.6	19.0	20.4
0	05	7.1	8.1	9.0	9.9	10.8	11.5	13.4	15.1	16.6	18.1	19.5
0	06	6.5	7.5	8.4	9.2	10.0	10.8	12.6	14.2	15.8	17.2	18.6
0	07	6.0	6.9	7.7	8.6	9.4	10.1	11.9	13.5	15.0	16.4	17.7
0	08	5.5	6.4	7.2	8.0	8.8	9.5	11.2	12.8	14.2	15.6	16.9
0	09	5.1	5.9	6.7	7.5	8.2	8.9	10.6	12.1	13.5	14.9	16.2
0	10	4.7	5.5	6.3	7.0	7.7	8.4	10.0	11.5	12.9	14.2	15.5
0	15	3.4	4.1	4.7	5.3	5.8	6.4	7.8	9.0	10.3	11.5	12.6
0	20	2.7	3.2	3.7	4.2	4.6	5.1	6.3	7.4	8.4	9.5	10.5
0	25	2.2	2.6	3.0	3.4	3.8	4.2	5.2	6.2	7.1	8.0	8.9
0	30	1.8	2.2	2.6	2.9	3.2	3.6	4.4	5.3	6.1	6.9	7.7
0	35	1.6	1.9	2.2	2.5	2.8	3.1	3.9	4.6	5.3	6.0	6.7
0	40	1.4	1.7	1.9	2.2	2.5	2.8	3.4	4.1	4.7	5.4	6.0
0	45	1.2	1.5	1.7	2.0	2.2	2.5	3.1	3.6	4.2	4.8	5.4
0	50	1.1	1.3	1.6	1.8	2.0	2.2	2.8	3.3	3.8	4.4	4.9
0	55	1.0	1.2	1.4	1.6	1.8	2.0	2.5	3.0	3.5	4.0	4.5
1	00	0.9	1.1	1.3	1.5	1.7	1.9	2.3	2.8	3.2	3.7	4.1
1	10	0.8	1.0	1.1	1.3	1.4	1.6	2.0	2.4	2.8	3.2	3.6
1	20	0.7	0.8	1.0	1.1	1.3	1.4	1.8	2.1	2.4	2.8	3.1
1	30	0.6	0.8	0.9	1.0	1.1	1.2	1.6	1.9	2.2	2.5	2.8
1	40	0.6	0.7	0.8	0.9	1.0	1.1	1.4	1.7	2.0	2.2	2.5
1	50	0.5	0.6	0.7	0.8	0.9	1.0	1.3	1.5	1.8	2.0	2.3
2	00		0.6	0.7	0.7	0.8	0.9	1.2	1.4	1.6	1.9	2.1
2	30		0.5	0.5	0.6	0.7	0.8	0.9	1.1	1.3	1.5	1.7
3	00				0.5	0.6	0.6	0.8	0.9	1.1	1.3	1.4
3	30					0.5	0.5	0.7	0.8	0.9	1.1	1.2
4	00						0.5	0.6	0.7	0.8	0.9	1.1
4	30							0.5	0.6	0.7	0.8	0.9
5	00							0.5	0.6	0.7	0.8	0.8
6	00								0.5	0.5	0.6	0.7
7	00										0.5	0.6
8	00										0.5	0.5

TABLE 5-18(2): Distance by Vertical Angle From Horizon to Top of Object Beyond Horizon

Distance by Vertical Angle Measured Between Sea Horizon and Top of Object Beyond Sea Horizon
(Similar to *Bowditch* Table 15)   Sheet 3 of 3

Angle		Height of Top of Object Above Sea Level less Height of Eye of Observer (in Feet with Meters Below)										
Deg	Min	500	600	700	800	900	1000	1200	1400	1600	1800	2000
		152	183	213	244	274	305	366	427	488	549	610
0	05	20.8	23.2	25.4	27.5	29.5	31.4	34.8	38.0	41.0	43.8	46.5
0	06	19.8	22.3	24.5	26.6	28.5	30.4	33.8	37.0	40.0	42.8	45.4
0	07	19.0	21.4	23.6	25.6	27.6	29.4	32.9	36.0	39.0	41.8	44.4
0	08	18.2	20.5	22.7	24.7	26.7	28.5	31.9	35.1	38.0	40.8	43.4
0	09	17.4	19.7	21.9	23.9	25.8	27.6	31.0	34.1	37.1	39.8	42.5
0	10	16.7	19.0	21.1	23.1	25.0	26.8	30.1	33.2	36.2	38.9	41.5
0	11	16.0	18.3	20.4	22.3	24.2	26.0	29.3	32.4	35.3	38.0	40.6
0	12	15.4	17.6	19.6	21.6	23.4	25.2	28.5	31.5	34.4	37.1	39.7
0	13	14.8	16.9	19.0	20.9	22.7	24.4	27.7	30.7	33.6	36.3	38.8
0	14	14.2	16.3	18.3	20.2	22.0	23.7	26.9	29.9	32.8	35.4	38.0
0	15	13.7	15.8	17.7	19.6	21.3	23.0	26.2	29.2	32.0	34.6	37.2
0	17	12.7	14.7	16.6	18.4	20.1	21.7	24.8	27.8	30.5	33.1	35.6
0	20	11.4	13.3	15.1	16.8	18.4	20.0	23.0	25.8	28.4	31.0	33.4
0	25	9.7	11.4	13.0	14.6	16.1	17.5	20.3	22.9	25.4	27.8	30.1
0	30	8.4	9.9	11.4	12.8	14.2	15.5	18.1	20.5	22.9	25.2	27.4
0	35	7.4	8.8	10.1	11.4	12.6	13.9	16.3	18.5	20.7	22.9	24.9
0	40	6.6	7.8	9.0	10.2	11.4	12.5	14.7	16.9	18.9	20.9	22.9
0	45	6.0	7.1	8.2	9.3	10.3	11.4	13.4	15.4	17.3	19.2	21.1
0	50	5.4	6.4	7.5	8.5	9.4	10.4	12.3	14.2	16.0	17.7	19.5
0	55	5.0	5.9	6.8	7.8	8.7	9.6	11.4	13.1	14.8	16.5	18.1
1	00	4.6	5.5	6.3	7.2	8.0	8.9	10.5	12.2	13.8	15.3	16.9
1	10	3.9	4.7	5.5	6.2	7.0	7.7	9.2	10.6	12.1	13.5	14.9
1	20	3.5	4.2	4.8	5.5	6.2	6.8	8.1	9.4	10.7	12.0	13.2
1	30	3.1	3.7	4.3	4.9	5.5	6.1	7.3	8.5	9.6	10.8	11.9
1	40	2.8	3.3	3.9	4.4	5.0	5.5	6.6	7.7	8.7	9.8	10.8
1	50	2.5	3.0	3.6	4.1	4.5	5.0	6.0	7.0	8.0	9.0	9.9
2	00	2.3	2.8	3.3	3.7	4.2	4.6	5.5	6.5	7.4	8.2	9.1
2	30	1.9	2.2	2.6	3.0	3.4	3.7	4.5	5.2	5.9	6.7	7.4
3	00	1.6	1.9	2.2	2.5	2.8	3.1	3.7	4.4	5.0	5.6	6.2
3	30	1.3	1.6	1.9	2.1	2.4	2.7	3.2	3.7	4.3	4.8	5.3
4	00	1.2	1.4	1.6	1.9	2.1	2.3	2.8	3.3	3.7	4.2	4.7
5	00	0.9	1.1	1.3	1.5	1.7	1.9	2.3	2.6	3.0	3.4	3.7
6	00	0.8	0.9	1.1	1.3	1.4	1.6	1.9	2.2	2.5	2.8	3.1
7	00	0.7	0.8	0.9	1.1	1.2	1.3	1.6	1.9	2.1	2.4	2.7
8	00	0.6	0.7	0.8	0.9	1.1	1.2	1.4	1.6	1.9	2.1	2.3
10	00	0.5	0.6	0.7	0.7	0.8	0.9	1.1	1.3	1.5	1.7	1.9
12	00		0.5	0.5	0.6	0.7	0.8	0.9	1.1	1.2	1.4	1.5
15	00				0.5	0.6	0.6	0.7	0.9	1.0	1.1	1.2
20	00							0.5	0.6	0.7	0.8	0.9
25	00								0.5	0.6	0.6	0.7
30	00									0.5	0.5	0.6

TABLE 5-18(3): Distance by Vertical Angle From Horizon to Top of Object Beyond Horizon

Height of Eye		Distance to Horizon			Height of Eye		Distance to Horizon		
Feet	Meters	Nautical Miles	Statute Miles	Kilometers	Feet	Meters	Nautical Miles	Statute Miles	Kilometers
1	0.3	1.2	1.3	2.2	86	26.2	10.8	12.5	20.1
2	0.6	1.7	1.9	3.1	90	27.4	11.1	12.8	20.5
3	0.9	2.0	2.3	3.7	96	29.3	11.5	13.2	21.2
4	1.2	2.3	2.7	4.3	100	30.5	11.7	13.5	21.6
5	1.5	2.6	3.0	4.8	107	32.6	12.1	13.9	22.4
6	1.8	2.9	3.3	5.3	113	34.4	12.4	14.3	23.0
7	2.1	3.1	3.6	5.7	120	36.6	12.8	14.7	23.7
8	2.4	3.3	3.8	6.1	126	38.4	13.1	15.1	24.3
9	2.7	3.5	4.0	6.5	134	40.8	13.5	15.6	25.1
10	3.0	3.7	4.3	6.8	140	43	13.8	15.9	25.6
11	3.4	3.9	4.5	7.2	150	46	14.3	16.5	26.5
12	3.7	4.0	4.7	7.5	160	49	14.8	17.0	27.4
13	4.0	4.2	4.9	7.8	170	52	15.2	17.5	28.2
14	4.3	4.4	5.0	8.1	180	55	15.7	18.0	29.0
15	4.6	4.5	5.2	8.4	190	58	16.1	18.5	29.8
16	4.9	4.7	5.4	8.7	200	61	16.5	19.0	30.6
17	5.2	4.8	5.5	8.9	210	64	16.9	19.5	31.4
18	5.5	5.0	5.7	9.2	220	67	17.3	20.0	32.1
19	5.8	5.1	5.9	9.4	230	70	17.7	20.4	32.8
20	6.1	5.2	6.0	9.7	250	76	18.5	21.3	34.2
21	6.4	5.4	6.2	9.9	260	79	18.8	21.7	34.9
22	6.7	5.5	6.3	10.2	280	85	19.6	22.5	36.2
24	7.3	5.7	6.6	10.6	290	88	19.9	22.9	36.9
25	7.6	5.8	6.7	10.8	310	94	20.6	23.7	38.1
26	7.9	6.0	6.9	11.0	330	101	21.2	24.4	39.3
28	8.5	6.2	7.1	11.5	350	107	21.9	25.2	40.5
30	9.1	6.4	7.4	11.9	370	113	22.5	25.9	41.6
31	9.4	6.5	7.5	12.1	390	119	23.1	26.6	42.8
33	10.1	6.7	7.7	12.4	410	125	23.7	27.2	43.8
35	10.7	6.9	8.0	12.8	430	131	24.2	27.9	44.9
37	11.3	7.1	8.2	13.2	460	140	25.1	28.9	46.4
39	11.9	7.3	8.4	13.5	480	146	25.6	29.5	47.4
41	12.5	7.5	8.6	13.9	510	155	26.4	30.4	48.9
44	13.4	7.8	8.9	14.4	540	165	27.2	31.3	50.3
46	14.0	7.9	9.1	14.7	570	174	27.9	32.1	51.7
49	14.9	8.2	9.4	15.2	600	183	28.6	33.0	53.0
52	15.8	8.4	9.7	15.6	640	195	29.6	34.0	54.8
55	16.8	8.7	10.0	16.1	680	207	30.5	35.1	56.5
58	17.7	8.9	10.2	16.5	720	219	31.4	36.1	58.1
61	18.6	9.1	10.5	16.9	760	232	32.2	37.1	59.7
65	19.8	9.4	10.8	17.5	800	244	33.1	38.0	61.2
68	20.7	9.6	11.1	17.9	850	259	34.1	39.2	63.1
72	21.9	9.9	11.4	18.4	890	271	34.9	40.1	64.6
76	23.2	10.2	11.7	18.9	950	290	36.0	41.5	66.7
81	24.7	10.5	12.1	19.5	1000	305	37.0	42.5	68.5

TABLE 5-19: Distance to Natural Horizon

Distance Object or Light Can Be Seen Over Horizon 1 of 2											
Height of Object or Light	**Height of Eye (Feet / Meters)**										
	7	10	13	16	20	23	26	30	33	36	39
	2	3	4	5	6	7	8	9	10	11	12
Ft **M**	**Nautical Miles**										
3 1	5.1	5.7	6.2	6.7	7.3	7.6	8.0	8.4	8.7	9.0	9.3
7 2	6.2	6.8	7.3	7.8	8.3	8.7	9.1	9.5	9.8	10.1	10.4
10 3	6.8	7.4	7.9	8.4	8.9	9.3	9.7	10.1	10.4	10.7	11.0
13 4	7.3	7.9	8.4	8.9	9.5	9.8	10.2	10.6	10.9	11.2	11.5
16 5	7.8	8.4	8.9	9.4	9.9	10.3	10.6	11.1	11.4	11.7	12.0
20 6	8.3	8.9	9.5	9.9	10.5	10.8	11.2	11.6	12.0	12.3	12.5
23 7	8.7	9.3	9.8	10.3	10.8	11.2	11.6	12.0	12.3	12.6	12.9
26 8	9.1	9.7	10.2	10.6	11.2	11.6	11.9	12.4	12.7	13.0	13.3
30 9	9.5	10.1	10.6	11.1	11.6	12.0	12.4	12.8	13.1	13.4	13.7
33 10	9.8	10.4	10.9	11.4	12.0	12.3	12.7	13.1	13.4	13.7	14.0
36 11	10.1	10.7	11.2	11.7	12.3	12.6	13.0	13.4	13.7	14.0	14.3
39 12	10.4	11.0	11.5	12.0	12.5	12.9	13.3	13.7	14.0	14.3	14.6
43 13	10.8	11.4	11.9	12.4	12.9	13.3	13.6	14.1	14.4	14.7	15.0
46 14	11.0	11.6	12.2	12.6	13.2	13.5	13.9	14.3	14.7	15.0	15.2
49 15	11.3	11.9	12.4	12.9	13.4	13.8	14.2	14.6	14.9	15.2	15.5
52 16	11.5	12.1	12.7	13.1	13.7	14.0	14.4	14.8	15.2	15.5	15.7
59 18	12.1	12.7	13.2	13.7	14.2	14.6	15.0	15.4	15.7	16.0	16.3
66 20	12.6	13.2	13.7	14.2	14.7	15.1	15.5	15.9	16.2	16.5	16.8
72 22	13.0	13.6	14.1	14.6	15.2	15.5	15.9	16.3	16.6	16.9	17.2
79 24	13.5	14.1	14.6	15.1	15.6	16.0	16.4	16.8	17.1	17.4	17.7
85 26	13.9	14.5	15.0	15.5	16.0	16.4	16.8	17.2	17.5	17.8	18.1
92 28	14.3	14.9	15.4	15.9	16.5	16.8	17.2	17.6	17.9	18.2	18.5
98 30	14.7	15.3	15.8	16.3	16.8	17.2	17.5	18.0	18.3	18.6	18.9
108 33	15.3	15.9	16.4	16.8	17.4	17.8	18.1	18.6	18.9	19.2	19.5
121 37	16.0	16.6	17.1	17.5	18.1	18.5	18.8	19.3	19.6	19.9	20.2
135 41	16.7	17.3	17.8	18.3	18.9	19.2	19.6	20.0	20.3	20.6	20.9
151 46	17.5	18.1	18.6	19.1	19.6	20.0	20.4	20.8	21.1	21.4	21.7
167 51	18.2	18.8	19.3	19.8	20.4	20.7	21.1	21.5	21.8	22.1	22.4
184 56	19.0	19.6	20.1	20.6	21.1	21.5	21.8	22.3	22.6	22.9	23.2
203 62	19.8	20.4	20.9	21.3	21.9	22.3	22.6	23.1	23.4	23.7	24.0
226 69	20.7	21.3	21.8	22.3	22.8	23.2	23.6	24.0	24.3	24.6	24.9
253 77	21.7	22.3	22.8	23.3	23.8	24.2	24.6	25.0	25.3	25.6	25.9
279 85	22.6	23.2	23.8	24.2	24.8	25.2	25.5	26.0	26.3	26.6	26.8
312 95	23.8	24.4	24.9	25.3	25.9	26.3	26.6	27.1	27.4	27.7	28.0
344 105	24.8	25.4	25.9	26.4	26.9	27.3	27.7	28.1	28.4	28.7	29.0
384 117	26.0	26.6	27.1	27.6	28.2	28.5	28.9	29.3	29.6	29.9	30.2
427 130	27.3	27.9	28.4	28.9	29.4	29.8	30.1	30.6	30.9	31.2	31.5
472 144	28.5	29.1	29.6	30.1	30.7	31.0	31.4	31.8	32.1	32.4	32.7
525 160	29.9	30.5	31.0	31.5	32.0	32.4	32.8	33.2	33.5	33.8	34.1
584 178	31.4	32.0	32.5	33.0	33.5	33.9	34.2	34.7	35.0	35.3	35.6
646 197	32.8	33.4	34.0	34.4	35.0	35.3	35.7	36.1	36.5	36.8	37.0
719 219	34.5	35.1	35.6	36.1	36.6	37.0	37.3	37.8	38.1	38.4	38.7
797 243	36.1	36.7	37.2	37.7	38.3	38.6	39.0	39.4	39.8	40.1	40.3
886 270	37.9	38.5	39.0	39.5	40.1	40.4	40.8	41.2	41.5	41.8	42.1
984 300	39.8	40.4	40.9	41.4	41.9	42.3	42.7	43.1	43.4	43.7	44.0

TABLE 5-20(1): Distance Object Can Be Seen Over Horizon

Distance Object or Light Can Be Seen Over Horizon 2 of 2												
Height of Object or Light		Height of Eye (Feet / Meters)										
		46 / 14	52 / 16	59 / 18	66 / 20	72 / 22	79 / 24	85 / 26	92 / 28	98 / 30	105 / 32	115 / 35
Ft	M	Nautical Miles										
3	1	10.0	10.5	11.0	11.5	12.0	12.4	12.8	13.2	13.6	14.0	14.6
7	2	11.0	11.5	12.1	12.6	13.0	13.5	13.9	14.3	14.7	15.1	15.6
10	3	11.6	12.1	12.7	13.2	13.6	14.1	14.5	14.9	15.3	15.7	16.2
13	4	12.2	12.7	13.2	13.7	14.1	14.6	15.0	15.4	15.8	16.2	16.8
16	5	12.6	13.1	13.7	14.2	14.6	15.1	15.5	15.9	16.3	16.7	17.2
20	6	13.2	13.7	14.2	14.7	15.2	15.6	16.0	16.5	16.8	17.2	17.8
23	7	13.5	14.0	14.6	15.1	15.5	16.0	16.4	16.8	17.2	17.6	18.2
26	8	13.9	14.4	15.0	15.5	15.9	16.4	16.8	17.2	17.5	18.0	18.5
30	9	14.3	14.8	15.4	15.9	16.3	16.8	17.2	17.6	18.0	18.4	19.0
33	10	14.7	15.2	15.7	16.2	16.6	17.1	17.5	17.9	18.3	18.7	19.3
36	11	15.0	15.5	16.0	16.5	16.9	17.4	17.8	18.2	18.6	19.0	19.6
39	12	15.2	15.7	16.3	16.8	17.2	17.7	18.1	18.5	18.9	19.3	19.9
43	13	15.6	16.1	16.7	17.2	17.6	18.1	18.5	18.9	19.3	19.7	20.2
46	14	15.9	16.4	16.9	17.4	17.9	18.3	18.7	19.2	19.5	19.9	20.5
49	15	16.1	16.6	17.2	17.7	18.1	18.6	19.0	19.4	19.8	20.2	20.7
52	16	16.4	16.9	17.4	17.9	18.4	18.8	19.2	19.7	20.0	20.4	21.0
59	18	16.9	17.4	18.0	18.5	18.9	19.4	19.8	20.2	20.6	21.0	21.5
66	20	17.4	17.9	18.5	19.0	19.4	19.9	20.3	20.7	21.1	21.5	22.1
72	22	17.9	18.4	18.9	19.4	19.9	20.3	20.7	21.2	21.5	21.9	22.5
79	24	18.3	18.8	19.4	19.9	20.3	20.8	21.2	21.6	22.0	22.4	22.9
85	26	18.7	19.2	19.8	20.3	20.7	21.2	21.6	22.0	22.4	22.8	23.3
92	28	19.2	19.7	20.2	20.7	21.2	21.6	22.0	22.4	22.8	23.2	23.8
98	30	19.5	20.0	20.6	21.1	21.5	22.0	22.4	22.8	23.2	23.6	24.1
108	33	20.1	20.6	21.1	21.7	22.1	22.6	22.9	23.4	23.7	24.1	24.7
121	37	20.8	21.3	21.9	22.4	22.8	23.3	23.7	24.1	24.5	24.9	25.4
135	41	21.5	22.0	22.6	23.1	23.5	24.0	24.4	24.8	25.2	25.6	26.1
151	46	22.3	22.8	23.4	23.9	24.3	24.8	25.2	25.6	26.0	26.4	26.9
167	51	23.1	23.6	24.1	24.6	25.0	25.5	25.9	26.3	26.7	27.1	27.7
184	56	23.8	24.3	24.9	25.4	25.8	26.3	26.7	27.1	27.5	27.9	28.4
203	62	24.6	25.1	25.7	26.2	26.6	27.1	27.5	27.9	28.3	28.7	29.2
226	69	25.5	26.0	26.6	27.1	27.5	28.0	28.4	28.8	29.2	29.6	30.1
253	77	26.5	27.0	27.6	28.1	28.5	29.0	29.4	29.8	30.3	30.6	31.2
279	85	27.5	28.0	28.5	29.0	29.5	29.9	30.3	30.8	31.1	31.5	32.1
312	95	28.6	29.1	29.7	30.2	30.6	31.1	31.5	31.9	32.2	32.7	33.2
344	105	29.6	30.1	30.7	31.2	31.6	32.1	32.5	32.9	33.3	33.7	34.2
384	117	30.9	31.4	31.9	32.4	32.9	33.3	33.7	34.1	34.5	34.9	35.5
427	130	32.1	32.6	33.2	33.7	34.1	34.6	35.0	35.4	35.8	36.2	36.7
472	144	33.4	33.9	34.4	34.9	35.3	35.8	36.2	36.6	37.0	37.4	38.0
525	160	34.7	35.2	35.8	36.3	36.7	37.2	37.6	38.0	38.4	38.8	39.4
584	178	36.2	36.7	37.3	37.8	38.2	38.7	39.1	39.5	39.9	40.3	40.8
646	197	38.2	38.7	39.2	39.7	40.1	40.5	41.0	41.3	41.7	41.3	42.3
719	219	39.3	39.8	40.4	40.9	41.3	41.8	42.2	42.6	43.0	43.4	43.9
797	243	41.0	41.5	42.0	42.5	43.0	43.4	43.8	44.3	44.6	45.0	45.6
886	270	42.3	42.8	43.8	44.3	44.8	45.2	45.6	46.0	46.4	46.8	47.4
984	300	44.6	45.1	45.7	46.2	46.6	47.1	47.5	47.9	48.3	48.7	49.2

TABLE 5-20(2): Distance Object Can Be Seen Over Horizon

Sine, Cosine, Tangent (1 of 2)						
Sin +	Sin +	Sin -	Sin -	\		
Cos +	Cos -	Cos -	Cos +	\< Function gets this sign		
Tan +	Tan -	Tan +	Tan -	/ (Instructions page 360)		
0°-45°	180°-135°	180°-225°	360°-315°	Sin	Cos	Tan
0	180	180	360	0.000	1.000	0.000
1	179	181	359	0.017	1.000	0.017
2	178	182	358	0.035	0.999	0.035
3	177	183	357	0.052	0.999	0.052
4	176	184	356	0.070	0.998	0.070
5	175	185	355	0.087	0.996	0.087
6	174	186	354	0.105	0.995	0.105
7	173	187	353	0.122	0.993	0.123
8	172	188	352	0.139	0.990	0.141
9	171	189	351	0.156	0.988	0.158
10	170	190	350	0.174	0.985	0.176
11	169	191	349	0.191	0.982	0.194
12	168	192	348	0.208	0.978	0.213
13	167	193	347	0.225	0.974	0.231
14	166	194	346	0.242	0.970	0.249
15	165	195	345	0.259	0.966	0.268
16	164	196	344	0.276	0.961	0.287
17	163	197	343	0.292	0.956	0.306
18	162	198	342	0.309	0.951	0.325
19	161	199	341	0.326	0.946	0.344
20	160	200	340	0.342	0.940	0.364
21	159	201	339	0.358	0.934	0.384
22	158	202	338	0.375	0.927	0.404
23	157	203	337	0.391	0.921	0.424
24	156	204	336	0.407	0.914	0.445
25	155	205	335	0.423	0.906	0.466
26	154	206	334	0.438	0.899	0.488
27	153	207	333	0.454	0.891	0.510
28	152	208	332	0.469	0.883	0.532
29	151	209	331	0.485	0.875	0.554
30	150	210	330	0.500	0.866	0.577
31	149	211	329	0.515	0.857	0.601
32	148	212	328	0.530	0.848	0.625
33	147	213	327	0.545	0.839	0.649
34	146	214	326	0.559	0.829	0.675
35	145	215	325	0.574	0.819	0.700
36	144	216	324	0.588	0.809	0.727
37	143	217	323	0.602	0.799	0.754
38	142	218	322	0.616	0.788	0.781
39	141	219	321	0.629	0.777	0.810
40	140	220	320	0.643	0.766	0.839
41	139	221	319	0.656	0.755	0.869
42	138	222	318	0.669	0.743	0.900
43	137	223	317	0.682	0.731	0.933
44	136	224	316	0.695	0.719	0.966
45	135	225	315	0.707	0.707	1.000

TABLE 5-21(1): Trigonometric Functions. See Instructions on page 360

Sine, Cosine, Tangent (2 of 2)						
Sin + Cos + Tan +	Sin + Cos - Tan -	Sin - Cos - Tan +	Sin - Cos + Tan -	< Function gets this sign (Instructions page 360)		
45°-90°	135°-90°	225°-270°	315°-270°	Sin	Cos	Tan
45	135	225	315	0.707	0.707	1.000
46	134	226	314	0.719	0.695	1.036
47	133	227	313	0.731	0.682	1.072
48	132	228	312	0.743	0.669	1.111
49	131	229	311	0.755	0.656	1.150
50	130	230	310	0.766	0.643	1.192
51	129	231	309	0.777	0.629	1.235
52	128	232	308	0.788	0.616	1.280
53	127	233	307	0.799	0.602	1.327
54	126	234	306	0.809	0.588	1.376
55	125	235	305	0.819	0.574	1.428
56	124	236	304	0.829	0.559	1.483
57	123	237	303	0.839	0.545	1.540
58	122	238	302	0.848	0.530	1.600
59	121	239	301	0.857	0.515	1.664
60	120	240	300	0.866	0.500	1.732
61	119	241	299	0.875	0.485	1.804
62	118	242	298	0.883	0.469	1.881
63	117	243	297	0.891	0.454	1.963
64	116	244	296	0.899	0.438	2.050
65	115	245	295	0.906	0.423	2.145
66	114	246	294	0.914	0.407	2.246
67	113	247	293	0.921	0.391	2.356
68	112	248	292	0.927	0.375	2.475
69	111	249	291	0.934	0.358	2.605
70	110	250	290	0.940	0.342	2.747
71	109	251	289	0.946	0.326	2.904
72	108	252	288	0.951	0.309	3.078
73	107	253	287	0.956	0.292	3.271
74	106	254	286	0.961	0.276	3.487
75	105	255	285	0.966	0.259	3.732
76	104	256	284	0.970	0.242	4.011
77	103	257	283	0.974	0.225	4.331
78	102	258	282	0.978	0.208	4.705
79	101	259	281	0.982	0.191	5.145
80	100	260	280	0.985	0.174	5.671
81	99	261	279	0.988	0.156	6.314
82	98	262	278	0.990	0.139	7.115
83	97	263	277	0.993	0.122	8.144
84	96	264	276	0.995	0.105	9.514
85	95	265	275	0.996	0.087	11.430
86	94	266	274	0.998	0.070	14.300
87	93	267	273	0.999	0.052	19.081
88	92	268	272	0.999	0.035	28.635
89	91	269	271	1.000	0.017	57.286
90	90	270	270	1.000	0.000	

TABLE 5-21(2): Trigonometric Functions. See Instructions on page 360

Trigonometric Table instructions

Table 5-21 on page 358 gives the sine, cosine, and tangent for angles through 360 degrees. Enter the table in one of the first four columns to find angle you are looking for then read across to the right to find the sine, cosine, or tangent. The sign (+ or −) for the answer is read from the top of the column in which the angle was found.

For example say you wanted to find the cosine of 202 degrees. 202 degrees is found in the third column and reading across yields 0.927 for the cosine. Moving to the top of the third column you find the sign for a cosine is "−" so the final answer is cosine(202°) = −0.927

DISTANCES BETWEEN PORTS

Comments regarding the distance tables:

*   Great Lakes and Mississippi distances are taken from NOAA publication Distances Between United States Ports, for ports listed therein. This publication is available for free download at the NOAA website mentioned earlier. For ports not listed, distances are scaled from charts.

*   The Atlantic and Pacific Coast tables show distances staying close to shore and generally from port to port similar to how a recreational boater might travel. For this reason total distance for a long run, such as from Cape Flattery Washington to Panama, is greater than the distance found in the NOAA or NIMA Publications.

*   In the Caribbean, distances along the Windward Isles follow along the islands. Distances along the North coast of South America tend to follow the coastline. Distances across the Caribbean are approximate shortest distances. Most Caribbean distances are scaled from charts.

*   Distances for the Atlantic Ocean, the Pacific Ocean, the Indian Ocean, and the Mediterranean Sea are taken from NIMA Pub 151 Distances between Ports, for ports listed therein. For ports not listed, distances are scaled on charts from the nearest listed ports. Publication 161 is available for free download at the NIMA website mentioned earlier in this chapter.

	Montreal QC	Ogdensburg NY	Thousand Isles NY	Kingston ON	Trenton ON	Toronto ON	Oswego NY	Rochester NY	Port Colbourne ON	Buffalo NY	Erie PA	Cleveland OH	Toledo OH	Detroit MI	Port Severn ON	Bay City MI	Chicago IL	Milwaukee WI	Green Bay WI	Sault Ste Marie MI	Houghton MI	Duluth MN
Thunder Bay On	1217	1094	1052	1032	925	903	1016	977	965	848	795	658	604	505			621	560			116	195
Duluth MN	1339	1216	1174	1154	1099	1025	1138	1087	970	917	987	834	780	726	627	808	743	682	560	394	179	
Houghton MI	1165	1042	1000	980		925	851	964	913	796	743	796	660	606	552	453	570	509	221	273		
Sault St Marie MI	944	821	779	759				703	630	743	692	575	522	575	385	331	232	349	288			
Green Bay WI	1120	997	955	935				806	919	868	751	698	751	561	507	407	255	180				
Milwaukee WI	1181	1058	1016	941					980	929	812	759	676	622	513	452	85					
Chicago IL	1246	1123	1081	1061						932	877	824	741	687	568	534						
Bay City MI	837	714	672	652				521	583	466	415	332	278	224	265							
Port Severn ON	941	818	776	756					627	689	572	517	380	326								
Detroit MI	613	490	448	373		412			299	261		108	54									
Toledo OH	606	483	441	366		405		354		261	191	96										
Cleveland OH	529	406	364	328		292	237	176	160	102	54											
Erie PA	434	311	269	249		215	182	120	65	78												
Buffalo NY	391	268	226	206		120	139	77	22													
Port Colbourne ON	369	246	204	184		55	168	117														
Rochester NY	271	148	106	86		95	59															
Oswego NY	232	109	67	47		145																
Toronto ON	342	219	177	157	98																	
Trenton ON	258	135	93	73																		
Kingston ON	185	62	20																			
Thousand Isles NY	165	43																				
Ogdensburg NY	123																					

Most distances are from *NOAA Distances Between U.S. Ports.* Some distances are scaled from charts.

TABLE 5-22: *Distances Between Ports. Great Lakes (statute miles).*

	Montreal QC	Ogdensburg NY	Thousand Isles NY	Kingston ON	Trenton ON	Toronto ON	Oswego NY	Rochester NY	Port Colbourne ON	Buffalo NY	Erie PA	Cleveland OH	Toledo OH	Detroit MI	Port Severn ON	Bay City MI	Chicago IL	Milwaukee WI	Green Bay WI	Sault St Marie MI	Houghton MI	Duluth MN
Thunder Bay On	1959	1761	1693	1661	1572	1453	1635	1553	1365	1392	1279	1146	972	813	1059	1064	1104	999	901	439	187	314
Duluth MN	2155	1957	1889	1857	1769	1650	1831	1749	1561	1588	1476	1342	1168	1009	1255	1260	1300	1196	1098	634	288	
Houghton MI	1875	1677	1609	1577	1489	1370	1551	1469	1281	1196	1062	888	729	620	916	975	1022	917	819	356		
Sault St Marie MI	1519	1321	1254	1221	1133	1014	1196	1114	925	953	840	707	533	373	560	619	666	562	463			
Green Bay WI	1802	1605	1505	1416	1327	1322	1479	1397	1209	1236	1123	990	816	655	500	470	410	290				
Milwaukee WI	1901	1703	1603	1514	1425	1420	1577	1495	1307	1334	1221	1088	914	753	598	525	137					
Chicago IL	2005	1807	1740	1708	1619	1500	1682	1411	1439	1326	1193	1019	859	430	650	426						
Bay City MI	1347	1149	1081	1049	958	838	1020	899	750	781	668	534	360	287	612							
Port Severn ON	1514	1316	1249	1217	1128	1009	1191	1020	938	945	832	698	570	525								
Detroit MI	987	789	721	689	600	481	663	581	393	420	307	164	87									
Toledo OH	975	777	710	678	589	470	652	570	381	409	298	154										
Cleveland OH	851	653	586	554	465	346	528	446	257	283	164											
Erie PA	698	501	433	401	312	193	375	293	105	126												
Buffalo NY	629	431	364	332	243	124	306	224	35													
Port Colbourne ON	594	396	328	296	208	89	270	188														
Rochester NY	436	238	171	138	106	153	95															
Oswego NY	373	175	108	76	135	233																
Toronto ON	550	352	287	253	158																	
Trenton ON	415	217	150	117																		
Kingston ON	298	100	32																			
Thousand Isles NY	266	69																				
Ogdensburg NY	198																					

Most distances are from *NOAA Distances Between U.S. Ports*. Some distances are scaled from charts.

TABLE 5-23: Distances Between Ports. Great Lakes (kilometres).

	Head of Passes	New Orleans	Baton Rouge	Natchez	Memphis	JN OH/MS	Mobile	Pickwick Landg	Chattanooga	Knoxville	Paducah	Cincinnati	Pittsburgh	Cape Girardeau	St Louis	JN MO/MS	Kansas City	Omaha	JN IL/MS	Peoria	Chicago (Lake)	Dubuque
Minneapolis MN	1807	1712	1578	1444	1073	853	1558	1106	1363	1547	899	1362	1834	801	673	658	1021	1273	635	793	968	273
Dubuque IA	1534	1439	1305	1171	800	580	1285	833	1090	1274	626	1089	1561	528	400	385	748	1000	362	520	695	
Chicago (Lake) IL	1505	1410	1276	1142	771	551	1256	804	1061	1245	597	1060	1532	499	371	356	719	971	333	175		
Peoria IL	1330	1235	1101	967	596	376	1081	629	886	1070	422	885	1357	324	196	181	544	796	158			
JN IL/MS Rivers	1172	1077	943	809	438	218	923	471	728	912	264	727	1199	166	38	23	386	638				
Omaha NE	1764	1669	1535	1401	1030	810	1515	1063	1320	1504	856	1319	1791	758	630	615	252					
Kansas City MO	1512	1417	1283	1149	778	558	1263	811	1068	1252	604	1067	1539	506	378	363						
JN MO/MS Rivers	1149	1054	920	786	415	195	900	448	705	889	241	704	1176	143	15							
St Louis MO	1134	1039	905	771	400	180	885	433	690	874	226	689	1161	128								
Cape Girardeau MO	1006	911	777	643	272	52	757	305	562	746	98	561	1033									
Pittsburgh PA	1935	1840	1706	1572	1201	981	1594	1142	1399	1583	935	472										
Cincinnati OH	1463	1368	1234	1100	729	509	1122	670	927	1111	463											
Paducah KY	1000	905	771	637	266	46	659	207	464	648												
Knoxville TN	1648	1553	1419	1285	914	694	893	441	184													
Chattanooga TN	1464	1369	1235	1101	730	510	709	257														
Pickwick Landg TN	1207	1112	978	844	473	253	452															
Mobile AL	1659	1564	1430	1296	925	705																
JN OH/MS Rivers	954	859	725	591	220																	
Memphis TN	734	639	505	371																		
Natchez MS	363	268	134																			
Baton Rouge LA	229	134																				
New Orleans LA	95																					

Most distances are from *NOAA Distances Between U.S. Ports*. All distances are by river, not shortest distance (e.g. Mobile to New Orleans is not by Gulf or Inland Waterway).

TABLE 5-24: Distances Between Ports. Mississippi River system (statute miles).

	Miami	Nassau	Ft Myers	Stuart	Jacksonville	Savannah	Charleston	Myrtle Beach	Wilmington	Norfolk	Washington	Baltimore	Philadelphia	New York	Boston	Portland	Bangor	Saint John	Halifax	St John's	Charlottetown	Quebec
Montreal QC	2525	2625	2716	2310	2252	2146	2086	2013	1932	1674	1542	1555	1492	1444	1305	1224	1210	1085	1071	1150	693	139
Quebec QC	2386	2577	2668	2171	2113	2007	1947	1874	1793	1535	1403	1416	1353	1305	1162	1085	1071	946	894	1011	554	
Charlottetown PE	1880	2071	2162	1665	1607	1501	1441	1368	1297	1039	907	920	857	799	657	579	565	430	249	698		
St John's NL	2162	2353	2444	1947	1889	1783	1723	1650	1579	1321	1189	1202	1139	1081	939	861	847	712	531			
Halifax NS	1631	1822	1913	1416	1358	1252	1192	1119	1048	790	658	671	608	550	408	330	316	256				
Saint John NB	1577	1768	1859	1362	1304	1198	1138	1065	994	736	604	617	554	496	354	276	195					
Bangor ME	1492	1683	1774	1277	1219	1113	1053	980	909	651	519	532	469	411	269	128						
Portland ME	1382	1573	1664	1167	1109	1003	943	870	799	541	409	422	369	301	111							
Boston MA	1321	1512	1603	1106	1048	942	868	795	738	470	338	417	369	240								
New York NY	1110	1301	1392	895	837	731	657	584	498	259	177	306	212									
Philadelphia PA	1063	1254	1345	848	790	684	610	537	480	369	237	306										
Baltimore MD	1000	1191	1282	785	727	621	547	474	417	177	190											
Washington DC	1013	1204	1295	798	740	634	560	481	430	298												
Norfolk VA	881	1072	1163	666	608	502	428	349	223													
Wilmington NC	602	793	884	387	329	223	149	89														
Myrtle Beach SC	542	733	594	327	269	163	88															
Charleston SC	467	658	519	252	194	94																
Savannah GA	409	600	461	194	136																	
Jacksonville FL	311	502	333	235																		
Stuart FL	285	448	128																			
Ft Myers FL	222	364																				
Nassau Bahamas	191																					

Distances follow close to coast from port to port, and are not shortest distances. Via Cabot Strait Via Cape Cod Canal. Most distances scaled from charts.

TABLE 5-25: Distances Between Ports. Atlantic Coast North America (nautical miles).

	Panama City	Cancun	Cayman Islands	Jamaica	Aruba	Curacao	Bonaire	Maracaibo	Caracas	Trinidad	Grenada	St. Vincent	Barbadoes	Martinique	Guadeloupe	Antigua	St Kitts	Tortola	St Thomas	Puerto Rico	Havana	Nassau
Miami Florida	1257	498	605	797	1179	1069	1224	1294	1334	1364	1209	1456	1301	1405	1250	1396	1241	1051	1026	960	225	176
Nassau Bahamas	1191	605	774	667	1139	1179	1289	1334	1391	1427	1352	1521	1301	1405	1250	1391	1241	1073	1048	982	322	
Havana Cuba	1039	280	449	752	970	581	489	721	793	561	544	472	550	430	262	211	156	995	970	805		
San Juan Puerto Rico	1047	1252	670	583	561	511	489	721	793	561	544	472	478	358	262	211	156	97	72			
St Thomas USVI	1086	1291	709	581	536	514	489	746	514	489	453	478	333	262	126	75	65	25				
Tortola BVI	1111	1316	734	606	536	514	489	746	514	489	453	478	333	211	126	75	20					
Basseterre St Kitts	1231	1447	865	496	474	460	566	706	460	366	332	297	212	177	116	65						
St. John's Antiqua	1262	1502	920	527	568	527	505	737	505	331	298	263	177	116	81							
Basse-Terre Guadeloupe	1233	1516	934	498	568	476	505	708	476	344	263	182	122	96								
Fort-de-France Martinique	1256	1539	957	521	582	521	460	731	423	260	166	168	132									
Bridgetown Barbadoes	1357	1557	1077	957	622	600	832	478	284	190	122	122										
Kingstown St. Vincent	1247	1548	1227	966	512	490	722	368	174	122	80											
St George's Grenada	1205	1557	1236	975	470	448	680	326	174	100												
Port of Spain Trinidad	1223	1609	1288	1027	558	466	698	378	344													
Caracas Venezuela	903	1289	968	707	268	216	168	378														
Maracaibo Venezuela	811	1197	876	615	146	146	216															
Krajendjik Bonaire	781	1167	846	585	116	46																
Willemstad Curacao	741	1057	806	545	76																	
Oranjestad Aruba	671	1057	736	475																		
Kingston Jamaica	597	630	309																			
Georgetown Cayman Islands	653	327																				
Cancun Cancun	864																					

Distances are scaled from charts. Distances are not shortest distance and tend to follow coastlines and the Windward Isles.

TABLE 5-26: Distances Between Ports. Caribbean (nautical miles).

	Panama City Panama	Havana Cuba	Georgetown Cayman	Cancun Mexico	Brownsville TX	Corpus Christi TX	Freeport TX	Houston TX	Galveston TX	Port Arthur LA	Lake Charles LA	New Orleans LA	Gulfport MS	Mobile AL	Pensacola FL	Panama City FL	Port St Joe FL	Tampa FL	St Petersburg FL	Fort Myers FL	Stuart FL	Key West FL
Miami FL	1257	225	498	1017	1031	967	970	926	940	748	695	605	593	443	374							151
Key West FL	1107	102	356	880	880	816	819	775	789	597	544	454	442	292							223	
Fort Myers FL	1198	223	433	792	847	838	816	769	739	511	435	316	303	122					128			
Stuart FL via Okeechobee	1326	351	561	975	966	897	897	859	867	639	563	444	431							250		
St Petersburg FL	1239	290	462	813	797	729	733	690	697	459	401	252	240					18				
Tampa FL	1252	299	475	826	810	742	746	703	710	472	413	265					252					
Port St Joe FL	1334	440	526	695	671	604	605	562	568	308	235					42						
Panama City FL	1356	467	545	684	659	593	593	550	545	295	206				139							
Pensacola FL	1382	520	557	643	618	552	553	509	517	253				89								
Mobile AL	1441	556	577	629	605	538	539	496	504	236			98									
Gulfport MS	1432	573	568	632	607	540	542	493	491			238										
New Orleans LA	1448	612	584	599	574	508	510	471			298											
Lake Charles LA	1521	745	657	387	347	166	172	128		83												
Port Arthur TX	1508	750	644	347	249	126	132		89													
Galveston TX	1526	773	662	304	207	84		47														
Houston TX	1573	820	709	348	250		127															
Freeport TX	1529	790	665	258		160																
Corpus Christi TX	1582	872	1022	718	154																	
Brownsville TX	1538	851	986	674																		
Cancun Mexico	867	280	327																			
Georgetown Cayman	653	449																				
Havana Cuba	1039																					

Distances between U.S. Ports from NOAA *Distances Between U.S. Ports*. Distances to foreign ports scaled from charts.

TABLE 5-27: Distances Between Ports. Gulf of Mexico (nautical miles).

	Panama City	Puntarenas	Acapulco	Puerto Vallarta	Mazatlan	Guaymas	La Paz	Cabo San Lucas	Ensenada	San Diego	Los Angeles	San Fransisco	Eureka	Portland	Seattle	Bellingham	Victoria	Vancouver	Campbell River	Port Hardy	Prince Rupert	Juneau
Anchorage AK	4893	5634	3468	3086	2908	2530	2686	2785	3130	3086	2861	2479	2125	2748	1895	1661	1592	1554	1457	1348	1079	741
Juneau AK	4555	5226	3130	2748	2570	2192	2348	2447	2790	2752	2521	2139	1384	1592	1154	920	851	813	716	607	338	
Prince Rupert BC	4286	4855	3118	2861	2748	2374	2265	2479	2447	1786	1517	1363	1046	1254	816	582	513	475	378	269		
Port Hardy BC	4177	4869	2752	2370	2412	2521	2790	2178	1517	1290	1254	1199	777	985	547	313	244	206	109			
Campbell River BC	4122	2886	2412	2357	2214	2323	2014	2069	1408	1283	1254	668	877	438	204	135	97					
Vancouver BC	4039	2697	2315	2210	2159	2014	1353	1270	1199	613	530	383	777	383	129	83						
Victoria BC	4147	2614	2232	2127	1931	1378	1283	1116	828	530	300	613	244	135	80							
Bellingham WA	4163	2722	2340	2398	2200	2055	1394	1190	745	408	204	313	129	80								
Seattle WA	3946	2738	2356	2382	2184	2039	1378	1206	989	638	383	438	232									
Portland OR	3526	2521	2139	2181	1838	1983	1274	1190	652	530	436	436										
Eureka CA	3294	2101	1719	1761	1563	1418	757	1200	569	232	232											
San Fransisco CA	2934	1869	1487	1529	1331	1186	525	826	455	371												
Los Angeles CA	2839	2526	1509	1127	1022	971	876	826	165	95												
San Diego CA	2795	2431	1414	1032	1074	1030	971	731	70													
Ensenada Mexico	2738	2387	1370	988	832	1030	876	687														
Cabo San Lucas Mexico	2108	1700	683	301	196	235	145															
La Paz Mexico	2207	1799	782	384	249	343																
Guaymas Mexico	2363	1955	938	547	381																	
Mazatlan Mexico	2006	1598	581	178																		
Puerto Vallarta Mexico	1880	1472	455																			
Acapulco Mexico	1425	1017																				
Puntarenas Costa Rica	474																					

All distances from ports south of Cape Flattery Washington, to ports north, are via the inside passage. Most distances are scaled from charts.

TABLE 5-28: Distances Between Ports. West Coast North America (nautical miles).

	Magellan Strait	Valparaiso	Lima	Panama City	Mazatlan	Los Angeles	San Francisco	Seattle	Vancouver	Anchorage	Honolulu	Suva	Sydney	Auckland	Melbourne	Perth	Cape Gd Hope	Port Said	Bombay	Manila	Hong Kong
Tokyo, Japan	9285	9280	8418	7692	5782	4849	4546	4255	4262	3455	3407	3977	4340	4789	5045	5818	8510	7924	5330	1768	1585
Hong Kong, China	9202	9710	9945	9347	8321	7307	6530	6380	6044	5768	4949	4787	4541	4048	3481	2966	6971	6489	3895	631	
Manila, Philippines	9482	9945	13055	10505	9347	8731	7353	7062	7078	6344	5881	4867	4730	4275	3950	2235	6742	6365	3771		
Singapore, Singapore	12066	12386	13055	12846	11172	10308	7353	5959	5784	5015	4650	4505	4340	3855	2235	5679	5035	2441	1330		
Bombay, India	14626	14977	15615	15540	13766	12902	10308	9503	9794	8785	8322	7886	7088	7033	6157	3998	4554	3046			
Port Said, Suez Canal	12005	14980	12791	12846	13737	13101	12618	12097	11965	11379	11045	10916	9671	9418	7886	6322	5340				
Cape of Good Hope	4262		12791	15305	13737	13103	12388	12634	12113	9519	10916	7618	7033	6157	4767						
Perth, Australia	7022	8353	8514	10994	9426	8792	8856	8872	9273	9045	8322	3805	2242	1690							
Melbourne, Australia	6790	6790	7046	7928	7203	6970	6448	6826	7348	7000	5556	2157	1690								
Sydney, Australia	5459	5247	7415	7674	6766	6448	6170	6810	6455	6175	4420	1738									
Auckland, New Zealand	4814	5759	5995	6516	5719	5658	5719	5162	6810	4942	2242	1149									
Suva, Fiji Islands	4848	5834	5995	5051	6511	6810	5162	4409	4942	2776	1280										
Honolulu, Hawaii	6370	6812	7046	2859	7032	7332	2091	2409	2576	582											
Anchorage, Alaska	7941	5919	5161	3224	2228	1701	1314	1249	796												
Vancouver, British Columbia	6978	5928	5742	2115	1144	812	126														
Seattle, Washington	6964	5919	4776	2099	1128	126															
San Francisco, California	6188	6812	4764	1337	1011																
Los Angeles, California	5871	4808	3989	1350																	
Mazatlan, Mexico	8533	3930	3655	2765																	
Panama City, Panama	3932	2616	1350																		
Lima, Peru	2671	1306																			
Valparaiso, Chile	1432																				

Most distances are from NIMA *Pub. 151 Distances Between Ports.* Some distances are scaled from charts.

TABLE 5-29: Distances Between Ports. Pacific and Indian Oceans (nautical miles).

From \ To	Cape Gd Hope	Gibralter	Lisbon	Calais	Amsterdam	London	Dublin	Belfast	Glasgow	Copenhagen	Stockholm	Oslo	Magellan Strait	Buenos Aires	Rio De Janeiro	Caracas	Panama City	Hamilton	Miami	New York	Boston	Halifax
Montreal, Canada	7134	3405	2708	3014	3162	3094	2587	2675	2603	3183	3267	3095	7527	6455	5268	3204	2885	1413	2050	1516	1309	958
Halifax, Nova Scotia	6507	2998	2500	2874	3038	2958	2870	2587	2675	3222	3241	3267	6799	5737	4660	2328	2050	756	1413	697	380	
Boston, United States	6722	3180	2817	3250	3270	3182	3038	2897	2897	3547	3528	3701	6916	5889	4738	2200	2016	704	1301	240		
New York, United States	6814	3270	2980	3418	3350	3250	3126	3065	3065	3701	3223	3510	6918	5871	4770	1860	1981	697	1090			
Miami, Florida	6685	3967	3604	4115	4047	3889	3764	3720	3764	4437	3510	3701	5810	5211	4110	1151	1257	956				
Hamilton, Bermuda	6169	3102	2693	3038	3182	2962	2895	2897	2895	3720	3223	3547	6287	5531	3572	1327	1702					
Panama Canal Junction	6466	4721	4351	4869	4801	4558	4642	4519	4642	5199	4519	4763	4770	4738	4110	903						
Caracas, Venezuela	5563	4120	3503	4189	4189	4007	4091	4091	4091	4642	4763	5389	3932	4110	3572							
Rio De Janeiro, Brazil	3267	4869	4180	5259	5259	5268	5289	5289	5289	5806	5972	5991	2238	1151								
Buenos Aires, Argentina	3815	5327	5270	6280	6360	6267	6349	6349	6349	6408	6408	7091	1394									
Magellan Strait, Chile	4262	7451	6398	7383	7340	7339	7421	7421	7339	7969	7969	8765										
Oslo, Norway	8087	1864	1901	634	989	1005	1251	650	650	272	683											
Stockholm, Sweden	8580	2066	2318	989	1102	1441	1358	922	965	603												
Copenhagen, Denmark	8163	1649	1630	685	704	941	984	704	683													
Glasgow, Scotland	6192	1371	1112	735	815	735	801	114														
Belfast, N. Ireland	6110	1289	1030	653	733	195	112															
Dublin, Ireland	6022	1201	942	565	645	208																
London, England	6143	1315	1063	92	208																	
Amsterdam, Netherlands	6211	1383	1131	222																		
Calais, France	6067	1239	987																			
Lisbon, Portugal	5152	284																				
Gibraltar, Mediterranean	5082																					

Most distances are from NIMA *Pub. 151 Distances Between Ports.* Some distances are scaled from charts.

TABLE 5-30: Distances Between Ports. Atlantic Ocean (nautical miles).

	Port Said	Alexandria	Haifa	Beirut	Cyprus	Iraklion	Odessa	Istanbul	Athens(Pireas)	Tripoli	Venice	Palermo	Naples	Genoa	Tunis	Cagliari	Nice (Monaco)	Marseille	Palma	Barcelona	Algiers	Valencia
Gibraltar	1943	1679	1822	2034	1953	1516	2169	1821	1451	1093	1691	940	1001	820	750	788	711	534	471	437	403	403
Valencia Spain	1514	1393	1559	1770	1651	1252	1906	1558	1174	831	1428	656	513	512	492	461	432	282	146	165	230	
Algiers Algeria	1600	1482	1645	1602	1703	1584	1834	1486	1022	665	1281	574	531	448	336	379	459	271	189	140		
Barcelona Spain	1555	1435	1596	1648	1529	1130	1784	1446	1091	762	1323	582	559	356	435	336	363	170	140			
Palma Balearic Isles	1518	1398	1576	1627	1529	1133	1794	1446	1049	708	1264	559	531	435	336	336	363	300				
Marseille France	1456	1346	1457	1576	1481	1012	1731	1383	988	745	1220	495	520	204	476	336	116					
Nice (Monaco) France	1255	1136	1333	1576	1457	1218	1627	1279	920	740	1173	520	369	89	465	354						
Cagliari Sardinia	1172	1051	1260	1263	1144	745	1481	1050	738	435	940	221	193	313	169							
Tunis Tunisia	1426	1305	1442	1445	1326	820	1481	1133	680	322	970	369	272	472								
Genoa Italy	1316	1206	1395	1398	1279	981	1639	1291	896	719	872	626	338									
Naples Italy	1116	1005	1194	1198	1079	982	1329	1073	586	516	460	170										
Palermo Sicily	1061	950	1139	1194	1024	681	1050	981	516	460	763											
Venice Italy	1317	1208	1359	1356	1237	872	1073	926	719	931												
Tripoli Libya	998	866	1129	1106	1128	818	940	953	640													
Athens(Pireas) Greece	599	515	650	647	566	175	436	364														
Istanbul Turkey	804	742	849	896	766	436	352															
Odessa Ukraine	1152	1090	1197	1194	1075	793																
Iraklion Crete	455	372	522	526	407																	
Cyprus	297	222	246	112																		
Beirut Lebanon	230	341	76																			
Haifa Israel	171	295																				
Alexandria Egypt	164																					

Most distances are from NIMA *Pub. 151 Distances Between Ports*. Some distances are scaled from charts.

TABLE 5-31: Distances Between Ports. Mediterranean (nautical miles).

6 ROPES, LINES AND KNOTS (MARLINESPIKE SEAMANSHIP)

ROPE AND LINES

ROPE

Rope Construction Materials

Historically, rope was made from naturally occurring materials such as hemp, manila, or flax and was laid in three strands twisted together. Most rope today is made from *nylon*, *polyester*, or *polypropylene*, which produces a product far superior to the ropes made from the natural materials. Other far stronger synthetic ropes, made from materials such as *Kevlar* or *Spectra*, are becoming available.

Nylon rope is the most common in marine applications and is characterized by its superior strength and elasticity (it stretches). Three-strand nylon rope is three times stronger than manila rope and double-braided nylon is about four times stronger (see strength tables at the end of this chapter). For some applications, such as anchoring and mooring, the ability to stretch is a plus, but for other uses such as sheets and halyards, nylon's stretchiness is an undesirable characteristic.

Polyester rope is about as strong as nylon but doesn't stretch nearly as much. It is commonly used for running rigging on sailboats.

Polypropylene rope is about twice the strength of manila and breaks down in sunlight. Its main virtue is that it floats (unlike the other two types), which makes it useful for towing water-skiers or a dinghy (because it won't get tangled in your propeller).

All three of the synthetic materials are highly resistant to rot, which is a major advantage over the natural materials. Table 6-1 on the next page compares these materials.

The newer high tech materials like Spectra are about eight times stronger than manila and are much less elastic than even polyester. This makes them suitable for applications such as standing rigging, where only wire rope would suffice heretofore.

	Nylon	**Polyester**	**Polypropylene**
Tensile strength	Highest	Almost as high as nylon	Lowest
Elasticity	Most elastic	Not elastic	Somewhat
Shock loading	Best	Intermediate	Worst
Abrasion resistance	Best	Good	Good
Weight	Intermediate	Heaviest	Lightest
Buoyancy	Sinks	Sinks	Floats
Sun resistance	Best	Intermediate	Poorest
Rot	Very good	Very good	Very good

TABLE 6-1: Characteristics of Rope Making Materials

Types of Rope

The two basic types of rope construction are either ***three-strand*** or ***braided***.

Three-Strand Rope

Three-strand rope is the traditional type and consists of fibers twisted into yarns, which are twisted into three strands, which in turn are twisted into rope. Figure 6-1 shows construction of three-strand rope.

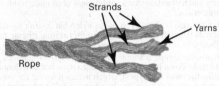

FIGURE 6-1: Three-Strand Rope

Three-strand rope tends to hold knots better, is somewhat more elastic, and is easy to splice.

Braided Rope

Braided rope is (as you might expect) braided instead of twisted and is either single-braided or double-braided. Double-braided rope has a braided outer sheath and an inner braided core. Figure 6-2 shows a typical double-braided rope. Generally, only very small ropes are single-braided.

Braided rope is stronger than three-strand, easier on the hands, and less likely to kink.

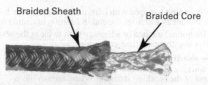

Braided Sheath   Braided Core

FIGURE 6-2: Double-Braided Rope
Compare Three-Strand and Braided Rope

	Three-Strand	**Braided**
Strength	Weaker	Stronger
Elasticity	More	Less
Flexibility	More rigid	More flexible
Wear resistance	Best	Good
Knots	Hold better	Not as good holding
Splicing	Easy	More difficult
Splice to steel cable	Yes	No
Handling	Harder on hands	Easier on hands
Unraveling	Unravels easily	Less easily but still will unravel

TABLE 6-2: Compare Three-Strand and Braided Rope

LINES

> Once a rope is cut and placed into service aboard a vessel, it is no longer a *rope*; instead it is a *line*. One should, almost always, use the term line instead of rope when on or around boats.

Taking Care of Lines

Just because the lines are synthetic, and therefore stronger and more rot-resistant than the natural variety, doesn't mean they don't require care.

Whipping

A *whipping* is a wrapping of twine or tape around the end of a line to prevent the line from unraveling. A cut line must immediately be whipped since it will begin to unravel even as it is being cut. Better yet, whip the line before cutting it.

Electrical or masking tape is quite commonly used for whipping; heat shrink tubing is another good alternative. In addition, the end of synthetic line is usually melted to further prevent fraying. When buying rope at the store, the rope will usually be first wrapped with tape, and then cut with a hot knife that melts and fuses the end in addition to cutting it.

The traditional method of whipping with twine is the best, but it is also the most time-consuming.

Allowable Working Load of Lines

The working load of a line should be no greater than 20 percent of the breaking strength. Where human life is involved, 5 to 10 percent of the breaking strength should be the maximum load.

If a line is stressed to more than 65 or 75 percent of its breaking strength it has been over-stressed and should be removed from service.

Knots can weaken lines by as much as 50 percent and therefore must be taken into account when sizing lines. A good splice can retain up to 90 percent of breaking strength and is therefore the preferred method of permanently joining two lines together. As with knots, the splice must be considered when sizing lines.

Chafing also reduces breaking strength, and care must be taken to guard against it. Chafing gear made specifically for the purpose is available from marine supply stores. Some boaters use garden hose slit along one side to place around the rope at chafe points.

Lines Through Blocks, Sheaves, and Fairleads

Major changes in direction should be by means of blocks (pulleys) and not through fairleads, although small direction changes through fairleads are acceptable. A fairlead is a ring, eye or fitting through which a line is passed to guide it in a required direction. The line should feed straight onto the sheave and not touch the sides of the block. The sheave diameter should be at least eight times the diameter of the line for the three synthetics discussed here. Some newer materials require larger diameter sheaves.

Stowing Lines

Lines should be rinsed with fresh water to remove salt, dirt, and other corrosive or abrasive material. *Do not* wash lines in a washing machine or dry in a dryer.

Lines should be stowed by coiling them and hanging them in a well ventilated place. Leaving lines lying loose on deck is a mark of poor seamanship and can be downright dangerous.

KNOTS

INTRODUCTION

Terminology

When a line is looped back on itself as in figure 6-3, the loop and doubled back portion is termed a *bight*. Some consider a bight to be loop that is open (the free end does not cross back over the standing part).

FIGURE 6-3: Parts of a Line Used In Making Knots

If the line crosses back over itself it is called a *loop*. In most of the reading I've done, loop and bight are used fairly interchangeably.

The *free end* is the end that is unattached and not under tension and that is used in making the knot.

The *working part* is the section of line that actually ends up being part of the knot.

The *standing part* is the part of the rope that is attached to something and usually under tension when in use.

A *turn* is a loop around some object, such as a piling, cleat, or line. A *round turn* is a turn with two loops around the object.

Capsize a knot refers to the changing of the structure of the knot when it is placed under load. Many knots, such as the reef knot, will come undone when capsized.

To *seize* a knot is to bind the free end to the standing part by wrapping it with several turns of twine.

Seven Basic Knots

The seven most basic knots that every skipper and deckhand should know are as follows:

1. Cleat hitch (on page 382)
2. Figure 8 knot (on page 376)
3. Reef (square) knot (on page 378)
4. Sheetbend (on page 380)
5. Bowline (on page 390)
6. Round turn and two half hitches (on page 387)
7. Clove hitch (on page 383)

Table 6-3 lists several of the most common knots and their effect on the breaking strength of the line they are tied in. For example, two lines joined by a sheet bend would only have about 55 percent of the breaking strength of the line with no knot. These were compiled as an average from several sources and should just be considered a guide to compare one knot to another.

Knot	Strength Percent
Reef Knot	45%
Sheet bend	55%
Carrick bend	58%
Anchor bend -ring	68%
Anchor bend -post	80%
Two half hitches	66%
Bowline	66%
Short splice	87%
Eye splice	88%

TABLE 6-3: Relative Strength of Common Knots

Most of these basic knots include some diagrams of how to tie the knot, whereas other simple knots are deemed self-explanatory.

STOPPER AND END KNOTS

A **stopper knot** is any of several types of knots tied at the free end of a line to prevent the line from running through a block or other small opening.

Overhand Knot

The simplest of all knots, the overhand knot is often used as a stopper knot, although the figure 8 knot below is better, since the overhand knot can be hard to untie particularly when wet. It is sometimes used instead of whipping as a quick and dirty way to keep lines from unraveling. This is not a recommended knot for boaters.

Figure 8 Knot

The figure 8 knot, so called because it looks like a figure 8, is the most common stopper knot used by boaters. It's easier to untie than the overhand knot.

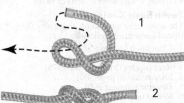

Heaving Line Knot

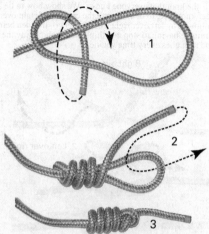

The heaving line knot is used to add weight to the end of a line, which can be useful when heaving a line.

KNOTS USED TO JOIN TWO LINES (BENDS)
Carrick Bend

The carrick bend is typically used to join large diameter lines such as hawsers and steel rope. If the ends are seized it will be much easier to untie after being placed under load since it will not capsize so easily.

Reef Knot (Square Knot)

This is the knot that everyone knows. We show how to tie the reef knot here, to demonstrate the concept of right over left followed by left over right (or vice-versa), the idea being to eliminate having to stop and think about which way the second turn goes every time you tie it.

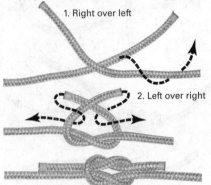

1. Right over left

2. Left over right

The reef knot is also called the square knot. This is the most common knot for joining two lines together. Note how, in the completed knot, the free ends come out of the knot adjacent to and parallel to the standing parts. Also the free ends should end up on the same side of the knot. You should be able to tie this knot blindfolded or behind your back with just a couple of minutes practice. It is commonly used for tying around something, as around the reefed part of a sail. This is not a good knot for joining two different size lines. Also, the reef knot is not good for joining two lines under heavy load since it can capsize and come undone.

Granny Knot (the unReef Knot)

The granny knot slips easily and is of no use on a boat; it's only included here to show what a reef knot should not look like. Note how the free end is not adjacent to and parallel to the standing part as in the reef knot shown above. If your reef knot ends up looking like this, then quickly undo it and retie it before anyone else sees it!

Reef Knot—Slippery

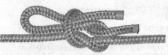

The slippery reef knot is easier to untie than a reef knot. It is used for a temporary knot that might need to be undone quickly. Note that this is actually half the knot you tie in your shoelace.

Sheepshank

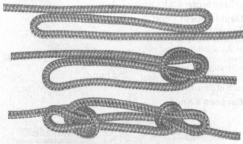

The sheepshank is used to substantially shorten a length of rope or to temporarily isolate a damaged portion of rope. Make sure the bights at each end are long enough that the loops won't slip off them. Consider this a temporary knot.

Knotted Sheepshank

This version of the sheepshank cannot come undone like the ordinary sheepshank since the half hitches can't slip off the end of the bights they are looped around. Although it's more dependable, it's much harder to undo.

Sheet Bend

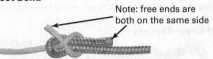

Note: free ends are
both on the same side

The sheet bend is a good knot for joining two lines under heavy load since it tightens up rather than capsizing like the reef knot. It is also used to join two unequal size ropes together as shown in the illustration. This knot will be stronger if both free ends are on the same side of the standing parts. This can also be used to join a line to an eye or loop (the line being the larger line to the right above), in which case it is called a *becket hitch*.

Double Sheet Bend

The double sheet bend is
used for the same purposes
as the sheet bend, but is
more secure, particularly
with slippery nylon line. It
is made with an additional
turn of the smaller rope.

2nd turn

Surgeon's Knot

The surgeon's knot is similar to the reef knot, except an extra turn is taken that helps keeps the line from slipping under light load until the second set of turns is taken. To balance the knot, the second part of the knot should contain the same number of turns as the first part. This knot is also called a suture knot and is used by surgeons to join stitching. It's more secure than a reef knot.

KNOTS FOR TYING TO OBJECTS (HITCHES)

Anchor Bend

This is called the anchor bend because it is commonly used to attach a line to an anchor. It is also good for securing docklines. Note the first hitch passes back through the round turn. This is a more secure knot than the round turn and

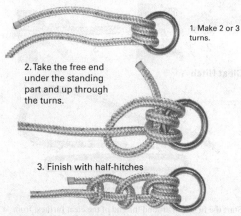

1. Make 2 or 3 turns.

2. Take the free end under the standing part and up through the turns.

3. Finish with half-hitches

two half hitches and is less likely to work loose; however, it is difficult if not impossible to tie if there is tension on the standing part. For more security seize the free end to the standing part.

Buntline Hitch

This is one of the more useful hitches, and it is easy to tie and is secure. Unlike the clove hitch, the buntline can be tied with tension on the standing part.

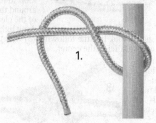

1.

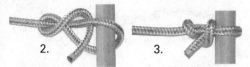

Cleat Hitch

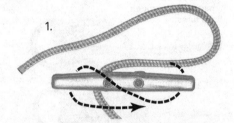

Start the first turn around the end of the cleat furthest from the direction of pull on the standing part. Continue turns until the line looks like the illustration (2) below.

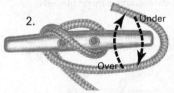

Now twist the bight on the end so the free end passes underneath and then slip the loop so formed around the end of the cleat and draw tight. The finished hitch should look like the following (3) with the two lines adjacent and parallel in the center.

The cleat hitch is used for securing a line to a cleat. It is mostly used for dock-lines, halyards, and sheets.

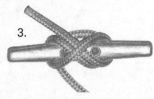

Clove Hitch

The clove hitch is well known, but it is not particularly secure since it will work loose

if not constantly loaded. It's good for round poles but won't hold on a square post. This knot can't be tied under load and is hard to untie under heavy load.

Clove Hitch and Two Half Hitches

Adding two half hitches to the clove hitch as shown makes it a much more secure knot.

Double Clove Hitch

Adding additional turns to the clove hitch makes it a much more secure knot. You can add as many turns as needed. Obviously this won't work if there is a load on the standing part.

Constrictor Hitch

This is good knot for binding things together and can be drawn very tight. Once it's tight, it is quite difficult to undo. Like the clove hitch, this can't be tied with the standing part under tension. This is a better knot than the reef knot for many applications where the reef knot is commonly used.

1.

2.

Half Hitch

The half hitch is
a very basic knot
that is typically
to control the
free end from
other knots, such
as the clove hitch.
Shown here is
a turn with a
double half hitch.

Highwayman's Hitch

Although this knot needs some explanation as to how to tie
it, it is actually very quick to tie and unties by simply pulling
on the free end. It was used by highwaymen in centuries past
to tether their horses for a quick getaway. It doesn't come
undone with tugging and pulling (like a horse would do), so
it makes a good dinghy tie up.

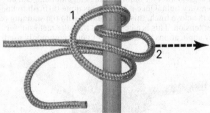

First make a bight and bring it around the post to position (1).
Reach through the bight and pull a loop of the standing part
(2) through. Next make a bight of the free end (3) and bring it
through the loop just formed.

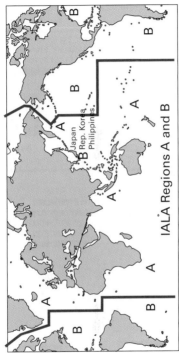

FIGURE Q-1: IALA Regions for Aids to Navigation . As the map shows, North and South America are in IALA Region B.

Most of the illustrations for aids to navigation are from United States Coast Guard publications. Canadian aids are fairly similar so they are not duplicated unless they are different enough to be confusing, as is the case with day beacons. Notes are included to point out differences from the United States system. Most differences have to do with flashing light characteristics and are fairly minor.

LATERAL SYSTEM IALA "B"(Entering From Seaward)

■ Green Light Only   PORT SIDE MARKS

PREFERRED CHANNEL TO STARBOARD
TOPMOST BAND GREEN
Keep mark to port to stay in preferred channel

Composite Group Flashing (2+1) ▮▮ ▮ ▮▮ ▮ (1)

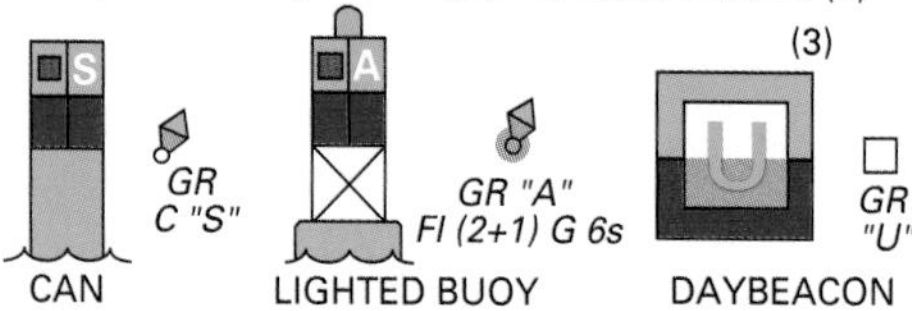

S
GR
C "S"
CAN

A
GR "A"
Fl (2+1) G 6s
LIGHTED BUOY

(3)
U
GR
"U"
DAYBEACON

(1) Canada uses Fl (2+1) 6s or Fl (2+1) 10s

PORT SIDE
ODD NUMBERED AIDS

FLASHING (2) ▮▮▮▮▮▮▮▮▮▮▮
FLASHING ▮ ▮ ▮ ▮ ▮ (2)
OCCULTING ▮▮ ▮▮ ▮▮
QUICK FLASHING ▮▮▮▮▮▮▮▮▮▮ (2)
ISO ▮▮ ▮▮ ▮▮

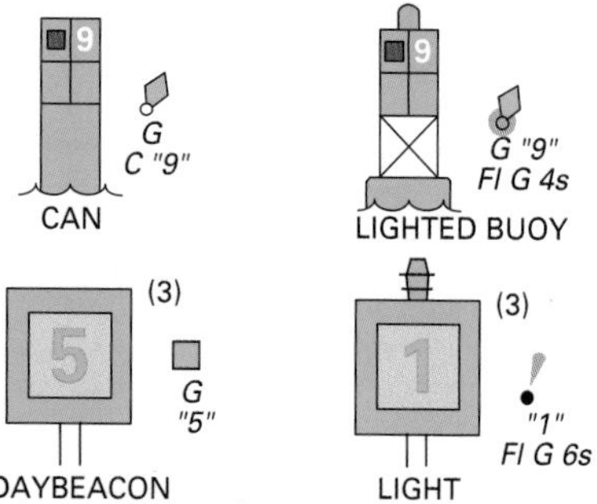

9
G
C "9"
CAN

9
G "9"
Fl G 4s
LIGHTED BUOY

(3)
5
G
"5"
DAYBEACON

(3)
1
"1"
Fl G 6s
LIGHT

(2) Canada uses Fl 4s or Q 1s
(3) See plate for Canadian Standard Daybeacons

FIGURE Q-2: Port Side Marks

LATERAL SYSTEM IALA "B" (Entering From Seaward)

STARBOARD SIDE MARKS ■ Red Light Only

PREFERRED CHANNEL TO PORT
TOPMOST BAND RED
Keep mark to starboard to in preferred channel
Composite Group Flashing (2+1) (1)

RG
"G"

RG "B"
Fl (2+1) R 6s

RG
N "C"

DAYBEACON   LIGHTED BUOY   NUN

(1) Canada uses Fl (2+1) 6s or Fl (2+1) 10s

STARBOARD SIDE
EVEN NUMBERED AIDS

FLASHING (2)
FLASHING (2)
OCCULTING
QUICK FLASHING (2)
ISO

R "8"
Fl R 4s

R
N "6"

LIGHTED BUOY   NUN

"2"
Fl R 6s

R
"2"

LIGHT   DAYBEACON

(2) Canada uses Fl 4s or Q 1s
(3) See plate for Canadian Standard Daybeacons

FIGURE Q-3: Starboard Side Marks

Canadian Standard Daybeacons

PORT BIFURCATION / JUNCTION	STARBOARD BIFURCATION /JUNCTION

DESCRIPTION
Green reflective square on a white diamond with a red reflecting border

DESCRIPTION
Red reflective triangle on a white diamond with a red reflecting border.

USER'S GUIDE ◆
Marks a point where the channel divides and may be passed on either side. If the preferred channel is desired (right), the daybeacon should be kept on the vessel's port (left) side.

USER'S GUIDE ◆
Marks a point where the channel divides and may be passed on either side. If the preferred channel is desired (left), the daybeacon should be kept to the vessel's starboard (right) side.

UPSTREAM

PORT HAND

 Black or Green

STARBOARD HAND

DESCRIPTION
Black or green square centered on a white background with a green reflecting border. may display an odd number.

DESCRIPTION
A red triangle centered on a white background with a red reflecting border. May display an even number.

USER'S GUIDE ▣
When proceeding upstream, a port hand daybeacon must be kept on the vessel's port (left) side.

USERS' GUIDE ▲
When proceeding upstream, must be kept on the vessel's starboard (right) side.

FIGURE Q-4: Canada Daybeacons

IALA MARITIME BUOYAGE SYSTEM
CARDINAL MARKS REGIONS A AND B

Top marks are always fitted (when practicable).
Buoy shapes are pillar or spar.

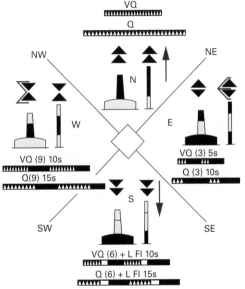

Lights, when fitted, are white, Very Quick Flashing or Quick Flashing: a South mark also has a Long Flash immediately following the quick flashes.

A north buoy indicates the best water is to the north and danger to the south. Similarly for E, S, and W.

Mnemonic -note the lights have 3 flashes at the 3 o'clock position, 6 at 6, and 9 at 9 o'clock. Also note the red W and E above for West and East.

FIGURE Q-5: Cardinal Marks

ISOLATED DANGER
NO NUMBERS -- MAY BE LETTERED
☐ White light only

Fl (2) 5s ▐▌ ▐ ▌▐▐ ▌▐▐ ▌ (1)

BR "A"
Fl (2) 5s

A

C

BR "C"

LIGHTED

UNLIGHTED

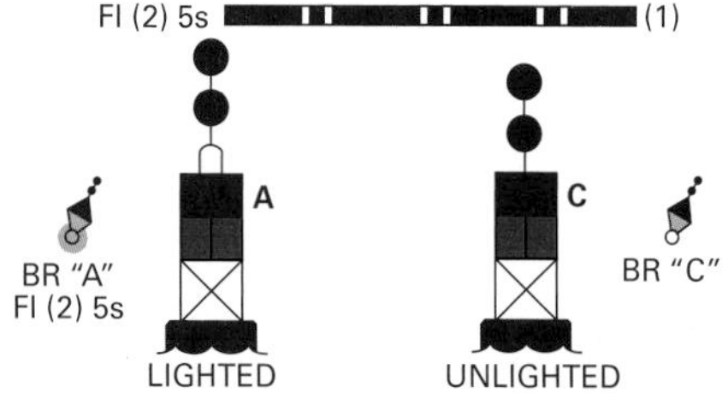

These aids indicate an isolated danger which may be
passed on all sides. Do not approach closely.

(1) Canada also uses Fl (2) 10s

SAFE WATER
NO NUMBERS -- MAY BE LETTERED
☐ White light only   Morse code

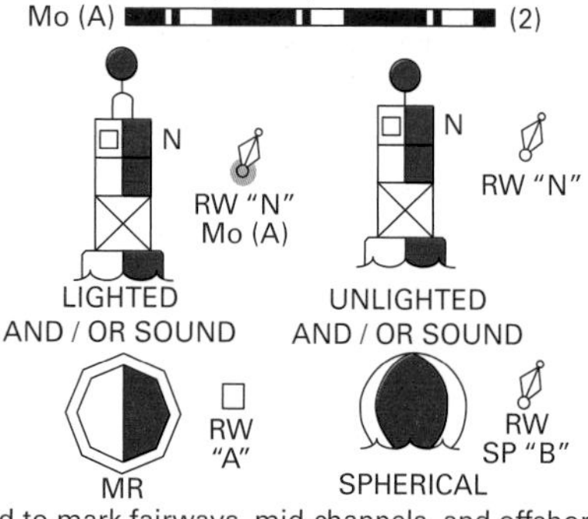

Mo (A) ▐▌ ▐ ▌▐▐ ▌▐ (2)

RW "N"
Mo (A)

N

N

RW "N"

LIGHTED
AND / OR SOUND

UNLIGHTED
AND / OR SOUND

☐ RW
"A"

MR

RW
SP "B"

SPHERICAL

Used to mark fairways, mid-channels, and offshore
approach points, and have unobstructed water on all
sides. Buoys may show a red top mark.

(2) Canada also uses LF (1) 10s

FIGURE Q-6: Isolated Danger and Safe Water Marks

RANGE DAYBOARDS -- MAY BE LETTERED

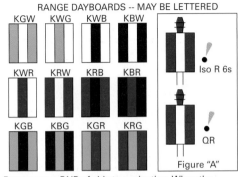

Ranges are a PAIR of aids to navigation. When the dayboards and/or lights appear to be in line with each other (figure "A"), it assists the vessel operator in maintaining a safe course within the navigable channel. The appropriate nautical chart must be consulted when using ranges to determine whether the range marks the centerline of the navigable channel and also what section of the range may be safely traversed. Ranges are generally, but not always, lighted, and display rectangular dayboards of various colors. Ranges which are lit 24 hous a day may not have dayboards. In Canada range dayboards can be different shapes and are not necessarily rectangular.

INLAND (STATE) WATERS OBSTRUCTION MARK

State Water Obstruction Mark is a black/white vertically striped buoy used to indicate to a vessel operator that an obstruction to navigation extends from the nearest shore to the buoy. This means "do not pass between the buoy and shore."

MOORING BUOY

Mooring Buoys are white with a blue horizontal band. This distinctive color scheme is used to facilitate identification and to avoid confusion with aids to navigation.

FIGURE Q-7: Range Dayboards

DAYBOARDS HAVING NO LATERAL SIGNIFICANCE
May be lettered   White light only ☐

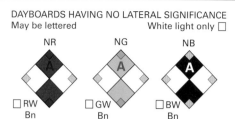

NR   NG   NB

☐ RW   ☐ GW   ☐ BW
Bn   Bn   Bn

These diamond shaped dayboards can be used to help
the vessel operator determine his/her location. They are
like the "X's" on shopping mall maps "You Are Here".
An appropriate nautical chart must be consulted to
determine location.

SPECIAL MARKS -- MAY BE LETTERED
☐ Yellow light only   Fixed ▬▬▬▬
                       Flashing ▤▤▤▤

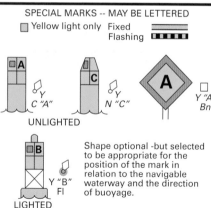

Y
C "A"
UNLIGHTED

Y
N "C"

☐ Y "A"
Bn

Y "B"
Fl
LIGHTED

Shape optional -but selected
to be appropriate for the
position of the mark in
relation to the navigable
waterway and the direction
of buoyage.

These aids are not intended to assist in navigation,
but rather to alert the vessel operator to a special
feature of area (anchoring, traffic separation, fish
net area, cable or pipeline, military exercise areas,
jetties, etc.

FIGURE Q-8: Dayboards and Special Marks

TYPICAL INFORMATION AND REGULATORY MARKS

When lighted, information and regulatory marks may display any light rhythm except quick flashing and flashing (2).

White light only

Exclusion Area   Restricted Operations   Danger

W Bn

Buoy used to display regulatory markers

May show white light. Canada shows yellow light Fl 4s.

EXAMPLES

Explanation may be placed outside the crossed diamond shape, such as dam, rapids, swim area, etc.

The nature of danger may be indicated inside the diamond shape, such as rock, wreck, shoal, dam, etc.

Type of control is indicated in the circle, such as slow, no wake, anchoring, etc.

Information -for displaying information such as directions, distances, locations, etc.

FIGURE Q-9: Information and Regulatory Marks

INTRACOASTAL WATERWAY MARKS

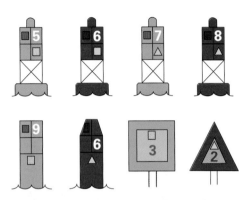

The ICW runs parallel to the Atlantic and gulf coasts from Manasquan Inlet, New Jersey to the Mexican border. The conventional direction of buoyage in the ICW is north to south down the Atlantic coast and westward across the gulf to Mexico. Aids to navigation marking the ICW display unique yellow symbols to distinguish them from aids marking other waters. Yellow triangles indicate aids should be passed by keeping them on the starboard side of the vessel. Yellow squares indicate aids should be passed by keeping them on the port side of the vessel. A yellow horizontal band provides no lateral information, but simply identifies aids to navigation as marking the ICW.

When following the ICW from New Jersey through Texas, keep yellow triangles to starboard, yellow squares to port, <u>regardless</u> of the color of the navigation aid they appear on.

FIGURE Q-10: Intracoastal Waterway Marks

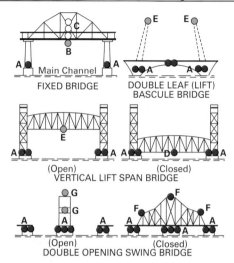

FIGURE Q-11: Bridge Lighting. Additional information on bridges is found on page 305

Bridge Lighting: In U.S. waters, the Coast Guard prescribes certain combinations of fixed lights for bridges and structures extending over waterways. In general, red lights (A) are used to mark piers and supports, and green lights (B) mark the centerline of the navigable channel through a fixed bridge. if there is more than one channel through the bridge, the preferred route is marked by three white lights (C) placed vertically. Red lights (D) are also used on some lift bridges to indicate the lift is closed, and green lights (E) to indicate that the lift is open to vessel traffic. Double-opening swing bridges are lighted with three lights on top of the span structure so that when viewed from an approaching vessel the swing span will display three red lights (F), and when open for navigation will display two green lights (G).

FIGURE Q-11: Bridge Lighting. Additional information on bridges is found on page 305

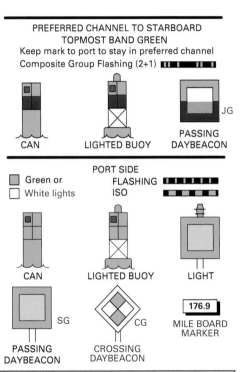

WESTERN RIVERS MARKING SYSTEM
(Entering From Seaward)
PORT Side Marks or Right Descending Bank

PREFERRED CHANNEL TO STARBOARD
TOPMOST BAND GREEN
Keep mark to port to stay in preferred channel
Composite Group Flashing (2+1)

CAN

LIGHTED BUOY

PASSING DAYBEACON — JG

PORT SIDE
FLASHING
ISO

■ Green or
□ White lights

CAN

LIGHTED BUOY

LIGHT

PASSING DAYBEACON — SG

CROSSING DAYBEACON — CG

176.9
MILE BOARD MARKER

The term "Western Rivers" refers to the Mississippi River and it's tributaries, not rivers in the western U.S.

FIGURE Q-12: Western Rivers Port Side Marks

WESTERN RIVERS MARKING SYSTEM
(Entering From Seaward)
STARBOARD Side Marks or Left Descending Bank

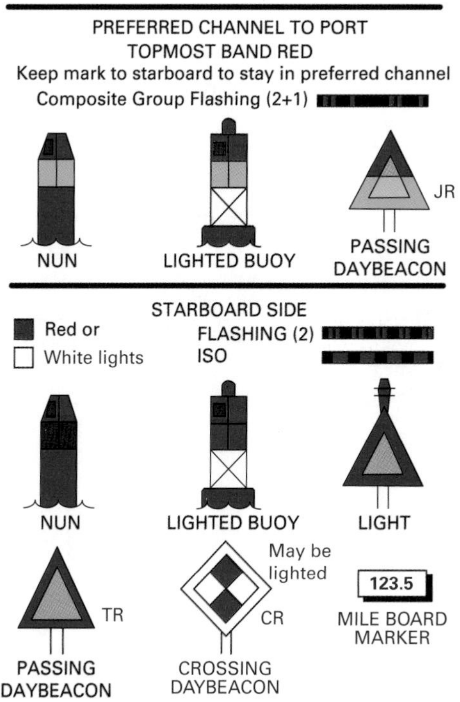

PREFERRED CHANNEL TO PORT
TOPMOST BAND RED
Keep mark to starboard to stay in preferred channel
Composite Group Flashing (2+1) ▮▮ ▮ ▮▮ ▮

NUN

LIGHTED BUOY

JR

PASSING
DAYBEACON

■ Red or
□ White lights

STARBOARD SIDE
FLASHING (2) ▮▮ ▮▮ ▮▮
ISO ▮ ▮ ▮ ▮

NUN

LIGHTED BUOY

LIGHT

TR

PASSING
DAYBEACON

May be
lighted

CR

CROSSING
DAYBEACON

123.5

MILE BOARD
MARKER

See the USCG discussion on the Western Rivers
Marking System in the Piloting and Navigation chapter.

FIGURE Q-13: Western Rivers Starboard Side Marks

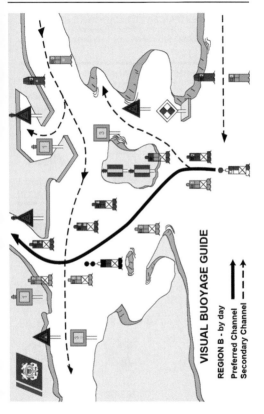

FIGURE Q-14: Visual Buoyage Guide by Day

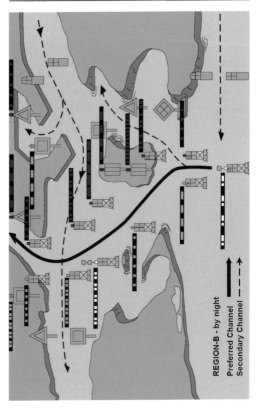

FIGURE Q-15: Visual Buoyage Guide by Night

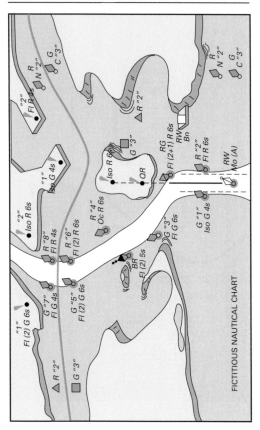

FIGURE Q-16: Buoyage Guide —Fictitious Nautical Chart

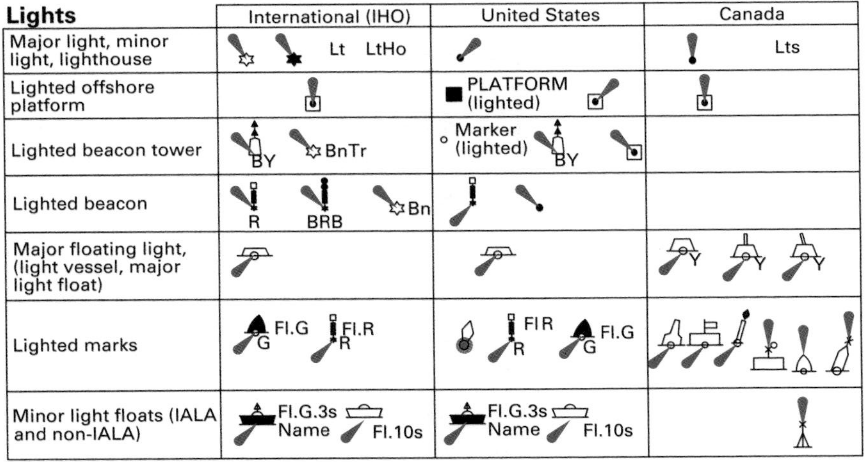

Lights	International (IHO)	United States	Canada
Major light, minor light, lighthouse	Lt LtHo		Lts
Lighted offshore platform		PLATFORM (lighted)	
Lighted beacon tower	BnTr	Marker (lighted) BY	
Lighted beacon	BRB R Bn		
Major floating light, (light vessel, major light float)			
Lighted marks	Fl.G G · Fl.R R	Fl.R R · Fl.G G	
Minor light floats (IALA and non-IALA)	Fl.G.3s Name Fl.10s	Fl.G.3s Name Fl.10s	

FIGURE Q-17: Chart Symbols Used For Lights

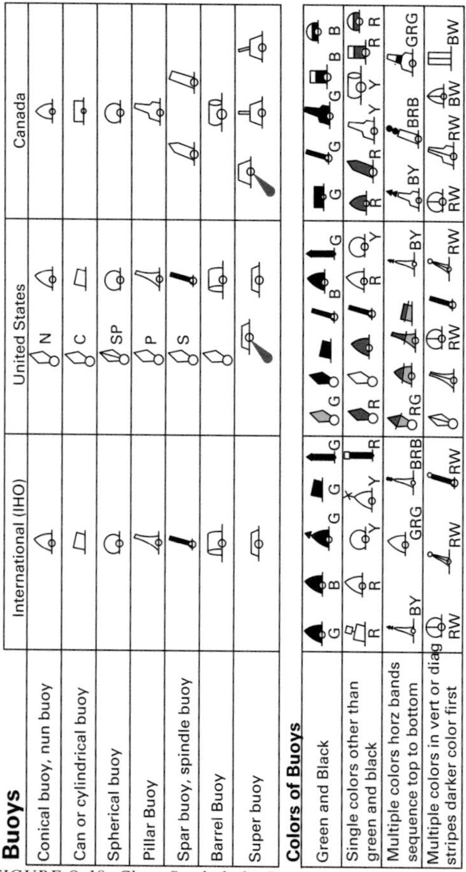

Buoys

Buoys	International (IHO)	United States	Canada
Conical buoy, nun buoy		N	
Can or cylindrical buoy		C	
Spherical buoy		SP	
Pillar Buoy		P	
Spar buoy, spindle buoy		S	
Barrel Buoy			
Super buoy			

Colors of Buoys

Colors of Buoys	International (IHO)	United States	Canada
Green and Black	G B	G B	G G B B
Single colors other than green and black	R R	R Y	R R
Multiple colors horz bands sequence top to bottom	GRG BRB	RG ORG	BY BRB GRG
Multiple colors in vert or diag stripes darker color first	BY RW RW	RW RW	RW BW BW

FIGURE Q-18: Chart Symbols for Buoys

Supplementary National	United States	Canada		
Starboard hand buoy	R "2"	R R R R R R R		
Port Hand Buoy	RW	G G G G G RW RW RW RW		
Mid channel, safe water buoy	RW	RGR RGR RGR RGR BW BW BW		
Starboard bifurcation or junction buoy (preferred channel to port)	RG	GRG GRG GRG GRG Fl (2+1)R RGR		
Port bifurcation or junction buoy (preferred channel to starboard)	GR	RB RB RB RB RB RB Fl (2+1)G GRG		
Junction, middle ground		RB RB RB RB B B B		
Starboard beacon	R Bn	Fixed	Floating	
Port beacon	G Bn	Fixed ▣	Floating ▣	
Starboard bifurcation or junction beacon (preferred channel to port)	RG Bn	Fixed ◆	Floating ◆	
Port bifurcation or junction beacon (preferred channel to starboard)	GR Bn	Fixed ◆	Floating ◆	
Isolated danger	BR	BRB	BRB	

FIGURE Q-19: Chart Symbols for Buoys -Supplemental

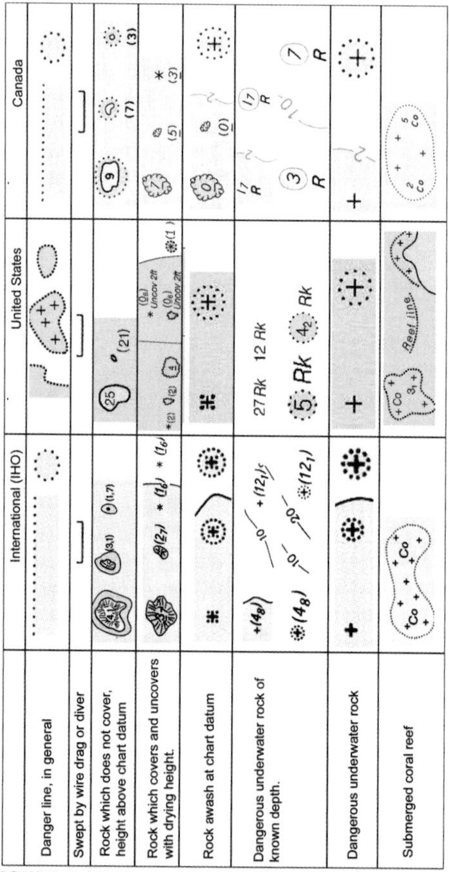

FIGURE Q-20: Commonly Used Chart Symbols

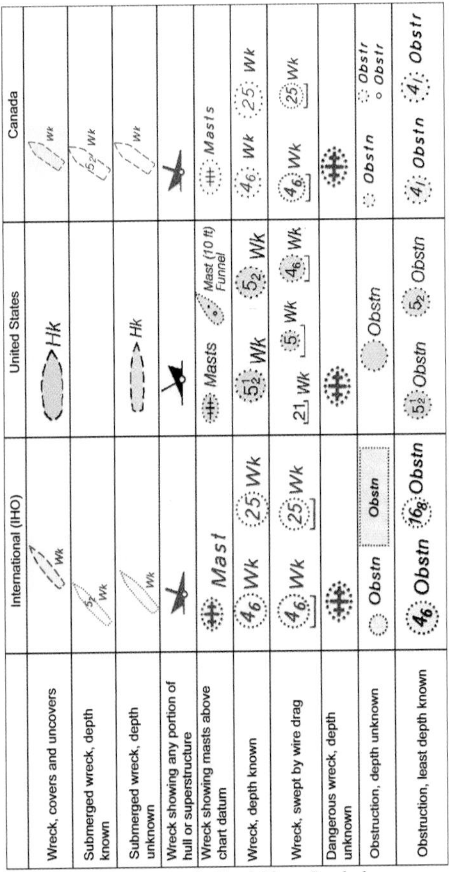

	International (IHO)	United States	Canada
Wreck, covers and uncovers	*Wk*	*Hk*	*Wk*
Submerged wreck, depth known	5₂ *Wk*		5₂ *Wk*
Submerged wreck, depth unknown	*Wk*	*Hk*	*Wk*
Wreck showing any portion of hull or superstructure			
Wreck showing masts above chart datum	*Mast*	*Masts*	*Masts*
Wreck, depth known	4₆ *Wk* 25 *Wk*	5₁ *Wk* Mast (10 ft) Funnel 21₂ *Wk* 5 *Wk* 5₂ *Wk* 4₆ *Wk*	4₆ *Wk* 25 *Wk* 4₆ *Wk* 25 *Wk*
Wreck, swept by wire drag	4₆ *Wk*		
Dangerous wreck, depth unknown			
Obstruction, depth unknown	Obstn Obstn	Obstn	Obstn Obstn
Obstruction, least depth known	4₆ *Obstn* 16₈ *Obstn*	5₂ *Obstn* 5 *Obstn*	4₁ *Obstn*

FIGURE Q-21: Commonly Used Chart Symbols

LATERAL SYSTEM IALA "A" (Entering From Seaward)

■ Red light only   PORT SIDE MARKS

PREFERRED CHANNEL TO STARBOARD
TOPMOST BAND RED
Keep mark to port to stay in preferred channel

Lights when fitted are
COMPOSITE GROUP
FLASHING (2+1)

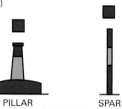

| CAN | PILLAR | SPAR |

PORT HAND

Lights, when fitted, may have any phase characteristic
other than that used for preferred channels

QUICK FLASHING
FLASHING
LONG FLASHING
GROUP FLASHING

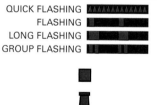

| CAN | PILLAR | SPAR |

Topmark (if any): Single can

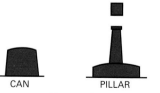

FIGURE Q-22: IALA Region A Port Side Marks

LATERAL SYSTEM IALA "A" (Entering From Seaward)

■ Green light only   STARBOARD SIDE MARKS

PREFERRED CHANNEL TO PORT
TOPMOST BAND GREEN
Keep mark to starboard to stay in preferred channel

Lights when fitted are
COMPOSITE GROUP
FLASHING (2+1)

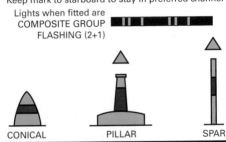

CONICAL   PILLAR   SPAR

STARBOARD HAND

Lights, when fitted, may have any phase characteristic
other than that used for preferred channels

QUICK FLASHING

FLASHING

LONG FLASHING

GROUP FLASHING

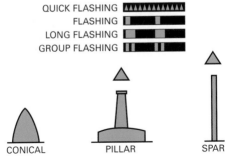

CONICAL   PILLAR   SPAR

Topmark (if any): Single cone point upward

FIGURE Q-23: IALA Region A Starboard Side Marks

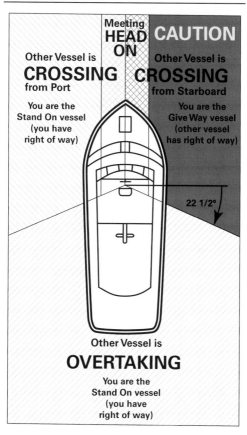

FIGURE Q-24: Crossing Zones

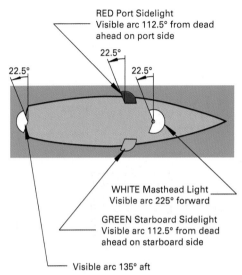

RED Port Sidelight
Visible arc 112.5° from dead
ahead on port side

22.5°   22.5°

22.5°

WHITE Masthead Light
Visible arc 225° forward

GREEN Starboard Sidelight
Visible arc 112.5° from dead
ahead on starboard side

Visible arc 135° aft

The navigation lights arcs of visibility correspond to the
crossing zones shown on the previous page.

- The sternlight will only be visible from aft when neither
  of the sidelights or the masthead light will be visible. You
  are overtaking.
- *When only the red port sidelight and masthead lights are
  visible on the other vessel then you are in a crossing situation. You must give way to the other vessel.*
- When only the GREEN starboard sidelight and masthead
  lights on the other vessel are visible you are in a crossing
  situation and you are the stand-on vessel (you have right
  of way).
- If both sidelights (RED and GREEN) and the masthead
  lights are visible, then you are in a head on situation.

FIGURE Q-25: Navigation Lights

SOUND SIGNALS:	Short Blast = 1 second ■ Long Blast = 5 seconds ■■■■■

Danger = 5 short blasts ■ ■ ■ ■ ■
The danger signal is also used to signal disagreement
with a proposed method of passing or crossing.

I am operating power astern = 3 short blasts ■ ■ ■

RESTRICTED VISIBILITY
Vessel under power underway
1 long blast every 2 minutes   ■■■■

Vessel stopped
2 long every 2 minutes   ■■■■ ■■■■

Vessel under sail
1 long, 2 short every 2 minutes   ■■■■ ■ ■

One short blast (one whistle)

Head on situation - normally pass port to port
Two short blasts (two whistle)

Head on situation - can pass starboard to starboard
if proper signals are exchanged.

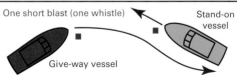

One short blast (one whistle)   Stand-on vessel

Give-way vessel

Crossing situation -the vessel with the other to starboard
is the give way vessel and must keep out of the way of
the stand on vessel.

FIGURE Q-26: Crossing Situations and Sound Signals

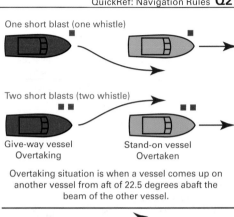

One short blast (one whistle)

Two short blasts (two whistle)

Give-way vessel
Overtaking

Stand-on vessel
Overtaken

Overtaking situation is when a vessel comes up on another vessel from aft of 22.5 degrees abaft the beam of the other vessel.

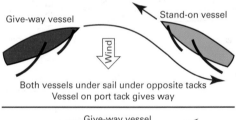

Give-way vessel

Stand-on vessel

Wind

Both vessels under sail under opposite tacks
Vessel on port tack gives way

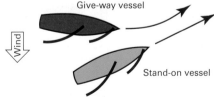

Give-way vessel

Wind

Stand-on vessel

Both vessels under sail on same tacks
Vessel to windward gives way

FIGURE Q-27: Crossing Situations and Sound Signals

International Signal Flags

 ALFA; Diver down; keep well clear at slow speed

 BRAVO; Loading, discharging or carrying dangerous cargo

 CHARLIE; Yes or affirmative

 DELTA; I am maneuvering with difficulty; keep clear

 ECHO; I am changing my course to starboard

 FOXTROT; I am disabled; communicate with me

 GOLF; I require a pilot.

 HOTEL; I have a pilot on board.

 INDIA; I am changing my course to port.

 JULIET; I am on fire and have dangerous cargo; keep clear

 KILO; I wish to communicate with you

 LIMA; You should stop your vessel immediately

 MIKE; My vessel is stopped; making no way

 NOVEMBER; No or negative

 OSCAR; Man overboard

 PAPA; About to leave port; return to ship

 QUEBEC; Request pratique; ship meets health regs.

 ROMEO; No code

 SIERRA; Moving astern

 TANGO; Keep clear

FIGURE Q-28: International Signal Flags

International Signal Flags

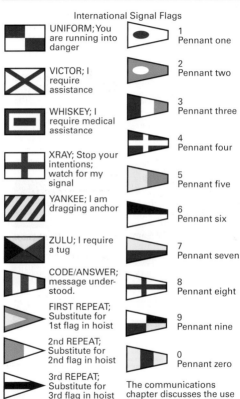

UNIFORM; You are running into danger

VICTOR; I require assistance

WHISKEY; I require medical assistance

XRAY; Stop your intentions; watch for my signal

YANKEE; I am dragging anchor

ZULU; I require a tug

CODE/ANSWER; message understood.

FIRST REPEAT; Substitute for 1st flag in hoist

2nd REPEAT; Substitute for 2nd flag in hoist

3rd REPEAT; Substitute for 3rd flag in hoist

4th REPEAT; Substitute for 4th flag in hoist

1 Pennant one

2 Pennant two

3 Pennant three

4 Pennant four

5 Pennant five

6 Pennant six

7 Pennant seven

8 Pennant eight

9 Pennant nine

0 Pennant zero

The communications chapter discusses the use of signal flags, including the use of two letter signals.

FIGURE Q-29: International Signal Flags

National Flags

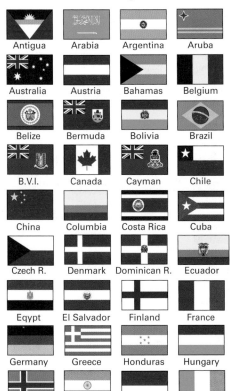

Antigua	Arabia	Argentina	Aruba
Australia	Austria	Bahamas	Belgium
Belize	Bermuda	Bolivia	Brazil
B.V.I.	Canada	Cayman	Chile
China	Columbia	Costa Rica	Cuba
Czech R.	Denmark	Dominican R.	Ecuador
Eqypt	El Salvador	Finland	France
Germany	Greece	Honduras	Hungary
Iceland	India	Indonesia	Ireland

FIGURE Q-30: National Flags

National Flags

FIGURE Q-31: National Flags

Diver flag - stay well clear. Rules vary by state.

Special Flags

Small craft advisory to force 7 Wind to 33 knots

Storm warning Force 10 - 11 Wind 48 - 63 knots

Gale Force 8 - 9 Wind 34 - 47 knots

Hurricane Force 12 Wind > 64 knots

Organization Flags

U.S. Yacht Ensign

U.S. Coast Guard

Canada Coast Guard

U.S. Coast Guard Auxiliary

Canada Coast Guard Auxiliary

U.S. Power Squadrons

Canadian Power Squadrons

FIGURE Q-32: Special Flags and Organization Flags

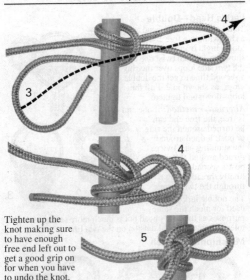

Tighten up the knot making sure to have enough free end left out to get a good grip on for when you have to undo the knot. Try tugging on the standing part.

You'll find this doesn't come undone easily except by pulling on the free end.

Lark's Head or Ring Knot

The lark's head is often used to tie through grommets or fasten to a ring. There must be equal tension on both lines otherwise the knot slips. It stays tight when under load but unties very easily when the tension is released. This should be considered a temporary knot.

Lark's Head—Double

To tie a double lark's head around
a ring without a free end, first
loop a bight over the ring as
shown in 1. Then twist one of
the two side loops over the ring
a second time to get the double
loops, as shown in 2. Pull the
loops down and tighten.

Alternative method: if one end
is free, the free end can
be turned around the ring
or post; looped around
the standing part twice;
turned around the ring or
post a second time; and
finally threaded down
through the two loops.

The double lark's head is
used for much the same
purposes as the lark's head but is much more secure and will
tolerate some unequal tension on the two lines.

Midshipman's Hitch

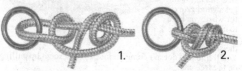

The midshipman's hitch is useful for binding things together
since it can be made and then slipped tight. It is commonly
used to secure pulley blocks.

Mooring Hitch

This is a quick-release knot used
to temporarily moor a small boat.
The knot will hold fast under
tension.

Rolling Hitch

The rolling hitch is used to fasten a line to another larger line or a post for purposes of pulling parallel to the line. It can be used to pull the larger line without slipping in the direction shown by the arrow. This hitch will slip if pulled at right angles to the post or line.

Start by making two turns spiraling toward the direction the larger rope is to be pulled. Then finish with a turn with the free end tucked

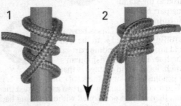

under itself on the opposite side (top above) of the standing part. This can be made much more secure by tying a second rolling hitch with the free end.

Round Turn and Two Half Hitches

The round turn and two half hitches are often used to attach an already loaded line to an object.

Common uses are securing to pilings or hanging fenders from railings. This is easier to tie and untie than the clove hitch and two half hitches, particularly when the standing part is tensioned, and is just about as secure.

Slippery Hitch

The slippery hitch is a temporary knot often used to moor small boats. It unties easily for a quick departure by pulling on the free end.

Tautline Hitch

The tautline hitch is somewhat similar to a midshipman's hitch except it has two turns around the standing part before finishing with a single half hitch. This is basically a rolling hitch tied with the free end around the standing part of the line. Like the midshipman's hitch, its main advantage is that it is adjustable, since the knot can slide along the standing part so as to adjust the length of line and then remain positioned without sliding backward. This hitch is quite often used for tent guy lines.

Timber Hitch

The timber hitch is most commonly used to attach a rope to timber (a log). After a turn around the log, pass the free end around the standing part, then wrap the free end around itself two or more times. This knot will tighten under load but is very easy to untie when tension is released.

Timber Hitch and a Half Hitch (Killick Hitch)

See top of next page. The killick hitch is used to actually tow or drag the log. It is basically a timber hitch with a half hitch further down the log in the direction the log is to be towed.

Trucker's Hitch—No Slip Type

The trucker's hitch is used to bind down a load with a two-to-one tensioning advantage. If the small loop is made with a figure 8 knot on a bight instead of an overhand knot it will be much easier to untie. The far end of the standing part of the line is secured on the opposite side of the load using a suitable knot such as a bowline. The free end is cinched tight and fastened to something with another knot—perhaps a couple of half hitches.

Trucker's Hitch—Slip Type

The slip type trucker's hitch to the right is used for the same purposes as the no-slip trucker's hitch above; however, when the free end is released back through the eye, the knot unties. It is also a little quicker to tie.

LOOP KNOTS

Bowline

The bowline is one of the stronger knots, it doesn't slip or capsize, and it can be easily untied. It can be tied around objects in any size loop and can be used as a rescue sling to lift a

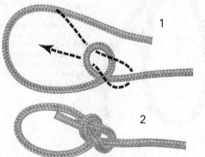

man out of the water. A bowline on the end of each of two lines is also a good way to join two lines together since not only does it not slip but it is also one of the stronger knots.

Bowline on the Bight

The three illustrations below show how to tie a bowline on the bight.

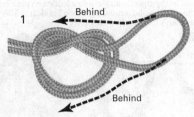

Form an overhand knot from a bight leaving a generous loop of the bight out as shown above. Pass the bight around and behind the overhand knot as shown. When the bight is pulled back along behind the standing part it should end up as shown in the next illustration. Now, pull the bight out to

make the bowline loop as shown by the arrows above. The finished bowline on the bight is shown below.

Like the ordinary bowline, the bowline on the bight is a strong knot and easy to untie. The double loop makes it easy on the hands for gripping and pulling.

Butterfly Knot

Because the lines come out of the knot perpendicular to
the loop, the butterfly knot is used to make a perpendicular
attachment loop perpendicular to a line loaded on both ends.
One of the stronger and more secure loop knots. It is also
called lineman's loop or alpine butterfly.

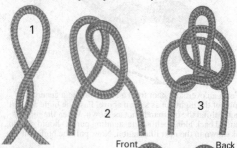

Front   Back

Tie the knot as follows: (1)
make a bight and twist it
around as shown, (2) fold
the bight down to the front,
(3) pass the bight back and
up through the center, and
(4) tighten the knot.

The two figures to the right
show the front and back view
of the tightened butterfly
knot.

Crabber's Eye Knot

When loose,
the loop and
standing part of
the crabber's eye
knot slip easily
but hold fast
when tightened.
It is also called
the crossed running knot or the crabbin's eye knot.

Loop Knot (Left)

This is just an overhand knot in a bight and is the easiest way to form a loop along a line. Note that this knot is often used as part of the nonslip trucker's hitch. The figure on the right shows the knot from the back.

Loop Knot—Figure 8 Version (Right)

This uses a figure 8 knot tied in the bight to form a loop. This is a better knot than the loop knot above since it is stronger and easier to untie after being under load.

Triple Crown

The triple crown knot is used to form a double loop in a line. This is a secure knot and the loops are independent of each other. It is difficult to untie after supporting a heavy weight.

First, form two loops as shown in (1) and lay the two ends back up across the base of the right hand loop. These two loops will become the two loops in the final knot. Next fold the right hand loop down and across the front as shown in (2).

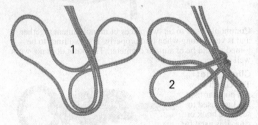

Referring to the next page, next bring the upper left loop down through the bottom double loop (3) , and pull the knot tight (4).

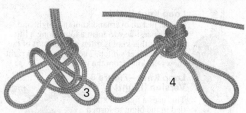

FISHING KNOTS
Blood Knot

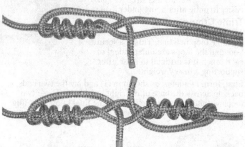

Commonly used to tie two pieces of monofilament together and is very strong when tied properly. The two lines to be joined should be of similar diameter. This knot does not work well on rope.

Clinch Knot

The clinch knot is a popular fishing knot used to secure a hook or ring. It is used for small diameter line and is not useful for rope.

Pass the line through the eye

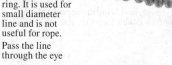

of the hook, then wrap the free end around the standing part about five times. Then pass the free end through the first loop and back through its own loop. Slide the wraps tight to the eye. Note that when done, this is like half of a blood knot.

Dropper Loop

The dropper loop is used to form a loop in a fishing line so another line or hook can be attached. This knot doesn't slip, and it maintains the strength of the line better than the butterfly knot.

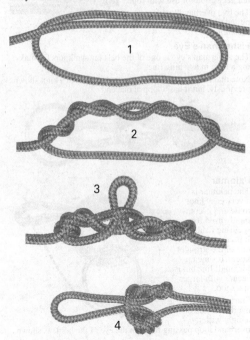

Fisherman's Knot (also Angler's Knot or Water Knot)

This knot is suited to small line such as fishing line and is popular with fishermen. It's very easy to tie, but is suitable for small diameter line only and not very good for use with rope.

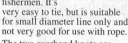

The two overhand knots are pulled tight together to finish the knot.

Fisherman's Eye

The fisherman's eye is one of the best known knots for making a loop in a fishing line.

Note that this is actually the same as fisherman's knot shown previously, but it has a loop at one end.

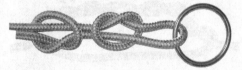

Palomar

The palomar is a very easy knot to tie and is commonly used for securing fishhooks. It is considered one of the stronger knots. It's meant for small line but is secure with larger sizes too.

Start by tying an overhand loop on a bight with the overhand loop passing through the eye of the hook as shown.

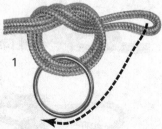

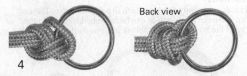

Bring the bight down and loop it all the way around the hook to end up looking like (3). Pull the knot tight as shown in (4).

Back view

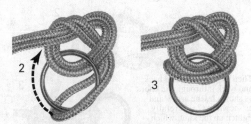

Perfection Loop

This is a fishing knot used to make a loop at the end of a leader. This is a strong and secure knot when tied correctly.

Tie a loose overhand knot in the standing part and thread the free end through the eye and back parallel to itself through the overhand knot.

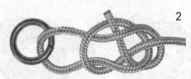

Then loop the free end back
and work it through the knot
as shown by the arrow and
as shown in (2). Carefully
tighten up the knot, which
should end up looking like
(3).

Uni Knot

This is commonly used to attach to a fishhook eye. The uni
can leave the loop open or can be tightened right up to the
eye of the hook. Note that this is like one-half of the double

uni knot. Wind the free end at least four or five turns around
both the parallel lines. Tighten up the loops, sliding them
together, then trim the free end.

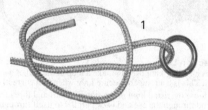

Double Uni Knot

The double uni knot is a strong knot used to join two fishing lines of the same or different diameters. Each half of the double uni knot is tied like the uni knot above. Although this knot works with rope, it really is meant for smaller line.

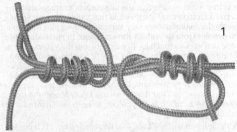

Start with the two lines to be joined overlapped and parallel. First the free end of one of the lines is looped back toward and over itself; then four or five successive wraps are taken around the two parallel lines as shown. Repeat the operation for the second line. When the knot is tightened up the knots should look like those in (2). When tension is applied to the standing part of both lines, the knots will come together as in (3).

REFERENCE TABLES FOR ROPE

Strength of Ropes

The tables that follow show breaking strengths and working loads of synthetic and wire ropes to illustrate their differences relative to one another.

It is important to note that the tables show averages that are derived from several sources and that values for rope from a particular manufacturer may vary as much as plus or minus 20 percent from the values shown herein. In particular, wire rope can vary as much as 40 percent from the values shown. Therefore, these tables should only be used as a reference for comparative purposes only. *Do not rely on these tables to select a rope size for your application! You must use the data provided by the manufacturer of the rope you purchase to select rope for your needs.* Also, a knot reduces the rope strength by as much as 55 percent, so keep this in mind when selecting a rope.

Although you wouldn't use manila rope today, it is included in the synthetic rope table for comparative purposes. At the bottom of the synthetic rope tables is a row with the percent that the rope typically stretches when tensioned to 30 percent of its breaking strength.

The wire rope table shows 316 stainless and 304 stainless wire rope to highlight their relative difference in strength. Because it is more corrosion-resistant than type 304, 316 stainless is preferred in saltwater applications, particularly in warm moist climates. Type 316 is also more expensive.

The weight of wire rope is also shown since it is sometimes used as anchor rode, particularly in the Pacific Northwest.

Note that each table is duplicated, one showing strengths in pounds and the other in kilograms.

Diameter		Manila 3 Strand	Nylon 3 Strand	Nylon Braid	Polyester Braid	Polypropylene Braid	New Tech [1] Braid
(in)	(mm)	(lb)	(lb)	(lb)	(lb)	(lb)	(lb)
Average Breaking Strength							
1/4	6	490	1670	2140	2220	1280	5890
5/16	8	880	2660	3390	3060	1940	8180
3/8	10	1320	3840	4900	4270	2690	11040
1/2	12	2350	6810	8680	7820	4450	18440
5/8	16	3600	10580	13500	12860	6570	28070
3/4	20	5050	15140	19330	19400	9040	39950
7/8	22	6710	20500	26200	27440	11860	54060
1	25	8570	26650	34090	36970	15040	70410
Working load at 5:1 Safety Factor							
1/4	6	100	330	430	440	260	1180
5/16	8	180	530	680	610	390	1640
3/8	10	260	770	980	850	540	2210
1/2	12	470	1360	1740	1560	890	3690
5/8	16	720	2120	2700	2570	1310	5610
3/4	20	1010	3030	3870	3880	1810	7990
7/8	22	1340	4100	5240	5490	2370	10810
1	25	1710	5330	6820	7390	3010	14080
Working load at 9:1 Safety Factor							
1/4	6	50	190	240	250	140	650
5/16	8	100	300	380	340	220	910
3/8	10	150	430	540	470	300	1230
1/2	12	260	760	960	870	490	2050
5/8	16	400	1180	1500	1430	730	3120
3/4	20	560	1680	2150	2160	1000	4440
7/8	22	750	2280	2910	3050	1320	6010
1	25	950	2960	3790	4110	1670	7820
Stretch [2]			16.0%	6.5%	2.4%	3.3%	1.0%
[1] Average of various new technology synthetics such as Spectra							
[2] Stretch % is at 30% of breaking strength.							

TABLE 6-4: Strength of Synthetic Rope (Pounds)

Diameter		Manila 3 Strand	Nylon 3 Strand	Nylon Braid	Polyester Braid	Poly-propyl-ene Braid	New Tech [1] Braid
(in)	(mm)	(kg)	(kg)	(kg)	(kg)	(kg)	(kg)
Average Breaking Strength							
1/4	6	220	760	970	1010	580	2670
5/16	8	400	1210	1540	1390	880	3710
3/8	10	600	1740	2220	1940	1220	5010
1/2	12	1070	3090	3940	3550	2020	8360
5/8	16	1630	4800	6120	5830	2980	12730
3/4	20	2290	6870	8770	8800	4100	18120
7/8	22	3040	9300	11880	12450	5380	24520
1	25	3890	12090	15460	16770	6820	31940
Working load at 5:1 Safety Factor							
1/4	6	40	150	190	200	120	530
5/16	8	80	240	310	280	180	740
3/8	10	120	350	440	390	240	1000
1/2	12	210	620	790	710	400	1670
5/8	16	330	960	1220	1170	600	2550
3/4	20	460	1370	1750	1760	820	3620
7/8	22	610	1860	2380	2490	1080	4900
1	25	780	2420	3090	3350	1360	6390
Working load at 9:1 Safety Factor							
1/4	6	20	80	110	110	60	300
5/16	8	40	130	170	150	100	410
3/8	10	70	190	250	220	140	560
1/2	12	120	340	440	390	220	930
5/8	16	180	530	680	650	330	1410
3/4	20	250	760	970	980	460	2010
7/8	22	340	1030	1320	1380	600	2720
1	25	430	1340	1720	1860	760	3550
Stretch [2]			16.0%	6.5%	2.4%	3.3%	1.0%

[1] Average of various new technology synthetics such as Spectra®
[2] Stretch % is at 30% of breaking strength.

TABLE 6-5: Strength of Synthetic Rope (Kilograms)

Diameter		316 Stainless	304 Stainless	304 Stainless	Galvanized	wt / 1000 ft
		1 x 19	1 x 19	7 x 19	7 x 19	
(in)	(mm)	(lb)	(lb)	(lb)	(lb)	(lb)
Average Breaking Strength						
3/32	2	890	1140	770	1120	16
1/8	3	1760	2130	1700	1940	29
5/32	4	2800	3330	2720	2910	45
3/16	5	4010	4740	3820	4040	64
1/4	6	6940	8180	6260	6780	111
9/32	7	8660	10210	7600	8380	140
5/16	8	10550	12450	9020	10150	171
3/8	10	14830	17550	12090	14150	243
1/2	12	25440	30250	19210	24070	425
Working load at 5:1 Safety Factor						
3/32	2	180	230	150	220	16
1/8	3	350	430	340	390	29
5/32	4	560	670	540	580	45
3/16	5	800	950	760	810	64
1/4	6	1390	1640	1250	1360	111
9/32	7	1730	2040	1520	1680	140
5/16	8	2110	2490	1800	2030	171
3/8	10	2970	3510	2420	2830	243
1/2	12	5090	6050	3840	4810	425
Working load at 9:1 Safety Factor						
3/32	2	100	130	90	120	16
1/8	3	200	240	190	220	29
5/32	4	310	370	300	320	45
3/16	5	450	530	420	450	64
1/4	6	770	910	700	750	111
9/32	7	960	1130	840	930	140
5/16	8	1170	1380	1000	1130	171
3/8	10	1650	1950	1340	1570	243
1/2	12	2830	3360	2130	2670	425

TABLE 6-6: Strength of Wire Rope (Pounds)

Diameter		316 Stainless	304 Stainless	304 Stainless	Galvanized	wt / 1000 m
		1 x 19	1 x 19	7 x 19	7 x 19	
(in)	(mm)	(kg)	(kg)	(kg)	(kg)	(kg)
Average Breaking Strength						
3/32	2	400	520	350	510	24
1/8	3	800	970	770	880	43
5/32	4	1270	1510	1230	1320	67
3/16	5	1820	2150	1730	1830	95
1/4	6	3150	3710	2840	3080	165
9/32	7	3930	4630	3450	3800	208
5/16	8	4790	5650	4090	4600	254
3/8	10	6730	7960	5480	6420	362
1/2	12	11540	13720	8710	10920	632
Working load at 5:1 Safety Factor						
3/32	2	80	100	70	100	24
1/8	3	160	190	150	180	43
5/32	4	250	300	250	260	67
3/16	5	360	430	350	370	95
1/4	6	630	740	570	620	165
9/32	7	790	930	690	760	208
5/16	8	960	1130	820	920	254
3/8	10	1350	1590	1100	1280	362
1/2	12	2310	2740	1740	2180	632
Working load at 9:1 Safety Factor						
3/32	2	40	60	40	60	24
1/8	3	90	110	90	100	43
5/32	4	140	170	140	150	67
3/16	5	200	240	190	200	95
1/4	6	350	410	320	340	165
9/32	7	440	510	380	420	208
5/16	8	530	630	450	510	254
3/8	10	750	880	610	710	362
1/2	12	1280	1520	970	1210	632

TABLE 6-7: Strength of Wire Rope (Kilograms)

7 WEATHER

INTRODUCTION

It doesn't matter much where you do your boating; sooner or later you will encounter weather that will, at the very least, be quite unpleasant, and at the extreme, life threatening to both your vessel and the personnel on it. Conditions of little or no concern to the average motorist can be a chief concern to the recreational boater.

Weather is of major importance to any mariner and having a basic understanding and appreciation of weather and its causes and consequences will go a long way to ensuring safety underway. The main goal is to avoid adverse weather as much as possible, which requires some form of forecasting the weather in advance.

This book will present a few basic facts about weather, which I hope will encourage the reader to pursue further education on the subject. The U.S. and Canadian Power Squadrons offer excellent introductory courses and seminars on weather forecasting, which are informative and interesting.

Note: Some tables in this chapter show only miles per hour or knots for wind speeds. Table 5-15 on page 344 can be used to convert between differing speed units by simply substituting speed for distance in the table.

WEATHER SYSTEMS

The sun ultimately provides the energy that drives all weather on earth, with factors such as the earth's rotation, land and sea masses, and topography all having an effect on how the weather ultimately behaves.

GENERAL ATMOSPHERIC CIRCULATION

The net result of these forces is a general circulation of air at the earth's surface in the directions shown by the arrows in figure 7-1. Since most North American boaters do their boating between 30 and 60 degrees north latitude, the zone of prevailing westerlies and the behavior of weather within that zone are of most interest to us.

As most of us in our latitudes are well aware, and as figure 7-1 on the next page shows, the winds and consequently the weather, move generally from west to east.

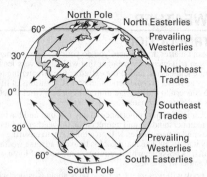

FIGURE 7-1: General Circulation of the Earth's Atmosphere

ATMOSPHERIC PRESSURE

Atmospheric pressure is measured with a barometer. Standard atmospheric pressure at sea level is 29.92 inches (760 mm) of mercury (traditional), which is equal to 1013.25 millibars (current accepted usage). This is also equal to 101.325 kPa, or 14.696 psi.

Pressure and Elevation

As elevation increases air pressure decreases so that air pressure at 5000 feet is only about 840 millibars, or 17 percent less. A barometer used at a higher elevation must be corrected for elevation to read what it would read if it was at sea level. Stated another way, the barometer at 5000 feet where pressure is actually 840 millibars is adjusted so it reads 1013.25 millibars.

Pressure and Wind

Difference in air pressure is associated with wind. If pressure varies slowly over a considerable distance, then winds will be light. When pressure difference is large over relatively short distances, high wind is expected.

Highs and Lows

Within our temperate zone of prevailing westerlies, areas of high and low barometric pressure form and move generally in the eastward direction of the prevailing westerlies. Note that winds are named for the direction they blow *from*, so a west wind is a wind *from* the west that blows to the east.

The centers of highs and lows are marked on **surface analysis maps** (weather maps) with "H" or "L."

Generally speaking, highs tend to be associated with stability and clear

Counterclockwise Inward

Clockwise Outward

FIGURE 7-2: Circulation of Air Around Highs and Lows

air, whereas lows tend to be associated with instability and foul weather. Air flows down and outward from highs and in the northern hemisphere moves in a clockwise direction as it flows outward. Conversely, air spirals counterclockwise inward and then upward into lows in the northern hemisphere (see figure 7-2). If you hold your right hand with fingers curled and thumb up, you will describe a low, and with thumb down a high.

The air moving into the low is relatively warm and moist, and as it rises it cools, which results in condensation (clouds) and precipitation.

Speed of Advance of Lows
During boating season (the summer) lows tend to move at approximately 500 miles (800 km) per day and during winter over 700 miles (1100 km) per day. This is very approximate, since a low can actually become stationary for a time, or move much more quickly.

Buys-Ballot Law
The phenomenon of counterclockwise circulation around lows leads to the **Buys-Ballot Law**, which states that if you face the wind, the low pressure is to your right. This is true only for the northern hemisphere; the low will be to the left in the southern hemisphere.

Here is an example of applying the Buys-Ballot law to make a simple forecast: If the wind is from the south (you face south), then the low is generally to the west (to your right). This means there is a good chance the weather will deteriorate since the low will move in a generally eastward direction (toward you).

WARM AND COLD FRONTS

Fronts are associated with low pressure areas, with the warm front moving eastward ahead of the cold front as shown in figure 7-3. Usually the warm and cold fronts start far apart, then move closer together as the entire system moves to the east. Eventually, the cold front overtakes the warm front, which forms an *occluded front*. Note: The symbols, such as the triangles and semi-circles on the fronts in figure 7-3, are explained in the weather map symbols at the end of this chapter.

The numbers on the contour lines are the barometric pressure in millibars. The contour lines themselves are termed *isobars*, since they represent lines of equal barometric pressure.

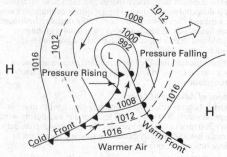

FIGURE 7-3: Warm and Cold Fronts on a Surface Analysis Map.

As the low and the fronts move eastward toward you, the barometric pressure falls, with the pressure falling faster toward the center of the low (which means higher winds). As the low passes, the pressure increases.

This leads to another simple forecasting example: If the barometer is falling, then wet weather is probably on the way. If the barometer is rising then expect fair weather. Note that it is the *change* in barometric pressure that indicates a change in weather. A constant barometric pressure reading doesn't really indicate much of anything.

Warm Front

The *warm front* consists of warmer air riding up over colder air with the front sloping forward and upward as shown schematically in figure 7-4. The leading edge of the front at over 30,000 feet (9000 m) can be up to 500 miles (800 km) ahead of the front at ground level.

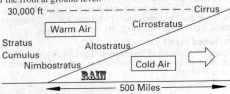

FIGURE 7-4: Schematic Section of Warm Front

The cirrus and cirrostratus clouds preceding the front at ground level give a good indication that a front warm front can be expected to pass within the next day or two.

Note: Definitions and pictures of the various cloud types are included later in this chapter.

The warm front will typically bring rain from nimbostratus clouds, but if the air masses are unstable thunderstorms can occur. As the warm front passes the wind will veer from southeast to south or south to southwest. If the system is fairly stable, rain may continue. Rain should eventually diminish as the temperature increases.

Cold Front

The *cold front* consists of colder air overtaking warmer air. Since the cold air is heavier than the warm air it tends to push under the warm air. Figure 7-5 shows a side view of a cold front.

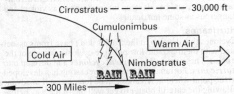

FIGURE 7-5: Schematic Section of Cold Front

The cold front usually produces precipitation and may produce violent thunderstorms.

Squall lines are produced out of strong, fast moving cold fronts and actually precede the fronts, which can produce unusually violent thunderstorms as well as tornadoes. As the front passes the wind veers quickly from southwest to west or northwest. The weather should clear fairly quickly with a few remaining cumulus clouds remaining and the barometer should start rising, indicating fair weather coming.

Occluded Front

Figure 7-6 depicts a cold occlusion. The clouds and precipitation in an occlusion are a combination of those from warm and cold fronts.

FIGURE 7-6: Schematic Section of Occluded Front

After the occluded front passes, expect similar conditions to those after the passing of a cold front.

SEVERE WEATHER

Cyclones

A *cyclone* refers to the winds surrounding a low pressure system, which, as we have seen previously, rotate counterclockwise in the northern hemisphere. These aren't necessarily violent storms, but they certainly can develop into them, often very quickly and without warning. Cyclonic systems formed outside of the tropics are called *extratropical cyclones* and can develop into storms just as violent and dangerous as some hurricanes.

Hurricanes

Cyclones that develop in the tropics don't have fronts associated with them like the low pressure cyclones outside of the tropics. These are called *tropical cyclones* and develop into *hurricanes*. Fortunately, weather forecasting has developed to the point where hurricanes can be forecast well in advance, allowing the careful boater to get well out of the way before it hits.

As a hurricane moves, its forward speed is added to the speed of the rotational winds on one side of the storm track and subtracted from the speed of the rotational winds on the other side. In the northern hemisphere, since the rotational winds are counterclockwise, the navigable semicircle is to the left of the track and the dangerous semicircle is to the right. Figure 7-7 shows this.

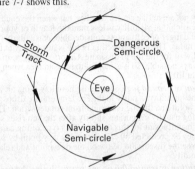

FIGURE 7-7: Hurricane Dangerous and Navigable Areas

For example, if a hurricane has developed rotational winds of, say, 70 knots and it is moving along the track at 25 knots, then the winds on the dangerous side could be 70 kn + 25 kn = 95 knots, as compared to 70 kn − 25 kn = 45 knots on the navigable side. Note that 70 knot winds are barely into the hurricane category and 130 knot winds are not unheard of.

Hurricane season lasts from about June through the end of October. Toward each end of this interval, hurricanes are less likely to occur.

Thunderstorms

The danger from thunderstorms is twofold: The obvious danger is from lightning strikes, but less obvious is the possibility of severe wind squalls that can capsize a boat. Hail can cause damage as well. There is a short discussion on lightning protection in the electrical chapter of this book.

Always keep aware of approaching fronts that can cause thunderstorms and keep checking the VHS weather channels for your area (see the section on communications in this book).

Cumulus clouds beginning to build in height provide a good indicator of developing thunderstorms. When it looks like a thunderstorm is unavoidable, start preparations well in advance; don't wait until the last moment hoping the storm will miss you. When you first think about reefing the sails, it's time to reef the sails—now.

Fog

Fog may not seem like severe weather, but when the conditions are such that visibility is less than the length of your boat, the danger of collision is considerable, particularly without radar. The best protection in fog is just to stay at the pier and wait for the fog to dissipate. Unfortunately, waiting isn't always possible, so it is helpful to have an idea when the fog might lift.

Radiation or *ground fog* occurs at night in low-lying areas where the humidity is fairly high. The temperature drops to the dew point and the fog is formed from condensation. This type of fog usually evaporates shortly after the sun rises so you can usually wait for this to clear. This type of fog can sometimes be predicted by calculating the dew point by some means; see the discussion below on the dew point and relative humidity.

Precipitation or *frontal fog* occurs mostly during the passing of a front. Rain falls from warmer air down to cooler air. Again, condensation of water vapor causes the fog. In this case, the fog should clear when the front has passed. The weather forecast and/or a current surface map will help decide when this fog will dissipate.

Advection fog is caused by winds ranging from a light to fresh breeze moving warmer moisture laden air to a colder surface such as a lake or the sea. This type of fog is also termed *marine fog* because it primarily forms over water, and it can persist for a long time until the wind either increases or changes direction.

Sea fog or *steam fog* is somewhat the opposite of advection fog, in that it forms when colder air comes in contact with warmer water. The water will often look like it is steaming, hence the name. This is often found on the Mississippi and its tributaries at dawn and dusk. This type of fog is also common off the north east coast where it can cover large areas and be very thick. It is hard to predict the persistence of this type of coastal fog.

The Dew Point and Relative Humidity

The *dew point* is the temperature at which water vapor will condense into water droplets, which is when fog forms. Knowing the current temperature and relative humidity allows us to calculate the dew point with reasonable accuracy.

A *wet bulb thermometer* is a thermometer with a dampened piece of gauze wrapped around the bulb. The effect of water evaporating from the gauze causes the thermometer to read a lower temperature than an ordinary dry bulb thermometer. The amount that the temperature is depressed is greater when the air has less relative humidity and less when the humidity is higher. This fact can be used to calculate the relative humidity and dew point.

To enhance the cooling effect, a device called a *sling psychrometer* is used; it is a device containing both a dry and wet bulb thermometer that can be swung around in a circle. The dry and wet bulb temperatures are noted. Dew point tables are included at the end of this chapter, which can be entered using the dry and wet bulb temperatures obtained from the psychrometer.

A *humidistat* is an instrument for measuring humidity, but these have not been particularly accurate in the past, hence the use of the sling psychrometer. Nowadays, however, digital electronic humidistats are available that are fairly accurate. If one of these is used, just enter the dew point tables with the dry bulb temperature and relative humidity and read the dew point.

Dew point can be measured directly by placing a thermometer in a glass of water and adding ice cubes, one at a time. When condensation occurs on the outside of the glass, quickly read the temperature, which will be the dew point. This method can also be used to determine relative humidity if a psychrometer or humidistat is not available. Just enter the tables with the dry bulb temperature and the dew point and read the humidity from the same line.

CLOUDS

Clouds occurring at differing heights have differing prefixes and words assigned as follows:

- *Cirro* for high clouds from about 18,000 feet (5500 m) up to 45,000 feet (14,000 m). *Cirrus* is used as a standalone name to describe high clouds with no prefix. These high clouds are composed of ice particles.
- *Alto* is used for clouds in the intermediate elevations from approximately 6000 to 23,000 feet (1800 to 7000 m).
- Below 6000 to 7000 feet (2100 m) no prefix is used to describe height. These clouds are water particles.

Prefixes and names used to describe shape are:

- *Cumulo* or *cumulus* describes clouds that are puffy in shape.
- *Strato* or *stratus* refers to clouds occurring in horizontal or flat layers.
- *Nimbo* or word *nimbus* is used to describe clouds that produce rain.

These words are combined to describe 10 different types of clouds. The descriptions that follow are arranged approximately in order of base height.

HIGH LEVEL CLOUDS
Cirrus (Ci)

Cirrus clouds are very high, wispy strands that are sometimes called *mare's tails*. These usually precede a warm front by a few hundred miles and thus serve to forecast the front arriving in the next day or two.

Cirrostratus (Cs)

Cirrostratus clouds are cirrus clouds that form a continuous sheet covering the entire sky. They look almost like a translucent silk veil and produce a halo around the sun or moon. Cirrostratus clouds are seen after cirrus clouds when a warm front is approaching or just after the passing of a cold front.

Cirrocumulus (Cc)

Cirrocumulus clouds are more clearly outlined than cirrus clouds and have some of the puffy appearance associated with cumulus type clouds. They appear as a thin layer with grains and ripples without shadows.

MID-LEVEL CLOUDS (WATER DROPLETS)
Altostratus (As)

Altostratus appear as a grayish or bluish veil or sheet. These clouds are caused by warm air riding over cold air. Altostratus clouds usually follow cirrostratus clouds as a warm front gets close. Initially the sun will be just visible but the clouds will ultimately thicken and rain or snow will begin.

Altocumulus (Ac)

Altocumulus clouds have a gray, flattened, thick, and puffy appearance. They often appear somewhat like wet sand ripples on a beach and will form a layer or sheet with this appearance. They are sometimes confused with cirrocumulus but have more mass and cast shadows. These are not usually associated with precipitation.

LOW-LEVEL CLOUDS

The base of these clouds is low—less than 6000 or 7000 feet (1800 or 2100 m)—but they may develop vertically into intermediate and high regions.

Cumulus (Cu)

Cumulus clouds are the large puffy clouds with vertical development that look like balls of cotton with distinct edges. They often have a cauliflower or popcorn appearance. Usually cumulus clouds are associated with fair weather following a front, but in some circumstances they develop vertically into a cumulonimbus cloud and ultimately into a thunderstorm.

Stratocumulus (Sc)

Stratocumulus clouds are solid layers with little vertical development and somewhat puffy undersides. Sometimes they will appear in long parallel rolls and move in a direction perpendicular to the rolls like waves on the water. These are sometimes formed from the remains of cumulus clouds.

Stratus (St)

Stratus clouds are a uniform fairly flat layer of clouds with no vertical development indicating stable air. They can be quite thick so as to appear quite dark from below. The base is often less than 1000 feet (300 m). Fine drizzle is possible but unlikely.

Nimbostratus (Ns)

Nimbostratus clouds are your usual rain clouds, layered but rendered indistinct by the fact that continuous rain or drizzle (or snow) is falling from them. These almost always obscure the sun. Often lower wisps or shreds of cloud are found just beneath these.

Cumulonimbus (Cb)

Commonly called a thunder cloud, cumulonimbus are huge clouds that have developed vertically and produce rain or hail. From a distance they look something like a snow-covered mountain. Quite often they have an anvil-shaped top. These can develop into thunderheads as high as 50,000 feet (15,000 m) even though the base is low enough to classify this as a low-level cloud.

WIND AND WAVES

The sea state is directly related to the speed of the wind and as a result, it is possible to predict sea conditions if the anticipated wind speed is known. Conversely, by observing the sea state, the wind speed can be estimated. The amount of sea disturbance is related to three main factors:

1. The wind speed. Higher wind speed causes greater sea movement.
2. The duration of the wind. The longer the wind blows the greater the motion of the sea until a maximum sea state is reached.
3. The fetch. The fetch is the distance over which the wind acts on the sea. The longer the fetch the greater the sea state can be. With a short fetch, the sea state will be relatively small.

Table 7-1 on the next page shows the effect of these factors on wave height.

Beaufort force of wind	Theoretical maximum wave height (ft) unlimited duration and fetch	Duration of winds (hours), with unlimited fetch, to produce percent of maximum wave height indicated			Fetch (nautical miles), with unlimited duration of blow, to produce percent of maximum wave height indicated		
		50%	75%	90%	50%	75%	90%
3	2	1.5	5	8	3	13	25
5	8	3.5	8	12	10	30	60
7	20	5.5	12	21	22	75	150
9	40	7	16	25	55	150	280
11	70	9	19	32	85	200	450

TABLE 7-1: Wave Heights Produced by Various Combinations of Wind Force, Duration, and Fetch (From Bowditch)

The Beaufort Wind Force Scale

The Beaufort Wind Force Scale was originally developed in 1805 by Sir Francis Beaufort of England as an aid to determining how much sail a ship could carry. Table 7-2 enumerates the Beaufort force numbers from 1 through 12 along with the wind speed for each along with a description of sea and land states.

Force	Effects of Wind
Force 0 < 1 kn Calm	SEA: Sea like a mirror LAND: Calm, smoke rises vertically
Force 1 1-3 kn Calm	SEA: Wave height 0.1 m (0.25 ft); scaly ripples, no foam crests LAND: Smoke drift indicates wind direction, still wind vanes
Force 2 4-6 kn Light Air	SEA: Wave height 0.2–0.3 m (0.5–1 ft); small wavelets, crests glassy, not breaking LAND: Wind felt on face, leaves rustle, vanes begin to move
Force 3 7-10 kn Gentle Breeze	SEA: Wave height 0.6–1 m (2-3 ft); Large wavelets, crests begin to break, scattered whitecaps LAND: Leaves and small twigs constantly moving, light flags extended
Force 4 11-16 kn Moderate Breeze	SEA: Wave height 1–1.5 m (3.5–5 ft); small waves becoming longer, numerous whitecaps LAND: Dust, leaves, and loose paper lifted, small tree branches move
Force 5 17-21 kn Fresh Breeze	SEA: Wave height 2–2.5 m (6–8 ft); Moderate waves, taking longer form, many whitecaps, some spray LAND: Small trees in leaf begin to sway

Force	Effects of Wind
Force 6 22-27 kn Strong Breeze	SEA: Wave height 3-4 m (9.5-13.5 ft); larger waves forming, whitecaps everywhere, more spray LAND: Larger tree branches moving, whistling in wires
Force 7 28-33 kn Near Gale	SEA: Wave height 4-5.5 m (13.5-19 ft); sea heaps up, white foam starts from breaking waves LAND: Whole trees moving, resistance felt walking against wind
Force 8 34-40 kn Gale	SEA: Wave height 5.5-7.5 m (18-25 ft); moderately high waves of greater length, edges of crests begin to break into spindrift, foam is blown in well marked streaks LAND: Whole trees in motion, resistance felt walking against wind
Force 9 41-47 kn Strong Gale	SEA: Wave height 7-10 m (23-32 ft); high waves, sea begins to roll, dense streaks of foam, spray may reduce visibility LAND: Slight structural damage occurs, slate blows off roofs
Force 10 48-55 kn Storm	SEA: Wave height 9-12.5 m (29-41 ft); very high waves with overhanging crests, sea white with densely blown foam, rolling is heavy and shock-like, visibility is reduced LAND: Seldom experienced on land, trees broken or uprooted, "considerable structural damage"
Force 11 56-63 kn Violent Storm	SEA: Wave height 11.5-16 m (37-52 ft); exceptionally high waves, sea covered with white foam patches, visibility still more reduced.
Force 12 >64 knots Hurricane	SEA: Wave height more than 16 m (52 ft); Air filled with foam, sea completely white with driving spray, visibility greatly reduced

TABLE 7-2: Beaufort Wind Force Scale

Saffir-Simpson Hurricane Scale

The Saffir-Simpson Hurricane Scale assigns a rating of from 1 to 5 based on the hurricane's wind speed. This is useful for estimating expected storm surge (flooding) and damage to boats and other property. Table 7-3 specifies the five hurricane categories and some of the characteristics of each. Most of the descriptive information is from the National Oceanic and Atmospheric Administration (NOAA).

Cat- egory	Characteristics
1	Winds 74-95 mph (64-82 kt or 119-153 km/hr). Storm surge generally 4-5 ft above normal. No real damage to building structures. Damage primarily to unanchored mobile homes, shrubbery, and trees. Also, some coastal road flooding and minor pier damage.

Cat-egory	Characteristics
2	Winds 96–110 mph (83–95 kt or 154–177 km/hr). Storm surge generally 6–8 feet above normal. Some roofing material, door, and window damage of buildings. Considerable damage to shrubbery and trees with some trees blown down. Considerable damage to mobile homes, poorly constructed signs, and piers. Coastal and low-lying escape routes flood 2–4 hours before arrival of the hurricane center. Small craft in unprotected anchorages break moorings.
3	Winds 111–130 mph (96–113 kt or 178–209 km/hr). Storm surge generally 9–12 ft above normal. Some structural damage to small residences and utility buildings with a minor amount of curtainwall failures. Damage to shrubbery and trees with foliage blown off trees and large trees blown down. Mobile homes and poorly constructed signs are destroyed. Low-lying escape routes are cut by rising water 3–5 hours before arrival of the center of the hurricane. Flooding near the coast destroys smaller structures with larger structures damaged by battering from floating debris. Terrain continuously lower than 5 ft above mean sea level may be flooded inland 8 miles (13 km) or more. Evacuation of low-lying residences with several blocks of the shoreline may be required.
4	Winds 131–155 mph (114–135 kt or 210–249 km/hr). Storm surge generally 13–18 ft above normal. More extensive curtainwall failures with some complete roof structure failures on small residences. Shrubs, trees, and all signs are blown down. Complete destruction of mobile homes. Extensive damage to doors and windows. Low-lying escape routes may be cut by rising water 3–5 hours before arrival of the center of the hurricane. Major damage to lower floors of structures near the shore. Terrain lower than 10 ft above sea level may be flooded requiring massive evacuation of residential areas as far inland as 6 miles (10 km).
5	Winds greater than 155 mph (135 kt or 249 km/hr). Storm surge generally greater than 18 ft above normal. Complete roof failure on many residences and industrial buildings. Some complete building failures with small utility buildings blown over or away. All shrubs, trees, and signs blown down. Complete destruction of mobile homes. Severe and extensive window and door damage. Low-lying escape routes are cut by rising water 3–5 hours before arrival of the center of the hurricane. Major damage to lower floors of all structures located less than 15 ft above sea level and within 500 yards of the shoreline. Massive evacuation of residential areas on low ground within 5–10 miles (8–16 km) of the shoreline may be required.

TABLE 7-3: Saffir-Simpson Hurricane Scale

WEATHER MAP SYMBOLS

In addition to the isobars and fronts discussed earlier, surface weather maps include *station weather plots*. The use of symbols and numbers helps to convey a large amount of information visually without words. There are well over a hundred different symbols used by NOAA, most of which are reproduced here.

Figure 7-10 on the next page shows a hypothetical station plot. Note how the data on the plot is basically organized into three rows and three columns.

Symbols for Fronts

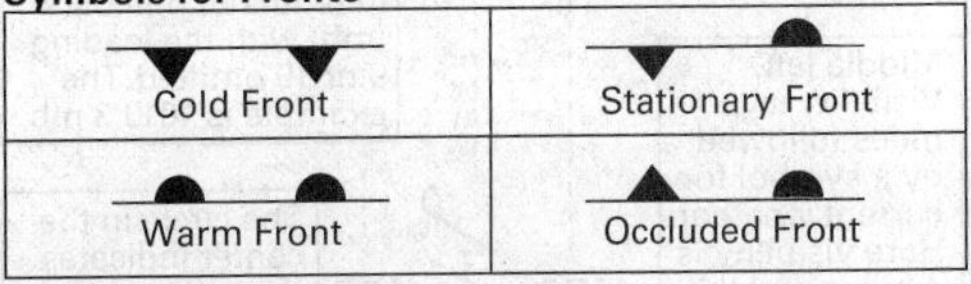

Cold Front	Stationary Front
Warm Front	Occluded Front

FIGURE 7-8: Symbols Used for Fronts

Sky Cover Symbols

Note: Sky obscured is used when fog or precipitation obscures view of the cloud cover.

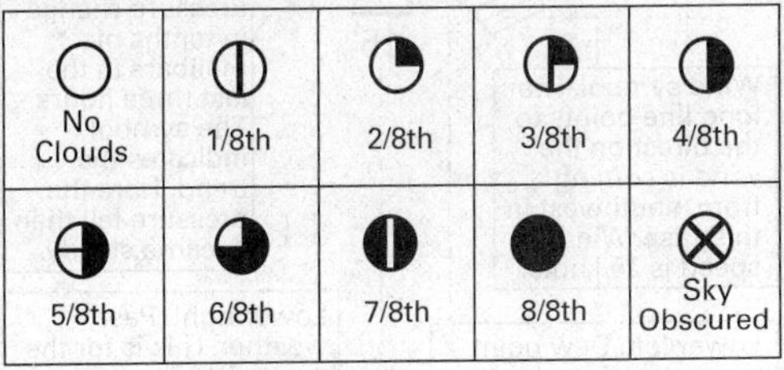

No Clouds	1/8th	2/8th	3/8th	4/8th
5/8th	6/8th	7/8th	8/8th	Sky Obscured

FIGURE 7-9: Sky Cover Symbols

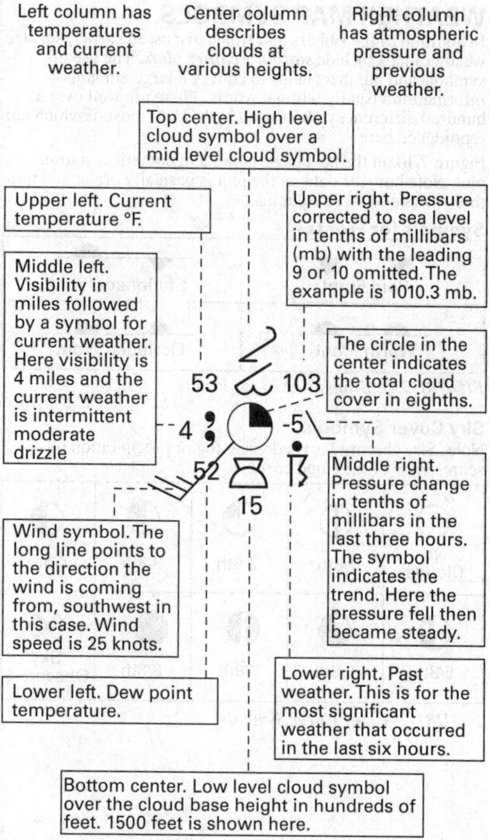

Left column has temperatures and current weather.

Center column describes clouds at various heights.

Right column has atmospheric pressure and previous weather.

Top center. High level cloud symbol over a mid level cloud symbol.

Upper left. Current temperature °F.

Upper right. Pressure corrected to sea level in tenths of millibars (mb) with the leading 9 or 10 omitted. The example is 1010.3 mb.

Middle left. Visibility in miles followed by a symbol for current weather. Here visibility is 4 miles and the current weather is intermittent moderate drizzle

The circle in the center indicates the total cloud cover in eighths.

53   103

4   -5

52   15

Middle right. Pressure change in tenths of millibars in the last three hours. The symbol indicates the trend. Here the pressure fell then became steady.

Wind symbol. The long line points to the direction the wind is coming from, southwest in this case. Wind speed is 25 knots.

Lower right. Past weather. This is for the most significant weather that occurred in the last six hours.

Lower left. Dew point temperature.

Bottom center. Low level cloud symbol over the cloud base height in hundreds of feet. 1500 feet is shown here.

FIGURE 7-10: Station Weather Plot. See figures 7-8 through 7-15 for explanations of symbols

HIGH LEVEL CLOUDS Typical base > 18,000 feet.		Cirrostratus (Cs)	⌐
Cirrus (Ci) Filaments	⌐	Cirrostratus Converging Bands	2
Cirrus Dense in Patches	⌐	Cirrostratus Veil	2⌐
Cirrus Dense	⌐	Cirrostratus Partial Sky Cover	⌐
Cirrus Hooked Shape	⌐	Cirrocumulus (Cc)	2

MID LEVEL CLOUDS Base 8,000 - 18,000 feet.		Altocumulus Bands Thickening	⌐
Altostratus (As)	∠	Altocumulus from Spreading Cu or Cb	⋉
Altostratus (As) / Nimbostratus (Ns)	⫽	Altocumulus Layered or Thick	6⌐
Altocumulus (Ac) Thin	∽	Altocumulus Tufts or Turrets	⋔
Altocumulus Thin in Patches	6	Altocumulus Chaotic Sky	6⌐

LOW LEVEL CLOUDS Typical base < 8,000 feet.		Stratocumulus Not fr Cu spreading	∽
Cumulus (Cu) Fair Weather	⌂	Stratus (St) or Stratus Fractus	—
Cumulus Developing	⌂	Stratus of Bad Weather	- - -
Cumulonimbus (Cb) Vertically Developed	⌂	Stratocumulus over Cumulus	⋈
Stratocumulus (Sc) Bands or Rolls	⊙	Cumulonimbus Fibrous or Anvil Top	⊠

FIGURE 7-11: Symbols for Clouds

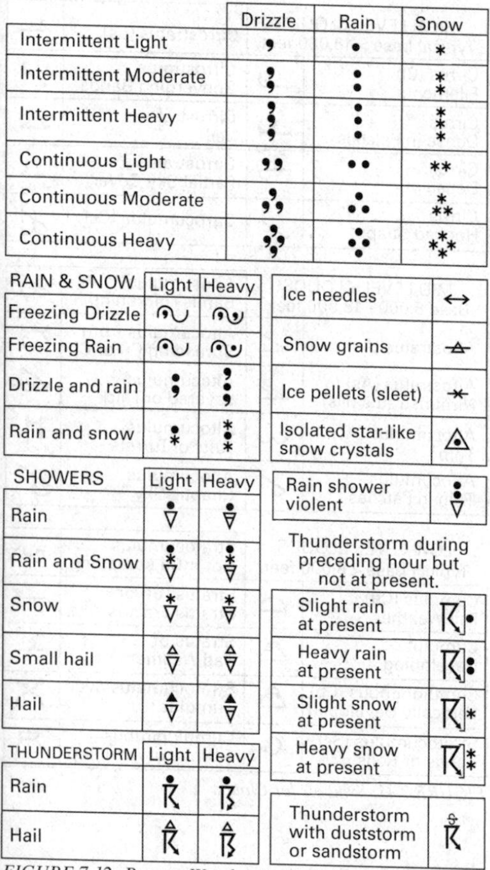

	Drizzle	Rain	Snow
Intermittent Light	'	•	✳
Intermittent Moderate	;	• •	✳✳
Intermittent Heavy	;	• • •	✳✳✳
Continuous Light	''	• •	✳✳
Continuous Moderate	;'	• • •	✳✳✳
Continuous Heavy	;;	• • • •	✳✳✳

RAIN & SNOW	Light	Heavy
Freezing Drizzle	∩	∩
Freezing Rain	∩	∩•
Drizzle and rain	;	;
Rain and snow	• ✳	• ✳✳

SHOWERS	Light	Heavy
Rain	▽	▽
Rain and Snow	▽	▽
Snow	▽	▽
Small hail	▽	▽
Hail	▽	▽

THUNDERSTORM	Light	Heavy
Rain	℞	℞
Hail	℞	℞

Ice needles	↔
Snow grains	⊸
Ice pellets (sleet)	⚹
Isolated star-like snow crystals	△

Rain shower violent	▽

Thunderstorm during preceding hour but not at present.	
Slight rain at present	℞•
Heavy rain at present	℞:
Slight snow at present	℞✳
Heavy snow at present	℞✳

Thunderstorm with duststorm or sandstorm	℞

FIGURE 7-12: Present Weather Symbols for Precipitation

NO PRECIPITATION AT STATION		Precip in sight not reaching ground	⦁
Visibility reduced by smoke	⌒	Precip in sight reaching ground > 3 mi	)•(
Haze	∞	Precip in sight reaching ground > 3 mi	(•)
Lightning visible, no thunder heard	⟨	Squalls in sight during past hour	▽
Funnel /Tornado within last hour	)(	Thunder heard no precip at station	⊼

•]	A square left facing parentheses means the condition ended in the past hour. Here light intermittent rain ended in the past hour.

⊨ |S ≡ S|	A vertical bar to the left of a fog or sand-storm symbol indicates the condition has increased within the past hour. A bar to the right indicates the condition has decreased.

DUST OR SAND		FOG	
Dust or sand whirls	⥁	Mist	=
Suspended Dust	S	Fog patches < 6 ft thick	≡≡
Wind raised sand or dust	$	Fog continuous < 6 ft thick	≡≡
Storm at distance within sight.	(S)	Fog at distance but not at station	(≡)
Slight or moderate sand or dust storm	S	Fog patches	≡≡
Severe sand or dust storm	S	Fog, sky visible	≡

DRIFTING SNOW	Light	Heavy	Fog, sky obscured	≡
Below eye level	+	⇸	Fog depositing rime ice, sky visible	ⱱ
Above eye level	+	⇸	Fog depositing rime ice, sky obscured	ⱱ

FIGURE 7-13: Present Weather Symbols—General Group

CHANGE DURING LAST THREE HOURS		Steady, same as 3 hours ago	—
Rising, then falling	∧	Falling, then rising	∨
Rising then steady, or rising, then rising more slowly	⌐	Falling, then steady, or falling then falling more slowly	⌐
Rising steadily, or unsteadily	╱	Falling steadily, or unsteadily	╲
Falling or steady then rising, or rising then rising more quickly	✓	Steady or rising, then falling, or falling, then falling more quickly	∧

FIGURE 7-14: Barometric Tendency

The wind symbol points to the direction the wind is coming from. Each long stroke represents 10 knots and each short stroke represents 5 knots. The solid black triangle is used to indicate 50 knots. With these three shapes, any wind speed can be indicated to the nearest 5 knots. The examples below demonstrate how this works.

5 knots	⌐	20 knots	╲╲	35 knots	╲╲╲
50 knots	▲	85 knots	▲╲╲╲	115 knots	▲▲╲

FIGURE 7-15: Wind Symbols

WEATHER TABLES AND CHARTS
Cold Water Survival Time

Water Temp °F	Water Temp °C	Exhaustion or Unconsciousness	Expected Survival Time
<32	<0	< 15 min	< 15–45 min
32.5–40	0–44	15–30 min	30–90 min
40–50	4–10	30–60 min	1–3 hrs
50–60	10–16	1–2 hrs	1–6 hrs
60–70	16–21	2–7 hrs	2–40 hrs
70–80	21–27	3–12 hrs	3 hrs–indefinite
>80	>80	Indefinite	Indefinite

TABLE 7-4: Cold Water Survival Time

Wind Chill Chart

The Wind Chill Chart was updated in 2001 by the National Weather Service and the Meteorological Services of Canada. It gives the perceived temperature (how cold it really feels) at various actual temperatures and wind speeds.

	Wind Speed (mph)											
	5	10	15	20	25	30	35	40	45	50	55	60
°F	Perceived Temperature °F											
40	36	34	32	30	29	28	28	27	26	26	25	25
35	31	27	25	24	23	22	21	20	19	19	18	17
30	25	21	19	17	16	15	14	13	12	12	11	10
25	19	15	13	11	9	8	7	6	5	4	4	3
20	13	9	6	4	3	1	0	-1	-2	-3	-3	-4
15	7	3	0	-2	-4	-5	-7	-8	-9	-10	-11	-11
10	1	-4	-7	-9	-11	-12	-14	-15	-16	-17	-18	-19
5	-5	-10	-13	-15	-17	-19	-21	-22	-23	-24	-25	-26
0	-11	-16	-19	-22	-24	-26	-27	-29	-30	-31	-32	-33
-5	-16	-22	-26	-29	-31	-33	-34	-36	-37	-38	-39	-40
-10	-22	-28	-32	-35	-37	-39	-41	-43	-44	-45	-46	-48
-15	-28	-35	-39	-42	-44	-46	-48	-50	-51	-52	-54	-55
-20	-34	-41	-45	-48	-51	-53	-55	-57	-58	-60	-61	-62
-25	-40	-47	-51	-55	-58	-60	-62	-64	-65	-67	-68	-69
-30	-46	-53	-58	-61	-64	-67	-69	-71	-72	-74	-75	-76
-35	-52	-59	-64	-68	-71	-73	-76	-78	-79	-81	-82	-84
-40	-57	-66	-71	-74	-78	-80	-82	-84	-86	-88	-89	-91
-45	-63	-72	-77	-81	-84	-87	-89	-91	-93	-95	-97	-98
°C	Perceived Temperature °C											
4	2	1	0	-1	-2	-2	-2	-3	-3	-3	-4	-4
2	-0	-3	-4	-4	-5	-6	-6	-7	-7	-7	-8	-8
-1	-4	-6	-7	-8	-9	-9	-10	-11	-11	-11	-12	-12
-4	-7	-9	-11	-12	-13	-13	-14	-14	-15	-16	-16	-16
-7	-11	-13	-14	-16	-16	-17	-18	-18	-19	-19	-19	-20
-9	-14	-16	-18	-19	-20	-21	-22	-22	-23	-23	-24	-24
-12	-17	-20	-22	-23	-24	-24	-26	-26	-27	-27	-28	-28
-15	-21	-23	-25	-26	-27	-28	-29	-30	-31	-31	-32	-32
-18	-24	-27	-28	-30	-31	-32	-33	-34	-34	-35	-36	-36
-21	-27	-30	-32	-34	-35	-36	-37	-38	-38	-39	-39	-40
-23	-30	-33	-36	-37	-38	-39	-41	-42	-42	-43	-43	-44
-26	-33	-37	-39	-41	-42	-43	-44	-46	-46	-47	-48	-48
-29	-37	-41	-43	-44	-46	-47	-48	-49	-50	-51	-52	-52
-32	-40	-44	-46	-48	-50	-51	-52	-53	-54	-55	-56	-56
-34	-43	-47	-50	-52	-53	-55	-56	-57	-58	-59	-59	-60
-37	-47	-51	-53	-56	-57	-58	-60	-61	-62	-63	-63	-64
-40	-49	-54	-57	-59	-61	-62	-63	-64	-66	-67	-67	-68
-43	-53	-58	-61	-63	-64	-65	-68	-69	-71	-72	-72	
Frostbite time				30 min				10 min			5 min	

TABLE 7-5: Wind Chill Chart

Heat Index Table

The Heat Index is similar to the Wind Chill Factor in that it gives the temperature the body "feels" when the effect of humidity is taken into account. Table 7-6 (data from NOAA) gives the perceived temperatures at various relative humidity's for various actual (dry bulb) temperatures.

Actual Temp	Relative Humidity					
	40%	50%	60%	70%	80%	90%
°F	Perceived Temperature °F					
80	79	80	81	82	84	85
85	84	86	90	92	96	101
90	90	94	99	105	113	121
95	98	105	113	122	133	
100	109	118	129	142		
105	121	133	148			
110	135					
°C	Perceived Temperature °C					
27	26	27	27	28	29	29
29	29	30	32	33	36	38
32	32	34	37	41	45	49
35	37	41	45	50	56	
38	43	48	54	61		
41	49	56	64			
43	57					

TABLE 7-6: Heat Index

Important: Add 15 degrees Fahrenheit (8 degrees Celsius) to perceived temperature for exposure to direct sunlight.

80 – 90 °F (27 – 32 °C)	Fatigue possible with prolonged exposure and physical activity
90 – 105 °F (32 – 41°C)	Sunstroke, heat cramps and heat exhaustion possible.
105 – 130 °F (41 – 54 °C	Sunstroke, heat cramps, and heat exhaustion likely, and heat stroke possible.
130 °F (54 °C)	Heat stroke highly likely with continued exposure.

TABLE 7-7: Perceived Temperatures and the Likely Health Disorders That Will Result

Air Pressure Conversion Table

m bar	in hg	mm hg	m bar	in hg	mm hg	m bar	in hg	mm hg	m bar	in hg	mm hg
900	26.58	675.1	945	27.91	708.8	990	29.23	742.6	1035	30.56	776.3
901	26.61	675.8	946	27.94	709.6	991	29.26	743.3	1036	30.59	777.1
902	26.64	676.6	947	27.96	710.3	992	29.29	744.1	1037	30.62	777.8
903	26.67	677.3	948	27.99	711.1	993	29.32	744.8	1038	30.65	778.6
904	26.70	678.1	949	28.02	711.8	994	29.35	745.6	1039	30.68	779.3
905	26.72	678.8	950	28.05	712.6	995	29.38	746.3	1040	30.71	780.1
906	26.75	679.6	951	28.08	713.3	996	29.41	747.1	1041	30.74	780.8
907	26.78	680.3	952	28.11	714.1	997	29.44	747.8	1042	30.77	781.6
908	26.81	681.1	953	28.14	714.8	998	29.47	748.6	1043	30.80	782.3
909	26.84	681.8	954	28.17	715.6	999	29.50	749.3	1044	30.83	783.1
910	26.87	682.6	955	28.20	716.3	1000	29.53	750.1	1045	30.86	783.8
911	26.90	683.3	956	28.23	717.1	1001	29.56	750.8	1046	30.89	784.6
912	26.93	684.1	957	28.26	717.8	1002	29.59	751.6	1047	30.92	785.3
913	26.96	684.8	958	28.29	718.6	1003	29.62	752.3	1048	30.95	786.1
914	26.99	685.6	959	28.32	719.3	1004	29.65	753.1	1049	30.98	786.8
915	27.02	686.3	960	28.35	720.1	1005	29.68	753.8	1050	31.01	787.6
916	27.05	687.1	961	28.38	720.8	1006	29.71	754.6	1051	31.04	788.3
917	27.08	687.8	962	28.41	721.6	1007	29.74	755.3	1052	31.07	789.1
918	27.11	688.6	963	28.44	722.3	1008	29.77	756.1	1053	31.10	789.8
919	27.14	689.3	964	28.47	723.1	1009	29.80	756.8	1054	31.12	790.6
920	27.17	690.1	965	28.50	723.8	1010	29.83	757.6	1055	31.15	791.3
921	27.20	690.8	966	28.53	724.6	1011	29.85	758.3	1056	31.18	792.1
922	27.23	691.6	967	28.56	725.3	1012	29.88	759.1	1057	31.21	792.8
923	27.26	692.3	968	28.59	726.1	1013	29.91	759.8	1058	31.24	793.6
924	27.29	693.1	969	28.61	726.8	1014	29.94	760.6	1059	31.27	794.3
925	27.32	693.8	970	28.64	727.6	1015	29.97	761.3	1060	31.30	795.1
926	27.34	694.6	971	28.67	728.3	1016	30.00	762.1	1061	31.33	795.8
927	27.37	695.3	972	28.70	729.1	1017	30.03	762.8	1062	31.36	796.6
928	27.40	696.1	973	28.73	729.8	1018	30.06	763.6	1063	31.39	797.3
929	27.43	696.8	974	28.76	730.6	1019	30.09	764.3	1064	31.42	798.1
930	27.46	697.6	975	28.79	731.3	1020	30.12	765.1	1065	31.45	798.8
931	27.49	698.3	976	28.82	732.1	1021	30.15	765.8	1066	31.48	799.6
932	27.52	699.1	977	28.85	732.8	1022	30.18	766.6	1067	31.51	800.3
933	27.55	699.8	978	28.88	733.6	1023	30.21	767.3	1068	31.54	801.1
934	27.58	700.6	979	28.91	734.3	1024	30.24	768.1	1069	31.57	801.8
935	27.61	701.3	980	28.94	735.1	1025	30.27	768.8	1070	31.60	802.6
936	27.64	702.1	981	28.97	735.8	1026	30.30	769.6	1071	31.63	803.3
937	27.67	702.8	982	29.00	736.6	1027	30.33	770.3	1072	31.66	804.1
938	27.70	703.6	983	29.03	737.3	1028	30.36	771.1	1073	31.69	804.8
939	27.73	704.3	984	29.06	738.1	1029	30.39	771.8	1074	31.72	805.6
940	27.76	705.1	985	29.09	738.8	1030	30.42	772.6	1075	31.74	806.3
941	27.79	705.8	986	29.12	739.6	1031	30.45	773.3	1076	31.77	807.1
942	27.82	706.6	987	29.15	740.3	1032	30.47	774.1	1077	31.80	807.8
943	27.85	707.3	988	29.18	741.1	1033	30.50	774.8	1078	31.83	808.6
944	27.88	708.1	989	29.21	741.8	1034	30.53	775.6	1079	31.86	809.3

TABLE 7-8: Convert Pressure Millibars, Inches Mercury, Millimeters Mercury

Temperature Conversion Tables

$$°C = (°F - 32) \times \frac{9}{5}$$

°F	°C	°F	°C	°F	°C	°F	°C	°F	°C	°F	°C
-50	-45.6	-10	-23.3	30	-1.1	70	21.1	110	43.3	216	102
-49	-45.0	-9	-22.8	31	-0.6	71	21.7	112	44.4	229	109
-48	-44.4	-8	-22.2	32	0.0	72	22.2	114	45.4	242	117
-47	-43.9	-7	-21.7	33	0.6	73	22.8	116	46.5	256	125
-46	-43.3	-6	-21.1	34	1.1	74	23.3	118	47.6	271	133
-45	-42.8	-5	-20.6	35	1.7	75	23.9	120	48.7	287	142
-44	-42.2	-4	-20.0	36	2.2	76	24.4	122	49.8	304	151
-43	-41.7	-3	-19.4	37	2.8	77	25.0	124	51.0	322	161
-42	-41.1	-2	-18.9	38	3.3	78	25.6	126	52.1	341	172
-41	-40.6	-1	-18.3	39	3.9	79	26.1	128	53.3	361	183
-40	-40.0	0	-17.8	40	4.4	80	26.7	130	54.5	382	195
-39	-39.4	1	-17.2	41	5.0	81	27.2	132	55.8	405	207
-38	-38.9	2	-16.7	42	5.6	82	27.8	135	57.0	428	220
-37	-38.3	3	-16.1	43	6.1	83	28.3	137	58.3	454	234
-36	-37.8	4	-15.6	44	6.7	84	28.9	139	59.6	480	249
-35	-37.2	5	-15.0	45	7.2	85	29.4	142	60.9	508	265
-34	-36.7	6	-14.4	46	7.8	86	30.0	144	62.2	538	281
-33	-36.1	7	-13.9	47	8.3	87	30.6	146	63.6	570	299
-32	-35.6	8	-13.3	48	8.9	88	31.1	149	65.0	603	317
-31	-35.0	9	-12.8	49	9.4	89	31.7	151	66.4	639	337
-30	-34.4	10	-12.2	50	10.0	90	32.2	154	67.8	676	358
-29	-33.9	11	-11.7	51	10.6	91	32.8	157	69.2	716	380
-28	-33.3	12	-11.1	52	11.1	92	33.3	159	70.7	758	403
-27	-32.8	13	-10.6	53	11.7	93	33.9	162	72.2	803	428
-26	-32.2	14	-10.0	54	12.2	94	34.4	165	73.7	850	454
-25	-31.7	15	-9.4	55	12.8	95	35.0	168	75.3	900	482
-24	-31.1	16	-8.9	56	13.3	96	35.6	170	76.9	953	511
-23	-30.6	17	-8.3	57	13.9	97	36.1	173	78.5	1008	542
-22	-30.0	18	-7.8	58	14.4	98	36.7	176	80.1	1068	575
-21	-29.4	19	-7.2	59	15.0	99	37.2	179	81.8	1130	610
-20	-28.9	20	-6.7	60	15.6	100	37.8	182	83.5	1197	647
-19	-28.3	21	-6.1	61	16.1	101	38.3	185	85.2	1267	686
-18	-27.8	22	-5.6	62	16.7	102	38.9	188	86.9	1341	727
-17	-27.2	23	-5.0	63	17.2	103	39.4	192	88.7	1420	771
-16	-26.7	24	-4.4	64	17.8	104	40.0	195	90.5	1504	818
-15	-26.1	25	-3.9	65	18.3	105	40.6	198	92.4	1592	867
-14	-25.6	26	-3.3	66	18.9	106	41.1	202	94.2	1685	919
-13	-25.0	27	-2.8	67	19.4	107	41.7	205	96.1	1784	974
-12	-24.4	28	-2.2	68	20.0	108	42.2	208	98.1	1889	1032
-11	-23.9	29	-1.7	69	20.6	109	42.8	212	100.0	2000	1093

TABLE 7-9: Fahrenheit to Celsius Conversion

$$°F = (\frac{°C \times 9}{5}) - 32$$

°C	°F	°C	°F	°C	°F	°C	°F	°C	°F
-50	-58.0	-10	14.0	30	86.0	70	158.0	163	325.6
-49	-56.2	-9	15.8	31	87.8	71	159.8	171	340.3
-48	-54.4	-8	17.6	32	89.6	72	161.6	180	355.8
-47	-52.6	-7	19.4	33	91.4	73	163.4	189	372.0
-46	-50.8	-6	21.2	34	93.2	74	165.2	198	389.1
-45	-49.0	-5	23.0	35	95.0	75	167.0	208	407.0
-44	-47.2	-4	24.8	36	96.8	76	168.8	219	425.8
-43	-45.4	-3	26.6	37	98.6	77	170.6	230	445.6
-42	-43.6	-2	28.4	38	100.4	78	172.4	241	466.3
-41	-41.8	-1	30.2	39	102.2	79	174.2	253	488.1
-40	-40.0	0	32.0	40	104.0	80	176.0	266	511.0
-39	-38.2	1	33.8	41	105.8	81	177.8	279	535.0
-38	-36.4	2	35.6	42	107.6	82	179.6	293	560.2
-37	-34.6	3	37.4	43	109.4	83	181.4	308	586.7
-36	-32.8	4	39.2	44	111.2	84	183.2	324	614.5
-35	-31.0	5	41.0	45	113.0	85	185.0	340	643.7
-34	-29.2	6	42.8	46	114.8	86	186.8	357	674.4
-33	-27.4	7	44.6	47	116.6	87	188.6	375	706.6
-32	-25.6	8	46.4	48	118.4	88	190.4	394	740.5
-31	-23.8	9	48.2	49	120.2	89	192.2	413	776.0
-30	-22.0	10	50.0	50	122.0	90	194.0	434	813.3
-29	-20.2	11	51.8	51	123.8	91	195.8	456	852.5
-28	-18.4	12	53.6	52	125.6	92	197.6	479	893.6
-27	-16.6	13	55.4	53	127.4	93	199.4	503	936.8
-26	-14.8	14	57.2	54	129.2	94	201.2	528	982.2
-25	-13.0	15	59.0	55	131.0	95	203.0	554	1029.9
-24	-11.2	16	60.8	56	132.8	96	204.8	582	1079.9
-23	-9.4	17	62.6	57	134.6	97	206.6	611	1132.5
-22	-7.6	18	64.4	58	136.4	98	208.4	642	1187.6
-21	-5.8	19	66.2	59	138.2	99	210.2	674	1245.6
-20	-4.0	20	68.0	60	140.0	100	212.0	708	1306.5
-19	-2.2	21	69.8	61	141.8	105	221.0	744	1370.4
-18	-0.4	22	71.6	62	143.6	110	230.5	781	1437.5
-17	1.4	23	73.4	63	145.4	116	240.5	820	1508.0
-16	3.2	24	75.2	64	147.2	122	250.9	861	1582.0
-15	5.0	25	77.0	65	149.0	128	261.9	904	1659.7
-14	6.8	26	78.8	66	150.8	134	273.4	950	1741.4
-13	8.6	27	80.6	67	152.6	141	285.5	997	1827.1
-12	10.4	28	82.4	68	154.4	148	298.2	1047	1917.1
-11	12.2	29	84.2	69	156.2	155	311.6	1100	2011.6

TABLE 7-10: Celsius to Fahrenheit Conversion

Dew Point Table

Dry °F	Dry °C	Wet °F	Wet °C	Rel Hum %	Dew point °F	Dew point °C
34	1.1	33	0.6	90%	31	-0.3
34	1.1	32	0.0	81%	29	-1.8
36	2.2	35	1.7	91%	34	0.9
36	2.2	34	1.1	82%	31	-0.6
36	2.2	33	0.6	73%	28	-2.2
36	2.2	32	0.0	64%	25	-3.9
38	3.3	37	2.8	91%	36	2.0
38	3.3	36	2.2	82%	33	0.6
38	3.3	35	1.7	74%	30	-0.9
38	3.3	34	1.1	65%	27	-2.5
38	3.3	33	0.6	57%	24	-4.3
38	3.3	32	0.0	49%	21	-6.4
40	4.4	39	3.9	92%	38	3.2
40	4.4	38	3.3	83%	35	1.9
40	4.4	37	2.8	75%	33	0.4
40	4.4	36	2.2	67%	30	-1.1
40	4.4	35	1.7	59%	27	-2.8
40	4.4	34	1.1	51%	24	-4.7
40	4.4	33	0.6	44%	20	-6.8
40	4.4	32	0.0	36%	15	-9.3
42	5.6	41	5.0	92%	40	4.4
42	5.6	40	4.4	84%	38	3.1
42	5.6	39	3.9	76%	35	1.7
42	5.6	38	3.3	69%	32	0.2
42	5.6	37	2.8	61%	30	-1.4
42	5.6	36	2.2	54%	26	-3.1
42	5.6	35	1.7	46%	23	-5.1
42	5.6	34	1.1	39%	19	-7.3
42	5.6	33	0.6	32%	14	-9.9
42	5.6	32	0.0	25%	9	-13.0
44	6.7	43	6.1	92%	42	5.5
44	6.7	42	5.6	85%	40	4.3
44	6.7	41	5.0	77%	37	3.0
44	6.7	40	4.4	70%	35	1.6
44	6.7	39	3.9	63%	32	0.1
44	6.7	38	3.3	56%	29	-1.6
44	6.7	37	2.8	49%	26	-3.4
44	6.7	36	2.2	42%	22	-5.4
44	6.7	35	1.7	35%	18	-7.8
44	6.7	34	1.1	28%	13	-10.5
44	6.7	33	0.6	21%	7	-13.8
44	6.7	32	0.0	15%	-1	-18.1
46	7.8	45	7.2	93%	44	6.7
46	7.8	44	6.7	85%	42	5.5
46	7.8	43	6.1	78%	40	4.2
46	7.8	42	5.6	71%	37	2.9
46	7.8	41	5.0	64%	35	1.5
46	7.8	40	4.4	57%	32	-0.1
46	7.8	39	3.9	51%	29	-1.8
46	7.8	38	3.3	44%	25	-3.7
46	7.8	37	2.8	38%	22	-5.8
46	7.8	36	2.2	31%	17	-8.2
46	7.8	35	1.7	25%	12	-11.0
46	7.8	34	1.1	19%	6	-14.5
46	7.8	33	0.6	13%	-3	-19.3
46	7.8	32	0.0	6%	-16	-26.7
48	8.9	47	8.3	93%	46	7.8
48	8.9	46	7.8	86%	44	6.7
48	8.9	45	7.2	79%	42	5.5
48	8.9	44	6.7	72%	40	4.2
48	8.9	43	6.1	66%	37	2.8
48	8.9	42	5.6	59%	34	1.4
48	8.9	41	5.0	53%	32	-0.2
48	8.9	40	4.4	46%	28	-2.0
48	8.9	39	3.9	40%	25	-3.9
48	8.9	38	3.3	34%	21	-6.1
48	8.9	37	2.8	28%	17	-8.6
48	8.9	36	2.2	22%	11	-11.6
48	8.9	35	1.7	16%	4	-15.4
48	8.9	34	1.1	10%	-5	-20.5
48	8.9	33	0.6	5%	-21	-29.2
50	10.0	49	9.4	93%	48	8.9
50	10.0	48	8.9	86%	46	7.8
50	10.0	47	8.3	80%	44	6.7
50	10.0	46	7.8	73%	42	5.5
50	10.0	45	7.2	67%	40	4.2
50	10.0	44	6.7	61%	37	2.8
50	10.0	43	6.1	55%	34	1.3
50	10.0	42	5.6	49%	31	-0.3
50	10.0	41	5.0	43%	28	-2.1
50	10.0	40	4.4	37%	25	-4.1
50	10.0	39	3.9	31%	21	-6.4
50	10.0	38	3.3	25%	16	-9.0
50	10.0	37	2.8	20%	10	-12.1
50	10.0	36	2.2	14%	3	-16.1
50	10.0	35	1.7	9%	-7	-21.8
50	10.0	34	1.1	3%	-26	-32.2
52	11.1	51	10.6	93%	50	10.1
52	11.1	50	10.0	87%	48	9.0
52	11.1	49	9.4	81%	46	7.9
52	11.1	48	8.9	74%	44	6.7
52	11.1	47	8.3	68%	42	5.5
52	11.1	46	7.8	62%	40	4.2
52	11.1	45	7.2	56%	37	2.8

TABLE 7-11: Dry and Wet Bulb Temperatures to Dew Point

Dry °F	°C	Wet °F	°C	Rel Hum %	Dew point °F	°C	Dry °F	°C	Wet °F	°C	Rel Hum %	Dew point °F	°C
52	11.1	44	6.7	51%	34	1.2	58	14.4	57	13.9	94%	56	13.5
52	11.1	43	6.1	45%	31	-0.4	58	14.4	56	13.3	88%	55	12.5
52	11.1	42	5.6	39%	28	-2.2	58	14.4	55	12.8	83%	53	11.5
52	11.1	41	5.0	34%	24	-4.3	58	14.4	54	12.2	77%	51	10.5
52	11.1	40	4.4	28%	20	-6.6	58	14.4	53	11.7	72%	49	9.4
52	11.1	39	3.9	23%	15	-9.3	58	14.4	52	11.1	66%	47	8.2
52	11.1	38	3.3	18%	9	-12.6	58	14.4	51	10.6	61%	45	7.0
52	11.1	37	2.8	12%	2	-16.9	58	14.4	50	10.0	56%	42	5.7
52	11.1	36	2.2	7%	-10	-23.1	58	14.4	49	9.4	51%	40	4.3
52	11.1	35	1.7	2%	-33	-35.9	58	14.4	48	8.9	46%	37	2.8
54	12.2	53	11.7	94%	52	11.1	58	14.4	47	8.3	41%	34	1.2
54	12.2	52	11.1	87%	50	10.2	58	14.4	46	7.8	36%	31	-0.5
54	12.2	51	10.6	81%	48	9.1	58	14.4	45	7.2	31%	28	-2.5
54	12.2	50	10.0	75%	46	8.0	58	14.4	44	6.7	26%	24	-4.6
54	12.2	49	9.4	69%	44	6.8	58	14.4	43	6.1	22%	19	-7.2
54	12.2	48	8.9	64%	42	5.5	58	14.4	42	5.6	17%	14	-10.2
54	12.2	47	8.3	58%	40	4.2	58	14.4	41	5.0	13%	7	-13.9
54	12.2	46	7.8	52%	37	2.8	58	14.4	40	4.4	8%	-2	-18.9
54	12.2	45	7.2	47%	34	1.2	58	14.4	39	3.9	4%	-17	-27.2
54	12.2	44	6.7	41%	31	-0.5	60	15.6	59	15.0	94%	58	14.6
54	12.2	43	6.1	36%	28	-2.3	60	15.6	58	14.4	89%	57	13.7
54	12.2	42	5.6	31%	24	-4.4	60	15.6	57	13.9	83%	55	12.7
54	12.2	41	5.0	26%	20	-6.8	60	15.6	56	13.3	78%	53	11.7
54	12.2	40	4.4	21%	15	-9.6	60	15.6	55	12.8	72%	51	10.6
54	12.2	39	3.9	16%	8	-13.1	60	15.6	54	12.2	67%	49	9.5
54	12.2	38	3.3	11%	0	-17.6	60	15.6	53	11.7	62%	47	8.3
54	12.2	37	2.8	6%	-12	-24.4	60	15.6	52	11.1	57%	45	7.1
54	12.2	36	2.2	1%	-42	-41.2	60	15.6	51	10.6	52%	42	5.8
56	13.3	55	12.8	94%	54	12.4	60	15.6	50	10.0	47%	40	4.4
56	13.3	54	12.2	88%	52	11.4	60	15.6	49	9.4	43%	37	2.9
56	13.3	53	11.7	82%	51	10.3	60	15.6	48	8.9	38%	34	1.3
56	13.3	52	11.1	76%	49	9.2	60	15.6	47	8.3	33%	31	-0.5
56	13.3	51	10.6	71%	47	8.1	60	15.6	46	7.8	29%	28	-2.5
56	13.3	50	10.0	65%	44	6.9	60	15.6	45	7.2	24%	24	-4.6
56	13.3	49	9.4	59%	42	5.6	60	15.6	44	6.7	20%	19	-7.3
56	13.3	48	8.9	54%	40	4.2	60	15.6	43	6.1	16%	13	-10.3
56	13.3	47	8.3	49%	37	2.8	60	15.6	42	5.6	12%	6	-14.2
56	13.3	46	7.8	44%	34	1.2	60	15.6	41	5.0	7%	-3	-19.5
56	13.3	45	7.2	38%	31	-0.5	60	15.6	40	4.4	3%	-19	-28.5
56	13.3	44	6.7	33%	28	-2.4	62	16.7	61	16.1	94%	60	15.8
56	13.3	43	6.1	28%	24	-4.6	62	16.7	60	15.6	89%	59	14.9
56	13.3	42	5.6	24%	19	-7.0	62	16.7	59	15.0	84%	57	13.9
56	13.3	41	5.0	19%	14	-9.9	62	16.7	58	14.4	78%	55	12.9
56	13.3	40	4.4	14%	8	-13.5	62	16.7	57	13.9	73%	53	11.9
56	13.3	39	3.9	9%	-1	-18.3	62	16.7	56	13.3	68%	51	10.8
56	13.3	38	3.3	5%	-14	-25.8	62	16.7	55	12.8	63%	49	9.7
56	13.3	37	2.8	0%	-60	-51.1	62	16.7	54	12.2	59%	47	8.5

TABLE 7-11: Dry and Wet Bulb Temperatures to Dew Point

Dry °F	Dry °C	Wet °F	Wet °C	Rel Hum %	Dew °F	Dew °C	Dry °F	Dry °C	Wet °F	Wet °C	Rel Hum %	Dew °F	Dew °C
62	16.7	53	11.7	54%	45	7.3	66	18.9	53	11.7	40%	41	4.8
62	16.7	52	11.1	49%	43	5.9	66	18.9	52	11.1	35%	38	3.3
62	16.7	51	10.6	44%	40	4.5	66	18.9	51	10.6	31%	35	1.6
62	16.7	50	10.0	40%	37	3.0	66	18.9	50	10.0	28%	32	-0.2
62	16.7	49	9.4	36%	34	1.4	66	18.9	49	9.4	24%	28	-2.3
62	16.7	48	8.9	31%	31	-0.4	66	18.9	48	8.9	20%	24	-4.6
62	16.7	47	8.3	27%	28	-2.4	66	18.9	47	8.3	16%	19	-7.3
62	16.7	46	7.8	23%	24	-4.7	66	18.9	46	7.8	12%	13	-10.6
62	16.7	45	7.2	19%	19	-7.3	66	18.9	45	7.2	9%	5	-14.8
62	16.7	44	6.7	14%	13	-10.5	66	18.9	44	6.7	5%	-5	-20.8
62	16.7	43	6.1	10%	6	-14.5	66	18.9	43	6.1	2%	-26	-32.3
62	16.7	42	5.6	7%	-4	-20.0	68	20.0	67	19.4	95%	66	19.2
62	16.7	41	5.0	3%	-22	-29.9	68	20.0	66	18.9	90%	65	18.3
64	17.8	63	17.2	95%	62	16.9	68	20.0	65	18.3	85%	63	17.4
64	17.8	62	16.7	89%	61	16.0	68	20.0	64	17.8	80%	62	16.5
64	17.8	61	16.1	84%	59	15.1	68	20.0	63	17.2	76%	60	15.6
64	17.8	60	15.6	79%	57	14.1	68	20.0	62	16.7	71%	58	14.6
64	17.8	59	15.0	74%	56	13.1	68	20.0	61	16.1	67%	56	13.6
64	17.8	58	14.4	69%	54	12.1	68	20.0	60	15.6	62%	55	12.5
64	17.8	57	13.9	65%	52	11.0	68	20.0	59	15.0	58%	53	11.4
64	17.8	56	13.3	60%	50	9.9	68	20.0	58	14.4	54%	51	10.3
64	17.8	55	12.8	55%	48	8.7	68	20.0	57	13.9	49%	48	9.1
64	17.8	54	12.2	51%	45	7.4	68	20.0	56	13.3	45%	46	7.8
64	17.8	53	11.7	46%	43	6.1	68	20.0	55	12.8	41%	44	6.5
64	17.8	52	11.1	42%	40	4.7	68	20.0	54	12.2	37%	41	5.0
64	17.8	51	10.6	38%	38	3.1	68	20.0	53	11.7	33%	38	3.5
64	17.8	50	10.0	33%	35	1.5	68	20.0	52	11.1	30%	35	1.8
64	17.8	49	9.4	29%	31	-0.4	68	20.0	51	10.6	26%	32	-0.1
64	17.8	48	8.9	25%	28	-2.4	68	20.0	50	10.0	22%	28	-2.2
64	17.8	47	8.3	21%	24	-4.7	68	20.0	49	9.4	19%	24	-4.5
64	17.8	46	7.8	17%	19	-7.4	68	20.0	48	8.9	15%	19	-7.3
64	17.8	45	7.2	13%	13	-10.6	68	20.0	47	8.3	12%	13	-10.6
64	17.8	44	6.7	10%	6	-14.7	68	20.0	46	7.8	8%	5	-14.9
64	17.8	43	6.1	6%	-5	-20.5	68	20.0	45	7.2	5%	-6	-21.0
64	17.8	42	5.6	2%	-24	-31.1	68	20.0	44	6.7	2%	-28	-33.2
66	18.9	65	18.3	95%	64	18.0	70	21.1	69	20.6	95%	68	20.0
66	18.9	64	17.8	90%	63	17.2	70	21.1	68	20.0	90%	67	19.4
66	18.9	63	17.2	85%	61	16.1	70	21.1	67	19.4	86%	65	18.6
66	18.9	62	16.7	80%	60	15.3	70	21.1	66	18.9	81%	64	17.7
66	18.9	61	16.1	75%	58	14.3	70	21.1	65	18.3	76%	62	16.8
66	18.9	60	15.6	70%	56	13.3	70	21.1	64	17.8	72%	61	15.8
66	18.9	59	15.0	66%	54	12.3	70	21.1	63	17.2	67%	59	14.9
66	18.9	58	14.4	61%	52	11.2	70	21.1	62	16.7	63%	57	13.8
66	18.9	57	13.9	57%	50	10.1	70	21.1	61	16.1	59%	55	12.8
66	18.9	56	13.3	52%	48	8.9	70	21.1	60	15.6	55%	53	11.7
66	18.9	55	12.8	48%	46	7.6	70	21.1	59	15.0	51%	51	10.5
66	18.9	54	12.2	44%	43	6.3	70	21.1	58	14.4	47%	49	9.3

TABLE 7-11: Dry and Wet Bulb Temperatures to Dew Point

Dry °F	Dry °C	Wet °F	Wet °C	Rel Hum %	Dew °F	Dew °C
70	21.1	57	13.9	43%	46	8.0
70	21.1	56	13.3	39%	44	6.7
70	21.1	55	12.8	35%	41	5.2
70	21.1	54	12.2	32%	39	3.7
70	21.1	53	11.7	28%	36	2.0
70	21.1	52	11.1	25%	32	0.1
70	21.1	51	10.6	21%	28	-2.0
70	21.1	50	10.0	18%	24	-4.4
70	21.1	49	9.4	14%	19	-7.1
70	21.1	48	8.9	11%	13	-10.5
70	21.1	47	8.3	8%	5	-14.8
70	21.1	46	7.8	5%	-6	-21.1
70	21.1	45	7.2	1%	-29	-33.9
72	22.2	71	21.7	95%	71	21.4
72	22.2	70	21.1	90%	69	20.6
72	22.2	69	20.6	86%	68	19.7
72	22.2	68	20.0	81%	66	18.9
72	22.2	67	19.4	77%	64	18.0
72	22.2	66	18.9	73%	63	17.1
72	22.2	65	18.3	68%	61	16.1
72	22.2	64	17.8	64%	59	15.1
72	22.2	63	17.2	60%	57	14.1
72	22.2	62	16.7	56%	54	13.1
72	22.2	61	16.1	52%	54	12.0
72	22.2	60	15.6	48%	51	10.8
72	22.2	59	15.0	45%	49	9.6
72	22.2	58	14.4	41%	47	8.3
72	22.2	57	13.9	37%	44	6.9
72	22.2	56	13.3	34%	42	5.5
72	22.2	55	12.8	30%	39	3.9
72	22.2	54	12.2	27%	36	2.2
72	22.2	53	11.7	23%	33	0.3
72	22.2	52	11.1	20%	29	-1.8
72	22.2	51	10.6	17%	24	-4.2
72	22.2	50	10.0	14%	19	-7.0
72	22.2	49	9.4	10%	13	-10.4
72	22.2	48	8.9	7%	5	-14.7
72	22.2	47	8.3	4%	-6	-21.1
72	22.2	46	7.8	1%	-30	-34.3
74	23.3	73	22.8	95%	73	22.5
74	23.3	72	22.2	91%	71	21.7
74	23.3	71	21.7	86%	70	20.9
74	23.3	70	21.1	82%	68	20.1
74	23.3	69	20.6	78%	67	19.2
74	23.3	68	20.0	73%	65	18.3
74	23.3	67	19.4	69%	63	17.4
74	23.3	66	18.9	65%	62	16.4
74	23.3	65	18.3	61%	60	15.4
74	23.3	64	17.8	57%	58	14.4
74	23.3	63	17.2	53%	56	13.3
74	23.3	62	16.7	50%	54	12.2
74	23.3	61	16.1	46%	52	11.1
74	23.3	60	15.6	42%	50	9.8
74	23.3	59	15.0	39%	47	8.6
74	23.3	58	14.4	35%	45	7.2
74	23.3	57	13.9	32%	42	5.7
74	23.3	56	13.3	29%	39	4.1
74	23.3	55	12.8	25%	36	2.4
74	23.3	54	12.2	22%	33	0.5
74	23.3	53	11.7	19%	29	-1.6
74	23.3	52	11.1	16%	25	-4.0
74	23.3	51	10.6	13%	20	-6.8
74	23.3	50	10.0	10%	14	-10.2
74	23.3	49	9.4	7%	6	-14.6
74	23.3	48	8.9	4%	-6	-21.0
74	23.3	47	8.3	1%	-30	-34.3
76	24.4	75	23.9	95%	75	23.7
76	24.4	74	23.3	91%	73	22.9
76	24.4	73	22.8	87%	72	22.1
76	24.4	72	22.2	82%	70	21.2
76	24.4	71	21.7	78%	69	20.4
76	24.4	70	21.1	74%	67	19.5
76	24.4	69	20.6	70%	65	18.6
76	24.4	68	20.0	66%	64	17.7
76	24.4	67	19.4	62%	62	16.7
76	24.4	66	18.9	58%	60	15.7
76	24.4	65	18.3	55%	58	14.7
76	24.4	64	17.8	51%	56	13.6
76	24.4	63	17.2	47%	55	12.5
76	24.4	62	16.7	44%	52	11.4
76	24.4	61	16.1	40%	50	10.1
76	24.4	60	15.6	37%	48	8.8
76	24.4	59	15.0	34%	45	7.5
76	24.4	58	14.4	31%	43	6.0
76	24.4	57	13.9	27%	40	4.4
76	24.4	56	13.3	24%	37	2.7
76	24.4	55	12.8	21%	30	0.8
76	24.4	54	12.2	18%	30	-1.3
76	24.4	53	11.7	15%	25	-3.7
76	24.4	52	11.1	12%	20	-6.5
76	24.4	51	10.6	9%	14	-9.9
76	24.4	50	10.0	7%	6	-14.3
76	24.4	49	9.4	4%	-5	-20.7
76	24.4	48	8.9	1%	-29	-33.9

TABLE 7-11: Dry and Wet Bulb Temperatures to Dew Point

Dry		Wet		Rel Hum	Dew point	
°F	°C	°F	°C	%	°F	°C
78	25.6	77	25.0	96%	77	24.8
78	25.6	76	24.4	91%	75	24.0
78	25.6	75	23.9	87%	74	23.2
78	25.6	74	23.3	83%	72	22.4
78	25.6	73	22.8	79%	71	21.6
78	25.6	72	22.2	75%	69	20.7
78	25.6	71	21.7	71%	68	19.8
78	25.6	70	21.1	67%	66	18.9
78	25.6	69	20.6	63%	64	18.0
78	25.6	68	20.0	59%	63	17.0
78	25.6	67	19.4	56%	61	16.1
78	25.6	66	18.9	52%	59	15.0
78	25.6	65	18.3	49%	57	14.0
78	25.6	64	17.8	45%	55	12.8
78	25.6	63	17.2	42%	53	11.7
78	25.6	62	16.7	39%	51	10.4
78	25.6	61	16.1	35%	48	9.1
78	25.6	60	15.6	32%	46	7.8
78	25.6	59	15.0	29%	43	6.3
78	25.6	58	14.4	26%	40	4.7
78	25.6	57	13.9	23%	37	3.0
78	25.6	56	13.3	20%	34	1.1
78	25.6	55	12.8	17%	30	-1.0
78	25.6	54	12.2	15%	26	-3.4
78	25.6	53	11.7	12%	21	-6.2
78	25.6	52	11.1	9%	15	-9.6
78	25.6	51	10.6	6%	7	-14.0
78	25.6	50	10.0	4%	-5	-20.3
78	25.6	49	9.4	1%	-28	-33.1
80	26.7	79	26.1	96%	79	25.9
80	26.7	78	25.6	91%	77	25.1
80	26.7	77	25.0	87%	76	24.4
80	26.7	76	24.4	83%	74	23.6
80	26.7	75	23.9	79%	73	22.7
80	26.7	74	23.3	75%	71	21.9
80	26.7	73	22.8	71%	70	21.1
80	26.7	72	22.2	68%	68	20.2
80	26.7	71	21.7	64%	67	19.3
80	26.7	70	21.1	60%	65	18.3
80	26.7	69	20.6	57%	63	17.4
80	26.7	68	20.0	53%	61	16.4
80	26.7	67	19.4	50%	60	15.4
80	26.7	66	18.9	47%	58	14.3
80	26.7	65	18.3	43%	56	13.2
80	26.7	64	17.8	40%	54	12.0
80	26.7	63	17.2	37%	51	10.8
80	26.7	62	16.7	34%	49	9.5

Dry		Wet		Rel Hum	Dew point	
°F	°C	°F	°C	%	°F	°C
80	26.7	61	16.1	31%	47	8.1
80	26.7	60	15.6	28%	44	6.6
80	26.7	59	15.0	25%	41	5.0
80	26.7	58	14.4	22%	38	3.3
80	26.7	57	13.9	19%	35	1.4
80	26.7	56	13.3	17%	31	-0.7
80	26.7	55	12.8	14%	26	-3.1
80	26.7	54	12.2	11%	21	-5.9
80	26.7	53	11.7	9%	15	-9.2
80	26.7	52	11.1	6%	8	-13.5
80	26.7	51	10.6	4%	-4	-19.8
80	26.7	50	10.0	1%	-26	-32.1
82	27.8	81	27.2	96%	81	27.0
82	27.8	80	26.7	92%	79	26.3
82	27.8	79	26.1	87%	78	25.5
82	27.8	78	25.6	84%	76	24.7
82	27.8	77	25.0	80%	75	23.9
82	27.8	76	24.4	76%	74	23.1
82	27.8	75	23.9	72%	72	22.3
82	27.8	74	23.3	68%	71	21.4
82	27.8	73	22.8	65%	69	20.5
82	27.8	72	22.2	61%	67	19.6
82	27.8	71	21.7	58%	66	18.7
82	27.8	70	21.1	54%	64	17.7
82	27.8	69	20.6	51%	62	16.7
82	27.8	68	20.0	48%	60	15.7
82	27.8	67	19.4	45%	58	14.6
82	27.8	66	18.9	41%	56	13.5
82	27.8	65	18.3	38%	54	12.3
82	27.8	64	17.8	35%	52	11.1
82	27.8	63	17.2	32%	50	9.8
82	27.8	62	16.7	30%	47	8.4
82	27.8	61	16.1	27%	45	7.0
82	27.8	60	15.6	24%	42	5.4
82	27.8	59	15.0	21%	39	3.7
82	27.8	58	14.4	19%	35	1.8
82	27.8	57	13.9	16%	31	-0.3
82	27.8	56	13.3	13%	27	-2.7
82	27.8	55	12.8	11%	22	-5.5
82	27.8	54	12.2	8%	16	-8.8
82	27.8	53	11.7	6%	8	-13.1
82	27.8	52	11.1	4%	-2	-19.2
82	27.8	51	10.6	1%	-23	-30.8
84	28.9	83	28.3	96%	83	28.2
84	28.9	82	27.8	92%	81	27.4
84	28.9	81	27.2	88%	80	26.3
84	28.9	80	26.7	84%	79	25.9

TABLE 7-11: Dry and Wet Bulb Temperatures to Dew Point

Dry °F	Dry °C	Wet °F	Wet °C	Rel Hum %	Dew °F	Dew °C	Dry °F	Dry °C	Wet °F	Wet °C	Rel Hum %	Dew °F	Dew °C
84	28.9	79	26.1	80%	77	25.1	86	30.0	66	18.9	33%	53	11.8
84	28.9	78	25.6	76%	76	24.3	86	30.0	65	18.3	30%	51	10.5
84	28.9	77	25.0	73%	74	23.5	86	30.0	64	17.8	27%	49	9.2
84	28.9	76	24.4	69%	73	22.6	86	30.0	63	17.2	25%	46	7.7
84	28.9	75	23.9	66%	71	21.8	86	30.0	62	16.7	22%	43	6.1
84	28.9	74	23.3	62%	70	20.9	86	30.0	61	16.1	20%	40	4.4
84	28.9	73	22.8	59%	68	20.0	86	30.0	60	15.6	17%	37	2.6
84	28.9	72	22.2	55%	66	19.0	86	30.0	59	15.0	15%	33	0.5
84	28.9	71	21.7	52%	65	18.1	86	30.0	58	14.4	13%	29	-1.8
84	28.9	70	21.1	49%	63	17.1	86	30.0	57	13.9	10%	24	-4.6
84	28.9	69	20.6	46%	61	16.1	86	30.0	56	13.3	8%	18	-7.8
84	28.9	68	20.0	43%	59	15.0	86	30.0	55	12.8	6%	11	-11.9
84	28.9	67	19.4	40%	57	13.9	86	30.0	54	12.2	4%	0	-17.6
84	28.9	66	18.9	37%	55	12.7	86	30.0	53	11.7	1%	-18	-27.8
84	28.9	65	18.3	34%	53	11.5	88	31.1	87	30.6	96%	87	30.4
84	28.9	64	17.8	31%	50	10.2	88	31.1	86	30.0	92%	85	29.7
84	28.9	63	17.2	28%	48	8.8	88	31.1	85	29.4	88%	84	28.9
84	28.9	62	16.7	26%	45	7.3	88	31.1	84	28.9	85%	83	28.2
84	28.9	61	16.1	23%	42	5.7	88	31.1	83	28.3	81%	81	27.4
84	28.9	60	15.6	20%	39	4.0	88	31.1	82	27.8	77%	80	26.6
84	28.9	59	15.0	18%	36	2.2	88	31.1	81	27.2	74%	79	25.9
84	28.9	58	14.4	15%	32	0.1	88	31.1	80	26.7	70%	77	25.1
84	28.9	57	13.9	13%	28	-2.3	88	31.1	79	26.1	67%	76	24.2
84	28.9	56	13.3	11%	23	-5.0	88	31.1	78	25.6	64%	74	23.4
84	28.9	55	12.8	8%	17	-8.3	88	31.1	77	25.0	60%	73	22.5
84	28.9	54	12.2	6%	9	-12.5	88	31.1	76	24.4	57%	71	21.6
84	28.9	53	11.7	4%	-1	-18.4	88	31.1	75	23.9	54%	69	20.7
84	28.9	52	11.1	1%	-21	-29.4	88	31.1	74	23.3	51%	68	19.8
86	30.0	85	29.4	96%	85	29.3	88	31.1	73	22.8	48%	66	18.8
86	30.0	84	28.9	92%	83	28.5	88	31.1	72	22.2	45%	64	17.8
86	30.0	83	28.3	88%	82	27.8	88	31.1	71	21.7	42%	62	16.8
86	30.0	82	27.8	84%	81	27.0	88	31.1	70	21.1	40%	60	15.7
86	30.0	81	27.2	80%	79	26.3	88	31.1	69	20.6	37%	58	14.6
86	30.0	80	26.7	77%	78	25.5	88	31.1	68	20.0	34%	56	13.5
86	30.0	79	26.1	73%	76	24.7	88	31.1	67	19.4	32%	54	12.2
86	30.0	78	25.6	70%	75	23.8	88	31.1	66	18.9	29%	52	10.9
86	30.0	77	25.0	66%	73	23.0	88	31.1	65	18.3	26%	49	9.6
86	30.0	76	24.4	63%	72	22.1	88	31.1	64	17.8	24%	47	8.1
86	30.0	75	23.9	60%	70	21.3	88	31.1	63	17.2	21%	44	6.5
86	30.0	74	23.3	56%	69	20.4	88	31.1	62	16.7	19%	41	4.9
86	30.0	73	22.8	53%	67	19.4	88	31.1	61	16.1	17%	37	3.0
86	30.0	72	22.2	50%	65	18.5	88	31.1	60	15.6	14%	34	0.9
86	30.0	71	21.7	47%	63	17.5	88	31.1	59	15.0	12%	30	-1.4
86	30.0	70	21.1	44%	62	16.4	88	31.1	58	14.4	10%	25	-4.1
86	30.0	69	20.6	41%	60	15.4	88	31.1	57	13.9	8%	19	-7.2
86	30.0	68	20.0	38%	58	14.2	88	31.1	56	13.3	6%	12	-11.3
86	30.0	67	19.4	35%	56	13.1	88	31.1	55	12.8	4%	2	-16.8

TABLE 7-11: Dry and Wet Bulb Temperatures to Dew Point

Dry		Wet		Rel Hum	Dew point		Dry		Wet		Rel Hum	Dew point	
°F	°C	°F	°C	%	°F	°C	°F	°C	°F	°C	%	°F	°C
88	31.1	54	12.2	2%	-15	-26.2	92	33.3	80	26.7	59%	76	24.2
90	32.2	89	31.7	96%	89	31.5	92	33.3	79	26.1	56%	74	23.3
90	32.2	88	31.1	92%	87	30.8	92	33.3	78	25.6	53%	72	22.4
90	32.2	87	30.6	88%	86	30.1	92	33.3	77	25.0	50%	71	21.5
90	32.2	86	30.0	85%	85	29.3	92	33.3	76	24.4	47%	69	20.6
90	32.2	85	29.4	81%	83	28.6	92	33.3	75	23.9	45%	67	19.6
90	32.2	84	28.9	78%	82	27.8	92	33.3	74	23.3	42%	66	18.6
90	32.2	83	28.3	74%	81	27.0	92	33.3	73	22.8	39%	64	17.6
90	32.2	82	27.8	71%	79	26.3	92	33.3	72	22.2	37%	62	16.5
90	32.2	81	27.2	68%	78	25.5	92	33.3	71	21.7	34%	60	15.4
90	32.2	80	26.7	64%	76	24.6	92	33.3	70	21.1	32%	58	14.3
90	32.2	79	26.1	61%	75	23.8	92	33.3	69	20.6	29%	55	13.1
90	32.2	78	25.6	58%	73	22.9	92	33.3	68	20.0	27%	53	11.8
90	32.2	77	25.0	55%	72	22.0	92	33.3	67	19.4	25%	51	10.4
90	32.2	76	24.4	52%	70	21.1	92	33.3	66	18.9	22%	48	9.0
90	32.2	75	23.9	49%	68	20.2	92	33.3	65	18.3	20%	45	7.4
90	32.2	74	23.3	46%	67	19.2	92	33.3	64	17.8	18%	42	5.8
90	32.2	73	22.8	44%	65	18.2	92	33.3	63	17.2	16%	39	3.9
90	32.2	72	22.2	41%	63	17.2	92	33.3	62	16.7	14%	35	1.9
90	32.2	71	21.7	38%	61	16.1	92	33.3	61	16.1	12%	31	-0.3
90	32.2	70	21.1	35%	59	15.0	92	33.3	60	15.6	10%	27	-2.9
90	32.2	69	20.6	33%	57	13.9	92	33.3	59	15.0	8%	21	-6.0
90	32.2	68	20.0	30%	55	12.6	92	33.3	58	14.4	6%	14	-9.8
90	32.2	67	19.4	28%	52	11.3	92	33.3	57	13.9	4%	5	-14.9
90	32.2	66	18.9	25%	50	10.0	92	33.3	56	13.3	2%	-9	-23.0
90	32.2	65	18.3	23%	47	8.5	92	33.3	55	12.8	0%	-79	-61.6
90	32.2	64	17.8	21%	45	7.0	94	34.4	93	33.9	96%	93	33.8
90	32.2	63	17.2	18%	42	5.3	94	34.4	92	33.3	93%	91	33.1
90	32.2	62	16.7	16%	38	3.5	94	34.4	91	32.8	89%	90	32.3
90	32.2	61	16.1	14%	35	1.4	94	34.4	90	32.2	85%	89	31.6
90	32.2	60	15.6	12%	30	-0.9	94	34.4	89	31.7	82%	88	30.9
90	32.2	59	15.0	10%	26	-3.5	94	34.4	88	31.1	79%	86	30.2
90	32.2	58	14.4	8%	20	-6.6	94	34.4	87	30.6	75%	85	29.4
90	32.2	57	13.9	6%	13	-10.6	94	34.4	86	30.0	72%	84	28.6
90	32.2	56	13.3	4%	3	-15.9	94	34.4	85	29.4	69%	82	27.9
90	32.2	55	12.8	2%	-12	-24.6	94	34.4	84	28.9	66%	81	27.1
92	33.3	91	32.8	96%	91	32.6	94	34.4	83	28.3	63%	79	26.3
92	33.3	90	32.2	92%	89	31.9	94	34.4	82	27.8	60%	78	25.4
92	33.3	89	31.7	89%	88	31.2	94	34.4	81	27.2	57%	76	24.6
92	33.3	88	31.1	85%	87	30.5	94	34.4	80	26.7	54%	75	23.7
92	33.3	87	30.6	82%	86	29.7	94	34.4	79	26.1	51%	73	23.0
92	33.3	86	30.0	78%	84	29.0	94	34.4	78	25.6	48%	72	21.9
92	33.3	85	29.4	75%	83	28.2	94	34.4	77	25.0	46%	70	21.0
92	33.3	84	28.9	71%	81	27.5	94	34.4	76	24.4	43%	68	20.1
92	33.3	83	28.3	68%	80	26.7	94	34.4	75	23.9	40%	66	19.1
92	33.3	82	27.8	65%	79	25.9	94	34.4	74	23.3	38%	64	18.0
92	33.3	81	27.2	62%	77	25.0	94	34.4	73	22.8	35%	63	17.0

TABLE 7-11: Dry and Wet Bulb Temperatures to Dew Point

Dry °F	Dry °C	Wet °F	Wet °C	Rel Hum %	Dew point °F	Dew point °C
94	34.4	72	22.2	33%	61	15.9
94	34.4	71	21.7	31%	58	14.7
94	34.4	70	21.1	28%	56	13.5
94	34.4	69	20.6	26%	54	12.2
94	34.4	68	20.0	24%	52	10.9
94	34.4	67	19.4	22%	49	9.4
94	34.4	66	18.9	20%	46	7.9
94	34.4	65	18.3	17%	43	6.2
94	34.4	64	17.8	15%	40	4.4
94	34.4	63	17.2	13%	36	2.4
94	34.4	62	16.7	11%	32	0.2
94	34.4	61	16.1	9%	28	-2.3
94	34.4	60	15.6	6%	22	-5.3
94	34.4	59	15.0	6%	16	-9.0
94	34.4	58	14.4	4%	7	-13.9
94	34.4	57	13.9	2%	-6	-21.4
94	34.4	56	13.3	0%	-44	-42.4
96	35.6	95	35.0	96%	95	34.9
96	35.6	94	34.4	93%	94	34.2
96	35.6	93	33.9	89%	92	33.5
96	35.6	92	33.3	86%	91	32.8
96	35.6	91	32.8	82%	90	32.0
96	35.6	90	32.2	79%	88	31.3
96	35.6	89	31.7	76%	87	30.6
96	35.6	88	31.1	72%	86	29.8
96	35.6	87	30.6	69%	84	29.1
96	35.6	86	30.0	66%	83	28.3
96	35.6	85	29.4	63%	81	27.5
96	35.6	84	28.9	60%	80	26.7
96	35.6	83	28.3	58%	79	25.9
96	35.6	82	27.8	55%	77	25.0
96	35.6	81	27.2	52%	75	24.2
96	35.6	80	26.7	49%	74	23.3
96	35.6	79	26.1	47%	72	22.4
96	35.6	78	25.6	44%	71	21.4
96	35.6	77	25.0	42%	69	20.5
96	35.6	76	24.4	39%	67	19.5
96	35.6	75	23.9	37%	65	18.5
96	35.6	74	23.3	34%	63	17.4
96	35.6	73	22.8	32%	61	16.3
96	35.6	72	22.2	30%	59	15.1
96	35.6	71	21.7	27%	57	13.9
96	35.6	70	21.1	25%	55	12.7
96	35.6	69	20.6	23%	52	11.3
96	35.6	68	20.0	21%	50	9.9
96	35.6	67	19.4	19%	47	8.4
96	35.6	66	18.9	17%	44	6.7

Dry °F	Dry °C	Wet °F	Wet °C	Rel Hum %	Dew point °F	Dew point °C
96	35.6	65	18.3	15%	41	4.9
96	35.6	64	17.8	13%	37	3.0
96	35.6	63	17.2	11%	33	0.8
96	35.6	62	16.7	9%	29	-1.7
96	35.6	61	16.1	7%	24	-4.6
96	35.6	60	15.6	6%	17	-8.2
96	35.6	59	15.0	4%	9	-12.9
96	35.6	58	14.4	2%	-4	-19.8
96	35.6	57	13.9	0%	-32	-35.6
98	36.7	97	36.1	96%	97	36.0
98	36.7	96	35.6	93%	96	35.3
98	36.7	95	35.0	89%	94	34.6
98	36.7	94	34.4	86%	93	33.9
98	36.7	93	33.9	83%	92	33.2
98	36.7	92	33.3	79%	90	32.5
98	36.7	91	32.8	76%	89	31.7
98	36.7	90	32.2	73%	88	31.0
98	36.7	89	31.7	70%	86	30.3
98	36.7	88	31.1	67%	85	29.5
98	36.7	87	30.6	64%	84	28.7
98	36.7	86	30.0	61%	82	27.9
98	36.7	85	29.4	58%	81	27.1
98	36.7	84	28.9	56%	79	26.3
98	36.7	83	28.3	53%	78	25.5
98	36.7	82	27.8	50%	76	24.6
98	36.7	81	27.2	48%	75	23.7
98	36.7	80	26.7	45%	73	22.8
98	36.7	79	26.1	43%	71	21.9
98	36.7	78	25.6	40%	70	20.9
98	36.7	77	25.0	38%	68	19.9
98	36.7	76	24.4	35%	66	18.9
98	36.7	75	23.9	33%	64	17.8
98	36.7	74	23.3	31%	62	16.7
98	36.7	73	22.8	29%	60	15.6
98	36.7	72	22.2	27%	58	14.4
98	36.7	71	21.7	25%	56	13.1
98	36.7	70	21.1	22%	53	11.8
98	36.7	69	20.6	20%	51	10.4
98	36.7	68	20.0	18%	48	8.9
98	36.7	67	19.4	17%	45	7.2
98	36.7	66	18.9	15%	42	5.5
98	36.7	65	18.3	13%	38	3.5
98	36.7	64	17.8	11%	34	1.4
98	36.7	63	17.2	9%	30	-1.1
98	36.7	62	16.7	7%	25	-3.9
98	36.7	61	16.1	6%	19	-7.4
98	36.7	60	15.6	4%	11	-11.8

TABLE 7-11: Dry and Wet Bulb Temperatures to Dew Point

8 MECHANICAL

SPEED AND HORSEPOWER

INTRODUCTION

Although it is beyond the scope of this book to accurately estimate power needed to drive a boat at specific speeds, I will provide some simple rules of thumb and tables to get a reasonable approximation of power requirements. This should enable one to estimate what to expect from a boat being considered for purchase. Is it underpowered? Does it go as fast as it should given the installed engine size? If I repower with a bigger engine, what should I expect?

For a more comprehensive treatment of this subject, obtain the *Propeller Handbook* by Dave Gerr, which provides information on boat horsepower requirements along with substantial detail on propeller types, sizing, and selection (Dave Gerr, *Propeller Handbook*. Camden: International Marine, 2001)

As discussed in the chapter on boat design, a boat can operate at displacement, semi-displacement, and planing speeds. In each of these regimes the methods for determining power requirements are different. For example, at slow displacement speeds, friction on the wetted surface area will be the major form of resistance, whereas at higher displacement speeds, wave motion becomes the dominant force. At planing speeds, the boat is subject to a different form of resistance and air resistance also starts to become more significant. To keep things simple, in this book we only consider formulas for estimating horsepower at displacement speeds and at planing speeds.

HORSEPOWER AT DISPLACEMENT SPEEDS

The chapter at the beginning of this book entitled *Boat Types, Design, and Construction*, describes the speed to length ratio (SLR) on page 21 and the displacement to length ratio (DLR) on page 34. As mentioned in that section, at SLRs of up to around 1.34, the boat is considered to be in displacement mode, although this is not an absolute number.

In the *Propeller Handbook*, Gerr provides an equation relating the SLR to displacement and shaft horsepower for boats traveling at displacement speeds, which is restated here on the next page as equation 8-1.

$$SLR = \frac{10.665}{\left(\frac{D(lbs)}{SHP(hp)}\right)^{1/3}} = \frac{9.036}{\left(\frac{D(kg)}{SHP(kW)}\right)^{1/3}}$$

Where: SLR = Speed to length ratio
D = Displacement
SHP = Shaft horsepower

EQUATION 8-1: SLR Versus Displacement and Shaft Horsepower. See horsepower definitions on page 450 for explanation of shaft horsepower (Equation Courtesy Dave Gerr)

Table 8-1 evaluates equation 8-1 for typical SLR values.

SLR	lb/SHP	kg/kW	SLR	lb/SHP	kg/kW
0.90	1660	1010	1.30	550	340
0.95	1410	860	1.35	490	300
1.00	1210	740	1.40	440	270
1.05	1050	640	1.45	400	240
1.10	910	550	1.50	360	220
1.15	800	490	1.55	330	200
1.20	700	430	1.60	300	180
1.25	620	380	1.65	270	160

TABLE 8-1: Speed to Length Ratio Versus Displacement to Horsepower

Inspection of table 8-1 shows that to travel at SLR=1.35 (hull speed) a boat will need approximately 1 shaft horsepower for every 490 pounds of displacement (1 kilowatt for every 300 kilograms of displacement). Here's a rule of thumb:

A typical boat will require about 1 shaft horsepower per 500 pounds of displacement to drive it at hull speed. This works out to a little over 4 horsepower per displacement ton.

Take this for what it is—a gross estimate of horsepower requirement. For example, the displacement to length ratio (DLR) described in chapter 1 is also related to achievable SLRs at displacement speeds. Everything else being equal, a lower DLR will allow a higher speed than a higher DLR. In particular, the so-called hull speed will be higher for the lower DLR, which describes a longer more slender hull. Equation 8-1 provides estimates for boats with DLRs of around 300 to 350.

A boat with a DLR of just 150 could have a maximum SLR as high as 1.6, which shows that long thin boats can go faster than short fat ones (at displacement speeds).

Also keep in mind this is for calm seas. You will need additional power to drive into wind and waves.

If the speed to length equation 1-1 from chapter 1 page 21 is substituted into equation 8-1 then solved for shaft horsepower, we get equation 8-2.

$$SHP(hp) = \frac{D(lb) \times S(kn)^3}{1213 \times LWL(ft)^{3/2}}$$

$$\frac{D(kg) \times S(kn)^3}{4385 \times LWL(m)^{3/2}}$$

Where: SHP = Shaft horsepower
   D = Displacement
   S = Speed in knots
   LWL = Length at waterline

EQUATION 8-2: Horsepower at Displacement Speeds From Displacement, Speed, and Length

With equation 8-2 and a scientific calculator you can solve for approximate shaft horsepower required for any displacement boat.

Table 8-2 on the next two pages evaluates equation 8-2 for various sample boat sizes and speeds. Note: The table does not take into account the effect of varying DLRs as described previously as it is only meant to give an approximate idea of power needed for various sizes of boats.

HORSEPOWER AT PLANING SPEEDS

At speeds higher than SLR 2.0, the boat can be considered to be planing. Approximate horsepower required at planing speeds can be calculated using the Crouch formula shown in equation 8-3 on page 448.

The value of C in the formula will be around 150 for an average planing boat. A high performance, lighter hull with little superstructure may have a C value of 200. A longer hull for a given displacement will tend to have a higher C value also.

Some observations:

1. The horsepower at planing speeds increases as the square of the speed whereas the horsepower at displacement speeds increases as the cube of the speed.
2. Length is not a variable in the Crouch formula like it is in the formula for displacement speeds. It follows that

LWL		Disp		Speed		Horsepower			
				S/L 1.0	S/L 1.34	S/L 1.0		S/L 1.34	
(ft)	(M)	(lb)	(Kg)	(kn)	(kn)	(hp)	(kW)	(hp)	(kW)
15	4.6	760	340	3.9	5.2	0.6	0.5	1.5	1.1
15	4.6	1130	510	3.9	5.2	0.9	0.7	2.2	1.7
15	4.6	1510	680	3.9	5.2	1.2	0.9	3.0	2.2
15	4.6	1890	860	3.9	5.2	1.6	1.2	3.7	2.8
15	4.6	2270	1030	3.9	5.2	1.9	1.4	4.5	3.4
15	4.6	2650	1200	3.9	5.2	2.2	1.6	5.3	3.9
15	4.6	3020	1370	3.9	5.2	2.5	1.9	6.0	4.5
15	4.6	3400	1540	3.9	5.2	2.8	2.1	6.7	5.0
15	4.6	3780	1710	3.9	5.2	3.1	2.3	7.5	5.6
18	5.5	1300	590	4.2	5.7	1.1	0.8	2.6	1.9
18	5.5	2000	910	4.2	5.7	1.6	1.2	4.0	3.0
18	5.5	2600	1180	4.2	5.7	2.1	1.6	5.2	3.8
18	5.5	3300	1500	4.2	5.7	2.7	2.0	6.5	4.9
18	5.5	3900	1770	4.2	5.7	3.2	2.4	7.7	5.8
18	5.5	4600	2090	4.2	5.7	3.8	2.8	9.1	6.8
18	5.5	5200	2360	4.2	5.7	4.3	3.2	10	7.7
18	5.5	5900	2680	4.2	5.7	4.9	3.6	12	8.7
18	5.5	6500	2950	4.2	5.7	5.4	4.0	13	9.6
22	6.7	2400	1100	4.7	6.3	2.0	1.5	4.8	3.6
22	6.7	3600	1600	4.7	6.3	3.0	2.2	7.1	5.2
22	6.7	4800	2200	4.7	6.3	4.0	3.0	9.5	7.2
22	6.7	6000	2700	4.7	6.3	4.9	3.7	12	8.8
22	6.7	7200	3300	4.7	6.3	5.9	4.5	14	11
22	6.7	8300	3800	4.7	6.3	6.8	5.1	16	12
22	6.7	9500	4300	4.7	6.3	7.8	5.8	19	14
22	6.7	10700	4900	4.7	6.3	8.8	6.6	21	16
22	6.7	11900	5400	4.7	6.3	9.8	7.3	24	18
26	7.9	3900	1800	5.1	6.8	3.2	2.4	7.7	5.9
26	7.9	5900	2700	5.1	6.8	4.9	3.7	12	8.8
26	7.9	7900	3600	5.1	6.8	6.5	4.9	16	12
26	7.9	9800	4400	5.1	6.8	8.1	6.0	19	14
26	7.9	11800	5400	5.1	6.8	9.7	7.3	23	18
26	7.9	13800	6300	5.1	6.8	11	8.5	27	21
26	7.9	15700	7100	5.1	6.8	13	9.6	31	23
26	7.9	17700	8000	5.1	6.8	15	11	35	26
26	7.9	19700	8900	5.1	6.8	16	12	39	29
32	9.8	7000	3200	5.7	7.6	5.8	4.3	14	10
32	9.8	11000	5000	5.7	7.6	9.1	6.8	22	16
32	9.8	15000	6800	5.7	7.6	12	9.2	30	22
32	9.8	18000	8200	5.7	7.6	15	11	36	27
32	9.8	22000	10000	5.7	7.6	18	14	44	33
32	9.8	26000	11800	5.7	7.6	21	16	52	38
32	9.8	29000	13200	5.7	7.6	24	18	58	43
32	9.8	33000	15000	5.7	7.6	27	20	65	49
32	9.8	37000	16800	5.7	7.6	31	23	73	55

TABLE 8-2(1): Horsepower at Displacement Speeds From Displacement and Speed to Length

LWL		Disp		Speed		Horsepower			
				S/L 1.0	S/L 1.34	S/L 1.0		S/L 1.34	
(ft)	(M)	(lb)	(Kg)	(kn)	(kn)	(hp)	(kW)	(hp)	(kW)
36	11.0	10000	4500	6.0	8.0	8.2	6.1	20	15
36	11.0	16000	7300	6.0	8.0	13	9.9	32	24
36	11.0	21000	9500	6.0	8.0	17	13	42	31
36	11.0	26000	11800	6.0	8.0	21	16	52	38
36	11.0	31000	14100	6.0	8.0	26	19	61	46
36	11.0	37000	16800	6.0	8.0	31	23	73	55
36	11.0	42000	19100	6.0	8.0	35	26	83	62
36	11.0	47000	21300	6.0	8.0	39	29	93	69
36	11.0	52000	23600	6.0	8.0	43	32	103	77
45	13.7	20000	9000	6.7	9.0	16	12	40	29
45	13.7	31000	14000	6.7	9.0	26	19	61	46
45	13.7	41000	19000	6.7	9.0	34	26	81	62
45	13.7	51000	23000	6.7	9.0	42	31	101	75
45	13.7	61000	28000	6.7	9.0	50	38	121	91
45	13.7	71000	32000	6.7	9.0	59	43	141	104
45	13.7	82000	37000	6.7	9.0	68	50	163	121
45	13.7	92000	42000	6.7	9.0	76	57	182	137
45	13.7	102000	46000	6.7	9.0	84	62	202	150
54	16.5	35000	16000	7.3	9.8	29	22	69	52
54	16.5	53000	24000	7.3	9.8	44	33	105	78
54	16.5	71000	32000	7.3	9.8	59	43	141	104
54	16.5	88000	40000	7.3	9.8	73	54	175	130
54	16.5	106000	48000	7.3	9.8	87	65	210	157
54	16.5	123000	56000	7.3	9.8	101	76	244	183
54	16.5	141000	64000	7.3	9.8	116	87	280	209
54	16.5	159000	72000	7.3	9.8	131	98	315	235
54	16.5	176000	80000	7.3	9.8	145	108	349	261
64	19.5	59000	27000	8.0	10.7	49	37	117	88
64	19.5	88000	40000	8.0	10.7	73	54	175	130
64	19.5	117000	53000	8.0	10.7	96	72	232	173
64	19.5	147000	67000	8.0	10.7	121	91	292	218
64	19.5	176000	80000	8.0	10.7	145	108	349	261
64	19.5	206000	93000	8.0	10.7	170	126	409	303
64	19.5	235000	107000	8.0	10.7	194	145	466	349
64	19.5	264000	120000	8.0	10.7	218	163	524	391
64	19.5	294000	133000	8.0	10.7	242	180	583	434
78	23.8	106000	48000	8.8	11.8	87	65	210	157
78	23.8	159000	72000	8.8	11.8	131	98	315	235
78	23.8	213000	97000	8.8	11.8	176	131	423	316
78	23.8	266000	121000	8.8	11.8	219	164	528	395
78	23.8	319000	145000	8.8	11.8	263	197	633	473
78	23.8	372000	169000	8.8	11.8	307	229	738	551
78	23.8	425000	193000	8.8	11.8	350	262	843	629
78	23.8	478000	217000	8.8	11.8	394	294	948	708
78	23.8	531000	241000	8.8	11.8	438	327	1053	786

TABLE 8-2(2): Horsepower at Displacement Speeds From Displacement and Speed to Length

$$SHP(hp) = \frac{D(lb) \times S(kn)^2}{C^2}$$

$$SHP(kW) = \frac{D(kg) \times S(kn)^2}{C^2 \times 0.60827}$$

Where: SHP = Shaft horsepower
D = Displacement
S = Speed in knots
C = Coefficient from 150 to 200

EQUATION 8-3: Horsepower at Planing Speeds From Displacement and Speed

displacement to length ratio is a greater factor at displacement speeds than at planing speeds.

3. Horsepower requirements go up dramatically if you wish to drive a boat at planing speeds. Consider a 40-foot boat weighing 26,000 pounds (11800 kg). The approximate horsepower required to drive it is shown in table 8-3.

Speed (kn)	SLR	Horsepower (hp)	Horsepower (kW)
6	1.00	21	16
8	1.34	52	38
13	2.00	185	138
19	3.00	416	310
25	4.00	740	551
38	6.00	1664	1241
51	8.00	2958	2206

FIGURE 8-3: 40-Foot 26,000-Pound Boat at Various Speeds

Table 8-4 on the next page uses the formula to calculate horsepower at some representative speeds and displacements and for C values of 150 and 200.

ENGINES

INTRODUCTION

In this section, two- and four-stroke gasoline and diesel engines are discussed and compared with the intent of helping to match engines with boating applications. Additionally, the information is meant to assist normal preventative maintenance procedures and to help debug engine problems. Having a basic understanding of how the engine operates will help in reasoning through starting and running problems.

Displacement				Horsepower							
C=150	C=150	C=200	C=200	20 knots		30 knots		40 knots		50 knots	
(lb)	(Kg)	(lb)	(Kg)	(hp)	(kW)	(hp)	(kW)	(hp)	(kW)	(hp)	(kW)
1000	450	1800	800	18	13	40	30	71	50	110	80
1100	500	2000	890	20	15	44	30	78	60	120	90
1300	590	2300	1050	23	17	52	40	92	70	140	110
1400	640	2500	1140	25	19	56	40	100	70	160	120
1600	730	2800	1300	28	21	64	50	110	90	180	130
1800	820	3200	1460	32	24	72	50	130	100	200	150
2000	910	3600	1620	36	27	80	60	140	110	220	170
2200	1000	3900	1780	39	29	88	70	160	120	240	180
2500	1130	4400	2010	44	33	100	70	180	130	280	210
2800	1270	5000	2260	50	37	110	80	200	150	310	230
3100	1410	5500	2510	55	41	120	90	220	160	340	260
3500	1590	6200	2830	62	46	140	100	250	190	390	290
3900	1770	6900	3150	69	52	160	120	280	210	430	320
4400	2000	7800	3560	78	58	180	130	310	230	490	370
4900	2220	8700	3950	87	65	200	150	350	260	540	410
5500	2490	9800	4430	98	73	220	160	390	290	610	450
6200	2810	11000	5000	110	82	250	180	440	330	690	510
6900	3130	12000	5560	120	91	280	210	490	370	770	570
7800	3540	14000	6080	140	100	310	230	550	410	870	650
8700	3950	15000	7300	150	120	350	260	620	460	970	720
9800	4450	17000	7910	170	130	390	290	700	520	1100	810
11000	4990	20000	9120	200	150	440	330	780	580	1200	910
12000	5440	21000	9730	210	160	480	360	850	640	1300	990
14000	6350	25000	11600	250	190	560	420	1000	740	1600	1160
15000	6800	27000	12200	270	200	600	450	1100	790	1700	1240
17000	7710	30000	14000	300	230	680	510	1200	900	1900	1410
19000	8620	34000	15200	340	250	760	570	1400	1010	2100	1570
22000	9980	39000	17600	390	290	880	660	1600	1170	2400	1820
24000	10900	43000	19500	430	320	960	720	1700	1270	2700	1990
27000	12200	48000	21900	480	360	1100	800	1900	1430	3000	2230
30000	13600	53000	24300	530	400	1200	890	2100	1590	3300	2480
34000	15400	60000	27400	600	450	1400	1010	2400	1800	3800	2810
38000	17200	68000	30400	680	500	1500	1130	2700	2010	4200	3140
43000	19500	76000	34700	760	570	1700	1280	3100	2280	4800	3560
48000	21800	85000	38900	850	640	2000	1430	3400	2550	5300	3980
54000	24500	96000	43800	960	720	2200	1610	3800	2860	6000	4480
60000	27200	110000	48700	1100	790	2400	1790	4300	3180	6700	4970
68000	30800	120000	54700	1200	900	2700	2030	4800	3600	7600	5630
76000	34500	140000	61400	1400	1010	3000	2270	5400	4030	8400	6200
85000	38600	150000	68000	1500	1130	3400	2540	6000	4510	9400	7050
95000	43100	170000	76600	1700	1260	3800	2830	6800	5040	10600	7870
110000	49900	200000	88000	2000	1460	4400	3280	7600	5830	12200	9120
120000	54400	210000	96700	2100	1590	4700	3580	8500	6360	13300	9940
130000	59000	230000	104600	2300	1720	5200	3880	9400	6900	14400	10780
140000	68000	270000	121000	2700	1960	6000	4470	10700	7950	16700	12420

TABLE 8-4: Horsepower Required at Planing Speeds for Various Displacements and Speeds

Understanding how the engine works can also be very helpful when talking to an engine technician about problems with your boat.

Both gas and diesel are *internal combustion* engines that burn an air-fuel mixture inside the engine cylinders to provide motive power.

HORSEPOWER DEFINITIONS

There are several measures of horsepower, and it is important to understand the differences.

Horsepower is usually measured at the engine flywheel as *brake horsepower* (**BHP**) or at the propeller as *shaft horsepower* (**SHP**). BHP is measured on an engine without any peripherals such as alternators. BHP is what is normally specified by the engine manufacturer. SHP will usually be about 96 to 97 percent of BHP.

Horsepower *ratings* are defined for different types of boat operation and different manufacturers often use different sets of ratings. Most use three ratings, while others use as many as five different ratings. Here we define the most common ratings.

Continuous duty horsepower refers to the power that can be maintained indefinitely without overheating or straining the engine and is usually at around 80 percent of maximum RPM. If available this is the power rating you should use when comparing boats. For a given rating, this rating specifies the lowest horsepower.

Medium duty rating where maximum RPM and horsepower are used less than 50 percent of the time.

High output where the engine is run at maximum less than one hour per eight hours of operation (10 to 15 percent of operating hours). This rating specifies the highest horsepower for a given engine.

For example, a specific engine might have ratings of:

- Continuous duty: 103 horsepower (77 kW)
- Medium duty: 115 horsepower (86 kW)
- High output: 126 horsepower (94 kW)

GASOLINE ENGINES

Gasoline powered engines are considered *spark ignition* internal combustion engines since they use an electrical spark (spark plug) to ignite a air-fuel mixture.

Inboard and Stern Drive Gasoline Engines

Inboard and stern drive (inboard/outboard) gasoline engines are typically an automobile engine block that has been adapted for marine use (*marinized*). Marinization includes modifying such items as pistons, valves, carburetor, fuel injection, spark protection, cooling systems, etc., for the marine environment. Because these engines are based on car engines, they only come in the same general horsepower range as car engines, ranging from about 80 to 400 horsepower, which limits their use to certain sizes and types of boats (more on this later). The only practical way to significantly increase gasoline engine power beyond this is to install two engines.

For purposes of comparison, commonly available marinized auto engine sizes are shown in table 8-5. Note: These numbers vary from one manufacturer to another and some of the entries in this table are averages of two or more engines.

Power			No.Cyls	Displ.		Wt		Ratios			
hp	kW	RPM		CID	L	Lbs	Kg	hp /cui	hp /lb	kW /L	kW /kg
135	101	4600	4	181	3.0	600	183	0.75	0.23	34	0.55
190	142	4600	6	262	4.3	800	244	0.73	0.24	33	0.58
220	164	4800	8	305	5.0	900	274	0.72	0.24	33	0.60
280	209	4400	8	350	5.7	900	274	0.80	0.31	37	0.76
320	239	4800	8	377	6.2	948	289	0.85	0.34	39	0.83
375	280	4400	8	496	8.1	1120	341	0.76	0.33	35	0.82

TABLE 8-5: Displacement and Power of Gasoline Inboard Engines

Note: *Displacement* refers to engine displacement and is defined later in this chapter.

Mercury MerCruiser, *Volvo Penta*, and *Crusader* are the primary makes of inboard and sterndrive gasoline engines available for sale in North America.

Outboard Engines

Outboard engines are designed specifically for marine use and range from very small (2 hp/1.5kW) to medium sized (250 hp/190 kW). These come in both two- and four-stroke (cycle) versions. Table 8-6 shows some representative outboard engine specifications.

Note: The weights can't be directly compared to the weights for inboard and diesel engines since outboards include the entire unit including propellers. Even so the power to displacement ratios and the power to weight ratios are generally higher for the outboard engines. Also the power ratings are at the propeller shaft and not at the engine.

In table 8-6, observe how the two-stroke outboards have higher power to displacement and power to weight ratios than the four-stroke outboards.

Propshaft			No Cyls	Strokes	Fuel Del.	Displ.		Wt		Ratios			
HP	kW	RPM				CID	L	Lbs	kg	hp /cui	hp /lb	kW /L	kW /kg
2	1	5500	1	4	C	3.4	0.1	27	8	0.59	0.07	26	0.18
4	3	4500	1	4	C	8.4	0.1	55	17	0.48	0.07	22	0.18
8	6	5000	2	2	C	10	0.2	58	18	0.80	0.14	36	0.34
8	6	5000	2	4	C	14	0.2	98	30	0.59	0.08	27	0.20
15	11	5500	2	2	C	16	0.3	74	23	0.96	0.20	44	0.50
15	11	5000	2	4	C	21	0.4	101	31	0.70	0.15	32	0.36
30	22	5000	2	2	C	32	0.5	117	36	0.94	0.26	43	0.63
30	22	5800	2	4	C	36	0.6	212	65	0.82	0.14	37	0.35
50	37	5000	2	2	C	45	0.7	195	59	1.11	0.26	51	0.63
50	37	6200	3	4	I	50	0.8	240	73	1.01	0.21	46	0.51
115	86	5500	4	2	I	105	1.7	369	112	0.99	0.31	50	0.76
115	86	5500	4	4	I	137	2.3	496	151	0.84	0.23	38	0.57
150	112	5000	6	2	I	158	2.6	419	128	0.95	0.36	43	0.88
150	112	5500	4	4	I	144	2.4	478	146	1.04	0.31	48	0.77
225	168	5750	6	2	I	200	3.3	524	160	1.13	0.43	51	1.05
225	168	5500	6	4	I	212	3.5	588	179	1.06	0.38	48	0.94
250	186	5750	6	2	I	200	3.3	524	160	1.25	0.48	57	1.17

Fuel Del.: I=Injection, C=Carburetor

TABLE 8-6: Typical Outboard Engines Horsepower and Displacement

As with inboard engines, the only practical way to get more power from outboards is to install two (or even three) engines.

In North America, *Evinrude, Honda, Johnson, Mercury, Nissan, Suzuki, Tohatsu,* and *Yamaha* engines are the primary makes of outboard engines. Both Evinrude and Johnson are owned by Bombardier Corporation. Mercury is owned by Brunswick Corporation.

Specialized engines for jet drives also come in both two- and four-stroke versions. Two-stroke engines have been used in personal watercraft (PWC) applications but are increasingly being supplanted by four-stroke engines to reduce both noise and exhaust pollution.

Safety

Gasoline fumes are heavier than air and will concentrate in spaces that are enclosed on the bottom and sides (which, by the way, is a good description of a boat's bilge and engine room). This isn't an issue with automobiles since the engine compartment is open on the bottom and any fumes simply descend downward and then dissipate. Since gasoline fumes are explosive in certain concentrations, this presents a potentially dangerous situation for the boater.

Ignition systems and any other electrical gear for marine use that creates, or has the potential to create, sparks, must be enclosed to prevent sparks and gasoline fumes from coming into contact with one another. In addition, spark arrestors are required by law to be installed on engine air intakes of gasoline powered inboard and stern drive engines. U.S. and Canadian regulations also require both natural ventilation and exhaust blowers for enclosed engine and fuel tank compartments.

Although gasoline engines are regarded as unsafe by many boaters, they are quite safe if proper precautions are taken when refueling and starting the engines. When refueling, all openings into the boat are kept closed so gasoline fumes cannot flow into and down to the bilge and engine compartments. Portable fuel tanks are always removed from the boat and refilled on the dock.

Once refueling is complete and before any engine startup, the engine room exhaust fans are run for at least two minutes, preferably more like five minutes. Before starting up, sniff for fumes in the engine room or compartment. Gasoline fume detectors are available for less that $200 and give extra protection and piece of mind.

Four-Cycle Gas Engine

The four-cycle (or four-stroke) gasoline engine is used in automobiles and also in boats with inboard and stern drive power trains. Note that the terms cycle and stroke are pretty much synonymous in that a cycle is essentially one up stroke or one downstroke of the piston. In a four-cycle engine the power stroke is one stroke of every four strokes.

The two figures on the next page show a four-stroke gasoline engine working through its four cycles.

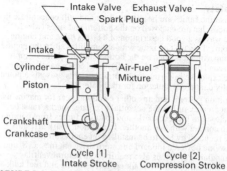

FIGURE 8-1: Four-Cycle Intake and Compression Cycles.

The four-stroke cycle begins with the intake stroke (1). The piston moves down from ***top dead center*** (**TDC**) with the intake valve open. As the piston moves downward, the air-fuel mixture is drawn into the cylinder. The compression stroke (2) then compresses the or air-fuel mixture. The ratio of the uncompressed mix to the compressed mix is known as the compression ratio and ranges from about 8:1 to 10:1. Higher ratios are found in higher performance engines.

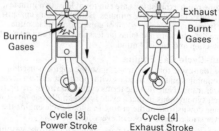

FIGURE 8-2: Four-Cycle Power and Exhaust Cycle

The third cycle (3) is the power stroke down. When the cylinder is just past TDC the spark plug ignites the compressed air-fuel mixture and the resulting controlled explosion pushes the piston down. When the piston reaches the bottom of the power stroke, the exhaust valve opens and then the burnt gases are expelled by the piston moving up (4). When the piston reaches the top again, the four cycles have been completed and the entire process is then repeated. Note that the crankshaft has completed two complete revolutions (720 degrees) to complete the four cycles.

The air-fuel mixture is provided by either a **carburetor** or a **fuel-injection** system. In a carburetor, air passes through a venturi, which lowers the air pressure such that fuel can be drawn into the intake air stream. Note: A venturi is a tube that narrows in the center which causes gases to flow faster which in turn results in lowered pressure at the center of the tube. A fuel injector actually *injects* a measured amount of fuel into the intake air stream (kind of like a hypodermic needle). Injection systems are becoming more prevalent because they allow more precise metering of the amount of fuel injected and they are more suitable for use with computerized engine control systems, with the net result being less emissions and more power. (There is a more complete discussion of fuel injection in the diesel engine topic later.)

The mechanism for opening and closing the valves at the correct times is the camshafts, which may be either overhead at the top of the engine near the valves, or down in the crankcase. Overhead cams are driven by timing belts or chains from the crankshaft, and the crankcase style cams are usually driven by gears from the crankshaft. Push rods through the engine block from the crankcase cams up to rocker arms operate the valves. Overhead cams have been found to be lighter and more efficient, and today are the preferred method of operating the valves in gasoline engines.

A four-cycle engine lubricates the cylinders with oil from the crankcase and pumps oil to the top of the engine to lubricate the valves.

Two-Cycle Gas Engine

The two-cycle (or two-stroke) gasoline engine has traditionally been used in most outboards and also in PWCs and some jet boats. In a two-cycle engine the power stroke is one stroke out of two strokes.

The four-cycle engine accomplishes one function per stroke, while the two-cycle engine accomplishes two functions per stroke in a rather ingenious way. The following four schematics show how a two-stroke gasoline engine accomplishes all the functions of a four-cycle engine in just two cycles.

The first schematic (figure 8-3), shows how both intake and compression are combined. Intake of air-fuel mixture into the cylinder is completed at the bottom of the downstroke by the piston uncovering the inlet port so that the pressurized air-fuel mix is expelled from the crankcase below the piston up into the cylinder above the piston 8-3(A). The air-fuel mix moving into the cylinder also forces the last of the exhaust gases out of the exhaust port.

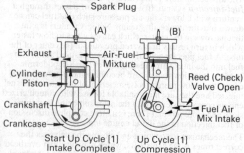

FIGURE 8-3: Two-Stroke Intake and Compression Cycle

In figure 8-3(B) we see both the input and exhaust ports are covered by the piston moving up, which causes the mixture to be compressed. At the same time, the next charge of air-fuel mix is being drawn into the crankcase through the Reed valve (a one-way check valve) by the vacuum induced by the upward moving piston.

In figure 8-4(A), the piston has reached the top and is just starting down, the mix is fully compressed, and the spark plug fires and the mixture is ignited. The ignition forces the piston downward providing power to the crankshaft.

As the piston passes the exhaust port, as in 8-4(B) the pressurized burnt gases escape through the open exhaust port as shown. Also as the piston moves downward, the Reed valve is closed by the pressure and the air-fuel mix in the crankcase is compressed in preparation for charging the upper cylinder.

On the way down, the cylinder inlet port is uncovered, and the pressurized air-fuel mix moves up from the crankcase. When the cylinder reaches bottom the two cycles have been

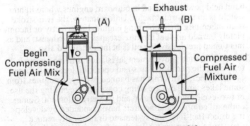

FIGURE 8-4: Two-Stroke Ignition and Exhaust Cycle

completed and the whole process repeats itself. In the two-cycle engine the complete power cycle is accomplished with one up and one downstroke and the crankshaft has turned through just one complete turn (360 degrees).

The crankcase is part of the air-fuel intake system so the oil bath can't be used like it is in the four-cycle engine. The usual method of lubricating the two-cycle engine is to mix the fuel with the lubricating oil in the gas tank so that the mix actually lubricates the moving parts as it passes through the engine. The ratio of the fuel oil mix is about 1 part oil to 40 parts gasoline. As you might expect, the oil gets burned along with the gasoline, which results in more atmospheric emissions than gasoline alone.

Direct injection systems have been developed to try to reduce the emissions from two-cycle engines while increasing power output. In a direct injection system, fuel injectors inject a precisely controlled amount of fuel just before ignition, and oil is injected into the crankcase rather than being mixed with the fuel. This results in oil consumption being reduced to about 1 part oil to 80 parts gasoline.

Compare Four-Cycle Gas Engines With Two-Cycle Gas Engines

The two-cycle engine is much simpler than a four-cycle engine since there are no valves that require a complex mechanical system to operate properly. As a result the two-stroke is cheaper to build, easier to maintain, is lighter and has a higher power to weight ratio than the four-stroke. For this reason, two-cycle engines are used extensively in hand held power tools and in outboard engines where lighter weight is an important factor. Unfortunately, the two-stroke is an inherently dirtier burning engine. Imperfectly or incompletely burned air-fuel mixture escapes in the exhaust, and as mentioned previously, the oil is being exhausted also.

As a result, much government legislation is being enacted regarding the permitted uses and operating locations of two-cycle engines. California has banned two-cycle engines from some lakes, and laws are being considered regarding the use of two-cycle engines in lawn and garden equipment. Some outboard engine manufacturers have responded by developing direct fuel-injection systems to dramatically reduce two-stroke emissions while others have converted their entire line of engines to four-strokes. Some are producing both. Where this will all end up is anyone's guess, although we can be sure the environmental regulations will get tougher as time goes on.

Four-cycle engines are just the opposite. They are more complex, more expensive to build, heavier, and have a lower power to weight ratio. But, they are inherently cleaner burning. Although the power to weight ratio of a four-stroke is less, the fuel efficiency is better so you get more miles to the gallon. Also, two-stroke oil isn't cheap so this will also add to your cruising cost. Last but not least, oil distribution in the four-stroke is far better resulting in a longer lasting engine, although this is somewhat offset by the greater complexity which increases the odds of something breaking.

DIESEL ENGINES

Introduction to Diesel Engines

The diesel engine is a *compression ignition* internal combustion engine, meaning that ignition of the air-fuel mixture is by means of compression to high pressure and temperature. This process is based on the thermodynamic principle that compressing a gas causes its temperature to rise. In the case of the diesel engine the compression has to be enough to raise the gas temperatures enough to initiate ignition. Compression ratios for diesel engines range from about 15:1 to 25:1, although some have been built with even higher ratios.

Diesel engines are used in inboard and stern drive applications and come in a much wider range of size and power than the four-cycle gasoline engines available for these applications. Many diesel engines used in boats are marinized versions of car or truck engines while others are designed specifically for marine use from the start.

The major makers of marine diesel engines are *Alaska Diesel* (*Lugger*), *American Diesel, Caterpillar, Cummins, Detroit Diesel, John Deere, Volvo Penta, Perkins*, and *Yanmar*.

Table 8-7 lists specifications for some randomly selected engines from various manufacturers. The RPM given is the RPM for the rated horsepower.

Power			No.Cyls	Aspirate	Displ.		Wt		Ratios			
hp	kW	RPM			CID	L	Lbs	Kg	hp/cui	hp/lb	kW/L	kW/kg
8	6	3400	1	N	19	0.3	167	51	0.41	0.05	19	0.12
10	7	3600	2	N	28	0.5	247	75	0.36	0.04	17	0.10
10	7	3200	2	N	28	0.5	247	75	0.36	0.04	17	0.10
55	41	3000	4	N	134	2.2	558	170	0.41	0.10	19	0.24
63	47	2600	4	N	183	3.0	579	176	0.34	0.11	16	0.27
70	52	2500	4	N	212	3.5	787	240	0.33	0.09	15	0.22
75	56	2400	4	N	276	4.5	961	293	0.27	0.08	12	0.19
101	75	2200	4	N	425	7.0	1710	521	0.24	0.06	11	0.14
105	78	2200	6	N	414	6.8	1194	364	0.25	0.09	12	0.22
140	104	2200	6	T	414	6.8	1194	364	0.34	0.12	15	0.29
158	118	3100	4	T	211	3.5	805	245	0.75	0.20	34	0.48
208	155	2300	6	T	414	6.8	1399	426	0.50	0.15	23	0.36
230	172	3900	6	T	219	3.6	534	163	1.05	0.43	48	1.05
254	189	2400	6	T	442	7.2	1812	552	0.57	0.14	26	0.34
325	242	2100	6	T	674	11.0	2400	732	0.48	0.14	22	0.33
375	280	1900	6	T	766	12.5	2695	821	0.49	0.14	22	0.34
415	309	2750	6	T	452	7.4	1815	553	0.92	0.23	42	0.56
480	358	2600	6	T	444	7.3	2304	702	1.08	0.21	49	0.51
510	380	1800	12	T	1649	27.0	6257	1907	0.31	0.08	14	0.20
615	459	2100	6	T	740	12.1	1400	427	0.83	0.44	38	1.07
700	522	1800	6	T	1413	23.2	5525	1684	0.50	0.13	22	0.31
825	615	2300	6	T	855	14.0	4240	1292	0.96	0.19	44	0.48
1000	746	1800	8	T	2105	34.5	11500	3505	0.48	0.09	22	0.21
Aspirate: N=Natural, T = Turbocharge												

TABLE 8-7: Typical Diesel Engine Specifications

Notice the large variation of the RPM, horsepower to displacement (hp/cui) and horsepower to engine weight (hp/lb) for the different engines. These ratios have implications relating to engine longevity that will directly affect matching the engine to the boating application. In general a slower turning engine with lower power to displacement and lower power to weight ratios will be the longer lasting engine. The faster turning higher ratio engines are performance engines that would be used in planing craft where weight is a prime consideration.

Four-Cycle Diesel Engine

The basic operating principle of the four-cycle engine is similar to the gasoline four-cycle engine except for a few fundamental differences. The similarity is that the four cycles are the same, these being intake, compression, ignition (power), and exhaust. The differences are the use of compression instead of spark ignition, direct fuel injection (explained below), and much higher operating temperatures and pressures.

Figure 8-5 and 8-6 show the four cycles of the diesel engine.

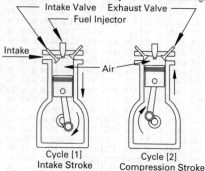

FIGURE 8-5: Diesel Engine Intake and Compression Cycle

The intake stroke (1) draws pure air in rather than a air-fuel mixture like a gas engine. The compression stroke (2) compresses the air to a much higher pressure and temperature than the gas engine does. At 15:1 to 25:1 compression ratios, pressures of over 500 psi (3450 kPa) and temperatures of 1000 degrees Fahrenheit (540 degrees C) can be achieved.

With the piston near the top, the injector injects fuel into the high temperature air and ignition occurs. The combustion induced high pressure pushes the piston down in the power stroke (3), the same as in the gas engine. The exhaust stroke (4) will then exhaust the burnt gases through the exhaust valve.

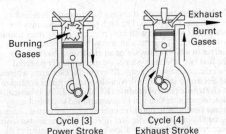

FIGURE 8-6: Diesel Engine Power and Exhaust Cycle

Two-Cycle Diesel Engine

The two-cycle diesel engine was popularized by Detroit Diesel and saw widespread use in the past. These are no longer being produced for use in pleasure craft although some might still be found in older boats. Since these are discontinued, I won't spend more than a paragraph on them here.

They are similar to the two-cycle gas engine with the same functions of intake, compression, power, and exhaust being combined into two strokes. They differ, however, in their means of getting fuel and air into the engine. Instead of an air-fuel mixture being forced up from the crankcase, the air is blown in the open port by a low boost blower, and the fuel is injected at the appropriate time just like in a four-cycle diesel. Lubrication takes place by pumping oil through the engine as in the four-cycle system.

Advantages are similar to those for the two-cycle gasoline engine and so are the disadvantages of higher emissions and less fuel economy. The higher emissions are the main reasons these engines have fallen out of favor.

Diesel Fuel Injection

If the engine fails to operate, odds are 90 percent that it's a problem in the fuel-injection system. If you're going to fix the problem yourself, ,it is important to understand how the injection system functions.

The fuel-injection system basically consists of a *low pressure pump*, a *high pressure pump*, and the *injectors*. There is also a *return line* to scavenge unused fuel from the injectors and return it to the fuel tanks.

The low pressure pump transfers fuel from the fuel tank to the high pressure pump. The high pressure pump may be located on the engine with high pressure supply lines running to the individual injectors, or it may be integrated with the injector in a ***direct injector*** or an ***electronic fuel injector***. The first two injector systems are mechanically powered from the engine using gears, lifters and rocker arms whereas the electronic injector is driven electrically under control of an ***electronic control module*** (**ECM**). An ECM is basically a microcomputer that can be programmed to control many engine functions to optimize operation under various operating conditions. Electronic fuel injector systems are becoming more prevalent since they allow more precise control of the injection process, which, in turn, results in less emissions and better engine performance.

The injector itself has either a ***nozzle*** with multiple holes, or a ***pintle*** with a single hole, through which finely atomized fuel is delivered to the cylinder. A ***nozzle valve*** held shut by an injector spring keeps the holes sealed until fuel is needed. The high pressure pump activates just before the piston reaches top dead center, and when the pressure is high enough to overcome the spring, the injector will release and inject the fuel into the cylinder.

The high pressure pump and the injectors have very fine tolerances so that even the smallest particle of dirt can disable them. If air is present in the fuel they won't function. Water in the fuel can vaporize in the high heat and stop operation also. Bacteria that like to grow in diesel fuel will clog the system and cause it to fail.

For this reason, the wise boat owner will be fanatical about buying only clean, contaminant-free fuel, and installing and maintaining filters and fuel cleaning and polishing systems. If the fuel is clean and the engine has been properly maintained then, aside from overheating, it's highly unlikely you'll ever experience an engine failure.

Diesel Air Supply and Turbocharging

Traditionally, diesel engines used natural aspiration to supply air to the cylinder. This simply means that the piston moving down on the intake stroke creates a vacuum that draws air in at atmospheric pressure. This engine is said to be a ***naturally aspirated*** engine.

In a naturally aspirated engine there is a limit to the amount of fuel that can be injected and burned in a cylinder of specific displacement and configuration, the limiting factor being the amount of air available to burn all the fuel. To increase the horsepower of a naturally aspirated engine, we must increase the displacement, which, in turn, increases the size and weight of the engine.

An alternative is to boost the intake air pressure above normal atmospheric pressure to force more air into the cylinder, which allows the injection and burning of more fuel, which in turn increases the horsepower produced by the engine. The *turbocharger* accomplishes this task without adding much weight to the engine, and in fact, this is what turbocharging is all about. In planing boats, getting more horsepower without increasing weight is a critical design consideration.

Turbocharging can also improve overall efficiency (i.e., miles per gallon) and with improved burning, lower emissions. For these reasons, turbocharged engines are increasing their market share and may be your only choice in the not too distant future.

The turbocharger is basically a blower that has a turbine at one end that is powered by exhaust gases from the engine, connected by a shaft to a turbine at the other end that boosts intake air pressure. The result is more air and fuel burn in the cylinder to produce more power. The amount of increased pressure above atmospheric pressure is known as *boost*.

This sounds quite simple but unfortunately it gets more complex pretty quickly:

1. Burning more fuel and air means more heat and pressure, which places more load on an engine that may not have been designed to take it. There is no question that turbocharging reduces engine life.
2. The turbocharger will actually impede engine performance at slower speeds since there will not be enough exhaust gas to drive it effectively. This means turbocharging is not a good idea if you plan to run frequently at below cruising speeds.
3. The turbine runs at speeds up to 100,000 RPM and more. This is a very high speed, and it means another high maintenance item has been added that is subject to failure if everything is not just right because of its precise tolerances.
4. When a gas is compressed it heats up, which, in turn, expands it—exactly the opposite of what we want to happen in the turbocharger. In a sense, the turbo is working against itself. In addition, the exhaust gases used to

drive it are adding even more heat, which compounds the problem.

5. To counteract the heating problem and cool the air going to the turbocharger, an *intercooler* is commonly used, particularly in larger engines. The intercooler is a heat exchanger (much like a radiator) that uses raw (sea) water to cool the air.

ENGINE COOLING AND EXHAUST SYSTEMS

Cooling Systems

The engine cooling and exhaust systems are similar for both gasoline and diesel engines however diesel engines require more cooling capacity because of their higher operating temperatures. Gasoline engines are much more tolerant of overheating than diesel engines. Failure of the cooling system in a diesel can lead to an overheat condition and total engine failure in less than a minute, so monitoring and shutdown systems must be meticulously maintained.

Raw Water Cooling

Raw water cooling refers to the practice of circulating seawater directly through the engine block to cool the engine. Since salt water is quite corrosive, this is usually an undesirable way to cool the engine unless the boat is used exclusively in fresh water. The resulting corrosion will tend to reduce circulation and ultimately lead to the engine running hotter, which ultimately reduces engine life.

Outboard engines, most gasoline stern drives, and some gasoline inboards use raw water cooling. Generally, diesel installations don't use raw water cooling systems.

A raw water cooled boat that is hauled out of saltwater after each use needs to be flushed with fresh water each time. For boats that are left in the (salt) water, raw water cooling is just not recommended, since there is no practical way to flush the engines with fresh water. Outboard engines are designed to drain all the water after each use, which should help, but a good flushing is still recommended after each use in saltwater.

The most common type of raw water pump, uses a rubber vane type impeller. The raw water is circulated continuously by the raw water pump with a thermostat controlling the actual flow through the engine. When the thermostat is closed the water bypasses the engine and is discharged into the hot engine exhaust gases to cool them. When the thermostat is open, the raw water passes through the engine and is then also discharged into the exhaust.

In climates where freezing temperatures are expected, the raw water system must be completely drained of all water, usually from several points on the engine block and the cooling system.

Closed Circuit Cooling with Heat Exchanger

In the closed circuit cooling system, the raw water circulates through a heat exchanger that cools a water-antifreeze mix, which is then circulated in a closed circuit through the engine. The raw water is continuously circulating and is discharged into the exhaust the same as with the raw water system (if the boat has a wet exhaust system).

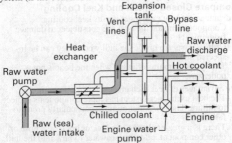

FIGURE 8-7: Closed Circuit Engine Cooling

The *heat exchanger* usually consists of a number of parallel tubes around which the closed circuit mixture circulates. The raw water passes through the inside of the tubes where the heat exchange actually takes place.

A thermostat regulates closed circuit coolant flow through the engine block as needed. Freezing temperatures are not such an issue as they are with the raw water system since the water-antifreeze mixture doesn't freeze. There still may be concerns with water in the raw water side of the system, particularly in the pump.

In general, the closed circuit cooling system is going to be both more expensive and more work to maintain than the raw water system, since there are more parts involved. However, this is more than offset by the harmful effects of circulating saltwater through the engine.

Closed Circuit Cooling With Keel Coolers

With a keel cooling system, the coolant in the closed circuit is run through a **keel cooler**, which is essentially a flat heat exchanger mounted on the outside of the hull. In this case, the cooling is by direct contact with the surrounding seawater.

Keel cooling is often favored for ocean crossing vessels because its simplicity contributes to reliability.

Keel cooling makes the most sense if combined with a dry exhaust system (described next). If a wet exhaust system is used, raw water must still be pumped into the boat, which negates one of the main advantages of using the keel cooler (eliminating the raw water pump).

Compare Closed Circuit and Keel Cooling

Advantages of heat exchanger versus keel cooling:

- Components inside the boat are not subject to damage from impact.
- Critical parts are inside the hull where they can be inspected and maintained.
- The system remains efficient when the boat is not underway.

Disadvantages of heat exchanger versus keel cooling:

- The heat exchanger system has more components subject to failure. The raw water pump is particularly prone to failure.
- There is a greater chance of a leak or break in a hose or other component, allowing seawater to flow into the boat.

Advantages of keel cooler versus heat exchanger:

- No raw water pump is needed, which eliminates a common failure point. This is considered the primary advantage of keel cooling.
- Substantially less maintenance that raw water cooling with a heat exchanger.

Disadvantages of keel cooler versus heat exchanger:

- The keel cooler is on the outside where it is subject to damage from impact. Also it is subject to fouling, which can reduce its efficiency.
- It can increase hull resistance to forward motion.
- It loses efficiency when the boat is not making way since there is no flow of seawater over the tubes.

Exhaust Systems

Exhaust systems are generally classified as either wet or dry exhaust systems.

The *dry exhaust* system discharges the hot exhaust gases directly, first through a muffler, then up vertically through the boat to a smoke stack. These gases are very hot, typically on the order of 1000 degrees Fahrenheit (540 degrees Celsius).

The *wet exhaust* system relies on the discharge of raw cooling water, used to cool the engine, into the exhaust to cool the engine exhaust gases to below 200 degrees Fahrenheit (93 degrees Celsius), where they can be discharged from the boat through noninsulated hoses and pipes.

Dry Exhaust

Dry exhaust systems are used on most commercial boats and are found on some recreational boats (e.g., Nordhavn) that are designed specifically for crossing oceans. As a general rule, dry exhaust systems won't be found on recreational boats of less than 40 feet (12 m).

Relative to a wet exhaust system, the dry exhaust system is basically simpler in design since it has no moving parts. As a result, it requires considerably less maintenance and is much less prone to catastrophic failure. By catastrophic failure I mean failure that can stop the engine and damage it—to the extent that it needs to be rebuilt or replaced—or setting the boat on fire. Proper design and installation of the dry exhaust system is critical since failure will generally result in a boat fire. If it is designed and installed correctly, however, the probability of fire caused by a dry exhaust is near zero.

A dry exhaust system is quite often installed along with keel cooling systems, thus completely eliminating the need for any raw water pumps in critical systems.

Because of the high temperatures involved, the use of thick insulation and special materials such as stainless steel are required to isolate the hot stack from the parts of the boat through which it passes. In addition a large muffler is required to minimize exhaust noise. All this takes up much more interior room in the boat both in the engine room and right up through the center of the boat. On a boat of less than 40 feet (12 m), the space taken is prohibitive, but on a boat over 50 feet (15 m), it may be acceptable.

Disadvantages of dry exhaust relative to wet exhaust:

- As mentioned previously, it uses substantially more space.
- It is more expensive because of the need to use components that withstand the high temperature.
- It requires a smoke stack, which can't be lowered to clear overhead obstructions such as bridges.

- It can emit carbon and ash particulates that settle back on to the boat, particularly when starting.
- It radiates more heat into the boat.

Advantages of dry exhaust:
- There is less maintenance; it generally just requires periodic inspection.
- It is less likely to fail. This is the major reason dry exhaust is installed in boats that will be crossing oceans, or passagemakers.

Wet Exhaust

Wet exhaust systems are found on virtually all boats under 40 feet (12 m) and most recreational boats over 40 feet. All outboards and gasoline engines use wet exhaust systems.

The raw cooling water is the discharge from the heat exchanger in the case of a closed circuit cooling system, or the discharge from the engine block in a raw water cooling system. In the case of a keel cooling system, the raw water will be drawn directly from the sea. In all these cases the water circulation depends on a raw water pump.

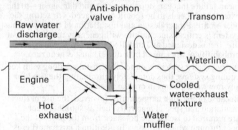

FIGURE 8-8: Wet Exhaust System Schematic

The hot exhaust discharge pipe must be capable of withstanding the high temperature exhaust (1000 degrees Fahrenheit/540 degrees Celsius) gases; however, once the exhaust gases mix with the discharge water, they are cooled to temperatures less than 200 degrees Fahrenheit (93 degrees Celsius), which allows the use of rubber and fiberglass piping to route the cooled mixture from the muffler out through the transom.

The gooseneck in the cooled exhaust discharge line is to prevent seawater from flowing back down into the engine through the exhaust system. The anti-siphon device is designed to prevent siphoning of water back through the exhaust system. The heights and sizing of the various components must be correct and within certain limits or the system will not function correctly, so the design of a wet exhaust system should be left to a professional.

The water-exhaust mix is a heated blend of acidic exhaust gases and saltwater. This is a very corrosive combination, so the components from the water injection point onward corrode rather quickly. A five-year life is about all one might expect for some of these components.

Close and frequent monitoring and inspection of this system is an absolute necessity since failure can cause devastating results. There are plenty of anecdotal estimates by diesel engine technicians suggesting that *wet exhaust cooling system failures ultimately are responsible for 40 to 75 percent of all engine failures.*

Sensors can be placed in strategic places to monitor the system and warn of failure. Flow sensors can be placed in the raw water line, and temperature sensors can be placed in the cooled exhaust pipe. High temperature probes can be placed in the hot exhaust pipe. All of these combined with gauges and alarms, and lots of attention to preventative maintenance, will negate most of the disadvantages of the wet exhaust system.

Disadvantages of wet exhaust:

- If the raw water pump (impeller) fails, then without cooling water the high temperature exhaust gases enter the muffler and components made of rubber and fiberglass. Within less than a minute, there's going to be a fire in the engine room if you don't stop the engine in time.
- If the anti-siphon valve or vent fails, water can be siphoned back into the engine. Water in the cylinders may not total the engine if the situation is corrected quickly, but if left for a longer period a rebuild or new engine will likely be required.
- When the engine is shut down, salt-laden gases can back into the high temperature exhaust pipe causing more rapid than usual corrosion. Failure here will allow hot exhaust gases into the engine room and most likely result in a fire.
- The relative complexity and the severe penalty for failure imply relatively high maintenance costs.

Advantages of wet exhaust:

- Wet exhaust systems are cheaper to build since high temperature materials and insulation are not required throughout.
- They use much less space.
- The water muffler is much smaller and does a better job of reducing exhaust noise.
- They are quite safe if the correct precautions and maintenance are carried out. That's a big if, since most boaters tend to neglect this critical area even more than they neglect maintaining their engine.
- When the wet exhaust system is functioning correctly, there is probably less chance of fire than with dry exhaust.

GASOLINE AND DIESEL ENGINE COMPARISON AND SELECTION

Horsepower

From the engine specification tables (8-5, 8-6 and 8-7) starting on page 451, we see that inboard gasoline engines range from about 135 to 375 horsepower, outboards from 2 to 250 horsepower, and diesels from 8 to 1000 (and larger) horsepower. One major factor in comparison will simply be size: If more than 750 (375 x 2 engines) horsepower is required, then the diesel is all that's available.

Safety

As we are all aware, gasoline fumes are dangerous since they are explosive. Consequently, this is a significant consideration, although with proper maintenance and operating procedures in place, this shouldn't be a major factor in engine selection. Keep in mind that diesel fuel, although not normally explosive, is definitely a fuel and it can burn fiercely. The flash point of diesel fuel is in the range of 140 degrees Fahrenheit (60 degrees C), which is the temperature where explosive vapors are given off, so diesel explosions can occur too, they're just much less likely.

Expense

Diesel engines are expensive to buy and maintain. The largest gasoline engine runs about $8000 and is roughly equivalent to a $20,000 diesel engine. And, if anything goes wrong with the diesel, the cost of parts will be typically be twice as much as a gasoline engine. Offsetting this is the fact that the diesel uses less fuel. Diesel fuel was generally about 50 cents cheaper per gallon than gasoline up to 2005 but now it costs more then gasoline. It is going to take several years to make up the difference in engine cost of $12,000.

Operating Life

Diesels have achieved a reputation for operating up to 20,000 hours without major overhauls and this is often compared to a typical gasoline engine operating life of around 2000 hours. These high engine operating hours are achieved by working boats that operate high hours per year operating day in and day out. These are engines that produce low horsepower relative to engine displacement and weight.

Horsepower to engine displacements ratios for these long lived engines typically run at less than 0.3 horsepower/cubic inch (23 kW/L). Horsepower to weight ratios would run less than 0.1 horsepower/pound (0.3 kW/kg).

By way of comparison, a typical gasoline engine produces approximately 0.75 horsepower/cubic inch (34 kW/L) and 0.3 hp/lb (0.75 kW/kg). One major reason for this difference is that diesel engines run at much higher temperatures and pressures than gasoline engines, and therefore must be built much heavier if they are going to last as long. To get an extraordinarily long life, they must be even heavier.

In general the lower the ratios of horsepower to engine displacement and weight, the longer the engine can be expected to operate.

Unfortunately, many recreational boats aren't getting any more hours with diesels than with gasoline engines for several reasons:

- Many of the new turbocharged high performance diesels are achieving horsepower to engine displacement ratios of over 1.0 horsepower/cui, which is even higher than that of gasoline engines. Look back at table 8-7 to see some examples. These engines are designed this way for high-speed planing boats as a matter of necessity, since light weight and high horsepower are the critical factors in planing boat performance.
- To achieve this high performance they also operate at much higher RPMs—in the 3500 to 4000 range.
- Diesel engines are suited to continuous running at around 80 percent of full power and running at idle speeds for extended periods of time lessens engine life especially with turbocharged engines, this being primarily because of carbon build up in the cylinders. Regrettably, a lot of recreational boat diesel engines are run in just this way.

- Diesel engines are not suited to infrequent use. Diesel fuel is somewhat acidic and the byproducts will corrode internal engine surfaces when they are left unused for extended periods.

Keep in mind, a 2000-hour operating life is not necessarily a bad thing. An average weekend boater might use his boat six hours per weekend for 25 weekends for a net 150 hours per year. At this rate, if the gasoline or high performance engine is properly maintained you'll get 2000/150 or 13 years out of it.

If you are passagemaking, putting on thousands of hours per year with a low horsepower to weight engine, you can expect to get 20,000 engine hours just like the workboats. This is assuming you do the proper preventative maintenance.

Which Engine for Which Boat?

Small diesels are generally the best choice for auxiliary engines for cruising sailboats, if only because they are located deep in the unventilated bilge area where gasoline fumes can be particularly dangerous. On a cruising sailboat, this engine may be used for extended operating periods, which is where the diesels have the edge. Reliability is an important factor too.

The smallest boats, up to about 17 feet (5 m) are generally going to be outboard powered since these are the only engines small enough for these boats. This includes small sailboats. Outboards are also found on boats up to around 32 feet (10 m) long and 15,000 pounds (6800 kg) displacement. These larger, outboard-driven boats will usually be some kind of sport fisherman, which is a planing boat where light engine weight is important. Fishermen tend to like outboards because they can mount a second smaller outboard for trolling on the same transom.

Gasoline inboard and stern drive engines span the range from about 16 feet (5 m) to 40 feet (12 m). At the higher end, performance will likely be limited to semi-displacement speeds.

Diesels can be found in power boats from around 25 feet (8 m) and up. A diesel in a planing boat will be a higher performance engine, which involves accepting a lower engine life. A diesel for a displacement boat should be a heavier, slower turning (1800 to 2400 RPM) engine.

The question of gas versus diesel only arises for boats in the range of from about 25 feet (8 m) to 40 feet (12 m) in length. If the boat is only going to run 150 hours or less, then the gas engine makes sense because it's much cheaper to buy, and it's more suited to infrequent use. Extended use at idle or slow speeds also points to a gas engine.

Extended cruising, such as doing the "great loop" around the East Coast, suggests the use of a diesel, although gasoline would work. The great loop is about 6000 miles and requires 1000 engine hours to complete at 6 knots.

If you're passagemaking, then diesel is the only way to go, both for range and reliability.

SURVEYING USED ENGINES

Many buyers, when buying a used boat, have a boat survey done and assume that the boat survey includes the engines. Normally a boat surveyor is not an engine surveyor and when buying a used boat, particularly larger boats (over, say, 28 feet or 9 meters), an engine survey is highly recommended since the nonprofessional will find it difficult to evaluate the internal condition of the engines. Even a professional can't always find all the problems.

You probably will find that most owners haven't bothered to keep detailed maintenance logs, so when you do find a meticulously kept log, this is a good indication the owner also took meticulous care of the engines. In addition, well-kept logs will help pinpoint developing problems. It follows that any owner should keep a good maintenance log as it not only enhances the value of the boat when it comes time to sell it, but it is invaluable in analyzing and troubleshooting engine and mechanical problems. A sample maintenance log is included at the end of this chapter.

The most obvious thing to look for in the engine room is just plain old cleanliness. A filthy engine room is a pretty obvious indication that the owner didn't like being in the "holy place" and hasn't taken care of it.

Even without a survey there are some basic things the prospective owner can check. The normal pretrip fluid level checks, visual checks of belts and filters, etc., are obviously minimum checks. Some sample mechanical checklists are included at the end of this chapter.

Here are some simple checks to make. The engine should be cold (as in not run since yesterday) before starting these checks

- When the dipstick is pulled, smell for diesel or gas in the oil. Observe the condition of the oil. Is it dirty black or clear?

- Check the coolant for contaminants and/or rust. Check the antifreeze level with a hydrometer.
- Squeeze the hoses. They should be firm, not soft and not hardened.
- Look everywhere for signs of corrosion. Look for signs of painting over corrosion.
- Look for oil (or fuel) leaks
- If possible run a compression test on each cylinder.
- Start the cold engine. Listen carefully for any strange or irregular sounds.
- Watch and record oil pressure as the engine warms up. It should remain steady and not fluctuate once the engine is warmed up.
- Look for smoke both when the engine is cold and when it's warming up. Note the color of the smoke. Smoke when cold is not unusual if it's not excessive.
- Get the boat out to sea so it can be run at cruising speed for at least an hour or two. During that time the engine should be taken to maximum throttle for at least a few minutes. Now check again for temperature, pressure, smoke, vibrations, and strange noises.
- Check the dipsticks again. See if the oil feels gritty between the fingers. It probably won't, but if it does there's something seriously wrong—something is abrading or wearing off inside the engine. A far better idea is to have a sample of the oil analyzed for contaminants, although if the oil has recently been changed this might not show problems.

ENGINE MAINTENANCE AND TROUBLESHOOTING

Maintenance

With any marine engine, it is essential that the manufacturer's preventative maintenance schedules be followed. This is true for gasoline engines and it is absolutely critical for diesel engines.

Certain checks should always be carried out before starting the engine. These should be in your engine manual. Samples of periodic checklists are at the end of this chapter. Pay particular attention to the cooling system and the exhaust system. Always be on the alert for leaks in these systems. Any leaks should be fixed immediately. Every cooler should be inspected and cleaned at least once per year even if it's not required in the engine maintenance schedule.

Alarm systems need to be checked frequently. These need to be in working order if there is a failure in the cooling or exhaust systems. As mentioned previously, if you don't have exhaust temperature gauges and alarms installed, get them installed sooner rather than later. The alarm system must include loud sound alarms as well as lights. Adhere to the manufacturer's recommendations for oil weight and quality, and follow the oil and filter change schedule. Install vacuum gauges on fuel filters to indicate when filters need to be changed.

Introduction to Troubleshooting

Make it a habit to always put on safety goggle or glasses when in the engine room. If they are prescription eyeglasses, make sure they are the kind with side protection as well.

In this topic we only consider engine starting problems without going into a great deal of detail. The purpose is primarily to introduce a generalized approach to troubleshooting engine problems.

I caution you not to rely on this book for troubleshooting engine problems; you should have the shop manual for your engine onboard. Normally this will be supplied with a new boat, but with a used boat it may be long gone. If it is gone, then get one, as it will save you a lot of trouble in the long run. It will describe in great detail how you go about fixing problems with your engine and will tell you what all those gizmos attached to it are. The manual will also contain detailed preventative maintenance schedules, fluid specifications and capacities, and a wealth of other information specific to your engine.

A set of tools should be onboard any boat with an engine. Larger boats and boats that travel offshore should have a more comprehensive set of tools and spares. A suggested set of tools is listed at the end of this chapter.

Troubleshooting Both Gasoline and Diesel Engines

Engine won't turn over at all when starting
Before doing anything, put on your safety goggles.

Check that the ignition is turned on and the battery selector is switched to on. Keep in mind that starting problems are almost always electrical.

The most obvious and probable cause is dead batteries or bad battery connections (corroded battery terminals).

- Use a battery acid tester to check the specific gravity of the electrolyte. This is the easiest way to determine charge.
- A clicking noise (from the starter solenoid) is a good indicator of dead batteries, although if you don't get the clicking sound that just might mean the batteries are totally dead or the terminals are very badly corroded.
- With a volt-ohmmeter (every boat should have one onboard), check the voltage across the battery terminals before starting. This should read over 12 volts; if it's less, then the battery is almost certainly the problem. If it's over 12 volts the battery still could be the culprit.
- Measure the voltage as you try to start. If the voltage drops way down (below 9 volts), when the starter is engaged, then the battery needs charging.

If the batteries are good then the problem may be the ignition switch, a bad starter motor, a seized engine, or possibly water in one or more cylinders.

- Check voltage to the starter motor terminals with the starter button pressed. No voltage indicates a problem in the starting circuit.
- If you have a booster battery (that you know is good), you can try connecting it directly to the starter motor to see if that will turn the engine over. Use heavy duty jumper cables.
- With a large wrench on the crankshaft, try turning the engine in its normal direction of rotation (clockwise from front) by hand. If you can turn it over then the engine is not seized and does not have water in the cylinders. The problem is most likely to be the starter motor if you're sure the starter circuit and batteries are okay. Note that you may not be able to turn the engine over by hand, particularly with a large engine.
- If you were able to turn it part way and then it stops, that's a pretty good indication that you have water in the cylinder(s).
- If you can't turn it over by hand and you don't have your shop manual for further advice, then perhaps it's time to turn this over to professionals.
- If you are a real do-it-yourself type, then the next step is to relieve the compression by removing the injectors or spark plugs and then turning the motor with the wrench again. If you still can't turn it, then either the engine is seized or you need to start lifting weights. If there was water in the

cylinder(s), then it will probably come out the spark plug or injector holes.

- If there's water in the cylinder, you might be able to siphon it with a small tube and work it out by continuing to turn the engine over with the wrench (don't use the starter). If the water has been in the cylinder(s) for a long time then the cylinders and valves will be rusted and the engine will have to be overhauled. Even if it's recent, you should probably get a professional to check things out and remove any remaining water.
- If you insist on doing this yourself or you're stuck at sea, then you must be sure that all water is out of the oil circulation system. If water has gone any further than the cylinder it will travel down past the pistons into the crankcase so check the crankcase for water. If water is present in the oil, then a complete oil change is required before starting the engine—although the oil should be changed as soon as possible regardless. Change the oil again after running the engine at operating temperature for a few minutes. Continue to check for water over the next few days. If all the water isn't removed, the engine is going to fail in the near future.
- Make at least two full turns of the crankshaft to be sure the engine turns freely through all four cycles.

Troubleshooting Gasoline Engines

Engine turns over but won't start
Before doing anything, put on your safety goggles.

- Never crank an engine more than 10 to 20 seconds, and wait two minutes before cranking again to prevent the starter motor from overheating.
- If the engine usually starts quickly but now won't start with continued cranking, don't keep cranking.
- Before continuing, be sure that the area is well ventilated to remove gasoline fumes, since some of the tests may produce sparks.
- In the marine environment, corrosion of electrical components, loose connections, and broken wires are commonplace and most problems like this are likely to be electrical.
- If the engine has been getting harder and harder to start over time, then that raises the probability that the problem may be in the fuel system but the ignition system is still the most likely culprit.
- Look for the obvious things first, such as loose ignition wires, detached tubes or hoses, fuel leaks, clogged air

filter, etc. Check fuses. (You did check that there is gas in the fuel tank, didn't you?)

- If the engine has a distributor, remove the ignition coil wire from the distributor cap and hold it a little more than 1/8 inch (3 mm) from a good ground. Turn the engine over and look for a good spark. If there's no spark then the coil or the ignition coil wire are likely to be the problem. Work backwards, first to the coil, and then check for power to the coil. This is about as far as you can go without the shop manual.
- If there is a spark, then remove the spark plug wires one by one, and do the same test at each spark plug to see if there's a spark.
- If there is a good spark at the plugs then remove the plugs one by one. Inspect each one for carbon or oil build up.
- If the spark plugs are very dirty, replace them. In an emergency, clean off any deposits.
- With the plug removed, reattach the spark plug wire and hold it against a good ground while cranking the engine. If all the spark plugs are clean and produce a good spark then the ignition is most likely okay. There still may a timing problem but that's beyond our discussion here; for that you'll want the shop manual.
- If the electrical system checks out then the air and fuel delivery systems are the remaining suspects.
- Fuel should be fresh. Old, stale, or contaminated fuel is the primary cause of fuel system problems.
- Check all fuel filters to make sure they are not clogged. Look for contaminants in the filters.
- Carbureted engines: Check to see that fuel is getting to the carburetor. *With the ignition turned off* and the spark arrestor removed, if you move the throttle back and forth, you might be able to see a stream of fuel being pumped into the barrel. If no fuel is getting to the carburetor then the fuel pump is likely at fault. Use the shop manual for troubleshooting the fuel pump.
- Fuel-injected engines: *Do not try to see if the fuel is being injected by looking down the barrel while cranking the engine. Flames can explode out of the barrel when the spark arrestor is removed causing serious injury.* You can often tell if a fuel pump is running by feeling it. It should run for a brief time when the ignition is first turned on, and it should run when cranking the engine.

Diesel Engine Troubleshooting

Engine turns over but won't start
Before doing anything, put on your safety goggles.

- Never crank an engine more than 10 to 15 seconds, and wait two minutes before cranking again to prevent the starter motor from overheating.
- If there is air and fuel being delivered to the cylinder and compression is good, a diesel should start. Some lower compression engines will require glow plugs to initiate combustion, particularly in cold weather.
- Remember, most diesel engine problems can be traced to fuel problems. Even the smallest of contaminants can clog the injection nozzles. Water in the fuel will also stop the injectors from operating. Air will most likely stop injection also.
- The easiest thing to check is air intake. Are there any obstructions to airflow such as a clogged air filter?
- Next check for fuel delivery to the injector. Loosen the fuel delivery line one by one, at each injector. Crank the engine and watch for good fuel delivery. Watch for bubbles in the fuel, which indicate the presence of air in the lines. If you just changed a filter that may have introduced the air. Crank the engine until the bubbles are cleared. If air is found in one injector, repeat the process at each injector until all are cleared.
- If the bubbles persist then air is leaking into the fuel supply somewhere before the high pressure pump. Check to see that the low pressure pump is working. If it is, the leak is likely before the low pressure pump. Look for leaks at all filters, connections, gaskets, etc. Make sure the pickup in the fuel tank is actually immersed completely in fuel.
- If there is no air in the fuel and fuel is being delivered to the injectors then remove the injectors one by one, reattach them to their delivery line, and check to see that they actually spray fuel from the pintle or nozzle. *Be careful here; the fuel is sprayed at extremely high pressures and can easily penetrate skin. Again: Make sure you are wearing safety goggles!*
- If the injectors are at fault, you might be able to clean them, but most likely they will have to go into the diesel shop.
- If the engine is getting both fuel and air, then the remaining check is the glow plugs, if they are present. Remove them one by one and hold the body against a good ground while cranking the engine. They should glow red hot.

- If the injectors are injecting, and there is plenty of air, inadequate compression is likely the problem. You will not be able to be able to do much about that.
- *The use of starting fluid in diesel engines is strongly discouraged. It can ignite on the upstroke and cause serious damage to the engine. It will probably void your warranty too.* The factory manual may have something to say on this subject.

PROPELLERS

INTRODUCTION

Accurately selecting and sizing a propeller for your boat is beyond the scope of this book, but you should be able to at least determine if you are over-propped or under-propped with the information contained herein.

It's necessary to first develop some definitions and terminology.

PROPELLER TERMINOLOGY

A *right-hand* propeller rotates clockwise as viewed from aft (facing forward). A *left-hand* propeller rotates counter-clockwise as viewed from aft.

Propellers are usually specified by their diameter and pitch, for example 14x21, where 14 is the diameter in inches and 21 is the pitch in inches, but there is a lot more to propeller design that just these two items (although these two are the most important).

The *diameter* is simply the diameter in inches of a circle that circumscribes the outside edges (tips) of the propeller. As diameter increases, the amount of horsepower needed to drive the propeller increases.

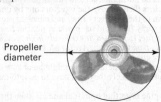

Propeller diameter

FIGURE 8-9: Propeller Diameter

Pitch is the distance in inches the propeller would move forward through a solid in one complete revolution.

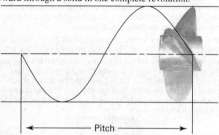

FIGURE 8-10: Propeller Pitch

The ***pitch ratio*** is the ratio of pitch to diameter. As the pitch increases the horsepower required increases.

$$PR = \frac{P}{D}$$

Where: PR = Pitch ratio
P = Pitch
D = Diameter

EQUATION 8-4: Propeller Pitch Ratio

In water the propeller actually moves forward a distance less than the pitch and the difference between the pitch and the actual distance moved is defined as the ***slip***. ***Slip percent*** is the slip divided by the pitch = (slip/pitch) x 100.

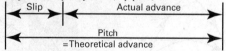

FIGURE 8-11: Propeller Slip

The ***hub*** is the cylinder at the center of the propeller with a hole bored to allow installing on the propeller shaft.

The ***leading edge*** is the front edge of the blade that is cutting through the water. The ***trailing edge*** is the back edge of the blade where water leaves the blade. The ***blade face*** (also termed the ***suction side***) is the surface that faces forward (to the front of the boat). The ***blade back*** (also termed ***pressure*** *side* or *pitch side*) is the surface that faces aft. The **blade root** is where the blade meets the hub. The **blade tip** is the outside edge of the blade furthest from the center of the hub. When the propeller rotates, the blade tip circumscribes the circle that defines the propeller diameter.

Cup is a curve aft in the trailing edge of the blade. A cup acts to reduce slip and has the effect of increasing effective pitch.

A **pitch line** is a line on the blade back from the leading edge to the trailing edge, which is a constant distance (radius) from the shaft centerline. Pitch lines may be drawn at any distance (radius) from the shaft centerline. The **pitch angle** or **blade angle** is the angle between a pitch line and a plane perpendicular to the shaft.

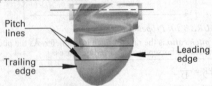

Pitch lines

Leading edge

Trailing edge

FIGURE 8-12: Propeller Pitch Lines

To maintain a **constant** or **fixed-pitch**, the pitch angle must decrease as the pitch line moves outward from the hub. Figure 8-13 illustrates graphically the helical paths followed by a point at the hub and a point at the tip. Note how the pitch angle at the hub and tip are aligned to follow those paths.

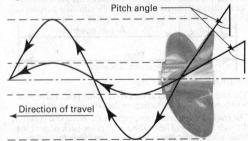

Pitch angle

Direction of travel

FIGURE 8-13: Propeller Pitch Angle (Blade Angle)

The pitch can be related to the pitch angle with an equation as follows.

$$P = \frac{Tan(A)}{2 \times \pi \times R}$$

Where: P = Pitch
      A = Pitch or face angle
      R = Radius (distance from the
             centerline to the pitch line)

EQUATION 8-5: Pitch Versus Pitch Angle

Most propellers are fixed pitch but there are other types, these being:

- *Variable-pitch*, where the pitch varies with the radius.
- *Progressive-pitch*, where the pitch varies from the leading edge to the trailing edge.
- *Controllable-pitch*, where the pitch angle can be changed mechanically. Controllable pitch propellers are often (erroneously) referred to as variable pitch propellers.

The *disk area* is the area of the circle circumscribing the propeller blade tips.

Disk area is the
shaded area
in the circle

FIGURE 8-14: Propeller Disk Area

The formula for calculating disk area is:

$$DA = \pi \times r^2 = \frac{\pi \times D^2}{4}$$

Where: DA = Disk area
      π = Pi = 3.1415
      r = Radius of propeller
      D = Diameter of propeller

EQUATION 8-6: Calculation of Disk Area

Developed or *expanded area* (**Ad**) is the actual area of all the blades combined. If a blade could be removed and flattened out it would occupy the developed area for that one blade. The developed area for the propeller is the developed area of a single blade times the number of blades. You can determine area of a propeller blade by using some paper cross ruled with one-quarter inch squares. Place the paper flat on a blade and trim it to fit the blade. Count the number of quarter-inch squares and divide the count by 16 to get the developed blade area in square inches.

If a light is placed in line with the shaft a good distance away, the area of the shadow projected by the blades is termed the *projected area*.

Developed area ratio (**DAR**) is simply the developed area divided by the disk area.

$$DAR = \frac{Ad}{DA}$$

Where: DAR = Developed area ratio
Ad = Developed or expanded area
DA = Disk area

EQUATION 8-7: Developed Area Ratio (DAR).

Cavitation can occur if the DAR of a propeller is too low. On the forward or suction side of the blade a vacuum is created as the blade rotates. If there is too much vacuum created, the water vaporizes (boils) and forms bubbles of water vapor. This phenomenon is known as *cavitation*. The small bubbles pop as they collapse back into liquid form which can cause pitting of the blades. Some high speed propellers are designed specifically to operate as *cavitating propellers* (sometimes called *supercavitating propellers*).

Ventilation is when surface air or exhaust gases are drawn into the propeller which can cause loss of power and also allow the engine to over speed. Ventilation is quite often confused with cavitation, although they are distinctly different phenomena.

The propeller blade can slope forward or aft. A blade sloping aft has *positive rake* and a blade sloping forward has *negative rake*.

If the blade centerline curves away from the direction of rotation, it is said to be *skewed*.

PROPELLER SELECTION AND SIZING
Maximum or Design RPM
The propeller is sized based on the engine operating at design RPM at wide open throttle. In other words, with the throttle wide open (WOT); the engine should turn at the design specified RPM, if the propeller is correctly sized.

If the engine RPM at WOT is higher than design RPM then the boat is ***underpropped***, with a propeller that has too small a pitch or diameter. If the engine cannot reach design RPM then the boat is ***overpropped***, with a propeller that has too much pitch or diameter.

Operating an underpropped boat is analogous to operating a car in a lower gear. Operating an overpropped boat is analogous to operating a car in too high a gear.

Boaters will often deliberately underprop their boat to "get out of the hole" more quickly when towing water skiers. This is okay, but if this is done, care must be taken never to exceed design RPM. Underpropping yields additional acceleration but will result in a loss of top speed.

The boat should *never* be overpropped, since doing so results in the engine always operating under additional strain, adversely affecting engine life. Overpropping will not get more top speed since the engine can never get to design RPM and develop maximum horsepower. *Along with wet exhaust problems, improper propeller sizing ranks right up there as one of the major causes of premature engine failure.*

> A general rule of thumb is that increasing pitch by 1 inch (2.5 cm) will result in a drop of 100 to 200 RPM.

Figure 8-15 shows a typical engine power curve. The curve labeled engine power shows the horsepower produced by the engine versus engine speed. The curve immediately below it, labeled shaft power shows the SHP delivered at the propeller after losses through the gearing. The propeller power curve shows the horsepower used by a typical propeller at various engine speeds.

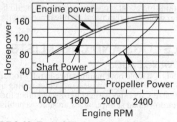

FIGURE 8-15: Typical Engine Power Curve

Unfortunately, the propeller power curve doesn't match the engine power curve and at lower RPMs the propeller draws less power than the engine is able to produce. There is no cure for this; it's just the way it is. The propeller is selected so that the propeller curve meets the shaft power curve at the engine's maximum rated horsepower and RPM. In this way, we can deliver the most power to the propeller when it is needed. Normally, the engine will be run around 80 percent of maximum RPM, so the engine will have reserve power available and will operate under much less strain. Also, the excess engine power is available for additional uses such as driving alternators or hydraulic systems.

Overpropping moves the propeller curve upward on the graph so that the intersection with the shaft power curve moves to the left and down, with the result that maximum horsepower and RPM achievable have been reduced.

Sizing the Propeller

Propeller sizing is beyond the scope of this little book and in general is a subject best left to the pros.

If you are getting different opinions on your propeller or are an avid do-it-yourselfer, get the *Propeller Handbook* by Dave Gerr, mentioned earlier in this chapter. It is the best text on the subject for the layman, and it explains in detail both the Crouch method and the more precise Bp-δ (Bp-delta) method. The Bp-δ method is the way to go if you want accuracy so get that book if you have reason to do these calculations yourself.

There are some computer programs on the market as well, and the propeller manufacturers have online forms you can fill out on their websites.

If you are thinking about repropping then you should have a (reputable) professional or naval architect perform the calculations.

SAMPLE LOGS AND CHECKLISTS

MAINTENANCE LOGS

Figure 8-16 is a sample boat maintenance log. It's too small to be useable but it should provide a model for setting up your own. A full size Excel spreadsheet of this and other forms are available for download at http://www.anchorcovepublishing. com.

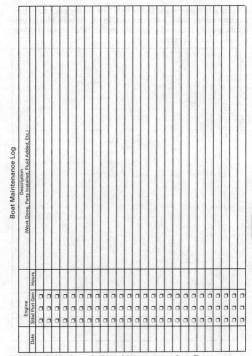

FIGURE 8-16: Sample Boat Maintenance Log Form

The log shown in figure 8-16 is designed for use for all boat maintenance including two engines and a generator. With this form you check the engine or generator being worked on, write in the date and engine hours, and describe the work.

You may wish to use separate sheets for each engine (as in figure 8-17 on the next page), or keep special sheets for oil, fuel, maintenance, etc.; everyone has his or her own preference.

An entry is made in the figure 8-17 engine log each day the engine runs or work is carried out. In the "levels/added" columns specify the level ("full," "down 2," etc.) or the amount of fluid added (2 qts).

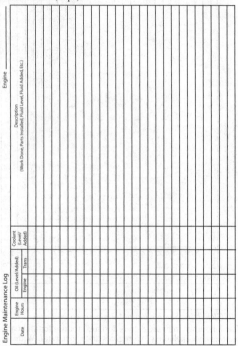

FIGURE 8-17: Sample Engine Maintenance Log Form

Following are some reasons keeping detailed maintenance logs is a good idea:

- No one's memory is perfect, especially with so many disparate pieces of equipment to maintain. Can you actually remember for sure whether you changed the oil filter last fall?

- Keeping it will act as your conscience; having to omit a log entry because you didn't do the scheduled work will, hopefully, tend to make you feel guilty (and therefore maybe get the work done).
- A detailed log will really help when it comes time to sell the boat. This will prove to the buyer that this boat was conscientiously and meticulously maintained.
- If you are actually doing all the scheduled maintenance work, the time it takes to make the entries is miniscule compared to the time it takes to do the work.

TOOLS AND SPARES

Any boat needs to have a minimum set of tools and spare parts. Here is a list of some of the more common tools that should be kept onboard permanently, grouped approximately by boat length. This list should be viewed as a minimum required list, since there will be many additional specialized tools for specific hardware and equipment on a particular boat.

Many of these tools are available in stainless steel from marine supply stores and are not much more expensive than good tools from your local hardware store. A complete set of tools like those recommended here is not particularly expensive, and with tools, unlike lot of consumer goods, quality is generally correlated with price. A cheap tool that breaks might end being the most expensive tool you ever bought when you need it to do an emergency repair at sea.

A list of suggested electrical tools is given separately in the electrical chapter.

Example Onboard Toolkit

Tool	< 25ft 8m	< 40ft 12m	> 40ft 12m	Off-shore
#1 phillips screwdriver	❑	❑	❑	❑
#2 phillips screwdriver	❑	❑	❑	❑
#3 phillips screwdriver			❑	❑
#4 phillips screwdriver				❑
#1 phillips stubby screwdriver		❑	❑	❑
#2 phillips stubby screwdriver		❑	❑	❑
#3 phillips stubby screwdriver		❑	❑	❑
3/16" slotted screwdriver	❑	❑	❑	❑
1/4" slotted screwdriver	❑	❑	❑	❑

Tool	< 25ft 8m	< 40ft 12m	> 40ft 12m	Off-shore
5/16" slotted screwdriver			❑	❑
3/8" slotted screwdriver				❑
3/16" slotted stubby screwdriver		❑	❑	❑
1/4" slotted stubby screwdriver		❑	❑	❑
5/16" slotted stubby screwdriver			❑	❑
8" slip-joint pliers	❑	❑	❑	❑
10" groove-joint (waterpump) pliers	❑	❑	❑	❑
6-1/2" needlenose pliers	❑	❑	❑	❑
6-1/2" diagonal (side-cut) pliers		❑	❑	❑
7" linemans pliers		❑	❑	❑
snap-ring (inside) pliers			❑	❑
snap-ring (outside) pliers			❑	❑
6" adjustable (crescent) wrench	❑	❑	❑	❑
8" adjustable (crescent) wrench		❑	❑	❑
10" adjustable (crescent) wrench			❑	❑
12" adjustable (crescent) wrench				❑
15" adjustable (crescent) wrench				❑
6" vise grip long nose wrench	❑	❑	❑	❑
7" vise grip wrench		❑	❑	❑
10" vise grip wrench			❑	❑
14" pipe wrench			❑	❑
18" pipe wrench				❑
5/16"–3/4" combination (box/open) wrench		❑		
5/16"–1" combination (box/open) wrench			❑	❑
10–19mm combination (box/open) wrench		❑		
10–26mm combination (box/open) wrench			❑	❑
3/8" drive ratchet wrench		❑	❑	❑
1/2" drive ratchet wrench			❑	❑
5/16"–3/4" american (imperial) socket set		❑	❑	
5/16"–1" american (imperial) socket set				❑
10–19mm metric socket set		❑	❑	
10–26mm metric socket set				❑
spark plug sockets for your engines		❑	❑	❑
1/16"–3/8" allen wrench set		❑	❑	❑
1.5–10mm allen wrench set		❑	❑	❑
oil filter wrench		❑	❑	❑

Tool	< 25ft 8m	< 40ft 12m	> 40ft 12m	Off-shore
fuel filter wrench		❏	❏	❏
claw hammer	❏	❏	❏	❏
ballpeen hammer			❏	❏
utility (drywall) knife	❏	❏	❏	❏
6" standard knife	❏	❏	❏	❏
25' steel measuring tape	❏	❏	❏	❏
hacksaw		❏	❏	❏
scissors	❏	❏	❏	❏
tin snips			❏	❏
pulley puller			❏	❏
propeller puller			❏	❏
battery connector puller			❏	❏
>12 V cordless drill			❏	❏
1/16"–1/2" drill bits			❏	
1/16"–1" drill bits				❏
vise				❏
clamps				❏
level				❏
woodworking chisels				❏
cold chisels				❏
duct tape	❏	❏	❏	❏
feeler gauge set				❏
files				❏
sandpaper, wet or dry 140 – 400 grit			❏	❏
emery cloth		❏	❏	❏
tap & die set				❏
tapered punches				❏
straight punches				❏
WD-40		❏	❏	❏
hand cleaner		❏	❏	❏
silicon seal	❏	❏	❏	❏
fiberglass patch kit			❏	❏
magnetic part retriever		❏	❏	❏
plastic wire ties			❏	❏

Example Spare Parts List

Item	
Engines	
Engine oil	❏
Oil filters	❏

Item	
Transmission fluid	❏
Fuel filters	❏
Cooling pump impellers	❏
Cooling pump gaskets	❏
Gasket cement	❏
Engine thermostats	❏
Engine belts	❏
Spare injectors & nozzles	❏
Electrical	
Spare alternator	❏
Alternator parts	❏
Spare voltage regulator	❏
Brushes for Motors & Generators	❏
Fuses —spares for all	❏
Bulbs —spares for all	❏
Miscellaneous Other	
Greases	❏
Silicone grease	❏
Lithium grease	❏
Grease gun	❏
WD-40	❏
Silicone spray	❏
Spare zincs	❏
Spare hoses	❏
Wooden plugs	❏
Hose clamps for all hoses	❏
Assortment stainless nuts, bolts, screws	❏

Maintenance Checklists

These lists are provided only as samples. The boat owner should make his own preventative maintenance schedule based on the engine and other manuals provided with the boat.

These sample checklists associate 50 hours with a month regardless of the maintenance task, which is not what is actually encountered. For example, the manufacturer may recommend the engine oil be changed every 100 hours or every six months, but the pump impeller checked every 300 hours or six months.

All inspection should be noted as carried out in the maintenance log. All fluid additions or changes should be logged. Any repairs and/or parts installed should be logged.

Before Starting / Daily

Check these items at least once per day or on the first engine start of the day. For each engine including the generator.

Check oil level (if any added log hours and amount)	❏
Check hydraulic fluid	❏
Check coolant level (if any added log hours and amount)	❏
Check transmission oil (if any added log hours and amount)	❏
Check secondary fuel filter	❏
Check primary fuel filter	❏
Check any other fuel filters	❏
Check sea strainers	❏
Check for any fluid leaks	❏
Check stuffing boxes	❏
Belts visual check (powder, floppiness) —log changes	❏
Bilge water level	❏
Visual inspection all around engine	❏
Visual inspection engine room	❏

Periodic Checks While Underway

Bridge

Check these items every 1 or 2 hours and enter readings in a log. You might opt to keep a separate day log for these entries rather than keeping them in your primary maintenance log. When the engine is new or recently repaired or overhauled, do this even more frequently, like twice an hour.

Engine Temperature (check and log temperature)	❏
Oil Pressure (check and log pressure)	❏
Exhaust temperature (check and log temperature)	❏
Any other critical gauges (check and log)	❏

Engine Room

This is just a quick visual looking for anything unusual. Set a schedule such as every 1 or 2 hours. Enter in the log that the check was made.

Smoke	❏
Belts visual check (powder, floppiness) —log changes	❏
Bilge water level	❏
Check for any fluid leaks	❏
Unusual noises	❏
Vacuum gauges	❏

25 Hours or Weekly

Carry out these every 25 hours or every week, whichever comes first. Note: This list is not for use. It is a sample to provide a starting point for a checklist customized to your boat. Maintenance intervals recommended by your engine builder should be used rather than the intervals shown here.

Close visual inspection of wet exhaust system when cold	❏
Check wet exhaust for leaks underway	❏
Check all fuel lines for leaks	❏
Check oil lines for leaks	❏
Check raw water lines for leaks	❏
Check fresh water cooling lines for leaks	❏
Check for leaks anywhere else you can think of	❏
If engines have not been run for a week, run them for 5 to 10 minutes at 1600 to 1800 RPM	❏

50 Hours or Monthly

Carry out these every 50 hours or every month, whichever comes first. Note: This list is not for use. It is a sample to provide a starting point for a checklist customized to your boat. Maintenance intervals recommended by your engine builder should be used rather than the intervals shown here.

Remove and test all engine alarm lights	❏
Test engine audible alarms	❏
Check hoses for hardening or softening or other damage	❏
Propeller shaft coupling check	❏
Check battery electrolyte level	❏

150 Hours / 3 months

Carry out these every 150 hours or every 3 months, whichever comes first. Note: This list is not for use. It is a sample to provide a starting point for a checklist customized to your boat. Maintenance intervals recommended by your engine builder should be used rather than the intervals shown here.

Inspect anti-siphon on raw water discharge to exhaust	❏
Engine zinc inspect	❏
Operate all sea cocks	❏

300 Hours / 6 months	
Carry out these every 300 hours or every 6 months, whichever comes first. Note: This list is not for use. It is a sample to provide a starting point for a checklist customized to your boat. Maintenance intervals recommended by your engine builder should be used rather than the intervals shown here.	
Change engine oil	❏
Change engine oil filter	❏
Change primary fuel filter element	❏
Replace air cleaner	❏
Remove cover and inspect raw water impeller	❏
Remove cover and inspect fresh water pump	❏

600 Hours / 1 Year	
Carry out these every 600 hours or every year, whichever comes first. Note: This list is not for use. It is a sample to provide a starting point for a checklist customized to your boat. Maintenance intervals recommended by your engine builder should be used rather than the intervals shown here.	
Check belt tension and wear	❏
Check valve clearances —adjust if necessary	❏
Clean crankcase vent tube	❏
Change secondary fuel filter element	❏
Check injectors	❏
Replace raw water impeller	❏
Flush fresh water cooling circuit and change coolant	❏
Engine alarm system test (probably requires a professional)	❏

1200 Hours / 2 Years	
Carry out these every 1200 hours or every 2 years, whichever comes first. Note: This list is not for use. It is a sample to provide a starting point for a checklist customized to your boat. Maintenance intervals recommended by your engine builder should be used rather than the intervals shown here.	
Wet exhaust system, disassemble, inspect	❏
Fuel cooler disassemble, inspect, clean	❏
Heat exchanger disassemble, inspect, clean	❏
Intercooler disassemble, inspect, clean	❏
Oil cooler disassemble, inspect, clean	❏
Transmission cooler, disassemble, inspect, clean	❏
Check fuel injection pump	❏

Winterize or Long-Term Layup

These are basic tasks that should be carried as a part of winterizing or before a long-term layup. This is by no means a complete list. Consider doing many of the things you normally do in the spring when recommissioning.

Engine

Gasoline —if possible drain and run carburetor dry. If not use stabilizer	❏
Change engine oil before long term layup —don't wait until spring	❏
Change transmission oil before long term layup —don't wait until spring	❏
Flush and change coolant (antifreeze) in the freshwater circuit -don't wait until spring	❏
Drain the raw water circuit completely	❏
Remove, inspect, clean, gap, spark plugs	❏
Spray oil into air intake while cranking the engine. Don't start the engine while doing this. Gasoline engines can remove spark plugs and squirt oil directly into cylinders	❏
Grease all grease fittings and parts	❏
Cover engine openings including exhaust	❏

Shaft and Propeller

Remove, clean, inspect, propeller (repair if necessary)	❏
Inspect shaft for excessive play, check for stuffing box leaks	❏

Other Systems

Add fuel stabilizer if not draining fuel	❏
Drain entire fresh water system including water heater. Use propylene glycol if antifreeze is used	❏
Drain and flush blackwater system.	❏
Test the bilge pumps especially if the boat is staying in the water	❏

Electrical / Electronics

Remove electronics —they will winter better in your house than in the salt air. Less likelihood of theft too	❏
Fully charge batteries. Batteries must be topped up once per month while laid up or be on continuous maintenance charge	❏

Recommission after Long-Term Layup

These are tasks that should be carried out as a part of recommissioning after a long-term layup. This is by no means a complete list. Consider doing many of these things when laying up for the winter.

Engine

Uncover all the engine openings covered at layup	❑
Change engine oil if you didn't do it before layup like you should have	❑
Change transmission oil if not done before layup	❑
Change coolant (antifreeze) in the freshwater circuit if not done before layup	❑
Clean carburetor, adjust linkages	❑
Change air filter	❑
Remove spark plugs, inspect and clean	❑
Raw water pump remove cover. Remove, inspect, light grease raw water impeller. Consider replacing with a new one, regardless of condition, it's cheap insurance	❑
Check and clean raw water intake strainers	❑
Remove cover and inspect fresh water pump	❑
Check fuel lines for cracks, leaks, wear, etc.	❑
Check, clean or replace fuel filters	❑
Check all hoses for condition. Replace if soft, worn, cracked or otherwise damaged	❑
Inspect all belts, replace if necessary	❑
Inspect exhaust system closely (particularly wet exhaust)	❑
Grease any grease fittings	❑
Control cables and pulleys, inspect, adjust, lubricate	❑
Check propeller shaft coupling	❑

Other Systems

Check the log to see what might have been missed when laying up. Carry out the omitted tasks.	❑
Steering cables and pulleys, inspect, adjust and lubricate	❑
Steering hydraulics, inspect, test, top up fluid	❑
Check for worn hoses and clamps	❑
Check bilge and engine room exhaust blower	❑
Check bilge pump screens	❑
Check operation of all bilge pumps, lift floats to test	❑
Check all openings and intakes for spider, insect, or animal nests.	❑
Inspect all through-hulls	❑
Operate all seacocks	❑
Drain antifreeze, inspect water tanks and system	❑
Test operate heads	❑
Test run all mechanical equipment	❑

Recommission after Long-Term Layup	
Safety	
Check inventory of safety equipment	❏
Fire extinguishers, check expiration and charge	❏
Test sound signaling equipment	❏
Flares, check expiration, replace if necessary	❏
Test gasoline fume detectors	❏
Test carbon monoxide detectors	❏
Electrical	
Batteries fully charged	❏
Check battery electrolyte level, top-up	❏
Terminal posts clean and greased	❏
Inspect all electrical connections and wiring	❏
Charging system check	❏
Test run all electrical systems	❏
Test run all electronics	❏

9 ELECTRICAL

INTRODUCTION

This chapter attempts to give the reader a basic understanding of marine electrical systems and to give an appreciation of how they differ from electrical systems in a house or automobile. Wiring a house doesn't qualify a person for wiring a boat, and I hope to help the reader see and appreciate that fact.

Understanding a boat's electrical systems should:
- Assist in solving basic electrical problems underway.
- Help you communicate better with your electrician and know what standards to expect from him or her.
- Help in evaluating the quality of the electrical installation on a boat you are thinking of buying.
- Make you more aware of potentially dangerous or unsafe conditions.

What this chapter does *not* do is qualify anyone to carry out marine electrical work.

The *U.S. Code of Federal Regulations* (CFR) contains regulations pertaining to electrical systems on gasoline powered boats in *Title 33 CFR Sections 183.401-183.460*. The first section states,"This subpart applies to all boats that have gasoline engines, except outboard engines, for electrical generation, mechanical power, or propulsion," and although this statement limits the legal applicability, it would be a good idea to think of these regulations as setting a minimum standard for any boat with electrical systems onboard.

These actual regulations can be found at www.gpoaccess.gov/cfr/index.html. The U.S. Coast Guard has also produced an 86-page Adobe Acrobat .pdf document that provides a good explanation of these regulations. It can be downloaded at no cost from http://www.uscgboating.org/safety/boatbuilder/electrical/electrical.htm. Much of the material in this section is derived from these documents.

If you are actually planning on some do-it-yourself boat wiring, it should conform to the standards established by the *American Boat and Yacht Council* (ABYC). This is an organization of boat builders and various other marine related individuals and firms that sets standards that are generally accepted as requirements for building recreational boats. They offer for purchase part or all of their standards and several books, including the three mentioned below. You can join the ABYC and enjoy substantial discounts on their materials and books. Their website is http://www.abycinc. org/ and their phone number is 410-956-1050.

In Canada, a government publication entitled *Construction Standards for Small Vessels, Section 8: Electrical Systems* can be found and downloaded for free at http://www.tc.gc. ca/MarineSafety/tp/TP1332/section8.htm. The Canadian standards are quite similar to U.S. standards.

Obtain, read, and thoroughly understand one or more or the following publications:

*   *Boatowner's Mechanical and Electrical Manual* by Nigel Calder (Camden, Maine: International Marine, 1996), $49.95. Thoroughly covers all boat systems, not just electrical.
*   *Boatowners Illustrated Handbook of Wiring* by Charlie Wing (Camden, Maine: International Marine, 1993), $29.95.
*   *Boating Magazine's Powerboater's Guide to Electrical Systems* by Ed Sherman (International Marine/Ragged Mountain Press, 2000), $22.95.

Finally, get a qualified person to coach you and inspect your work

ELECTRICITY BASICS

INTRODUCTION

This section deals with the essentials of electricity, and starts with explanations of volts, amperes, and resistance, and then works through explanations of how solenoids, motors, generators, transformers, and other basic electrical devices work. Understanding these fundamentals will help you follow the discussions on 12-volt and 120-volt electrical systems later on.

Basic Principles

Current, Voltage, and Resistance

The three fundamental units used in working with electricity circuits are the volt, ampere, and ohm. A helpful analogy in explaining these three units compares electricity flowing through a wire to water flowing through a pipe.

Amperes, commonly called *amps*, are a measure of the amount of electricity or current flowing through the wire. You can think of the *current* (**I**) as the electricity flowing through a wire just as water flows through a pipe. The amp is the measure of the amount of current flowing, just as gallons per minute is the measure of the water flowing.

To get water to actually flow through a pipe you need pressure produced by something like gravity or a pump. Water pressure is measured in units such as pounds/square inch (kg/sq m or P). Electrical current also needs an equivalent to pressure to make it flow, and that equivalent is electrical *potential* (pressure) or *voltage* (**V**) and it is measured in *volts*. A battery, generator, or alternator is the most common means of inducing a voltage to get an electrical current flow.

When water flows through a pipe it encounters resistance, and the smaller the pipe the greater the resistance to water flowing through it. The electrical analogy is also called *resistance* (**R**) and it is measured in *ohms*, and just as in a pipe, the smaller the wire the greater the resistance to flow (of current). The voltage (in volts) pushes the current (in amps) through the wire or device, which resists (in ohms) the flow.

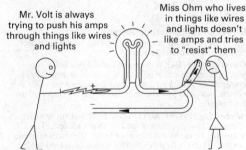

Mr. Volt is always trying to push his amps through things like wires and lights

Miss Ohm who lives in things like wires and lights doesn't like amps and tries to "resist" them

FIGURE 9-1: Mr. Volt and Miss Ohm

Current, voltage, and resistance are related by equation 9-1, which is known as Ohm's law. Note: In many texts "E" (for electromotive force) is used instead of "V" to represent volt-

$$I = \frac{V}{R}$$

Where: I = Current in Amperes (A)
V = Voltage or potential in Volt (V)
R = Resistance in Ohms (Ω)

EQUATION 9-1: Ohm's Law

age in equations. We'll use "V" in this book since it's more intuitive.

From the equation, it follows that current is proportional to voltage and inversely proportional to resistance and 1 volt will push 1 amp of current through 1 ohm of resistance.

We can solve equation 9-1 for V, knowing I and R:

$$V = I \times R$$

Or R, knowing V and I

$$R = \frac{V}{I}$$

Example using equation 9-1: A light bulb at a voltage of 120 V (volt) with a resistance of 145 Ω (ohms) will have a current flow of:

$$I = \frac{V}{R} = \frac{120V}{145\Omega} = 0.83A$$

Direct and Alternating Current

There are two kinds of electrical current, which are direct current and alternating current.

Direct current (**DC**) is electrical current that flows constantly in one direction only, from positive to negative (by convention). A boat's 12-volt electrical system uses DC current produced by either batteries or the alternator on the boat engine.

Alternating current (**AC**) refers to electrical current that alternates flow direction several times per second. The 120 V current we use in our houses or boats, alternates 60 times per second (50 in Europe), so that within each 1/60 second the flow is forward and backward once. The number of cycles per second is named the *Hertz* (**Hz**), so that our 120 V current that alternates at 60 times per second is called 60 Hertz current. The traditional name used for this unit was *cycles per second* (**cps**) and this is still sometimes used. Often the reference to per second is dropped and a shortened form is used, as in 60 cycle electricity or 60 cycle power, so be prepared to read or hear any or all of these terms and know that they mean the same thing.

BASIC ELECTRICAL CIRCUITS
Closed and Open Circuits

Here is where the analogy with water through a pipe starts to break down. Whereas the water can pass through a circuit of pipes, valves, and pumps, and then discharge from the end of the circuit (an open circuit), the electrical current must always run through a *closed circuit* that is a closed or continuous loop (figure 9-2).

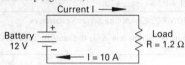

FIGURE 9-2: A Closed Circuit

Current is considered to flow from the *positive* (+) side of a power source to the *negative* (−) side.

On a boat, the *loads* can be lights, heaters, electric motors, or electronic devices. When current passes through a load, there is a *voltage drop* from one side to the other which can be calculated using the V = I x R formula. In figure 9-2, the voltage drop over the load is V = I x R = 10 A x 1.2 Ω = 12 V.

In figure 9-3 a switch has been introduced that is off (*open*). The circuit is an *open circuit* and no current will flow.

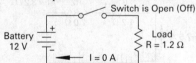

FIGURE 9-3: An Open Circuit

Series Connections of Loads

A *series* connection refers to the connection of sources or loads in sequence, one after the other. Any number of devices

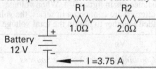

FIGURE 9-4: Loads Connected in Series

may be connected in the series. Figure 9-4 on the previous page shows two resistors connected in series so that current flows from one to the other.

Total resistance of all the resistors in series is simply the sum of all the resistances. This makes intuitive sense, and in the water analogy, corresponds to two restrictions in a pipe circuit, which present more resistance than just one.

$$Rt = R1 + R2 + \ldots\ldots\ldots + Rn$$

EQUATION 9-2: Combining Series Resistances

The amount of current flowing is the same throughout the circuit and is:

$$I = \frac{V}{Rt} = \frac{V}{R1 + R2 + \ldots\ldots Rn}$$

Example using values from figure 9-4 on the previous page.

Series Connection of Voltage Sources

$$I = \frac{12V}{1.2\Omega + 2.0\Omega} = \frac{12V}{3.2\Omega} = 3.75A$$

Next we'll look at connecting voltage sources, such as batteries, in series.

In figure 9-5 there are now two batteries connected in series

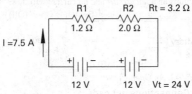

FIGURE 9-5: Voltage Sources Connected in Series

with the same resistances as in figure 9-4. When voltage sources, such as batteries, are connected in series, the voltages are simply added together to obtain the total voltage.

$$Vt = V1 + V2 + \ldots\ldots + Vn$$

EQUATION 9-3: Combining Series Voltage Sources

Current will now be calculated as:

$$I = \frac{Vt}{Rt} = \frac{V1 + V2 + \dots + Vn}{R1 + R2 + \dots + Rn}$$

Example using values from figure 9-5:

$$I = \frac{12V + 12V}{1.2\Omega + 2.0\Omega} = \frac{24V}{3.2\Omega} = 7.5A$$

Parallel Connection of Loads

If a circuit path divides into two or more paths and loads are placed in each path then the loads are said to be connected in *parallel*. Figure 9-6 shows the same two resistances as before now connected in parallel.

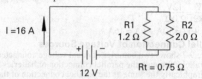

FIGURE 9-6: Loads Connected in Parallel

Although only two loads are shown, any number may be connected in parallel which is usually the case in boat circuitry. For example, several cabin lights are connected in parallel in one circuit.

As one might intuitively expect, two resistances connected in parallel will have less resistance to current flow than the lowest resistance connected. The equation for combining multiple parallel resistances into an equivalent or total resistance is:

$$Rt = \frac{1}{\frac{1}{R1} + \frac{1}{R2} + \dots + \frac{1}{Rn}}$$

EQUATION 9-4: Combining Parallel Resistances

There are a couple of ways to calculate the current flowing in the main circuit, as well as through the two branches. One alternative is calculate the combined resistance Rt and then use Ohm's law to solve for the main circuit current.

Here's the example for that approach:

$$Rt = \frac{1}{\dfrac{1}{1.2\Omega} + \dfrac{1}{2.0\Omega}} = \frac{1}{0.8333\Omega + 0.5\Omega} = \frac{1}{1.3333\Omega} = 0.75\Omega$$

$$I = \frac{V}{Rt} = \frac{12V}{0.75\Omega} = 16A$$

The other alternative is to figure the current through each branch of the parallel circuit and then add the currents together. The voltage across the top and bottom of the parallel branches is 12 volts, so this same voltage can be applied to each load to find the current through each branch.

$$I1 = \frac{V}{R1} = \frac{12V}{1.2\Omega} = 10A$$

$$I2 = \frac{V}{R2} = \frac{12V}{2.0\Omega} = 6A$$

$$I = I1 + I2 = 10A + 6A = 16A$$

Parallel Connection of Voltage Sources

Figure 9-7 shows two batteries of equal voltage connected in parallel. Although the parallel connection of batteries is topographically the same as the parallel connection of the loads we just considered, the calculations are quite different. First, the batteries on each branch of a parallel circuit must be of equal voltage, since any difference will result in the higher voltage battery trying to charge the lower voltage battery, which is not a good thing.

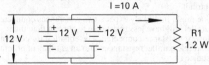

FIGURE 9-7: Voltages Sources Connected in Parallel

Second, the combined voltage is simply the same as the single battery voltage. So, the voltage applied to the resistance is 12 volts, just like in figure 9-2 on page 503, and the current is the same at 10 amps. By connecting two batteries in parallel, we are doubling the capacity or length of time the batteries will operate on a charge, while leaving current flow the same as with a single battery. Even if we connect 10 batteries in parallel, the current flow will still remain the same, but the batteries will last 10 times as long.

Combining Series and Parallel Loads

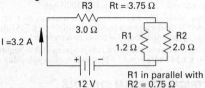

FIGURE 9-8: Combining Series and Parallel Loads

To calculate combined circuits, first combine the parallel resistances into equivalent resistances. In this case R1 and R2 were combined to R = 0.75 Ω using equation 9-4 from the previous page.

Now the series resistances can be added up. In the example, we add 3.0 Ω + 0.75 Ω to get 3.75 Ω.

With Ohm's law, the current is calculated as
I = V / R = 12 V / 3.75 Ω = 3.2 A.

Once the current is known, the voltage drop over each resistance can be calculated.
Over R3 V = I x R = 3.2 A x 3.0 Ω = 9.6 V.
Over R1 | R2 V = I x R = 3.2 A x 0.75 Ω = 2.4 V.

The sum of the voltage drops 9.6 V + 2.4 V = 12 V should match the battery voltage of 12 V, and it does.

ELECTRICAL POWER AND HORSEPOWER

When electricity flows through a load, either heat is generated or mechanical work is performed. The power used in any electrical device is calculated as the voltage drop across the device times the current flow through the device and is termed the *watt* (**W**).

$$P = V \times I = \frac{V^2}{R} = I^2 \times R$$

Where: P = Power in watts
V = Voltage drop in volts
I = Current in amperes

EQUATION 9-5: Calculation of Electrical Power in Watts

The light bulb discussed earlier draws 0.83 A with a voltage drop of 120 V so the power used by the bulb is:
P = 120 V × 0.83 A = 100 W

Kilowatts (**kW**) is the electrical (and metric) equivalent of horsepower and 1 kilowatt is equal to 1000 watts.

To convert from kilowatts to horsepower multiply by 1.341. To convert from horsepower to watts multiply by 0.7457 (0.75 is a good approximation and is easier to remember).

Example: To power a generator that produces 10 kW requires a 10 kW x 1.341 hp/kW = 13.4 hp diesel engine, assuming no losses.

ELECTRICAL DIAGRAM SYMBOLS

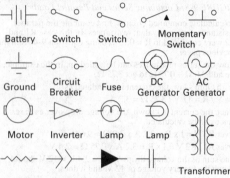

Battery   Switch   Switch   Momentary Switch

Ground   Circuit Breaker   Fuse   DC Generator   AC Generator

Motor   Inverter   Lamp   Lamp   Transformer

Resistor   Connector   Diode   Capacitor

FIGURE 9-9: Commonly Used Electrical Symbols

ELECTROMAGNETISM AND BASIC ELECTRICAL DEVICES
Electromagnetic Force

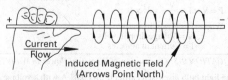

Current Flow

Induced Magnetic Field (Arrows Point North)

FIGURE 9-10: Magnetic Field Around a Current Carrying Wire

A current passing through a wire induces a magnetic field around the wire. Figure 9-10 shows how the field circles the wire.

If the right hand is held around the wire with the thumb pointing in the direction of current flow (from + to −), then the fingers point in the north direction of the induced field.

If the wire is formed into a circle, the magnetic field will still surround the wire but will be concentrated in the center of the circle. If the wire is formed into a helix (many circles) like that shown in figure 9-11, we have constructed a solenoid. The magnetic field is concentrated in the center of the solenoid and is weaker on the outside.

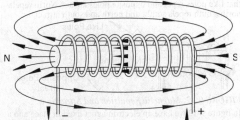

FIGURE 9-11: Solenoid

If an iron bar (*core*) is fixed in the center, as shown, the magnetic field will be strengthened several hundred fold, and as long as current flows we will have the equivalent of a bar magnet known as an *electromagnet*, with a north pole at one end and south pole at the other.

Electric Relay

The solenoid principle is used in electrical *relays* where a small electric control current is applied to the solenoid to close a contact, to complete a circuit that carries much higher current than the control circuit. A relay can be used to control high current devices, such as a starter motor, to alleviate running large diameter cables from the starter to the bridge and back. The relay is basically a switch that is controlled electrically by a solenoid.

Solenoids

The more common use of the term *solenoid* is to describe an electromechanical device based on the principal of the solenoid described above. If the iron core in figure 9-11 is free to slide back and forth, and we move the core partly out one end and then apply current to the coil, the core will be drawn back to the center position with considerable force. This phenomenon is used in the devices we commonly call solenoids and are used to operate such things as solenoid valves or doorbell chimes. Of particular interest to the boater is the solenoid used in the starter to engage the flywheel when starting the engine on the boat. Solenoids are also used to actuate the electronic fuel injectors used in some diesel engines.

Electric Motors

Anyone who has played with a couple of magnets knows that like poles repel and opposite poles attract. North repels north, south repels south, and north and south attract.

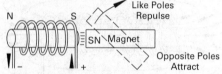

FIGURE 9-12: Magnetic Repulsion and Attraction.

In figure 9-12 we have an electromagnet fixed in place and a regular bar magnet near it that is free to move. If the electromagnet is energized with the south pole of the magnet near the south pole of the electromagnet it will push the magnet away. Conversely, if the electromagnet is energized with the north pole of the magnet near the south pole of the electromagnet it will pull the magnet toward itself.

Of course, if the magnet is fixed in place and the electromagnet is free to move, then it is the electromagnet that will be pushed away or pulled toward the magnet.

Figure 9-13 shows a schematic of a simple DC motor with a rotating electromagnet (*armature*). Power is supplied via stationary *brushes* that contact the *commutator*, which is a copper slip ring attached to the rotating shaft. The armature windings connect to the commutator.

The figure shows the north pole of the armature being repulsed by the north field magnet, and likewise the south poles, which propels the armature clockwise. As the armature rotates further clockwise, its north pole approaches the south field magnet and the mutual attraction reinforces the clockwise rotation.

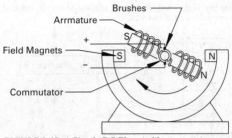

FIGURE 9-13: A Simple DC Electric Motor

But once the armature north passes the south field magnet, the two opposites will still be attracting, which acts to impede continued rotation. The solution to this problem is to split the commutator into segments so that the polarity of the armature can be reversed as the north and south poles pass each other. This way the north pole of the armature changes to a south pole as it passes the south field magnet and the repulsion acts to continue clockwise rotation.

Keep in mind this is just an illustration to explain basic concepts. A real electric motor won't look much like our illustration. For example, in most motors, electromagnets are used instead of permanent field magnets and also there will be more poles. In addition, the field can be the rotating part in the center while the armature is stationary on the outside.

In an AC motor the reversing back and forth of the armature field is taken care of by the fact that the current is alternating back and forth already. When the motor is running at the correct speed, the changing of N-S orientation is synchronized with the passing of the field poles. Because of this, the AC motor usually runs at a constant speed that is some multiple of 60 cycles. Common AC electric motor speeds are 1800 and 3600 RPM.

Induced Voltage

If an electrical conductor is moved within a magnetic field (or a magnetic field is moved past a conductor), a voltage is induced, which causes a current to flow if the circuit is closed. Stated differently, a change in the strength of a magnetic field near a conductor will induce a voltage in the conductor. If the conductor is part of a closed circuit, induced voltage will cause a current to flow.

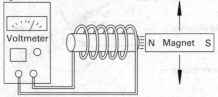

FIGURE 9-14: Induced Voltage

In figure 9-14 we have the same coil around an iron core as before, except now we connect it to a volt meter instead of a battery. As the permanent magnet is moved back and forth as shown, a voltage will be indicated on the voltmeter, with the highest voltage being induced as the permanent magnet pole passes the centerline of the coil. If the movement is stopped, the voltage drops to zero.

Generators and Alternators

At this point you might be thinking that we can make a generator much like the motor in figure 9-13, and you would be correct. The principal is much the same except now we are applying an external force to rotate the shaft and armature past field magnets to induce a voltage, and the current produced is taken off the armature with the brushes. A generator such as this with a rotating armature is usually called just that—a generator.

A generator with the field magnets rotating within stationary current-producing windings (the *stator*) is usually termed an *alternator*.

A generator can produce either DC or AC, depending how the commutator is set up. Since on an alternator the current is taken off the stationary windings around the circumference of the generator, a commutator can't be used and the alternator can only produce alternating current (maybe that's why it's called an alternator).

In a 12-volt car or boat electrical system, the alternator AC output is *rectified* into DC using a system of *diodes*, which are electric devices similar to transistors that only allow electricity to pass in one direction. Here's an analogy: A diode is to electricity as a check valve is to water.

In a generator or alternator, the field magnets are electromagnets powered by direct current that usually is rectified current supplied from the armature or stator output. The output of the generator can be controlled by metering the amount of current allowed through the field windings with a voltage regulator. If too much current is flowing, the voltage regulator will decrease the field strength by decreasing the current to the field windings, and just the opposite if too little current is flowing. In some cases, the voltage regulator is installed in or on the alternator and in other cases as a separate unit.

Transformers

Consider two windings around the same core as shown in figure 9-15. The winding connected to a power source is called the *primary* winding and the other winding connected to a load (voltmeter in this case) is called the *secondary* winding.

When the switch is closed with a DC power source, the primary coil produces a magnetic field in the core and as

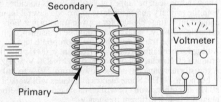

FIGURE 9-15: A Simple Transformer

the field is increasing in strength, a voltage is induced in the secondary coil and there will be a momentary reading on the voltmeter. Once the field has reached full strength and is no longer increasing, the induced voltage falls back to zero.

If, instead of direct current, alternating current is applied to the primary, the magnetic field will be constantly increasing or decreasing at the frequency of the applied current. As one might expect, the cycling magnetic field induces alternating current in the secondary windings at the same frequency.

If the number of windings in the primary and secondary are the same, the voltage and current induced in the secondary, will be the same as in the primary; however, if there are twice as many windings in the secondary, the voltage in the secondary will be doubled and the current halved.

Conversely, if there are half the windings in the secondary, the voltage will be halved and the current doubled.

This, of course, is why a **_transformer_** is called a transformer; it can transform voltage and current up or down to any desired ratio.

Some other things to note about transformers:

- The fact that only alternating current can be transformed is a major reason for our everyday use of AC power instead of DC power.
- A transformer will not allow DC to pass. This is of considerable interest when connecting to shorepower, which is discussed later.
- A transformer can be around 97 to 99 percent efficient, so there is a small power loss in the form of heat.
- The windings won't actually be configured as shown in figure 9-15, rather they might be wound one over the other or interleaved in layers to increase efficiency.
- The windings can be tapped at various points on either or both the primary and secondary, to provide several input and output voltage choices for a given transformer. For example, 120 VAC shorepower could be transformed up to 240 VAC if the transformer has the appropriate taps.
- A transformer cannot transform frequency; 60 Hz in will produce 60 Hz out. In Europe the power is 220 V, 50 Hz. A transformer can convert the power from 220 V to 110 V but not to 60 Hz. Some electrical devices will work at 50 Hz and others won't or will be damaged. Check before plugging in to a different frequency.

Inverters

On a boat, inverters are used to transform 12 VDC to 120 VAC. An **_inverter_** uses solid state electronics to first convert the DC input to AC, then uses a transformer to increase the voltage.

ELECTRICAL CABLING

INTRODUCTION

Conductors and Insulators

A **_conductor_** is material that has very low resistance to the flow of electricity. An **_insulator_** is material that has very high resistance to the flow of electricity. Copper is a conductor that has very low resistance along with other properties that make it the best choice for electrical wiring in boats. Essentially, there's no choice: The regulations specify that conductors used in boats must be made of copper and that's that.

Boat Cable

Electrical cables used in boats encounter an environment far more severe than that of a house or even a car. In the marine environment, the cable must be able to withstand constant flexing and vibration, high ambient temperatures, and exposure to oil, fuel, and saltwater.

U.S. federal regulations specify that *each conductor must be insulated, stranded copper.* The regulations go on to specify the type of insulation allowed, based on such factors as operating voltage and temperature.

Stranded cable is specified because solid copper cable will harden and break from constant flexing. Stranded cable is available as types 2 and 3 where type 3 contains more strands than type 2 and is therefore more flexible. Type 3 cable is used where vibration is excessive, as on engines and generator sets.

Better quality boat cable has been **tinned**, where each conductor has a thin coating of tin applied. Tinned cable is not a requirement but is highly recommended, because it provides much better protection from corrosion.

Rather than hunting around to find cable that meets all the requirements, the best approach is to just go to a reputable marine supply store and acquire marine electrical cable there. *Do not use automobile or house wire or cable for boat wiring!*

Cable Connections

Most problems with wiring occur at connections and rarely in the cables themselves. Electrical cables should be terminated with crimp type connectors, rather than soldered. Note that *U shape connectors should not be used* unless they are the locking or flanged type shown. *Wire nuts should not be used. Set screws should not be used* unless they are the indirect bearing type. *Wire should not be secured directly to a bolt or screw.* See figure 9-16 on the next page for examples of acceptable connectors.

Like cable, the connectors should be specifically for marine use and the best way to ensure this is to buy them from a trustworthy marine supply. The connectors come in different sizes to match different wire sizes. To do a proper crimp, a good ratcheting crimper that matches the type of connector should be used, especially if you're an amateur. Also cables should be stripped to the correct length using a good wire stripper, *not* a pocket knife.

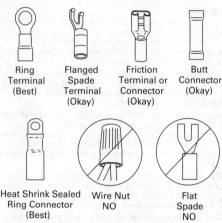

FIGURE 9-16: Cable Terminals and Connectors

Use nylon insulated rather than PVC-insulated connectors, since nylon withstands crimping better, or use connectors with heat-shrink sealed insulation.

Double crimp connectors are available from companies, such as Ancor, that have a second crimp that crimps onto the insulation to give a better grip. Good ratcheting crimping tools cost anywhere from $50 to $140, but they are well worth it if you are doing more than a couple of connections. Test crimps by trying to pull the wire out of the connector.

Solder should not be used as the sole means of connecting cable, because constant flexing can cause the soldered connection to break; however, there are differences of opinion as to whether solder should be used on crimped connectors. The argument for using solder is that it seals the end of the wire against moisture. The argument against is that if too much solder is applied it will flow up the wire and solidify it, thus making it susceptible to failure from flexing. A better alternative to soldering is probably to use the heat-shrink sealed connectors although they cost almost three times as much.

If you do decide to solder, you must use rosin rather than acid flux and use a good grade of solder with about 50 percent tin to 50 percent lead.

AC Terminations and Connections

For safety reasons all AC terminations must be enclosed in an electrical box, much as they are in house wiring.

Color Coding

The ABYC has set standards that stipulate specific wire colors for specific circuits, which makes it easier to trace those circuits and lessen the chance of error. Unless you are totally rewiring your boat, you probably want to stick with the generally accepted practice for general wiring, since it will be impractical to keep all those colors of wire on hand.

For DC 12-volt wiring the convention is:

Positive	Red
Negative	Yellow (not black)
Ground	Green

For AC wiring the convention is:

Hot wire (120 V or 240 V)	Black
Second hot wire (240 V only)	Red
Neutral (120 V or 240 V)	White
Ground (120 V or 240 V)	Green or bare

In the past black was used for negative conductors in DC wiring, which is also the color used for the hot conductor in AC circuits. This creates the possibility for confusion between the two and for this reason yellow is now used rather than black. You may find black DC negative return conductors in older boats.

Duplex (2 conductor) wire for DC use, sold at marine supply stores, follows this convention and will contain a red and a yellow conductor.

Triplex wire (3 conductor) wire for AC use, also available at marine supply stores, follows this convention too and will contain black, white, and green conductors. Note that although this color standard is the same as for house wiring, stranded type 2 or 3 marine cable must be used in boats.

Cable Routing

AC cabling should be bundled separately from DC cabling and all cables should be supported every foot or so or continuously with tray or conduit. If conduit must be used it should have drain holes at any low spots.

The regulations state that *each conductor or group of conductors that passes through a bulkhead, structural member, junction box, or other rigid surface must be protected from abrasion*. Generally, any means that will accomplish this is acceptable. Grommets, bushings, caulking, hose, etc., are all ways to do this. Cable grip devices designed specifically for the purpose are available too.

If at all possible, avoid running cable through the bilge. If the cable has to be run through the bilge ensure it is above water at all points and try to avoid having any connections in the bilge. If there are any connections in the bilge they must be completely sealed.

Route cables well away from moving parts and exhaust systems. To avoid the possibility of cables falling onto an engine or exhaust system, don't run cables above them.

Take the time now to label both ends of every cable you run. A couple of years from now, when you're trying to debug some weird electrical problem, you'll thank yourself for doing it. Labels for this purpose are usually available from any electrical parts supplier or marine supply store. If you are doing a lot of work, labeling systems from Dymo or Brother work quite well and produce waterproof labels. In *Boatowner's Mechanical and Electrical Manual*, Nigel Calder suggests the use of transparent heat shrink tubing over the labels to prevent their working loose, which sure seems like a good idea if you've gone to the trouble of putting the labels on in the first place.

Cable Sizing

Wire Gauge

Wire must be sufficiently large that the resistance of the wire is small compared to the load. Resistance of wire is proportional to its length and inversely proportional to its cross-sectional area.

Wire is sized by *gauge*, where larger gauge numbers correspond to smaller wire diameters. There are differing standards for wire gauge, the two most prevalent in North America being *American Wire Gauge* (**AWG**) and *Society of Automotive Engineers* (**SAE**) with wire of the same gauge number in SAE having a slightly smaller diameter than wire of the same gauge number in AWG. In the United States, the regulations state that AWG gauge wire must be used for 50 volt and above systems, and either AWG or SAE may be used below 50 volts.

The gauge system was devised so that a decrease of three gauge numbers (e.g., 15 to 12) results in an approximate doubling of cross-sectional area, which corresponds to a doubling of current carrying capacity. It's also handy to know that a decrease of two gauge numbers will result in approximately 1.6 times or 60 percent more current carrying capacity. So going from 14 to 12 gauge will add 60 percent to

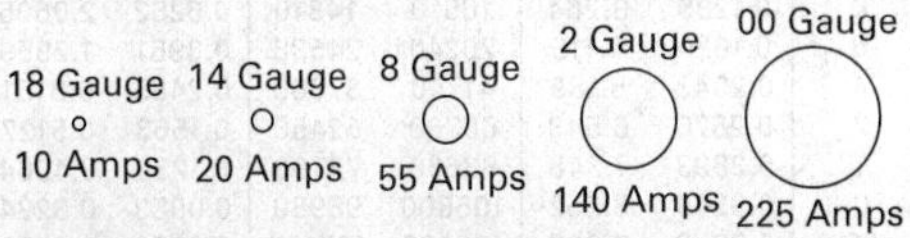

18 Gauge	14 Gauge	8 Gauge	2 Gauge	00 Gauge
10 Amps	20 Amps	55 Amps	140 Amps	225 Amps

FIGURE 9-17: Actual Wire Sizes (Scaled to Actual Size)

allowable current. Figure 9-17 shows some typical wire sizes taken from table 9-1 on the next page and current carrying capacity (ampacity) at 60 degrees Celsius taken from table 9-2 on page 522.

The Circular Mil

The cross-sectional area of wire is usually specified as circular mils rather than square inches or millimeters. A *mil* is

$$CM = D^2 \times 10^6 = D^2 \times 1,000,000$$
Where: CM = Circular Mils
D = Diameter in inches

EQUATION 9-6: Calculation of Circular Mils

1/1000 of 1 inch or 0.001 inches. A *circular mil* (**CM**) is the area of a circle that has a diameter of 1 mil (0.001 in). With some manipulation we arrive at equation 9-6 for calculating circular mils from diameter:

In equation 9-6 use 1550 instead of 1,000,000 if you have the diameter in millimeters.

The use of the circular mil for measuring cross-sectional area eliminates the need to use pi or divide the diameter by 2 to get radius when doing area calculations.

Standard Wire Sizes

Table 9-1 lists standard wire sizes along with their cross-sectional areas and resistance per unit length.

Wire	Diameter		X-Section Area (Circular Mils)		Resistance @ 20° C (AWG)	
	AWG		AWG	SAE	Ω/	Ω/
Gauge	in	mm	CM	CM	1000 ft	km
18	0.0403	1.024	1620	1537	6.3850	20.9428
16	0.0508	1.290	2580	2336	4.0160	13.1725
14	0.0641	1.628	4110	3702	2.5250	8.2820
12	0.0808	2.052	6530	5833	1.5880	5.2086
10	0.1019	2.588	10380	9343	0.9989	3.2764
8	0.1285	3.264	16510	14810	0.6282	2.0605
6	0.1620	4.115	26240	24538	0.3951	1.2959
4	0.2043	5.189	41740	37360	0.2485	0.8151
2	0.2576	6.543	66360	62450	0.1563	0.5127
1	0.2893	7.348	83690	77790	0.1239	0.4064
0	0.3249	8.252	105600	98980	0.0983	0.3224
00	0.3648	9.266	133100	125100	0.0779	0.2555
000	0.4096	10.404	167800	158600	0.0618	0.2027
0000	0.4600	11.684	211600	205500	0.0490	0.1607

TABLE 9-1: Standard Wire Sizes and Specifications

Current Carrying Capacity Limited by Wire Heating

The first step in selecting a conductor size is to determine the continuous or steady state current that it will carry without overheating. Note that surges higher than continuous for short periods of time are allowed. The most common example of current surge occurs during the starting of an electric motor.

The top half of table 9-2 on page 522 contains the allowable amperages for no more than two conductors bundled, as specified in *U.S. 33 CFR 183.425*. Note: The top half of table 9-2 and the factors for use in engine spaces and correction factors for the number of current carrying conductors are the same as in tables in *U.S. 33 CFR 183.425*, in *ABYC standards* and in *Transport Canada Standards for Small Vessels*.

To use the table first enter the table in the column with the conductor insulation temperature rating of the cable you propose to use. This rating should be printed on the cable. Then proceed down the column until an amperage is reached that is greater than or equal to the desired continuous current and read the wire gauge from the left-hand column. This is the *minimum* diameter wire that may be used to carry that amperage.

Halfway down the table is a line that gives factors for inside engine spaces. These factors are provided as part of the regulations and they correct the amperages in the top table if the conductor is to be in an engine space. To spare you the calculation, the corrected values are provided in the bottom half of the table.

The regulation goes on to specify bundling correction factors for more than two conductors in a cable carrying 50 volts or more as follows:

- 3 conductors   0.70
- 4 to 6 conductors   0.60
- 7 to 24 conductors   0.50
- 25 or more conductors 0.40

For example, if you have a cable with five conductors operating at 120 volts, the allowable amperage in table 9-2 must be further corrected downward by multiplying by 0.60.

The four tables 9-3 through 9-6 on pages 523 to 526 have calculated the allowable amperages for each of the four correction factors so you can go directly to the appropriate table and directly determine your conductor size without having to perform the correction calculation.

A couple more things from the regulations to note:

- No conductors are to be smaller than 18 AWG if bundled with other conductors, and no smaller than 16 AWG if it is a single conductor.
- The regulations exempt from these rules such things as navigation equipment, electronic circuitry with currents less than 1 amp, high voltage ignition circuitry, and cranking motor conductors.

Example:

Assume we have an appliance that draws 30 amps at 12 volts. We will run 2 conductors together, inside the engine room. The cable we wish to use is rated 105 degrees Celsius.

Use table 9-2 for no more than 2 conductors. Enter the bottom half of the table for engine room spaces, find the column for 105 degrees Celsius and read down the column to find the first amperage greater than 30 amps which is 38.3 amps. In the right most column read the required wire gauge of 12 AWG.

	No more than 2 conductors bundled, any voltage						
Wire Size AWG	Temperature rating of conductor insulation						
	60° C	75° C	80° C	90° C	105° C	125° C	200° C
	140° F	167° F	176° F	194° F	221° F	257° F	392° F
	Allowable Amperage of Conductors Outside Engine Spaces at Ambient 30° C (86° F)						
18	10	10	15	20	20	25	25
16	15	15	20	25	25	30	35
14	20	20	25	30	35	40	45
12	25	25	35	40	45	50	55
10	40	40	50	55	60	70	70
8	55	65	70	70	80	90	100
6	80	95	100	100	120	125	135
4	105	125	130	135	160	170	180
3	120	145	150	155	180	195	210
2	140	170	175	180	210	225	240
1	165	195	210	210	245	265	280
0	195	230	245	245	285	305	325
00	225	265	285	285	330	355	370
000	260	310	330	330	385	410	430
0000	300	360	385	385	445	475	510
	Factor for Inside Engine Spaces						
	0.6	0.8	0.8	0.8	0.9	0.9	1.0
	Allowable Amperage of Conductors Inside Engine Spaces at Ambient 50° C (122° F)						
18	5.8	7.5	11.7	16.4	17.0	22.3	25
16	8.7	11.3	15.6	20.5	21.3	26.7	35
14	11.6	15.0	19.5	24.6	29.8	35.6	45
12	14.5	18.8	27.3	32.8	38.3	44.5	55
10	23.2	30.0	39.0	45.1	51.0	62.3	70
8	31.9	48.8	54.6	57.4	68.0	80.1	100
6	46.4	71.3	78.0	82.0	102.0	111.3	135
4	60.9	93.8	101.4	110.7	136.0	151.3	180
3	69.6	108.8	117.0	127.1	153.0	173.6	210
2	81.2	127.5	136.5	147.6	178.5	200.3	240
1	95.7	146.3	163.8	172.2	208.3	235.8	280
0	113.1	172.5	191.1	200.9	242.3	271.4	325
00	130.5	198.8	222.3	233.7	280.5	315.9	370
000	150.8	232.5	257.4	270.6	327.3	364.9	430
0000	174.0	270.0	300.3	315.7	378.3	422.8	510
	Table derived from data per 33 CFR 183.425						

TABLE 9-2: Allowable Amperage, Two or Less Conductors.

Wire Size AWG	3 Conductors Bundled, > 50 V -Factor 0.70						
	Temperature rating of conductor insulation						
	60° C	75° C	80° C	90° C	105° C	125° C	200° C
	140° F	167° F	176° F	194° F	221° F	257° F	392° F
	Allowable Amperage of Conductors Outside Engine Spaces at Ambient 30° C (86° F)						
18	7.0	7.0	10.5	14.0	14.0	17.5	17.5
16	10.5	10.5	14.0	17.5	17.5	21.0	24.5
14	14.0	14.0	17.5	21.0	24.5	28.0	31.5
12	17.5	17.5	24.5	28.0	31.5	35.0	38.5
10	28.0	28.0	35.0	38.5	42.0	49.0	49.0
8	38.5	45.5	49.0	49.0	56.0	63.0	70.0
6	56.0	66.5	70.0	70.0	84.0	87.5	94.5
4	73.5	87.5	91.0	94.5	112.0	119.0	126.0
3	84.0	101.5	105.0	108.5	126.0	136.5	147.0
2	98.0	119.0	122.5	126.0	147.0	157.5	168.0
1	115.5	136.5	147.0	147.0	171.5	185.5	196.0
0	136.5	161.0	171.5	171.5	199.5	213.5	227.5
00	157.5	185.5	199.5	199.5	231.0	248.5	259.0
000	182.0	217.0	231.0	231.0	269.5	287.0	301.0
0000	210.0	252.0	269.5	269.5	311.5	332.5	357.0
	Factor for Inside Engine Spaces						
	0.6	0.8	0.8	0.8	0.9	0.9	1.0
	Allowable Amperage of Conductors Inside Engine Spaces at Ambient 50° C (122° F)						
18	4.1	5.3	8.2	11.5	11.9	15.6	17.5
16	6.1	7.9	10.9	14.4	14.9	18.7	24.5
14	8.1	10.5	13.7	17.2	20.8	24.9	31.5
12	10.2	13.1	19.1	23.0	26.8	31.2	38.5
10	16.2	21.0	27.3	31.6	35.7	43.6	49.0
8	22.3	34.1	38.2	40.2	47.6	56.1	70.0
6	32.5	49.9	54.6	57.4	71.4	77.9	94.5
4	42.6	65.6	71.0	77.5	95.2	105.9	126.0
3	48.7	76.1	81.9	89.0	107.1	121.5	147.0
2	56.8	89.2	95.5	103.3	125.0	140.2	168.0
1	67.0	102.4	114.7	120.5	145.8	165.1	196.0
0	79.2	120.8	133.8	140.6	169.6	190.0	227.5
00	91.3	139.1	155.6	163.6	196.3	221.2	259.0
000	105.6	162.8	180.2	189.4	229.1	255.4	301.0
0000	121.8	189.0	210.2	221.0	264.8	295.9	357.0
Table derived from data per 33 CFR 183.425							

TABLE 9-3: Allowable Amperage, Three Conductors.

	\multicolumn{7}{c|}{4 to 6 Conductors are Bundled, > 50 V - Factor 0.60}						
Wire Size AWG	\multicolumn{7}{c|}{Temperature rating of conductor insulation}						
	60° C	75° C	80° C	90° C	105° C	125° C	200° C
	140° F	167° F	176° F	194° F	221° F	257° F	392° F
	\multicolumn{7}{c|}{Allowable Amperage of Conductors Outside Engine Spaces at Ambient 30° C (86° F)}						
18	6.0	6.0	9.0	12.0	12.0	15.0	15.0
16	9.0	9.0	12.0	15.0	15.0	18.0	21.0
14	12.0	12.0	15.0	18.0	21.0	24.0	27.0
12	15.0	15.0	21.0	24.0	27.0	30.0	33.0
10	24.0	24.0	30.0	33.0	36.0	42.0	42.0
8	33.0	39.0	42.0	42.0	48.0	54.0	60.0
6	48.0	57.0	60.0	60.0	72.0	75.0	81.0
4	63.0	75.0	78.0	81.0	96.0	102.0	108.0
3	72.0	87.0	90.0	93.0	108.0	117.0	126.0
2	84.0	102.0	105.0	108.0	126.0	135.0	144.0
1	99.0	117.0	126.0	126.0	147.0	159.0	168.0
0	117.0	138.0	147.0	147.0	171.0	183.0	195.0
00	135.0	159.0	171.0	171.0	198.0	213.0	222.0
000	156.0	186.0	198.0	198.0	231.0	246.0	258.0
0000	180.0	216.0	231.0	231.0	267.0	285.0	306.0
	\multicolumn{7}{c|}{Factor for Inside Engine Spaces}						
	0.6	0.8	0.8	0.8	0.9	0.9	1.0
	\multicolumn{7}{c|}{Allowable Amperage of Conductors Inside Engine Spaces at Ambient 50° C (122° F)}						
18	3.5	4.5	7.0	9.8	10.2	13.4	15.0
16	5.2	6.8	9.4	12.3	12.8	16.0	21.0
14	7.0	9.0	11.7	14.8	17.8	21.4	27.0
12	8.7	11.3	16.4	19.7	22.9	26.7	33.0
10	13.9	18.0	23.4	27.1	30.6	37.4	42.0
8	19.1	29.3	32.8	34.4	40.8	48.1	60.0
6	27.8	42.8	46.8	49.2	61.2	66.8	81.0
4	36.5	56.3	60.8	66.4	81.6	90.8	108.0
3	41.8	65.3	70.2	76.3	91.8	104.1	126.0
2	48.7	76.5	81.9	88.6	107.1	120.2	144.0
1	57.4	87.8	98.3	103.3	125.0	141.5	168.0
0	67.9	103.5	114.7	120.5	145.3	162.9	195.0
00	78.3	119.3	133.4	140.2	168.3	189.6	222.0
000	90.5	139.5	154.4	162.4	196.3	218.9	258.0
0000	104.4	162.0	180.2	189.4	226.9	253.7	306.0
	\multicolumn{7}{c|}{Table derived from data per 33 CFR 183.425}						

TABLE 9-4: Allowable Amperage, four to six Conductors

Wire Size AWG	7 to 24 Conductors are Bundled, > 50 V - Factor 0.50 Temperature rating of conductor insulation						
	60° C 140° F	75° C 167° F	80° C 176° F	90° C 194° F	105° C 221° F	125° C 257° F	200° C 392° F
	Allowable Amperage of Conductors Outside Engine Spaces at Ambient 30° C (86° F)						
18	5.0	5.0	7.5	10.0	10.0	12.5	12.5
16	7.5	7.5	10.0	12.5	12.5	15.0	17.5
14	10.0	10.0	12.5	15.0	17.5	20.0	22.5
12	12.5	12.5	17.5	20.0	22.5	25.0	27.5
10	20.0	20.0	25.0	27.5	30.0	35.0	35.0
8	27.5	32.5	35.0	35.0	40.0	45.0	50.0
6	40.0	47.5	50.0	50.0	60.0	62.5	67.5
4	52.5	62.5	65.0	67.5	80.0	85.0	90.0
3	60.0	72.5	75.0	77.5	90.0	97.5	105.0
2	70.0	85.0	87.5	90.0	105.0	112.5	120.0
1	82.5	97.5	105.0	105.0	122.5	132.5	140.0
0	97.5	115.0	122.5	122.5	142.5	152.5	162.5
00	112.5	132.5	142.5	142.5	165.0	177.5	185.0
000	130.0	155.0	165.0	165.0	192.5	205.0	215.0
0000	150.0	180.0	192.5	192.5	222.5	237.5	255.0
	Factor for Inside Engine Spaces						
	0.6	0.8	0.8	0.8	0.9	0.9	1.0
	Allowable Amperage of Conductors Inside Engine Spaces at Ambient 50° C (122° F)						
18	2.9	3.8	5.9	8.2	8.5	11.1	12.5
16	4.4	5.6	7.8	10.3	10.6	13.4	17.5
14	5.8	7.5	9.8	12.3	14.9	17.8	22.5
12	7.3	9.4	13.7	16.4	19.1	22.3	27.5
10	11.6	15.0	19.5	22.5	25.5	31.2	35.0
8	16.0	24.4	27.3	28.7	34.0	40.0	50.0
6	23.2	35.6	39.0	41.0	51.0	55.6	67.5
4	30.4	46.9	50.7	55.3	68.0	75.7	90.0
3	34.8	54.4	58.5	63.5	76.5	86.8	105.0
2	40.6	63.8	68.3	73.8	89.3	100.1	120.0
1	47.8	73.1	81.9	86.1	104.1	117.9	140.0
0	56.5	86.3	95.5	100.4	121.1	135.7	162.5
00	65.3	99.4	111.2	116.8	140.3	158.0	185.0
000	75.4	116.3	128.7	135.3	163.6	182.4	215.0
0000	87.0	135.0	150.2	157.8	189.1	211.4	255.0
Table derived from data per 33 CFR 183.425							

TABLE 9-5: Allowable Amperage, seven to 24 Conductors

Wire Size AWG	Temperature rating of conductor insulation						
	60° C	75° C	80° C	90° C	105° C	125° C	200° C
	140° F	167° F	176° F	194° F	221° F	257° F	392° F

25 or More Conductors are Bundled, > 50 V - Factor 0.40

Wire Size AWG	Allowable Amperage of Conductors Outside Engine Spaces at Ambient 30° C (86° F)						
18	4.0	4.0	6.0	8.0	8.0	10.0	10.0
16	6.0	6.0	8.0	10.0	10.0	12.0	14.0
14	8.0	8.0	10.0	12.0	14.0	16.0	18.0
12	10.0	10.0	14.0	16.0	18.0	20.0	22.0
10	16.0	16.0	20.0	22.0	24.0	28.0	28.0
8	22.0	26.0	28.0	28.0	32.0	36.0	40.0
6	32.0	38.0	40.0	40.0	48.0	50.0	54.0
4	42.0	50.0	52.0	54.0	64.0	68.0	72.0
3	48.0	58.0	60.0	62.0	72.0	78.0	84.0
2	56.0	68.0	70.0	72.0	84.0	90.0	96.0
1	66.0	78.0	84.0	84.0	98.0	106.0	112.0
0	78.0	92.0	98.0	98.0	114.0	122.0	130.0
00	90.0	106.0	114.0	114.0	132.0	142.0	148.0
000	104.0	124.0	132.0	132.0	154.0	164.0	172.0
0000	120.0	144.0	154.0	154.0	178.0	190.0	204.0

Factor for Inside Engine Spaces							
	0.6	0.8	0.8	0.8	0.9	0.9	1.0

Wire Size AWG	Allowable Amperage of Conductors Inside Engine Spaces at Ambient 50° C (122° F)						
18	2.3	3.0	4.7	6.6	6.8	8.9	10.0
16	3.5	4.5	6.2	8.2	8.5	10.7	14.0
14	4.6	6.0	7.8	9.8	11.9	14.2	18.0
12	5.8	7.5	10.9	13.1	15.3	17.8	22.0
10	9.3	12.0	15.6	18.0	20.4	24.9	28.0
8	12.8	19.5	21.8	23.0	27.2	32.0	40.0
6	18.6	28.5	31.2	32.8	40.8	44.5	54.0
4	24.4	37.5	40.6	44.3	54.4	60.5	72.0
3	27.8	43.5	46.8	50.8	61.2	69.4	84.0
2	32.5	51.0	54.6	59.0	71.4	80.1	96.0
1	38.3	58.5	65.5	68.9	83.3	94.3	112.0
0	45.2	69.0	76.4	80.4	96.9	108.6	130.0
00	52.2	79.5	88.9	93.5	112.2	126.4	148.0
000	60.3	93.0	103.0	108.2	130.9	146.0	172.0
0000	69.6	108.0	120.1	126.3	151.3	169.1	204.0

Table derived from data per 33 CFR 183.425

TABLE 9-6: Allowable Amperage 25 or More Conductors

Effect of Voltage Drop on Conductor Sizing

Having determined a conductor size adequate to carry the specified current, we must also determine the size of conductor to keep voltage drop over its length to less than a specified amount (usually 3 percent or 10 percent). The final conductor size is the larger (smallest gauge number) of the two determinations.

Many electrical devices will work fine with a 10 percent voltage drop but others, particularly some electric motors and some electronic equipment, will suffer. It is preferable to wire for a 3 percent maximum drop wherever possible, and only use the 10 percent maximum drop where absolutely necessary in situations with very high current draw, such as operating bow thrusters or a windlass (assuming they have motors that can tolerate the lower voltage).

Equation 9-7 relates voltage drop to length and cross-sectional area of a conductor.

$$V = I \times (\frac{K \times L}{A}) \quad (1) \quad \text{or rearranged} \quad A = \frac{K \times L \times I}{V} \quad (2)$$

Where: V = Voltage drop across the length of conductor (volts)
 I = Current flow (amperes)
 L = Length of conductor (feet or meters)
 A = Cross sectional area of conductor (circular mils)
 K = Constant relating resistance to length and area of conductor
  = 10.75 for L in feet
  = 35.26 for L in meters

EQUATION 9-7: Conductor Area for Voltage Drop and Length

With equation 9-7(2) we can determine the area in circular mils (CM) that corresponds to a given length (L) of conductor and current (I). The constant K varies with temperature and for boat calculations K = 10.75 is the standard used by the ABYC and Transport Canada).

Example:

Assume we have an appliance that draws 30 amps at 12 volts. The distance from the source to the appliance is 12 feet. We want to limit the voltage drop to 3 percent.

Total conductor length out to appliance and back L = 12 x 2 = 24 feet. Allowed voltage drop = 3% x 12 V = 0.36 V

A = (K x L x I) / V = (10.75 x 24 ft x 30 A) / 0.36 V = 21,500 CM

So we need a cable of at least 21,500 circular mils area. From table 9-1 on page 520 we find the smallest conductor with an area larger than 21,500 CM is a 6 gauge conductor with an area of 26400 CM which is the cable we would select.

Tables 9-7 through 9-9 are provided on the following pages, calculated from equation 9-7, for determining the wire gauge to carry a specified current over a specified distance, at voltage drops of either 3 percent or 10 percent. So you have the option of calculating wire gauge using the formula or using the tables.

To use the tables:
1. First pick the appropriate table for the operating voltage and percent voltage drop.
2. Then enter the table in the first column and go down until you reach the first round trip distance that is greater than your required round trip distance.
3. Then move to the right across that line until amperage is found that is greater than or equal to your required amperage. If there is no amperage found in the line greater than your required amperage, then you only have to consider current carrying capacity, as per table 9-2.
4. Move up that column to the top of the table to read the size of conductor required.

Example:

Repeating the example we just solved by the equation method, use table 9-8 for 3 percent drop and 12 volts. In the Round Trip Distance column, the line with 25 feet is the first line greater than the 24 foot length of the conductor.

Moving to the right across the line, 35 A is the first amperage greater than our design amperage of 30 A.

This is in the 6 gauge column so our answer is 6 gauge.

Checking table 9-2 on page 522; at 105 degrees Celsius our conductor has a permissible amperage of 120 A so 6 gauge is okay and is our final answer

Some other things to note about these tables

- For 6 V circuits, multiply the amperages in the 12-volt tables by 0.5 and for 24 V circuits, multiply the amperages by 2.0.
- 120 V tables are given, but most of the time the current carrying capacity rather than voltage drop will be what determines the conductor size.

3% Voltage Drop - 110 Volts - K=10.75 - 1 of 2							
Round Trip Distance	AWG Wire Gauge						
ft m	18	16	14	12	10	8	6
	Amperage						

ft	m	18	16	14	12	10	8	6
21	6.4	24						
23	7.0	22	34					
25	7.6	20	32					
27	8.2	18	29					
29	8.8	17	27	44				
31	9.4	16	26	41				
33	10.1	15	24	38				
36	11.0	14	22	35				
39	11.9	13	20	32	51			
42	12.8	12	19	30	48			
45	13.7	11	18	28	45			
49	14.9	10	16	26	41	65		
52	15.8	9.6	15	24	39	61	97	
57	17.4	8.7	14	22	35	56	89	
61	18.6	8.2	13	21	33	52	83	132
66	20.1	7.5	12	19	30	48	77	122
71	21.6	7.0	11	18	28	45	71	113
76	23.2	6.5	10	17	26	42	67	106
82	25.0	6.1	9.7	15	24	39	62	98
89	27.1	5.6	8.9	14	23	36	57	91
96	29.3	5.2	8.3	13	21	33	53	84
103	31.4	4.8	7.7	12	19	31	49	78
111	33.8	4.5	7.1	11	18	29	46	73
120	36.6	4.1	6.6	11	17	27	42	67

3% Voltage Drop - 110 Volts - K=10.75 - 2 of 2							
Round Trip Distance	AWG Wire Gauge						
ft m	4	2	1	0	00	000	0000
	Amperage						

ft	m	4	2	1	0	00	000	0000
71	21.6	180						
76	23.2	169						
82	25.0	156						
89	27.1	144	229					
96	29.3	133	212	268				
103	31.4	124	198	249	315			
111	33.8	115	184	231	292	368		
120	36.6	107	170	214	270	340	429	

TABLE 9-7: Allowable Amperage for 3% Voltage Drop, 110 Volts, AWG 18 to AWG 0000 Gauge Cable

3% Voltage Drop - 12 Volts - K=10.75 - 1 of 2							
Round Trip Distance		**AWG Wire Gauge**					
ft	m	18	16	14	12	10	8	6
		Amperage						
10	3.0	5.4	8.6	14	22	35	55	88
11	3.4	4.9	7.9	13	20	32	50	80
12	3.7	4.5	7.2	11	18	29	46	73
13	4.0	4.2	6.6	11	17	27	43	68
14	4.3	3.9	6.1	9.8	16	25	39	63
15	4.6	3.6	5.8	9.2	15	23	37	59
16	4.9	3.4	5.4	8.6	14	22	35	55
17	5.2	3.2	5.1	8.1	13	20	33	52
18	5.5	3.0	4.8	7.6	12	19	31	49
20	6.1	2.7	4.3	6.9	11	17	28	44
21	6.4	2.6	4.1	6.6	10	17	26	42
23	7.0	2.4	3.8	6.0	9.5	15	24	38
25	7.6	2.2	3.5	5.5	8.7	14	22	35
27	8.2	2.0	3.2	5.1	8.1	13	20	33
29	8.8	1.9	3.0	4.7	7.5	12	19	30
31	9.4	1.8	2.8	4.4	7.1	11	18	28
33	10.1	1.6	2.6	4.2	6.6	11	17	27
36	11.0	1.5	2.4	3.8	6.1	9.7	15	24
39	11.9	1.4	2.2	3.5	5.6	8.9	14	23
42	12.8	1.3	2.1	3.3	5.2	8.3	13	21
45	13.7	1.2	1.9	3.1	4.9	7.7	12	20
49	14.9	1.1	1.8	2.8	4.5	7.1	11	18
52	15.8	1.0	1.7	2.6	4.2	6.7	11	17
57	17.4	1.0	1.5	2.4	3.8	6.1	9.7	15
61	18.6	0.9	1.4	2.3	3.6	5.7	9.1	14
66	20.1	0.8	1.3	2.1	3.3	5.3	8.4	13
71	21.6	0.8	1.2	1.9	3.1	4.9	7.8	12
76	23.2	0.7	1.1	1.8	2.9	4.6	7.3	12
82	25.0	0.7	1.1	1.7	2.7	4.2	6.7	11
89	27.1	0.6	1.0	1.5	2.5	3.9	6.2	9.9
96	29.3	0.6	0.9	1.4	2.3	3.6	5.8	9.2
103	31.4	0.5	0.8	1.3	2.1	3.4	5.4	8.5
111	33.8	0.5	0.8	1.2	2.0	3.1	5.0	7.9
120	36.6	0.5	0.7	1.1	1.8	2.9	4.6	7.3

TABLE 9-8(1): Allowable Amperage for 3% Voltage Drop, 12 Volts, AWG 18 to AWG 6 Gauge Cable

3% Voltage Drop - 12 Volts - 2 of 2								
Round Trip Distance		AWG Wire Gauge						
ft	m	4	2	1	0	00	000	0000
		Amperage						
10	3.0	140	222	280				
11	3.4	127	202	255	321			
12	3.7	116	185	234	295			
13	4.0	108	171	216	272	343		
14	4.3	100	159	200	253	318	401	506
15	4.6	93	148	187	236	297	375	472
16	4.9	87	139	175	221	279	351	443
17	5.2	82	131	165	208	262	331	417
18	5.5	78	123	156	196	248	312	394
20	6.1	70	111	140	177	223	281	354
21	6.4	67	106	133	168	212	268	337
23	7.0	61	97	122	154	194	244	308
25	7.6	56	89	112	141	178	225	283
27	8.2	52	82	104	131	165	208	262
29	8.8	48	77	97	122	154	194	244
31	9.4	45	72	90	114	144	181	229
33	10.1	42	67	85	107	135	170	215
36	11.0	39	62	78	98	124	156	197
39	11.9	36	57	72	91	114	144	182
42	12.8	33	53	67	84	106	134	169
45	13.7	31	49	62	79	99	125	157
49	14.9	29	45	57	72	91	115	145
52	15.8	27	43	54	68	86	108	136
57	17.4	25	39	49	62	78	99	124
61	18.6	23	36	46	58	73	92	116
66	20.1	21	34	42	54	68	85	107
71	21.6	20	31	39	50	63	79	100
76	23.2	18	29	37	47	59	74	93
82	25.0	17	27	34	43	54	69	86
89	27.1	16	25	31	40	50	63	80
96	29.3	15	23	29	37	46	59	74
103	31.4	14	22	27	34	43	55	69
111	33.8	13	20	25	32	40	51	64
120	36.6	12	19	23	29	37	47	59

TABLE 9-8(2): Allowable Amperage for 3% Voltage Drop, 12 Volts, AWG 4 to AWG 0000 Gauge Cable

10% Voltage Drop - 12 Volts - K=10.75 - 1 of 2								
Round Trip Distance		**AWG Wire Gauge**						
ft	m	18	16	14	12	10	8	6
				Amperage				
10	3.0	18	29					
11	3.4	16	26	42				
12	3.7	15	24	38				
13	4.0	14	22	35				
14	4.3	13	21	33	52			
15	4.6	12	19	31	49			
16	4.9	11	18	29	46			
17	5.2	11	17	27	43	68		
18	5.5	10	16	25	40	64		
20	6.1	9.0	14	23	36	58	92	
21	6.4	8.6	14	22	35	55	88	
23	7.0	7.9	13	20	32	50	80	127
25	7.6	7.2	12	18	29	46	74	117
27	8.2	6.7	11	17	27	43	68	108
29	8.8	6.2	9.9	16	25	40	64	101
31	9.4	5.8	9.3	15	24	37	59	94
33	10.1	5.5	8.7	14	22	35	56	89
36	11.0	5.0	8.0	13	20	32	51	81
39	11.9	4.6	7.4	12	19	30	47	75
42	12.8	4.3	6.9	11	17	28	44	70
45	13.7	4.0	6.4	10.2	16	26	41	65
49	14.9	3.7	5.9	9.4	15	24	38	60
52	15.8	3.5	5.5	8.8	14	22	35	56
57	17.4	3.2	5.1	8.0	13	20	32	51
61	18.6	3.0	4.7	7.5	12	19	30	48
66	20.1	2.7	4.4	7.0	11	18	28	44
71	21.6	2.5	4.1	6.5	10	16	26	41
76	23.2	2.4	3.8	6.0	9.6	15	24	39
82	25.0	2.2	3.5	5.6	8.9	14	22	36
89	27.1	2.0	3.2	5.2	8.2	13	21	33
96	29.3	1.9	3.0	4.8	7.6	12	19	31
103	31.4	1.8	2.8	4.5	7.1	11	18	28
111	33.8	1.6	2.6	4.1	6.6	10	17	26
120	36.6	1.5	2.4	3.8	6.1	9.7	15	24

TABLE 9-9(1): Allowable Amperage for 10% Voltage Drop, 12 Volts, AWG 18 to AWG 6 Gauge Cable

10% Voltage Drop - 12 Volts - 2 of 2								
Round Trip Distance		AWG Wire Gauge						
ft	m	4	2	1	0	00	000	0000
		Amperage						
10	3.0							
11	3.4							
12	3.7							
13	4.0							
14	4.3							
15	4.6							
16	4.9							
17	5.2							
18	5.5							
20	6.1							
21	6.4							
23	7.0							
25	7.6							
27	8.2	173						
29	8.8	161						
31	9.4	150	239					
33	10.1	141	224					
36	11.0	129	206	260				
39	11.9	119	190	240	302			
42	12.8	111	176	222	281	354		
45	13.7	104	165	208	262	330	416	
49	14.9	95	151	191	241	303	382	482
52	15.8	90	142	180	227	286	360	454
57	17.4	82	130	164	207	261	329	414
61	18.6	76	121	153	193	244	307	387
66	20.1	71	112	142	179	225	284	358
71	21.6	66	104	132	166	209	264	333
76	23.2	61	97	123	155	195	246	311
82	25.0	57	90	114	144	181	228	288
89	27.1	52	83	105	132	167	210	265
96	29.3	49	77	97	123	155	195	246
103	31.4	45	72	91	114	144	182	229
111	33.8	42	67	84	106	134	169	213
120	36.6	39	62	78	98	124	156	197

TABLE 9-9(2): Allowable Amperage at 10% Voltage Drop, 12 Volts, AWG 4 to AWG 0000 Gauge Cable

DC ELECTRICAL SYSTEMS
DC GROUNDING AND CABLING
Grounding

For our purposes, ***ground*** refers to an electrical connection to the surrounding earth or water with the express purpose of ensuring the connected part of the electrical circuit stays at the same electrical potential (voltage) as the surrounding earth or water.

One side of a power source, such as a battery, can be connected to ground to keep it at ground potential. In the case of a boat's DC system, this connection is from the negative side of the battery to the negative terminal of the engine block or the main boat ground bus, which provides a connection to the water outside the hull via the propeller shaft or a ground plate installed on the outer hull. This keeps the negative or return side of the system that is connected to the negative side of the battery at ground potential. This is a ***negative ground*** system.

DC Cabling

DC cabling is sized and connected as per the earlier topic on cabling.

A circuit doesn't always consist of wire; part of it can be any conductor such as earth, water, a metal framework, or even your body (not good). If a circuit uses a metal framework or chassis to complete the circuit back to the power source, it said to have a ***ground return***. This is commonly used in automobiles but *is not used in boats* (not even metal boats). Exception: Electrical equipment on the engine block, such as starters and alternators, often but not always use the engine block itself as a negative ground return.

DC cabling on boats requires both a positive conductor and negative return conductor for each device on each circuit. Marine duplex cable used for DC cabling has a red conductor for positive and a yellow conductor for the negative return. On some older boats you may find black instead of yellow for the negative return conductor. The return conductor must be as large as the positive supply conductor; the use of duplex cable guarantees this.

The red conductor may or not connect to a switch, and then must connect to a circuit breaker or fuse on the DC distribution panel. The negative or yellow conductor is connected directly to a negative bus which in turn connects to the negative battery terminal. The negative side of DC circuits always connects directly to the bus with no intervening switches, breakers, or fuses.

BATTERIES

Introduction

Batteries tend to be one of those things that receive little or no attention on the average recreational boat, which results in substantially shortened operating life and premature failure—usually at the worst possible time. Often batteries are bought and installed without any thought as to what they are to be used for and how much capacity is needed. The result is batteries mismatched to the application and often undersized for the actual loads encountered.

The type of battery used on boats is a **lead-acid** battery, so named because of the use of lead in the electrodes and acid in the electrolyte.

How the Battery Charges and Discharges

Figure 9-18 shows a schematic representation of a lead-acid battery cell under charge. The **electrodes** are conductors of current that enters or leaves the electrolyte and the **electrolyte** is a conductive solution of acid.

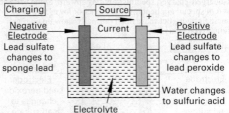

FIGURE 9-18: Charging a Lead-Acid Battery

When the charging current is applied the lead sulfate in the positive electrode changes to lead peroxide, the lead sulfate in the negative electrode changes to sponge lead, and water is changed to sulfuric acid. Note: Sponge lead is just lead that has a porous physical structure like a sponge.

As charging nears completion, hydrogen gas begins forming at the negative plate, and oxygen at the positive plate. This happens because there is too much charging current for the remaining lead sulfate and the excess current ionizes the water in the electrolyte. Ionizing refers to the separation of water (H2O) into its constituent elements of hydrogen (H) and oxygen (O). This phenomenon is referred to as *gassing* or *venting*.

Concentrated sulfuric acid has a specific gravity of around 1.83, so the electrolyte in a charged cell with a higher acid concentration has a higher specific gravity than a discharged cell. Also as one might expect, a fully charged battery, not under load, will have a higher voltage across the electrodes. Table 9-10 shows specific gravities and no load voltages found in normal lead-acid batteries.

Condition	Discharged	Charged
Specific Gravity	1.12	1.7
Voltage 1 cell	1.8	2.1
Voltage 6 cells	11.7	12.7

TABLE 9-10: Lead-Acid Battery Specific Gravity and Voltage

Note: The condition of the electrodes is what determines the charge, and adding sulfuric acid to the battery doesn't increase the battery's charge; rather it just moves the range of discharged-charged specific gravities upward. Some batteries used in special applications use higher or lower ranges of specific gravity but these don't normally show up on recreational type boats.

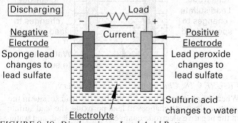

FIGURE 9-19: Discharging a Lead-Acid Battery

In figure 9-19 we see that discharging the battery is just the opposite process as charging, converting both electrodes back to lead sulfate.

Battery Construction

The lead-acid battery has a number of cells connected together in series so that the voltage of the battery is 2.1 volts per cell times the number of cells. Thus a 12-volt battery will have six cells.

The cells are constructed of a hard plastic or rubber material and contain positive and negative electrodes that are in the form of flat plates interleaved with one another, such that every positive plate has a negative plate on either side. The plates are kept from touching each other by separators.

Starting batteries are designed to deliver a very high current for a short period of time and are the type found in automobiles and in boats for engine starting. They deliver higher current by having many thin plates that increase internal plate surface area, which permits higher current flow.

Some batteries are designed with fewer thicker plates that allow the battery to function longer, which effectively gives the battery greater capacity (i.e., more stored energy). These are known as a *deep-cycle battery*, and they are meant to deliver lower amperage over longer periods of time to a deeper discharge level than starting batteries.

Battery Specifications and Ratings

There are several different measures used to describe battery characteristics.

The *20-hour rate* is the continuous amperage that the battery can supply for 20 hours at 80° Fahrenheit (27° C). An alternate way to state this: The 20-hour rate is the continuous current needed to fully discharge the battery over 20 hours.

The battery's capacity is measured in *amp-hours* (**Ah**) and is a measure of the energy the battery can be expected to deliver under standardized condition. The amp-hour rating is defined as the 20-hour rate (amps) times 20 hours. For example a battery that can supply 5 amps continuously over the 20-hour period is a 5 A x 20 h = 100 Ah battery.

The amp-hour rating is the rating of interest for almost all applications except engine starting.

If a battery is discharged at a faster rate than the 20-hour rate, the amp-hours produced will be less than the rated amp-hours. Conversely, if the battery is discharged at a lower rate, then the amp-hours produced will be greater than the rated amp-hours. For example, if a battery with a 20-hour rate of 5 amps is discharged at 25 amps it will produce only around 70 percent of the rated amp-hours.

Cold cranking amps (**CCA**) is defined as the number of amps a battery can deliver for 30 seconds at 0 degrees Fahrenheit (–18 degrees C) with an ending voltage of at least 7.2 V while still cranking.

Marine cranking amps (**MCA**) is defined as the number of amps a battery can deliver for 30 seconds at 32 degrees Fahrenheit (0 degrees C) with an ending voltage of at least 7.2 V. MCA will always be higher than CCA.

CCA or MCA is the measure of most interest for engine starting applications.

The *reserve capacity* is the number of minutes a battery can be discharged at 25 amps at 0 degrees Fahrenheit (–18 degrees C) and maintain a voltage of at least 10.5 volts while still under discharge.

Battery Types

There are three types of lead-acid batteries used in recreational boats, these being *wet-cell*, *gel*, and *absorbed glass mat* (**AGM**).

Wet-Cell Battery

The flooded or wet-cell lead-acid battery is the conventional type that we are used to in our cars and uses a liquid sulfuric acid electrolyte. The wet-cell battery has vents at the top of each cell and may lose electrolyte during the venting process, which requires checking and topping up the electrolyte from time to time.

Wet-cell advantages:

- There is a lower initial cost.
- There is better deep-cycle performance.
- With proper maintenance and charging regimens, higher quality wet-cell cell batteries should achieve more than a thousand charge-discharge cycles.

Wet-cell disadvantages:

- Maintenance is required.
- Liquid battery acid can be spilled.
- Gases are released during charging.
- Quality varies considerable among different manufacturers. The expected number of charge-discharge cycles ranges anywhere from 500 to 2000 cycles.
- They have a high self-discharge rate—greater than 6 percent per month.
- Something most people don't realize is that if a wet-cell battery is left totally discharged for more than a couple

of weeks, the battery will sustain serious damage or fail completely.

Gel-Cell Battery

The gel-cell has the acid electrolyte in gel rather than liquid form and the cell is sealed although it has pressure release valves to vent any excess gas. The slightly higher internal pressure causes any vented oxygen and hydrogen to recombine into water which keeps the gel from drying out.

Gel-cell advantages:

- There is virtually no maintenance.
- It can't spill or leak.
- If charged correctly, there is no gas release.
- There is low self-discharge of around 3 percent per month.
- It is faster charging.

Gel-cell disadvantages:

- The charging process must be more closely controlled since too much gassing in the last part of the charging process will result in drying out the gel and ruining the battery.
- The maximum charging voltage of 14.2 volts may require specialized charging equipment.
- There is a higher initial cost.
- Too much gassing will ruin electrolyte.

Absorbed Glass Mat Battery

Absorbed glass mat (AGM) batteries have a glass mat separator tightly packed between the positive and negative plates. Just enough electrolyte is in these plates to activate the battery. The tight packing lowers internal resistance to allow higher starting currents in a battery that is also a deep-cycle battery. As with the gel-cell, the oxygen and hydrogen gases are recombined into water.

AGM advantages:

- It is maintenance free.
- It is shock and vibration resistant.
- There is little or no gas release under charge.
- It is good for both deep-cycle and starting.

AGM disadvantages:

- It has the highest initial cost.
- It is heavier than wet-cell type for same capacity.
- It requires very controlled charging cycle.
- Too much gassing will ruin electrolyte.

Comparing Battery Costs

Batteries of each type were randomly selected from various vendors and the prices averaged for each type in table 9-11. Note that prices differed widely for various vendors and brands so just consider these as a rough comparison.

Type	Usage	Volts	$ / Ah	CCA / $
AGM	Deep-cycle	12	2.00	3.27
Gel	Deep-cycle	12	2.25	2.54
Wet-cell	Deep-cycle	12	1.18	4.23
Wet-cell	Deep-cycle—golf cart	6	0.83	3.96
Wet-cell	Starting	12	n/a	12.12

TABLE 9-11: Comparative Cost of Battery Types

Because of charging considerations (which we'll discuss further on) AGM, gel-cell and wet-cell batteries can't be mixed together. Once the decision on battery type is made, that should be the only type of battery on the boat, including the starting battery.

Matching Batteries to the Application (Starting or Deep-Cycle)

Usually on a small boat like a runabout, only a starting battery is installed, and its only function is to start the engine, although it may run some very low power devices such as a bilge pump or radio from time to time. Obviously, a starting type battery makes the most sense, since a deep-cycle battery with enough cold cranking amps to start the engine would be excessively large and expensive. A quick look at table 9-11 shows how you get a lot more CCAs per dollar with a starting battery.

Many smaller boats are outfitted for fishing with an electric trolling motor that requires battery power while the main engine is stopped. Obviously you don't want to be discharging the starter battery to run that trolling motor or you may end up rowing those fish back to shore. The solution is to provide a second battery for powering the trolling motor, which allows the starting battery to be used exclusively for engine starting. The second battery should be a deep-cycle battery, which is suited to being deeply discharged as is likely in this situation.

In addition to deep-cycle and starting batteries, there are dual-purpose batteries designed to perform both functions. If a second battery is to be used as a back up starting battery, this could provide an argument for it being a ***dual-purpose*** battery, if a deep-cycle battery can't provide the necessary CCAs.

When you trade in your runabout for a 30-foot express cruiser, you are most likely getting a boat with plenty of added house electrical loads, like cabin lights or a refrigerator. Many of these will be loads you expect to use when the engine is turned off, when you'll be relying entirely on the batteries (assuming you don't have an AC system with generator or a shorepower connection). If the starter battery is used to run these loads overnight, most likely the engine isn't going to start in the morning —the same situation as with the trolling motor.

Here's where you start thinking about a second battery or bank of batteries so you can save the starter battery for starting. This second bank (called *house batteries*) will be deep-cycle batteries since, starting batteries just aren't designed for continuous use and deep discharges.

Deep-cycle batteries say deep-cycle on the label and provide instructions for charging. Read the labels on those marine batteries at your local warehouse store to make sure you're getting what you really want; starting or deep-cycle.

On even larger boats, you start thinking about enough battery power to run an inverter that can provide AC power for appliances such as televisions and microwave ovens. Here the possibilities start to multiply. The usual and probably best approach is to have dedicated starting batteries and a separate bank of deep-cycle batteries, just like we did on the express cruiser.

An alternative is to go with two banks of house batteries and use one bank for engine starting and the other for the house power. This is acceptable, provided the total CCAs meet the requirements specified by the engine builder, even if it doesn't make a lot of economic sense.

Yet another plan is one starting bank and two house banks where use of the house banks alternates from one day to the next, the idea being that the batteries will last twice as long.

Nigel Calder makes a good detailed argument in his book that if you want to double the capacity like this, you would be better off to have all the batteries in one bank discharging them only half as much each time.

To summarize matching batteries to the application: *Use starting batteries for starting and deep-cycle batteries for everything else!*

Estimating Required Battery Capacity

Starter Battery Capacity

Engine starting batteries are sized by cold cranking ampere (CCA) rating and not the ampere hour (Ah) rating. The engine manufacturer specifies the CCA requirement and you simply need to meet this requirement. If necessary, two or more batteries can be wired in parallel to increase the CCAs available.

Actual Capacity Realized from House Batteries

The number of times a battery can be expected to be completely charged and discharged is usually specified by the manufacturer and depending on the quality and type of battery can range anywhere from 300 to 1000 full cycles. The number of times a battery can be cycled has an inverse relationship to the percent it is discharged. Thus, a battery that is only partially discharged in each cycle can be cycled more times than a battery that is fully discharged each cycle.

It is generally accepted that a 50 percent discharge gives the best balance between achieving useful capacity and useful battery life, and this number should be used to calculate expected capacity.

However, there is some controversy as to the amount of charging that has to take place. Some argue that it is unlikely that more than an 80 percent charge will be achieved during a day's run, so that's all you should plan for. Others argue that you must charge to 100 percent if you are to expect maximum battery life. If you use the 80 percent figure, you are now only getting 80% − 50% = 30% of the rated capacity.

The number that seems to have fairly general acceptance is 25 percent, so *figure on obtaining 25 percent of the battery's rated capacity in ampere-hours (Ah) each day.*

Estimating Power Usage

To estimate the required battery capacity, we must first estimate daily power usage. This is a reasonably straightforward process that involves listing all the power loads on the boat, along with their current draw and length of time they will be used each day. Multiplying the current (amps) by the time (hours) for each load yields the ampere-hours, which are then totaled up with all the other loads to give the total estimated daily power requirement in ampere-hours.

A form for estimating the boat's power requirement can be drawn up on a scratch pad (or spreadsheet) with column headings similar to the sample in table 9-12.

Equipment	Volts	Watts	Amps @ 12V	Hrs/ Day	Amp- Hrs
Bilge Pump	12	75	6.3	0.5	3
Fan	12	25	2.1	8	17
Light	12	25	2.1	4	8
Microwave	120	1500	125.0	0.2	25
Hair Dryer	120	1200	100.0	0.1	10
Etc.	...	...	...	...	...
Total					135

TABLE 9-12: Example Ampere-Hour Tabulation

An explanation of the columns is as follows:

- Equipment—This lists every piece of equipment that consumes electrical power on board.
- Volts (12 or 120)—Not necessary for this calculation, but it's useful information.
- Watts—The actual wattage from the equipment label.
- Amps (12-volt basis)—This is watts divided by 12 regardless of whether this item operates at 120 V or not. If you just have the amperage for a 120 V piece of equipment, then multiply the amperage by 10 to get the amperage on a 12 V basis.
- Hours/day—Estimated hours per day the item will operate.
- Amp hours—This is amps multiplied by hours/day. This is totaled at the bottom to get the final answer.

Our example totals up to 135 ampere-hours. Since batteries only supply 25 percent, or 1/4 of their capacity, multiply 135 × 4 to get 540 amp-hours of battery capacity is needed for the house batteries.

Table 9-13 on the next page lists some typical equipment that might be found onboard and ranges of power requirements for each. This table could be used for a guesstimate, but the watts or amperes should be determined from the actual equipment labels or manuals.

Equipment	Watts		Amps (12 V Basis)	
	From	To	From	To
Anchor Light	10	12	0.8	1.0
Anchor windlass	400	4000	33.3	333.3
Bilge blower	20	50	1.7	4.2
Bilge pump	50	500	4.2	41.7
Fan	10	200	0.8	16.7
Fresh water pump	50	100	4.2	8.3
Light	5		0.4	
Light	10		0.8	
Light	25		2.1	
Light	50		4.2	
Shower pump	50	100	4.2	8.3
Clothes dryer	4000	5000	333.3	416.7
Clothes washer	400	600	33.3	50.0
Water heater	700	2000	58.3	166.7
Air Conditioner	1000	2000	83.3	166.7
Electric drill	300	500	25.0	41.7
Hair Dryer	1000	1300	83.3	108.3
Color TV 10"	35	45	2.9	3.8
Color TV 19"	70	90	5.8	7.5
Computer	100	150	8.3	12.5
Satellite Reciever	15	30	1.3	2.5
Stereo	30	100	2.5	8.3
VCR	15	30	1.3	2.5
Blender	150	300	12.5	25.0
Coffeemaker (brew)	700	1300	58.3	108.3
Electric frypan	1000	1500	83.3	125.0
Icemaker	100	200	8.3	16.7
Microwave	500	1500	41.7	125.0
Refrigerator	50	500	4.2	41.7
Toaster	800	1200	66.7	100.0

Note: Amps on a 12 volt basis are watts divided by 12 regardless of operating voltage

TABLE 9-13: Typical Equipment Power Draw

Battery Cabling

Assuming your boat has a 12-volt DC system, all 12-volt batteries will be wired in parallel, never in series. Six-volt golf cart batteries are often used for house batteries because they are cheap and have good deep-cycle characteristics. In a 12-volt system, two golf cart batteries must be wired in series to produce 12 volts.

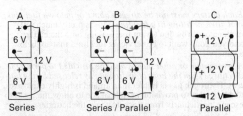

FIGURE 9-20: Battery Wiring Examples

In figure 9-20, B would have twice the amp-hour capacity of A but voltage is the same at 12 volts. C shows two 12-volt batteries hooked together to double the capacity but leave the voltage at 12 volts.

Battery Installation

According to 33 CFR 183.420, *a battery must not move more than one inch in any direction when a pulling force of 90 pounds or twice the battery weight, whichever is less, is applied through the center of gravity of the battery.* If batteries weighing 50 pounds and more are able to slide back and forth an inch in rough seas, eventually something is going to break. *The batteries should be fixed in place so as to be totally immobile in all directions including vertical.*

The battery must be installed so that metal objects cannot come in contact with the ungrounded battery terminals. This can be accomplished by covering the connection with an insulating boot or installing the battery in a covered battery box.

Each metallic fuel line and fuel system component within 12 inches and above the horizontal plane of the battery top surface as installed must be shielded with dielectric material. What the heck does that mean? Basically it means that any metal fuel system component that is above the battery and within 12 inches of the battery in any direction must be insulated. The purpose is to allow the battery to be installed or removed without the terminals contacting the metal and sparking. The author would like to suggest that it's going to be quite awkward to install or remove a heavy battery with an obstruction only 12 inches above it and that neither fuel lines nor anything else should be within 3 feet of the top of a battery.

Each battery must not be directly above or below a fuel tank, fuel filter, or fitting in a fuel line. This is pretty much self-explanatory. You don't want fuel leaking onto the battery, and you don't want to be servicing fuel lines that are below a battery.

A vent system or other means must be provided to permit the discharge from the boat of hydrogen gas released by the battery. Hydrogen gas is lighter than air and is highly explosive and will rise, so provision must be made to allow the gases to escape, particularly from pockets above the batteries.

Each battery terminal must not depend on spring tension for its mechanical connection to the terminal. This means the terminal must either clamp on to the battery post or be secured by a nut or bolt.

Battery Charging

Introduction

Batteries on a boat are usually charged using the alternator attached to the main engine or with a battery charger powered by 120 VAC. The AC power for the charger is supplied either from a shore connection or an onboard generator. Other alternatives such as solar and wind power are used, particularly on cruising sailboats, to charge the batteries while underway without the engine running. Here discussion is limited to charging with alternators and AC chargers.

The alternator supplied with a gasoline or diesel boat engine is usually a small frame alternator designed to generate just enough power to charge a starting battery, and will not be capable of continuous operation at rated maximum output. Similarly, the voltage regulator supplied with the engine is designed for the same purpose and will be incapable of properly charging the deep-cycle house batteries we just discussed.

Voltage Regulators and Battery Chargers

Earlier we established that the output of the alternator can be controlled by metering the amount of current allowed through the field windings with a *voltage regulator*. We want a voltage regulator that will allow the alternator to charge the batteries as fast as possible, but without excessive gassing, and without overcharging them.

The same qualities are also desirable in an AC-powered battery charger, so both will be discussed at the same time.

Cheaper regulators, like the one that came on the boat engine and automobile type battery chargers, usually provide a *one stage* charge that begins charging with a high current that drops rapidly so charging time is lengthened considerably. The dotted lines on figure 9-21 show how the voltage and current behave over the charging cycle with a single stage regulator or charger.

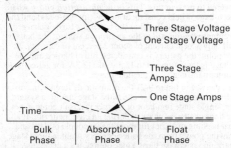

FIGURE 9-21: One and Three Stage Charging

The curves in figure 9-21 are not for any particular battery; rather they are just for illustrating the concept of three stage charging. Actual curves vary by battery model and manufacturer and also will be different for wet-cell, gel-cell, and AGM battery types.

A *three stage* charger or regulator manages the charging process in three separate stages or phases in order to charge the battery in the minimum amount of time but without excessive gassing or overcharging. The solid lines on figure 9-21 show how the voltage and current behave over the charging cycle with a three stage regulator or charger.

A battery is capable of accepting a current of approximately 25 to 40 percent of its amp-hour capacity rating until it reaches about 75 percent of full charge. Initial charging at this rate is termed the *bulk phase*. During the bulk phase the charging voltage is raised to maintain the constant current flow until the voltage reaches 14.4 volts for a wet-cell or 14.1 volts for a gel-cell.

Note that although the battery might accept current up to 40 percent of capacity, that is probably excessive and it would be advisable to limit bulk current to a maximum of 25 percent of capacity. Charging at somewhere from 15 to 25 percent of capacity is a reasonable target. Fifteen percent gets you from 50 percent charged to 75 percent charged in a little under two hours.

At this point the battery begins excessive gassing if the high current flow is maintained, so the charging current must be lowered to prevent this. This is the *absorption phase* where the voltage is held constant at 14.4 V (for wet-cells) and the charging current falls off as the battery is further charged. Eventually, while still at the absorption voltage, the battery will only accept current of about 2 percent of capacity. At this point, the battery is considered fully charged and the voltage is then dropped to 13.3 volts (13.7 V for gel-cells) to maintain the charge in the float phase.

One can see in figure 9-21 the dramatic difference in current delivery from a one stage and three stage charging system. The single stage regulator or charger just isn't going to get the house batteries charged during an eight hour run. If a boat is going to be out for more than a couple of days and drawing power from the batteries every night, a three stage charging system isn't just a nice option, it's a necessity.

THE ALTERNATOR

Now that the charging current has been established as somewhere in the range of 15 percent to 25 percent of battery bank capacity, the required alternator output can be determined.

An alternator heats up when producing and also will be running continuously in a hot engine space which will cause it to run even hotter. At higher temperatures, the output is reduced by as much as 20 to 25 percent, so this should be allowed for when sizing the alternator. If the desired charging rate is 20 percent of bank capacity, then the alternator size is 125% x 20% = 25% of bank capacity.

Another item to consider is that alternator output decreases as RPMs decrease. For example, an alternator that produces 110 A at 6000 RPM will only produce 75 A at 2500 RPM. If you think a lot of charging will be done at anchor with the engine running at idle, then an even larger alternator is indicated. Be sure the regulator can control current delivery to the battery bank.

Alternators are available as small frame alternators, similar in size and mounting configuration to an automobile alternator, and as large frame alternators that operate at higher outputs. Small frame alternators can replace the existing alternator while large frame alternators may require additions or modifications to the engine to be mounted properly. Generally large frame alternators will run cooler and therefore will be more efficient. Small frame alternators are available in outputs up to about 160 A. To achieve more than that, you either need to install two alternators or install a large frame alternator.

If you replace an existing alternator, keep the old one as a spare. Another option is to keep the existing alternator in service to charge the starting battery and use the new high capacity alternator to charge the house bank.

One last consideration: The alternator uses horsepower produced by the main engine and this could be a significant consideration with a very small engine. A 160 amp alternator would draw around 3 horsepower from the engine.

AC SYSTEMS

INTRODUCTION

These days AC electrical systems are becoming more and more commonplace on smaller and smaller boats. The impetus driving this trend is the desire to have power microwave ovens, refrigerators, color televisions, kitchen appliances, power tools, and all the other comforts of home, onboard. Many of these items aren't available at all for 12 VDC operation or the ones that are available cost two or three times more than their 120-volt brethren, further fueling the move to AC.

In many cases, inverters are retrofitted to older boats that didn't have a 120 V system to start with, often with little or no regard for proper wiring or grounding—a dangerous practice, to say the least. One-hundred-twenty volts is 10 times greater than 12 volts, which means it can push 10 times the current through your body with sometimes fatal results. Add in the fact that saltwater is an excellent electrical conductor, and you have a greater chance of receiving a serious or even fatal shock than in your home.

At the beginning of this electrical chapter it was emphasized that *this book will in no way qualify anyone to carry out electrical work on their boat*, and this bears repeating. You should hire an electrician with actual marine electrical experience if you wish to have electrical work done on your boat, keeping in mind that even a journeyman electrician qualified to work on house or even industrial wiring is not automatically qualified to work on boat electrical systems. Again, if you insist on being a do-it-yourselfer, obtain, read, and thoroughly understand one or more of the publications mentioned at the beginning of this electrical chapter. Purchase the appropriate standards from the ABYC and get a qualified person to coach you and inspect your work.

AC CABLING AND CONNECTIONS

AC cabling is sized and connected as per the earlier topic on cabling.

Polarity

As mentioned previously, triplex cable for marine AC wiring has three conductors as follows; black for hot, white for neutral, and green for ground. Four conductor cable for 240 VAC has an additional hot conductor with red insulation.

Correct polarity must be maintained throughout the AC system. When connecting to any electrical device or receptacle:

- The black hot conductor connects to the brass or copper colored terminal.
- The white conductor connects to the silver terminal.
- The ground connects to the ground terminal, usually marked with green.

Get one of these gizmos from your local hardware store for checking correct polarity of AC receptacles, then go ahead and check all the receptacles on your boat regardless of who did the wiring. It will only take five minutes and it could save you a lot of grief.

Figure 9-22 shows color pinouts for standard 3 prong 125 V wall receptacles. These are polarized receptacles designed to ensure that anything plugged into them will maintain correct polarity. Note the wider slot that ensures that a polarized plug with just two blades will only plug in with the correct

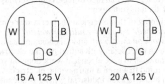

15 A 125 V   20 A 125 V

FIGURE 9-22: AC 125 V Receptacle Pinouts

orientation. These receptacles have the same design and polarity as the ones in your house (except they are marine grade) so everyday household appliances can be plugged into them safely.

In your house, the neutral and ground connectors are connected at the main junction box where the power comes into your house. On a boat, the neutral must only connect to ground at the power source and nowhere else. Make sure neutral is not connected to ground in any appliances onboard. To check this with an ohmmeter, the resistance from white (neutral) to green (ground) should be infinity.

Receptacles for household use are not suitable for marine use and are definitely not designed to connect to stranded wire, so all 125 V receptacles onboard should be of a type approved for marine use. They seem ridiculously expensive at more than 20 bucks a pop, but if you own a boat you are already painfully aware that everything for boats costs a lot more, so hopefully you've already learned to live with it.

Ground Fault Circuit Interrupters

A ground fault circuit interrupter is a circuit breaker that can detect current leakage to ground and trip when it does so. The operating principle is to trip if the return current is less than the supply current—the difference is assumed to be leaking to ground. This usually provides reasonable protection from electric shocks.

Receptacles located in deck areas, galleys, heads, and machinery spaces are supposed to have ground fault circuit interruption (GFCI) installed. Consider installing GFCI for all AC circuits on the boat. A GFCI receptacle must be the first one installed in a series to protect all the downstream receptacles.

Distribution Panel

All AC circuits originate from individual breakers installed on the AC distribution panel. Double pole breakers that open both the hot and neutral circuits are preferred, but single pole breakers on just the hot black conductors are acceptable if the system is properly polarized throughout.

The neutral white wire is connected to a neutral bus and the green ground wire is connected to an AC ground bus. Neutral and ground must not be connected here (like they are in your house). It bears repeating that *neutral and ground are only connected together at one place and that is at the power source, be it ashore at the marina, or at your onboard generator or inverter.*

AC Grounding

The ground conductor circuits must not be able to be disconnected in any way and must not have any installed breakers, fuses, or switches.

The AC ground from AC distribution panels is connected to a single AC ground bus, which in turn is connected to the negative engine terminal or the boat main ground bus. This effectively grounds the AC ground to the surrounding water either through the propeller shaft or an external grounding plate.

If this AC electrical system ground connection is somehow disconnected, you may someday find yourself or your first mate performing a rather unpleasant role that is much better performed by said ground connection. *Severing the AC ground connection in the hope of eliminating stray dockside currents or for any other reason is downright dangerous and should not be done!* You cannot rely only on shorepower ground for protection.

AC SOURCES

Introduction

There are three ways to provide AC electricity to a boat:
1. Plug into a source ashore using a shorepower cable.
2. Generate power onboard using a diesel or gas powered generator.
3. Use an inverter to convert 12 VDC current to 120 VAC current.

Wiring must be such that individual circuits can only be connected to one of these sources at a time, although it's possible to use more than one these power sources at a time, as long as no individual circuits can be connected to more than one power source. In other words, some circuits may be powered by source 1, while other circuits are powered by source 2, and yet others by source 3, as long as the wiring is such that no circuit can be connected to more than one source at a time.

Any power source must have sufficient capacity to power all the circuits that can be connected to it. For example, if the inverter is capable of powering several circuits, not including the air conditioning system, then the wiring must be such that the inverter cannot be connected to the air conditioning system.

Shorepower

Shorepower Receptacles

Today most marinas provide some kind of shorepower although the voltage and current vary. Typical hookups are: 120 volt/20 amps, 120 volt/30 amps, 120 volt/50 amps and 240 volt/50 amps. The standard locking receptacles used for dock outlets are shown in figure 9-23 along with the conductor color pinouts used to maintain correct polarity.

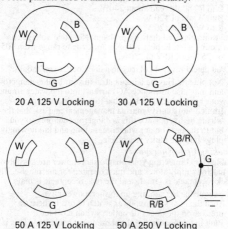

20 A 125 V Locking   30 A 125 V Locking

50 A 125 V Locking   50 A 250 V Locking

FIGURE 9-23: Shorepower Receptacle Pinouts

Note how the 250 V receptacle shows B/R and R/B on two of the prongs. This just means that the B/R prong can be connected to either black or red and the R/B prong must be connected to the other color (i.e., if the B/R prong is connected to red then the R/B prong must be connected to black).

Knowing the pinout, it's easy to check for correct polarity before plugging in.

With 125 V receptacles:

- W to G should read 0 V. If W to G is around 120 V then polarity has been reversed. If W to G is greater than 0 V

but less than 100 V then polarity isn't necessarily reversed but there's a problem somewhere.
- W to B should read approximately 120 V.

With 250 V receptacles:
- W to G should read 0 V. If W to G is around 120 V then polarity has been reversed. If W to G is greater than 0 V but less than 100 V, then polarity isn't necessarily reversed but there's a problem somewhere.
- B to R should read about 240 V.
- B to W about 120 V.
- R to W about 120 V.

Anything else and there's a problem. Note that voltage can vary quite a bit. Expect voltages dockside to range from 105 V to 125 V or 210 V to 250 V.

If you detect reverse polarity in a dock outlet you should:
- Not plug in. Having a hot neutral in your boat is dangerous and may also introduce AC currents into the water around your boat, which can be lethal to a nearby swimmer.
- Immediately notify marina management and ask that the wiring be fixed, since this is dangerous not only to you, but to the next boater who comes along and unknowingly plugs into the faulty receptacle.

Hooking Up to Shorepower
Cables for connecting your boat to shorepower are available at marine supply stores and must be rated for marine use. The dock receptacle is female and the boat receptacle is male.

The sequence for hooking up to shorepower is:
1. Turn the boat's shore power switch to off. If there's a breaker on the dockside outlet, switch it off too.
2. Plug in the boat end of the shorepower cable first. This is to ensure you don't drop a "hot" cable into the water.
3. Plug in to the shore outlet.
4. Check your polarity indicator on your main panel. If it's on then polarity is wrong and you stop here. If it is off continue.
5. Turn the boat's shore power switch to on.

To disconnect:
1. Turn the boat's shore power switch to off.
2. Disconnect from the shore outlet first.
3. Disconnect the boat end of the cable.

The Shorepower Circuit
The circuit diagram in figure 9-24 is for a shorepower hookup, and it shows the essential parts of the connection.

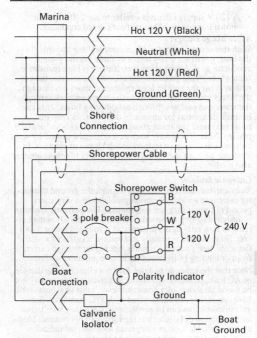

FIGURE 9-24: Shorepower Circuit 240 V

Things to note about this hookup:

- Neutral is connected to ground only at the source, in this case the marina.
- Polarity is maintained throughout.
- A 3 pole breaker that breaks all three current carrying conductors is required near the shorepower inlet.
- The galvanic isolator prevents stray currents from flowing through the ground wire.
- There are no breakers or switches in the ground conductors.
- The AC ground (green) is grounded inside the boat.

- A 120 V supply circuit is similar to the 240 V circuit shown in figure 9-24 but without the red conductor.

AC Leakage Danger

With this setup, if there is AC current leaking aboard the boat, it will normally return to shore via the ground conductor as it should. However, if there is high resistance somewhere in the ground connection to the marina, the current, seeking the path of least resistance, flows out through the boat's ground and returns to the marina source through the water and perhaps through neighboring boats. This can be quite dangerous for anyone in the water, so keep that in mind next time you think about letting your kids swim at the marina. Note: There have been several deaths caused by stray currents paralyzing swimmers around boats in marinas. In at least one case, an individual who jumped in to rescue another also died.

Galvanic Isolator

Stray currents entering the boat through the ground conductor can cause serious corrosion problems in a very short period of time if they are not stopped. The *galvanic isolator* is designed to stop these stray currents by only allowing currents to flow only in the presence of a voltage greater than 1 volt. Stray current is usually at a voltage less than 1 volt and therefore won't pass the isolator, but higher voltage current from grounding of live conductors or equipment will pass.

Note that the galvanic isolator does not eliminate the danger of AC leakage mentioned above. A galvanic isolator may not be found on some older boats; however, most new boats will have one if they are constructed to ABYC standards. Some galvanic isolators can be problematic since they won't give any indication of failure, leaving the boat unprotected. Models are available with an integrated monitor that indicates whether or not the unit is working properly.

Cost of a galvanic isolator is from about $150 for a 30-amp unit with no monitor, to around $350 for a 50-amp unit with monitor. The incremental cost of the integrated monitor is about $100.

Isolation Transformer

A much better alternative to the galvanic isolator is an *isolation transformer*, which severs the ground connection to the marina completely, leaving no possibility of stray currents from that source.

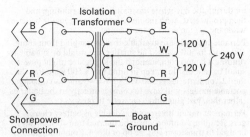

FIGURE 9-25: Isolation Transformer

The shorepower ground ends at the transformer. The secondary of the transformer acts as an independent source, and therefore the neutral is attached to boat ground there. Since the two windings are not electrically connected, no stray current can pass the isolation transformer.

For 240-volt input only the red and black conductors need be attached to the primary. The secondary is tapped in the center to provide two separate 120-volt circuits.

This arrangement keeps the neutral at ground potential and at the same time provides a return path for AC leakage, through the ground conductor back to the secondary. This way no AC leakage currents will leave the boat as they always seek to return to their source. An added bonus is that your boat will not be able to act as a ground return for the boat next to you, since you are not connected to shorepower ground.

Another advantage of an isolation transformer is that reverse polarity on the shorepower side of a 120-volt transformer doesn't matter, since the secondary sets its own polarity by attaching neutral to ground.

It's pretty clear that this is the way to go especially if your boat spends a lot of time plugged in at the marina. The only problem is, it's not cheap and it's relatively heavy. Figure on about $1000 for a 30-amp unit and around $2000 for a 50-amp unit. A 50-amp transformer capable of voltage boosting goes for approximately $4000 and weighs over 200 pounds.

Inverter

A boat *inverter* is designed to convert (invert) electricity from 12-volt DC to 120-volt AC. The general idea behind inverter use is to charge the house batteries from the alternator during the day while the main engine is running, and then produce AC with the inverter drawing from the batteries while the engine is off in the evening.

Portable Inverters are available in sizes ranging from about 100 watts to 500 watts. The smaller size would be suitable for running a laptop computer and the larger size might power small hand tools. Just keep in mind that a 500 watt draw on the 12-volt batteries is 500-W / 12 V = 40 amps so the larger portable models will have to connect directly to the batteries rather than just plug into a cigarette lighter.

Permanent mount inverters that double as battery chargers are quite common since the internal transformer can be used to transform voltage up or down. Combining the two functions like this in an inverter/charger saves both space and money, although installation should be done by a professional.

Inverter Output Wave Forms

Earlier, AC was described as current that changes direction back and forth, at its frequency of 60 hertz (60 times per second). Actually, AC comes in a couple of different flavors, which need to be understood.

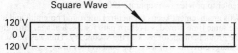

FIGURE 9-26: Square Wave AC

Figure 9-26 shows how we might imagine what AC looks like. Voltage would alternate back and forth from +120 V to –120 V as the current changes direction 60 times per second and the average absolute value of voltage would be 120 V. This is the current waveform that would be produced by a very simple inverter.

The power delivered by the public utility system or a generator actually takes the form of a sine wave and looks more like the waveform in figure 9-27.

Here, the voltage increases smoothly to a peak value of approximately 170 volts and then smoothly down to a reversed 170 volts at 60 cycles per second. The average and *root mean square* (**RMS**) voltage will be 120 V as it was for the square wave voltage above. We don't need to know why all this is so, we just need to know that electrical devices are designed to

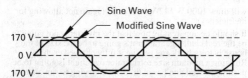

FIGURE 9-27: Sine Wave and Modified Sine Wave AC

work with the sine wave form of AC and that some devices just don't work well with square wave current.

Marine inverters are available that produce either *true sine wave* (TSW) or *modified sine wave* (MSW) output. The modified sine wave attempts to approximate the sine wave through a series of steps as shown in figure 9-27. The modified sine wave is better than the square wave, but not as desirable as a true sine wave. Electronics such as television sets and stereo systems tend to be quite sensitive to the waveform and will work best with TSW. Microwave ovens may not work very efficiently with MSW but they should work. Heat-producing appliances, such as light bulbs, toasters, and electric frying pans, don't care about the wave form at all.

As you might expect, a TSW inverter costs more than a MSW inverter. Browsing through a marine equipment catalog, I found 2000-watt TSW inverter/chargers priced around $1600 to $1800 and a 2000-watt MSW inverter/charger at about $1300.

Inverter Size

Inverters are sized by watts, so wattages for all the 120-volt loads on the inverter need to be tabulated. Keep in mind that some of the loads will be continuous and some higher loads will be for relatively short periods. For example, starting an electric motor usually requires a power surge more than double the running wattage. Other examples of short period loads include a microwave oven or a hair dryer. It is important to distinguish between the two because inverters have both a continuous and peak rating.

Inverters are available up to 2000 or even 3000 watts (5000 W or 8000 W surge) capacity. Figure 3000 watts is about equivalent to 110 V shorepower of 3000 W/ 110 V ≅ 30 amps. Without even allowing for efficiency losses this will translate to more than a 300 amp draw on the house batteries! Just running a 1000 watt microwave for five minutes will draw 1000 W / 12 V = 83 amps (again not allowing for inefficiency).

It should be apparent by now that the inverter is not going to be the real challenge; rather it's going to be the size of the house battery bank and getting it fully charged each day. Running a medium size refrigerator overnight is going to be pushing it. And don't even think about trying to run air-conditioning from an inverter. Actually, you can do it, but you'll need an awful lot of batteries.

Generator

Once power needs go much beyond 2000 watts, the inverter just doesn't cut it and a generator becomes the only real option when you're away from the dock. Unfortunately it's not a cheap option. A standalone diesel powered generating system will likely be the single most expensive item on the boat after the main engine.

A boat generating system consists of an armature or alternator type generator driven by a dedicated diesel engine. The generator produces 120 VAC or 240 VAC power directly and may also have a battery charging alternator attached.

The output wave form is sinusoidal (which is the preferred form) and can be produced at a frequency of 50 or 60 hertz. The output frequency depends on the engine RPM and 60 hertz power is usually produced at 1200, 1800, or 3600 RPM. The slower turning engine is the quietest, but is larger and heavier. 1800 RPM is probably the best compromise between noise and size. Also keep in mind that the 3600 RPM engine will have a shorter operating life.

The generators' diesel engine cooling and exhaust systems will usually be of the same type as the main engine systems, however they should be entirely separate from the main engine cooling and exhaust systems. In particular, the generator wet exhaust should never be run into the main engine wet exhaust system because water can be forced back into the main engine cylinders.

As with the main engine cooling system, avoid raw water cooling in favor of a closed circuit cooling system.

The system should be sized so the generator will run at 40 to 70 percent of full power when it is running. If running for extended periods at less than 40 percent is anticipated, consider installing two smaller size generators.

Combining the Inverter and Generator

The main objection to onboard generating systems is the noise and exhaust they produce. Often nearby boaters will find either or both of these objectionable, particularly if the system is left on all night.

Unless there's a need to keep the air conditioning running all night, a system that combines both an inverter and generator might be the best alternative. The generator is used in the early evening when using equipment that draws lots of power such as microwaves, clothes washers and dryers, electric skillets, hair dryers and curling irons, etc. Then the inverter is used just to keep the refrigerator, lights, and television going through the night.

BONDING AND CORROSION

BONDING

Bonding refers to the electrical connection of all metal frames and hardware on the boat to a common ground that is connected electrically to the surrounding water, so as to maintain the voltage potential of everything connected to the bonding system at the ground potential of the surrounding water.

The items to be connected include such diverse metal items as, fuel and water tanks, seacocks, propeller shafts, etc. Electrical equipment enclosures that are not otherwise grounded should also be connected to the bonding system. This should include all DC equipment enclosures since there is no grounding conductor in DC cabling (even though the negative return conductor is ultimately connected to ground).

Any of the aforementioned metal pieces of equipment or hardware has the potential to become electrically charged by contact with something like a loose or bare wire, so that they leak stray currents, or even worse, shock someone who comes in contact with them. Bonding prevents this possibility by providing any spurious currents a low resistance path to ground.

The physical installation of a bonding system consists of a long copper bus that runs the length of the boat, with each piece of equipment connected to this bus. A copper bar or copper pipe is usually used for this purpose and connections to it are made by drilling, tapping, and installing screws. The bonding system is grounded to the engine negative (ground) terminal for grounding through the propeller shaft or the boat's main ground bus, which is grounded either through the propeller shaft or to a ground plate on the outside of the hull.

Through-hulls, such as seacocks and the propeller shaft, may or may not be connected to the bonding system. Reasons for bonding or not bonding are discussed later in the topic on corrosion.

GROUNDING

A circuit doesn't always consist of wire; part of it can be any conductor such as earth, water, a metal framework, or even your body (not good). If a circuit uses a metal framework or chassis to complete the circuit back to the power source, it said to have a ground return. As mentioned previously this is commonly used in automobiles but not in boats—except on the engine block.

For our purposes, ground refers to the potential of the surrounding earth or water.

A wire that connects to a power source can be also connected to ground to keep it at the same potential (voltage) as ground. In the case of a boat this connection is to the surrounding water and the wire or conductor that is connected to ground is said to be grounded. In 12-volt DC systems it is the negative side of the battery that is grounded. Grounding is extremely important in boats and is also discussed in the sections on 12-volt and 120-volt systems.

The DC ground, AC ground, and bonding system must all be connected to the engine negative terminal or to the main ground bus that is connected to the engine negative terminal.

GALVANIC CORROSION

Galvanic Series

Figure 9-28 shows an experiment that anyone can set up and perform at home. Suspend two different metals in a saline solution and connect the two together with a wire and a voltmeter as shown. The voltmeter will read a voltage. In this case with one electrode of zinc and the other of copper a voltage of about 0.6 V should register on the voltmeter. I did this and registered a reading of approximately 0.8 V.

What's happening here? The zinc and copper have differing electrical voltage potentials, which induce a current flow if the two metals are connected and immersed in an electrolyte. This device we constructed for the experiment is known as a **_voltaic cell_** and is a specific example of the fact that two metals of differing potential will have a current flow between

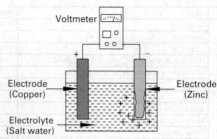

FIGURE 9-28: Demonstration of Galvanic Potential Using a Voltaic Cell

them it they are connected and immersed in an electrolyte. Note that if the two electrodes are of the same metal, there is no voltage difference and therefore no current flow.

If the cell if left connected and a current continues to flow, it will eventually become evident that the zinc is being eaten away, and if left long enough the zinc will completely disappear. This process is known as **galvanic corrosion**. There is a chemical reaction involved that explains why this is happening, but here all we need know is that when two different metals are joined and immersed in an electrolyte such as water, the metal with the lower voltage potential will corrode away.

Note that the two different metals don't have be joined by a wire as in our experiment; they just have to be in contact with one another while immersed in the electrolyte, in order to produce the same effect. The strength of this reaction is far more pronounced in saltwater, since saltwater is a much better electrolyte than fresh water,

Table 9-14 lists some common metals ranked in descending order of their voltage potential so that metals at the top of the list have more positive voltage and metals near the bottom more negative voltage relative to each other. This ranking is known as a **Galvanic Series**. The values in the right-hand column are the galvanic potential (voltage) and are averaged from four different tables (No two tables match but they are all close).

The metals at the top of the list are termed **cathodic** or **more noble** while metals further down the list are termed **anodic**

	Alloy	Volts
Cathodic or More Noble = Least Active >>	Graphite	0.3
	Platinum	0.2
	Titanium	0.0
	18-8-3 stainless steel, type 316 (passive)	-0.0
	18-8 stainless steel, type 304 (passive)	-0.1
	Monel	-0.1
	Silver	-0.1
	Nickel (passive)	-0.2
	Inconel (passive)	-0.2
	Silver solder	-0.2
	70-30 cupro-nickel	-0.2
	Lead	-0.2
	400 series stainless steels (passive)	-0.3
	Bronze Type M and G	-0.3
	Manganese bronze	-0.3
	Silicon bronze	-0.3
	Admiralty brass	-0.3
	Tin	-0.3
	Red brass	-0.3
	Aluminum bronze	-0.3
	Naval brass	-0.4
	Yellow brass	-0.4
	Copper	-0.4
	Inconel (active)	-0.4
	18-8-3 stainless steel, type 316 (active)	-0.4
	400 series stainless steels (active)	-0.4
	18-8 stainless steel, type 304 (active)	-0.5
	13 percent chromium stainless steel, type 410 (active)	-0.5
	Mild steel	-0.6
	Cast iron	-0.6
	Cadmium	-0.7
	Aluminum alloys	-0.8
Anodic = Less Noble = More Active <<	Zinc	-1.0
	Magnesium	-1.6

TABLE 9-14: The Galvanic Series

or *less noble*. Since the least noble metal is the one with the most negative voltage potential, it is the least noble metal that will corrode when the two metals are joined in an electrolyte. The less noble metals are more active and more susceptible to corrosion.

To get an idea of the potentials involved, the difference in voltage potential from platinum at the top of the list to zinc near the bottom of the list is approximately –1.8 volts. That is to say, zinc is negative 1.8 volts relative to platinum and current flow through the connection will be from the platinum (+) to the zinc (–). Another example would be zinc at 1.3 V less than copper.

In general, metals far apart on the series can be expected to produce more galvanic corrosion and metals close together very little galvanic corrosion.

Galvanic Corrosion on Boats

For example, if an aluminum propeller is mounted on a stainless steel shaft and immersed in seawater, the aluminum prop will experience galvanic corrosion since aluminum is further down the table than stainless steel.

This of course, is not good; we need to find a way to stop the galvanic corrosion of the propeller. It turns out that if three, rather than two, metals are linked together in our galvanic cell, only the least noble of the three metals experiences galvanic corrosion and the two more noble metals don't corrode and are protected (at least until the less noble metal has completely corroded away). This applies to any number of metals connected together; only the least noble metal will experience galvanic corrosion.

This explains the zincs we see mounted on propeller shafts, rudders, hulls, etc. They are near the bottom of the galvanic series and being lower down than the steels, bronzes, and aluminums, serve to protect by sacrificing themselves, thus the term *sacrificial zincs* or *anodes*. Zincs must be inspected and replaced periodically, since they corrode, and they must never be painted if they are to function as intended.

Something to note: Galvanic corrosion occurs without the presence of electricity from any external source; it is entirely self-generated by the action between dissimilar metals connected together in an electrolyte. It can be experienced just as easily on a sail boat with no installed electrical systems, as on a fully electrified powerboat.

If all metal through-hulls are bonded together with an internal bonding circuit then galvanic currents can develop between these through-hulls. For example, a bronze seacock forward on the hull that is bonded (connected) internally to a steel propeller shaft aft can induce galvanic corrosion of the steel shaft (assuming no zincs on the shaft).

Galvanic corrosion can even occur between differing metals on neighboring boats if the boats are connected electrically to each other, such as via a shorepower cable grounding wire.

Internal Corrosion

Almost all metals used on boats are an alloy of two or more metals. Stainless steel, brass, bronze, and sometimes aluminum are all alloys. These metals can be susceptible to internal galvanic currents in the presence of seawater, which leads to galvanic corrosion of the least noble metal in the alloy.

Brass is a case in point. Brass is very "shippy." You find nicely polished brass fittings all over the place onboard ships and yachts, so you might conclude that brass is a good metal for use in a marine environment. In fact, brass is copper alloyed with up to 40 percent zinc, so if brass fittings are used below the waterline the zinc is going to corrode away just like the sacrificial zinc anodes we just talked about in a process called *dezincification*. The remaining copper will crumble and fail and well, there goes your seacock, leaving a 2-inch hole in the bottom of your boat. *Never use brass valves or fittings below the waterline.* Always use marine grade bronze.

Another somewhat different example is stainless steel. Stainless steel is alloyed with metals such as nickel and chromium, and develops an oxidized layer that actually requires the presence of oxygen to stay intact. When stainless is deprived of oxygen, corrosion begins and it's not so stainless anymore. Where this causes the most problem is in crevices such as the space around a stainless bolt in a hole, under deck fittings, or around a propeller shaft, where this is little or no oxygen available. When you see rust stains coming from stainless steel fittings like this, you are seeing evidence of *crevice corrosion*. When stainless steel experiencing crevice corrosion it is said to be *active* and is much lower in the galvanic series than stainless steel in a *passive* state.

Much the same process occurs with aluminum. Whereas aluminum will work fine as hull material, it suffers from crevice corrosion when used for fuel tanks with no breathing space around them or that sit on a damp surface.

STRAY CURRENT CORROSION
Corrosion of Electrodes by Applied Electrical Current

Figure 9-29 shows the same voltaic cell as figure 9-28 on page 563, but the voltmeter has been replaced by a battery with its positive terminal connected to the copper (+) electrode.

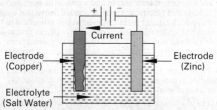

FIGURE 9-29: Electrical Current Induced Corrosion

In this case, the battery is working against galvanic potential, and if the battery voltage is sufficient to overcome the galvanic potential difference between the two electrodes, a current will flow in the reverse direction to the galvanic current and cause the copper electrode to corrode, even though it is more noble and has a higher galvanic potential then the zinc.

This little experiment demonstrates that:

* A metal electrode can be corroded by an applied current.
* Corrosion from applied electric currents is independent of and in fact can operate in the reverse direction of galvanic corrosion.
* The corrosion occurs in the electrode that has the current flowing out of it (i.e., the electrode on the positive side of the electrical source).

A couple of other things to know about corrosion from applied electric current:

* The positive and negative metal electrodes can be either the same metal or different metals. The corrosion occurs regardless.
* Corrosion from stray currents can occur at much higher rates than galvanic corrosion due to the higher voltages and currents involved.
* If the positively charged electrode that is being made to corrode consists of more than one metal connected together, the least noble metal will corrode first.

Stray Electrical Currents in Boats

Stray current corrosion has grown from being a relatively unknown phenomenon 40 years ago to a significant problem today. This is because of the proliferation of electrical hardware and systems on boats, along with the almost universal use of shorepower at all marinas.

Stray currents are usually generated by faulty electrical wiring and equipment both within and without the boat, and act like the applied electrical currents described above that cause corrosion to the metal parts (the electrodes) immersed in the surrounding water (the electrolyte). Stray current generation inside the boat is usually caused by leaks to ground from such things as frayed insulation, saltwater, or salt bridges between positive terminations and ground, or current leaks into bilge water. Undersized wiring can create unbalanced potentials in grounding systems, which also can lead to generation of stray currents.

Sources of stray current outside the boat include faulty marina wiring and faulty wiring in your neighbor's boat. Stray currents can affect your boat even if you aren't connected to shorepower, in that they can enter your boat via a metal through-hull and exit elsewhere via a metal through-hull if they are bonded together.

In general, stray currents are much stronger than galvanic currents and will therefore cause corrosion to proceed at a much faster rate.

As noted above, if two or more metals are joined as part of the same corroding electrode, the least noble metal will corrode first so those zincs do provide some measure of protection. Keep in mind, though, that strong stray current may cause loss of zincs in a matter of hours instead of the months you would expect from galvanic corrosion. Once the zincs are gone, expect the next metal down the series to follow the zincs.

BONDING VERSUS NONBONDING OF THROUGH-HULLS

Unbonded Through-Hulls

Bonding all through-hulls together electrically helps protect them from corrosion due to current leakages inside the boat, since the bonding system provides a path of least resistance for the current to return to the source.

Figure 9-30 shows what can happen when a metal through-hull is not bonded. A stray current leakage has developed

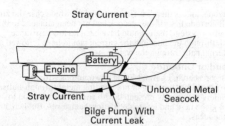

FIGURE 9-30: Internal Stray Current Leakage From an Unbonded Through-Hull

from a bilge pump located near a nonbonded seacock. The stray current flows out through the seacock, through the saltwater (electrolyte) to the propeller shaft, which is the path of least resistance back to the source. The result: The seacock is going to corrode.

If the seacock had been bonded, the current would found its way directly back to the source through the bonding system and the seacock corrosion prevented. This is the primary argument for bonding all metal parts that are in contact with seawater.

Bonded Through-Hulls

Unfortunately, there's also a downside to bonding all the metal through-hulls together. The bonding system provides a path of least resistance for external stray currents either from your neighbor's boat or leakage from the shorepower system itself.

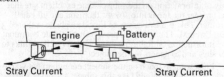

FIGURE 9-31: External Stray Currents Through Bonded Through-Hulls

Figure 9-31 gives an example of this case. A stray current seeking to return to its source follows a path, in through the seacock, through the bonding system, back to the engine, and out through propeller. In this case, the propeller will corrode, unless there's a zinc installed, in which case the zinc will corrode first. If the seacock had not been attached to the bonding system, there would have been no low resistance path through the boat and the current would have followed an external path through the water.

Bond or Unbond?

In my research, I haven't found any opinions strongly favoring either bonding or not bonding metal through-hulls. Readers are usually presented with similar information to that given here and left to decide for themselves. But here are some ideas.

If your boat's electrical system is in excellent condition with adequate size conductors and all electrical devices have a dedicated ground return conductor, then you might consider unbonding your through-hulls. If your boat spends a lot of time around marinas where you would expect to find lots of external stray currents, then you might also consider unbonding through-hulls.

Conversely, if you've bought an older boat with questionable wiring, then the wise thing would probably be to bond all the through-hulls. Of course, it would be even wiser not to buy that boat in the first place.

If the boat spends most of its time at sea, and is rarely near other boats and shorepower, then bonding is probably the better way to go.

LIGHTNING PROTECTION

There is plenty of literature on the subject of lightning protection for small boats, both in book form and on the internet. Google *lightning protection small boats*, and you'll turn up plenty of information on the subject. One excellent site that turns up near the top is http://www.thomson.ece.ufl.edu/lightning/. This is a University of Florida website authored by Dr. Ewen M. Thomson that provides up-to-date common sense information on lightning protection, as well as links to other sites and to papers on the subject.

Here, I just want to touch on the subject enough to get you to appreciate that you should take this subject seriously and do a little more research on it. There's not enough information here to allow you to design and install a lightning protection system; the idea is to just understand the basic concepts involved.

In general, boats of aluminum or steel construction are less likely to be seriously damaged by a lightning strike since the metal hull provides a path to ground. That doesn't mean a metal boat is invulnerable to lightning damage, however; masts, stays, electric, antennas, and electronic gear are all susceptible. So are people on the outside of the boat.

A fiberglass boat hit by lightning normally sustains far more serious damage than a metal-hulled boat. Lightning can travel down a metal mast, straight down through the center of the boat, and out through a hole that it blasts in the bottom of the hull. If it finds the bonding system it can pass through it to all grounded through-hulls and may end up melting those out. If you're on deck anywhere near a stay and holding on to the tiller, you yourself become an excellent path to ground.

The Protection System

The basic design of a small craft lightning protection system is fairly simple in principle. It consists basically of a #4 AWG copper conductor or its equivalent leading from the top of a mast of adequate height, down as straight a path as possible, through the boat to a grounding plate of at least 1 square foot affixed to the outside of the hull. The mast must be high enough to provide a cone or zone of protection that extends downward and outward at a 45-degree angle that encompasses the entire boat. Figure 9-32 illustrates the basic concept.

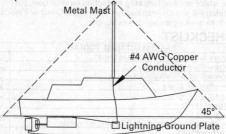

FIGURE 9-32: Elements of a Lightning Protection System

This system is not attached to the boat's grounding system inside the boat, but the grounding system may connect to the external lightning grounding plate. With the protective system in place, the lightning has a path to ground that doesn't necessitate blowing holes in your hull. More important, if all the stays and metal objects on deck are tied in to the system, some measure of protection is provided to personnel who don't have sense enough to get below when there's lightning around.

There are several guidelines published as to minimum turning radius of the main down conductor, minimum size of copper strands, acceptable connections, proximity to other equipment, methods of isolating electronic equipment, etc. The three books mentioned at the beginning of this chapter, the ABYC, and Dr. Thomson's website all provide detailed installation related information and requirements.

Is Lightning Protection a Good Idea?

As we've seen, a lightning protection does not prevent lightning strikes; rather it provides a relatively safe path through your boat for the strike to reach ground. There are those who say that installation of a lightning protection system increases the chances of being struck by lightning. Virtually all the experts dispute this, stating there is no reason for this to be so and no statistical evidence to the support this view.

In the very first sentence on his website, Dr. Thomson states, "The only benefit of not protecting a yacht from lightning is saving the cost of the protection system."

I hope this discussion will persuade you to analyze further the whole issue of lightning protection on your boat, particularly if you do your boating on the East Coast or Florida (where most lightning strikes occur).

CHECKLIST

BASIC ELECTRICAL TOOLKIT	
Spare fuses (if your boat uses them)	❏
Screwdrivers -slotted	❏
Screwdrivers -phillips	❏
Needlenose pliers	❏
Linemans pliers	❏
Wire stripper	❏
Crimping tool	❏
Selection of marine grade crimping terminals	❏
Electrical tape	❏
Heat shrink tubing	❏
Multimeter	❏
Spare wire in various sizes (marine grade)	❏
Battery testing hydrometer	❏
110 V receptacle polarity tester	❏
Battery terminal puller	❏
Soldering iron and rosin core solder	❏

10 COMMUNICATIONS

INTRODUCTION

SAFETY

Possibly one of the best ways to ensure your safety when on the water is to have appropriate communications equipment onboard with the ability to communicate easily with other vessels and shore stations when the need arises. It could be argued that anyone who operates a boat almost anywhere should be required to have a radio onboard and know how to use it.

Sound and whistle signals, discussed in the *Navigation Rules* chapter, are okay for negotiating agreement on passing or crossing situations with other vessels; however, using a radio for this purpose is a safer way and has become common practice. And when you need to make that emergency call for help; a radio call is much more intrusive and more likely to get attention than a signal flare, which requires someone to just happen to be looking in your direction. A handheld VHF radio can be had for as little as $99, so there's really no excuse for not having one onboard.

TYPES OF MARINE COMMUNICATIONS EQUIPMENT

These days there are lots of choices when it comes to types of marine two-way communication equipment, what with marine radiotelephones, citizen's band radios, cellular phones, satellite phones, satellite radios, etc. Of course, the one thing all these have in common is they are all, at heart, a type of radio.

All these communication devices can be somewhat arbitrarily lumped within one of two broad categories that we'll define here as:

- *Point-to-point communications*: The everyday telephone in our houses, the cell phone and the satellite phone are all examples of point-to-point communication devices. You call a specific location and talk only to the person at that location. No one else hears the conversation (at least they're not supposed to).
- *Two-way broadcast communications*: Marine purposed VHF and SSB radios and also CB radios fall within this category. When you transmit, you are heard by everyone who is within range and has similar equipment tuned to

the frequency you transmit on. Similarly, when someone responds, they are also heard by everyone in range.

Two-way broadcast equipment is what should be on any vessel, even if cell or satellite phones are available. Specifically, a marine VHF radio should be installed or available, and for cruising offshore a SSB shortwave radio should also be installed. (Note: VHF and SSB are described later.)

Here are some reasons for using VHF or SSB rather than a cell phone:

1. The Coast Guard continuously monitors VHF channel 16 in all areas (and so does everyone else) so that a transmission on channel 16 will be heard by the Coast Guard. SSB frequency 2182 KHz is also monitored by the Coast Guard.

2. Everyone in your area will also hear your VHF 16 transmission, so if it's an emergency call for help, vessels nearby can respond and come to your aid. A cell phone call to the Coast Guard might get through but those nearby vessels won't hear it.

3. In an emergency situation the Coast Guard can, if necessary, home in on your VHF signal to help locate you.

4. VHF range is from 5 to 25 miles. Digital cell phone range is not much greater than 5 miles.

This chapter is confined to discussion of the most commonly used types of marine two-way communications and does not address many one-way (receive only) services such as weather fax broadcasts, email services, NAVTEX, and the myriad other information services available to the serious cruiser. New services seem to be starting up at an every increasing rate so there will be even more choices over the next few years.

TWO-WAY BROADCAST COMMUNICATIONS
INTRODUCTION
There are several types of two-way radio communications available to the recreational boater. These include:

- VHF marine radio
- SSB MF/HF marine radio
- CB (citizens band) radio
- FRS (family radio system) radio
- Ham shortwave radio

Of these, the VHF radio is the most relevant to the average recreational boater and will be covered in some detail here. The SSB marine radio is of importance to those cruising offshore, and I'll describe what this is and how it works, but I won't get into too much detail. CB and FRS, although not designed for marine use, can also be handy to have, so I've included few remarks on both of them. Information on the ham radio is omitted since an onboard ham radio station is not likely to be of interest to anyone but an already licensed ham radio operator.

VHF MARINE RADIO

Regulations

Much of the information in this chapter on U.S. regulations regarding radio licensing was found at wireless.fcc. gov/marine.

Who Is Required to Have a Radio?

The VHF radio is the workhorse marine radio that every boater should have whether it's legally required or not. In the United States, any recreational vessel over 20 meters (65.6 ft) in length is required to carry a radio, as are most commercial vessels. These are known as *compulsory ships* because they are compelled to carry a radio. Recreational vessels less than 20 meters are not required to carry a radio, but may do so, and if they do are known as *voluntary ships*.

Radio Licensing—United States

Any vessels that have a SSB radio installed, or a satellite communications system installed, must have a ship *radio station license*. In the United States, a recreational vessel is not required to have a station license for a VHF radio, radar, or EPIRB on a voluntary ship unless the vessel voyages to a foreign country (including to Canada). Note that this requirement is as per U.S. FCC regulations, and that the foreign country to be visited will usually expect you to be licensed also. If your vessel is licensed, all communications equipment onboard is authorized under a single ship radio station license.

If you plan to dock in a foreign port you must also have a *Restricted Radiotelephone Operator Permit*, also referred to as an *individual license*. The ship radio station license and the restricted radiotelephone operator permit are both obtained by filing FCC Form 159 and 605 with the FCC. No test is required.

Forms are available by any of the following:

- Call the FCC Forms Distribution Center at 800-418-FORM (3676).
- FCC Fax-On-Demand system. Call 202-408-0177 from the handset of your fax machine. Follow the recorded instructions to have forms 150 and 605 faxed to you.
- On the Internet, go to www.fcc.gov/formpage.html.

Radio Licensing—Canada

In Canada, a vessel is not required to have a ship radio station license if the vessel is operated only within Canada or the United States and if the radio equipment onboard can only operate on frequencies allocated to maritime communications. This applies to vessels with SSB equipment as well.

If the vessel operates in any other foreign countries then a station license is required. Application for the license is to your local Industry Canada Office (there are far too many to list here—the Ontario Region number is 416-973-5000).

A Restricted Radiotelephone Operator Certificate (ROC) is required in Canada for anyone who operates marine radio equipment, regardless of whether a station license is required. You must pass the Industry Canada exam for the ROC. The Canadian Power and Sail Squadrons are the designated authority for issuing the ROC to recreational boaters.

How VHF Works

Most VHF communications are *simplex* (*push-to-talk*) where only one station transmits while the other listens. The person transmitting pushes a button to transmit and releases it when finished transmitting. This is necessary because a single radio frequency does not support simultaneous two-way communication.

Simultaneous two-way, or duplex, communications, like you have on your home phone or cell phone, requires the use of two separate frequencies, so that conversation in one direction uses one frequency and conversation in the opposite direction uses the other frequency.

VHF radios are available in both *fixed-mount* or *handheld* units. Fixed-mount radios are limited by regulation to a maximum of 25 watts transmit power, whereas handhelds are limited to a maximum of 6 watts. All VHF radios are required to also be able to transmit at low power or 1 watt.

VHF radio operates on a line of sight basis, which means the communication range between two stations is limited by the earth's horizon. Thus the effective range is determined by the height of the two antennas and the maximum transmission power of 25 watts.

VHF Permitted Communications

What VHF is Used For

Use of VHF radio is restricted to certain types of conversations that must relate to safety, distress, vessel operations, or public correspondence (marine operator).

Bridge-to-bridge conversations concerning maneuvering (to avoid collision) are considered *safety communications* as are broadcasts of weather and other safety-related bulletins.

Distress communications include Mayday, Pan-pan, or any other type of calls requesting help or indicating distress.

Planning a rendezvous location, discussing navigation, acquiring berthing instructions, reserving a slip, and arranging for repairs are all examples of *vessel operations communications*.

Public correspondence communications are VHF calls patched through to the land-based public telephone system and are arranged with a shore-based marine operator.

What VHF Is Not Used For

VHF communications concerning anything other that the above types of communications are prohibited by law.

Some communications the regulations explicitly disallow:

- It is unlawful to intentionally transmit a false distress alert, or to unintentionally transmit a false distress alert without taking steps to cancel that alert.
- Messages containing obscene, indecent, or profane words or meaning.
- Transmission from land. *This means you may not use your handheld VHF radio from land to communicate with your vessel.* In addition, if your vessel is on land, you may not transmit from the vessel's fixed-mount VHF.

Betting on this afternoon's ballgame, swapping recipes, social chitchatting, etc., are all definitely prohibited.

VHF Channels

Calling Channels and Working Channels

Certain channels are designated as *calling channels* and the others are some form of *working channel*. The idea is that all vessels monitor the calling channel to listen for calls. Once contact is established on the calling channel, the parties

Communication Type	Channels		
	United States	Canada	
		West	East
International distress, safety, and calling: Used to get the attention of another station (calling) or for emergencies. Ships carrying a radio maintain a listening watch on this channel. The Coast Guard monitors this channel.	16		
Supplemental calling channel for recreational boaters: Assigned by FCC to relieve congestion on channel 16.	09	---	
Working channels: these channels may be used as working channels by recreational boaters for vessel operations communications.	09 68 69 71 72 78 {79} {80}	{65A} 66A 67 {68} 69 71 72 73 74	{09} 10 {66A} {68} {71} 72 74
Navigation Safety (Bridge to Bridge): passing, meeting, overtaking, etc.	13 {67}	13	
Intership Safety: Intership safety messages & search and rescue messages.	06		
Coast Guard Liason: Used to talk to the Coast Guard (after calling on 16).	22A		
Maritime Safety Information Broadcasts: Canada: Continuous Marine Safety Broadcast (CMB).	22A	Wx1 Wx2 Wx3 21B {25B} {28B} {83B}	
Weather: National Oceanic and Atmospheric Administration (NOAA) broadcasts.	Wx1-Wx7		
Public Correspondence: used to call the marine operator at a public coast station to make and receive calls to shore based (public phone system) telephones.	24-28 84-87 {88}	01-03 23-28 60 64 84 86	24 26 27 85 87 88
Digital Selective Calling (DSC): -automated calling by radios equipped with DSC.	70		
Channels in { } See Table 10-1 Channel Notes On Next Page			

TABLE 10-1: Summary of Channels Available for Recreational Boaters

switch to an agreed upon working channel to continue the communication.

Channel Numbers and Frequencies

VHF channels are numbered in two series of consecutive numbers, the first from 1 through 28 and the second from 60 through 88. Channels 60 through 88 use frequencies interleaved with the frequencies of channels 1 through 28 so that the channels in order of increasing frequency are; 60, 01, 61, 02, 62, 03, 63, etc. Table 10-6 at the end of this chapter shows these channels and their frequencies. Additional channels, designated Wx1, through Wx7, are used for transmitting weather and other information.

All the channels are assigned frequencies in the range from 156 MHz to 163 MHz, and the frequencies are assigned in increments of 0.025 MHz which is also shown in table 10-6. The frequencies are provided in the table mainly for the curious, since the VHF operator only needs to know the channel numbers (as with a television set) and which channels are to be used for what purpose.

Channel Assignments

Only channels available to recreational boaters are summarized in table 10-1. Table 10-7 at the end of this chapter shows all the channels and the geographic regions where they are used in both the United States and Canada.

Table 10-1: Channel Notes { }

- Canada East includes East Coast, St. Lawrence River, and Great Lakes
- {09}{25B}{28B}{83B} East Coast and St. Lawrence up to Montreal only
- {65A} Alberta, Saskatchewan, and Manitoba—except Lake Winnipeg and Red River only
- {66A} Excluding St. Lawrence River and Great Lakes
- {67} Lower Mississippi only
- {68} Marinas and yacht clubs
- {71} Marinas and yacht clubs—including Lake Winnipeg
- {79}{80} Great Lakes only
- {88} Near Canadian border only

General notes regarding table 10-1:

- U.S. channels are derived from FCC chart at wireless. fcc.gov, which is based on FCC rules 47 CFR 80.371 & 80.373.

- Canadian channels are derived from Schedule IV of Industry Canada Publication RIC-13, Section 8, Schedule IV (available on the Internet).

Digital Selective Calling (DSC)

Digital Selective Calling is a new automated calling system designed to replace the current voice calling system on channel 16. It also will work on newer MF/HF SSB radios. DSC allows automated calling of a particular station, or a group of stations, or all stations in an area.

A nine-digit *maritime mobile service identity* (**MMSI**) must be obtained and programmed into each DSC capable radio before using it for DSC transmission.

If your vessel requires a station radio license, the MMSI is obtained at the same time the radio license is obtained. If no station license is required, BoatUS, Sea Tow Service International, or MariTel are authorized to issue a MMSI. In Canada, the MMSI is obtained from your Industry Canada local office.

To make a DSC call, you set your radio to the working channel you wish to use, then key in the MMSI of the station you wish to call. If the receiving station answers, DSC will set the receiving station to the working channel and ring an alert to tell the receiving operator that he has a call.

The most important feature of a DSC capable radio is the ability to send a distress alert call by pressing a distress button for five seconds. Your radio sends the distress alert on channel 70 identifying you by the MMSI and also transmitting your latitude and longitude (only if your GPS is connected). If you are able to stay by the radio after sending the DSC distress alert, you should then monitor and communicate on channel 16 to further clarify your emergency.

Since DSC currently is in the implementation process, Coast Guard monitoring of DSC distress calls may not work reliably in all areas. The USCG states on its website, "Until this system is installed, the Coast Guard cannot reliably receive VHF DSC distress calls." The current schedule calls for completion of the system by 2006.

VHF Operation

Monitor 16

You are required to always monitor channel 16 when underway. Although channel 09 has been designated a calling channel for recreational boaters in the U.S., channel 16 should be monitored if your VHF is only capable of monitoring one channel. If it can monitor two channels then monitor both 16 and 09. The reason for this is that distress calls and Coast Guard alerts will always be on channel 16.

Voice Calling Procedure for Nondistress Calls

If you have DSC and your friend has DSC, and you both have obtained your MMSI (like you should have), then by all means use DSC to make calls between you. This will help free up overcrowded channel 16. Always try to make first contact at low power (1 watt).

If calling a coast station, call on their assigned channel unless you don't know it. Call other vessels on channel 16.

When initiating a call you must not call for more than 30 seconds. If there is no reply, you must wait at least two minutes before calling again. After three tries you must wait at least 15 minutes before calling again.

To Make a Call

1. Select the calling channel (usually 16).
2. Listen and wait until the channel is quiet.
3. Assume here the calling vessel is "Wandering Star" and the vessel being called is the "Puffin."
4. Press the transmit button and say, "Puffin, Puffin, this is Wandering Star." Include your call sign at the end if applicable. The name of the vessel being called or your vessel name can be repeated up to three times although once should be enough if you speak slowly and clearly.
5. If Puffin hears you, Puffin responds, "This is Puffin, switch to 72." This means Puffin is asking you to switch to working channel 72.
6. You reply, "Roger Puffin 72" to indicate you understand and are switching to 72.
7. You both switch to 72 and carry out the communications.
8. At the end of the communication, you say "Wandering Star out," Puffin says "Puffin out," and you both switch back to 16.

Some other points to consider when communicating by radio:

- Don't use CB terminology such as "do you read me?" or "come to me." *"Ten" radio codes are not used.*
- *Over* is used to end each transmission, although this is often left unsaid, since it's usually apparent when the other station has released the talk button.
- *Out* is used to sign off and end the communication.
- *Roger* means that the transmission is understood. It doesn't signify agreement.

- *Wilco* means the transmission is understood and you will comply. Roger wilco is redundant since roger is implied in wilco.
- *Affirmative* means yes.
- *Negative* means no.
- Only use the radio alphabet when it's important to get the letters correct. For example, use W-A-1-2-3-4 instead of Whiskey-Alpha-1-2-3-4 for a call sign, but if you are sending your MMSI to someone to program into their radio, use the radio alphabet to ensure accuracy.
- The radio alphabet is listed in table 10-5 on page 592 at the end of the chapter.
- Be careful to press the talk button *before* you start talking.
- When you are dreaming up names for your boat, you might want to consider that you will often be using your boat's name when using the radio, and an easily pronounced and understood name will be to your advantage.

Emergency Distress Calls
The spoken international emergency signals are:

Mayday is used to indicate that the vessel or persons onboard are threatened by grave and imminent danger and request immediate assistance.

Pan-pan is the urgency signal used when the safety of the ship or person is in jeopardy.

Securite (pronounced saycuritay) is used for safety or navigation messages or important weather warnings.

Figure 10-1 gives an example format for an emergency Mayday call. Post this or a similar form near the VHF so that anyone onboard can make the emergency call if need be. A larger size Adobe .pdf copy of this form can be downloaded from www.anchorcovepublishing.com.

Figure 10-2 is an example of a vessel information form that will be useful when a description of your vessel is requested. This should also be posted near the radio.

Latitude and longitude are the preferred way to describe your position.

SSB MARINE RADIO
Introduction
Whereas VHF radio range is limited to approximately 30 miles; *MF/HF* (**medium frequency/high frequency**) Marine radio range is measured in hundreds or even thousands of miles. MF/HF overcomes the horizon line of sight limita-

MAYDAY Call Procedure

Use the MAYDAY call only when you are in distress.
Distress is a situation where you or your boat are
threatened by grave or immediate danger.

1. If within VHF range use VHF rather than MF/HF radio.
2. Make sure the radio is ON.
3. Set VHF channel 16 or MF/HF 2182 kHz
4. Transmit: MAYDAY   MAYDAY   MAYDAY
5. This is: _____ _____ _____   Boat Name   Boat Name   Boat Name

6. Our position is: Latitude ___ deg ___ min N
   or   Longitude ___ deg ___ min W
 Our position is _____ _____ _____
     Distance   Direction   Navaid or
     (miles, ft,   (NE, SW,   Landmark
     km, m, etc.   or bearing
              deg)

7. State problem: _____
     We are sinking, on fire,
     or have a heart attack, etc.

8. State urgency _____   How long you can stay afloat, etc.

9. We need: _____
     Describe assistance required,
     pumps, tow, medical, etc.

10. Number of persons on board is ____ and ____   adults   children   The number of injured is: _____
11. Our vessel is a _____ foot powerboat / sailboat
12. OVER
13. Release transmit and listen for a reply
If no-one answers repeat steps 4-13

FIGURE 10-1: Mayday Example Call Procedure

Vessel Description

Vessel Name: _____

Home Port:			
Make and Year:			
Country / Flag			
Registration / Documentation / License No.			

Length:		Displacement	
Color: Hull	Cabin		Trim
Type: Sail ☐ Power☐		Fuel: Diesel ☐ Gas☐	
Drive: Inboard ☐	Outdrive☐	Outboard ☐	

Communication Equipment			
Type	Freq / Number	Type	Freq / Number
VHF		Cell Phone	
DSC		Sat Phone	
SSB		CB	

Navigation Equipment				
Compass ☐	GPS ☐	Charts ☐	Radar ☐	Loran ☐

Survival Equipment

Life Jackets ☐	Horn ☐
Flares ☐	Dinghy / raft ☐
Mirror ☐	Paddles ☐
Smoke Signal ☐	EPIRB 121.5 / 243.0 ☐
Anchor ☐	EPIRB 406 ☐
Flashlights ☐	EPIRB 406 w. GPS ☐

FIGURE 10-2: Example Vessel Description

tion, by using frequencies that allow radio signals to bounce off the ionosphere and back to earth. The MF/HF radio is also commonly called a **SSB (single side band) radiotelephone** or **marine radio**.

FIGURE 10-3: MF/HF Radio Waves and the Ionosphere

The MF/HF radio is actually a shortwave radio designed specifically for marine use and has selectable channels much like a VHF radio.

A MF/HF radio should be considered a necessity by anyone venturing offshore even though some form of satellite communications might also be available. Marine safety bulletins, weather broadcasts, and even weather faxes can be received with a HF radio. In addition to the safety aspect, marine nets have become commonplace, where like-minded cruisers discuss topics of mutual interest at sea.

Email services are also available for HF, although they are slow and need favorable conditions. If you can afford it, some form of satellite communications is a better alternative for email.

MF/HF Channels

Use of the MF/HF radio is somewhat similar to the VHF radio, in that there are calling channels and working channels; however, the MF/HF radio differs in that there are a number of frequency bands with a number of channels in each band and within each band there are calling channels and working channels. The frequency bands used are 2 MHz, 4 MHz, 8 MHz, 12 MHz, 16 MHz, 18 MHz, 22 MHz, and 25 MHz. The 2 MHz band is a MF band and the 4 MHz through 25 MHz bands are HF bands.

Channels numbers are constructed by appending a number, that increments sequentially starting from 01, to the one or 2 digit band number. For example in the 4 MHz band the channels would be numbered 401, 402, 403, etc. The channels in the 16 MHz band would look like 1601, 1602, 1603, etc.

In the MF band the international distress channel (similar to VHF 16) is at frequency 2182 kHz (2.182 MHz). The Coast Guard monitors this channel but at some time in the future may discontinue monitoring it in favor of DSC. As of February 1, 1999, commercial ships were required to have DSC radio equipment operational and were no longer required to monitor the 2182 kHz distress channel after that date.

The Coast Guard also monitors the following HF channels:

ITU Channel Number	Coast Transmit	Ship Transmit
424	4426 kHz	4134 kHz
601	6501 kHz	6200 kHz
816	8764 kHz	8240 kHz
1205	13,089 kHz	12,242 kHz
1625	17,314 kHz	16,432 kHz

TABLE 10-2: Coast Guard Monitored HF Channels

Channels and frequencies for each channel are listed in the radio operating instructions and are not detailed here.

Distance Versus Frequency
In general, the lower frequency bands are used for communicating over shorter distances, and the higher bands are used over longer distances.

The maximum communication distance varies with the seasons, with day and night, and with sunspot activity. Approximate distance ranges associated with various frequency bands are:

Freq From	Freq To	Min. Distance	Max. Distance
2 MHz	6 MHz	200 nm	800 nm
4 MHz	12 MHz	800 nm	1500 nm
6 MHz	22 MHz	1500 nm	

TABLE 10-3: MF/HF Communications Range

There are charts and graphs available that indicate the best frequencies to try, depending on the time of day and desired communication range.

Installation and Cost of HF Radio
Installation of HF radio equipment is far more difficult than a VHF installation. Proper antenna selection and installation

is critical for successful HF radio operation. Even more critical is the installation of a proper grounding system, which consists of a long copper strip along the outside of the hull. Ideally, this work is done as the boat is being built.

MF/HF marine radio purchase cost is in the range of $1000 to $3000 (not including installation) but unlike satellite communications, once it's installed, there is no operating cost.

CB RADIO

A *citizens band* (**CB**) radio is a fixed mount radio similar to an installed VHF radio; however, it is not meant for marine communications and is not monitored by the Coast Guard or other boaters and thus is not suitable for distress related communications.

It can be useful, however, for nonoperations conversations of a type not allowed on the VHF radio. Here you can discuss the fish you caught, exchange recipes, organize a party, etc. Of course, the boat you communicate with must have one installed too, so CB will be most useful among two or more boats similarly equipped and traveling together. Aside from this, a CB is not a particularly useful thing to have on a boat.

The CB can transmit at up to 4 watts and has a whip antenna so range will be a little less than a VHF radio. There are 40 channels available for CB radios that are distributed from 26.965 MHz to 27.405 MHz. Channel 09 is reserved for emergency communications or traveler assistance. There are no officially designated calling or working channels.

FRS RADIO

Family Radio System (**FRS**) radios are handheld radios that look much like a handheld VHF radio or walkie talkie. Since you are not allowed to use a handheld VHF radio on shore, an FRS radio provides an ideal means of communication between a vessel and someone on shore. It also provides a means of communicating between vessels cruising together, and unlike VHF allows for idle chitchat of a nonoperational nature.

Since these can be used on land, they are also useful for hikers, skiers, hunters, or even for maintaining contact between two cars traveling together.

FRS radios have 14 channels and transmit at a maximum of 0.5 watts. No license is required to operate these. Transmitting at 0.5 watts will give you a range of about 2 miles over water. Table 10-4 shows the channels and frequencies for the 14 FRS channels.

Many FRS radios also include *General Mobile Radio Service* (**GMRS**) capability. FRS/GMRS radios have channels as shown in table 10-4. GMRS allows greater transmit power but requires an FCC license to operate. A five-year renewable license is currently $75 and is obtained by filing FCC Form 605 or filing online with the FCC Universal Licensing System (ULS) found at http://wireless.fcc.gov/uls/ .

Channel	Type	Frequency (MHz)	Typical Power (Watts)
1	GMRS/FRS	462.5625	1 to 5
2	GMRS/FRS	462.5875	1 to 5
3	GMRS/FRS	462.6125	1 to 5
4	GMRS/FRS	462.6375	1 to 5
5	GMRS/FRS	462.6625	1 to 5
6	GMRS/FRS	462.6875	1 to 5
7	GMRS/FRS	462.7125	1 to 5
8	FRS	467.5625	0.5
9	FRS	467.5875	0.5
10	FRS	467.6125	0.5
11	FRS	467.6375	0.5
12	FRS	467.6625	0.5
13	FRS	467.6875	0.5
14	FRS	467.7125	0.5
15	GMRS	462.5500	1 to 5
16	GMRS	462.5750	1 to 5
17	GMRS	462.6000	1 to 5
18	GMRS	462.6250	1 to 5
19	GMRS	462.6500	1 to 5
20	GMRS	462.6750	1 to 5
21	GMRS	462.7000	1 to 5
22	GMRS	462.7250	1 to 5

TABLE 10-4: FRS and GMRS Channels (United States)

Note that in Canada, use of FRS was legal, but GMRS was not until September of 2004. For more information go to http://strategis.ic.gc.ca/epic/internet/insmt-gst.nsf/en/sf08145e.html, or if you don't want to type all that in, just do a search on "Canada gmrs frs regulations."

POINT-TO-POINT COMMUNICATIONS
CELL PHONES
It's a good idea to have a cell phone onboard any boat, but not as a substitute for a VHF marine radio.

The original cell phone system was analog and some of the car phones and the old "bag" phones operated at 3 watts, while most cell phones sold now are digital and transmit at a maximum power of 0.6 watts. Most digital cell phones revert to analog mode if a digital signal is not available, but they still are limited to 0.6 watt power. With this low power you'll be lucky to get a digital cell phone to operate more than 5 miles from the nearest cell phone tower which is, of course, located on the shore somewhere. As you know from personal experience, once you get far away from towns or highways, the chances of hooking up are slim.

You can purchase cell phone amplifiers and antennas that will considerably improve your communication range and quality with cell phones. Just the use of a good antenna mounted high on the boat will improve operation considerably and adding an amplifier that can boost the signal to 3 watts (the legal limit) can increase useful range to 10 or 15 miles and maybe a little beyond.

SATELLITE COMMUNICATIONS
Introduction

Discussions herein are limited to two-way communications systems; broadcast radio and television communications are not covered.

INMARSAT, *Iridium*, and *Globalstar* are the leading providers of two-way satellite communications services of interest to recreational boaters. INMARSAT has been providing service since the late 1980s and uses four high earth orbit geosynchronous satellites whereas the newer providers, both Iridium and Globalstar, use many low earth orbit satellites.

There are other suppliers currently in this market and more are entering all the time. Change is taking place so rapidly, particularly with respect to Internet access, that any discussion beyond the big three providers is likely be obsolete by the time this book gets published, so we'll restrict ourselves to a brief discussion of these three.

Anyone planning to invest in a satellite communications phone needs to understand that each of these systems has definite strengths and weaknesses, and the homework needs to be done before committing to any particular system. Example prices shown here are from various Internet sites and are current as of 2005. Prices are generally trending downward for all the satellite services, so expect to do as well or better for any of these services in the future.

Inmarsat

This is the original satellite system designed to provide point-to-point, voice and data marine communications, and has about 90 percent market share in the marine satellite communications business. Various versions of the system have been implemented as INMARSAT A, B, C, D, E, and M. Inmarsat A through D are suitable only for ships or larger yachts. Inmarsat Mini-M is designed to use smaller equipment suitable for use on smaller size vessels and is the system of interest to off shore cruisers.

Inmarsat claims to be the most truly global system with virtually no dead spots in the areas it covers. Almost all the earth to 75 degrees latitude is covered. Because geosynchronous satellites are stationary (relative to any location on earth) calls are not dropped as often they are with low earth orbit systems, as satellites move out of view to be replaced by others.

A Mini-M portable phone can be purchased for about $2400 and an installed system from $3000 to $5000 and up. The portable phone is the size of a small laptop computer and weighs in at about 5 pounds and like all portable satellite phones must almost always be used outdoors. Since the Inmarsat geosynchronous satellites are 22,000 miles high versus just a few hundred miles for the Iridium and Globalstar systems, the equipment is heavier, has a larger antenna, and requires more power to operate. The Mini-M voice phones also support data and fax at 2400 baud.

Call pricing is about $1.75/minute for calls within a zone that includes the United States, Canada, and Europe. A worldwide pricing plan is about $2.15/minute. These are pay-as-you-go plans since there are no monthly minimums or fees with either plan.

Iridium

The Iridium system consists of 66 satellites plus 6 backup satellites in low earth orbit (about 500 miles). When you make a call, you will be routed through one of the nearest satellites, then through other satellites to the ground station nearest your call destination. As the nearest satellite moves away, your call is transferred to another satellite much as you are transferred from tower to tower with a cell phone. Additionally, as with a cell phone, calls are sometimes dropped during the transfer attempt.

Theoretically, the entire earth including the poles is covered; however, there are claims of a few spots where calls cannot be made.

Permanently installed phones are available for approximately $2500 and handheld phones are available for around $1100. As you might expect, the permanently installed phone will give considerably better service. The permanent install phone may be used with any standard desk or cordless phone connected via a standard RJ-11 phone jack.

The hand held phones weigh about 13 ounces, not as large as the original old-style cell phones but quite a bit larger than the typical modern cell phone. Iridium offers data at 2400 baud through the voice phones. Generally, handheld satellite phones must be used outdoors.

A typical monthly plan is $35/month plus $1.50/minute. Other higher volume plans can get this down to around $1/ minute. These rates are from anywhere in the world to a land phone anywhere else in the world.

Globalstar

Globalstar is also a low earth orbit system using 44 satellites plus 4 backup satellites; however, unlike Iridium, calls are routed through ground stations to the destination, rather than through other satellites. Similar to the Iridium system, calls can be dropped as satellites move overhead. Globalstar's website claims it has better voice quality and fewer dropped calls than other carriers. At the time of this writing, Globalstar provides service in North and South America (including the Caribbean), Europe, Russia, and Australia. The Middle East and China can expect coverage in the near future. Africa, India, and Indonesia are not currently covered. More than about 200 miles offshore are generally not covered so this is not a system for the high seas. However, this is an excellent system for use with coastal cruising.

A Globalstar phone for permanent mounting in your boat will cost about $1000 for voice only and $2300 to $2600 for a voice and data unit. The Globalstar fixed phone may be used with any standard desktop or cordless phone for access from anywhere in the vessel. Data transfer rates on these is 9600 baud.

A handheld phone is priced around $500 and weighs in at about 14 ounces and it also supports data at 9600 baud. These are tri-mode phones that can also be used as cell phones on CDMA 800 networks and the older AMPS analog networks; however, you will probably use your own cell phone company for these ground-based services and will need to have a different phone number (in the same phone). Like the Iridium handheld phone, this phone must usually be used outdoors.

Although Globalstar isn't truly global, they have generally cheaper rates if one is willing to commit to a monthly plan, much as one does with a cell phone. Examples of monthly plans for the United States and Caribbean zone include: 50 minutes for $50/month = $1/minute, 150 minutes for $65/month = $0.43/minute, or 4000 minutes for $550/month for a unit cost of $0.14/minute. Calls outside of the domestic zone (roaming) are about $1.39/minute and don't use up minutes from the monthly plan. This includes calls to and from Europe. Calls from Canada are just $0.75/minute.

Satellite Phone Rentals

All the three types of satellite phones are available for rental on a daily, weekly or monthly basis which may make sense for cruising less than a month a year. These are also handy if you need to make calls from a cruise ship as the rates are much cheaper than the ship's rates which can be over $10 per minute.

TABLES
THE RADIO ALPHABET

A	Alpha	N	November
B	Bravo	O	Oscar
C	Charlie	P	Papa
D	Delta	Q	Quebec
E	Echo	R	Romeo
F	Foxtrot	S	Sierra
G	Golf	T	Tango
H	Hotel	U	Uniform
I	India	V	Victor
J	Juliet	W	Whiskey
K	Kilo	X	X-ray
L	Lima	Y	Yankee
M	Mike	Z	Zulu

TABLE 10-5: The Radio Alphabet

VHF CHANNELS

Channel		Xmt MHz	Rec MHz	Channel		Xmt MHz	Rec MHz
	60	156.025	160.625	18A		156.900	156.900
1A		156.050	156.050		78A	156.925	156.925
1		156.050	160.650	19A		156.950	156.950
	61A	156.075	156.075		79A	156.975	156.975
2		156.100	160.700	20A		157.000	157.000
	62A	156.125	156.125	20		157.000	161.600
3		156.150	160.750		80A	157.025	157.025
	63A	156.175	156.175	21A		157.050	157.050
4A		156.200	156.200	21B			161.650
	64A	156.225	156.225		81A	157.075	157.075
	64	156.225	160.825	22A		157.100	157.100
5A		156.250	156.250		82A	157.125	157.125
	65A	156.275	156.275	23A		157.150	157.150
6		156.300	156.300	23		157.150	161.750
	66A	156.325	156.325		83A	157.175	157.175
7A		156.350	156.350	83		157.175	161.775
	67	156.375	156.375	83B			161.775
8		156.400	156.400	24		157.200	161.800
	68	156.425	156.425		84	157.225	161.825
9		156.450	156.450	25		157.250	161.850
	69	156.475	156.475	25B			161.850
10		156.500	156.500		85	157.275	161.875
	70	156.525	156.525	26		157.300	161.900
11		156.550	156.550		86	157.325	161.925
	71	156.575	156.575	27		157.350	161.950
12		156.600	156.600		87	157.375	161.975
	72	156.625	156.625	28		157.400	162.000
13		156.650	156.650	28B			162.000
	73	156.675	156.675		88A	157.425	157.425
14		156.700	156.700	88		157.425	162.025
	74	156.725	156.725	WX2			162.400
15			156.750	WX4			162.425
	75		156.775	WX5			162.450
16		156.800	156.800	WX3			162.475
	76		156.825	WX6			162.500
17		156.850	156.850	WX7			162.525
	77	156.875	156.875	WX1			162.550

TABLE 10-6: VHF Channel Frequency Assignments

Channel	United States	Canada	Key: Blank = service generally available in that country ✓ = service only in that area of that country X = service not available in that area P = service available in part of area Service
01A	U		Port Operations or VTS or Commercial Working
01		C	Public Correspondence (Marine Operator) duplex
02		C	Public Correspondence (Marine Operator) duplex
03		C	Public Correspondence (Marine Operator) duplex
04A		C	Canada Coast Guard Search & Rescue
		C	Working channel -commercial fishing only
05A	U	C	Port Operations or VTS
06	U	C	Search & rescue, Intership safety
07A	U	C	Working channel commercial
08	U	C	Working channel commercial (Intership only)
09	U		Working ch all vessels & Non-commercial calling
		C	Working channel all vessels & Ship movement
10	U		Working channel commercial
		C	Working channel all vessels & Ship movement
11	U		Working channel commercial, VTS some areas
		C	Working channel all vessels & Ship movement
12	U	C	Port Operations. VTS in selected areas.
13	U		Nav Safety (Bridge-to-bridge), locks, drawbridges
		C	Navigation Safety (Bridge-to-bridge)
14	U		Port Operations. VTS in selected areas, Locks
		C	Port Operations. pilot information & messages
15			Environmental (Receive only). Class C EPIRBs.
		C	All vessels, ship movement (1 Watt)
16	U	C	International Distress, Safety and Calling
17	U		State & Local maritime control
		C	Commercial & Non-comm. ship movement
18A	U	C	Working channel commercial
19A	U		Working channel commercial
		C	Canadian Coast Guard only
		C	Government use
20	U	C	Port Operations (duplex) ship to coast
20A	U		Port Operations
21A	U	C	U.S. & Canada Coast Guard only
21B		C	Safety-Continuous Marine Broadcast Svc (CMB)
22A	U	C	Coast Guard Liaison & in the U.S. Maritime Safety Information Broadcasts
23A	U		U.S. Coast Guard only
23		C	Public Correspondence (Marine Operator) duplex

TABLE 10-7(1a): VHF Channels Areas of Operation

Channel	United States								Canada				Xmt MHz	Rec MHz
	New Orleans	Lower Mississippi	Houston	Great Lakes	St Lawrence River	Seattle	Puget Sound	Str Juan de Fuca	Pacific Coast	Great Lakes (1)	St Lawrence River	Atlantic Coast (2)		
01A	✓	✓											156.050	156.050
01									✓				156.050	160.650
02									✓				156.100	160.700
03									✓				156.150	160.750
04A									✓	✓	P		156.200	156.200
05A	✓		✓			✓							156.250	156.250
06													156.300	156.300
07A													156.350	156.350
08													156.400	156.400
09											P	✓	156.450	156.450
10													156.500	156.500
10										✓	✓	✓	156.500	156.500
11													156.550	156.550
12													156.600	156.600
13													156.650	156.650
14										✓	✓	✓	156.700	156.700
15													--	156.750
15													156.750	156.750
16													156.800	156.800
17													156.850	156.850
18A													156.900	156.900
19A								X					156.950	156.950
19A									✓					
20													157.000	161.600
20A													157.000	157.000
21A													157.050	157.050
21B														161.650
22A													157.100	157.100
23A													157.150	157.150
23									✓				157.150	161.750

TABLE 10-7(1b): VHF Channels Areas of Operation

Channel	United States	Canada	Key: Blank = service generally available in that country ✔ = service only in that area of that country X = service not available in that area P = service available in part of area Service
24	U	C	Public Correspondence (Marine Operator) duplex
25	U	C	Public Correspondence (Marine Operator) duplex
25B		C	Safety -Continuous Marine Broadcast Service (CMB)
26	U	C	Public Correspondence (Marine Operator) duplex
27	U	C	Public Correspondence (Marine Operator) duplex
28	U	C	Public Correspondence (Marine Operator) duplex
28B		C	Safety -Continuous Marine Broadcase Service (CMB)
60	U	C	Public Correspondence (Marine Operator) duplex
61A		C	Canadian Coast Guard Only
		C	Working channel -commercial fishing only
62A		C	Canadian Coast Guard Only
		C	Working channel -commercial fishing only
63A	U		Working commercial or Port Operations or VTS
64		C	Public Correspondence (Marine Operator) duplex
64A		C	Working channel -commercial fishing only
65A	U		Port Operations
		C	Multiple use
66A	U	C	Port Operations (1 Watt max Canada)
		C	Working channel all vessels
67		U	Working channel commercial intership, & locks and drawbridges
	U		Navigational (Bridge-to-bridge)
		C	Working channel all vessels
		C	Working channel -commercial fishing
68		U	Working channel non-commercial
		C	Marinas and Yacht Clubs
69	U		Working channel non-commercial
		C	Working channel all vessels
		C	Working channel -commercial fishing
70	U	C	Digital Selective Calling (voice communications not allowed)
71		U	Working channel non-commercial
		C	Working channel all vessels, ship movement
		C	Marinas & Yacht Clubs -East Coast & Lake Winnipeg
72	U	C	Working channel non-commercial (Intership only)
		C	Working channel commercial (Intership only)

TABLE 10-7(2a): VHF Channels Areas of Operation

Channel	United States								Canada				Xmt MHz	Rec MHz
	New Orleans	Lower Mississippi	Houston	Great Lakes	St Lawrence River	Seattle	Puget Sound	Str Juan de Fuca	Pacific Coast	Great Lakes (1)	St Lawrence River	Atlantic Coast (2)		
24													157.200	161.800
25									✓				157.250	161.850
25B												✓		161.850
26													157.300	161.900
27													157.350	161.950
28									✓				157.400	162.000
28B												✓		162.000
60									✓				156.025	160.625
61A									✓	✓	✓	✓	156.075	156.075
62A									✓	✓	✓	✓	156.125	156.125
63A	P	P											156.175	156.175
64									✓				156.225	160.825
64A										✓	✓	✓	156.225	156.225
65A													156.275	156.275
66A										X	X		156.325	156.325
67		✓							✓	✓	✓	✓	156.375	156.375
68													156.425	156.425
69									✓	✓	✓	✓	156.475	156.475
70													156.525	156.525
71													156.575	156.575
71									✓				156.575	156.575
71										✓	✓	✓	156.575	156.575
72							✓	✓					156.625	156.625
72							✓	✓					156.625	156.625

TABLE 10-7(2b): VHF Channels Areas of Operation

Channel	United States	Canada	Key: Blank = service generally available in that country ✓ = service only in that area of that country X = service not available in that area P = service available in part of area Service
	U		Port Operations
73		C	Working channel all vessels, marinas north of Campbell River
		C	Working channel -commercial fishing
74	U		Port Operations
		C	Working channel all vessels, ship movement
75	U	C	Not available -guard band for channel 16
76	U	C	Not available -guard band for channel 16
77	U	C	Intership to pilots only
		C	Port Operations (1 Watt max)
78A	U		Working channel non-commercial
		C	Working channel commercial
79A	U	C	Working channel commercial
	U		Working channel non-commercial
80A	U	C	Working channel commercial
	U		Working channel non-commercial
81A	U		U.S. Government only - Environmental protection operations.
		C	Canada Coast Guard Use only
82A	U		U.S. Government only
		C	Canada Coast Guard Use only
83		C	Canada Coast Guard Use only (duplex)
83A	U		U.S. Coast Guard only
		C	Canada Coast Guard and Other Govt Agencies
83A		C	Safety -Continuous Marine Broadcase Svc (CMB)
84	U	C	Public Correspondence (Marine Operator) duplex
85	U	C	Public Correspondence (Marine Operator) duplex
86	U	C	Public Correspondence (Marine Operator) duplex
87	U	C	Public Correspondence (Marine Operator) duplex
88	U	C	Public Correspondence only near Canadian border.
88A	U		Working channel commercial intership
Wx1	U	C	NOAA Weather (CMB in Canada)
Wx2	U	C	NOAA Weather (CMB in Canada)
Wx3	U	C	NOAA Weather (CMB in Canada)
Wx4	U	C	NOAA Weather (CMB in Canada)
Wx5	U	C	NOAA Weather (CMB in Canada)
Wx6	U	C	NOAA Weather (CMB in Canada)
Wx7	U	C	NOAA Weather (CMB in Canada)

TABLE 10-7(3a): VHF Channels Areas of Operation

Channel	New Orleans	Lower Mississippi	Houston	Great Lakes	St Lawrence River	Seattle	Puget Sound	Str Juan de Fuca	Pacific Coast	Great Lakes (1)	St Lawrence River	Atlantic Coast (2)	Xmt MHz	Rec MHz
73									✔				156.675	156.675
										✔	✔	✔		
74													156.725	156.725
75														156.775
76														156.825
77									✔				156.875	156.875
										✔	✔			
78A													156.925	156.925
79A				X									156.975	156.975
				✔										
80A				X									157.025	157.025
				✔										
81A									✔	✔	✔		157.075	157.075
82A									✔	✔	✔		157.125	157.125
83									✔				157.175	161.775
83A										✔	✔	✔	157.175	157.175
83B										✔	✔	✔		161.775
84									✔				157.225	161.825
85										✔	✔	✔	157.275	161.875
86									✔				157.325	161.925
87										✔	✔	✔	157.375	161.975
88				✔	✔		✔	✔		✔	✔	✔	157.425	162.025
88A				X	X		X	X					157.425	157.425
Wx1														162.550
Wx2														162.400
Wx3														162.475
Wx4														162.425
Wx5														162.450
Wx6														162.500
Wx7														162.525

TABLE 10-7(3b): VHF Channels Areas of Operation

INTERNATIONAL CODE OF FLAG SIGNALS

The flags for the letters A to Z and numerals 0 to 9 are shown in the color plates on page Q28 in the Quick Reference color plates near the center of this book. Table 10-8 gives one-, two-, and three-letter (flag) codes and their meaning.

This table does not give all the signals specified in the *International Code of Signals*; only the more common signals are listed. The complete text of the *International Code of Signals* is available as an Adobe .pdf download of *Publication 102* from http://pollux.nss.nima.mil/pubs/.

Flags are hoisted so that the flags are read from the top down.

A complete set of flags includes only one flag for each letter and numeral. The three *substitute* or *repeater* flags are used to repeat letters or numerals where necessary. Letters are considered one *class* of flags and numbers are another *class*.

- The 1st substitute flag indicates a repeat of the 1st flag in the class of flags preceding the substitute.
- The 2nd substitute flag indicates a repeat of the 2nd flag in the class preceding.
- The 3rd substitute flag indicates a repeat of the 3rd flag in the class preceding.

Here are three examples of how this works taken from *Publication 102:*

The signal VV is made as follows:
» V
» 1st substitute

The signal 1100 is:
» 1
» 1st substitute in the class (of numbers)
» 0
» 3rd substitute to repeat the 3rd flag in the class

The signal L233 is:
» L
» 2
» 3
» 2nd substitute –repeats 2nd numeral class flag
» 0

The answering station responds with the code/answer flag.

The transmitting station hoists the answer flag after the last hoist of signals.

Note: For pictures of signal flags see page Q28 of the color plates.

Flags	Signals
A	Diver down; keep well clear at low speed.
B	Loading, discharging, or carrying dangerous cargo.
C	Yes or affirmative.
D	I am maneuvering with difficulty; keep clear.
E	I am changing my course to starboard.
F	I am disabled; communicate with me.
G	I require a pilot.
H	I have a pilot onboard.
I	I am changing my course to poet.
J	I am on fire and have dangerous cargo; keep clear.
K	I wish to communicate with you.
L	You should stop your vessel immediately.
M	My vessel is stopped; making no way.
N	No or negative.
O	Man overboard.
P	About to leave port; return to ship.
Q	Request pratique; ship meets health regulations.
R	No code.
S	Moving astern.
T	Keep clear.
U	You are running into danger.
V	I require assistance.
W	I require medical assistance.
X	Stop carrying out your intentions and watch for my signal.
Y	I am dragging anchor.
Z	I require a tug.
AC	I am abandoning my vessel.
AE	I must abandon my vessel.
AE1	I (or crew of vessel indicated) wish to abandon my (or their) vessel but have not the means.
AE2	I shall abandon my vessel unless you will remain by me, ready to assist.
AF	I do not intend to abandon my vessel.
AF1	Do you intend to abandon your vessel?
AN	I need a doctor.
BR	I require a helicopter urgently.
CB	I require immediate assistance.
CB4	I require immediate assistance; I am aground.
CB5	I require immediate assistance; I am drifting.
CB6	I require immediate assistance; I am on fire.
CB7	I require immediate assistance; I have sprung a leak.
CJ	Do you require assistance?

TABLE 10-8(1): International Code of Flag Signals

Flags	Signals
CK	Assistance is no longer required.
CV	I am unable to give assistance.
DX	I am sinking.
DV	I am drifting.
ED	Your distress signals are understood.
EF	SOS/Mayday has been cancelled.
FA	Will you give me my position?
GW	Man overboard.
IL	I can only proceed at slow speed.
IT	I am on fire.
IX	Fire is gaining.
IM	I request to be escorted until further notice.
IW	Fire is under control.
IZ	Fire has been extinguished.
JG	I am aground/in danger.
JH	I am aground. I am not in danger.
JI	Are you aground?
JL	You are running risk of going aground.
JO	I am afloat.
JW	I have sprung a leak.
JX	Leak is gaining rapidly.
KM	I can take you in tow.
KN	I cannot take you in tow.
LO	I am not in my correct position (used by light vessel).
MG	You should steer course...course follows.
NC	I am in distress and require immediate assistance.
NG	You are in a dangerous position.
NH	You are clear of all dangers.
PD	Your navigation lights are not visible.
PH	You should steer as indicated.
PI	You should maintain your present course.
PP	Keep well clear of me.
QD	I am going ahead.
QO	You should not come.
QP	I will come alongside.
QR	I cannot come alongside.
QT	You should not anchor; you are going to foul my anchor.
QQ	I require health clearance.
QU	Anchoring is prohibited.
QX	I request permission to anchor.
RA	My anchor is foul.
RB	I am dragging my anchor.

TABLE 10-8(2): International Code of Flag Signals

Flags	Signals
RN	My engines are out of action.
RY	You should proceed at slow speed when passing me (or vessel making signal).
RU	Keep clear of me; I am maneuvering with difficulty.
SC	I am underway.
SD	I am not ready to get underway.
SO	You should stop your vessel instantly.
SQ	You should stop or heave to.
UM	The harbor is closed to traffic.
UN	You may enter harbor immediately.
UO	You must not enter harbor.
UP	Permission to enter harbor is urgently requested. I have an emergency.
UW	I wish you a pleasant voyage.
VJ	Gale is expected from direction.
VK	Storm is expected from the direction indicated.
YU	I am going to communicate with your station with the International Code of Signals.
ZD1	Please report me to the Coast Guard, New York.
ZD2	Please report me to Lloyd's of London.
ZK	I cannot distinguish your signal. Please repeat it by...
ZL	You signal has been received but not understood.
ZM	You should send (or speak) more slowly.

TABLE 10-8(2): International Code of Flag Signals

INTERNATIONAL MORSE CODE

A	•—	R	•—•	9	————•
B	—•••	S	•••	0	—————
C	—•—•	T	—	,	——••——
D	—••	U	••—	;	—•—•—•
E	•	V	•••—	:	———•••
F	••—•	W	•——	.	•—•—•—
G	——•	X	—••—	?	••——••
H	••••	Y	—•——	'	•————•
I	••	Z	——••	-	—••••—
J	•———	1	•————	=	—•••—
K	—•—	2	••———	/	—••—•
L	•—••	3	•••——	(	—•——•—
M	——	4	••••—	)	—•——•—
N	—•	5	•••••	Error	••••••••
O	———	6	—••••	Wait	•—•••
P	•——•	7	——•••	End Msg	•—•—•
Q	——•—	8	———••	End Work	•••—•—

TABLE 10-9: International Morse Code

THE SEMAPHORE ALPHABET

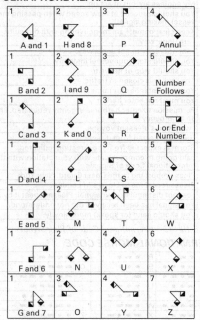

TABLE 10-10: The Semaphore Alphabet

The semaphore alphabet is shown here mostly as an interesting curiosity since no one except Boy Scouts uses it any more. The letters and numbers are shown here ordered here by their circles rather than in alphabetic order. The circle number is shown in the upper left hand corner of each box in figure 10-10. The circles are sequenced down the columns.

A number is sent by preceding the numbers with the "number follows" signal and following the numbers with the "end number" signal.

11 BOAT TRAILERING

INTRODUCTION

Most recreational boats are small enough to be trailerable, and although many are never trailered and are left in the water for the boating season, a large percentage is towed by owners to various boating locales. Accidents occur for various reasons but primarily because of improper loading, inadequate trailer maintenance, and driver error. Almost all of these accidents can be prevented by exercising proper care in selecting and maintaining the trailering equipment and by adjusting driving habits to allow for the extra weight of the trailer and its load behind the tow vehicle.

TRAILERING EQUIPMENT

THE BOAT TRAILER

Capacity

First and foremost, a boat trailer must be of sufficient capacity to carry the boat and all the supplies and equipment that are typically loaded into the boat. This means the capacity must be enough to allow for all that extra camping gear and other stuff you put in the boat.

If the trailer was purchased with the boat, there is a good chance the trailer is sized adequately for the unloaded boat but will not be up to the task when all the aforementioned supplies and hardware are loaded into the boat. If that's the case, then you must either be careful not to overload the boat or acquire a new adequately sized trailer. *Do not drive with an overloaded trailer!*

The total weight of the trailer with loaded boat is the ***gross trailer weight*** (**GTW**).

Single and Tandem Axle

Boat trailers usually come with one or two (tandem) axles, although three axles are found on some trailers for larger boats. Generally, tandem axle trailers tend to track better and are less prone to fishtailing. The extra wheels also provide a safety factor in the event of a blowout. The downside of tandem axle trailers is that they are harder to turn, which makes them difficult to maneuver by hand.

Trailer Weight Ratings

The *gross vehicle weight rating* (**GVWR**) is the maximum total allowable load including the trailer and the boat with everything loaded into it (i.e., the maximum allowable GTW).

The *gross axle weight rating* (**GAWR**) is the load capacity of a single axle and with a single axle trailer is equal to the GVWR for the trailer. The GVWR for a tandem axle trailer is two times the GAWR.

The GVWR and GAWR of the trailer must be specified on a plate attached to the frame somewhere near the front of the trailer.

Figure 11-1 shows a typical trailer rating plate for a tandem axle trailer. Note how the sum of the front GAWR plus the rear GAWR equals the GVWR.

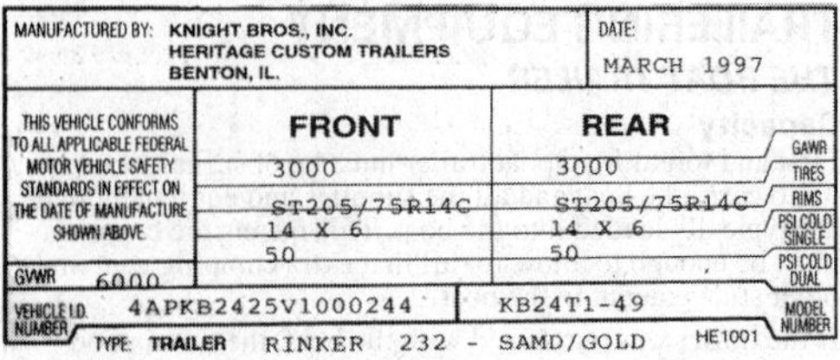

MANUFACTURED BY:	KNIGHT BROS., INC. HERITAGE CUSTOM TRAILERS BENTON, IL.		DATE: MARCH 1997	
THIS VEHICLE CONFORMS TO ALL APPLICABLE FEDERAL MOTOR VEHICLE SAFETY STANDARDS IN EFFECT ON THE DATE OF MANUFACTURE SHOWN ABOVE.	**FRONT**		**REAR**	GAWR
	3000		3000	TIRES
	ST205/75R14C		ST205/75R14C	RIMS
	14 X 6		14 X 6	PSI COLD SINGLE
	50		50	PSI COLD DUAL
GVWR 6000				
VEHICLE I.D. NUMBER	4APKB2425V1000244		KB24T1-49	MODEL NUMBER
TYPE: **TRAILER**	RINKER 232 - SAMD/GOLD			HE1001

FIGURE 11-1: Trailer Rating Plate

What Capacity Trailer Is Required?

If you own the boat but haven't bought the trailer yet, or are now purchasing the boat and have a choice of trailer capacities, consider specifying a trailer with a GVWR that is at least 15 percent greater than the combined weight of the trailer, the boat, and the anticipated extra load.

If you already have the trailer and boat, and you're not sure of the weight, a trip to the local truck scale is in order. You might find scales at the local gravel pit or landscaping supplier. To get an accurate weight, drive over the scale until only the trailer and swivel jack are over the scale and then disconnect the trailer from the tow vehicle. Don't forget to place trailer wheel chocks before disconnecting the trailer.

Ideally, you do the weighing both with the boat unloaded and loaded (GTW). If the unloaded weight is determined, then an estimate of the fully loaded (GTW) condition should be made, to compare to the trailer GVWR. Again, you're look-

FIGURE 11-2: Weighing the Boat and Trailer

ing for the rated GVWR to be at least 15 percent more than the full load (GTW).

Load Distribution

The *tongue weight* (**TW**) is the downward force exerted by the fully loaded trailer on the hitch ball by the trailer coupler.

In addition to the total load being less than the GTW, the load must also be properly distributed between the trailer wheels and trailer hitch. Ideally, the TW will be 5 to 10 percent of the GTW. If the TW is too little, the trailer will have a tendency to sway easily. If the TW is too heavy, too much stress is placed on the truck hitch and suspension.

If the boat and trailer are relatively heavy, the 5 percent figure will be fine. If the boat and trailer are of intermediate weight (say, 1500 to 3000 pounds [700 kg to 1400 kg]), then the 10 percent ratio will be more appropriate. A very light rig might have 15 percent or more of the weight at the tongue.

Determining TW Using the Public Truck Scale

The TW is most safely and easily determined at the truck scale by carrying out the following procedure:

Determine the GTW of the trailer and boat by using the procedure described earlier.

- Hook the trailer back to the towing vehicle and tow the trailer forward until only the trailer wheels are on the scale. Take down this weight. We'll call this the total axle weight.
- Subtract the total axle weight from the GTW to get the TW.

Note: *This procedure won't work with a weight-distributing hitch.* In this case, the trailer must be unhooked from the vehicle before weighing for the total axle weight. Alternatively, the TW can be directly determined on the scale with a vertical pipe from the inside of the coupler down to the scale.

Be sure to place chocks front and back on both sides of the trailer when doing this.

Determining TW With a Bathroom Scale

If you feel quite sure of the GTW and the GTW is fairly light, it's possible to check the TW using an ordinary bathroom scale. To do this, you should be fairly certain the tongue is less than the capacity of the scale—usually around 300 pounds (140 kg).

Before starting, make sure the trailer tongue can't move from side to side by securing the wheels on both sides with chocks tightly installed in both front and back of each wheel. You may want to place a board on the scale to protect it and distribute the weight. If the trailer is fairly long and the swivel jack is quite near the coupler, then the swivel jack can be used for the weighing. Otherwise, a vertical pipe from the inside of the coupler down to the scale should be used.

Redistributing the Weight

If the TW is either too light or too heavy, then the weight distribution is changed by either:

- Moving the boat forward or backward on the trailer. This is accomplished most easily by launching the boat, then moving the vertical winch standard forward or backward, and then reloading the boat back onto the trailer.
- Moving the trailer wheels forward or backward, as appropriate. For safety reasons, this should be done with the boat off the trailer and is best done by professionals.
- If the weight distribution is close to correct, then shifting the equipment and supplies inside the boat might do the trick.

Calculate How Far to Shift the Boat on the Trailer

How far does one need to shift the boat on the trailer to achieve the desired tongue weight? One approach, probably the most common one, is by trial and error, trying different positions until the desired TW is reached.

The alternative approach is to calculate how much to shift the boat so only one repositioning is required. Equation 11-1 gives a pretty good approximation of the amount to shift the boat to get a desired change in tongue weight. It works for metric or imperial units.

Example:

Distance axles to coupler = XT = 17 ft 4 in = 208 in = 528 cm

Boat weight = BW = 3800 lb = 1724 kg

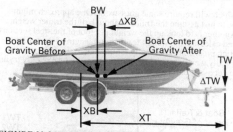

FIGURE 11-3: Dimensions Used to Calculate Amount to Shift Boat on Trailer

$$\Delta XB \times BW = \Delta TW \times XT$$

$$\Delta XB = \frac{\Delta TW \times XT}{BW}$$

Where: ΔXB = Distance to shift boat
ΔTW = Desired tongue weight change
XT = Distance from center of axles to coupler
BW = Boat weight

EQUATION 11-1: Calculate Amount to Shift Boat on Trailer to Achieve Desired Tongue Weight

Gross trailer weight = GTW = 4500 lb = 2041 kg

Tongue weight = TW = 200 lbs = 91 kg (4.4% of GTW)

This TW is too low. For this example, assume we want to get our TW to 7.5 percent of GTW or 338 lb (153 kg):

Desired change in tongue weight = ΔTW = 338 − 200 = 138 lb (62.6 kg)

ΔXB = (ΔTW x XT) / BW = (138 lb x 208 in) / 3800 lb = 7.6 in.

ΔXB = (ΔTW x XT) / BW = (62.6 kg x 528 cm) / 1724 kg = 19.2 cm

Calculate Distance to Shift Axles

Sometimes it will be more desirable to alter the TW by moving the wheels backward or forward. The following diagram and formula can be used to get an approximate distance to shift the wheels.

Note that in this case we must use the weight of the *boat plus the frame weight* (**BFW**) excluding the axles and wheels which will require some guesswork. One approach might be to just assume the frame is about half the trailer weight. Another is to look up the weight per foot of the steel sections and calculate the weight for the total length of the trailer. High precision is not really required here since the trailer usually weighs much less than the boat, and we're only trying to get in the ball park of the desired tongue weight.

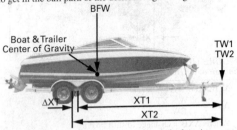

FIGURE 11-4: Dimensions Required to Calculate Amount to Shift Wheels on Trailer

$$\Delta XT = \frac{XT1 \times (TW2 - TW1)}{BFW - TW2}$$

Where: ΔXT = Distance to shift axles
  $TW1$ = Initial tongue weight
  $TW2$ = Desired tongue weight
  $XT1$ = Initial distance from center of axles to coupler
  BFW = Boat plus frame weight

EQUATION 11-2: Calculate Distance to Shift Wheels to Achieve Desired Tongue Weight

Example:

This example uses the same parameters as for the last example for shifting the boat. In this case we only show British units, but the equation works just as well for metric.

Distance axles to coupler = $XT1$ = 17 ft 4 in = 208 in

Boat weight = BW = 3800 lb

Gross trailer weight = GTW = 4500 lb

Average BW and GTW to get an estimate of boat and frame weight = BFW = (3800 + 4500) / 2 = 4150 lb

Initial tongue weight = $TW1$ = 200 lbs (4.4% of GTW)

This TW is too low. For this example, assume we want to get our TW to 7.5 percent of GTW or 338 lb = TW2

$$\Delta XT = (XT1 \times (TW2 - TW1)) / (BFW - TW2)$$
$$= (208 \text{ in} \times (338 \text{ lb} - 200 \text{ lb})) / (4150 \text{ lb} - 338 \text{ lb})$$
$$= 28704 \text{ in-lb} / 3812 \text{ lb}$$
$$= 7.5 \text{ in}$$

The wheels need to be shifted 7.5 inches aft.

Notice that the answer of 7.5 inches for shifting the wheels is essentially the same as the earlier answer of 7.6 inches for shifting the boat.

Wheels

Tires

Tires must be adequately rated to support the gross trailer weight. If the trailer has two wheels, each tire must support one-half the GTW. With four wheels, each tire must support one quarter of the GTW. Actually, the weight supported by the tires is a little less than GTW since some of the weight is taken up by the hitch but ignoring this provides a small safety factor.

As on an automobile, all the tires on the trailer must be matched as to size, load range, inflation, and ply type (radial or bias ply).

Quite often, trailer wheels and tire diameters are smaller than automobile tires, which results in a much higher wheel RPM at any given speed. This is much harder on the tires as well as the bearings, since both will run hotter. These smaller diameter tires need to be inflated to higher pressures than larger diameter tires to support the same loads without excessive flexing and overheating. For example, tires on those small 8-inch (20-cm) wheels are typically inflated to between 60 and 100 psi (410 and 690 kPa), whereas tire pressures for the same load rating on larger size tires might range from 35 to 50 psi (240 to 345 kPa). Therefore, the larger the tire diameter the better; if you have any choice in the matter, go for the trailer with the larger diameter tires.

The tires must be kept inflated to the maximum inflation pressure. Inflated properly they will run cooler, last longer, and have less rolling resistance resulting in better gas mileage.

Opinions vary as to whether trailers perform better with radial or bias ply tires. Each has its advantages. Bias ply tires are most common on trailers, since it is widely believed that their superior resistance to side wall rollover is more important on trailers, which can sometimes sway violently from side to side. On the other hand, radial tires generally improve traction, provide a softer ride, and wear longer. Trailer manufacturers all strongly recommend the use of trailer tires.

Spare Tire and Jack

A spare trailer wheel and tire of the same size and type as the others must be carried with the trailer. Normally this wheel is fastened well forward on the trailer frame. Some people carry this in the boat, but then there's the problem of where to put it when you launch the boat.

The spare tire won't do much good without a jack that works on the trailer. If you plan to use the towing vehicle's jack, try it out on the trailer first to make sure it works. If it doesn't, get one for the trailer that does work.

Bearings

The wheel bearing is, by far, the trailer part most likely to cause a complete breakdown while towing, and unlike a flat tire, cannot be changed out alongside the highway. Actually that's not quite true: Complete spare hub assemblies are available that bolt onto the trailer frame and can be changed out alongside the road just like the spare wheel and tire.

When bearings are immersed during launching, water tends to work its way into the bearings, which tends to flush out some of the grease. If the bearings are hot during launch this condition is exacerbated since the rapid cooling creates a vacuum that draws in even more water. In addition to washing out grease, the presence of water contributes to corrosion of the bearings and hubs. With less grease and corroded surfaces causing more friction, excessive heat builds up while running, which ultimately leads to complete failure (seizing or bearing failure).

To help alleviate this problem, most boat trailer bearings are equipped with Bearing Buddy caps. These replace original equipment dust caps and include a grease fitting and spring loaded internal plate that maintains a slight positive pressure on the bearing grease, which helps to keep water out. The grease fitting allows for easy addition of grease when required.

If your trailer is not equipped with Bearing Buddys, these or some equivalent are worth considering. Other bearing lubrication systems are manufactured by Fulton Performance Products, Liqua-Lube, Inc., and Tie Down Engineering. Both

Liqua-Lube and Tie Down produce systems that use oil baths instead of grease. Contact information for these companies is found in the boating organizations and companies chapter near the end of this book.

Brakes

Although some states don't require brakes on any trailers, you really should consider brakes as a necessity for any trailer with a GTW greater than 1500 pounds (680 kg).

Two main types of brakes are used on boat trailers. The most common are *hydraulic surge brakes*, which are activated by the braking of the tow vehicle. As the tow vehicle decelerates the force exerted on the coupler moves an actuator, which supplies hydraulic pressure to activate the brakes. These are preferred for boating applications because they are relatively insensitive to immersion in water.

The surge brake must be adjusted correctly so as not to brake too much or too little. Surge brakes that are oversensitive can apply themselves when traveling downhill because of the force of the trailer pushing into the tow vehicle. Surge brakes have a breakaway cable attached to the tow vehicle that activates the brakes in the event of the trailer breaking loose.

The other type of trailer brake is the *electric brake*, which is electronically linked to the towing vehicle. As the towing vehicle brakes, an electrical signal is sent to the trailer braking actuator to apply the hydraulic pressure needed for braking. Since this is an electrical system, it is much more sensitive to immersion in water than surge brakes.

For breakaway situations, trailers with electric brakes apply the brakes when the electrical circuit to the tow vehicle is broken.

The Trailer Hitch

On the tow vehicle, a *draw-bar* with a *hitch ball* fixed to the top slides into a *receiver* which is attached to the frame of the car or truck. The *coupler* on the trailer is designed to fit down over the ball and lock in place. Trailer hitches come in various sizes and capacities with variations in how they are mounted on the tow vehicle as well as different ball diameters. The coupler and hitch ball must be the same diameter. *A mismatch between the coupler and ball diameters is very dangerous and must be avoided.*

Hitch balls come in three sizes: 1-7/8 inches, 2 inches, and 2-5/16 inches.

Hitch Types

There are two main types of hitches for boat trailers: weight carrying and weight distributing. Weight-carrying hitches are what you normally encounter on boat trailers. A weight-carrying hitch simply has the full weight of the tongue on the ball, which in turn transmits the full load to the rear axle of the towing vehicle. This is the type of hitch most of us use.

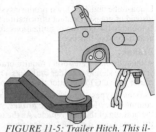

FIGURE 11-5: Trailer Hitch. This illustration shows the hitch just before dropping the hitch onto the ball. This hitch is on a trailer with surge brakes.

The load-distributing hitch has bars attached so as to place leverage on the tow vehicle to distribute some of the trailer weight forward to the front wheels (of the tow vehicle).

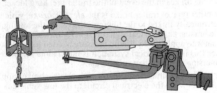

FIGURE 11-6: Weight-Distributing Hitch

In general, weight-distributing hitches are found only on the largest boat trailers. These are difficult to install and adjust; both tasks are best left to professionals.

Hitch Class

Trailer hitches are classified by hitch class depending on their load carrying capacity. Table 11-1 shows hitch classes with their associated capacities. The hitch installed on the trailer must have a maximum GTW capacity equal to or greater than the GVWR rating of the trailer, which in turn must be greater than the weight of the total tow load including all equipment and supplies in the boat (GTW).

Note that in table 11-1, the maximum TW is always 10 percent of the GTW.

Class	Capacity	
	Gross Trailer Weight (lbs)	**Tongue Weight (lbs)**
I	2000	200
II	3500	350
III	5000	500
IV	7500–12000	750–1200
Note: This table is only a guide. The weight and capacity are specific to each hitch.		

TABLE 11-1: Trailer Hitch Classes

Hitch Safety Chains

Safety chains from the trailer to the tow vehicle are required by law to keep the trailer from running away in the event of a hitch failure. An illustration showing how safety chains must be attached is shown later in the hooking up topic.

The chain used must have a strength rating, equal to or greater than the allowable GTW as specified in table 11-1.

THE TOW VEHICLE

The tow vehicle must be up to the task of towing the completely loaded boat and trailer. Determining this is a fairly straightforward process; you simply get the owner's manual out of the glove box of your truck and look up the tow rating for the vehicle.

If the maximum GTW specified in the manual is greater than that of your boat and trailer, then you're okay. If it's less, then you need to show this book page to your significant other to prove that you really do need to get a new truck, since it's obviously impractical to downsize to a smaller boat.

In general, a truck is needed to tow most boats, since most modern cars are of unibody construction and essentially lack a frame to which a good hitch needs to be attached. In addition, front-wheel drive presents a problem in that additional weight behind the rear axle takes weight off the front driving wheels which lessens traction. This can be problematic on a slippery boat ramp.

If the truck is towing a boat/trailer load, that is near the truck's towing capacity, it may be necessary to outfit the truck with such things as a heavy duty suspension and brakes, a larger radiator, and a transmission oil cooler. Even the rear differential ratio might need to be changed, particularly it the towing is to take place be in hilly or mountainous country.

TRAILER OPERATION
TRAVELING WITH THE BOAT TRAILER
Hooking Up
If you have someone helping guide you, make sure he or she is standing off to one side and not between the trailer and the tow vehicle. Back the tow vehicle until the hitch ball is directly underneath the coupler, and then lower the tongue until the coupler is completely seated over the ball. Lock the latching mechanism in place and visually inspect to be sure it's locked below the ball. *Don't check by sticking your fingers in there. Ouch!* Make sure the locking pin is inserted to ensure the latch won't come undone.

Attach the breakaway cable to the tow vehicle (the one that actuates the brakes in the event of accidental uncoupling). Attach the safety chains to the tow vehicle. They must be crossed underneath the tongue to support the tongue in case the trailer comes uncoupled. They should just be loose enough to allow for tight turns, but not so loose that the tongue can drag on the road. The hooks should be inserted with the hook opening facing backwards so they will not easily bounce out (figure 11-7).

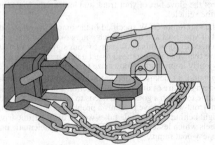

FIGURE 11-7: Hooking Up the Trailer Chains

Connect the electrical plug from the trailer to the receptacle on the tow vehicle. Check that the trailer lights function correctly with the tow vehicle (1) headlights on, (2) turn signals flashing, and (3) brake lights on. Check the tires for proper inflation and condition. Remove chocks from the trailer wheels and raise the swivel jack.

Make it a habit to before driving off to carry out a complete walk-around of the trailer and boat to make sure you haven't forgotten anything. Always use a checklist for hooking up. An example checklist is provided at the end of this chapter.

Driving

Backing Up

Back up slowly and carefully. Move the bottom of the steering wheel in the direction you want the trailer to go. Avoid excessive turns that may cause you to jackknife. The boat usually blocks your view of where you're going, so have someone on hand to help guide you.

If you're new to this, find a vacant lot or little-used road and practice backing up. Also practice 90-degree turns since you are likely to have to perform this maneuver somewhere someday. It's far better to perfect your skills here than on a busy launch ramp.

On the Highway

With the extra weight of the boat and trailer, stopping distance is increased substantially, so allow more distance for braking. Keep your speed down. In some states it's illegal to tow a trailer over 55 mph.

A few minutes into any trip, stop and inspect again. In particular check bearings for overheating and check the coupling and safety chains. Check that the boat is still properly secured and that everything in the boat is secure. On long trips make it a habit to stop and perform this check every couple of hours or so.

Unhooking

Detaching the trailer from the tow vehicle is essentially the reverse of hooking up. The main thing to remember is to securely place the chocks before starting to undo the hitch or anything else.

Before driving away from the trailer, walk around and inspect the trailer one last time. Drive away slowly in case something was inadvertently left connected.

Protecting the Boat and Trailer From Theft

Unfortunately, boat theft is a significant problem, and leaving a boat sitting out alone on a trailer in a public place is like an open invitation to the human trash who don't want to work for a living like the rest of us. The first line of defense is just to keep it out of sight or secured behind a locked gate.

Beyond that, keep some of the following in mind:

- Use locks anywhere you can. Buy a lock especially made for locking the hitch and use it. Lock your outboard to the transom. Although this won't stop a skilled and determined thief, it will certainly be a deterrent since thieves like to be hooked up and gone in a couple of minutes or less.
- There are devices used by professional thieves that clamp over the hitch so the lock won't be of any use. Chain at least one wheel to the frame, or if possible, chain the frame to a nearby tree.
- In hotel or marina parking lots, put the boat cover on.
- If you are leaving the trailer connected to the tow vehicle, use a locking receiver pin and chain the trailer to the vehicle frame.
- If you are leaving the boat for a period of time, take the wheels off and store them elsewhere.
- Remove small outboard motors and store in a safe place.
- Consider removing license plates and taillights, if possible.
- Remove the propellers, especially the expensive stainless steel kind.
- Some suggest painting the trailer in gaudy, bright colors. This might convince the thief to try stealing another boat instead of yours. It will certainly make it easier to describe your boat and trailer to the police.

BOAT LAUNCH AND HAUL-OUT

Launching

Prelaunch

Before you reach the ramp, as a matter of courtesy to others waiting to launch, get prepared as much as possible ahead of time.

Remove all tie-downs but *leave the winch connected to the bow-eye*. Remember to *replace the drain plug* because it will be really embarrassing if you don't. Disconnect the trailer lights. If they are left connected, the electrical system can be shorted and/or the bulbs can be burned out. Have a line attached to both the bow and stern to keep control of the boat.

Attach fenders to the side of the boat that will be against the launching dock (if there is one). Make sure the outboard or sterndrive is fully raised. If there is an outboard or sterndrive support installed for transport, remove it now. The ignition key should be inserted and ready to start the engine. It's better to find out you forgot your key now than once you're in the water. If you have an inboard gasoline engine, start the exhaust blower running now so you don't have to wait five minutes after you launch to start the engine.

Use the launch checklist provided at the end of this chapter to help you remember all these steps.

Launching the Boat
When everything is ready, proceed to the launch ramp. Have one person on the ramp to one side to help guide the driver.

Back down only as far as necessary. A trailer with slide type bunks usually needs to go far enough for the boat to float off the trailer. A trailer with rollers can stop when the water is deep enough to allow the boat to roll off safely. The winch should remain connected until the boat is nearly afloat since the boat can slide off the trailer as you are backing down the ramp, especially if you need to shift into forward to go back up the ramp. Boats sliding off on the ramp are a more common occurrence than one might think.

If the driver needs to leave the tow vehicle, the vehicle should be placed in park, the emergency brake pulled full on, and the engine shut off. Most boaters don't bother with a wheel chock, but this is a good idea and it only takes about five seconds to place it. Ensure that someone has control of both docklines.

Lower the engine or sterndrive, start the engine, and immediately check to see if cooling water is pumping. Move the boat promptly from the ramp area to make room for the next person.

Haul-Out

Retrieving the Boat
Essentially, retrieving the boat is the opposite of launching it.

Let everyone off the boat except the boat operator if the boat is to be driven onto the trailer. Once the boat is aligned with the trailer it can be winched up to the vertical winch post roller. Often when the trailer and boat are pulled up the ramp, the boat slides back a few inches, even though the winch was tightened as much as possible. To prevent this, a chain or turnbuckle can be attached to the bow-eye (in addition to the winch hook) before hauling the rig up the ramp.

Turn off the engine. Raise the sterndrive or outboard. Clear the ramp area as soon as possible and proceed to an area where you can take your time getting everything secured properly.

Post-Retrieve

Remove the drain plug and stow it in the boat. Install the sterndrive support. If you have an outboard and travel with it raised, install the engine support. Do not travel with an outboard engine in the raised position without bracing it with an engine support.

Always attach the safety tie downs before towing even a short distance. With runabouts this will usually consist of two straps running from eyes on the transom down to the frame. Sailboats will often be secured by gunnel straps over the boat. Reconnect the trailer lights and check them for proper operation.

Before driving off, do a complete walk around of the trailer and boat to make sure you haven't forgotten anything. Review the checklist for retrieval provided at the end of this chapter.

Considerations for Launching Sailboats

Launching a sailboat is similar to launching a powerboat albeit with a couple of significant differences.

The Sailboat Mast

The mast must be stepped either before or after launching, with stepping before launch being the much preferred option. With larger boats stepping the mast must be done ashore. Since this is preparatory work that takes anywhere from 30 minutes to an hour, it should be done away from the ramp. The most important thing here is to make sure there are no overhead power lines between the stepping location and the boat ramp.

The Keel and Rudder

If the rudder is removable or can be tilted up, this should be done during the preparatory work before going to the ramp.

Most sailboats, other than small daysailers, have a keel of some kind which needs to be given consideration when launching and retrieving the boat. For a centerboard or a daggerboard, the primary consideration is to make sure the keel is fixed in the raised position so that it doesn't drop as soon as the boat is off the trailer.

In the case of a fixed keel, no prelaunch preparation is required. A trailer tongue extender of some kind may be required for the actual launch in order to get the boat into deep enough water without immersing the back of the tow vehicle in the water. These are sometimes available at the launch ramp, but most of the time you will provide this yourself. If an extension didn't come with your trailer, you may need to have one fabricated at your local welding shop.

An alternative to the extension is as follows:

• Install a wheel forward on the trailer so the trailer can be rolled forward and backward without being hitched to a tow vehicle. This is a one-time operation at home or at the shop and would be a good use for your spare wheel and tire.

• Back the boat down the ramp until the wheels are almost at the water.

• Attach a length of chain between the trailer and the tow vehicle. This chain must of sufficient length that the boat and trailer can be backed into deep enough water without the truck wheels having to enter the water. For now this chain will lie loose on the ground.

• Chock the trailer wheels securely on both sides. Note that the safety chains should still be attached at this point. Unhook the tow vehicle and if the chocks hold securely, remove the safety chains.

• Drive the tow vehicle forward until the slack in the chain is taken up. Drive forward a little more to relieve the pressure on the chocks.

Remove the chocks, and back the trailer and boat into the water.

This may seem like an overly involved process, but at some relatively flat ramps this or some similar approach may be the only alternative.

TRAILER MAINTENANCE

Introduction

As mentioned earlier, the main causes of trailer failure are wheel bearing and tire failure. Brake failure, although less common, can be more dangerous in an emergency situation. Malfunctioning lights can result in the boat and trailer being rear-ended. All of these are preventable by doing some basic preventative maintenance on these systems. If you are paying to have the work done, use a trailer or boating shop rather than an automobile repair shop since the braking systems function differently and require specialized adjustments.

Hubs

As mentioned previously, some kind of hub lubrication device such as Bearing Buddy should be installed. Before each trip, it should just be necessary to check that the indicator rings are still pushed out, which indicates that grease is still in the hub and under pressure. If grease needs to be added, be careful; excess pressure may blow out the back seals, which will allow grease to leave and water to enter more easily. If no such device is installed, then the wheel bearings should be removed and repacked at least once per year.

If you do a lot of trailerboating and put on a lot of miles, then annual inspection and repacking is advised even if a lubrication device is installed.

Tires

It is crucial to keep tires inflated to the correct or recommended maximum pressure specified on the side of the tire. Tires can deteriorate with exposure to the sun, so covering them when they are left exposed for long periods of time will help prolong tire life.

When storing the boat and trailer for long periods, it is a good idea to jack up the trailer and place it on jack stands to take weight off the tires.

In most cases, boat trailer tires fail because of road and sunlight damage or just plain old rot, rather than from mileage. Cracking on the sidewalls is a good indicator that it's time to replace the tires. Waiting for boat trailer tire treads to wear out is just asking for failure on the road.

Watch for tread wear that is unusual, such as only on one side or just on the outside edges. Wear on one side indicates a possible alignment problem of some kind. Wear on both edges of the tread is probably because of under-inflation or overloading.

Brakes

Maintenance of brakes tends to be overlooked because it's often hard to tell if they are working correctly—at least until a hard emergency stop demonstrates that they're not. As with the hubs, if the trailer is used frequently, the brakes should be inspected and adjusted once yearly. If they start squealing or otherwise acting out the ordinary, then they should be repaired as soon as possible.

After every immersion in saltwater the brakes, wheels, and everything else that was immersed should be thoroughly flushed with fresh water as soon as possible.

General

Chips in paint and rust spots should be sanded and repainted at least yearly. Structural members that allow accumulation of water internally should be inspected to ensure that drain holes are clear and draining properly. Check the winch to be sure it is secure and working properly. In particular check the condition of the strap. If it appears worn or frayed, replace it. On trailers with rollers, replace any rollers that are cracked or broken.

Lights

Trailer lights should be checked in advance of every time the trailer is towed. Burnt-out bulbs should be replaced immediately. Spares for all bulbs should be carried on trips. Again, always unplug the lights before immersing the trailer in water.

Next time the bulbs need replacing or the light fixture is damaged, consider replacing them with the LED lights that are now available. They are virtually indestructible and supposedly last upwards of 100,000 hours.

Protect the electrical plug and receptacle when disconnected with a plastic cover. Wipe a small amount of light waterproof grease or petroleum jelly on the contact surfaces to protect them from moisture and oxidation.

TRAILER CONNECTOR WIRING GUIDE

This section is meant to be of assistance for debugging trailer wiring problems.

Hints

If you are having a receptacle installed on a tow vehicle, consider installing a seven-way connector, even if only four of the connections are being used. Plug-in adapters are available to convert from seven-way to any of the other configurations; so doing this will give you the flexibility to connect other trailer plugs (and hence other trailers) rather than just the kind on your own boat trailer.

Connections on a trailer are susceptible to vibration and corrosion from moisture just as wiring on the boat is. All electrical connections should be completely sealed with heat shrink tubing (marine grade, if possible).

Some trailers do not have the white ground wire connected, instead relying on the trailer hitch to provide a ground return to the tow vehicle. This provides a poor connection and is often the cause of intermittent problems with the lights. If you have one of these, connect a white wire from the (white) pin to the trailer frame to ensure a good ground.

Warnings

Incorrect wiring on some types of tow vehicles can cause severe (and very expensive) damage to the vehicle's electrical system. For this reason, the installation of wiring and receptacles on the tow vehicle should be left to experienced professionals.

The wiring color indexes shown here are for trailers not for the tow vehicle. The installation of wiring and receptacles on the tow vehicle should be left to experienced professionals since incorrect wiring can damage your car.

The color coding shown is standard, but there are trailers out there that are not wired this way so be careful.

Seven-Way Trailer Wiring

The colors shown are for the trailer, not the truck or car. Note that the color index used for trailers with seven-way connectors differs from the colors used for other connectors.

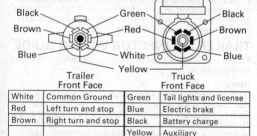

White	Common Ground	Green	Tail lights and license
Red	Left turn and stop	Blue	Electric brake
Brown	Right turn and stop	Black	Battery charge
		Yellow	Auxiliary

FIGURE 11-8: Seven-Way Trailer Connector Wiring and Color Index for Seven-Way Trailer Connectors

6-Way Trailer Wiring

The colors shown are for the trailer, not the truck or car. Note that the color index used for trailers with six-way connectors differs from the colors used for seven-way connectors.

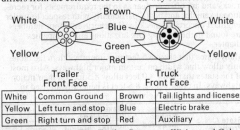

Trailer
Front Face

Truck
Front Face

White	Common Ground	Brown	Tail lights and license
Yellow	Left turn and stop	Blue	Electric brake
Green	Right turn and stop	Red	Auxiliary

FIGURE 11-9: Six-Way Trailer Connector Wiring and Color Index for Six-Way Trailer Connectors. Use this index for five-way and four-way connectors as well.

Four-Way and Five-Way Trailer Wiring

The colors shown are for the trailer, not the truck or car. Note that the color index used for trailers with four-way connectors is the same as for six-way connectors except only four of the colors are used.

The flat five-way connector is not very common. The flat four-way connector is found on most boat trailers.

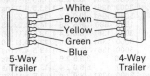

5-Way
Trailer

4-Way
Trailer

FIGURE 11-10: Five-Way and Four-Way Flat Trailer Connector Wiring. Use the color index from figure 11-9, above.

RULES AND REGULATIONS FOR TOWING TRAILERS

Rules for trailers tend to be based on rules derived from large trucks and are often unclear as to the requirements for recreational vehicles and boats, particularly with respect to trailer length. If uncertain, check local authorities. Phone numbers are found in the Boating Organizations and Companies chapter.

Many states that show 8.5 feet maximum width in the table, only allow that width on certain major highways. Also most of the states that show 8.0 feet allow 8.5 feet on their major highways. In other words, 8.5 feet is generally allowed in most states on major highways.

State / Province	Trailer Brakes Required Over		Maximum Trailer Dimensions						Safety Chains
			Width		Height		Length		
	lbs	kg	ft	m	ft	m	ft	m	
United States									
Alabama	3000	1361	8.0	2.4 1	13.5	4.11	40	12.2	Yes
Alaska	5000	2268	8.5	2.6	14.0	4.27	40	12.2	Yes
Arizona	3000	1361	8.0	2.4 1	13.5	4.11	40	12.2	ns
Arkansas	3000	1361 2	8.5	2.6	13.5	4.11	53	16.3	Yes
California	1500	680	8.5	2.6	14.0	4.27	40	12.2	Yes
Colorado	3000	1361	8.5	2.6	13.0	3.96	ns		Yes
Connecticut	3000	1361	8.5	2.6	13.5	4.11	ns		Yes
Delaware	4000	1814	8.5	2.6	13.5	4.11	40	12.2	Yes
Dist of Columbia	3000	1361	8.0	2.4	13.5	4.11	ns		Yes
Florida	3000	1361	8.5	2.6	13.5	4.11	40	12.2	Yes
Georgia	3000	1361	8.5	2.6 1	13.5	4.11	ns		Yes
Hawaii	3000	1361	9.0	2.7	14.0	4.27	40	12.2	Yes
Idaho	1500	680	8.5	2.6	14.0	4.27	48	14.6	ns
Illinois	3000	1361	8.0	2.4 1	13.5	4.11	60	18.3	Yes
Indiana	3000	1361	8.5	2.6	13.5	4.11	40	12.2	Yes
Iowa	3000	1361	8.0	2.4 1	13.5	4.11	ns		Yes
Kansas	40/20	3	8.5	2.6	14.0	4.27	ns		Yes
Kentucky	note	5	8.0	2.4	13.5	4.11	ns		Yes
Lousiana	3000	1361	8.0	2.4 1	13.5	4.11	30	9.1	Yes
Maine	3000	1361	8.5	2.6	13.5	4.11	48	14.6	Yes
Maryland	3000	1361	8.5	2.6	13.5	4.11	40	12.2	Yes
Massachusetts	10000	4536	8.5	2.6	13.5	4.11	33	10.1	Yes
Michigan	3000	1361	8.5	2.6	13.5	4.11	45	13.7	ns
Minnesota	3000	1361	8.5	2.6	13.5	4.11	45	13.7	ns
Mississippi	2000	907	8.5	2.6	13.5	4.11	40	12.2	Yes
Missouri	ns	6	8.0	2.4 1	13.5	4.11	ns		Yes
Montana	3000	1361	8.5	2.6	14.0	4.27	ns		Yes
Nebraska	3000	1361	8.5	2.6	14.5	4.42	40	12.2	Yes
Nevada	1500	680	8.5	2.6	14.0	4.27	ns		Yes

State / Province	Trailer Brakes Required Over		Maximum Trailer Dimensions						Safety Chains
			Width		Height		Length		
	lbs	kg	ft	m	ft	m	ft	m	
United States									
New Hampshire	30/20	4	8.5	2.6	13.5	4.11	48	14.6	Yes
New Jersey	ALL		8.0	2.4	13.5	4.11	40	12.2	Yes
New Mexico	3000	1361	8.5	2.6	14.0	4.27	40	12.2	Yes
New York	3000	1361	8.0	2.4 1	13.5	4.11	ns		Yes
North Carolina	1000	454	8.5	2.6	13.5	4.11	ns		Yes
North Dakota	All		8.5	2.6	14.0	4.27	53	16.2	Yes
Ohio	2000	907	8.5	2.6	13.5	4.11	40	12.2	Yes
Oklahoma	3000	1361	8.5	2.6	13.5	4.11	40	12.2	Yes
Oregon	note	5	8.5	2.6	14.0	4.27	45	13.7	Yes
Pennsylvania	3000	1361	8.5	2.6	13.5	4.11	ns		Yes
Rhode Island	4000	1814	8.5	2.6	13.5	4.11	ns		ns
South Carolina	3000	1361	8.5	2.6	13.5	4.11	48	14.6	Yes
South Dakota	3000	1361	8.5	2.6	14.0	4.27	ns		Yes
Tennessee	3000	1361	8.5	2.6	13.5	4.11	40	12.2	Yes
Texas	4500	2041	8.5	2.6	14.0	4.27	ns		Yes
Utah	40/20	3	8.5	2.6	14.0	4.27	40	12.2	Yes
Vermont	3000	1361	8.5	2.6	13.5	4.11	53	16.2	Yes
Virginia	3000	1361	8.5	2.6	13.5	4.11	ns		Yes
Washington	3000	1361	8.5	2.6	14.0	4.27	ns		Yes
West Virginia	3000	1361	8.0	2.4 1	13.5	4.11	40	12.2	Yes
Wisconsin	3000	1361	8.5	2.6	13.5	4.11	45	13.7	Yes
Wyoming	40/20	3	8.5	2.6	14.0	4.27	ns		ns
Canada									
Alberta	2982	909	8.5	2.6	12.6	3.85	41	12.5	-
British Columbia	4593	1400	8.5	2.6	13.6	4.15	41	12.5	Yes
Manitoba	2986	910	8.5	2.6	13.6	4.15	41	12.5	Yes
New Brunswick	4921	1500	8.5	2.6	13.6	4.15	41	12.5	-
Newfoundland	14763	4500	8.5	2.6	13.6	4.15	41	12.5	Yes
Nova Scotia	5905	1800	8.5	2.6	13.6	4.15	41	12.5	Yes
Nunavik	ns		8.5	2.6	13.8	4.20	-		-
Northwest Territories	4462	1360	8.5	2.6	13.8	4.20	-		-
Ontario	4462	1360	8.5	2.6	13.6	4.15	41	12.5	Yes
Prince Edward Island	4921	1500	8.5	2.6	13.6	4.15	41	12.5	Yes
Quebec	4265	1300	8.5	2.6	13.6	4.15	48	14.7	Yes
Saskatchewan	4462	1360	8.5	2.6	13.6	4.15	41	12.5	Yes
Yukon	2986	910	8.5	2.6	14.8	4.50	41	12.5	Yes

(1) 8.5 ft (2.6 m) on designated roads
(2) New trailers over 1500 lbs (460 kg) must have brakes
(3) Brakes must stop in less than 40 ft from 20 mph
(4) Brakes must stop in less than 30 ft from 20 mph
(5) Brakes must stop in less than statute specified distance
(6) Some roads have a 13.5 height limit

TABLE 11-2: State and Provincial Rules for Trailers

TOWING—TRIP DEPARTURE CHECKLIST	
Trailer Pre Trip	
Tire pressure at rated pressure	❑
Tire condition —rot, cracking, wear	❑
All wheel lugs for correct torque, missing lugs	❑
Trailer brakes —hydraulic fluid reservoir topped off, brakes working correctly	❑
Wheel bearings greased.	❑
Test lights and wiring	❑
Checklist —Trailering Supplies and Tools	❑
Boat Pre Trip	
Boat snugged up to bow roller	❑
Boweye attached to winch, winch secure	❑
Safety chain or turnbuckle —boweye to trailer frame	❑
Transom tie downs in place	❑
Gunnel tie downs in place	❑
Equipment & supplies in boat secured	❑
Drain plug removed and stored in boat	❑
Bimini or other covers in down position and secured	❑
Boat cover stored inside boat and secured (best not to travel with the cover on, flapping canvas damages gelcoat)	❑
Outboards or sterndrives braced in raised position	❑
Checklist in Rules & Regs —All safety equipment aboard	❑
Sailboat Pretrip Additional	
Mast and rigging lowered and fully secured	❑
Red flag on aft end of mast / remove wind direction indicator	❑
Rudder tilted up or removed	❑
Centerboard or daggerboard released to rest on trailer bunk	❑
Hook—up and Depart	
Draw bar secured with hitch pin or lock	❑
Lower hitch completely onto ball, fully engage coupler lever in the down position	❑
Check for ball clamp under ball	❑
Insert coupler locking pin or padlock	❑
Connect safety chains, crossed over, hooks front to back	❑
Connect breakaway switch and lanyard —trailers with brakes	❑
Raise swivel / tongue jack	❑
Connect electrical cable to tow vehicle	❑
Check functioning of all lights on trailer	❑
Remove chocks	❑
Complete trailer/boat walk around and inspect	❑

TRAILERING SUPPLIES AND TOOLS	
Spare trailer tire	❏
Trailer lug wrench	❏
Trailer jack	❏
Wheel chocks	❏
Road flares	❏
Emergency reflectors (triangles)	❏
Spare signal bulbs	❏
Jack stands	❏
Extension mirrors	❏
Extra chain for locking trailer	❏
Locks for motors, trailer, etc	❏

EN ROUTE CHECKLIST	
On The Road	
30 minutes into trip, stop and do a quick visual of everything on the departure checklist. Most importantly, check hitch, bearing temperature, and tires	❏
Every 2 hours, stop and do a quick visual of everything on the departure checklist. Most importantly check hitch, bearing temperature, and tires	❏
Hotel Parking Lots Overnight	
Install boat cover	❏
Install hitch lock	❏
Lock trailer to vehicle frame or tree	❏
Lock at least one wheel to frame	❏
Remove license plate	❏
Remove propellers	❏
Do some of the checks from the departure checklist so you don't have to do them in the morning	❏
Leaving Next Morning	
Repeat the relevant items from the trip departure checklist	❏
As always—Complete trailer/boat walk around and inspect	❏

BOAT LAUNCH	
Pre Launch (away from ramp)	
Checklist in Rules & Regs—All safety equipment aboard	❏
Gasoline inboards and sterndrives—turn exhaust blower on	❏
Disconnect trailer lights	❏
Remove transom or gunnel tie downs	❏
Remove bow-eye turnbuckle or chain	❏
Leave winch connected to bow-eye	❏
Install drain plug	❏
Attach line to bow and stern for controlling boat	❏
Fasten fenders if there is a launch dock	❏
Check that outboard or sterndrive is in raised position	❏
Remove outboard or sterndrive supports	❏
Outboard—hook up gas tank and prime fuel line	❏

BOAT LAUNCH	
Insert ignition key without turning it on	❏
Boat toolbox onboard	❏
Food / beverage loaded	❏
Check clothing, jackets, shoes, bathing suits, etc. are onboard	❏
Cell phones, cameras, GPS, other electronics onboard	❏
Take a minute and think about anything else you might need	❏
Sailboat —step mast	❏
Sailboat —fix centerboard or daggerboard in raised position	❏
Sailboat —remove/raise rudder	❏
Sailboat —overhead powerline check	❏
Launch	
Back down until boat is almost afloat	❏
Make sure someone on shore has control of the dock lines	❏
Release winch hook	❏
Back further down if necessary and float boat off	❏
Lower engine and start	❏
Check for cooling water discharge immediately after start	❏
Power or pull the boat away from ramp area	❏

BOAT HAUL-OUT	
Haul-out	
Winch hook attached to bow—eye	❏
Power or winch boat up to bow roller	❏
Safety chain or turnbuckle —boweye to trailer frame —tighten	❏
Turn engine off	❏
Raise sterndrive or outboard	❏
Sailboat —remove or raise rudder	❏
Clear the ramp area	❏
Post Haul—out	
Remove drain plug, stow onboard	❏
Install outboard or sterndrive brace	❏
Transom tie downs in place	❏
Gunnel tie downs in place	❏
Equipment & supplies in boat secured	❏
Bimini or other covers in down position and secured	❏
Connect electrical cable to tow vehicle	❏
Check functioning of all lights on trailer	❏
Complete trailer/boat walkaround and inspect	❏
Sailboat mast and rigging lowered and fully secured	❏
Sailboat —red flag on aft end of mast / remove wind direction indicator	❏
Sailboat —centerboard or daggerboard released to rest on trailer bunk	❏

12 GENERAL REFERENCE TABLES

TIME ZONES

City	Z	City	Z
United States		New York, New York	-5
Albuquerque, N.Mexico	-7	Oklahoma City, Oklahoma	-6
Anchorage, Alaska	-9	Omaha, Nebraska	-6
Atlanta, Georgia	-5	Pensacola, Florida	-6
Baltimore, Maryland	-5	Philadelphia, Pennsylvania	-5
Bangor, Maine	-5	Phoenix, Arizona	-7
Bismarck, North Dakota	-6	Pittsburgh, Pennsylvania	-5
Boise, Idaho	-7	Portland, Maine	-5
Boston, Massachussets	-5	Portland, Oregon	-8
Buffalo, New York	-5	Rochester, New York	-5
Charleston, West Virginia	-5	Salt Lake City, Utah	-7
Chesapeake, Virginia	-5	San Diego, California	-8
Cheyenne, Wyoming	-7	San Francisco, California	-8
Chicago, Illinois	-6	Sault St Marie, Michigan	-5
Cincinnati, Ohio	-5	Savannah, Georgia	-5
Cleveland, Ohio	-5	Seattle, Washington	-8
Dallas, Texas	-6	Sioux Falls, South Dakota	-6
Denver, Colorado	-7	St Louis, Missouri	-6
Des Moines, Iowa	-6	Toledo, Ohio	-5
Detroit, Michigan	-5	Tucson, Arizona	-7
Duluth, Wisconsin	-6	Washington, D.C.	-5
Erie, Pennsylvania	-5	Wichita, Kansas	-6
Honolulu, Hawaii	-10	**Canada**	
Houston, Texas	-6	Calgary, Alberta	-7
Indianapolis, Indiana	-5	Charlottetown, P.E.I.	-4
Jackson, Mississippi	-6	Edmonton, Alberta	-7
Jacksonville, Florida	-5	Halifax, Nova Scotia	-4
Juneau, Alaska	-9	Kingston, Ontario	-5
Kansas City, Missouri	-6	Montreal, Quebec	-5
Las Vegas, Nevada	-8	Port Colbourne, Ontario	-5
Little Rock, Arkansas	-6	Quebec, Quebec	-5
Los Angeles, California	-8	Regina, Saskatchewan	-6
Louisville, Kentucky	-5	Saint John, New Brunswick	-4
Memphis, Tennessee	-6	St John's, Newfoundland	-3.5
Miami, Florida	-5	Thunder Bay, Ontario	-5
Milwaukee, Wisconsin	-6	Toronto, Ontario	-5
Minneapolis, Minnesota	-6	Vancouver, British Columbia	-8
Mobile, Alabama	-6	Victoria, British Columbia	-8
New Orleans, Louisianna	-6	Winnipeg, Manitoba	-6
(-) = subtract from UTC, (+) = add to UTC, to get local time			

TABLE 12-1: United States And Canada Standard Time Differences from UTC. For Daylight Savings Add 1 Hour

City	Z	City	Z
Acapulco, Mexico	-6	Marseille, France	1
Alexandria, Egypt	2	Mazatlan, Mexico	-7
Algiers, Algeria	1	Melbourne, Australia	10
Amsterdam, Netherlands	1	Mexico City, Mexico	-6
Athens, Greece	2	Montevideo, Uruguay	-3
Auckland, New Zealand	12	Moscow, Russia	3
Barcelona, Spain	1	Naples, Italy	1
Basselterre, St Kitts	-4	Nassau, Bahamas	-5
Basse-Terre, Guadeloupe	-4	Nicosia, Cyprus	2
Beirut, Lebanon	2	Odessa, Ukraine	2
Belfast, N. Ireland	0	Oranjestad, Aruba	-4
Berlin, Germany	1	Oslo, Norway	1
Bombay, India	5.5	Palermo, Sicily	1
Bridgetown, Barbadoes	-4	Panama City, Panama	-5
Brussels, Belgium	1	Paris, France	1
Buenos Aires, Argentina	-3	Perth, Australia	8
Calais, France	1	Port of Spain, Trinidad	-4
Cancun, Mexico	-6	Port Said, Suez Canal	2
Cape Horn, Argentina	-3	Port-au-Prince, Haiti	-5
CapeTown, South Africa	2	Puntarenas, Costa Rica	-6
Caracas, Venezuela	-4	Rio de Janeiro, Brazil	-3
Copenhagen, Denmark	1	Rome, Italy	1
Dublin, Ireland	0	San Juan, Puerto Rico	-4
Edinburgh, Scotland	0	Santiago, Chile	-4
Ensenada, Mexico	-8	Seoul, South Korea	9
Fort-de-France, Martinque	-4	Singapore, Singapore	8
Genoa, Italy	1	St George's, Grenada	-5
Georgetown, Cayman Islands	-5	St Thomas, USVI	-4
Gibralter, Gibralter	1	St. John's, Antigua	-4
Hamilton, Bermuda	-4	Stockholm, Sweden	1
Havana, Cuba	-5	Suva, Fiji Islands	12
Hong Kong, China	8	Sydney, Australia	10
Istanbul, Turkey	2	Tel Aviv, Israel	2
Kingston, Jamaica	-5	Tokyo, Japan	9
Kingstown, St. Vincent	-4	Tortola, BVI	-4
Kralendijk, Bonaire	-4	Tripoli, Libya	1
Lima, Peru	-5	Valparaiso, Chile	-4
Lisbon, Portugal	0	Venice, Italy	1
London, England	1	Vienna, Austria	1
London, England	0	Vladivostok, Russia	10
Madrid, Spain	1	Wellington, New Zealand	12
Manila, Philippines	8	Willemstad, Curacao	-4
Maracaibo, Venezuela	-4	Zurich, Switzerland	1
(-) = subtract from UTC, (+) = add to UTC, to get local time			

TABLE 12-2: World Cities Standard Time Differences from UTC. For Daylight Savings Add 1 Hour

NATIONAL HOLIDAYS

United States Holidays

Federal holidays in the United States are observed by all federal offices including the post office. Most of the individual states have adopted these as legal state holidays. In addition, most states have one or more state specific holidays in addition to those shown in the table.

Holiday	Date
New Year's Day	1-Jan
Martin Luther King Day	3rd Monday in January
President's Day	3rd Monday in February
Good Friday	Friday before Easter
Easter	Sunday as defined by explanation in note 1 below. Next 8 years are: 16Apr06 08Apr07 23Mar08 12Apr09 04Apr10 24Apr11 08Apr12 31Mar13
Memorial Day	Last Monday in May
Independence Day	4-Jul
Labor Day	1st Monday in September
Columbus Day	2nd Monday in October
Veteran's Day	11-Nov
Thanksgiving Day	4th Thursday in November
Christmas Day	December 25th

1. Easter falls on the 1st Sunday following the 1st ecclesiastical full moon that occurs on or after the day of the vernal equinox which is March 21st. Note that the ecclesiastical full moon is determined from tables and is not always exactly equal to the astronomical full moon. Easter always occurs between March 22 and April 25.

TABLE 12-3: U. S. Holidays

Canadian Holidays

The following table lists Canadian holidays at the national level. Individual provinces will have at least one additional holiday, most of which are scheduled during August.

Holiday	Date
New Year's Day	1-Jan
Good Friday	Friday before Easter
Easter	(See Easter for the U.S. Above)
Victoria Day	Monday preceding May 25
Canada Day	July 1. July 2 if July 1 is a Sunday
Labor Day	1st Monday of September
Thanksgiving Day	2nd Monday of October
Remembrance Day	11-Nov
Christmas	25-Dec
Boxing Day	26-Dec

TABLE 12-4: Canadian Holidays

AIR AND WATER VERSUS ELEVATION

Elevation		Pressure			H2O Boil Temp.	
(ft)	(m)	(psi)	(mbar)	(in Hg)	(°F)	(°C)
0	0	14.70	1013.2	29.92	212.0	100.0
100	30	14.64	1009.6	29.81	211.8	99.9
200	61	14.59	1005.9	29.71	211.7	99.8
300	91	14.54	1002.3	29.60	211.5	99.7
400	122	14.48	998.7	29.49	211.3	99.6
500	152	14.43	995.1	29.38	211.1	99.5
600	183	14.38	991.5	29.28	210.9	99.4
700	213	14.33	987.9	29.17	210.8	99.3
800	244	14.28	984.3	29.07	210.6	99.2
900	274	14.22	980.7	28.96	210.4	99.1
1000	305	14.17	977.2	28.86	210.2	99.0
1200	366	14.07	970.1	28.65	209.9	98.8
1400	427	13.97	963.0	28.44	209.5	98.6
1600	488	13.87	956.0	28.23	209.2	98.4
1800	549	13.76	949.0	28.03	208.8	98.2
2000	610	13.66	942.1	27.82	208.4	98.0
2500	762	13.42	925.0	27.31	207.5	97.5
3000	914	13.17	908.1	26.82	206.6	97.0
3500	1067	12.93	891.5	26.33	205.7	96.5
4000	1219	12.69	875.1	25.84	204.8	96.0
4500	1372	12.46	859.0	25.37	203.9	95.5
5000	1524	12.23	843.1	24.90	203.0	95.0
5500	1676	12.00	827.4	24.43	202.0	94.5
6000	1829	11.78	812.0	23.98	201.1	94.0
6500	1981	11.56	796.8	23.53	200.2	93.4
7000	2134	11.34	781.9	23.09	199.3	92.9
7500	2286	11.13	767.1	22.65	198.3	92.4
8000	2438	10.92	752.6	22.23	197.4	91.9
8500	2591	10.71	738.3	21.80	196.4	91.4
9000	2743	10.50	724.3	21.39	195.5	90.8
9500	2896	10.30	710.4	20.98	194.6	90.3
10000	3048	10.11	696.8	20.58	193.6	89.8
10500	3200	9.91	683.4	20.18	192.6	89.2
11000	3353	9.72	670.2	19.79	191.7	88.7
11500	3505	9.53	657.2	19.41	190.7	88.2
12000	3658	9.35	644.4	19.03	189.8	87.6
12500	3810	9.16	631.8	18.66	188.8	87.1
13000	3962	8.98	619.4	18.29	187.8	86.6
13500	4115	8.81	607.2	17.93	186.8	86.0
14000	4267	8.63	595.2	17.58	185.9	85.5

TABLE 12-5: Characteristics of Air and Pure Water Versus Elevation

SOUND DECIBEL RATINGS

Description of Sound	Decibels	Description of Sound	Decibels
Perforated eardrum	160	Hair dryer	75
30M from jet aircraft	140	Quiet car interior at 60mph	70
Gunshot	135	Easy listening music background	
Pain threshold	130	Noisy	60
Diesel engine -loud		Normal human voice at 5 feet	
Almost intolerable	120	Dishwasher	55
Rock band		Electric shaver	
Chainsaw	110	Sewing machine	
Auto horn		Clearly audible	50
Circular saw at operator		Quiet conversation	
Chainsaw at operator		Library	45
Rock concert	105	Subdued	40
Extremely noisy	100	Whisper	
Disco		Average residence	
Diesel engine —quiet		Quiet bedroom at night	
Osha mandated hearing protection	85	Extremely quiet	30
Lawn mower		Personal computer	
Noisy restaurant		Whispering at 5 feet	25
Bus interior		Barely audible	20
Very noisy	80	Background in tv studio	
Side of busy road		Ambient background wilderness	15
Vacuum cleaner		Quiet recording studio	10
Heavy traffic	75	Rustling leaves	
Flush toilet		Threshold of hearing	0

TABLE 12-6: Loudness of Typical Sounds in Decibels

Duration of Exposure (hrs/day)	Sound Level (dB)	Duration of Exposure (hrs/day)	Sound Level (dB)
16	85	1	105
8	90	1/2	110
4	95	1/4	115*
2	100	1/8	—

TABLE 12-7: OSHA Allowable Exposure Times Without Ear Protection for Various Sound Levels

* No exposure to noise in excess of 115 dB is allowed.

BLOOD ALCOHOL PERCENTAGES

Weight		Standard Drinks											
lbs	kg	1	2	3	4	5	6	7	8	9	10	11	12
		Blood Alcohol Percent (Male)											
100	45	0.04	0.07	0.11	0.14	0.18	0.21	0.25	0.29	0.32	0.36	0.39	0.43
110	50	0.03	0.07	0.10	0.13	0.16	0.20	0.23	0.26	0.29	0.33	0.36	0.39
120	54	0.03	0.06	0.09	0.12	0.15	0.18	0.21	0.24	0.27	0.30	0.33	0.36
130	59	0.03	0.05	0.08	0.11	0.14	0.17	0.19	0.22	0.25	0.28	0.30	0.33
140	64	0.03	0.05	0.08	0.10	0.13	0.15	0.18	0.20	0.23	0.26	0.28	0.31
150	68	0.02	0.05	0.07	0.10	0.12	0.14	0.17	0.19	0.21	0.24	0.26	0.29
160	73	0.02	0.04	0.07	0.09	0.11	0.13	0.16	0.18	0.20	0.22	0.25	0.27
170	77	0.02	0.04	0.06	0.08	0.11	0.13	0.15	0.17	0.19	0.21	0.23	0.25
180	82	0.02	0.04	0.06	0.08	0.10	0.12	0.14	0.16	0.18	0.20	0.22	0.24
190	86	0.02	0.04	0.06	0.08	0.09	0.11	0.13	0.15	0.17	0.19	0.21	0.23
200	91	0.02	0.04	0.05	0.07	0.09	0.11	0.13	0.14	0.16	0.18	0.20	0.21
210	95	0.02	0.03	0.05	0.07	0.09	0.10	0.12	0.14	0.15	0.17	0.19	0.20
220	100	0.02	0.03	0.05	0.07	0.08	0.10	0.11	0.13	0.15	0.16	0.18	0.20
230	104	0.02	0.03	0.05	0.06	0.08	0.09	0.11	0.12	0.14	0.16	0.17	0.19
240	109	0.01	0.03	0.04	0.06	0.07	0.09	0.10	0.12	0.13	0.15	0.16	0.18
250	113	0.01	0.03	0.04	0.06	0.07	0.09	0.10	0.11	0.13	0.14	0.16	0.17

Weight		Standard Drinks											
lbs	kg	1	2	3	4	5	6	7	8	9	10	11	12
		Blood Alcohol Content (Female)											
90	41	0.05	0.09	0.14	0.19	0.24	0.28	0.33	0.38	0.42	0.47	0.52	0.56
100	45	0.04	0.08	0.13	0.17	0.21	0.25	0.30	0.34	0.38	0.42	0.47	0.51
110	50	0.04	0.08	0.12	0.15	0.19	0.23	0.27	0.31	0.35	0.39	0.42	0.46
120	54	0.04	0.07	0.11	0.14	0.18	0.21	0.25	0.28	0.32	0.35	0.39	0.42
130	59	0.03	0.07	0.10	0.13	0.16	0.20	0.23	0.26	0.29	0.33	0.36	0.39
140	64	0.03	0.06	0.09	0.12	0.15	0.18	0.21	0.24	0.27	0.30	0.33	0.36
150	68	0.03	0.06	0.08	0.11	0.14	0.17	0.20	0.23	0.25	0.28	0.31	0.34
160	73	0.03	0.05	0.08	0.11	0.13	0.16	0.19	0.21	0.24	0.26	0.29	0.32
170	77	0.02	0.05	0.07	0.10	0.12	0.15	0.17	0.20	0.22	0.25	0.27	0.30
180	82	0.02	0.05	0.07	0.09	0.12	0.14	0.16	0.19	0.21	0.24	0.26	0.28
190	86	0.02	0.04	0.07	0.09	0.11	0.13	0.16	0.18	0.20	0.22	0.25	0.27
200	91	0.02	0.04	0.06	0.08	0.11	0.13	0.15	0.17	0.19	0.21	0.23	0.25
210	95	0.02	0.04	0.06	0.08	0.10	0.12	0.14	0.16	0.18	0.20	0.22	0.24
220	100	0.02	0.04	0.06	0.08	0.10	0.12	0.13	0.15	0.17	0.19	0.21	0.23
230	104	0.02	0.04	0.06	0.07	0.09	0.11	0.13	0.15	0.17	0.18	0.20	0.22
240	109	0.02	0.04	0.05	0.07	0.09	0.11	0.12	0.14	0.16	0.18	0.19	0.21

TABLE 12-8: Blood Alcohol Percent Versus Number of Drinks

Table 12-8 provides only a rough estimate of blood alcohol content since metabolism and other factors vary substantially from one individual to the other. The table is based on information from the National Highway Traffic Safety Administration (NHTSA).

The body metabolizes alcohol in the range of 0.10 to 0.20 percent per hour depending on the individual. This percent times the number of hours over which the alcohol is consumed is deducted from the percent derived from the tables to arrive at an estimated blood alcohol percent at any time.

Note: A standard drink is defined as a drink containing 1/2 ounce of pure alcohol. This would be equivalent to one ounce of 100 proof liquor, or one 5-ounce glass of wine or one 12-ounce beer.

The blood alcohol limit in most states is 0.08 or 0.10 percent and in Canada 0.08. Some states have lesser penalties set at 0.05 percent. Note: the blood alcohol percent is not truly a percentage, but is actually grams of alcohol per 100 milliliters of blood.

BOAT LOAN INTEREST

Table 12-9 on the following two pages show monthly loan payments for a $1000 loan for terms of 1 to 20 years. To calculate the monthly payment for any boat multiply the cost of the boat in thousands of dollars times the monthly payment from the table.

For example a boat costing 140,000 over 10 years at 6.00% interest would have payments of 140 x $11.10 = $1554 per month.

Yrs >	1	2	3	4	5
Interest			monthly payment		
5.00%	85.61	43.87	29.97	23.03	18.87
5.25%	85.72	43.98	30.08	23.14	18.99
5.50%	85.84	44.10	30.20	23.26	19.10
5.75%	85.95	44.21	30.31	23.37	19.22
6.00%	86.07	44.32	30.42	23.49	19.33
6.25%	86.18	44.43	30.54	23.60	19.45
6.50%	86.30	44.55	30.65	23.71	19.57
6.75%	86.41	44.66	30.76	23.83	19.68
7.00%	86.53	44.77	30.88	23.95	19.80
7.25%	86.64	44.89	30.99	24.06	19.92
7.50%	86.76	45.00	31.11	24.18	20.04
7.75%	86.87	45.11	31.22	24.30	20.16
8.00%	86.99	45.23	31.34	24.41	20.28
8.25%	87.10	45.34	31.45	24.53	20.40
8.50%	87.22	45.46	31.57	24.65	20.52
8.75%	87.34	45.57	31.68	24.77	20.64
9.00%	87.45	45.68	31.80	24.89	20.76
9.25%	87.57	45.80	31.92	25.00	20.88
9.50%	87.68	45.91	32.03	25.12	21.00
9.75%	87.80	46.03	32.15	25.24	21.12
10.00%	87.92	46.14	32.27	25.36	21.25
Yrs >	6	7	8	9	10
Interest			monthly payment		
5.00%	16.10	14.13	12.66	11.52	10.61
5.25%	16.22	14.25	12.78	11.64	10.73
5.50%	16.34	14.37	12.90	11.76	10.85
5.75%	16.46	14.49	13.02	11.88	10.98
6.00%	16.57	14.61	13.14	12.01	11.10
6.25%	16.69	14.73	13.26	12.13	11.23
6.50%	16.81	14.85	13.39	12.25	11.35
6.75%	16.93	14.97	13.51	12.38	11.48
7.00%	17.05	15.09	13.63	12.51	11.61
7.25%	17.17	15.22	13.76	12.63	11.74
7.50%	17.29	15.34	13.88	12.76	11.87
7.75%	17.41	15.46	14.01	12.89	12.00
8.00%	17.53	15.59	14.14	13.02	12.13
8.25%	17.66	15.71	14.26	13.15	12.27
8.50%	17.78	15.84	14.39	13.28	12.40
8.75%	17.90	15.96	14.52	13.41	12.53
9.00%	18.03	16.09	14.65	13.54	12.67
9.25%	18.15	16.22	14.78	13.68	12.80
9.50%	18.27	16.34	14.91	13.81	12.94
9.75%	18.40	16.47	15.04	13.94	13.08
10.00%	18.53	16.60	15.17	14.08	13.22
Payment is for $1000 loan principal					

TABLE 12-9(1): Loan Payments Table

Yrs >	11	12	13	14	15
Interest			monthly payment		
5.00%	9.86	9.25	8.73	8.29	7.91
5.25%	9.99	9.37	8.86	8.42	8.04
5.50%	10.11	9.50	8.99	8.55	8.17
5.75%	10.24	9.63	9.12	8.68	8.30
6.00%	10.37	9.76	9.25	8.81	8.44
6.25%	10.49	9.89	9.38	8.95	8.57
6.50%	10.62	10.02	9.51	9.08	8.71
6.75%	10.75	10.15	9.65	9.22	8.85
7.00%	10.88	10.28	9.78	9.35	8.99
7.25%	11.02	10.42	9.92	9.49	9.13
7.50%	11.15	10.55	10.05	9.63	9.27
7.75%	11.28	10.69	10.19	9.77	9.41
8.00%	11.42	10.82	10.33	9.91	9.56
8.25%	11.55	10.96	10.47	10.06	9.70
8.50%	11.69	11.10	10.61	10.20	9.85
8.75%	11.82	11.24	10.75	10.34	9.99
9.00%	11.96	11.38	10.90	10.49	10.14
9.25%	12.10	11.52	11.04	10.64	10.29
9.50%	12.24	11.66	11.19	10.78	10.44
9.75%	12.38	11.81	11.33	10.93	10.59
10.00%	12.52	11.95	11.48	11.08	10.75

Yrs >	16	17	18	19	20
Interest			monthly payment		
5.00%	7.58	7.29	7.03	6.80	6.60
5.25%	7.71	7.42	7.17	6.94	6.74
5.50%	7.84	7.56	7.30	7.08	6.88
5.75%	7.98	7.69	7.44	7.22	7.02
6.00%	8.11	7.83	7.58	7.36	7.16
6.25%	8.25	7.97	7.72	7.50	7.31
6.50%	8.39	8.11	7.87	7.65	7.46
6.75%	8.53	8.25	8.01	7.79	7.60
7.00%	8.67	8.40	8.16	7.94	7.75
7.25%	8.81	8.54	8.30	8.09	7.90
7.50%	8.96	8.69	8.45	8.24	8.06
7.75%	9.10	8.83	8.60	8.39	8.21
8.00%	9.25	8.98	8.75	8.55	8.36
8.25%	9.40	9.13	8.90	8.70	8.52
8.50%	9.54	9.28	9.05	8.85	8.68
8.75%	9.69	9.43	9.21	9.01	8.84
9.00%	9.85	9.59	9.36	9.17	9.00
9.25%	10.00	9.74	9.52	9.33	9.16
9.50%	10.15	9.90	9.68	9.49	9.32
9.75%	10.30	10.05	9.84	9.65	9.49
10.00%	10.46	10.21	10.00	9.81	9.65
Payment is for $1000 loan principal					

TABLE 12-9(2): Loan Payments Table

CURRENCY CONVERSION TABLE

Some exchange rates are very volatile; use these exchange rates only as a general guide. Tables are current as of December 2006.

To convert from any of the five currencies across the top, to any of the currencies down the left side; move down the column of the "from" currency to the row of the "to" currency and read the multiplier there.

For example, to convert from $50.00 USD to CAD, multiply by 1.13 to get $56.50 CAD.

Comments regarding currency exchange:

- To convert in the opposite direction, from currencies in the left column to currencies across the top; divide (instead of multiply) by the value in the intersecting cell. For example, to convert from $50.00 AUD to USD, divide by 1.28 to get $39.06.
- The Euro is the currency used in the Euro zone countries, which include Austria, Belgium, Finland, France, Germany, Greece, Ireland, Italy, Luxembourg, Netherlands, Portugal, and Spain. For this reason, most of these countries are not listed in the currency conversion table.
- Up-to-date rate conversions can be found at many web sites, including the following (a Google search will find plenty of others): http://www.oanda.com/

From →	USD	CAD	GBP	EUR	JPY
To ↓	Multiply By				
U.S. $ (USD)	1	0.882	1.95	1.32	0.0086
Canada $ (CAD)	1.13	1	2.21	1.49	0.0098
British Pound (GBP)	0.51	0.45	1	0.68	0.0044
Euro (EUR)	0.76	0.67	1.48	1	0.0065
Japan Yen (JPY)	116	102	226	153	1
Argentine Peso	3.07	2.71	5.99	4.05	0.026
Australia $ (AUD)	1.28	1.13	2.49	1.68	0.011
Bahamian Dollar	0.99	0.87	1.90	1.30	0.0085
Barbados Dollar	1.97	1.74	3.84	2.60	0.017
Belize Dollar	1.88	1.66	3.66	2.47	0.016
Bermudian Dollar	0.99	0.87	1.93	1.30	0.0085
Brazilian Real	2.18	1.92	4.24	2.87	0.019
Cayman Islands $	0.82	0.72	1.59	1.08	0.007
Chilean Peso	529	466	1030	697	4.56
Chinese Yuan	7.82	6.87	15.29	10.32	0.0674
Costa Rican Colon	498	439	971	656	4.29
Cuban Peso	22.2	19.6	43.3	29.3	0.19
Danish Krone	5.66	4.99	11.00	7.45	0.049
Ecuador Sucre	25000	21950	48850	32980	215
Egyptian Pound	5.66	4.99	11.00	7.45	0.049
El Salvador Colon	8.38	7.39	16.30	11.00	0.072
Fiji Dollar	1.67	1.47	3.25	2.20	0.014
Gibraltar Pound	0.51	0.45	1.00	0.68	0.0044
Hong Kong $	7.78	6.83	15.20	10.28	0.0670
Iceland Krona	69	61	134	91	0.59
Israeli New Shekel	4.26	3.76	8.31	5.61	0.037
Jamaican Dollar	66.7	58.8	130	87.90	0.575
Kuwaiti Dinar	0.29	0.25	0.56	0.38	0.0025
Mexican Peso	11.00	9.70	21.00	15.00	0.0949
New Zealand Dollar	1.47	1.30	2.87	1.94	0.0127
Norwegian Kroner	6.27	5.53	12.20	8.27	0.0541
Panamanian Balboa	0.97	0.85	1.88	1.27	0.0083
Paraguay Guarani	5180	4570	10100	6830	44.7
Peruvian Nuevo Sol	3.19	2.81	6.22	4.20	0.0275
Philippine Peso	49	43	97	65	0.428
Russian Rouble	26	23	51	35	0.227
Saudi Riyal	3.75	3.31	7.31	4.94	0.323
Singapore Dollar	1.55	1.36	3.01	2.04	0.0133
South African Rand	7.12	6.28	13.90	9.38	0.0614
Swiss Franc	1.21	1.06	2.35	1.59	0.0104
Korean Won	921	912	1800	1210	7.94
Sri Lanka Rupee	108	95	210	142	0.93
Swedish Krona	6.90	6.08	13.50	9.08	0.0594
Taiwan Dollar	32.50	28.70	63.40	42.80	0.28
Trinidad/Tobago Dollar	6.15	5.42	12.00	8.10	0.053
Venezuelan Bolivar	2150	1890	4190	2830	18.5
Vietnamese Dong	15800	14000	30900	20900	136

TABLE 12-10: Currency Conversions (December 2006)

NUMBERED DAYS OF THE YEAR

1-Jan 1	2-Jan 2	3-Jan 3	4-Jan 4	5-Jan 5
6-Jan 6	7-Jan 7	8-Jan 8	9-Jan 9	10-Jan 10
11-Jan 11	12-Jan 12	13-Jan 13	14-Jan 14	15-Jan 15
16-Jan 16	17-Jan 17	18-Jan 18	19-Jan 19	20-Jan 20
21-Jan 21	22-Jan 22	23-Jan 23	24-Jan 24	25-Jan 25
26-Jan 26	27-Jan 27	28-Jan 28	29-Jan 29	30-Jan 30
31-Jan 31	1-Feb 32	2-Feb 33	3-Feb 34	4-Feb 35
5-Feb 36	6-Feb 37	7-Feb 38	8-Feb 39	9-Feb 40
10-Feb 41	11-Feb 42	12-Feb 43	13-Feb 44	14-Feb 45
15-Feb 46	16-Feb 47	17-Feb 48	18-Feb 49	19-Feb 50
20-Feb 51	21-Feb 52	22-Feb 53	23-Feb 54	24-Feb 55
25-Feb 56	26-Feb 57	27-Feb 58	28-Feb 59	1-Mar 60
2-Mar 61	3-Mar 62	4-Mar 63	5-Mar 64	6-Mar 65
7-Mar 66	8-Mar 67	9-Mar 68	10-Mar 69	11-Mar 70
12-Mar 71	13-Mar 72	14-Mar 73	15-Mar 74	16-Mar 75
17-Mar 76	18-Mar 77	19-Mar 78	20-Mar 79	21-Mar 80
22-Mar 81	23-Mar 82	24-Mar 83	25-Mar 84	26-Mar 85
27-Mar 86	28-Mar 87	29-Mar 88	30-Mar 89	31-Mar 90
1-Apr 91	2-Apr 92	3-Apr 93	4-Apr 94	5-Apr 95
6-Apr 96	7-Apr 97	8-Apr 98	9-Apr 99	10-Apr 100
11-Apr 101	12-Apr 102	13-Apr 103	14-Apr 104	15-Apr 105
16-Apr 106	17-Apr 107	18-Apr 108	19-Apr 109	20-Apr 110
21-Apr 111	22-Apr 112	23-Apr 113	24-Apr 114	25-Apr 115
26-Apr 116	27-Apr 117	28-Apr 118	29-Apr 119	30-Apr 120
1-May 121	2-May 122	3-May 123	4-May 124	5-May 125
6-May 126	7-May 127	8-May 128	9-May 129	10-May 130
11-May 131	12-May 132	13-May 133	14-May 134	15-May 135
16-May 136	17-May 137	18-May 138	19-May 139	20-May 140
21-May 141	22-May 142	23-May 143	24-May 144	25-May 145
26-May 146	27-May 147	28-May 148	29-May 149	30-May 150
31-May 151	1-Jun 152	2-Jun 153	3-Jun 154	4-Jun 155
5-Jun 156	6-Jun 157	7-Jun 158	8-Jun 159	9-Jun 160
10-Jun 161	11-Jun 162	12-Jun 163	13-Jun 164	14-Jun 165
15-Jun 166	16-Jun 167	17-Jun 168	18-Jun 169	19-Jun 170
20-Jun 171	21-Jun 172	22-Jun 173	23-Jun 174	24-Jun 175
25-Jun 176	26-Jun 177	27-Jun 178	28-Jun 179	29-Jun 180
30-Jun 181				

TABLE 12-11(1): Numbered Days of the Year—Julian Calendar. Leap Years Add One Day After February 28th

	1-Jul 182	2-Jul 183	3-Jul 184	4-Jul 185
5-Jul 186	6-Jul 187	7-Jul 188	8-Jul 189	9-Jul 190
10-Jul 191	11-Jul 192	12-Jul 193	13-Jul 194	14-Jul 195
15-Jul 196	16-Jul 197	17-Jul 198	18-Jul 199	19-Jul 200
20-Jul 201	21-Jul 202	22-Jul 203	23-Jul 204	24-Jul 205
25-Jul 206	26-Jul 207	27-Jul 208	28-Jul 209	29-Jul 210
30-Jul 211	31-Jul 212	1-Aug 213	2-Aug 214	3-Aug 215
4-Aug 216	5-Aug 217	6-Aug 218	7-Aug 219	8-Aug 220
9-Aug 221	10-Aug 222	11-Aug 223	12-Aug 224	13-Aug 225
14-Aug 226	15-Aug 227	16-Aug 228	17-Aug 229	18-Aug 230
19-Aug 231	20-Aug 232	21-Aug 233	22-Aug 234	23-Aug 235
24-Aug 236	25-Aug 237	26-Aug 238	27-Aug 239	28-Aug 240
29-Aug 241	30-Aug 242	31-Aug 243	1-Sep 244	2-Sep 245
3-Sep 246	4-Sep 247	5-Sep 248	6-Sep 249	7-Sep 250
8-Sep 251	9-Sep 252	10-Sep 253	11-Sep 254	12-Sep 255
13-Sep 256	14-Sep 257	15-Sep 258	16-Sep 259	17-Sep 260
18-Sep 261	19-Sep 262	20-Sep 263	21-Sep 264	22-Sep 265
23-Sep 266	24-Sep 267	25-Sep 268	26-Sep 269	27-Sep 270
28-Sep 271	29-Sep 272	30-Sep 273	1-Oct 274	2-Oct 275
3-Oct 276	4-Oct 277	5-Oct 278	6-Oct 279	7-Oct 280
8-Oct 281	9-Oct 282	10-Oct 283	11-Oct 284	12-Oct 285
13-Oct 286	14-Oct 287	15-Oct 288	16-Oct 289	17-Oct 290
18-Oct 291	19-Oct 292	20-Oct 293	21-Oct 294	22-Oct 295
23-Oct 296	24-Oct 297	25-Oct 298	26-Oct 299	27-Oct 300
28-Oct 301	29-Oct 302	30-Oct 303	31-Oct 304	1-Nov 305
2-Nov 306	3-Nov 307	4-Nov 308	5-Nov 309	6-Nov 310
7-Nov 311	8-Nov 312	9-Nov 313	10-Nov 314	11-Nov 315
12-Nov 316	13-Nov 317	14-Nov 318	15-Nov 319	16-Nov 320
17-Nov 321	18-Nov 322	19-Nov 323	20-Nov 324	21-Nov 325
22-Nov 326	23-Nov 327	24-Nov 328	25-Nov 329	26-Nov 330
27-Nov 331	28-Nov 332	29-Nov 333	30-Nov 334	1-Dec 335
2-Dec 336	3-Dec 337	4-Dec 338	5-Dec 339	6-Dec 340
7-Dec 341	8-Dec 342	9-Dec 343	10-Dec 344	11-Dec 345
12-Dec 346	13-Dec 347	14-Dec 348	15-Dec 349	16-Dec 350
17-Dec 351	18-Dec 352	19-Dec 353	20-Dec 354	21-Dec 355
22-Dec 356	23-Dec 357	24-Dec 358	25-Dec 359	26-Dec 360
27-Dec 361	28-Dec 362	29-Dec 363	30-Dec 364	31-Dec 365

TABLE 12-11(2): Numbered Days of the Year—Julian Calendar. Leap Years Add One Day After February 28th

MEASUREMENT CONVERSION TABLES

INCH FRACTIONS TO DECIMAL INCHES AND MILLIMETERS

Inches				Inches			
1/64	Fract	Decimal	mm	1/64	Fract	Decimal	mm
1		0.015625	0.396875	33		0.515625	13.096875
2	1/32	0.03125	0.79375	34	17/32	0.53125	13.49375
3		0.046875	1.190625	35		0.546875	13.890625
4	1/16	0.0625	1.5875	36	9/16	0.5625	14.2875
5		0.078125	1.984375	37		0.578125	14.684375
6	3/32	0.09375	2.38125	38	19/32	0.59375	15.08125
7		0.109375	2.778125	39		0.609375	15.478125
8	1/8	0.125	3.175	40	5/8	0.625	15.875
9		0.140625	3.571875	41		0.640625	16.271875
10	5/32	0.15625	3.96875	42	21/32	0.65625	16.66875
11		0.171875	4.365625	43		0.671875	17.065625
12	3/16	0.1875	4.7625	44	11/16	0.6875	17.4625
13		0.203125	5.159375	45		0.703125	17.859375
14	7/32	0.21875	5.55625	46	23/32	0.71875	18.25625
15		0.234375	5.953125	47		0.734375	18.653125
16	1/4	0.25	6.35	48	3/4	0.75	19.05
17		0.265625	6.746875	49		0.765625	19.446875
18	9/32	0.28125	7.14375	50	25/32	0.78125	19.84375
19		0.296875	7.540625	51		0.796875	20.240625
20	5/16	0.3125	7.9375	52	13/16	0.8125	20.6375
21		0.328125	8.334375	53		0.828125	21.034375
22	11/32	0.34375	8.73125	54	27/32	0.84375	21.43125
23		0.359375	9.128125	55		0.859375	21.828125
24	3/8	0.375	9.525	56	7/8	0.875	22.225
25		0.390625	9.921875	57		0.890625	22.621875
26	13/32	0.40625	10.31875	58	29/32	0.90625	23.01875
27		0.421875	10.715625	59		0.921875	23.415625
28	7/16	0.4375	11.1125	60	15/16	0.9375	23.8125
29		0.453125	11.509375	61		0.953125	24.209375
30	15/32	0.46875	11.90625	62	31/32	0.96875	24.60625
31		0.484375	12.303125	63		0.984375	25.003125
32	1/2	0.5	12.7	64	1	1	25.4

TABLE 12-12: Convert Fractions to Decimal

Dec	64	32	16	8	4	Dec	64	32	16	8	4
0.01	1/64	0/32				0.51	33/64	16/32			
0.02			0/16			0.52			8/16		
0.03	2/64	1/32				0.53	34/64	17/32			
0.04	3/64			0/8		0.54				4/8	
0.05						0.55	35/64				
0.06	4/64	2/32	1/16			0.56	36/64	18/32	9/16		
0.07					0/4	0.57					2/4
0.08	5/64					0.58	37/64				
0.09	6/64	3/32				0.59	38/64	19/32			
0.10						0.6					
0.11	7/64					0.61	39/64				
0.12	8/64	4/32	2/16	1/8		0.62	40/64	20/32	10/16	5/8	
0.13						0.63					
0.14	9/64					0.64	41/64				
0.15	10/64	5/32				0.65	42/64	21/32			
0.16						0.66					
0.17	11/64					0.67	43/64				
0.18	12/64	6/32	3/16			0.68	44/64	22/32	11/16		
0.19						0.69					
0.20	13/64					0.70	45/64				
0.21						0.71					
0.22	14/64	7/32				0.72	46/64	23/32			
0.23	15/64					0.73	47/64				
0.24						0.74					
0.25	16/64	8/32	4/16	2/8	1/4	0.75	48/64	24/32	12/16	6/8	3/4
0.26	17/64					0.76	49/64				
0.27						0.77					
0.28	18/64	9/32				0.78	50/64	25/32			
0.29	19/64					0.79	51/64				
0.30						0.8					
0.31	20/64	10/32	5/16			0.81	52/64	26/32	13/16		
0.32						0.82					
0.33	21/64					0.83	53/64				
0.34	22/64	11/32				0.84	54/64	27/32			
0.35						0.85					
0.36	23/64					0.86	55/64				
0.37	24/64	12/32	6/16	3/8		0.87	56/64	28/32	14/16	7/8	
0.38						0.88					
0.39	25/64					0.89	57/64				
0.40	26/64	13/32				0.9	58/64	29/32			
0.41	27/64					0.91					
0.42						0.92	59/64				
0.43						0.93					
0.44	28/64	14/32	7/16		2/4	0.94	60/64	30/32	15/16		4/4
0.45						0.95					
0.46	29/64					0.96	61/64				
0.47	30/64	15/32		4/8		0.97	62/64	31/32			8/8
0.48	31/64					0.98					
0.49			8/16			0.99	63/64		16/16		
0.50	32/64	16/32				1	64/64	32/32			

TABLE 12-13: Convert Decimal Inches to Fractions

Inch	0	1	2	3	4	5
0	0.0000	0.0833	0.1667	0.2500	0.3333	0.4167
1/32	0.0026	0.0859	0.1693	0.2526	0.3359	0.4193
1/16	0.0052	0.0885	0.1719	0.2552	0.3385	0.4219
3/32	0.0078	0.0911	0.1745	0.2578	0.3411	0.4245
1/8	0.0104	0.0938	0.1771	0.2604	0.3438	0.4271
5/32	0.0130	0.0964	0.1797	0.2630	0.3464	0.4297
3/16	0.0156	0.0990	0.1823	0.2656	0.3490	0.4323
7/32	0.0182	0.1016	0.1849	0.2682	0.3516	0.4349
1/4	0.0208	0.1042	0.1875	0.2708	0.3542	0.4375
9/32	0.0234	0.1068	0.1901	0.2734	0.3568	0.4401
5/16	0.0260	0.1094	0.1927	0.2760	0.3594	0.4427
11/32	0.0286	0.1120	0.1953	0.2786	0.3620	0.4453
3/8	0.0313	0.1146	0.1979	0.2813	0.3646	0.4479
13/32	0.0339	0.1172	0.2005	0.2839	0.3672	0.4505
7/16	0.0365	0.1198	0.2031	0.2865	0.3698	0.4531
15/32	0.0391	0.1224	0.2057	0.2891	0.3724	0.4557
1/2	0.0417	0.1250	0.2083	0.2917	0.3750	0.4583
17/32	0.0443	0.1276	0.2109	0.2943	0.3776	0.4609
9/16	0.0469	0.1302	0.2135	0.2969	0.3802	0.4635
19/32	0.0495	0.1328	0.2161	0.2995	0.3828	0.4661
5/8	0.0521	0.1354	0.2188	0.3021	0.3854	0.4688
21/32	0.0547	0.1380	0.2214	0.3047	0.3880	0.4714
11/16	0.0573	0.1406	0.2240	0.3073	0.3906	0.4740
23/32	0.0599	0.1432	0.2266	0.3099	0.3932	0.4766
3/4	0.0625	0.1458	0.2292	0.3125	0.3958	0.4792
25/32	0.0651	0.1484	0.2318	0.3151	0.3984	0.4818
13/16	0.0677	0.1510	0.2344	0.3177	0.4010	0.4844
27/32	0.0703	0.1536	0.2370	0.3203	0.4036	0.4870
7/8	0.0729	0.1563	0.2396	0.3229	0.4063	0.4896
29/32	0.0755	0.1589	0.2422	0.3255	0.4089	0.4922
15/16	0.0781	0.1615	0.2448	0.3281	0.4115	0.4948
31/32	0.0807	0.1641	0.2474	0.3307	0.4141	0.4974

TABLE 12-14(1): Convert Inches and Inch Fractions to Decimal Feet.

Example: 4-3/16 inches = 0.3490 feet

Inch	6	7	8	9	10	11
0	0.5000	0.5833	0.6667	0.7500	0.8333	0.9167
1/32	0.5026	0.5859	0.6693	0.7526	0.8359	0.9193
1/16	0.5052	0.5885	0.6719	0.7552	0.8385	0.9219
3/32	0.5078	0.5911	0.6745	0.7578	0.8411	0.9245
1/8	0.5104	0.5938	0.6771	0.7604	0.8438	0.9271
5/32	0.5130	0.5964	0.6797	0.7630	0.8464	0.9297
3/16	0.5156	0.5990	0.6823	0.7656	0.8490	0.9323
7/32	0.5182	0.6016	0.6849	0.7682	0.8516	0.9349
1/4	0.5208	0.6042	0.6875	0.7708	0.8542	0.9375
9/32	0.5234	0.6068	0.6901	0.7734	0.8568	0.9401
5/16	0.5260	0.6094	0.6927	0.7760	0.8594	0.9427
11/32	0.5286	0.6120	0.6953	0.7786	0.8620	0.9453
3/8	0.5313	0.6146	0.6979	0.7813	0.8646	0.9479
13/32	0.5339	0.6172	0.7005	0.7839	0.8672	0.9505
7/16	0.5365	0.6198	0.7031	0.7865	0.8698	0.9531
15/32	0.5391	0.6224	0.7057	0.7891	0.8724	0.9557
1/2	0.5417	0.6250	0.7083	0.7917	0.8750	0.9583
17/32	0.5443	0.6276	0.7109	0.7943	0.8776	0.9609
9/16	0.5469	0.6302	0.7135	0.7969	0.8802	0.9635
19/32	0.5495	0.6328	0.7161	0.7995	0.8828	0.9661
5/8	0.5521	0.6354	0.7188	0.8021	0.8854	0.9688
21/32	0.5547	0.6380	0.7214	0.8047	0.8880	0.9714
11/16	0.5573	0.6406	0.7240	0.8073	0.8906	0.9740
23/32	0.5599	0.6432	0.7266	0.8099	0.8932	0.9766
3/4	0.5625	0.6458	0.7292	0.8125	0.8958	0.9792
25/32	0.5651	0.6484	0.7318	0.8151	0.8984	0.9818
13/16	0.5677	0.6510	0.7344	0.8177	0.9010	0.9844
27/32	0.5703	0.6536	0.7370	0.8203	0.9036	0.9870
7/8	0.5729	0.6563	0.7396	0.8229	0.9063	0.9896
29/32	0.5755	0.6589	0.7422	0.8255	0.9089	0.9922
15/16	0.5781	0.6615	0.7448	0.8281	0.9115	0.9948
31/32	0.5807	0.6641	0.7474	0.8307	0.9141	0.9974

TABLE 12-15(2): Convert Inches and Inch Fractions to Decimal Feet

Example: 9-13/16 inches = 0.8177 feet

WEIGHT AND VOLUME OF LIQUIDS
Water Weight and Volume Conversion

From	To	Multiply By
cu feet H2O		
	gallons (Imperial) H2O	6.2288
	gallons (U.S.) H2O	7.4805
	kilograms H2O	28.317
	liters H2O	28.317
	pounds H2O	62.428
gallons (Imperial) H2O		
	cu feet H2O	0.16054
	gallons (U.S.) H2O	1.2009
	kilograms H2O	4.5461
	liters H2O	4.5461
	pounds H2O	10.022
gallons (U.S.) H2O		
	cu feet H2O	0.13368
	gallons (Imperial) H2O	0.83267
	kilograms H2O	3.7854
	liters H2O	3.7854
	pounds H2O	8.3454
kilograms H2O		
	cu feet H2O	0.035315
	gallons (Imperial) H2O	0.21997
	gallons (U.S.) H2O	0.26417
	liters H2O	1
	pounds H2O	2.2046
liters H2O		
	cu feet H2O	0.035315
	gallons (Imperial) H2O	0.21997
	gallons (U.S.) H2O	0.26417
	kilograms H2O	1
	pounds H2O	2.2046
pounds H2O		
	cu feet H2O	0.016019
	gallons (Imperial) H2O	0.099776
	gallons (U.S.) H2O	0.11983
	kilograms H2O	0.45359
	liters H2O	0.45359

TABLE 12-16: Weight and Volume of Water

Seawater Weight and Volume Conversion

From	To	Multiply By
cu feet seawater		
	gallons (Imperial) seawater	6.2288
	gallons (U.S.) seawater	7.4805
	kilograms seawater	29.043
	liters seawater	28.317
	pounds seawater	64.029
gallons (Imperial) seawater		
	cu feet seawater	0.16054
	gallons (U.S.) seawater	1.2009
	kilograms seawater	4.6627
	liters seawater	4.5461
	pounds seawater	10.279
gallons (U.S.) seawater		
	cu feet seawater	0.13368
	gallons (Imperial) seawater	0.83267
	kilograms seawater	3.8825
	liters seawater	3.7854
	pounds seawater	8.5594
kilograms seawater		
	cu feet seawater	0.034432
	gallons (Imperial) seawater	0.21447
	gallons (U.S.) seawater	0.25757
	liters seawater	0.975
	pounds seawater	2.2046
liters seawater		
	cu feet seawater	0.035315
	gallons (Imperial) seawater	0.21997
	gallons (U.S.) seawater	0.26417
	kilograms seawater	1.0256
	pounds seawater	2.2612
pounds seawater		
	cu feet seawater	0.015618
	gallons (Imperial) seawater	0.097282
	gallons (U.S.) seawater	0.11683
	kilograms seawater	0.45359
	liters seawater	0.44225

TABLE 12-17: Weight and Volume of Seawater

Diesel Fuel Weight and Volume Conversion

From	To	Multiply By
cu feet diesel		
	gallons (Imperial) diesel	6.2288
	gallons (U.S.) diesel	7.4805
	kilograms diesel	24.069
	liters diesel	28.317
	pounds diesel	53.064
gallons (Imperial) diesel		
	cu feet diesel	0.16054
	gallons (U.S.) diesel	1.2009
	kilograms diesel	3.8642
	liters diesel	4.5461
	pounds diesel	8.5191
gallons (U.S.) diesel		
	cu feet diesel	0.13368
	gallons (Imperial) diesel	0.83267
	kilograms diesel	3.2176
	liters diesel	3.7854
	pounds diesel	7.0936
kilograms diesel		
	cu feet diesel	0.041547
	gallons (Imperial) diesel	0.25879
	gallons (U.S.) diesel	0.31079
	liters diesel	1.1765
	pounds diesel	2.2046
liters diesel		
	cu feet diesel	0.035315
	gallons (Imperial) diesel	0.21997
	gallons (U.S.) diesel	0.26417
	kilograms diesel	0.85
	pounds diesel	1.8739
pounds diesel		
	cu feet diesel	0.018845
	gallons (Imperial) diesel	0.11738
	gallons (U.S.) diesel	0.14097
	kilograms diesel	0.45359
	liters diesel	0.53364

TABLE 12-18: Weight and Volume of Diesel Fuel

Gasoline Weight and Volume Conversion

From	To	Multiply By
cu feet gasoline		
	gallons (Imperial) gasoline	6.2288
	gallons (U.S.) gasoline	7.4805
	kilograms gasoline	21.201
	liters gasoline	28.317
	pounds gasoline	46.741
gallons (Imperial) gasoline		
	cu feet gasoline	0.16054
	gallons (U.S.) gasoline	1.2009
	kilograms gasoline	3.4037
	liters gasoline	4.5461
	pounds gasoline	7.504
gallons (U.S.) gasoline		
	cu feet gasoline	0.13368
	gallons (Imperial) gasoline	0.83267
	kilograms gasoline	2.8342
	liters gasoline	3.7854
	pounds gasoline	6.2484
kilograms gasoline		
	cu feet gasoline	0.047167
	gallons (Imperial) gasoline	0.29379
	gallons (U.S.) gasoline	0.35283
	liters gasoline	1.3356
	pounds gasoline	2.2046
liters gasoline		
	cu feet gasoline	0.035315
	gallons (Imperial) gasoline	0.21997
	gallons (U.S.) gasoline	0.26417
	kilograms gasoline	0.74872
	pounds gasoline	1.6506
pounds gasoline		
	cu feet gasoline	0.021395
	gallons (Imperial) gasoline	0.13326
	gallons (U.S.) gasoline	0.16004
	kilograms gasoline	0.45359
	liters gasoline	0.60583

TABLE 12-19: Weight and Volume of Gasoline

Gallons	20:1	24:1	28:1	32:1	40:1	50:1	100:1
1	6.4 oz / 190 ml	5.3 oz / 160 ml	4.6 oz / 140 ml	4 oz / 120 ml	3.2 oz / 90 ml	2.6 oz / 80 ml	1.3 oz / 40 ml
2	13 oz / 380 ml	11 oz / 330 ml	9 oz / 270 ml	8 oz / 240 ml	6.4 oz / 190 ml	5.1 oz / 150 ml	2.6 oz / 80 ml
3	19 oz / 560 ml	16 oz / 470 ml	14 oz / 410 ml	12 oz / 350 ml	9.6 oz / 280 ml	7.7 oz / 230 ml	3.8 oz / 110 ml
4	26 oz / 770 ml	21 oz / 620 ml	18 oz / 530 ml	16 oz / 470 ml	13 oz / 380 ml	10 oz / 300 ml	5.1 oz / 150 ml
5	1 qt / 0.9 l	27 oz / 800 ml	23 oz / 680 ml	20 oz / 590 ml	16 oz / 470 ml	13 oz / 380 ml	6.4 oz / 190 ml
6	1.2 qt / 1.1 l	1 qt / 0.9 l	27 oz / 800 ml	24 oz / 710 ml	19 oz / 560 ml	15 oz / 440 ml	7.7 oz / 230 ml
7	1.4 qt / 1.3 l	1.2 qt / 1.1 l	1 qt / 0.9 l	28 oz / 830 ml	22 oz / 650 ml	18 oz / 530 ml	9 oz / 270 ml
8	1.6 qt / 1.5 l	1.3 qt / 1.2 l	1.1 qt / 1.1 l	1 qt / 0.9 l	26 oz / 770 ml	20 oz / 590 ml	10 oz / 300 ml
9	1.8 qt / 1.7 l	1.5 qt / 1.4 l	1.3 qt / 1.2 l	1.1 qt / 1 l	29 oz / 860 ml	23 oz / 680 ml	12 oz / 350 ml
10	2 qt / 1.9 l	1.7 qt / 1.6 l	1.4 qt / 1.3 l	1.3 qt / 1.2 l	1 qt / 0.9 l	26 oz / 770 ml	13 oz / 380 ml
12	2.4 qt / 2.3 l	2 qt / 1.9 l	1.7 qt / 1.6 l	1.5 qt / 1.4 l	1.2 qt / 1.1 l	31 oz / 920 ml	15 oz / 440 ml
14	2.8 qt / 2.6 l	2.3 qt / 2.2 l	2 qt / 1.9 l	1.8 qt / 1.7 l	1.4 qt / 1.3 l	1.1 qt / 1 l	18 oz / 530 ml
16	3.2 qt / 3.1 l	2.7 qt / 2.5 l	2.3 qt / 2.2 l	2 qt / 1.9 l	1.6 qt / 1.5 l	1.3 qt / 1.2 l	20 oz / 590 ml
18	3.6 qt / 3.4 l	3 qt / 2.8 l	2.6 qt / 2.5 l	2.3 qt / 2.2 l	1.8 qt / 1.7 l	1.4 qt / 1.3 l	23 oz / 680 ml
20	4 qt / 3.8 l	3.3 qt / 3.1 l	2.9 qt / 2.7 l	2.5 qt / 2.4 l	2 qt / 1.9 l	1.6 qt / 1.5 l	26 oz / 770 ml
25	5 qt / 4.7 l	4.2 qt / 4 l	3.6 qt / 3.4 l	3.1 qt / 2.9 l	2.5 qt / 2.4 l	2 qt / 1.9 l	1 qt / 0.9 l
30	6 qt / 5.7 l	5 qt / 4.7 l	4.3 qt / 4.1 l	3.8 qt / 3.6 l	3 qt / 2.8 l	2.4 qt / 2.3 l	1.2 qt / 1.1 l
35	7 qt / 6.6 l	5.8 qt / 5.5 l	5 qt / 4.7 l	4.4 qt / 4.2 l	3.5 qt / 3.3 l	2.8 qt / 2.6 l	1.4 qt / 1.3 l
40	8 qt / 7.6 l	6.7 qt / 6.3 l	5.7 qt / 5.4 l	5 qt / 4.7 l	4 qt / 3.8 l	3.2 qt / 3.1 l	1.6 qt / 1.5 l
45	9 qt / 8.5 l	7.5 qt / 7.1 l	6.4 qt / 6.1 l	5.6 qt / 5.3 l	4.5 qt / 4.3 l	3.6 qt / 3.4 l	1.8 qt / 1.7 l
50	10 qt / 9.5 l	8.3 qt / 7.9 l	7.1 qt / 6.7 l	6.3 qt / 5.9 l	5 qt / 4.7 l	4 qt / 3.8 l	2 qt / 1.9 l
55	11 qt / 10 l	9.2 qt / 8.7 l	7.9 qt / 7.5 l	6.9 qt / 6.6 l	5.5 qt / 5.2 l	4.4 qt / 4.2 l	2.2 qt / 2.1 l
60	12 qt / 11 l	10 qt / 9.5 l	8.6 qt / 8.1 l	7.5 qt / 7.1 l	6 qt / 5.7 l	4.8 qt / 4.5 l	2.4 qt / 2.3 l
65	13 qt / 12 l	11 qt / 10 l	9.3 qt / 8.8 l	8.1 qt / 7.6 l	6.5 qt / 6.2 l	5.2 qt / 4.9 l	2.6 qt / 2.5 l
70	14 qt / 13 l	12 qt / 11 l	10 qt / 9.5 l	8.8 qt / 8.5 l	7 qt / 6.6 l	5.6 qt / 5.3 l	2.8 qt / 2.6 l
80	16 qt / 15 l	13 qt / 12 l	11 qt / 11 l	10 qt / 9.5 l	8 qt / 7.6 l	6.4 qt / 6.1 l	3.2 qt / 3.1 l
90	18 qt / 17 l	15 qt / 14 l	13 qt / 12 l	11 qt / 10 l	9 qt / 8.5 l	7.2 qt / 6.8 l	3.6 qt / 3.4 l
100	20 qt / 19 l	17 qt / 16 l	14 qt / 13 l	13 qt / 12 l	10 qt / 9.5 l	8 qt / 7.6 l	4 qt / 3.8 l

TABLE 12-20: Fuel/Oil Mixture for 2-Cycle Engines–U.S.

Liters	20:1	24:1	28:1	32:1	40:1	50:1	100:1
				Fuel / Oil Ratio			
1	50 ml / 1.7 oz	42 ml / 1.4 oz	36 ml / 1.2 oz	31 ml / 1 oz	25 ml / 0.8 oz	20 ml / 0.7 oz	10 ml / 0.3 oz
2	100 ml / 3.4 oz	83 ml / 2.8 oz	71 ml / 2.4 oz	63 ml / 2.1 oz	50 ml / 1.7 oz	40 ml / 1.4 oz	20 ml / 0.7 oz
3	150 ml / 5.1 oz	125 ml / 4.2 oz	107 ml / 3.6 oz	94 ml / 3.2 oz	75 ml / 2.5 oz	60 ml / 2 oz	30 ml / 1 oz
4	200 ml / 6.8 oz	167 ml / 5.6 oz	143 ml / 4.8 oz	125 ml / 4.2 oz	100 ml / 3.4 oz	80 ml / 2.7 oz	40 ml / 1.4 oz
5	250 ml / 8.5 oz	208 ml / 7 oz	179 ml / 6.1 oz	156 ml / 5.3 oz	125 ml / 4.2 oz	100 ml / 3.4 oz	50 ml / 1.7 oz
10	500 ml / 17 oz	417 ml / 14 oz	357 ml / 12 oz	313 ml / 11 oz	250 ml / 8.5 oz	200 ml / 6.8 oz	100 ml / 3.4 oz
15	750 ml / 25 oz	625 ml / 21 oz	536 ml / 18 oz	469 ml / 16 oz	375 ml / 13 oz	300 ml / 10 oz	150 ml / 5.1 oz
20	1 l / 1.1 qt	833 ml / 28 oz	714 ml / 24 oz	625 ml / 21 oz	500 ml / 17 oz	400 ml / 14 oz	200 ml / 6.8 oz
25	1.3 l / 1.3 qt	1 l / 1.1 qt	893 ml / 30 oz	781 ml / 26 oz	625 ml / 21 oz	500 ml / 17 oz	250 ml / 8.5 oz
30	1.5 / 1.6	1.3 / 1.3	1.1 l / 1.2 qt	938 ml / 32 oz	750 ml / 25 oz	600 ml / 20 oz	300 ml / 10 oz
35	1.8 / 1.9	1.5 / 1.5	1.3 / 1.3	1.1 l / 1.2 qt	875 ml / 30 oz	700 ml / 24 oz	350 ml / 12 oz
40	2 / 2.1	1.7 / 1.8	1.4 / 1.5	1.3 / 1.3	1 l / 1.1 qt	800 ml / 27 oz	400 ml / 14 oz
45	2.3 / 2.4	1.9 / 2	1.6 / 1.7	1.4 / 1.5	1.1 / 1.2	900 ml / 30 oz	450 ml / 15 oz
50	2.5 / 2.6	2.1 / 2.2	1.8 / 1.9	1.6 / 1.7	1.3 / 1.3	1 l / 1.1 qt	500 ml / 17 oz
55	2.8 / 2.9	2.3 / 2.4	2 / 2.1	1.7 / 1.8	1.4 / 1.5	1.1 / 1.2	550 ml / 19 oz
60	3 / 3.2	2.5 / 2.6	2.1 / 2.3	1.9 / 2	1.5 / 1.6	1.2 / 1.3	600 ml / 20 oz
65	3.3 / 3.4	2.7 / 2.9	2.3 / 2.4	2 / 2.1	1.6 / 1.7	1.3 / 1.4	650 ml / 22 oz
70	3.5 / 3.7	2.9 / 3.1	2.5 / 2.6	2.2 / 2.3	1.8 / 1.9	1.4 / 1.5	700 ml / 24 oz
75	3.8 / 4	3.1 / 3.3	2.7 / 2.8	2.3 / 2.5	1.9 / 2	1.5 / 1.6	750 ml / 25 oz
80	4 / 4.2	3.3 / 3.5	2.9 / 3	2.5 / 2.6	2 / 2.1	1.6 / 1.7	800 ml / 27 oz
90	4.5 / 4.8	3.8 / 4	3.2 / 3.4	2.8 / 3	2.3 / 2.4	1.8 / 1.9	900 ml / 30 oz
100	5 / 5.3	4.2 / 4.4	3.6 / 3.8	3.1 / 3.3	2.5 / 2.6	2 / 2.1	1 l / 1.1 qt
150	7.5 / 7.9	6.3 / 6.7	5.4 / 5.7	4.7 / 5	3.8 / 4	3 / 3.2	1.5 / 1.6
200	10 / 11	8.3 / 8.8	7.1 / 7.5	6.3 / 6.6	5 / 5.3	4 / 4.2	2 / 2.1
250	13 / 13	10 / 11	8.9 / 9.4	7.8 / 8.3	6.3 / 6.7	5 / 5.3	2.5 / 2.6
300	15 / 16	13 / 13	11 / 11	9.4 / 9.9	7.5 / 7.9	6 / 6.3	3 / 3.2
350	18 / 19	15 / 16	13 / 13	11 / 12	8.8 / 9.3	7 / 7.4	3.5 / 3.7
400	20 / 21	17 / 18	14 / 15	13 / 13	10 / 11	8 / 8.5	4 / 4.2

TABLE 12-21: Fuel/Oil Mixture for 2-Cycle Engines—Metric

13 CONVERSION TABLES

From	To	Multiply By
acres (area)		
	hectares	0.40469
	sections	ex 0.0015625
	sq feet	ex 43560
	sq kilometers	0.0040469
	sq meters	ex 4046.8564224
	sq miles	0.0015625
	sq rods	ex 160
	sq yards	ex 4840
atmospheres (pressure)		
	centimeters mercury	76
	inches mercury	29.921
	inches water	406.78
	kilograms/sq centimeter	1.0332
	kilograms/sq meter	10332
	kilopascals	101.33
	millibars	1013.3
	newtons/sq centimeter	10.133
	newtons/sq meter	101330
	pascals	101330
	pounds/sq inch	14.696
	tons/sq foot	1.0581
barrels (crude oil) (volume)		
	barrels (proof spirits)	ex 1.05
	cu meters	0.15899
	cups	ex 672
	gallons (Imperial)	34.972
	gallons (U.S.)	ex 42
	liters	158.99
	pints (Imperial)	279.78
	pints (U.S.)	ex 336
	quarts (Imperial)	139.89
	quarts (U.S.)	ex 168
barrels (proof spirits) (volume)		
	barrels (crude oil)	0.95238
	cu meters	0.15142
	cups	ex 640
	gallons (Imperial)	33.307
	gallons (U.S.)	ex 40

ex = exact conversion

From	To		Multiply By
barrels (proof spirits) (volume)			
	liters		151.42
	pints (Imperial)		266.46
	pints (U.S.)	*ex*	320
	quarts (Imperial)		133.23
	quarts (U.S.)	*ex*	160
BTUs (energy)			
	calories		252
	foot-pounds		778.17
	joules		1055.1
	kilowatt-hours		0.00029307
BTUs/minute (power)			
	foot-pounds/minute		778.17
	foot-pounds/second		12.969
	horsepower		0.023581
	joules/second		17.584
	kilowatts		0.017584
	watts		17.584
cables (distance)			
	fathoms	*ex*	120
	feet	*ex*	720
	kilometers	*ex*	0.219456
	meters	*ex*	219.456
	miles		0.13636
	miles (naut)		0.1185
	yards	*ex*	240
calories (energy)			
	BTUs		0.0039683
	foot-pounds		3.088
	joules		4.1868
	kilowatt-hours		1.1630E-6
centimeters (distance)			
	feet		0.032808
	inches		0.3937
	meters	*ex*	0.01
	millimeters	*ex*	10
	yards		0.010936
centimeters mercury (pressure)			
	atmospheres		0.013158
	inches mercury		0.3937
	inches water		5.3524
	kilograms/sq centimeter		0.013595

ex = exact conversion

From	To	Multiply By
centimeters mercury (pressure)		
	kilograms/sq meter	135.95
	kilopascals	1.3332
	millibars	13.332
	newtons/sq centimeter	0.13332
	newtons/sq meter	1333.2
	pascals	1333.2
	pounds/sq inch	0.19337
	tons/sq foot	0.013922
circular mils (area)		
	sq centimeters	5.0671E-6
	sq inches	7.8540E-7
	sq millimeters	0.00050671
	sq mils	0.7854
cu centimeters (volume)		
	cu inches	0.061024
	cu millimeters	*ex* 1000
	cups	0.0042268
	liters	*ex* 0.001
	milliliters	*ex* 1
	ounces (fluid)	0.033814
	pints (Imperial)	0.0017598
	pints (U.S.)	0.0021134
	quarts (Imperial)	0.00087988
	quarts (U.S.)	0.0010567
	tablespoons	0.067628
	teaspoons	0.20288
cu inches (volume)		
	cu centimeters	*ex* 16.387064
	cu millimeters	*ex* 16387.064
	cups	0.069264
	gallons (U.S.)	0.004329
	liters	*ex* 0.016387064
	milliliters	*ex* 16.387064
	ounces (fluid)	0.55411
	pints (Imperial)	0.028837
	pints (U.S.)	0.034632
	quarts (Imperial)	0.014419
	quarts (U.S.)	0.017316
	tablespoons	1.1082
	teaspoons	3.3247

ex = exact conversion

From	To		Multiply By
cu meters (volume)			
	barrels (crude oil)		6.2898
	barrels (proof spirits)		6.6043
	cups		4226.8
	gallons (Imperial)		219.97
	gallons (U.S.)		264.17
	liters		1000
	pints (Imperial)		1759.8
	pints (U.S.)		2113.4
	quarts (Imperial)		879.88
	quarts (U.S.)		1056.7
cu millimeters (volume)			
	cu centimeters	*ex*	0.001
	cu inches		6.1024E-5
	milliliters		0.001
	ounces (fluid)		3.3814E-5
	tablespoons		6.7628E-5
	teaspoons		0.00020288
cups (volume)			
	barrels (crude oil)		0.0014881
	barrels (proof spirits)	*ex*	0.0015625
	cu centimeters		236.59
	cu inches	*ex*	14.4375
	cu meters		0.00023659
	gallons (Imperial)		0.052042
	gallons (U.S.)	*ex*	0.0625
	liters		0.23659
	milliliters		236.59
	ounces (fluid)	*ex*	8
	pints (Imperial)		0.41634
	pints (U.S.)	*ex*	0.5
	quarts (Imperial)		0.20817
	quarts (U.S.)	*ex*	0.25
	tablespoons	*ex*	16
	teaspoons	*ex*	48
degrees (angles)			
	minutes	*ex*	60
	radians (π/180)		0.017453
	seconds	*ex*	3600
fathoms (distance)			
	cables		0.0083333
	feet	*ex*	6

ex = exact conversion

From	To	Multiply By
fathoms (distance)		
	kilometers	*ex* 0.0018288
	meters	*ex* 1.8288
	miles	0.0011364
	miles (naut)	0.00098747
	yards	*ex* 2
feet (distance)		
	cables	0.0013889
	centimeters	*ex* 30.48
	fathoms	0.16667
	furlongs	0.0015152
	inches	*ex* 12
	kilometers	*ex* 0.0003048
	meters	*ex* 0.3048
	miles	0.00018939
	miles (naut)	0.00016458
	millimeters	*ex* 304.8
	rods	0.060606
	yards	0.33333
feet/minute (speed)		
	feet/second	0.016667
	kilometers/hour	0.018288
	kilometers/second	*ex* 5.0800E-6
	knots	0.0098747
	meters/minute	*ex* 0.3048
feet/minute (speed)		
	meters/second	*ex* 0.00508
	miles/hour	0.011364
	miles/second	3.1566E-6
feet/second (speed)		
	feet/minute	*ex* 60
	kilometers/hour	*ex* 1.09728
	kilometers/second	*ex* 0.0003048
	knots	0.59248
	meters/minute	*ex* 18.288
	meters/second	*ex* 0.3048
	miles/hour	0.68182
	miles/second	0.00018939
feet/second/second (acceleration)		
	gravity-acceleration	0.031081
	meters/second/second	0.3048

ex = exact conversion

From	To	Multiply By
foot-pounds (energy)		
	BTUs	0.0012851
	calories	0.32383
	joules	1.3558
	kilowatt-hours	3.7662E-7
foot-pounds/minute (power)		
	BTUs/minute	0.0012851
	foot-pounds/second	0.016667
	horsepower	3.0303E-5
	joules/second	0.022597
	kilowatts	2.2597E-5
	watts	0.022597
foot-pounds/second (power)		
	BTUs/minute	0.077104
	foot-pounds/minute	60
	horsepower	0.0018182
	joules/second	1.3558
	kilowatts	0.0013558
	watts	1.3558
furlongs (distance)		
	feet	ex 660
	kilometers	0.20117
	meters	ex 201.168
	miles	ex 0.125
	rods	ex 40
gravity-acceleration (acceleration)		
	feet/second/second	32.174
	meters/second/second	9.8067
gallons (Imperial) (volume)		
	barrels (crude oil)	0.028594
	barrels (proof spirits)	0.030024
	cu meters	0.0045461
	cups	19.215
	gallons (U.S.)	1.2009
	liters	4.5461
	pints (Imperial)	ex 8
	pints (U.S.)	9.6076
	quarts (Imperial)	ex 4
	quarts (U.S.)	4.8038

ex = exact conversion

From	To	Multiply By
gallons (U.S.) (volume)		
	barrels (crude oil)	0.02381
	barrels (proof spirits)	*ex* 0.025
	cu inches	*ex* 231
	cu meters	0.0037854
	cups	*ex* 16
	gallons (Imperial)	0.83267
	liters	3.7854
	ounces (fluid)	*ex* 128
	pints (Imperial)	6.6614
	pints (U.S.)	*ex* 8
	quarts (Imperial)	3.3307
	quarts (U.S.)	*ex* 4
grams (weight/force)		
	kilograms	*ex* 0.001
	milligrams	*ex* 1000
	ounces	0.035274
	pounds	0.0022046
hectares (area)		
	acres	2.4711
	sections	0.003861
	sq feet	107640
	sq kilometers	*ex* 0.01
	sq meters	*ex* 10000
	sq miles	0.003861
	sq rods	395.37
	sq yards	11960
horsepower (power)		
	BTUs/minute	42.407
	foot-pounds/minute	33000
	foot-pounds/second	550
	joules/second	745.7
	kilowatts	0.7457
	watts	745.7
hundredweight (weight/force)		
	hundredweight (long)	0.89286
	kilograms	45.359
	metric tons	0.045359
	newtons	444.82
	pounds	*ex* 100
	tons	*ex* 0.05
	tons (long)	0.044643

ex = exact conversion

From	To		Multiply By
hundredweight (long) (weight/force)			
	hundredweight	*ex*	1.12
	kilograms		50.802
	metric tons		0.050802
	newtons		498.2
	pounds	*ex*	112
	tons		0.056
	tons (long)	*ex*	0.05
inches (distance)			
	centimeters	*ex*	2.54
	feet		0.083333
	meters	*ex*	0.0254
	millimeters	*ex*	25.4
	yards		0.027778
inches mercury (pressure)			
	atmospheres		0.033421
	centimeters mercury	*ex*	2.54
	inches water		13.595
	kilograms/sq centimeter		0.034532
	kilograms/sq meter		345.32
	kilopascals		3.3864
	millibars		33.864
	newtons/sq centimeter		0.33864
	newtons/sq meter		3386.4
	pascals		3386.4
	pounds/sq inch		0.49115
	tons/sq foot		0.035363
inches water (pressure)			
	atmospheres		0.0024583
	centimeters mercury		0.18683
	inches mercury		0.073556
	kilograms/sq centimeter		0.00254
	kilograms/sq meter		25.4
	kilopascals		0.24909
	millibars		2.4909
	newtons/sq centimeter		0.024909
	newtons/sq meter		249.09
	pascals		249.09
	pounds/sq inch		0.036127
	tons/sq foot		0.0026012

ex = exact conversion

From	To	Multiply By
joules (energy)		
	BTUs	0.00094782
	calories	0.23885
	foot-pounds	0.73756
	kilowatt-hours	2.7778E-7
joules/second (power)		
	BTUs/minute	0.056869
	foot-pounds/minute	44.254
	foot-pounds/second	0.73756
	horsepower	0.001341
	kilowatts	0.001
	watts	1
kilogram-meters (torque)		
	newton-meters	9.8067
	pound-feet	7.233
	pound-inches	86.796
kilograms (weight/force)		
	grams	*ex* 1000
	hundredweight	0.022046
	hundredweight (long)	0.019684
	metric tons	0.001
	milligrams	*ex* 1000000
	newtons	9.8067
	ounces	35.274
	pounds	2.2046
	tons	0.0011023
	tons (long)	0.00098421
kilograms/cubic meter (density)		
	kilograms/liter	*ex* 0.001
	pounds/cubic foot	0.062428
	pounds/gallon	0.0083454
	pounds/quart (U.S.)	2.0864
kilograms/liter (density)		
	kilograms/cubic meter	*ex* 1000
	pounds/cubic foot	62.428
	pounds/gallon	8.3454
	pounds/quart (U.S.)	2086.4
kilograms/sq centimeter (pressure)		
	atmospheres	0.96784
	centimeters mercury	73.556
	inches mercury	28.959
	inches water	393.7

ex = exact conversion

From	To	Multiply By
kilograms/sq centimeter (pressure)		
	kilograms/sq meter	1000
	kilopascals	98.066
	millibars	980.67
	newtons/sq centimeter	9.8066
	newtons/sq meter	98066
	pascals	98066
	pounds/sq inch	14.223
	tons/sq foot	1.0241
kilograms/sq meter (pressure)		
	atmospheres	9.6784E-5
	centimeters mercury	0.0073556
	inches mercury	0.0028959
	inches water	0.03937
	kilograms/sq centimeter	0.001
	kilopascals	0.0098066
	millibars	0.098067
	newtons/sq centimeter	0.00098066
	newtons/sq meter	9.8066
	pascals	9.8066
	pounds/sq inch	0.0014223
	tons/sq foot	0.00010241
kilometers (distance)		
	cables	4.5567
	fathoms	546.81
	feet	3280.8
	furlongs	4.971
	meters	*ex* 1000
	miles	0.62137
	miles (naut)	0.53996
	rods	198.84
	yards	1093.6
kilometers/hour (speed)		
	feet/minute	54.681
	feet/second	0.91134
	kilometers/second	0.00027778
	knots	0.53996
	meters/minute	16.667
	meters/second	0.27778
	miles/hour	0.62137
	miles/second	0.0001726

ex = exact conversion

From	To	Multiply By
kilometers/second (speed)		
	feet/minute	196850
	feet/second	3280.8
	kilometers/hour	*ex* 3600
	knots	1943.8
	meters/minute	*ex* 60000
	meters/second	*ex* 1000
	miles/hour	2236.9
	miles/second	0.62137
kilopascals (pressure)		
	atmospheres	0.0098692
	centimeters mercury	0.75006
	inches mercury	0.2953
	inches water	4.0146
	kilograms/sq centimeter	0.10197
	kilograms/sq meter	101.97
	millibars	*ex* 10
	newtons/sq centimeter	*ex* 0.1
	newtons/sq meter	*ex* 1000
	pascals	*ex* 1000
	pounds/sq inch	0.14504
	tons/sq foot	0.010443
kilowatt-hours (energy)		
	BTUs	3412.1
	calories	859850
	foot-pounds	2655200
	joules	3600000
kilowatts (energy)		
	BTUs/minute	56.869
	foot-pounds/minute	44254
	foot-pounds/second	737.56
	horsepower	1.341
	joules/second	1000
	watts	1000
knots (speed)		
	feet/minute	101.27
	feet/second	1.6878
	kilometers/hour	1.852
	kilometers/second	0.00051444
	meters/minute	30.867
	meters/second	0.51444
	miles/hour	1.1508
	miles/second	0.00031966

ex = exact conversion

From	To	Multiply By
liters (volume)		
	barrels (crude oil)	0.0062898
	barrels (proof spirits)	0.0066043
	cu centimeters	*ex* 1000
	cu inches	61.024
	cu meters	*ex* 0.001
	cu millimeters	*ex* 1000000
	cups	4.2268
	gallons (Imperial)	0.21997
	gallons (U.S.)	0.26417
	milliliters	*ex* 1000
	ounces (fluid)	33.814
	pints (Imperial)	1.7598
	pints (U.S.)	2.1134
	quarts (Imperial)	0.87988
	quarts (U.S.)	1.0567
	tablespoons	67.628
	teaspoons	202.88
meters (distance)		
	cables	0.0045567
	centimeters	*ex* 100
	fathoms	0.54681
	feet	3.2808
	furlongs	0.004971
	inches	39.37
	kilometers	*ex* 0.001
	miles	0.00062137
	miles (naut)	0.00053996
	millimeters	*ex* 1000
	rods	0.19884
	yards	1.0936
meters/minute (speed)		
	feet/minute	3.2808
	feet/second	0.054681
	kilometers/hour	*ex* 0.06
	kilometers/second	1.6667E-5
	knots	0.032397
	meters/second	0.016667
	miles/hour	0.037282
	miles/second	1.0356E-5

ex = exact conversion

From	To	Multiply By
meters/second (speed)		
	feet/minute	196.85
	feet/second	3.2808
	kilometers/hour	*ex* 3.6
	kilometers/second	*ex* 0.001
	knots	1.9438
	meters/minute	*ex* 60
	miles/hour	2.2369
	miles/second	0.00062137
meters/second/second (acceleration)		
	feet/second/second	3.2808
	gravity-acceleration	0.10197
metric tons (weight/force)		
	hundredweight	22.046
	hundredweight (long)	19.684
	kilograms	*ex* 1000
	newtons	9806.7
	pounds	2204.6
	tons	1.1023
	tons (long)	0.98421
miles (distance)		
	cables	7.3333
	fathoms	*ex* 880
	feet	*ex* 5280
	furlongs	*ex* 8
	kilometers	*ex* 1.609344
	meters	*ex* 1609.344
	miles (naut)	0.86898
	rods	*ex* 320
	yards	*ex* 1760
miles (naut) (distance)		
	cables	8.439
	fathoms	1012.7
	feet	6076.1
	kilometers	*ex* 1.852
	meters	*ex* 1852
	miles	1.1508
	yards	2025.4
miles/hour (speed)		
	feet/minute	*ex* 88
	feet/second	1.4667
	kilometers/hour	1.6093

ex = exact conversion

From	To	Multiply By
miles/hour (speed)		
	kilometers/second	ex 0.00044704
	knots	0.86898
	meters/minute	ex 26.8224
	meters/second	ex 0.44704
	miles/second	0.00027778
miles/second (speed)		
	feet/minute	316800
	feet/second	ex 5280
	kilometers/hour	5793.6
	kilometers/second	ex 1.609344
	knots	3128.3
	meters/minute	ex 96560.64
	meters/second	ex 1609.344
	miles/hour	ex 3600
millibars (pressure)		
	atmospheres	0.00098692
	centimeters mercury	0.075006
	inches mercury	0.02953
	inches water	0.40146
	kilograms/sq centimeter	0.0010197
	kilograms/sq meter	10.197
	kilopascals	0.1
	newtons/sq centimeter	0.01
millibars (pressure)		
	newtons/sq meter	ex 100
	pascals	ex 100
	pounds/sq inch	0.014504
	tons/sq foot	0.0010443
milligrams (weight/force)		
	grams	ex 0.001
	kilograms	ex 1.0000E-6
	ounces	3.5274E-5
	pounds	2.2046E-6
milliliters (volume)		
	cu centimeters	ex 1
	cu inches	0.061024
	cu millimeters	ex 1000
	cups	0.0042268
	liters	ex 0.001
	ounces (fluid)	0.033814
	pints (Imperial)	0.0017598

ex = exact conversion

From	To		Multiply By
milliliters (volume)			
	pints (U.S.)		0.0021134
	quarts (Imperial)		0.00087988
	quarts (U.S.)		0.0010567
	tablespoons		0.067628
	teaspoons		0.20288
millimeters (distance)			
	centimeters	*ex*	0.1
	feet		0.0032808
	inches		0.03937
	meters	*ex*	0.001
	yards		0.0010936
minutes (angle)			
	degrees		0.016667
	radians		0.00029089
	seconds	*ex*	60
newton-meters (torque)			
	kilogram-meters		0.10197
	pound-feet		0.73756
	pound-inches		8.8507
newtons (weight/force)			
	hundredweight		0.0022481
	hundredweight (long)		0.0020072
	kilograms		0.10197
	metric tons		0.00010197
	pounds		0.22481
	tons		0.0001124
	tons (long)		0.00010036
newtons/sq centimeter (pressure)			
	atmospheres		0.098692
	centimeters mercury		7.5006
	inches mercury		2.953
	inches water		40.146
	kilograms/sq centimeter		1.0197
	kilograms/sq meter		1019.7
	kilopascals	*ex*	10
	millibars	*ex*	100
	newtons/sq meter	*ex*	10000
	pascals	*ex*	10000
	pounds/sq inch		1.4504
	tons/sq foot		0.10443

ex = exact conversion

From	To	Multiply By
newtons/sq meter (pressure)		
	atmospheres	9.8692E-6
	centimeters mercury	0.00075006
	inches mercury	0.0002953
	inches water	0.0040146
	kilograms/sq centimeter	0.00010197
	kilograms/sq meter	0.10197
	kilopascals	*ex* 0.001
	millibars	*ex* 0.01
	newtons/sq centimeter	*ex* 0.0001
	pascals	*ex* 1
	pounds/sq inch	0.00014504
	tons/sq foot	1.0443E-5
ounces (weight)		
	grams	28.35
	kilograms	0.02835
	milligrams	28350
	pounds	*ex* 0.0625
ounces (fluid) (volume)		
	cu centimeters	29.574
	cu inches	*ex* 1.8046875
	cu millimeters	29574
	cups	*ex* 0.125
	gallons (U.S.)	0.0078125
	liters	0.029574
	milliliters	29.574
	pints (Imperial)	0.052042
	pints (U.S.)	*ex* 0.0625
	quarts (Imperial)	0.026021
	quarts (U.S.)	*ex* 0.03125
	tablespoons	*ex* 2
	teaspoons	*ex* 6
pascals (pressure)		
	atmospheres	9.8692E-6
	centimeters mercury	0.00075006
	inches mercury	0.0002953
	inches water	0.0040146
	kilograms/sq centimeter	0.00010197
	kilograms/sq meter	0.10197
	kilopascals	*ex* 0.001
	millibars	*ex* 0.01
	newtons/sq centimeter	*ex* 0.0001

ex = exact conversion

From	To	Multiply By
pascals (pressure)		
	newtons/sq meter	*ex* 1
	pounds/sq inch	0.00014504
	tons/sq foot	1.0443E-5
pints (Imperial) (volume)		
	barrels (crude oil)	0.0035743
	barrels (proof spirits)	0.003753
	cu centimeters	568.26
	cu inches	34.677
	cu meters	0.00056826
	cups	2.4019
	gallons (Imperial)	*ex* 0.125
	gallons (U.S.)	0.15012
	liters	0.56826
	milliliters	568.26
	ounces (fluid)	19.215
	pints (U.S.)	1.2009
	quarts (Imperial)	*ex* 0.5
	quarts (U.S.)	0.60047
	tablespoons	38.43
	teaspoons	115.29
pints (U.S.) (volume)		
	barrels (crude oil)	0.0029762
	barrels (proof spirits)	*ex* 0.003125
	cu centimeters	473.18
	cu inches	*ex* 28.875
	cu meters	0.00047318
	cups	*ex* 2
	gallons (Imperial)	0.10408
	gallons (U.S.)	*ex* 0.125
	liters	0.47318
	milliliters	473.18
	ounces (fluid)	*ex* 16
	pints (Imperial)	0.83267
	quarts (Imperial)	0.41634
	quarts (U.S.)	*ex* 0.5
	tablespoons	*ex* 32
	teaspoons	*ex* 96
pound-feet (torque)		
	kilogram-meters	0.13825
	newton-meters	1.3558
	pound-inches	*ex* 12

ex = exact conversion

From	To	Multiply By
pound-inches (torque)		
	kilogram-meters	0.011521
	newton-meters	0.11298
	pound-feet	0.083333
pounds (weight/force)		
	grams	_ex_ 453.59237
	hundredweight	_ex_ 0.01
	hundredweight (long)	0.0089286
	kilograms	_ex_ 0.45359237
	metric tons	0.00045359
	milligrams	_ex_ 453592.37
	newtons	4.4482
	ounces	_ex_ 16
	tons	_ex_ 0.0005
	tons (long)	0.00044643
pounds/cubic foot (density)		
	kilograms/cubic meter	16.018
	kilograms/liter	0.016018
	pounds/gallon	0.13368
	pounds/quart (U.S.)	0.03342
pounds/gallon (density)		
	kilograms/cubic meter	119.83
	kilograms/liter	0.11983
	pounds/cubic foot	7.4805
	pounds/quart (U.S.)	_ex_ 0.25
pounds/quart (U.S.) (density)		
	kilograms/cubic meter	479.31
	kilograms/liter	0.47931
	pounds/cubic foot	29.922
	pounds/gallon	_ex_ 4
pounds/sq inch (pressure)		
	atmospheres	0.068046
	centimeters mercury	5.1715
	inches mercury	2.036
	inches water	27.68
	kilograms/sq centimeter	0.070307
	kilograms/sq meter	703.07
	kilopascals	6.8948
	millibars	68.948
	newtons/sq centimeter	0.68948
	newtons/sq meter	6894.8
	pascals	6894.8
	tons/sq foot	0.072

ex = exact conversion

From	To	Multiply By
quarts (Imperial)		
	barrels (crude oil)	0.0071485
	barrels (proof spirits)	0.0075059
	cu centimeters	1136.5
	cu inches	69.355
	cu meters	0.0011365
	cups	4.8038
	gallons (Imperial)	*ex* 0.25
	gallons (U.S.)	0.30024
	liters	1.1365
	milliliters	1136.5
	ounces (fluid)	38.43
	pints (Imperial)	*ex* 2
	pints (U.S.)	2.4019
	quarts (U.S.)	1.2009
	tablespoons	76.861
	teaspoons	230.58
quarts (U.S.) (volume)		
	barrels (crude oil)	0.0059524
	barrels (proof spirits)	*ex* 0.00625
	cu centimeters	946.35
	cu inches	*ex* 57.75
	cu meters	0.00094635
	cups	*ex* 4
	gallons (Imperial)	0.20817
	gallons (U.S.)	*ex* 0.25
	liters	0.94635
	milliliters	946.35
	ounces (fluid)	*ex* 32
	pints (Imperial)	1.6653
	pints (U.S.)	*ex* 2
	quarts (Imperial)	0.83267
	tablespoons	*ex* 64
	teaspoons	*ex* 192
radians (angle)		
	degrees (180/π)	57.296
	minutes	3437.7
	seconds	206260

ex = exact conversion

From	To		Multiply By
rods (distance)			
	feet	ex	16.5
	furlongs	ex	0.025
	kilometers		0.0050292
	meters	ex	5.0292
	miles	ex	0.003125
seconds (angle)			
	degrees		0.00027778
	minutes		0.016667
	radians		4.8481E-6
sections (area)			
	acres	ex	640
	hectares		259
	sq feet	ex	27878400
	sq kilometers		2.59
	sq meters		2590000
	sq miles		1
	sq rods	ex	102400
	sq yards	ex	3097600
sq centimeters (area)			
	circular mils		197350
	sq feet		0.0010764
	sq inches		0.155
	sq meters	ex	0.0001
	sq millimeters	ex	100
	sq mils		155000
	sq yards		0.0001196
sq feet (area)			
	acres		2.2957E-5
	hectares	ex	9.2903E-6
	sections		3.5870E-8
	sq centimeters	ex	929.0304
	sq inches	ex	144
	sq kilometers	ex	9.2903E-8
	sq meters	ex	0.09290304
	sq miles		3.5870E-8
	sq millimeters	ex	92903.04
	sq rods		0.0036731
	sq yards		0.11111

ex = exact conversion

From	To	Multiply By
sq inches (area)		
	circular mils	1273200
	sq centimeters	*ex* 6.4516
	sq feet	0.0069444
	sq meters	*ex* 0.00064516
	sq millimeters	*ex* 645.16
	sq mils	1000000
	sq yards	0.0007716
sq kilometers (area)		
	acres	247.11
	hectares	*ex* 100
	sections	0.3861
	sq feet	10764000
	sq meters	*ex* 1000000
	sq miles	0.3861
	sq rods	39537
	sq yards	3588000
sq meters (area)		
	acres	0.00024711
	hectares	*ex* 0.0001
	sections	3.8610E-7
	sq centimeters	*ex* 10000
	sq feet	10.764
	sq feet	10.764
	sq inches	1550
	sq kilometers	*ex* 1.0000E-6
	sq miles	3.8610E-7
	sq millimeters	*ex* 1000000
	sq rods	0.039537
	sq yards	1.196
	sq yards	1.196
sq miles (area)		
	acres	*ex* 640
	hectares	259
	sections	*ex* 1
	sq feet	*ex* 27878400
	sq kilometers	2.59
	sq meters	2590000
	sq rods	*ex* 102400
	sq yards	*ex* 3097600

ex = exact conversion

From	To		Multiply By
sq millimeters (area)			
	circular mils		1973.5
	sq centimeters	*ex*	0.01
	sq feet		1.0764E-5
	sq inches		0.00155
	sq meters	*ex*	1.0000E-6
	sq mils		1550
	sq yards		1.1960E-6
sq mils (area)			
	circular mils		1.2732
	sq centimeters	*ex*	6.4516E-6
	sq inches	*ex*	1.0000E-6
	sq millimeters	*ex*	0.00064516
sq rods (area)			
	acres	*ex*	0.00625
	hectares		0.0025293
	sections		9.7656E-6
	sq feet	*ex*	272.25
	sq kilometers		2.5293E-5
	sq meters	*ex*	25.29285264
	sq miles		9.7656E-6
	sq yards		30.25
sq yards (area)			
	acres		0.00020661
	hectares		8.3613E-5
	sections		3.2283E-7
	sq centimeters	*ex*	8361.2736
	sq feet	*ex*	9
	sq feet	*ex*	9
	sq inches	*ex*	1296
	sq kilometers		2.7871E-7
	sq meters	*ex*	0.83612736
	sq miles		3.2283E-7
	sq millimeters	*ex*	836127.36
	sq rods		0.033058
tablespoons (volume)			
	cu centimeters		14.787
	cu inches		0.90234
	cu millimeters		14787
	cups	*ex*	0.0625
	liters		0.014787
	milliliters		14.787

ex = exact conversion

From	To		Multiply By
tablespoons (volume)			
	ounces (fluid)	*ex*	0.5
	pints (Imperial)		0.026021
	pints (U.S.)	*ex*	0.03125
	quarts (Imperial)		0.013011
	quarts (U.S.)	*ex*	0.015625
	teaspoons	*ex*	3
teaspoons (volume)			
	cu centimeters		4.9289
	cu inches		0.30078
	cu millimeters		4928.9
	cups		0.020833
	liters		0.0049289
	milliliters		4.9289
	ounces (fluid)		0.16667
	pints (Imperial)		0.0086737
	pints (U.S.)		0.010417
	quarts (Imperial)		0.0043368
	quarts (U.S.)		0.0052083
	tablespoons		0.33333
tons (weight/force)			
	hundredweight	*ex*	20
	hundredweight (long)		17.857
	kilograms		907.18
	metric tons		0.90718
	newtons		8896.4
	pounds	*ex*	2000
	tons (long)		0.89286
tons (long) (weight/force)			
	hundredweight	*ex*	22.4
	hundredweight (long)	*ex*	20
	kilograms		1016
	metric tons		1.016
	newtons		9964
	pounds	*ex*	2240
	tons	*ex*	1.12
tons/sq foot (pressure)			
	atmospheres		0.94508
	centimeters mercury		71.826
	inches mercury		28.278
	inches water		384.44
	kilograms/sq centimeter		0.97649

ex = exact conversion

From	To	Multiply By
tons/sq foot (pressure)		
	kilograms/sq meter	9764.9
	kilopascals	95.761
	millibars	957.61
	newtons/sq centimeter	9.5761
	newtons/sq meter	95761
	pascals	95761
	pounds/sq inch	13.889
watts (energy)		
	BTUs/minute	0.056869
	foot-pounds/minute	44.254
	foot-pounds/second	0.73756
	horsepower	0.001341
	joules/second	1
	kilowatts	0.001
yards (distance)		
	cables	0.0041667
	centimeters	*ex* 91.44
	fathoms	*ex* 0.5
	feet	*ex* 3
	inches	*ex* 36
	kilometers	*ex* 0.0009144
	meters	*ex* 0.9144
	miles	0.00056818
	miles (naut)	0.00049374
	millimeters	*ex* 914.4

ex = exact conversion

14 BOATING ORGANIZATIONS AND PUBLICATIONS

BOATING ORGANIZATIONS

COAST GUARD

U.S. Coast Guard

Homepage: http://www.uscg.mil/
National Response Center: 800-424-8802 or 202-267-2675
Public Affairs: 202-267-1587
Navigation Center (local notices to mariners):
703-313-5800
Boating Safety Education: 800-368-5647

The U.S. Coast Guard (USCG) currently operates as part of the Department of Homeland Security, but in times of war may serve under the Department of the Navy.

From a recreational boater's perspective, the most significant missions of the USCG are:

- Aiding mariners in distress (i.e., search and rescue)
- Enhancing marine safety by setting safe boating standards and regulations along with programs to help educate the boating public in safe boating practices

In addition, the USCG carries out a number of other duties, some of which relate to law enforcement and yet others related to mobility (marine navigation). Examples of enforcement activities include port and maritime security (a high priority today), drug and illegal alien interdiction, enforcement of environmental regulations, etc. Navigation operations include maintaining aids to navigation, administering bridges, traffic and waterway management, ice breaking, and other activities contributing to the safe and efficient movement of vessels through our waterways.

The USCG is organized into nine districts with headquarters in Washington, D.C. Each district is assigned a number from 1 to 17, so some numbers are not used. The districts are as follows:

Atlantic Area

Atlantic Area SOS—Emergency: 757-398-6390
1st District Boston, Massachusetts: http://www.uscg.mil/units.shtm
5th District Portsmouth, Virginia: http://www.uscg.mil/units.shtm
7th District Miami, Florida: http://www.uscg.mil/units.shtm
8th District New Orleans, Louisiana: http://www.uscg.mil/units.shtm Command Center (24 hours): 504-589-6225
9th District Cleveland, Ohio: http://www.uscg.mil/units.shtm

Pacific Area

Pacific Area SOS—Emergency: 510-437-3701
11th District Alameda, California: http://www.uscg.mil/units.shtm
13th District Seattle, Washington: http://www.uscg.mil/units.shtm Emergency contact: 800-982-8813
14th District Honolulu, Hawaii: http://www.uscg.mil/units.shtm General no: 808-541-2450
17th District Juneau, Alaska: http://www.uscg.mil/units.shtm Response Command Center: 907-463-2000

U.S. Coast Guard Auxiliary

Homepage: http://www.cgaux.org/ Coast Guard Customer Infoline: 877-875-6296

The U.S. Coast Guard Auxiliary (USCGA) is an organization of volunteers whose purpose is to assist the Coast Guard in nonenforcement activities, such as teaching boating safety, carrying out safety patrols and checks, and assisting with search and rescue operations.

On their website, the USCGA estimates that they save almost 500 lives annually and teach thousands of students in boating safety courses, which saves hundreds of millions of taxpayer dollars every year.

Similar to the Power Squadron, members of the auxiliary receive training in all aspects of boating and seamanship.

The USCGA and the Power Squadrons collaborated in developing *America's Boating Course*, an interactive course that can be completed over the Internet, by book, or on a CD. *America's Boating Course* has been approved by the National Association of State Boating Law Administrators.

Schedules of classroom-based courses the USCGA is holding in your area can be found online at the website mentioned above or by calling the Infoline number.

The USCGA is always looking for members, so if you want to get more involved and make a contribution to the boating community, while gaining valuable boating experience and education, you may wish consider the auxiliary. Members must be a U.S. citizen over 17 years of age.

Canadian Coast Guard

Homepage: http://www.ccg-gcc.gc.ca
General questions: 613-993-0999
Boating safety hotline: 800-267-6687

The Canadian Coast Guard (CCG) currently operates as a part of Fisheries and Oceans Canada.

The CCG programs that are most obvious to recreational boaters are search and rescue, and boating safety, among other programs. CCG also provides navigation services that include such activities as maintaining navigation aids, issuing notices to mariners, and providing communications and traffic services.

The CCG is headquartered in Ottawa, Ontario, and has five major regions:

Pacific Region:
http://www.ccg-gcc.gc.ca/regions_e.htm
General information: 604-775-8888

Central and Arctic Region:
http://www.ccg-gcc.gc.ca/regions_e.htm
General information: 204-983-5000

Quebec Region:
http://www.ccg-gcc.gc.ca/regions_e.htm
General information: 418-648-7747

Maritimes Region:
http://www.ccg-gcc.gc.ca/regions_e.htm
General information: 902-426-3550

Newfoundland Region:
http://www.ccg-gcc.gc.ca/regions_e.htm
General information: 709-772-4423

Other CCG Phone Numbers of Interest

Canadian Coast Guard Office of Boating Safety: This site
describes regulations including how to license or register
boats. It also has the Safe Boating Guide and some other
handy publications online:
http://www.tc.gc.ca/BoatingSafety/menu.htm
Inside Canada: 800-267-6687
Outside Canada: 613-991-9002

The Canadian Coast Guard Auxiliary

Homepage: http://www.ccga-gcac.com/
National information: 866-629-3292 or 613-991-5714
(Ottawa)

The Canadian Coast Guard Auxiliary (CCGA) is a volunteer
organization whose purpose is to assist the Canadian Coast
Guard with safe boating programs and education, as well as
assisting with search and rescue missions. Members typically
are pleasure craft operators and fishermen who volunteer
the use of their own vessels to help with the CCG missions.
The auxiliary conducts safe boating courses and conducts
courtesy safety checks of recreational vessels.

There are approximately 5000 members and 1600 vessels in
the CCGA at the current time. On their website, the CCGA
estimate they participate in about 25 percent of almost 7000
search and rescue incidents annually, which results in an
estimated 200 lives saved each year.

The CCGA is organized into regions that correspond to the
CCG regions and the most basic level of organization at
individual ports and towns is the unit. A number of units
make up a zone.

THE POWER (AND SAIL) SQUADRONS
U.S. Power Squadrons

Homepage: http://www.usps.org/
Phone: 919-821-0281

The U.S. Power Squadrons (USPS) were organized in 1914 as an organization to educate yacht club members in the safe operation of the then new-fangled motorboats (as opposed to sailboats). Shortly after World War I, the squadrons were re-organized to provide education to the general boating public.

Today the squadron is no longer limited to powerboating and has both sailors (about 40 percent) and powerboaters comprising a membership of approximately 60,000 boaters organized into about 450 squadrons.

The way the squadron education program works is that the more experienced members volunteer their time to instruct classes in various aspects of boating and then, with time and experience, the newly educated members will (hopefully) go on to be instructors themselves. Courses held include:

- The Public Boating Course—open to the public. Passing the exam for this course, qualifies the student to operate a boat in those states where certification is required, as well as in Canada. A pass in this or an equivalent course is required to join the USPS.
- Seamanship
- Piloting
- Advanced Piloting
- Junior Navigation (includes celestial navigation)
- Navigation
- Sail
- Weather
- Engine Maintenance
- Marine Electronics (and Electrical)
- Cruise Planning

There is even a squadron in Boulder, Colorado, of which I am proud to say I am a member. We have members who have sailed from California to the South Pacific and back; at least one who has circumnavigated (the world); those who have sailed the so-called Great Loop (up the eastern seaboard and back down the Mississippi); and others who keep boats on either coast. As I write this (June 2004), we have several members crossing the Atlantic in the Nordhavn Atlantic Rally 2004 from Florida to Gibraltar. Of course, being in Colorado, we also have members who canoe, sail, powerboat, and water-ski on our local lakes, rivers, and reservoirs.

The USPS and the USCGA collaborated in developing the *America's Boating Course*, as mentioned previously.

Social activities are also an important part of Power Squadron functions both on and off the water. The squadrons also organize boating trips together. In our case, we'll usually organize a rendezvous on one of the coasts every two years or so. Some members trailer their boats there, others charter, and others are fortunate enough to have boats already in place.

There are several other programs that the squadrons participate in, which are described at the website above.

Whether you are new to boating or experienced, consider joining a squadron near you. You won't regret it. You can even save money since many marine insurance companies offer significant discounts to boaters with certificates from advanced boating courses. Much of what is written in this book was learned first by the author in squadron courses.

The USPS maintains a close relationship with the Canadian Power Squadrons (described below) and many members are members of both organizations. A USPS member qualifies for, and may apply for, membership in the Canadian Power Squadrons.

Canadian Power and Sail Squadrons

Homepage: http://www.cps-ecp.ca
Phone: 416-293-2438

According to their website, the first Canadian Power Squadron was actually a USPS squadron formed in Windsor Ontario in 1938, which quickly grew and evolved into the Canadian Power Squadrons as an independent organization. The words "and sail" were added to change the name to the Canadian Power and Sail Squadrons (CPS) in 1985.

The CPS is organized into basic units of squadrons, much like the USPS, and the mission is similar—to educate members and the public in safe boating and to promote social fellowship among members. CPS offers a public boating course, which when completed along with successful passing of the associated exam, will qualify the student for a ***CCG Pleasure Craft Operator Card***. This card allows the boater to operate anywhere in Canada as well as those states now requiring certification of some sort. Completion of this course and exam or equivalent is required for membership in CPS.

Other courses offered by CPS to members include:

- Power Boating
- Sail

- Piloting
- Advanced Piloting
- Celestial Navigation
- Extended Cruising
- VHF Radio
- Marine Electronics
- Marine Maintenance
- Weather—Fundamental
- Weather—Global

Social activities include cruises, picnics, regular meetings, etc., much like those described previously for the USPS.

Substantial (up to 40 percent) insurance discounts are available to CPP members who have successfully completed advanced courses.

CPS maintains a close relationship with the USPS, and many people are members of both organizations. A CPS member qualifies for, and may apply for, membership in USPS.

OTHER ORGANIZATIONS
American Boat and Yacht Council

Homepage: http://www.abycinc.org/
Phone number: 410-956-1050

The American Boat and Yacht Council (ABYC) is the de-facto standards-setting body for the design and construction of recreational power and sail boats in the United States and Canada. This is an organization of more than 4000 boat builders and various other marine-related individuals and businesses that set standards generally accepted as requirements for building recreational boats. They offer for purchase part or all of their standards and several of the better books on boating. They also develop and offer education programs, along with marine technician certification.

Individuals like yourself can join the ABYC and enjoy substantial discounts on their materials and books. If you are considering doing work on your boat yourself, it would behoove you to purchase a copy of their standards relating to the work you plan to do. If you are contracting work to a boatyard, look for the boatyard to be an ABYC member and their technicians to be ABYC certified.

Look for the ABYC logo on boats you are considering for purchase as this indicates it has been designed and constructed to the rigorous standards set by the ABYC.

American Power Boat Association

Homepage: http://www.apba-racing.com
General information: 586-773-9700

The American Power Boat Association (APBA) was founded in 1903 and is the authority for UIM approved powerboat racing in the United States. UIM stands for Union Internationale Motonautique, which is the world boat racing authority based in Monaco. This organization is somewhat analogous to U.S. Sailing except it is more focused on racing. For more information, check the website or call the general information number.

America's Great Loop Cruisers' Association

Homepage: http://www.greatloop.com/
General Phone: 865/856-7888

This is an association for boaters who are interested in cruising America's Great Loop and associated waterways. The Great Loop is the continuous waterway that circumnavigates the eastern portion of North America —along the Atlantic Seaboard, across the Great Lakes, through the Mississippi and Tenn-Tom Rivers to the Gulf of Mexico, and around Florida.

The association disseminates information regarding the loop and provides a bimonthly newsletter, and a member directory to help keep in touch with other "loopers". 2 or 3 annual rendezvous are held that include seminars, information exchange, and socialization with other boaters.

If you are thinking about doing the Loop, this is the organization to join. Membership is about $33.00 per year.

BoatUS

Homepage: http://www.boatus.com/
General phone: 703-461-4666
Boating course information: 410-897-0512
Boat loans: 800-365-5636
Towing assistance: 800-391-4869
Insurance quotes: 800-283-2883
Insurance claims: 800-937-1937
MMSI ID number assignment: 800-563-1536 (VHF DSC)

This is an organization with over a half-million members; every boater should consider joining. BoatUS not only provides many services to members but also acts as an effective advocate for recreational boaters with local, state, and federal levels of government. The more members this organization has, the more the politicians will feel the need to listen.

BoatUS has boat towing services, boat insurance, a trailering club that offers trailer towing, and a boat loan program. Travel services include discounted hotels and auto rentals, as well as arranging boat charters. Members get substantial discounts on fuel, slip fees, and repairs at more than 700 marinas.

A basic membership runs about $19 per year and includes a subscription to BoatUS magazine.

Canadian Yachting Association

Homepage: http://www.sailing.ca/home.asp
General phone: 613-545-3044

The Canadian Yachting Association (CYA) is a nonprofit corporation and the governing body for sailing and sailboat racing in Canada. The CYA works with international sailing organizations such as the International Sailing Federation (ISAF).

The CYA has 10 affiliated Provincial Sailing Associations (PSA) that actually deliver the CYA programs and services in each province. Individual clubs and schools join a PSA and thereby become members of the CYA. To become a CYA member, individuals join a CYS/PSA member club rather than joining the CYA directly.

Activities are primarily related to racing, but programs and education are also available for those who just want to learn to sail or operate a powerboat. CYA affiliated clubs also offer instruction and certification for the Pleasure Craft Operator's Card. CYA places heavy emphasis on training afloat as well as in the classroom for both the learn to sail and learn to power boat courses. Training and certification is recognized by the ISAF, and includes training for instructors, coaches, and race officials. All types of sailing and racing at differing levels of expertise are taught.

Use the website to find a member club or school in your area or call the general information number. If you're a beginning boater, this is an excellent way to learn because of the on-water training emphasis.

U.S. Sailing

Homepage: http://www.ussailing.org/
General inquiries: 401-683-0800, extension 600

As the name implies, this is a sailing rather than a powerboat organization, and U.S. Sailing is, in fact, the governing body for sailing and sailboat racing in the United States. It is a nonprofit organization and currently has about 40,000 members.

Although U.S. Sailing is heavily involved in sailboat racing, it offers programs for sailors of all types, with varying levels of expertise. It also trains and certifies instructors, race officers, judges, and the like, and is involved in developing teaching curriculums and handicapping systems.

U.S. Sailing is involved in many other areas, including the U.S. Olympic and Paralympic sailing teams, and the International Sailing Federation (ISAF). There is also an insurance program for members.

The website can point you to an affiliated organization in your area if you are interested in learning to sail or race. You can also join U.S. Sailing online. Check out the website to get a better idea of how comprehensive its programs are.

PHONE NUMBERS
State Boating Offices and Police

Alabama http://www.dcnr.state.al.us/MP.html
Marine police: 334-242-3673
Highway patrol: 334-242-4128

Alaska http://www.dnr.state.ak.us/parks/boating/index.htm
Boating safety: 907-269-8705
State troopers: 907-269-5976

Arizona http://www.gf.state.az.us/outdoor_recreation/boating.shtml
Boating information: 602-942-3000
Highway patrol: 603-223-2000

Arkansas http://www.agfc.state.ar.us/index.html
Boating into: 501-223-6351
Registration: 501-223-6378
State police: 501-618-8000

California http://www.dbw.ca.gov/
Boating into: 916-445-6281
Registration: 916-657-8013
Highway patrol: 916-657-7261

Colorado http://parks.state.co.us/
Boating information and registration: 303-791-1954
State police: 303-239-4500

Connecticut http://dep.state.ct.us/rec/boating/
General information: 860-434-8638
Registration: 860-566-1556
State police: 860-685-8000

Delaware http://www.dnrec.state.de.us/dnrec2000/Boating.
asp
Boat registration: 302-739-3498
Enforcement: 302-739-3440
Hunting education and boating safety: 302-739-3486
State police: 302-739-5901

District of Columbia http://mpdc.dc.gov/info/season/harbor-
patrol.htm
Harbor patrol: 202-727-4582
Metropolitan police: 202-727-1000

Florida http://myfwc.com/law/boatsafe/
General information: 850-488-5600
Highway patrol: 850-487-3139

Georgia http://georgiawildlife.dnr.state.ga.us/
General information: 770-918-6408
Registration: 888-748-6887
State patrol: 770-528-3251

Hawaii http://www.state.hi.us/dlnr/dbor/dbor.html
Main office: 808-587-1966
State sheriff 808-538-5696

Idaho http://www.idahoparks.org/rec/boating.html
General information: 208-334-4199
State police: 208-884-7000

Illinois http://dnr.state.il.us/admin/systems/boats.htm
General information: 217-782-6302
Registration: 800-382-1696
State police: 217-782-2841

Indiana http://www.ai.org/nrc/boat_laws/
Law enforcement: 317-232-4010
Registration: 317-232-2821
State police: 317-232-8250

Iowa http://www.iowadnr.com/law/boating/index.html
General: 515-281-5918
Registration: 515-281-5267
State patrol: 515-281-5824

Kansas http://www.kdwp.state.ks.us/boating/boatinglaws.html
General information and registration: (620) 672-5911
Highway patrol: 785-296-6800

Kentucky http://www.kdfwr.state.ky.us
General information: 800-858-1549
State police: 502-695-6300

Louisiana http://www.wlf.state.la.us
General information: 504-765-2988
Registration: 504-765-2898
State police: 225-925-6325

Maine http://www.state.me.us/ifw/
General information: (207) 287-8000
Registration: 207-287-2043
State police: 207-624-7000

Maryland http://www.dnr.state.md.us/boating/
General information: 877-620-8367
State police: 301-644-4151

Massachusetts http://www.mass.gov/dfwele/
General information: 617-727-3905
Registration: 617-626-1610
State police: 508-820-2300

Michigan http://www.michigan.gov/dnr
General information: 517-335-3414
Registration: 517-322-1460
State police: 517-332-2521

Minnesota http://www.dnr.state.mn.us/regulations/boatwater/index.html
General information: 651-296-6157
Registration: 888-665-4236
State patrol: 651-282-6871

Mississippi http://www.mdwfp.com/lawenforcement_boating.asp
General information: 601-432-2182
Registration: 601-364-2032
Highway patrol: 601-987-1212

Missouri http://www.mswp.state.mo.us/
General information: 573-751-3333
Registration: 573-751-4509
Highway patrol: 573-751-3313

Montana http://www.fwp.state.mt.us/fishing/boatrestrictions.asp
General information: 406-444-2535
Registration: 406-846-1423
Highway patrol: 406-444-3780

Nebraska http://www.ngpc.state.ne.us/boating/boating.asp
General information and registration: 402) 471-0641
State patrol: 402-471-4545

Nevada http://www.boatnevada.org/
General information: 775-688-1500
Registration: 775-688-1500
Highway patrol: 775-684-4808

New Hampshire http://www.state.nh.us/safety/ss/links.html
General information: 603-293-2037
Registration: 603-271-2333
State police: 603-271-2575

New Jersey http://www.state.nj.us/mvc/
General information: 609-882-2000
Registration: 609-292-6500
State police: 609-882-2000

New Mexico http://www.emnrd.state.nm.us/NMParks
General information: 505-476-3369
Registration: 505-827-0612
State police: 505-827-9000

New York http://www.nysparks.com/boats/
General information: 518-474-0445
Registration: 518-473-5595
State police: 518-457-6811

North Carolina http://www.boatsafe.com/North_Carolina/
General information: 919-733-3391
Registration: 919-773-2800
Highway patrol: 919-733-7952

North Dakota http://www.state.nd.us/gnf/boating/
General information and licensing: 701-328-6300
Highway patrol: 701-328-2455

Ohio http://www.dnr.state.oh.us/watercraft/
General information & registration: 614-265-6480
Highway patrol: 614-466-2660

Oklahoma http://www.dps.state.ok.us/ohp/aboutlp.htm
General information: 405-521-3221
Registration: 405-521-2439
Highway patrol: 405-425-2424

Oregon http://www.marinebd.osmb.state.or.us/
General information and registration: 503-378-8587
State police: 503-378-3720

Pennsylvania http://www.fish.state.pa.us/
General information: 717-705-7930 717-705-7831
State police: 717-783-5599

Rhode Island http://www.state.ri.us/dem/programs/bpoladm/
manserv/hfb/index.htm
General information: 401-277-2284
Registration: 401-222-6647
State police: 401-444-1000

South Carolina http://water.dnr.state.sc.us/
General information: 803-734-3888
Registration: 803-734-3857
Highway patrol: 803-896-7920

South Dakota http://www.sdgfp.info/Wildlife/Boating/Index.
htm
General information: 605-773-3630
Registration: 605-773-3311
Highway patrol: 605-773-3105

Tennessee http://www.state.tn.us/twra/index.html
General information: 615-781-6682
Registration: 615-781-6522
Highway patrol: 615-251-5175

Texas http://www.tpwd.state.tx.us/
General information: (512) 389-4800
Registration: (800) 262-8755
Highway patrol: 512-424-2000

Utah http://parks.state.ut.us/parks/safety.htm
General information: 801-538-7220
Registration: 801-297-7780
Highway patrol: 801-965-4518

Vermont http://www.dps.state.vt.us/vtsp/boat_safe.html
General information: 802-244-8727
Registration: 802-828-2000
State police: 802-244-7345

Virginia http://www.dgif.state.va.us/boating/
General information: 804-367-1258
Registration: 877-898-2628
State police: 804-674-2000

Washington http://www.parks.wa.gov/boating.asp
General information: 360-586-6590
Registration: 360-902-3770
State patrol: 360-753-6540

West Virginia http://www.wvdnr.gov/lenforce/boating.shtm
General information: 304-558-2784
Registration: 800-642-9066
State police: 304-746-2100

Wisconsin http://www.dnr.state.wi.us/org/es/enforcement/
safety/boatsaf.htm
General information: 608-266-2141
Registration: 608-267-7799
State patrol: 608-266-3212

Wyoming http://gf.state.wy.us/fish/boating/index.asp
General information: 307-777-4600
Registration: 307-777-4575
Highway Patrol: 307-777-4305

Provincial Police

Boat licensing in Canada is handled by local offices of the
Canada Customs and Revenue Agency rather than by the
individual provinces; telephone directory blue pages list local
agency office numbers. Boating regulations are handled at
the federal level as well. For these reasons, there are no list-
ings here for boating authorities in the individual provinces
as for the individual U.S. states.

See the Canadian Coast Guard information and phone numbers above for information on boat licensing, registration,
and rules and regulations.

Ontario and Quebec have their own provincial police forces.
Provincial police service in all the other provinces is supplied by the RCMP.

Alberta
RCMP Edmonton HQ: 780-412-5424

British Columbia
RCMP Vancouver HQ: 604-264-3111

Manitoba
RCMP Winnipeg HQ: 204-983-5420

New Brunswick
Fredericton HQ: 506-452-3400

Newfoundland RCMP St. John's HQ: 709-772-5400	
Northwest Territories RCMP Yellowknife HQ: 867-669-5100	
Nova Scotia RCMP Halifax HQ: 902-426-3644	
Nunavut RCMP Igaluit HQ: 867-975-4409	
Ontario Provincial police: 888-310-1122	
Prince Edward Island RCMP Charlottetown HQ: 902-566-7112	
Quebec Provincial Police: 514-598-4141	
Saskatchewan RCMP Regina: 306-780-5560	
Yukon RCMP Whitehorse HQ: 867-633-8612	

Car Rental Phone Numbers

Advantage Rent-A-Car	800-777-5500; 210-344-4712
Alamo Rent-A-Car	800-462-5266; 954-320-4000
Avis	800-230-4898 (U.S.) 800-272-5871 (Canada)
Budget	800/527-0700 (U.S.) 800/268-8900 (Canada)
Dollar	800-800-3665
Enterprise	800-261-7331
Hertz	800-654-3131 (U.S.) 800-263-0600 (Canada)
National	800-227-7368;
Payless	800-729-5377; 727-321-6352
Thrifty	800-847-4389; 918-669-2168

Airline Phone Numbers

Aeroflot	800-736-4192
Aerolineas Argentinas	800-333-0276
Aeromexico	800-237-6639
Air Aruba	800-882-7822
Air Canada	888-247-2262
Air France	800-237-2747
Air India	800-223-7776
Air Jamaica	800-523-5585
Air New Zealand	800-262-1234
Alaska Airlines	800-426-0333
Alitalia	800-223-5730
All Nippon Airways	800-235-9262
Aloha Airlines	800-367-5250
America West	800-235-9292
American Airlines	800-433-7300
American Eagle	800-433-7300
Bahamas Air	800-222-4262
Big Sky Airlines	800-237-7788
British Airways	800-247-9297
CanJet	800-809-7777
Cathay Pacific	800-233-2742
Cayman Airways	800-441-3003
China Airlines	800-227-5118
Continental Airlines	800-525-0280
Delta Airlines	800-221-1212
Florida Coastal Airlines	888-435-9322
Frontier Airlines	800-432-1359
Great Lakes Airlines	800-554-5111
Hawaiian Airlines	800-367-5320
Hooters Air	888-359-4668
Icelandair	800-223-5500
Indian Airlines	866-435-9422 (U.S.) 866-770-7799 (Canada)
JAL Japan Airlines	800-525-3663
Korean Air	800-438-5000
LanChile Airways	800-735-5526

Lufthansa	800-645-3880
Mesa Airlines	800-637-2247
Mexicana	800-531-7921
Midwest Airlines	800-452-2022
Northwest Airlines	800-225-2525
Pan Am	800-359-7262
Philippine Airlines	800-435-9725
Polynesian Airlines	800-644-7659
Qantas Airways	800-227-4500
SAS Scandinavian Airlines	800-221-2350
Saudi Arabian Airlines	800-472-8342
South African	800-722-9675
Southwest Airlines	800-435-9792
Swiss	877-359-7947
TAM—Brazilian Airlines	888-235-9826
United Airlines	800-241-6522
US Airways	800-428-4322
Varig	800-468-2744
Virgin	800-862-8621

Lost Credit Card Phone Numbers

American Express	800-528-4800 or 336-393-1111
Diners Club/Carte Blanche	800-234-6377 or 303-799-1504
Discover	800-347-2683 or 801-902-3100
MasterCard	800-622-7747 or 636-722-7111
Visa	800-847-2911 or 410-581-9994

BOATING INFORMATION AND REFERENCES

BOOKS OF INTEREST

In the process of carrying out research for this book, I read a lot of books and perused countless others in libraries and bookstores. Like almost everything, there are poor books, good books, and just a few that really stand out. The few books of interest listed below are the books that really stood out.

Chapman Piloting: Seamanship and Small Boat Handling, 63rd ed. New York: Hearst Marine Books, 1999. This is generally considered the bible for recreational boaters. All but the most experienced boaters can benefit from this book, which covers all aspects of boating. Covers boat construction and ownership, safety, seamanship, regulations, weather, navigation, electronics, etc.

The Nature of Boats: Insights and Esoterica for the Nautically Obsessed by Dave Gerr. Camden, ME: International Marine, 1995. This is my favorite boating book that is just fun to read. It provides an interesting introduction to boat design and construction. It includes discussions on hull form, engines, propellers, sails, electrical systems, and construction materials and techniques. If you are thinking of acquiring a new boat, this might give you a different perspective on the alternatives available to you.

Cruising Handbook: The Essential Guide for Choosing, Equipping, and Sailing Coastal or Offshore Cruising Boats by Nigel Calder. Camden, ME: International Marine, 2001. Anyone considering buying and equipping a boat and then sailing it offshore should consider this book. It's oriented to sailboats, but there's plenty of valuable material for powerboaters.

Mid Size Power Boats: A Guide for Discriminating Buyers by David Pascoe. Destin, FL: D.H. Pascoe & Company, 2003. This is a comprehensive guide by an experienced marine surveyor to help the prospective buyer evaluate new or used boats. This book will help you get the right boat the first time and save you a lot of trouble and headaches.

The Weekend Navigator: Simple Boat Navigation with GPS and Electronics by Bob Sweet. Camden, ME: International Marine, 2005. This book has everything the recreational boater needs to know about navigation. Extensive discussions on using electronic navigation aids such as GPS and radar.

Reed's Nautical Companion: The Comprehensive Shipboard Reference. Boston: Thomas Reed Publications, 2002. This is a comprehensive reference book covering navigation rules, regulations, navigation, communications, weather, tides, and other subjects. Kind of like this reference book but with far more comprehensive treatment of many subjects. This is an excellent book to keep onboard. Note: This book also qualifies as a copy of the navigation rules required on vessels over 12 meters (39.4 ft).

Boatowner's Mechanical and Electrical Manual: How to Maintain, Repair, and Improve Your Boat's Essential Systems. By Nigel Calder. Camden ME: International Marine 1996. This is the most thorough and comprehensive book on boat mechanical and electrical systems. If you are a do-it-yourselfer, this is a must-have book.

Propeller Handbook: The Complete Reference for Choosing, Installing and Understanding Boat Propellers by Dave Gerr. Camden, ME: International Marine, 2001. This is the most comprehensive book on powering and propellers that can be understood by the layman.

INTERESTING INTERNET SITES
General Boating

Best Boating Web Pages http://www.bestboating.org/
Contains links to other boating-related sites rated as the best sites.

BoatingLinks.com http://www.boatinglinks.com/
Contains links to plenty of other boating-related sites.

Boatlinks.com http://www.boatlinks.com/
Contains links to other boating related sites. Very comprehensive.

BoatSafe http://www.boatsafe.com/
General safety information. Online boating courses. Lots of information and tips on boating

BoatUS http://www.boatus.com/
Boat Owners Association of the United States homepage.

Canada Tourist Information http://www.etourist.ca/travel/

Canadian Coast Guard http://www.ccg-gcc.gc.ca/main_e.htm Homepage

Discover Boating http://www.discoverboating.com/

Guide to Sailing and Cruising Stories http://cruisenews.net
Personal cruising stories make for interesting reading.
Articles on anything to do with boats.

Kasten Marine Design Inc http://www.kastenmarine.com/
This site contains several informative articles on boat design and building.

MarinePlanner http://www.marineplanner.com/
This site specializes in route planning tools, including downloadable charts and weather plots. Also has a "MariPedia," which has links to many other sites.

National Association of State Boating Law Administrators http://www.nasbla.org/ 859.225.9487

National Geospatial-Intelligence Agency http://pollux.nss.nima.mil/index/index.html Maritime Safety Information Page.

NIMA publications site http://pollux.nss.nima.mil/pubs/
Free downloads of *The American Practical Navigator* (*Bowditch*), *Publication 229, Chart No. 1*, light lists and other useful publications. You'll want a high-speed Internet connection for some of the larger downloads.

NOAA Charts http://chartmaker.ncd.noaa.gov/
Nautical charts, including free downloads of electronic chart data.

Open Directory -Boating Laws and Regulations http://dmoz.org/Recreation/Boating/Safety/Boating_Laws_and_Regulations/
This site has links to various state boating-related websites.

Pat's Boating in Canada http://boating.ncf.ca/
An excellent website with all kinds of information pertaining to boating in Canada, including regulations, safety, and other general interest information. Includes links to other sites.

Reed's Nautical Almanac http://www.reedsalmanac.com/
Home page.

SailNet http://www.sailnet.com/index.cfm
Store that carries almost everything but with an emphasis
on sailing.

Transport Canada Marine http://www.tc.gc.ca/marine/
menu.htm

US Coast Guard http://www.uscgboating.org/

US Coast Guard Mariner Licensing http://www.uscg.
mil/stcw/index.htm

US Naval Observatory (USNO) Astronomical Application
Department http://aa.usno.navy.mil/
Publications and software relating to celestial navigation.

USCG Boatbuilder's Handbook http://www.uscgboating.
org/safety/boatbuilder/index.htm

USCG Boating Safety http://www.uscgboating.org/
Homepage for recreational boating safety and regulations.

USCG Vessel Documentation Center http://www.uscg.
mil/hq/g-m/vdoc/nvdc.htm
Information on documenting your boat.

World Wide Boat Shows Calendar by NMMA http://
www.nmma.org/calendar

Yachtsurvey.com http://www.yachtsurvey.com/.
A collection of more than 150 articles on boats by David H.
Pascoe, marine surveyor. He also has some books for sale.
If you're thinking of buying a boat, these are books that
might just save you a lot of money and headaches.

BOAT AND EQUIPMENT SALES AND MANUFACTURING

Bearing Buddy http://www.bearingbuddy.com/
Produces boat trailer bearing lubrication system.

Boat Mall http://www.boatmall.com
Boat listing, links to boating organizations and boat manufacturers, marinas, and lots of other information.

Boat Manufacturer Directory http://www.rbbi.com/
links/pbl.htm A comprehensive listing of most powerboat
manufacturers.

Boat TraderOnline.com http://www.boattraderonline.com
Lists more than 100,000 boats for sale.

Bruce Roberts Yacht Design http://www.bruceroberts.
com/ This is for people interested in metal boats, sailboats,
and powerboats.

Celestaire http://www.celestaire.com/
This company specializes in sales of traditional navigation
equipment including a variety of sextants. They also have
the newer stuff like GPS. They are quite price competitive.
After shopping around, I ended up buying my own sextant
here.

Fulton Performance Products. http://www.fultonper-
formance.com Produces boat trailer bearing lubrication
system.

Liqua-Lube, Inc http://www.liqualube.com
Produces boat trailer oil bath lubrication system.

NADA Guides.com http://www.nadaguides.com/
Used car and boat price guide.

National Marine Manufacturers Association (NMMA)
http://www.nmma.org
More than 1400 companies belong to this organization.

Tie Down Engineering http://www.tiedown.com
Produces boat trailer oil bath lubrication system.

West Marine http://www.westmarine.com
The Home Depot of marine supplies and equipment. More
than 300 stores. Catalog and internet sales.

YachtWorld.com http://yachtworld.com/
More than 70,000 boats for sale.

MAGAZINES AND PERIODICALS

Boating Life Magazine http://www.boatinglifemag.com/	
Boating Magazine http://www.boatingmag.com/	
Cruising World http://www.cruisingworld.com	
Go Boating http://www.goboatingamerica.com	
Latitudes and Attitudes http://www.latsandatts.net/	
Motor Boat and Yachting http://www.mby.com/	
MotorBoating http://www.motorboating.com	

Multihulls Magazine http://www.multihullsmag.com/ for sailing multihulls
Ocean Navigator http://www.oceannavigator.com/ Emphasis on navigation and weather.
Passagemaker http://www.trawlertravel.com Sponsors of Trawler Fest and TrawlerPort at major boat shows.
Power and Motoryacht http://www.powerandmotoryacht.about.com/
Power of Multihulls http://www.powermultihulls.com
Powerboat Reports http://www.powerboat-reports.com/ This periodical reviews powerboats, and powerboat equipment and supplies. *Powerboat Reports* does not accept commercial advertising. Sister publication of *Practical Sailor*.
Practical Sailor http://www.practical-sailor.com/ This periodical reviews sailboats, and sailboat equipment and supplies. *Practical Sailor* does not accept commercial advertising. Sister publication of *Powerboat Reports*.
Sail http://www.sailmag.com/
Sailing World http://www.sailingworld.com/index.jsp
Sea http://www.goboatingamerica.com/sea/
Trailer Boats Magazine http://www.trailerboats.com/
Wooden Boat http://www.woodenboat.com/
Yachting http://www.yachtingnet.com/yachting/

BIBLIOGRAPHY

————. *Advanced Piloting.* Raleigh, NC: U.S. Power Squadrons, 1997.

Armstrong, Bob. *Getting Started in Powerboating,*. 2d ed. Camden, ME: International Marine, 1995.

————. *Basic Engine Maintenance and Advanced Engine Maintenance.* Raleigh, NC: U.S. Power Squadrons, 2002.

Bigon, Mario and Regazzoni, Guido. *The Morrow Guide to Knots.* New York: Quill/William Morrow, 1982.

————. *Boating Course.* 8th ed. Scarborough, Ontario: Canadian Power and Sail Squadrons, 1999.

Bowditch, Nathaniel (original author). *The American Practical Navigator: An Epitome of Navigation.* Bethesda, MD: National Imagery and Mapping Agency, 2002.

Calder, Nigel. *Boatowner's Mechanical and Electrical Manual: How to Maintain, Repair, and Improve Your Boat's Essential Systems.* Camden, ME: International Marine, 1996.

Calder, Nigel. *Cruising Handbook: The Essential Guide for Choosing, Equipping, and Sailing Coastal or Offshore Cruising Boats.* Camden, ME: International Marine, 2001

————. *Canada Chart No. 1 / Carte No. 1: Symbols Abbreviations Terms.* Canadian Hydrographic Service, 1996.

————. *Chapman Piloting: Seamanship & Small Boat Handling.* 63rd ed. New York: Hearst Marine Books, 1999.

————. *Chart Number One: United States of America: Nautical Chart Symbols Abbreviations & Terms.* Washington, DC: Department of Commerce, National Oceanic, and Atmospheric Administration, 1997

————. *Collision Regulations.* Ottawa: Transport Canada, 2000.

Compton, Peter. *Troubleshooting Marine Diesels.* Camden, ME: International Marine, 1998.

————. *Cruise Planning.* Raleigh, NC: U.S. Power Squadrons, 1997.

Cutler, Thomas J. *Dutton's Nautical Navigation*, 15th ed. Annapolis, MD: Naval Institute Press, 2004.

————. *Digest of Motor Laws.* Washington, DC: AAA Government Relations, 2004.

————. *Distances Between Ports*, 11th ed. Bethesda, MD: National Imagery and Mapping Agency, 2001.

Dodds, Don. *Modern Seamanship*. Guilford, CN: The Lyons Press, 2001

————. *Federal Requirements and Safety Tips for Recreational Boaters*. Washington, DC: U.S. Coast Guard, 2001.

Fleming, John. *Complete Guide to Diesel Marine Engines*. Harrisburg, PA: Bristol Fashion Publications, 2000.

Gerr, Dave. *Boat Strength for Builders, Designers, and Owners*. Camden, ME: International Marine, 2000.

Gerr, Dave. *Propeller Handbook: The Complete Reference for Choosing, Installing and Understanding Boat Propellers*. Camden, ME: International Marine, 2001.

Gerr, Dave. *The Nature of Boats: Insights and Esoterica for the Nautically Obsessed*. Camden, ME: International Marine, 1995.

Glover, Thomas J. *Pocket Ref*, 3rd ed. Littleton, CO: Sequoia Publishing, 2003.

Hamlin, Cyrus. *Preliminary Design of Boats and Ships*. Centreville, MD: Cornell Maritime Press, 1996.

Hubbard, Richard K. *Boater's Bowditch: The Small-Craft American Practical Navigator*. Camden, ME: International Marine, 2000.

Jobson, Gary. *Sailing Fundamentals*. New York: Fireside, Simon and Schuster, 1998.

————. *Junior Navigation*. Raleigh, NC: U.S. Power Squadrons, 2001.

Kay, H.F. *The Science of Yachts, Wind & Water*. Tuckahoe, NY: John de Graff, 1971.

Larsson, Lars and Eliasson, Rolf E. *Principles of Yacht Design*, 2nd ed. Camden, ME: International Marine, 2000

Lewis, Edward V. *Principles of Naval Architecture*: Volume II, Resistance, Propulsion and Vibration. Jersey City, NJ: The Society of Naval Architects and Engineers

Low, Charles T. *Boat Docking: Close Quarters Maneuvering for Small Craft*. Ontario: Harvey Island Enterprises, 1997.

————. *Marine Electronics*. Raleigh, NC: U.S. Power Squadrons, 2002.

Marshall, Roger. *All About Powerboats: Understanding Design and Performance*. Camden, ME: International Marine, 2002.

Monahan, Kevin. *The Radar Book*, 1st ed. Anacortes, WA: FineEdge.com LLC, 2004.

————. *Navigation Rules: International—Inland*. Washington, DC: U.S. Coast Guard, 1995.

————. *Navigation*. Raleigh, NC: U.S. Power Squadrons, 2002.

Nicolson, Ian. *Boat Data Book*. Dobbs Ferry, NY: Sheridan House, 1999.

Pascoe, David H. *Mid Size Power Boats: A Guide for Discriminating Buyers*. Florida: D. H. Pascoe and Company, 2003.

————. *Piloting*. Raleigh, NC: U.S. Power Squadrons, 1997.

————. *Reed's Nautical Companion*. Boston: Thomas Reed Publications, 2002.

Roberts-Goodson, Bruce. *The Complete Guide to Metal Boats*. Camden, ME: International Marine, 2001.

Royce, Patrick M. *Sailing Illustrated*. Ventura, CA: Western Marine Enterprises, 1985.

————. *Safe Boating Guide: Your Guide to Regulations and Responsible Recreational Boating*. Ottawa: Canadian Coast Guard, 2000.

————. *Sail 101 and Sail 102*. Raleigh, NC: U.S. Power Squadrons, 1998.

Scharff, Robert and Henderson, Richard and the Editors of Yacht Racing/Cruising. *Encyclopedia of Sailing*. New York: Harper and Row, 1971.

————. *Seamanship*. Raleigh, NC: United States Power Squadrons, 1994.

Skene, Norman L. *Elements of Yacht Design*. Dobbs Ferry, NY: Sheridan House, 2001.

Sorensen, Eric W. *Guide to Powerboats: How to Evaluate Design, Construction, and Performance.* Camden, ME: International Marine, 2002.

Sweet, Robert J. *GPS for Mariners*, 1st ed. Camden, ME: International Marine, 2003.

Sweet, Robert J. *The Weekend Navigator*, 1st ed. Camden, ME: International Marine, 2005.

———. *The Canadian Aids to Navigation System.* Ottawa: Fisheries and Oceans Canada, 2001.

———. *The Squadron Boating Course: Fundamental Boating Education for the Power and Sail Boater.* Raleigh, NC: U.S. Power Squadrons, 1998.

Toss, Brian. *Knots: A Chapman Nautical Guide.* New York: Hearst Books, 2000.

Traister, John E. Marine *Engine Troubleshooting and Repair.* Englewood Cliffs, NJ: Prentice-Hall, 1987.

———. *U.S. Aids to Navigation System.* Washington, DC: U.S. Coast Guard, 2001.

Vigor, John. *Boatowner's Handbook: Reference Data for Maintenance, Repair, Navigation, and Seamanship.* Camden, ME: International Marine, 2000.

———. *Weather: Supplemental Manual.* Raleigh, NC: U.S. Power Squadrons, 2002.

Williams, Jack. *The Weather Book: An Easy-to-Understand Guide to the USA's Weather.* New York: Vintage Books, Division of Random House, 1997.

Wing, Charlie. *Boatowner's Illustrated Handbook of Wiring.* Camden, ME: International Marine, 1993.

15 GLOSSARY

Abaft—a thing in a direction further aft (toward the stern) of some object on the boat is abaft of it. e.g. abaft the beam.

Abaft the beam—a direction between broad on the beam (90 degree relative bearing) and astern.

Abeam—something is abeam if it is to either side perpendicular (90 degree relative bearing) to the boat centerline.

Aboard—on or in the vessel.

Above deck—on deck but not over it.

Aft—toward the stern or near the stern.

Aground—a vessel that is touching or stuck on the bottom.

Ahead—in front of the bow, the forward direction.

Aid to navigation—A device or structure external to a craft, designed to assist in determination of position, to define a safe course, or to warn of dangers or obstructions. Includes buoys, daymarks, lights, etc.

Aloft—above the deck such as up in the rigging.

Amidships— the center part of a vessel.

Anchorage—an area where boats may anchor.

Anchor—n. a device used to anchor a boat to the sea floor. v. to use the anchor to secure to the sea floor.

Anemometer—a device for measuring wind velocity.

Aneroid barometer—a mechanical type of barometer.

Anode—the positive electrode of a battery or other electrochemical toward which negative ions are drawn.

Antenna—used to send or receive electromagnetic waves.

Anti-fouling paint used on the part of the hull below the waterline that repels marine organisms.

Apparent wind—the wind direction as perceived from a moving boat. It is a combination of the true (actual) wind and the wind created from the movement of the boat.

Note: Many of the definitions in this glossary of terms are quoted from Bowditch *(The American Practical Navigator).*

Astern—behind the stern, the backward direction.

Athwartships—Objects that are oriented across the boat are athwartships. That is at right angles to the centerline.

Auto pilot—a system used to steer a vessel automatically along a prescribed bearing without human assistance.

Awash—situated so that the top is intermittently washed by waves or tidal action. Applies to both objects afloat and fixed objects.

Azimuth—the horizontal direction or bearing of a celestial point from a terrestrial point.

Bar—a ridge or mound of sand, gravel, or other unconsolidated material below the high water level, especially at the mouth of a river or estuary.

Backing—refers to the wind changing direction in a counter-clockwise direction. In the southern hemisphere the wind backs in a clockwise directions. The opposite of veering wind.

Backstay—The aft stay (line) from the upper part of the mast down to a point on the boat abaft of the mast, the purpose of which is to hold (stay) the mast upright along with the shrouds (sidestays) and forestays.

Ballast—extra weight added to the keel or bottom of the hull to add stability. Lead is a preferred material for ballast because of its high density.

Barometer—an instrument used to measure atmospheric pressure.

Bathymetric chart—topographic chart of the seabed. i.e. a topo chart of water depth.

Batten down—refers to closing and securing of hatches and securing loose objects, usually in anticipation of bad weather.

Battens—strips of plastic or wood which are used to stiffen sails.

Baud—data transmission speed in bits/second.

Bay—a recess in the shore, on an inlet of a sea or lake between two capes or headlands, that may vary greatly in size but is usually smaller than a gulf but larger than a cove.

Beacon—fixed aid to navigation, attached to ground as opposed to a buoy which floats.

Beam—(1) the maximum width of the boat, (2) the direction perpendicular to the boat centerline.

Beam sea—waves moving in a direction approximately 90 degrees from the vessel's heading.

Bear off—to turn away from the wind.

Bearing—the horizontal direction of one terrestrial point from another, expressed as the angular distance from a reference direction. It is usually measured from 000° degrees at the reference direction clockwise through 360 degrees. Most often used to measure from the north.

Beating—tacking back and forth against the wind.

Beaufort wind scale—a numerical scale for indicating wind speed, devised by Admiral Sir Francis Beaufort in 1805. Beaufort numbers (or forces) range from force 0 (calm) to force 12 (hurricane).

Bend on—attaching a sail to the mast or stay in preparation for hoisting it.

Berth—a bed for sleeping, or a place where a boat can be secured.

Bifurcation—a division into two branches.

Bight—a loop in a rope or line

Bilge—the bottom inside of the hull.

Binnacle—a vertical post on which a compass and/or wheel is mounted.

Bitter end—the shipboard end of an anchor rode or the far end a line.

Block—a pulley or set of pulleys along with the plates that hold them together.

Boat—a small vessel.

Boat hook—a long hand held pole with a hook on the end. Can be used to fend off or hook a line.

Bollard—short vertical fitting to which lines are fastened. Used in mooring or towing. A post (usually steel or reinforced concrete) firmly secured on a wharf, quay, etc., for mooring vessels with lines.

Boom—a horizontal spar attached to the mast. On sailboats the foot of the sail is attached to the boom.

Boom vang (sailboat)—a tackle or hydraulic cylinder which runs from near the base of the mast to the boom and which serves to pull the boom down to help straighten the sail and leech.

Bore—diameter of a cylinder in an engine

Bow pulpit—a safety railing around the bow and partway aft on both sides. Also serves as the forward attachment point for the lifelines.

Bow—the front or forward end of the boat.

Bowditch—popular title for *The American Practical Navigator* (from which this definition was taken).

Bowsprit—a spar attached forward from the bow used for anchoring and to attach forestays on sailboats.

Bow wave—the wave set up by the bow of a vessel moving through the water.

Breakwater—a line of rocks, concrete, pilings, or other material that breaks the force of the sea at a particular place, forming a protected area. Often an artificial embankment built to protect the entrance to a harbor or to form an artificial harbor. See also Jetty.

Bridge—the area that contains the wheel (helm) and instruments used for the purpose of steering and controlling the boat.

Brightwork—polished metal fittings and accessories commonly made of brass, stainless steel, or chrome-plated steel.

Bristol—super clean, excellent condition, immaculate.

Bulkhead—a partition or wall running athwartships (across the hull).

Buoy—a float used as an aid to navigation or for mooring to.

Can—a buoy used as an aid to navigation that is cylindrical in shape. In North America it is colored green and odd numbered.

Cape—a relatively extensive land area jutting seaward from a continent, or large island, which prominently marks a change in or interrupts notably the coastal trend.

Capsize—to turn over a boat.

Capstan—a rotating drum (winch) that is usually used for raising and lowering anchors.

Cardinal heading—a heading in the direction of any of the cardinal points of the compass. That is N, E, S, or W.

Cardinal point—any of the four principal directions; north, east, south, or west.

Cast off—to let go or unfasten. Usually used when unfastening mooring lines before departure.

Catenary—the curve formed by a uniform line, chain, or cable supported only at its ends.

Catamaran—a two-hulled boat.

Cathode—the general term for a negative electrode. See also Anode.

Cavitation—bubbles of water vapor created underwater by pressure less than the vapor pressure of water. Usually caused by propellers.

Centerboard—a vertical plate that can be lowered down through the keel to provide a sailboat with additional resistance to leeway (sideways movement due to the wind).

Celsius temperature—the designation given to the temperature measured zero taken as the freezing point of water and 100 taken as the boiling point of water at sea level. Formerly called Centigrade temperature.

Centerline—the center dividing line of a vessel fore and aft that separates port from starboard.

Center of gravity—the point in any body at which the force of gravity may be considered to be concentrated.

Centigrade temperature—traditional term for Celsius. See Celsius temperature.

Chafing gear—a wrapping made of cloth or tubing to protect lines from chafing (wearing and abrading).

Chain locker—a locker below the capstan used to store the anchor rode (chain or line).

Channel—(1) a marked part of a waterway of known depth that is safe to navigate, (2) the deepest part of a river or other body of water, and (3) a large strait may be called a channel, the most well known being the English Channel.

Chart—maps for marine use.

Chart scale—the ratio between a distance on a chart and the corresponding distance represented as a ratio such as 1:80,000 (natural scale), or 30 miles to an inch (numerical scale).

Chine—the intersection of the side and bottom areas of the hull.

Chronometer—a very accurate clock used to set other clocks or watches by.

Chock—1. an opening or fitting which mooring or anchor lines pass through. 2. A triangular shaped block of wood, plastic or rubber that can be wedged under trailer wheels to prevent them rolling forward or backward.

Cleat—a device for fastening the end of a line to.

Clew (sail)—the lower aft corner of the sail.

Coaming—a vertical edge around a cockpit or hatch to prevent entry of water

Cockpit—the open area, generally aft, that is separated from the main cabin or saloon. Always aft in powerboats but sometimes midships in larger sailboats.

COLREGS—acronym for *International Regulations for Prevention of Collisions at Sea* (i.e., short for *Collision Regulations*). Commonly called the *Navigation Rules* in the United States.

Compass—an instrument for indicating a horizontal reference direction relative to the earth. A magnetic compass measures direction relative to magnetic north.

Compass rose—a circle graduated in degrees, clockwise from 0 degrees at the reference direction to 360 degrees, and sometimes also in compass points. Compass roses are placed at convenient locations on the Mercator chart or plotting sheet to facilitate measurement of direction.

Conformal projection—a map projection in which all angles around any point are correctly represented, In such a projection the scale in small areas is the same in all directions about any point. The Mercator projection is a conformal projection.

Contour or contour line—a line connecting points of equal elevation or equal depth.

Correcting—the process of applying corrections, particularly the process of converting compass to magnetic direction, or compass, magnetic, or gyro to true direction. The opposite is uncorrecting.

Cosine—the ratio of the length of the side adjacent to an acute angle of a plane right triangle to the length of the hypotenuse.

Cotangent—the reciprocal of the tangent or 1/tan.

Course—the direction in which a vessel is steered or intended to be steered, expressed as angular distance from north, usually from 000 degrees at north, clockwise through 360 degrees.

Course made good—a misnomer indicating the resultant direction from a point of departure to a point of arrival at any given time. The preferred term is track made good.

Course over ground—the direction of the path over the ground actually followed by a vessel. The preferred term is track. It is normally a somewhat irregular line. This is a misnomer in that courses are directions steered or intended to be steered through the water with respect to a reference meridian.

Cringle—a hole through a sail through which lines can be passed or attached. Usually reinforced with a metal or plastic ring.

Cunningham (sailboat)—a line through a cringle above the tack which can be pulled down to tighten the luff of the sail.

Current—a horizontal movement of water.

Daggerboard—a nonhinged centerboard that retracts vertically.

Davit—a horizontal device that may be fixed or swung out and used to raise and lower things out of a boat. Commonly used for dinghies.

Daybeacon—a fixed aid to navigation structure with attached daymark (dayboard) that is not lighted. If it is lighted, it is a light.

Dayboard—an aid to navigation signboard, attached to a fixed structure. May be lighted. Also termed a daymark.

Daymark—an aid to navigation signboard, attached to a fixed structure. May be lighted. Also termed a dayboard.

Dead ahead—directly or straight ahead.

Dead astern—directly or straight astern.

Dead reckoning—derived from deduced reckoning. Figuring position from only speed, time, and direction from a known starting position.

Deadrise—on a vee bottom hull the angle between the hull bottom and horizontal.

Deck—(1) the covering over the top of the hull, or (2) any floor.

Depth—distance from the surface of the water to the sea bottom.

Deviation—the angle between compass north and magnetic north. Caused by disturbing magnetic influences on the boat.

Dew point—the temperature below which water vapor in air will condense into dew.

Displacement (engine)—the volume of gas displaced by all the cylinders in an engine as they move from bottom to top. The most common units are liters, cubic centimeters, and cubic inches.

Displacement hull—a hull that is supported entirely by buoyancy when moving at speed as opposed to a planing hull that is supported by hydrodynamic lift.

Displacement—the weight of water displaced by a boat sitting still in the water = the weight of the boat and everything in it.

Diurnal—having a period or cycle of approximately one day.

Dock—n. an area where vessels are moored. Also commonly, but incorrectly, used to refer to a pier or wharf. Also used as a verb to describe the action of bringing a vessel into a pier, wharf or slip. v. To place (dock) at a pier, wharf, slip, etc.

Doldrums—the equatorial belt of calms or light variable winds, lying between the two trade wind belts.

Dolphin—several piles tied together. For mooring or for supporting aids to navigation.

Draft—the distance from the waterline to the deepest part of the boat.

Drift—(1) the speed of a current, (2) the distance a craft is moved by current and wind, and (3) the angular difference between a vessel's ground track and the water track.

Drogue—see Sea anchor.

Duplex—concurrent transmission and reception of radio signals, electronic data, or other information.

Ease—to let out or loosen a line.

Ebb—a tide that is receding or going out.

EPIRB—Emergency Position Indicating Radio Beacon. When activated, it will send an emergency radio distress signal via geostationary satellite.

Equator—the great circle perpendicular to the polar axis that lies mid way between the north and south poles.

Estimated position—the most probable position of a craft determined from incomplete data or data of questionable accuracy.

Estuary—an embayment of the coast in which fresh river water entering at its head mixes with the relatively saline ocean water.

Eye of the wind—the direction from which the wind is blowing

Eye splice—a loop permanently spliced in the end of a line.

Fahrenheit temperature—temperature based on a scale in which, under standard atmospheric pressure, water freezes at 32 degrees and boils at 212 degrees above zero.

Fairlead—a device through which a line passes and which changes the direction of the line.

Fairway—(1) the main thoroughfare of shipping in a harbor or channel, and (2) the middle of a channel.

Fast—describes a line or object that is secured to something.

Fathom—6 feet.

Fender—a soft, usually inflated, object placed on the sides of a boat to cushion the boat from hard contact with other boats or a pier.

Fiberglass—boat construction material consisting of glass fiber cloth or strands impregnated with epoxy.

Fid—a handheld pointed object used for separating strands of rope.

Fix—a position determined without reference to any former position; the common intersection of two or more lines of position obtained from simultaneous observations.

Flare—1. outward curve of the hull, particularly near the bow. 2. A pyrotechnic device used to attract attention in an emergency.

Flemish—spiral flat coiling of a line on a flat surface. Usually done for appearance sake.

Float—a deck or platform that floats on the water to which boats can be made fast.

Flood—tidal current moving toward land or up a tidal stream. The opposite is ebb.

Flotsam—floating articles that have not been thrown in deliberately (as jetsam), often the result of a shipwreck.

Flybridge—derived from the term "flying bridge." A bridge located on top of the vessel that is usually open and affords good visibility in all directions.

Flying bridge—see flybridge

Following Sea—seas (waves) moving in the same direction as the vessel.

Foot (sail)—the bottom edge of the sail.

Fore—located toward the front of a boat.

Forestay—a line running from the forward part of the boat to the upper part of the mast.

Forward—the direction toward the bow or near the bow

Fouled—an object that is stuck or entangled or dirty.

Founder—to fill with water and sink.

Fractional rig—a sailboat with a headsail that is attached below the top of the mast.

Freeboard—the minimum distance from the top of the gunwales to the surface of the water.

Gaff—a spar that supports the top edge of a sail.

Galley—the kitchen on a boat.

Gather way—to begin to move.

Genoa—a headsail of larger area than a jib, which when pulled straight aft, overlaps the mast.

Geostationary satellite—a earth satellite moving eastward in an equatorial, circular orbit at an altitude (approximately 35,900 kilometers) such that its period of revolution is exactly equal to and synchronous with the rotational period of the earth. Such a satellite will remain fixed over a point on the earth's equator. Although geostationary satellites are frequently called geosynchronous or synchronous satellites, the orbit of an eastward moving synchronous satellite must be equatorial if the satellite is to remain fixed over a point on the equator.

Giveway vessel—the vessel that must yield in meeting, crossing, or overtaking situations.

GLONASS—a satellite navigation system operated by Russia, analogous to the U.S. Global Positioning System (GPS).

Great circle—the intersection of a sphere and a plane through its center. The intersection of a sphere and a plane that does not pass through its center is called a small circle.

Gross tons—a measure of the total interior volume of a vessel including crew space. 1 gross ton = 100 cubic feet. This is a volume and not a weight like displacement tons.

Ground—to touch bottom or run aground.

Ground—a conducting connection between an electric circuit and the earth or some other conducting body of zero potential with respect to the earth.

Ground tackle—the anchors, anchor chains, fittings, etc., used for anchoring a vessel.

Gong—a sound signal producing a sound by the vibration of a resonant disc struck by a clapper.

Gulf—a major indentation of the sea into the land, usually larger than a bay.

Gunwale—the upper edge of the sides of the hull of the vessel often higher than the deck.

Gyrocompass—a compass having one or more gyroscopes as the directive element, and which is north-seeking.

Halyard—line running up the mast, through a block, and down to the head of a sail, used to raise and lower the sail. Also lines used to raise and lower flags.

Harbor—a safe anchorage that is protected from storms. A harbor may be manmade or natural.

Hard chine—a chine formed by the bottom and sides of the hull meeting at a sharp angle with no rounding.

Hatch—an opening in the deck providing access to the compartment below.

Head—(1) the top corner of the sail, (2) a boat toilet or bathroom, or (3) the bow.

Heading—the direction the vessel is oriented. The direction the bow points to. The horizontal direction in which a ship actually points or heads at any instant, expressed in angular units from a reference direction, usually from 000 degrees at the reference direction clockwise through 360 degrees. Heading is often designated as true, magnetic, compass, or grid. Heading should not be confused with course, which is the intended direction of movement through the water. At a specific instant the heading may or may not coincide with the course.

Headsail—the smaller sail forward of the boom.

Headstay—the most forward forestay (line) from the upper part of the mast down to a point on the boat forward of the mast, the purpose of which is to hold (stay) the mast upright along with the shrouds (sidestays) and backstays.

Headway—forward motion of the vessel.

Head sea—a sea in which the waves move in a direction approximately opposite to the heading.

Head wind—wind from ahead of the vessel.

Heave—the vertical (up and down) motion of the entire vessel. Not to be confused with pitch, yaw or roll.

Heave to—set the boat and sails in a position such that little or no headway is made. The boat is almost stationary.

Heel—to lean or tip toward one side.

Helm—the wheel or tiller used to control the rudder and steer the boat.

Hold—cargo carrying compartment below deck.

Holding tank—a tank used to hold sewage rather than dumping it overboard.

Hull—The main boat structure that floats in the water and upon which the deck and superstructure is built.

Hygrometer—an instrument for measuring the humidity of the air. The most common type is a psychrometer consisting of dry-bulb and wet-bulb thermometers.

IALA—International Association of Lighthouse Authorities.

Inlet—a narrow body of water extending into the land from a larger body of water.

Inboard—(1) an engine and drive-train that is contained inside the boat except for the shaft and propeller, or (2) toward the center of a boat.

Jacob's ladder—a rope ladder.

Jetsam—floating materials that have purposely been thrown overboard, often to lighten ship in an emergency.

Jetty—a structure usually of concrete or rocks extending out from the shore. A jetty is often used to protect a harbor.

Jib—a headsail that when the sail is pulled straight aft, has the leech and clew forward of the mast.

Jibe—to change direction from one tack to another with the wind aft (as opposed to tack which is changing direction with the wind forward).

Kedge—to move a boat by hauling on the anchor (rode). Also a type of anchor.

Keel—the center bottom part of the hull which serves as the main fore and aft structural component (the backbone) of the hull. The keel also serves as ballast and to assist keeping the boat on course. On sailboats the relatively large keel serves to keep the boat from making leeway (slipping sideways) in the wind.

Ketch—a sailboat with two masts, the smaller of which is aft but ahead of the rudder post.

Knot—1. a measure of velocity of one nautical mile per hour. 2. a fastening of a rope or string by looping and tying looping it around itself.

Landfall—the first sighting of land when approached from seaward. By extension, the term is sometimes used to refer to the first contact with land by any means, as by radar.

Landing—(1) a place where boats receive or discharge passengers, freight, etc., or (2) bringing of a vessel to a landing.

Landmark—a conspicuous artificial feature on land, other than an established aid to navigation, which can be used as an aid to navigation.

Large scale—a scale involving a relatively small reduction in size. A large scale chart is one covering a small area (in which small objects are larger) . The opposite is small scale.

Latitude—latitude is angular distance from the equator, measured northward or southward through 90 degrees and labeled N or S to indicate the direction of measurement.

Lee—the direction the wind is blowing toward. The downwind or sheltered side of an object.

Lee shore—the shore the wind is blowing your boat toward.

Leeboard—a board attached to the side of a sailboat that serves to stop the boat from making leeway. Similar in purpose to the sailboat keel.

Leech (sail)—the trailing or aft edge of the sail.

Leeward—the direction away from the wind or downwind.

Leeway—sideways movement away from the wind caused by the wind.

Left bank—the bank of a stream or river on the left of an observer facing downstream.

Length at waterline (**LWL**)—the length of the boat at the waterline.

Length overall (**LOA**)—the longest length of the boat including the hull.

Lifeline—lines usually made of plastic coated wire ropes that are stretched from bow to stern above the gunwales supported by intermediate posts and act as railings to keep persons from falling overboard.

Light—fixed aid to navigation that is lighted.

Line—a rope which has been put into use on a boat.

Line of position—a plotted line on which a vessel is located.

List—inclination to one side. List generally implies equilibrium in an inclined condition caused by uneven distribution of mass aboard the vessel itself, while heel implies either a continuing or momentary inclination caused by an outside force, such as the wind. The term roll refers to the oscillatory motion of a vessel rather than its inclined condition.

Locker—a storage space.

Log—(1) a device used to measure distance, somewhat analogous to the odometer on a car, Or (2) written journal of activities on a boat. Different logs may be used for logging weather, navigation, maintenance, etc.

Longitude—the angle at the pole, between the prime meridian and the meridian of a point on the earth measured eastward or westward from the prime meridian through 180 degrees, and labeled E or W to indicate the direction of measurement.

Lubber's line—the line marked on a compass parallel to the centerline of the vessel.

Luff (sail)—the leading or forward edge of the sail.

Magnetic bearing—bearing relative to magnetic north; compass bearing corrected for deviation.

Make way—to move through the water.

Mainsail—the primary sail, which is installed aft of the mast.

Marinize—the process of converting an engine or machine for marine use.

Marlinespike—pointed steel tool used for undoing knots and in separating strands of rope for splicing.

Mark—an artificial or natural object of easily recognizable shape or color, or both, situated in such a position that it may be identified on a chart.

Mast—a spar (pole) that extends above the boat and can be used for any of several purposes such as for flags, sails, navigation equipment, etc.

Masthead light—a fixed running light placed on the centerline of a vessel showing an unbroken white light over an arc of the horizon from dead ahead to 22.5 degrees abaft the beam on either side of the vessel.

Mercator projection—a conformal cylindrical map projection in which the surface of a sphere or spheroid, such as the earth, is developed on a cylinder tangent along the equator. Meridians appear as equally spaced vertical lines and parallels as horizontal lines drawn farther apart as the latitude increases, such that the correct relationship between latitude and longitude scales at any point is maintained. Since rhumb lines appear as straight lines and directions can be measured directly, this projection is widely used in navigation.

Meridian—a north-south reference line, particularly a great circle through the geographical poles of the earth.

Midships—near the center of a vessel, side to side, or fore and aft.

Mizzen mast—a shorter mast aft of the main mast.

Monohull—a single-hulled boat.

Moored—made fast to a pier or buoy, or anchored.

Mooring—v. the act of securing a craft to the ground, a wharf, pier, quay, etc. n. The place where a craft may be moored.

Multihull—a boat with two or more hulls.

Nautical Mile—the standard marine measurement of distance. A nautical mile corresponds to 1 minute of latitude and = 6076.12 ft = 1852 m = 1.15 statute miles.

NAVSTAR—Global Positioning System. A satellite navigation system. This is official name of the GPS system we all use.

Net tonnage—is gross tonnage less noncargo spaces such as crew space, engine rooms, etc. Net tons is a volume and 1 net ton = 100 cubic feet.

Nun—a buoy used as an aid to navigation that is tapered inward toward the top. In North America they are red and even numbered.

North Pole—the north geographical pole

Offshore—away from the shore.

Outboard—(1) toward or outside of the sides of a boat, or (2) a removable engine mounted on the transom of a boat.

Outdrive—propulsion system consisting of an engine mounted inside the boat, with the drive outside the boat. Also called an inboard/outboard or sterndrive.

Outhaul—line used to tension the foot of a sail.

Overboard—over the side of the vessel

Painter—a line to the bow for towing or making fast.

Parallel of latitude—a circle on the surface of the earth, parallel to the quator, and connecting points of equal latitude. Also called a parallel.

Pelorus—a dumb compass, or a compass card (called a pelorus card) without a directive element, suitably mounted and provided with vanes to permit observation of relative bearings. Like a protractor permanently affixed to the vessel with zero and 180 degrees aligned with the boat centerline.

Pennant—the line that attaches a mooring buoy to a boat.

PFD (Personal Flotation Device)—a personal flotation device is a type of life jacket. It may also be a throwable device such as a buoyant seat cushion.

Pier—a platform for landing or loading, extending from the shore. Usually constructed as a deck supported by pilings like a wharf, but can be solid concrete and fill construction as well.

Pile—a vertical pole driven by force into the bottom and used to support some structure above the water, such as a deck or bridge. A pile may be made of timber, concrete, or steel.

Pilot—a person who directs the movement of a vessel through pilot waters, usually a person who has demonstrated extensive knowledge of channels, aids to navigation, dangers to navigation, etc., in a particular area and is licensed in that area.

Pilothouse—the area of the boat containing the primary bridge for steering and controlling the boat. Also called the wheelhouse.

Piloting—navigation using surrounding (visible) objects as reference points.

Pitch—(1) theoretical propeller advance in one revolution, (2) up and down motion of the bow, or (3) caulking material used in wooden boats between planks.

Pitchpole—in very high seas, the action of a boat being thrown end over end, stern over bow.

Pivot point—the point around which a vessel rotates when it is turning. Usually in the forward half of the vessel.

Planing hull—a hull that when moving at speed is supported by hydrodynamic lift rather that by its buoyancy.

Poop—a short enclosed structure at the stern of a vessel, extending from side to side. It is covered by the poop deck, which is surrounded by the poop rail.

Port tack—sailing with the wind coming from the port side.

Port—the left side of the boat when looking forward to the bow.

Portuguese bridge—a protective railing aft of the bow area but in front of the main cabin, which wards off water breaking over the bow, and provides a protected area for personnel on deck.

Prime meridian—the 0 degrees meridian of longitude, used as the origin for measurement of longitude The meridian of Greenwich, England, is almost universally used for this purpose.

Psychrometer—a weather instrument with a dry and a wet bulb thermometer that is used to measure relative humidity and dew point.

PWC (personal water craft)—small jet-powered craft with a usual capacity of one to three people.

Quarter—the side of a vessel from midships aft.

Quay—a solid structure usually constructed of concrete, along the shoreline for berthing boats or ships.

Radar—from <u>ra</u>dio <u>d</u>etection <u>a</u>nd <u>r</u>anging. A radio system that measures distance and direction by measuring the time it takes for a radio signal to travel to, be reflected from, and return from a target whose position is to be determined.

Raft—to tie two or more vessels side to side when moored.

Range—two or more objects with known (charted) positions through which a line can be drawn to determine a line of position. A range is often set up to indicate the center line of a channel.

Reciprocal bearing or direction—a bearing or direction differing by 180 Degrees (i.e., a bearing measured in the opposite direction from the given bearing).

Reef—reducing of the sail area.

Relative bearing—bearing relative to the heading of a vessel expressed as the angular difference between the heading and the direction. It is usually measured from 000 degrees at the heading clockwise through 360 degrees, but is sometimes measured from 0 degrees at the heading either clockwise or counterclockwise through 180 degrees, when it is designated right or left.

Rigging—all the lines and hardware that support and control the masts and sails.

Right bank—the bank of a stream or river on the right of the observer when he or she is facing in the direction of flow, or downstream.

Roadstead or road—an open anchorage affording less protection than a harbor. Some protection may be afforded by reefs, shoals, etc.

Roll—side to side rolling motion of a boat.

Rope—made of either wire or fiber. When put into use on a boat is called a line.

RPM—revolutions per minute of an engine crankshaft or the propeller.

Rudder—flat vertical appliance mounted below the stern area which can be moved to port or starboard to steer the boat.

Running lights— navigation lights that must be on from dusk to dawn.

Running rigging—on a sailboat, the rigging that is moved, such as halyards for raising sails, sheets for controlling sails, etc.

Saloon—the area of the boat that corresponds roughly to your living room. Also called salon or cabin.

Schooner—a sailboat with more than one mast, with the forward mast shorter than the main mast.

Scope—the ratio of anchor rode (line) length to depth.

Screw—propeller.

Scuppers—drain channels and/or holes in the deck to drain away water.

Sea anchor—a device that looks somewhat like a parachute, used to slow a boat's drift before the wind.

Seacock—a through hull valve.

Semidiurnal—having a period or cycle of approximately one-half of a day. The predominating type of tide throughout the world is semidiurnal, with two high waters and two low waters each tidal day. The tidal current is said to be semidiurnal when there are two flood and two ebb periods each tidal day.

Set—the direction toward which a current flows.

Sextant—an instrument used to measure angles, usually from a star or other heavenly body down to the horizon.

Shackle—a connector shaped like a "U" closed with a pin or bolt.

Shaft horsepower—horsepower delivered to the propeller.

Sheave—a wheel or pulley over which line is run to change its directions.

Sheer—the line of the top of the gunnel running from bow to stern.

Sheet (sailboat)—the line running either from the aft end of the boom or the clew of a sail that is used to pull the sail in or let it out.

Ship—a large vessel, as opposed to a boat that is a small vessel. There is no exact definition relating to size or weight of what constitutes a ship. Collision Regulations differentiate between vessels greater than or less than 20 meters (65.6 ft) in length so that might be used as a definition.

Shoal—an area offshore where the depth is less than 96 feet (29 meters)

Shoe—an extension of the bottom of the keel aft, which affords protection for the propeller and rudder, and which can be used to mount the bottom of the rudder.

Sine—the ratio of the side opposite an angle of a plane right triangle to the hypotenuse.

Slack water—the state of a tidal current when its speed is near zero, especially the moment when a reversing current changes direction and its speed is zero.

Slip—a space between two piers or pilings for docking a boat bow to or stern to the main pier or float.

Sloop—single-masted sailboat with two sails, one fore and one main aft.

Small scale chart—a scale involving a relatively large reduction in size. A small scale chart usually covers a large area.

SOLAS—acronym for the standards set in the 1974 International Convention for the Safety Of Life At Sea.

Sole—the floor of a cabin, saloon, cockpit, etc.

Sonar—a system that determines distance and/or direction of an underwater object by measuring the interval of time between transmission of an underwater sonic or ultrasonic signal and the return of its echo. The name sonar is derived from the words sound navigation and ranging.

South pole—the south geographic pole.

Spar—a straight pole like structural member such as a mast or boom.

Spinnaker— a large headsail often made of nylon used for sailing downwind.

Spinnaker pole—a pole attached between the mast and clew of the spinnaker to hold the spinnaker out.

Spreader—a device used to spread the shrouds away from the mast the purpose of which is to lessen the tension on the upper shrouds.

Springline—(1) a docking line used to pivot a boat into a dock, or (2) a fore or aft line set to prevent a boat at dock from moving forward or backward.

Squadron—from the 16th century British Navy. Describes a small group of warships that could be commanded effectively by one officer.

Squall—a sudden, violent storm with high winds and often rain.

Stanchion—the metal poles that hold the lifelines up.

Standing rigging—rigging that is fixed, such as stays.

Stand-on vessel—the vessel that has right of way in a meeting, crossing, or overtaking situation.

Starboard tack— sailing with the wind from starboard

Starboard—the right side of the boat when looking forward to the bow.

Steerageway—the condition wherein a ship has sufficient way on to respond to rudder movements to maintain a desired course.

Stem—the forward center part of the hull.

Stern pulpit—a safety railing around the stern and partway forward on both sides of the boat. Also serves as the aft attachment point for lifelines.

Stern—the back or aft end of the boat.

Sternlight—a running light placed on the centerline of a vessel showing a continuous white light from dead astern to 67.5 degrees to either side.

Sternway—a boat moving backward in the water is said to have sternway.

Stroke—the distance a piston moves from top to bottom.

Survey—the inspection of a boat to determine its condition and seaworthiness.

Tack (sail)—the lower forward corner of the sail.

Tackle—as in block and tackle—two blocks with lines running between them use to gain mechanical advantage in pulling of lines.

Tangent—the ratio of the side opposite an acute angle of a plane right triangle to the shorter side adjacent to the same angle.

Thwart—a brace running athwartships (across the boat).

Tiller—a horizontal handle attached to the rudder post used for steering the boat. Also for turning an outboard motor.

Tide—the periodic rise and fall of the water resulting from gravitational interactions between the sun, moon, and earth.

Topping lift (sail)—a line running from near the top of the mast to the end of the boom to hold the boom up.

Topsides—above deck or on deck.

Track—(1) the intended or desired horizontal direction of travel with respect to the earth, (2) the path of intended travel with respect to the earth as drawn on the chart, or (3) the actual path of a vessel over the ground, such as may be determined by tracking.

Track made good—the single resultant direction from a point of departure to a point of arrival at any given time. The use of this term to indicate a single resultant direction is preferred to the use of the misnomer course made good.

Transom—the flat mostly vertical part of the hull at the stern. In smaller boats is used to mount the outboard motor.

Transceiver—a combination transmitter and receiver in a single housing, with some components being used by both parts.

Transducer—a device that converts one type of energy to another, such as the part of a depth sounder that changes electrical energy into acoustical energy.

Transponder—a component of a secondary radar system capable of accepting the interrogating signal, received from a radar set or interrogator, and in response automatically transmitting a signal that enables the transponder to be identified by the interrogating station. Also called transponder beacon.

Trim—fore and aft angular orientation of a boat relative to the horizontal.

Trimaran—a boat with three hulls.

Tripline—a line attached at or near the crown of an anchor used to free the anchor if it fouls.

True wind—the direction of the actual wind (i.e., the direction of the wind if the boat is not making way).

Underway—a boat that is moving as opposed to being anchored, moored or aground.

Variation—the difference between magnetic north and true north.

Veering—a clockwise change in wind direction. In the southern hemisphere a counterclockwise change. The opposite of a backing wind.

Way—movement of a boat through the water.

Weigh—the raise anchor or leave port.

Wharf—constructed from pilings covered by a deck usually parallel to or almost parallel to the shoreline. For berthing and loading boats or ships.

Wheel—wheel used for steering the boat.

Winch—a rotating drum powered either manually, electrically, or hydraulically, around which lines are wrapped to gain mechanical advantage.

Windward—the direction the wind is coming from.

Yar—1. level; a ship that is properly loaded so that she is level fore and aft, and side to side. 2. a trim, clean, responsive boat (usually sailboat) as in a yar boat.

Yaw—sideways rotation of a vessel relative to the direction of travel (i.e., the bow moving to port as the stern moves to starboard, or vice-versa).

Yawl—sailboat with two masts of which the smaller mizzen mast aft is stepped aft of the rudder post.

INDEX

Notes

_____

_____

_____

_____

_____

_____

_____

_____

_____

_____

_____

_____

_____

_____

_____

_____

_____

_____

_____

_____

Notes

Notes

Quick Order Form

Name:
Address:
City:
Zip:
Telephone:
Email:

Please send me one Boater's Pocket Reference at	$14.95
Plus freight	$2.10
Total (for orders outside Colorado)	$17.05
Colorado residents add sales tax at 5.1% (if you live in Colorado, both the sales tax and freight can probably be improved if you call us).	$0.76
Total (for orders inside Colorado)	$17.81

Order from our website or call us at the number on the next page to take advantage of quantity discounts. Discounts are available starting with two or more books, and freight per book is reduced also.

Payment: ❏ Check   ❏ Credit Card

Credit card numbers should be called or faxed in. Please don't send credit card numbers through the mail.

To Order the Boater's Pocket Reference You May:

Order from our website:

www.anchorcovepublishing.com

—Or—

Order by fax: 303-265-9119. Complete and fax the f
on the back side of this page, or fax a sheet with the
information requested on the form.

—Or—

Order by email: books@anchorcovepublishing.com.
Include the information requested on the form on the
back of this page.

—Or—

Order by mail: Complete and send the form on the previous page to:

> Anchor Cove Publishing
> P.O. Box 270588
> Littleton, CO 80127-0010

—Or—

Order by telephone : 303-972-0099

For more than one book, order from our website, or call
us at the number above to take advantage of quantity
discounts. Discounts are available for two or more books,
and freight per book is substantially reduced. For orders
to Canada, check our website or call us.